Juvenile Delinquency Law and Procedure

Juvenile Delinquency Law and Procedure

Jerry R. Foxhoven

EXECUTIVE DIRECTOR OF THE NEAL & BEA SMITH LEGAL CLINIC
PROFESSOR OF LAW, DRAKE LAW SCHOOL

A Lawyering Series Coursebook
Published in Collaboration with
Northeastern University School of Law

CAROLINA ACADEMIC PRESS

Durham, North Carolina

ISBN: 978-1-5310-0283-1
eISBN: 978-1-53100-284-8
LCCN: 2017942452

Carolina Academic Press, LLC
700 Kent Street
Durham, North Carolina 27701
Telephone (919) 489-7486
Fax (919) 493-5668
www.cap-press.com

Printed in the United States of America

Contents

Preface

It is no coincidence that the first edition of this book was published in 2017—fifty years since the United States Supreme Court rendered its decision of *In re Gault.* In that decision, the Court likened a juvenile delinquency proceeding to a felony prosecution of an adult and extended many of the rights of criminal defendants to juveniles in delinquency proceedings under the Due Process Clause of the United States Constitution. The *Gault* decision is still considered the seminal case in juvenile delinquency law by challenging the assumption that the juvenile justice system was a benevolent one not designed to punish youth but to give them a "guiding hand." The holding of the *Gault* decision should have been no surprise at the time. The United States Supreme Court had already held that juveniles were entitled to counsel at waiver proceedings. By the time of the *Gault* ruling, one-third of the states had statutes ensuring the right to counsel in juvenile proceedings, while other states provided such right by court rule. In the *Gault* decision, the United States Supreme Court rejected the extreme difference between the rights accorded an adult compared to those accorded to a child. The Court found that the Constitution "requires the guiding hand of counsel at every step in the proceedings against him." By 1979, just twelve years after *Gault*, the United States Supreme Court made the importance of counsel clear: "Whether it is a minor or an adult who stands accused, the lawyer is the one person to whom society as a whole looks as the protector of the legal rights of that person in his dealings with the police and the courts."

In addition to the rights relative to counsel, the *Gault* decision also granted juveniles other constitutional rights, including: (1) the right to constitutionally adequate notice of the precise nature of the charges; (2) the right to confront and cross-examine witnesses; and (3) the privilege against self-incrimination, as well as the right to be informed of that right. Many of the other rights guaranteed to adult criminal defendants were left for future cases. Once the *Gault* ruling was issued, a succession of cases continued to recognize basic rights for juveniles in delinquency proceedings. In 1970, the Court held that juveniles must be proven guilty beyond a reasonable doubt during the adjudicatory stage of delinquency cases. A year later, in 1971, the Court retreated somewhat, and held that the right to a jury trial is not required by the Constitution in delinquency cases. The Court later held that the Double Jeopardy Clause prevents a juvenile court from transferring a juvenile to the adult court after previously finding him or her delinquent.

There is still a tendency to hold juvenile delinquency courts to a lower standard than adult criminal courts because of the stated purpose of such courts as taking a *parens patria* approach to dealing with delinquent youth. Now, state and federal courts continue to examine, and often expand, the rights of youth involved in the juvenile justice system. As state legislatures began their "tough on crime" approach to dealing with both adults and juveniles committing crimes, more and more courts have seen the inequity of allowing juvenile courts to offer youth "the worst of both worlds" by denying them many of the fundamental rights of adults while, at the same time, imposing punishments that are akin to those imposed on adult criminal defendants.

Today, a lawyer who represents youth in a juvenile delinquency proceeding must be prepared to "push the envelope" by advocating that the client be guaranteed all of the elements of fundamental fairness. Full representation of a youth in juvenile delinquency proceedings requires that the attorney, just like a criminal defense attorney, protect the rights of his client from the very beginning of the youth's contact with authorities—long before formal charges are filed. Attorneys must be prepared to file motions to suppress evidence and confessions in much the same way that criminal defense lawyers conduct the defense of their clients.

It is essential that a lawyer understand the "evolution" of the juvenile justice system from the non-adversarial, paternalistic one that it was originally intended to be to the adversarial and punitive one that it has become. Only by understanding this change can a lawyer fully understand the need to advocate for an expansion of a client's rights in that system. It is one of the roles of a defense lawyer in a juvenile delinquency case to convince the court that this transformation of the juvenile justice system has, in fact, occurred so as to support the extension of the full panoply of rights accorded to adult criminal defendants to youth involved in this system.

This casebook takes a comprehensive approach to teaching law students all of the issues involved in representing a minor who has been accused of violating the law, including the history and evolution of the juvenile justice system, the rights of minors in interrogation, searches and monitoring both at home and at school, and the procedures and rights in delinquency court. The casebook follows the life of a juvenile delinquency case from the first contact with authorities through sentencing in either juvenile or adult court. This book is intended to make a law student fully prepared to be an effective advocate for clients charged with committing a delinquent act.

About the Series

Carolina Academic Press, in cooperation with Northeastern University School of Law, is pleased to offer a new series of teaching materials, the Lawyering Series. Professor Roger Abrams, Richardson Professor of Law at Northeastern School of Law, will serve as Series Editor.

Carolina Academic Press, an independent publisher, has a strong reputation for publishing innovative print and digital teaching materials for the law school community. Northeastern University School of Law has long been known as an innovator in legal education, with a national reputation for its Cooperative Legal Education (Co-op) Program and its rich clinical, internship, and externship offerings.

Over the last decade, the American Bar Association has urged American law schools to better prepare their students for the practice of law. Most recently, the ABA has enacted new Standards that require all law students to complete six credit hours of "experiential" courses. This requirement will commence for students beginning law school in fall 2016.

It is our sincere hope that the Lawyering Series will support law schools and law professors—both full-time and adjunct—as they search for more innovative and more practical teaching materials.

We welcome your comments and suggestions. Please contact Carolina Academic Press at manuscript@caplaw.com or Series Editor Roger Abrams at r.abrams@neu.edu.

Juvenile Delinquency Law and Procedure

Chapter I

The Creation and Evolution of Juvenile Courts

Overview: Juvenile delinquency courts have historically been operated very differently than adult criminal courts. In fact, even the language used is different. In juvenile delinquency courts, the trial is deemed an "adjudicatory hearing" and rather than being convicted, the juvenile is "adjudicated." Also, the sentencing hearing is called a "dispositional hearing" and rather than calling it a sentence, it is called a "disposition." Historically, juveniles were given very few of the rights that have been given to adults because advocates believed that juvenile courts were not adversarial in nature and that the purpose was not punishment but rehabilitation. Juvenile delinquency courts were believed to take an almost paternalistic approach. However, as the nature of juvenile delinquency courts evolved, they became more and more adversarial and punitive. A complete reworking of the rights of juveniles in juvenile delinquency courts was begun by the seminal case of *In re Gault.* Courts have now been faced with claims that the constitutional requirements in the Bill of Rights applied to juveniles as well as adults. While some of the traditional notions of juvenile court still exist, courts have been forced to determine whether or not the evolution of juvenile courts still justify a forfeiture of juvenile rights in delinquency proceedings. This chapter will focus on three issues: (1) how the juvenile courts were created with the idea that they would be "treatment" oriented for the benefit of the minor, requiring a less formal and adversarial approach for juvenile justice as opposed to the criminal justice system; (2) how the juvenile justice system has evolved to look more like the criminal justice system; and (3) how science shows that minors really are different than adults.

In re Gault: In *In re Gault,* the United States Supreme Court was faced with a case where the juvenile, 15-year-old Gerald Gault, was accused of participating in making obscene phone calls to a neighbor lady with another youth. Because of the paternalistic (and non-adversarial) approach under which juvenile courts were conceived and operated, Gerald Gault was afforded almost no rights. The court analyzed the evolution of juvenile courts (which have continued since 1967). The Court then determined that some due process protections were guaranteed for juveniles in juvenile delinquency courts. (The particular rights afforded to juveniles by *Gault* will be discussed later in this book.)

As you read *In re Gault,* look for the following:

1. Observe the historical role noted by the Court in terms of the traditional function and purposes of juvenile delinquency courts.

2. Consider whether the Court is finding that juvenile delinquency courts are not living up to the traditional views of the purpose and function of those courts.

In re Gault

387 U.S. 1, (1967)

Mr. Justice FORTAS delivered the opinion of the Court.

On Monday, June 8, 1964, at about 10 a.m., Gerald Francis Gault and a friend, Ronald Lewis, were taken into custody by the Sheriff of Gila County. Gerald was then still subject to a six months' probation order which had been entered on February 25, 1964, as a result of his having been in the company of another boy who had stolen a wallet from a lady's purse. The police action on June 8 was taken as the result of a verbal complaint by a neighbor of the boys, Mrs. Cook, about a telephone call made to her in which the caller or callers made lewd or indecent remarks. It will suffice for purposes of this opinion to say that the remarks or questions put to her were of the irritatingly offensive, adolescent, sex variety.

At the time Gerald was picked up, his mother and father were both at work. No notice that Gerald was being taken into custody was left at the home. No other steps were taken to advise them that their son had, in effect, been arrested. Gerald was taken to the Children's Detention Home. When his mother arrived home at about 6 o'clock, Gerald was not there. Gerald's older brother was sent to look for him at the trailer home of the Lewis family. He apparently learned then that Gerald was in custody. He so informed his mother. The two of them went to the Detention Home. The deputy probation officer, Flagg, who was also superintendent of the Detention Home, told Mrs. Gault 'why Jerry was there' and said that a hearing would be held in Juvenile Court at 3 o'clock the following day, June 9.

Officer Flagg filed a petition with the court on the hearing day, June 9, 1964. It was not served on the Gaults. Indeed, none of them saw this petition until the habeas corpus hearing on August 17, 1964. The petition was entirely formal. It made no reference to any factual basis for the judicial action which it initiated. It recited only that 'said minor is under the age of eighteen years, and is in need of the protection of this Honorable Court; (and that) said minor is a delinquent minor.' It prayed for a hearing and an order regarding 'the care and custody of said minor.' Officer Flagg executed a formal affidavit in support of the petition.

On June 9, Gerald, his mother, his older brother, and Probation Officers Flagg and Henderson appeared before the Juvenile Judge in chambers. Gerald's father was not there. He was at work out of the city. Mrs. Cook, the complainant, was not there. No one was sworn at this hearing. No transcript or recording was made. No memorandum or record of the substance of the proceedings was prepared. Our information about the proceedings and the subsequent hearing on June 15, derives entirely from the testimony of the Juvenile Court Judge, Mr. and Mrs. Gault and Officer Flagg at the habeas corpus proceeding conducted two months later. From this, it appears that at the June 9 hearing Gerald was questioned by the judge about the telephone call. There was conflict as to what he said. His mother recalled that Gerald said he only dialed Mrs. Cook's number and handed the telephone to his friend, Ronald. Officer Flagg recalled that Gerald had admitted making the lewd remarks. Judge McGhee testified that Gerald 'admitted making one of these (lewd) statements.' At the conclusion of the hearing, the judge said he would 'think about it.' Gerald was taken back to the Detention Home. He was not sent to his own home with his parents. On June 11 or 12, after having been detained since June 8, Gerald was released and driven home. There is no explanation in the record as to why he was kept in the Detention Home or why he was released. At 5 p.m. on the day of Gerald's release, Mrs. Gault received a note signed by Officer Flagg. It was on plain paper, not letterhead. Its entire text was as follows:

'Mrs. Gault:

'Judge McGHEE has set Monday June 15, 1964 at 11:00 A.M. as the date and time for further Hearings on Gerald's delinquency

'/s/ Flagg'

At the appointed time on Monday, June 15, Gerald, his father and mother, Ronald Lewis and his father, and Officers Flagg and Henderson were present before Judge McGhee. Witnesses at the habeas corpus proceeding differed in their recollections of Gerald's testimony at the June 15 hearing. Mr. and Mrs. Gault recalled that Gerald again testified that he had only dialed the number and that the other boy had made the remarks. Officer Flagg agreed that at this hearing Gerald did not admit making the lewd remarks. But Judge McGhee recalled that 'there was some admission again of some of the lewd statements. He-he didn't admit any of the more serious lewd statements.' Again, the complainant, Mrs. Cook, was not present. Mrs. Gault asked that Mrs. Cook be present 'so she could see which boy that done the talking, the dirty talking over the phone.' The Juvenile Judge said 'she didn't have to be present at that hearing.' The judge did not speak to Mrs. Cook or communicate with her at any time. Probation Officer Flagg had talked to her once — over the telephone on June 9.

At this June 15 hearing a 'referral report' made by the probation officers was filed with the court, although not disclosed to Gerald or his parents. This listed the charge as 'Lewd Phone Calls.' At the conclusion of the hearing, the judge committed Gerald as a juvenile delinquent to the State Industrial School 'for the period of his minority (that is, until 21), unless sooner discharged by due process of law.' An order to that effect was entered. It recites that 'after a full hearing and due deliberation the Court finds that said minor is a delinquent child, and that said minor is of the age of 15 years.'

At the habeas corpus hearing on August 17, Judge McGhee was vigorously cross-examined as to the basis for his actions. He testified that he had taken into account the fact that Gerald was on probation.

Asked about the basis for his conclusion that Gerald was 'habitually involved in immoral matters,' the judge testified, somewhat vaguely, that two years earlier, on July 2, 1962, a 'referral' was made concerning Gerald, 'where the boy had stolen a baseball glove from another boy and lied to the Police Department about it.' The judge said there was 'no hearing,' and 'no accusation' relating to this incident, 'because of lack of material foundation.' But it seems to have remained in his mind as a relevant factor. The judge also testified that Gerald had admitted making other nuisance phone calls in the past which, as the judge recalled the boy's testimony, were 'silly calls, or funny calls, or something like that.'

The Supreme Court of Arizona held that due process of law is requisite to the constitutional validity of proceedings in which a court reaches the conclusion that a juvenile has been at fault, has engaged in conduct prohibited by law, or has otherwise misbehaved with the consequence that he is committed to an institution in which his freedom is curtailed. This conclusion is in accord with the decisions of a number of courts under both federal and state constitutions.

This Court has not heretofore decided the precise question. Accordingly, while these cases relate only to restricted aspects of the subject, they unmistakably indicate that, whatever may be their precise impact, neither the Fourteenth Amendment nor the Bill of Rights is for adults alone.

We do not in this opinion consider the impact of these constitutional provisions upon the totality of the relationship of the juvenile and the state. We do not even consider the entire process relating to juvenile 'delinquents.' For example, we are not here concerned with the procedures or constitutional rights applicable to the pre-judicial stages of the juvenile process, nor do we direct our attention to the post-adjudicative or dispositional process. We consider only the problems presented to us by this case. These relate to the proceedings by which a determination is made as to whether a juvenile is a 'delinquent' as a result of alleged misconduct on his part, with the consequence that he may be committed to a state institution. As to these proceedings, there appears to be little current dissent from the proposition that the Due Process Clause has a role to play. The problem is to ascertain the precise impact of the due process requirement upon such proceedings.

From the inception of the juvenile court system, wide differences have been tolerated—indeed insisted upon—between the procedural rights accorded to adults and those of juveniles. In practically all jurisdictions, there are rights granted to adults which are withheld from juveniles. In addition to the specific problems involved in the present case, for example, it has been held that the juvenile is not entitled to bail, to indictment by grand jury, to a public trial or to trial by jury. It is frequent practice that rules governing the arrest and interrogation of adults by the police are not observed in the case of juveniles.

The history and theory underlying this development are well-known, but a recapitulation is necessary for purposes of this opinion. The Juvenile Court movement began in this country at the end of the last century. From the juvenile court statute adopted in Illinois in 1899, the system has spread to every State in the Union, the District of Columbia, and Puerto Rico. The constitutionality of juvenile court laws has been sustained in over 40 jurisdictions against a variety of attacks.

It is claimed that juveniles obtain benefits from the special procedures applicable to them which more than offset the disadvantages of denial of the substance of normal due process. As we shall discuss, the observance of due process standards, intelligently and not ruthlessly administered, will not compel the States to abandon or displace any of the substantive benefits of the juvenile process. But it is important, we think, that the claimed benefits of the juvenile process should be candidly appraised.

Certainly, these figures and the high crime rates among juveniles to which we have referred could not lead us to conclude that the absence of constitutional protections reduces crime, or that the juvenile system, functioning free of constitutional inhibitions as it has largely done, is effective to reduce crime or rehabilitate offenders. We do not mean by this to denigrate the juvenile court process or to suggest that there are not aspects of the juvenile system relating to offenders which are valuable.

While due process requirements will, in some instances, introduce a degree of order and regularity to Juvenile Court proceedings to determine delinquency, and in contested cases will introduce some elements of the adversary system, nothing will require that the conception of the kindly juvenile judge be replaced by its opposite, nor do we here rule upon the question whether ordinary due process requirements must be observed with respect to hearings to determine the disposition of the delinquent child.

Ultimately, however, we confront the reality of that portion of the Juvenile Court process with which we deal in this case. A boy is charged with misconduct. The boy is committed to an institution where he may be restrained of liberty for years. It is of no constitutional consequence—and of limited practical meaning—that the institution to which he is committed is called an Industrial School. The fact of the matter is that, however euphemistic the title, a 'receiving home' or an 'industrial school' for juveniles is an institution of confinement in which the child is incarcerated for a greater or lesser time. His world becomes 'a building with whitewashed walls, regimented routine and institutional hours …' Instead of mother and father and sisters and brothers and friends and classmates, his world is peopled by guards, custodians, state employees, and 'delinquents' confined with him for anything from waywardness to rape and homicide.

In view of this, it would be extraordinary if our Constitution did not require the procedural regularity and the exercise of care implied in the phrase 'due process.' Under our Constitution, the condition of being a boy does not justify a kangaroo court. The essential difference between Gerald's case and a normal criminal case is that safeguards available to adults were discarded in Gerald's case. The summary procedure as well as the long commitment was possible because Gerald was 15 years of age instead of over 18.

If Gerald had been over 18, he would not have been subject to Juvenile Court proceedings. For the particular offense immediately involved, the maximum punishment would have been a fine of $5 to $50, or imprisonment in jail for not more than two months. Instead, he was committed to custody for a maximum of six years. If he had been over 18 and had committed an offense to which such a sentence might apply, he would have been entitled to substantial rights under the Constitution of the United States as well as under Arizona's laws and constitution. The United States Constitution would guarantee him rights and protections with respect to arrest, search, and seizure, and pretrial interrogation. It would assure him of specific notice of the charges and adequate time to decide his course of action and to prepare his defense. He would be entitled to clear advice that he could be represented by counsel, and, at least if a felony were involved, the State would be required to provide counsel if his parents were unable to afford it. If the court acted on the basis of his confession, careful procedures would be required to assure its voluntariness. If the case went to trial, confrontation and opportunity for cross-examination would be guaranteed. So wide a gulf between the State's treatment of the adult and of the child requires a bridge sturdier than mere verbiage, and reasons more persuasive than cliche can provide. As Wheeler and Cottrell have put it, 'The rhetoric of the juvenile court movement has developed without any necessarily close correspondence to the realities of court and institutional routines.'

For the reasons stated, the judgment of the Supreme Court of Arizona is reversed and the cause remanded for further proceedings not inconsistent with this opinion. It is so ordered.

Judgment reversed and cause remanded with directions.

Mr. Justice BLACK, concurring.

The juvenile court laws of Arizona and other States, as the Court points out, are the result of plans promoted by humane and forward-looking people to provide a system of courts, procedures, and sanctions deemed to be less harmful and more lenient to children than to adults. For this reason such state laws generally provide less formal and less public methods for the trial of children. In line with this policy, both courts and legislators have shrunk back from labeling these laws as 'criminal' and have preferred to call them 'civil.' This, in part, was to prevent the full application to juvenile court cases of the Bill of Rights safeguards, including notice as provided in the Sixth Amendment, the right to counsel guaranteed by the Sixth, the right against self-incrimination guaranteed by the Fifth, and the right to confrontation guaranteed by the Sixth. The Court here holds, however, that these four Bill of Rights safeguards apply to protect a juvenile accused in a juvenile court on a charge under which he can be imprisoned for a term of years. This holding strikes a well-nigh fatal blow to much that is unique about the juvenile courts in the Nation.

The juvenile court planners envisaged a system that would practically immunize juveniles from 'punishment' for 'crimes' in an effort to save them from youthful indiscretions and stigmas due to criminal charges or convictions. I agree with the Court, however, that this exalted ideal has failed of achievement since the beginning of the system. Indeed, the state laws from the first one on contained provisions, written in emphatic terms, for arresting and charging juveniles with violations of state criminal laws, as well as for taking juveniles by force of law away from their parents and turning them over to different individuals or groups or for confinement within some state school or institution for a number of years. The latter occurred in this case. Young Gault was arrested and detained on a charge of violating an Arizona penal law by using vile and offensive language to a lady on the telephone. If an adult, he could only have been fined or imprisoned for two months for his conduct. As a juvenile, however, he was put through a more or less secret, informal hearing by the court, after which he was ordered, or more realistically, 'sentenced,' to confinement in Arizona's Industrial School until he reaches 21 years of age. Thus, in a juvenile system designed to lighten or avoid punishment for criminality, he was ordered by the State to six years' confinement in what is in all but name a penitentiary or jail.

Where a person, infant or adult, can be seized by the State, charged, and convicted for violating a state criminal law, and then ordered by the State to be confined for six years, I think the Constitution requires that he be tried in accordance with the guarantees of all the provisions of the Bill of Rights made applicable to the States by the Fourteenth Amendment. Undoubtedly this would be true of an adult defendant, and it would be a plain denial of equal protection of the laws—an invidious discrimination—to hold that others subject to heavier punishments could, because they are children, be denied these same constitutional safeguards.

Mr. Justice HARLAN, concurring in part and dissenting in part.

Each of the 50 States has created a system of juvenile or family courts, in which distinctive rules are employed and special consequences imposed. The jurisdiction of these courts commonly extends both to cases which the States have withdrawn from the ordinary processes of criminal justice, and to cases which involve acts that, if performed by an adult, would not be penalized as criminal. Such courts are denominated civil, not criminal, and are characteristically said not to administer criminal penalties. One consequence of these systems, at least as Arizona construes its own, is that certain of the rights guaranteed to criminal defendants by the Constitution are withheld from juveniles. This case brings before this Court for the first time the question of what limitations the Constitution places upon the operation of such tribunals. For reasons which follow, I have concluded that the Court has gone too far in some respects, and fallen short in others, in assessing the procedural requirements demanded by the Fourteenth Amendment.

The proper issue here is, however, not whether the State may constitutionally treat juvenile offenders through a system of specialized courts, but whether the proceedings in Arizona's juvenile courts include procedural guarantees which satisfy the requirements of the Fourteenth Amendment.

No more evidence of the importance of the public interests at stake here is required than that furnished by the opinion of the Court; it indicates that 'some 601,000 children under 18, or 2% of all children between 10 and 17, came before juvenile courts' in 1965, and that 'about one-fifth of all arrests for serious crimes' in 1965 were of juveniles. The Court adds that the rate of juvenile crime is steadily rising. All this, as the Court suggests, indicates the importance of these due process issues, but it mirrors no less vividly that state authorities are confronted by formidable and immediate problems involving the most fundamental social values. The state legislatures have determined that the most hopeful solution for these problems is to be found in specialized courts, organized under their own rules and imposing distinctive consequences. The terms and limitations of these systems are not identical, nor are the procedural arrangements which they include, but the States are uniform in their insistence that the ordinary processes of criminal justice are inappropriate, and that relatively informal proceedings, dedicated to premises and purposes only imperfectly reflected in the criminal law, are instead necessary.

It follows, for the reasons given in this opinion, that Gerald Gault was deprived of his liberty without due process of law, and I therefore concur in the judgment of the Court.

Mr. Justice STEWART, dissenting.

The Court today uses an obscure Arizona case as a vehicle to impose upon thousands of juvenile courts throughout the Nation restrictions that the Constitution made applicable to adversary criminal trials. I believe the Court's decision is wholly unsound as a matter of constitutional law, and sadly unwise as a matter of judicial policy.

Juvenile proceedings are not criminal trials. They are not civil trials. They are simply not adversary proceedings. Whether treating with a delinquent child, a neglected child, a defective child, or a dependent child, a juvenile proceeding's whole purpose and mission is the very opposite of the mission and purpose of a prosecution in a criminal court. The object of the one is correction of a condition. The object of the other is conviction and punishment for a criminal act.

In the last 70 years many dedicated men and women have devoted their professional lives to the enlightened task of bringing us out of the dark world of Charles Dickens in meeting our responsibilities to the child in our society. The result has been the creation in this century of a system of juvenile and family courts in each of the 50 States. There can be no denying that in many areas the performance of these agencies has fallen disappointingly short of the hopes and dreams of the courageous pioneers who first conceived them. For a variety of reasons, the reality has sometimes not even approached the ideal, and much remains to be accomplished in the administration of public juvenile and family agencies — in personnel, in planning, in financing, perhaps in the formulation of wholly new approaches.

The inflexible restrictions that the Constitution so wisely made applicable to adversary criminal trials have no inevitable place in the proceedings of those public social agencies known as juvenile or family courts. And to impose the Court's long catalog of requirements upon juvenile proceedings in every area of the country is to invite a long step backwards into the nineteenth century. In that era there were no juvenile proceedings, and a child was tried in a conventional criminal court will all the trappings of a conventional criminal trial. So it was that a 12-year-old boy named James Guild was tried in New Jersey for killing Catharine Beakes. A jury found him guilty of murder, and he was sentenced to death by hanging. The sentence was executed. It was all very constitutional.

I would dismiss the appeal.

Holdings of *In re Gault*: As is clear from the portions of the *Gault* opinion included here, the court held that certain Due Process rights are afforded to juveniles in juvenile delinquency court proceedings, even though the juvenile court systems were designed to be fundamentally different than adult criminal courts. (The rights afforded by *Gault* will be discussed later in this book.) The majority opinion (as well as the concurring and dissenting opinions) provide a good background for the evolution of juvenile court proceedings from an informal, paternalistic ("treatment") system to one that is more adversarial and formal.

Discussion Questions

Why were differences between the procedural rights accorded to adults and those of juveniles initially tolerated if not required?

What "benefits" were awarded to juveniles by the use of the less formal and adversarial system that exists in adult court?

In re L.M.

286 Kan. 460, 186 P.3d 164 (2008)

L.M. seeks review of the Court of Appeals decision affirming his juvenile adjudication for aggravated sexual battery and being a minor in possession of alcohol. L.M. claims that he should have received a jury trial and argues that sweeping changes to juvenile justice procedures in Kansas since 1984 merit renewed scrutiny under applicable constitutional protections.

Sixteen-year-old L.M. was charged and prosecuted as a juvenile offender on one count of aggravated sexual battery and one count of minor in possession of alcohol. The facts leading up to these charges involve a sexually suggestive confrontation between L.M. and a neighbor who was walking home. Further discussion of the facts is not relevant to the issue on appeal and will not be discussed herein. L.M. requested a jury trial, and the district court denied his request. After a trial to the bench, the district court found L.M. guilty as charged. The district court sentenced L.M. as a Serious Offender I to a term of 18 months in a juvenile correctional facility but stayed his sentence and ordered L.M. to be placed on probation until he was 20 years old. In addition, the district court ordered L.M. to complete sex offender treatment and register as a sex offender.

L.M. appealed to the Court of Appeals, claiming that he had a constitutional right to a jury trial, that his statements to police should have been suppressed, and that the evidence was insufficient to support his convictions.

L.M. is challenging the constitutionality of K.S.A.2006 Supp. 38-2344(d), which provides that a juvenile who pleads not guilty is entitled to a "trial to the court," and K.S.A.2006 Supp. 38-2357, and which gives the district court complete discretion in determining whether a juvenile should be granted a jury trial.

We begin our analysis by noting that the Kansas Legislature has significantly changed the language of the Kansas Juvenile Offender Code (KJOC) since the *Findlay* court decided this issue 24 years ago. The juvenile code is now called the Revised Kansas Juvenile Justice Code. L.M. asserts that these changes to the code negated the rehabilitative purpose set forth in the KJOC. According to L.M., the negating of the rehabilitative purpose is evidenced by the replacement of nonpunitive terminology with criminal terminology similar to the adult criminal code, the alignment of the KJJC sentencing provisions with the adult sentencing guidelines, and the removal of the protections that the *McKeiver* Court relied on to distinguish juvenile systems from the adult criminal systems.

In 1982, the KJOC was focused on rehabilitation and the State's parental role in providing guidance, control, and discipline. However, under the KJJC, the focus has shifted to protecting the public, holding juveniles accountable for their behavior and choices, and making juveniles more productive and responsible members of society. These purposes are more aligned with the legislative intent for the adult sentencing statutes, which include protecting the public by incarcerating dangerous offenders for a long period of time, holding offenders accountable by prescribing appropriate consequences for their actions, and encouraging offenders to be more productive members of society by considering their individual characteristics, circumstances, needs, and potentialities in determining their sentences.

In addition to being more aligned with the purpose of the criminal sentencing statutes, the KJJC also incorporates language similar to that found in the Kansas Criminal Code.

The legislature also emulated the structure of the Kansas Sentencing Guidelines when it established a sentencing matrix for juveniles based on the level of the offense committed and, in some cases, the juvenile's history of juvenile adjudications.

In addition to reflecting the provisions of the sentencing guidelines, the KJJC also establishes sentencing options that are similar to those available for adult offenders.

Besides amending the 1982 version of the KJOC to reflect the purpose and provisions included in the adult criminal code, the legislature has removed some of the protective provisions that made the juvenile system more child-cognizant and confidential, a key consideration in the *McKeiver* plurality decision. In 1982, juvenile proceedings were confidential. The official court file and all police records of any juvenile under the age of 16 were not open to the public. Likewise, any hearing involving a juvenile under the age of 16 was confidential and the court could exclude anyone except the juvenile; his or her parents; the attorneys of any interested parties; officers of the court; and any testifying witness.

However, under the KJJC, the official file must be open to the public unless a judge orders it to be closed for juveniles under the age of 14 based on finding that it is in the best interests of the juvenile. Similarly, law enforcement records and municipal court records for any juvenile age 14 and over are subject to the same disclosure restrictions as the records for adults. Only juveniles under the age of 14 may have their law enforcement and municipal records kept confidential. The legislature has also eliminated the presumption of confidentiality for hearings, opening all hearings to the public unless the juvenile is under the age of 16 and the judge concludes that a public hearing would not be in the juvenile's best interests.

These changes to the juvenile justice system have eroded the benevolent *parens patriae* character that distinguished it from the adult criminal system. The United States Supreme Court relied on the juvenile justice system's characteristics of fairness, concern, sympathy, and paternal attention in concluding that juveniles were not entitled to a jury trial. Likewise, this court relied on that *parens patriae* character in reaching its decision in *Findlay*. However, because the juvenile justice system is now patterned after the adult criminal system, we conclude that the changes have superseded the *McKeiver* and *Findlay* Courts' reasoning and those decisions are no longer binding precedent for us to follow. Based on our conclusion that the Kansas juvenile justice system has become more akin to an adult criminal prosecution, we hold that juveniles have a constitutional right to a jury trial under the Sixth and Fourteenth Amendments. As a result, K.S.A.2006 Supp. 38-2344(d), which provides that a juvenile who pleads not guilty is entitled to a "trial to the court," and K.S.A.2006 Supp. 38-2357, which gives the district court discretion in determining whether a juvenile should be granted a jury trial, are unconstitutional.

In reaching this conclusion, we are mindful of decisions in other jurisdictions rejecting the argument that changes to the juvenile justice system have altered its *parens patriae* character.

We are also mindful that many of the state courts that have addressed this issue in one form or another have declined to extend the constitutional right to a jury trial to juveniles.

While there is wide variability in the juvenile offender laws throughout the country, it nevertheless seems apparent to us that the KJJC, in its tilt towards applying adult standards of criminal procedure and sentencing, removed the paternalistic protections previously accorded juveniles while continuing to deny those juveniles the constitutional right to a jury trial. Although we do not find total support from the courts in some of our sister states, we are undaunted in our belief that juveniles are entitled to the right to a jury trial guaranteed to all citizens under the Sixth and Fourteenth Amendments to the United States Constitution.

Kansas Constitution

In addition to claiming a federal constitutional right to a jury trial, L.M. asserts that he has a right to a jury trial under the Kansas Constitution. L.M. relies on the Kansas Constitution Bill of Rights, Sections 1, 5, and 10, which provide:

> § 1. "All men are possessed of equal and inalienable natural rights, among which are life, liberty, and the pursuit of happiness."
>
> § 5. "The right of trial by jury shall be inviolate."
>
> § 10. "In all prosecutions, the accused shall be allowed to appear and defend in person, or by counsel; to demand the nature and cause of the accusation against him; to meet the witness face to face, and to have compulsory process to compel the attendance of the witnesses in his behalf, and a speedy public trial by an impartial jury of the county or district in which the offense is alleged to have been committed. No person shall be a witness against himself, or be twice put in jeopardy for the same offense." (Emphasis added.)

The plain language of § 10 extends the right to a jury trial to "all prosecutions." This court has previously interpreted the phrase "all prosecutions" to "mean all criminal prosecutions for violations of the laws of the state."

The KJJC repeatedly refers to its proceedings as a prosecution. In addition, proceedings under the KJJC are based on allegations that juveniles have violated the criminal laws of this State. Because the KJJC has lost the *parens patriae* character of the former KJOC and has transformed into a system for prosecuting juveniles charged with committing crimes, we conclude that the proceedings under the KJJC fit within the meaning of the phrase "all prosecutions" as set forth in § 10, and juveniles have a right to a jury trial under the Kansas Constitution. Consequently, K.S.A.2006 Supp. 38-2344(d) and K.S.A.2006 Supp. 38-2357 are also unconstitutional under the Kansas Constitution.

Because L.M. was tried without a jury, his adjudication is reversed and this matter is remanded to the district court for a new trial before a jury.

Reversed.

McFARLAND, C.J., dissenting:

I respectfully dissent from the majority's decision holding that changes to the juvenile offender system over the last couple of decades have eroded the protective, rehabilitative features of that system to the point that it has become akin to the adult criminal system and, therefore, juvenile offenders are now constitutionally entitled to a jury trial.

In *McKeiver v. Pennsylvania,* the United States Supreme Court held that the Due Process Clause of the Fourteenth Amendment does not require the states to provide a jury trial in a juvenile offender proceeding. The decision was based on the recognition that the juvenile system is fundamentally different from the adult criminal system in that its focus is rehabilitation, not punishment. This goal is pursued through less formal, more individualized, paternalistic, protective proceedings than those in the adult criminal system.

Thirteen years after *McKeiver*, the newly enacted Kansas Juvenile Offenders Code was the subject of a challenge similar to the one presently before the court.

The majority acknowledges this precedent, but holds that the benevolent, protective, *parens patriae* characteristics of the juvenile system that the United States Supreme Court relied on in *McKeiver* to distinguish it from adult criminal prosecutions have been so eroded by legislative changes over the years that the current system is more geared toward prosecuting and punishing juveniles in a manner akin to the adult criminal system. Thus, the rationale underlying *McKeiver* and *Findlay* no longer applies and juveniles therefore must be afforded the right to trial by jury under the Sixth and Fourteenth Amendments to the United States Constitution and under § 10 of the Kansas Constitution Bill of Rights.

I disagree. Although it cannot be disputed that in the 20-plus years since *Findlay*, the juvenile system has become more punitive and has incorporated some of the terminology and mechanisms of the adult criminal system, the majority overstates and overemphasizes the changes while ignoring the many features of the current system that remain consistent with the benevolent, protective, rehabilitative, child-cognizant characteristics that distinguish the juvenile system from the criminal system. The protective, rehabilitative focus that has distinguished the juvenile system from the punitive, retributive adult criminal system is still very much alive.

The majority contends that the current juvenile system has changed to be more in line with the adult criminal system in four ways: (1) the policy goals of the juvenile system have shifted from rehabilitation to protection of the public and accountability, goals more akin to those underlying the criminal system; (2) the current juvenile code uses language similar to that used in the criminal codes; (3) juveniles are now subject to determinative sentencing that closely resembles the sentencing guidelines for adults, and the sentencing options available for juvenile offenders are analogous to those available in the adult sentencing system; and (4) some of the protective confidentiality features of the former juvenile system have been eliminated.

First, the majority points to changes in the policy goals of the juvenile system. The majority contends the amendments in the stated goals evidence a shift from rehabilitation and the State's parental role in providing care, custody, guidance, control, and discipline to protecting the public, holding juveniles accountable, and making juveniles more productive and responsible members of society. What the majority disregards, however, is that in 1982, protection of the public, along with rehabilitation, was an express goal of the juvenile system.

Although the new statute is much more specific about how its goals will be accomplished, the basic goals of protecting the public and rehabilitating juvenile offenders, i.e., improving the ability of juveniles to live more productively and responsibly in the community, remain consistent.

That statute makes it clear that in the adult sentencing system, the focus is on the protection of the public through long terms of confinement for dangerous offenders, with imposition of lesser sanctions only where consistent with public safety and the welfare of the offender. There is no language suggesting that rehabilitation is one of the goals of the adult sentencing system.

The majority concludes that the current juvenile code incorporates language similar to that found in the adult system, thus stressing the similarities between juvenile and adult offenders over their differences.

Clearly some of the terminology has changed. And labels are important to some extent—hence the retention of the term adjudication instead of the term conviction. Nevertheless, form must not be placed over substance. If a change in terminology does not reflect any substantive change in the thing or process described, then too much emphasis should not be placed on that terminology. The facilities denominated as state youth centers, and now juvenile correctional facilities, are one and the same. Regardless of their names, these facilities have always been institutions where juvenile offenders are sent to serve a period of court-ordered confinement.

The majority contends that the sentencing scheme and the options available are now more like those in the adult criminal system. Specifically, the majority notes that juveniles now have determinate presumptive sentencing under a matrix that is based on the offense committed and the juvenile's unique adjudicatory history. And, the majority notes that, like the adult sentencing scheme under the guidelines grid, the current allows the juvenile judge to depart upward from the presumptive matrix upon finding that substantial and compelling reasons support departure. In determining whether to depart, the court may consider the nonexclusive list of aggravating factors set forth in the adult guidelines.

Significant differences remain between the two systems that are overlooked by the majority. First, the majority's analysis fails to take into account the difference in the severity of the sentences juveniles face under the matrix for the same crime committed by an adult offender. The KJJC also does not allow imposition of consecutive sentences. Additionally, the maximum term of commitment of any juvenile to a juvenile correctional facility is age 22 years, 6 months.

Second, in contrast to the adult sentencing guidelines, the sentences provided under the juvenile sentencing matrix are not mandatory. Commitment to a juvenile correctional facility for a term under the matrix is only one of a number of sentencing alternatives available to a juvenile judge. Thus, the judge has discretion in deciding whether to sentence a juvenile to a juvenile correctional facility. If that option is chosen, however, the court must impose the applicable sentence specified in the matrix. While the court may depart upward, downward departures are not authorized, presumably because a commitment to a juvenile correctional facility is discretionary in the first instance.

Another compelling difference is the power given to the juvenile judge to modify the sentence after it has been imposed—a power that does not exist under the adult sentencing guidelines.

The discretionary sentencing provisions and the modification provisions are unique to the juvenile system and are a clear expression of the legislature's continued belief in the juvenile system as an individualized, protective, and rehabilitative process.

Additionally, the majority notes that the current juvenile code imposes a term of aftercare on juveniles sentenced to a term of confinement under the matrix. This, the majority contends, reflects the adult sentencing guidelines postrelease provisions. A postrelease period of supervision is not new to the juvenile system.

The majority also mentions that the KJJC now provides the opportunity for good time credits, just like the adult system. I fail to see how providing a benefit to juveniles—even if it is the same benefit provided to incarcerated adult offenders—is really relevant to the issue of whether the new juvenile system is no longer the individualized, protective, re-habilitative system that it was when *Findlay* was decided. How would denying juveniles good time credits better serve a benevolent, paternalistic purpose?

The majority also fails to consider the importance of extended jurisdiction juvenile prosecution. Extended jurisdiction juvenile prosecution became effective in 1997 and is a mechanism whereby serious or repeat juvenile offenders who might otherwise have been waived up to adult court may remain in the juvenile sentencing system. In an extended jurisdiction juvenile prosecution, the court imposes both a juvenile and an adult sentence. The adult sentence is stayed as long as the juvenile complies with and completes the conditions of the juvenile sentence. If, however, the juvenile violates the conditions of the juvenile sentence, the juvenile sentence is revoked, the adult sentence is imposed, and the juvenile court transfers jurisdiction of the case to adult court. Because a juvenile in an extended jurisdiction prosecution may end up in adult court with an adult sentence, the right to trial by jury is provided by statute. Extended jurisdiction juvenile prosecution is important to the issue at hand because it evidences a last-ditch effort to extend the favorable protections of juvenile court and the benefits of its less severe sentences to juvenile offenders who previously would have been waived to adult court.

The majority contends that the sentencing options available to the juvenile judge are much more akin to those available for adult offenders. The court notes that juvenile offenders, like adult offenders, may be sentenced to probation; a community-based program; house arrest; a sanctions house, which the majority likens to conservation camps; placement in an out-of-home facility; and incarceration. In addition, the court may order both adults and juveniles to attend counseling; drug and alcohol evaluations; mediation; and educational programs. The court may also order both juveniles and adults to perform charitable or community service, pay restitution, and pay fines.

This broad overview overlooks the many unique features of the juvenile system that emphasize family and community involvement, early intervention diversionary procedures, flexibility to accommodate individualized needs of juveniles upon intake into the system, preference for noncustodial placements, graduated sanctions with preferences for the least-restrictive alternatives, and, above all, rehabilitation.

The juvenile system has unique pre-charge intake and intervention procedures: the Juvenile Intake and Assessment Program and the intermediate intervention program.

The importance of these unique intake and intervention procedures to the issue at hand cannot be dismissed. As Justice White noted in *McKeiver*: "To the extent that the jury is a buffer to the corrupt or overzealous prosecutor in the criminal law system, the distinctive intake policies and procedures of the juvenile court system to a great extent obviate this important function of the jury."

A dispositional feature unique to the juvenile system is its preference for maintaining the family unit. Under the KJJC, the court must make specific findings that reasonable efforts were made to maintain the family unit or that an emergency exists before a juvenile may be removed from the home, whether for detention, placement in the custody of the commissioner, or commitment to a juvenile correctional facility. An order removing a juvenile from the home may be made if the juvenile presents a risk to public safety.

It appears the legislature required these findings in an effort to comply with the provisions of the federal Adoption and Safe Families Act of 1997. However, it must be noted that this statutory preference for maintaining the family unit is consistent with the policy stated in K.S.A.1982 Supp. 38-1601: "[The code] shall be liberally construed to the end that each juvenile coming within its provisions shall receive the care, custody, guidance, control and discipline, preferably in the juvenile's own home, as will best serve the juvenile's rehabilitation and the protection of society."

In line with this emphasis on maintaining the family unit, the KJJC also requires that when a juvenile is placed out of the home, a permanency plan must be prepared which provides for reintegration or, if reintegration is not a viable option, for some other permanent placement. The court must conduct a review every 6 months of the progress being made toward permanency.

Another significant difference between the adult system and the juvenile system is the court-appointed special advocate (CASA). In 1994, the legislature provided for the appointment of a CASA—formerly a feature unique to child in need of care cases—in juvenile offender cases. The CASA's primary duty is to advocate for the juvenile's bests interests.

The addition of local citizen review boards to the juvenile process is also a feature not found in the adult criminal system. Under K.S.A.2006 Supp. 38-2308(a), judges may refer juvenile offender cases to the local citizen review board for the purpose of determining the progress that has been made toward rehabilitation and making recommendations regarding further actions on the case.

Additionally, and most importantly, the KJJC not only emphasizes, but requires, parental involvement in the entire process. Intake and assessment workers may require parents to participate in programs and services as a condition of the juvenile's release back home. The county or district attorney is authorized to require parents to be a part of any immediate intervention program. Parents served with a summons are required to attend all proceedings involving the juvenile unless excused by the court. The court has the power to require parents to participate in counseling, mediation, alcohol and drug evaluations and treatment programs, and parenting classes. The court also has the power to order parents to report violations of conditions of probation or conditional release and may order them to aid the court in enforcing the court's orders. Violation may result in contempt sanctions.

This emphasis on parental involvement is not merely incidental to the fact the juvenile offender is a child, but is, instead, part of the family and community centered approach to juvenile rehabilitation.

The majority also contends that juvenile proceedings and records no longer have the confidentiality protections they did in 1982. The majority points to provisions concerning public access to juvenile court hearings and confidentiality of records. With respect to juvenile hearings, there is little practical difference between the KJOC provisions in 1982 and the current KJJC provisions. The KJOC required that juvenile court hearings be open to the public if the juvenile was 16 years of age or older at the time of the alleged offense. For a juvenile under age 16, the court had discretion to close the hearing. Under the current KJJC, all hearings are open to the public, but in the case of juveniles under the age of 16, the court has discretion to close the hearing.

With respect to confidentiality of juvenile records, there are only two differences between the KJOC and the KJJC. First, the age of protection was lowered from 15 to 13.

Second, with respect to the official court file only, the file is now open for public inspection unless, in the case of a juvenile who is under age 14, the judge determines that public inspection is not in the juvenile's best interests. Previously, the official file of a juvenile under the age of 16 was privileged and not subject to disclosure to anyone other than the court, the parties and their attorneys, an agency or institution with custody of the juvenile, law enforcement, or upon court order.

The changes to the juvenile code cited by the majority have not so eroded the features of the juvenile system that distinguish it from the adult system that it can be said that the rationale underlying *McKeiver* and *Findlay* is no longer valid. The new system continues to further the goals that have always characterized the modern juvenile system: protection of the public and rehabilitation. As the Criminal Justice Coordinating Council's Juvenile Task Force noted in its report to the legislature in 1995, these two goals are not incompatible. Given the fact that the juvenile system must deal with serious, violent, and habitual offenders, it is entirely appropriate that the juvenile system balance rehabilitation with protection of the public.

The incorporation of certain aspects of the adult sentencing scheme for the most violent and chronic juvenile offenders is a critical part of meeting the obligation to protect the community from these offenders. However, the legislature, in choosing to make sentencing under the matrix a discretionary sentencing option, kept in place the individualized sentencing flexibility that has always been characteristic of the juvenile system. In addition, in creating extended juvenile jurisdiction, the legislature extended the protective net of the juvenile system as a last-ditch effort for those juveniles who would otherwise be prosecuted and sentenced as adults. These key features demonstrate the legislature's effort to carefully balance protection of the public with the goal of rehabilitating youthful offenders.

The dual goals of the juvenile system that commanded its process in 1982 are very much alive and well. The juvenile system still retains significant individualized, protective, rehabilitative, child-cognizant features that distinguish it from the adult system and which allow it to operate toward achieving those goals.

I must also note that the majority's decision is contrary to the weight of authority. The argument the majority accepts in this case has been rejected by the overwhelming majority of courts that have considered it.

With no persuasive authority from other jurisdictions, and a less than comprehensive analysis of the current system, the majority concludes that the Kansas juvenile justice system is the essential equivalent of the adult criminal justice system and, thus, the right to trial by jury must be afforded. To what end? As the United States Supreme Court recognized in *McKeiver*, imposing the constitutional right to trial by jury on the juvenile court system would not greatly strengthen the fact-finding function, but would erode the juvenile court's ability to function in a unique manner, and "remake the juvenile proceeding into a fully adversary process and ... put an effective end to what has been the idealistic prospect of an intimate, informal protective proceeding." "If the formalities of the criminal adjudicative system are to be superimposed upon the juvenile court system, there is little need for its separate existence."

The experiment has not failed. The majority has overlooked the most significant features of the juvenile system that distinguish it from the adult system — features that promote protection of the public while not only preserving, but furthering, the individualized, protective, rehabilitative character unique to the juvenile system. It does not embrace a purely punitive or retributive philosophy. Instead, it attempts to tread an equatorial line somewhere midway between the poles of rehabilitation and retribution.

For these reasons, I dissent.

Holdings of *In re L.M.*: The court held that the Kansas juvenile justice system has become more akin to an adult criminal prosecution, and, therefore, juveniles have a constitutional right to a jury trial under the Sixth and Fourteenth Amendment, as well as under the Kansas Constitution.

Discussion Questions

If the juvenile system really has moved away from a benevolent *parens patriae* system to a more adversarial system, should age alone be enough to deny the right to a jury trial?

―――――――――

Roper v. Simmons: In *Roper v. Simmons,* the United States Supreme Court was asked to revisit their ruling in the *Stanford* case. At the age of 17, when he was still a junior in high school, Christopher Simmons, committed murder. About nine months later, after he had turned 18, he was tried and sentenced to death. Before its commission, Simmons said he wanted to murder someone. He described his plan in detail to two friends, then aged 15 and 16 respectively, and assured his friends they could "get away with it" because they were minors. After confessing to the murder, Simmons was waived to adult court where he was charged with burglary, kidnaping, stealing, and murder in the first degree. A jury returned a guilty verdict of murder and Simmons was sentenced to death.

As you read *Roper v. Simmons,* look for the following:

1. Consider what science and psychology tells us about how minors and adults are different in ways that affect how they should be treated by the justice system.

Roper v. Simmons
543 U.S. 551 (2005)

Justice KENNEDY delivered the opinion of the Court.

This case requires us to address, for the second time in a decade and a half, whether it is permissible under the Eighth and Fourteenth Amendments to the Constitution of the United States to execute a juvenile offender who was older than 15 but younger than 18 when he committed a capital crime. In *Stanford v. Kentucky,* a divided Court rejected the proposition that the Constitution bars capital punishment for juvenile offenders in this age group. We reconsider the question.

At the age of 17, when he was still a junior in high school, Christopher Simmons, the respondent here, committed murder. About nine months later, after he had turned 18, he was tried and sentenced to death. There is little doubt that Simmons was the instigator of the crime. Before its commission Simmons said he wanted to murder someone. In chilling, callous terms he talked about his plan, discussing it for the most part with two friends, Charles Benjamin and John Tessmer, then aged 15 and 16 respectively. Simmons proposed to commit burglary and murder by breaking and entering, tying up a victim, and throwing the victim off a bridge. Simmons assured his friends they could "get away with it" because they were minors.

The three met at about 2 a.m. on the night of the murder, but Tessmer left before the other two set out. (The State later charged Tessmer with conspiracy, but dropped the charge in exchange for his testimony against Simmons.) Simmons and Benjamin entered the home of the victim, Shirley Crook, after reaching through an open window and unlocking the back door. Simmons turned on a hallway light. Awakened, Mrs. Crook called out, "Who's there?" In response Simmons entered Mrs. Crook's bedroom, where he recognized her from a previous car accident involving them both. Simmons later admitted this confirmed his resolve to murder her.

Using duct tape to cover her eyes and mouth and bind her hands, the two perpetrators put Mrs. Crook in her minivan and drove to a state park. They reinforced the bindings, covered her head with a towel, and walked her to a railroad trestle spanning the Meramec River. There they tied her hands and feet together with electrical wire, wrapped her whole face in duct tape and threw her from the bridge, drowning her in the waters below.

By the afternoon of September 9, Steven Crook had returned home from an overnight trip, found his bedroom in disarray, and reported his wife missing. On the same afternoon fishermen recovered the victim's body from the river. Simmons, meanwhile, was bragging about the killing, telling friends he had killed a woman "because the bitch seen my face."

The next day, after receiving information of Simmons' involvement, police arrested him at his high school and took him to the police station in Fenton, Missouri. They read him his Miranda rights. Simmons waived his right to an attorney and agreed to answer questions. After less than two hours of interrogation, Simmons confessed to the murder and agreed to perform a videotaped reenactment at the crime scene.

The State charged Simmons with burglary, kidnaping, stealing, and murder in the first degree. As Simmons was 17 at the time of the crime, he was outside the criminal jurisdiction of Missouri's juvenile court system. He was tried as an adult. At trial the State introduced Simmons' confession and the videotaped reenactment of the crime, along with testimony that Simmons discussed the crime in advance and bragged about it later. The defense called no witnesses in the guilt phase. The jury having returned a verdict of murder, the trial proceeded to the penalty phase.

The State sought the death penalty.

During closing arguments, both the prosecutor and defense counsel addressed Simmons' age, which the trial judge had instructed the jurors they could consider as a mitigating factor. Defense counsel reminded the jurors that juveniles of Simmons' age cannot drink, serve on juries, or even see certain movies, because "the legislatures have wisely decided that individuals of a certain age aren't responsible enough." Defense counsel argued that Simmons' age should make "a huge difference to [the jurors] in deciding just exactly what sort of punishment to make." In rebuttal, the prosecutor gave the following response: "Age, he says. Think about age. Seventeen years old. Isn't that scary? Doesn't that scare you? Mitigating? Quite the contrary I submit. Quite the contrary."

The jury recommended the death penalty after finding the State had proved each of the three aggravating factors submitted to it. Accepting the jury's recommendation, the trial judge imposed the death penalty.

After these proceedings in Simmons' case had run their course, this Court held that the Eighth and Fourteenth Amendments prohibit the execution of a mentally retarded person. Simmons filed a new petition for state postconviction relief, arguing that the reasoning of Atkins established that the Constitution prohibits the execution of a juvenile who was under 18 when the crime was committed.

The Missouri Supreme Court agreed. It held that since Stanford,

> "a national consensus has developed against the execution of juvenile offenders, as demonstrated by the fact that eighteen states now bar such executions for juveniles, that twelve other states bar executions altogether, that no state has lowered its age of execution below 18 since Stanford, that five states have legislatively

or by case law raised or established the minimum age at 18, and that the imposition of the juvenile death penalty has become truly unusual over the last decade."

On this reasoning it set aside Simmons' death sentence and resentenced him to "life imprisonment without eligibility for probation, parole, or release except by act of the Governor."

We granted certiorari, and now affirm.

A majority of States have rejected the imposition of the death penalty on juvenile offenders under 18, and we now hold this is required by the Eighth Amendment.

Three general differences between juveniles under 18 and adults demonstrate that juvenile offenders cannot with reliability be classified among the worst offenders.

First, as any parent knows and as the scientific and sociological studies respondent and his *amici* cite tend to confirm, "[a] lack of maturity and an underdeveloped sense of responsibility are found in youth more often than in adults and are more understandable among the young. These qualities often result in impetuous and ill-considered actions and decisions." It has been noted that "adolescents are overrepresented statistically in virtually every category of reckless behavior." Arnett, Reckless Behavior in Adolescence: A Developmental Perspective, 12 Developmental Rev. 339 (1992). In recognition of the comparative immaturity and irresponsibility of juveniles, almost every State prohibits those under 18 years of age from voting, serving on juries, or marrying without parental consent.

The second area of difference is that juveniles are more vulnerable or susceptible to negative influences and outside pressures, including peer pressure ("[Y]outh is more than a chronological fact. It is a time and condition of life when a person may be most susceptible to influence and to psychological damage"). This is explained in part by the prevailing circumstance that juveniles have less control, or less experience with control, over their own environment. See Steinberg & Scott, Less Guilty by Reason of Adolescence: Developmental Immaturity, Diminished Responsibility, and the Juvenile Death Penalty, 58 Am. Psychologist 1009, 1014 (2003) (hereinafter Steinberg & Scott) ("[A]s legal minors, [juveniles] lack the freedom that adults have to extricate themselves from a criminogenic setting").

The third broad difference is that the character of a juvenile is not as well formed as that of an adult. The personality traits of juveniles are more transitory, less fixed. See generally E. Erikson, Identity: Youth and Crisis (1968).

These differences render suspect any conclusion that a juvenile falls among the worst offenders. The susceptibility of juveniles to immature and irresponsible behavior means "their irresponsible conduct is not as morally reprehensible as that of an adult." Their own vulnerability and comparative lack of control over their immediate surroundings mean juveniles have a greater claim than adults to be forgiven for failing to escape negative influences in their whole environment. The reality that juveniles still struggle to define their identity means it is less supportable to conclude that even a heinous crime committed by a juvenile is evidence of irretrievably depraved character. From a moral standpoint it would be misguided to equate the failings of a minor with those of an adult, for a greater possibility exists that a minor's character deficiencies will be reformed. Indeed, "[t]he relevance of youth as a mitigating factor derives from the fact that the signature qualities of youth are transient; as individuals mature, the impetuousness and recklessness that may dominate in younger years can subside." see also Steinberg & Scott 1014 ("For most teens, [risky or antisocial] behaviors are fleeting; they cease with maturity as individual identity becomes settled. Only a relatively small proportion of adolescents who experiment in risky or illegal activities develop entrenched patterns of problem behavior that persist into adulthood").

In *Thompson,* a plurality of the Court recognized the import of these characteristics with respect to juveniles under 16, and relied on them to hold that the Eighth Amendment prohibited the imposition of the death penalty on juveniles below that age.

We conclude the same reasoning applies to all juvenile offenders under 18.

Once the diminished culpability of juveniles is recognized, it is evident that the penological justifications for the death penalty apply to them with lesser force than to adults. We have held there are two distinct social purposes served by the death penalty: "'retribution and deterrence of capital crimes by prospective offenders.'" As for retribution, we remarked in *Atkins* that "[i]f the culpability of the average murderer is insufficient to justify the most extreme sanction available to the State, the lesser culpability of the mentally retarded offender surely does not merit that form of retribution." The same conclusions follow from the lesser culpability of the juvenile offender. Whether viewed as an attempt to express the community's moral outrage or as an attempt to right the balance for the wrong to the victim, the case for retribution is not as strong with a minor as with an adult. Retribution is not proportional if the law's most severe penalty is imposed on one whose culpability or blameworthiness is diminished, to a substantial degree, by reason of youth and immaturity.

As for deterrence, it is unclear whether the death penalty has a significant or even measurable deterrent effect on juveniles, as counsel for petitioner acknowledged at oral argument. In general we leave to legislatures the assessment of the efficacy of various criminal penalty schemes. Here, however, the absence of evidence of deterrent effect is of special concern because the same characteristics that render juveniles less culpable than adults suggest as well that juveniles will be less susceptible to deterrence. In particular, as the plurality observed in *Thompson,* "[t]he likelihood that the teenage offender has made the kind of cost-benefit analysis that attaches any weight to the possibility of execution is so remote as to be virtually nonexistent." To the extent the juvenile death penalty might have residual deterrent effect, it is worth noting that the punishment of life imprisonment without the possibility of parole is itself a severe sanction, in particular for a young person.

In concluding that neither retribution nor deterrence provides adequate justification for imposing the death penalty on juvenile offenders, we cannot deny or overlook the brutal crimes too many juvenile offenders have committed. Certainly it can be argued, although we by no means concede the point, that a rare case might arise in which a juvenile offender has sufficient psychological maturity, and at the same time demonstrates sufficient depravity, to merit a sentence of death. Indeed, this possibility is the linchpin of one contention pressed by petitioner and his *amici.* They assert that even assuming the truth of the observations we have made about juveniles' diminished culpability in general, jurors nonetheless should be allowed to consider mitigating arguments related to youth on a case-by-case basis, and in some cases to impose the death penalty if justified. A central feature of death penalty sentencing is a particular assessment of the circumstances of the crime and the characteristics of the offender. The system is designed to consider both aggravating and mitigating circumstances, including youth, in every case. Given this Court's own insistence on individualized consideration, petitioner maintains that it is both arbitrary and unnecessary to adopt a categorical rule barring imposition of the death penalty on any offender under 18 years of age.

We disagree. The differences between juvenile and adult offenders are too marked and well understood to risk allowing a youthful person to receive the death penalty despite insufficient culpability. An unacceptable likelihood exists that the brutality or cold-blooded nature of any particular crime would overpower mitigating arguments based on youth as a matter of course, even where the juvenile offender's objective immaturity, vulnerability, and lack of true depravity should require a sentence less severe than death. In some cases a defendant's youth may even be counted against him. In this very case, as we noted above, the prosecutor argued Simmons' youth was aggravating rather than mitigating. While this sort of overreaching could be corrected by a particular rule to ensure that the mitigating force of youth is not overlooked, that would not address our larger concerns.

It is difficult even for expert psychologists to differentiate between the juvenile offender whose crime reflects unfortunate yet transient immaturity, and the rare juvenile offender whose crime reflects irreparable corruption. See Steinberg & Scott 1014–1016. As we understand it, this difficulty underlies the rule forbidding psychiatrists from diagnosing any patient under 18 as having antisocial personality disorder, a disorder also referred to as psychopathy or sociopathy, and which is characterized by callousness, cynicism, and contempt for the feelings, rights, and suffering of others. American Psychiatric Association, Diagnostic and Statistical Manual of Mental Disorders 701–706 (4th ed. text rev.2000); see also Steinberg & Scott 1015. If trained psychiatrists with the advantage of clinical testing and observation refrain, despite diagnostic expertise, from assessing any juvenile under 18 as having antisocial personality disorder, we conclude that States should refrain from asking jurors to issue a far graver condemnation—that a juvenile offender merits the death penalty. When a juvenile offender commits a heinous crime, the State can exact forfeiture of some of the most basic liberties, but the State cannot extinguish his life and his potential to attain a mature understanding of his own humanity.

Drawing the line at 18 years of age is subject, of course, to the objections always raised against categorical rules. The qualities that distinguish juveniles from adults do not disappear when an individual turns 18. By the same token, some under 18 have already attained a level of maturity some adults will never reach. For the reasons we have discussed, however, a line must be drawn. The plurality opinion in *Thompson* drew the line at 16. In the intervening years the *Thompson* plurality's conclusion that offenders under 16 may not be executed has not been challenged. The logic of *Thompson* extends to those who are under 18. The age of 18 is the point where society draws the line for many purposes between childhood and adulthood. It is, we conclude, the age at which the line for death eligibility ought to rest.

The Eighth and Fourteenth Amendments forbid imposition of the death penalty on offenders who were under the age of 18 when their crimes were committed. The judgment of the Missouri Supreme Court setting aside the sentence of death imposed upon Christopher Simmons is affirmed.

It is so ordered.

Justice O'CONNOR, dissenting.

The Court's decision today establishes a categorical rule forbidding the execution of any offender for any crime committed before his 18th birthday, no matter how deliberate, wanton, or cruel the offense. Neither the objective evidence of contemporary societal values, nor the Court's moral proportionality analysis, nor the two in tandem suffice to justify this ruling.

Although the Court finds support for its decision in the fact that a majority of the States now disallow capital punishment of 17-year-old offenders, it refrains from asserting that its holding is compelled by a genuine national consensus. Indeed, the evidence before us fails to demonstrate conclusively that any such consensus has emerged in the brief period since we upheld the constitutionality of this practice in *Stanford v. Kentucky.*

Instead, the rule decreed by the Court rests, ultimately, on its independent moral judgment that death is a disproportionately severe punishment for any 17-year-old offender.

I do not subscribe to this judgment. Adolescents as a class are undoubtedly less mature, and therefore less culpable for their misconduct, than adults. But the Court has adduced no evidence impeaching the seemingly reasonable conclusion reached by many state legislatures: that at least some 17-year-old murderers are sufficiently mature to deserve the death penalty in an appropriate case. Nor has it been shown that capital sentencing juries are incapable of accurately assessing a youthful defendant's maturity or of giving due weight to the mitigating characteristics associated with youth.

Seventeen-year-old murderers must be categorically exempted from capital punishment, the Court says, because they "cannot with reliability be classified among the worst offenders." That conclusion is premised on three perceived differences between "adults," who have already reached their 18th birthdays, and "juveniles," who have not. First, juveniles lack maturity and responsibility and are more reckless than adults. Second, juveniles are more vulnerable to outside influences because they have less control over their surroundings. And third, a juvenile's character is not as fully formed as that of an adult. Based on these characteristics, the Court determines that 17-year-old capital murderers are not as blameworthy as adults guilty of similar crimes; that 17-year-olds are less likely than adults to be deterred by the prospect of a death sentence; and that it is difficult to conclude that a 17-year-old who commits even the most heinous of crimes is "irretrievably depraved."

It is beyond cavil that juveniles as a class are generally less mature, less responsible, and less fully formed than adults, and that these differences bear on juveniles' comparative moral culpability. But even accepting this premise, the Court's proportionality argument fails to support its categorical rule.

First, the Court adduces no evidence whatsoever in support of its sweeping conclusion that it is only in "rare" cases, if ever, that 17-year-old murderers are sufficiently mature and act with sufficient depravity to warrant the death penalty. The fact that juveniles are generally less culpable for their misconduct than adults does not necessarily mean that a 17-year-old murderer cannot be sufficiently culpable to merit the death penalty. At most, the Court's argument suggests that the average 17-year-old murderer is not as culpable as the average adult murderer. But an especially depraved juvenile offender may nevertheless be just as culpable as many adult offenders considered bad enough to deserve the death penalty. Similarly, the fact that the availability of the death penalty may be less likely to deter a juvenile from committing a capital crime does not imply that this threat cannot effectively deter some 17-year-olds from such an act. Surely there is an age below which no offender, no matter what his crime, can be deemed to have the cognitive or emotional maturity necessary to warrant the death penalty. But at least at the margins between adolescence and adulthood—and especially for 17-year-olds such as respondent—the relevant differences between "adults" and "juveniles" appear to be a matter of degree, rather than of kind. It follows that a legislature may reasonably conclude that at least some 17-year-olds can act with sufficient moral culpability, and can be sufficiently deterred by the threat of execution, that capital punishment may be warranted in an appropriate case.

Indeed, this appears to be just such a case. Christopher Simmons' murder of Shirley Crook was premeditated, wanton, and cruel in the extreme. Well before he committed this crime, Simmons declared that he wanted to kill someone. On several occasions, he discussed with two friends (ages 15 and 16) his plan to burglarize a house and to murder the victim by tying the victim up and pushing him from a bridge. Simmons said they could "'get away with it'" because they were minors. In accord with this plan, Simmons and his 15-year-old accomplice broke into Mrs. Crook's home in the middle of the night, forced her from her bed, bound her, and drove her to a state park. There, they walked her to a railroad trestle spanning a river, "hog-tied" her with electrical cable, bound her face completely with duct tape, and pushed her, still alive, from the trestle. She drowned in the water below. One can scarcely imagine the terror that this woman must have suffered throughout the ordeal leading to her death. Whatever can be said about the comparative moral culpability of 17-year-olds as a general matter, Simmons' actions unquestionably reflect "'a consciousness materially more "depraved" than that of' … the average murderer." And Simmons' prediction that he could murder with impunity because he had not yet turned 18—though inaccurate—suggests that he did take into account the perceived risk of punishment in deciding whether to commit the crime. Based on this evidence, the sentencing jury certainly had reasonable grounds for concluding that, despite Simmons' youth, he "ha[d] sufficient psychological maturity" when he committed this horrific murder, and "at the same time demonstrate[d] sufficient depravity, to merit a sentence of death."

The Court's proportionality argument suffers from a second and closely related defect: It fails to establish that the differences in maturity between 17-year-olds and young "adults" are both universal enough and significant enough to justify a bright-line prophylactic rule against capital punishment of the former. The Court's analysis is premised on differences in the aggregate between juveniles and adults, which frequently do not hold true when comparing individuals. Although it may be that many 17-year-old murderers lack sufficient maturity to deserve the death penalty, some juvenile murderers may be quite mature. Chronological age is not an unfailing measure of psychological development, and common experience suggests that many 17-year-olds are more mature than the average young "adult." In short, the class of offenders exempted from capital punishment by today's decision is too broad and too diverse to warrant a categorical prohibition. Indeed, the age-based line drawn by the Court is indefensibly arbitrary—it quite likely will protect a number of offenders who are mature enough to deserve the death penalty and may well leave vulnerable many who are not.

For purposes of proportionality analysis, 17-year-olds as a class are qualitatively and materially different from the mentally retarded. "Mentally retarded" offenders, as we understood that category in *Atkins*, are defined by precisely the characteristics which render death an excessive punishment. A mentally retarded person is, "by definition," one whose cognitive and behavioral capacities have been proved to fall below a certain minimum. There is no such inherent or accurate fit between an offender's chronological age and the personal limitations which the Court believes make capital punishment excessive for 17-year-old murderers. Moreover, it defies common sense to suggest that 17-year-olds as a class are somehow equivalent to mentally retarded persons with regard to culpability or susceptibility to deterrence. Seventeen-year-olds may, on average, be less mature than adults, but that lesser maturity simply cannot be equated with the major, lifelong impairments suffered by the mentally retarded.

The proportionality issues raised by the Court clearly implicate Eighth Amendment concerns. But these concerns may properly be addressed not by means of an arbitrary, categorical age-based rule, but rather through individualized sentencing in which juries are required to give appropriate mitigating weight to the defendant's immaturity, his susceptibility to outside pressures, his cognizance of the consequences of his actions, and so forth.

I respectfully dissent.

Justice SCALIA, with whom THE CHIEF JUSTICE and Justice THOMAS join, dissenting.

Today's opinion provides a perfect example of why judges are ill equipped to make the type of legislative judgments the Court insists on making here. To support its opinion that States should be prohibited from imposing the death penalty on anyone who committed murder before age 18, the Court looks to scientific and sociological studies, picking and choosing those that support its position. It never explains why those particular studies are methodologically sound; none was ever entered into evidence or tested in an adversarial proceeding.

Moreover, the cited studies describe only adolescents who engage in risky or antisocial behavior, as many young people do. Murder, however, is more than just risky or antisocial behavior. It is entirely consistent to believe that young people often act impetuously and lack judgment, but, at the same time, to believe that those who commit premeditated murder are—at least sometimes—just as culpable as adults. Christopher Simmons, who was only seven months shy of his 18th birthday when he murdered Shirley Crook, described to his friends beforehand—"[i]n chilling, callous terms," as the Court puts it, the murder he planned to commit. He then broke into the home of an innocent woman, bound her with duct tape and electrical wire, and threw her off a bridge alive and conscious. In their *amici* brief, the States of Alabama, Delaware, Oklahoma, Texas, Utah, and Virginia offer additional examples of murders committed by individuals under 18 that involve truly monstrous acts. In Alabama, two 17-year-olds, one 16-year-old, and one 19-year-old picked up a female hitchhiker, threw bottles at her, and kicked and stomped her for approximately 30 minutes until she died. They then sexually assaulted her lifeless body and, when they were finished, threw her body off a cliff. They later returned to the crime scene to mutilate her corpse. Other examples in the brief are equally shocking. Though these cases are assuredly the exception rather than the rule, the studies the Court cites in no way justify a constitutional imperative that prevents legislatures and juries from treating exceptional cases in an exceptional way—by determining that some murders are not just the acts of happy-go-lucky teenagers, but heinous crimes deserving of death.

Holdings of *Roper v. Simmons:* The court held that, because of the inherent differences between minors and adults, the imposition of the death penalty on a youth who was a minor at the time of the offense constitutes cruel and unusual punishment and, therefore, violates the Eighth Amendment to the United States Constitution.

Discussion Questions

What are the three differences between Juveniles and adults that the court finds warrant a different holding for the two groups concerning the imposition of the death penalty (that they are not among the "worst offenders")?

How does the majority reason that the two justifications for the imposition of the death penalty (retribution and deterrence) are not as applicable to minors as to adults?

Key Concepts: The Creation and Evolution of Juvenile Courts

- Juvenile courts were created with the idea that they would be "treatment" oriented for the benefit of the minor, requiring a less formal and adversarial approach for juvenile justice as opposed to the criminal justice system.

- Juvenile justice systems have evolved to more resemble the criminal justice system. This evolution has led courts to hold that more formality and rights should be accorded to juveniles in juvenile court than were previously required.

- Brain science and sociological studies show that minors really are different than adults, justifying treating them different than adults when they break the law.

Chapter II

Status Offenses

Overview: A delinquent act is conduct by a minor that, if committed by an adult, would be a crime. Status offenses are offenses that are based on age: something that would not be a crime for an adult, but is only illegal because of the age of the actor. Recent statistics show that many status offenses lead to court involvement. One recent article published important statistics about status offenses. [Charles Puzzanchera and Sarah Hockenberry, *Juvenile Court Statistics, 2010* (National Center for Juvenile Justice, 2013)]. In 2010, courts were faced with approximately 137,000 cases involving status offenses. Of those cases, 36% were for truancy, 22% for liquor law violations, 12% for "ungovernability," 11% for runaway, 10% for curfew violations, and 9% for miscellaneous status violations. For these status offenses, approximately 10,400 cases resulted in the minor serving at least some time in detention, and in approximately 6,100 cases, the minor was ultimately placed in a longer-term placement in a residential facility.

The status offense that is subject to the greatest amount of litigation is the curfew violation. Many jurisdictions attempt to reduce criminal activity of juveniles by passing curfew ordinances that limit the right of juveniles to be in public during specified hours (usually the nighttime). However, curfew laws directly conflict with constitutional rights such as Freedom of Speech, Freedom of Association, and Freedom of Travel. Courts are required to answer the questions of whether or not the constitutional rights of minors are the same as the constitutional rights of adults and, if not, what are the extent of limitations acceptable on those rights. Curfews also conflict with what the courts have deemed a "fundamental right" of parents to control their children.

In 1974, the Juvenile Justice and Delinquency Prevention Act (JJDPA) was passed by the U.S. Congress. That law provided federal funds for states who prohibited contact between juvenile and criminal offenders in secure institutions and who prohibited placement of status offenders in detention. This law was seen as a barrier for juvenile court judges to enforce their orders with detention. The JJDPA was amended in 1980 in the "Valid Court Order" amendments allowing courts to subject status offenders to commitment to a secure confinement for violation of a court order.

QUTB v. Bartlett: In *QUTB v. Bartlett*, the federal court was faced with a challenge to a curfew ordinance in Dallas Texas. The Dallas curfew ordinance contained numerous exceptions, including when in the company of or on an errand for a parent or guardian, when travelling to employment-related activities, when participating in school, religious or civic functions and generally when exercising First Amendment rights. The city provided statistical evidence showing the rise in juvenile crime and the extent of crime that occurs at night, arguing that the ordinance is justified both to prevent juvenile crime and to protect juveniles from being victims of crimes. This case directly raises the issue of whether or not such a curfew ordinance violates: (1) Equal Protection rights of minors by treating minors differently than adults; (2) the "fundamental right" to move about freely by minors; and (3) the "fundamental right to privacy" for a parent to raise their child as the parent sees fit. The court is forced to determine the level of scrutiny to be afforded to a review of the statute and whether or not the ordinance is narrowly tailored to meet the state interests cited.

As you read *QUTB*, look for the following:

1. While the court quickly concludes that age is not a suspect classification, consider whether or not the court provided any guidance as to which constitutional rights of minors are preserved.

2. The exceptions or defenses in the Dallas ordinance allow the court to find that the ordinance was sufficiently tailored to pass strict scrutiny. Look at the exceptions contained in the ordinance and try to determine which are essential to the conclusion of the court that the ordinance passes strict scrutiny.

3. The court held that parents failed to provide "evidence" that the ordinance impermissibly impinged their rights as parents. Consider what kind of evidence the parent could provide to establish that an ordinance of this nature impinged their rights as a parent.

QUTB v. Bartlett
11 F.3d 488 (5th Cir. 1993)

This appeal presents a challenge to the constitutionality of a nocturnal juvenile curfew ordinance enacted by Dallas, Texas. The ordinance makes it a misdemeanor for persons under the age of seventeen to use the city streets or to be present at other public places within the city between certain hours. Several plaintiffs brought suit against the city to strike down the ordinance. The district court ruled for the plaintiffs, holding that the ordinance violated both the United States and the Texas Constitutions, and permanently enjoined enforcement of the ordinance. The city appeals. Because we conclude that this ordinance does not violate the United States or Texas Constitutions, we reverse the district court.

On June 12, 1991, in response to citizens' demands for protection of the city's youth, the Dallas City Council enacted a juvenile curfew ordinance. This ordinance prohibits persons under seventeen years of age from remaining in a public place or establishment from 11 p.m. until 6 a.m. on week nights, and from 12 midnight until 6 a.m. on weekends. As defined by the ordinance, a "public place" is any place to which the public or a substantial group of the public has access, and includes streets, highways, and the common areas of schools, hospitals, apartment houses, office buildings, transport facilities, and shops. "Establishment" is defined as "any privately-owned place of business operated for a profit to which the public is invited, including but not limited to any place of amusement or entertainment."

Although the ordinance restricts the hours when minors are allowed in public areas, the ordinance also contains a number of exceptions, or defenses. A person under the age of seventeen in a public place during curfew hours does not violate the ordinance if he or she is accompanied by a parent or guardian, or is on an errand for a parent or guardian. Likewise, minors would be allowed in public places if they are in a motor vehicle travelling to or from a place of employment, or if they are involved in employment related activities. Affected minors could attend school, religious, or civic organizational functions— or generally exercise their First Amendment speech and associational rights—without violating the ordinance. Nor is it a violation to engage in interstate travel, or remain on a sidewalk in front of the minor's home, or the home of a neighbor. And finally, the ordinance places no restrictions on a minor's ability to move about during curfew hours in the case of an emergency.

A minor violates the curfew if he or she remains in any public place or on the premises of any establishment during curfew hours, and if the minors' activities are not exempted from coverage. If a minor is apparently violating the ordinance, the ordinance requires police officers to ask the age of the apparent offender, and to inquire into the reasons for being in a public place during curfew hours before taking any enforcement action. An officer may issue a citation or arrest the apparent offender only if the officer reasonably believes that the person has violated the ordinance and that no defenses apply. If convicted, an offending party is subject to a fine not to exceed $500.00 for each separate offense.

Like minors who have violated the offense, a parent of a minor, or an owner, operator, or employee of a business establishment is also subject to a fine not to exceed $500 for each separate offense. A parent or guardian of a minor violates the ordinance if he or she knowingly permits, or by insufficient control allows, a minor child to remain in any public place or on the premises of any establishment during curfew hours. An owner, operator, or employee of a business establishment commits an offense by knowingly allowing a minor to remain upon the premises of the establishment during curfew hours.

The minor plaintiffs argue, *inter alia,* that the curfew ordinance violates the Equal Protection Clause of the Fourteenth Amendment. The Equal Protection Clause "is essentially a direction that all persons similarly situated should be treated alike." Only if the challenged government action classifies or distinguishes between two or more relevant groups must we conduct an equal protection inquiry. Here, it is clear that the curfew ordinance distinguishes between classes of individuals on the basis on age, treating those persons under the age of seventeen differently from those persons age seventeen and older. Because the curfew ordinance distinguishes between two groups, we must analyze the curfew ordinance under the Equal Protection Clause.

In this case, no one has argued, and correctly so, that a classification based on age is a suspect classification. The minor plaintiffs, however, have argued that the curfew ordinance impinges upon their "fundamental right" to move about freely in public. For purposes of our analysis, we assume without deciding that the right to move about freely is a fundamental right. We are mindful, however, that this ordinance is directed solely at the activities of juveniles and, under certain circumstances, minors may be treated differently from adults.

Because we assume that the curfew impinges upon a fundamental right, we will now subject the ordinance to strict scrutiny review. As stated earlier, to survive strict scrutiny, a classification created by the ordinance must promote a compelling governmental interest, and it must be narrowly tailored to achieve this interest. The city's stated interest in enacting the ordinance is to reduce juvenile crime and victimization, while promoting juvenile safety and well-being. The Supreme Court has recognized that the state "has a strong and legitimate interest in the welfare of its young citizens, whose immaturity, inexperience, and lack of judgment may sometimes impair their ability to exercise their rights wisely." In this case, the plaintiffs concede and the district court held that the state's interest in this case is compelling. Given the fact that the state's interest is elevated by the minority status of the affected persons, we have no difficulty agreeing with the parties and with the district court.

In the light of the state's compelling interest in increasing juvenile safety and decreasing juvenile crime, we must now determine whether the curfew ordinance is narrowly tailored to achieve that interest.

Before the district court, the city presented the following statistical information:

1. Juvenile crime increases proportionally with age between ten years old and sixteen years old.

2. In 1989, Dallas recorded 5,160 juvenile arrests, while in 1990 there were 5,425 juvenile arrests. In 1990 there were forty murders, ninety-one sex offenses, 233 robberies, and 230 aggravated assaults committed by juveniles. From January 1991 through April 1991, juveniles were arrested for twenty-one murders, thirty sex offenses, 128 robberies, 107 aggravated assaults, and 1,042 crimes against property.

3. Murders are most likely to occur between 10:00 p.m. and 1:00 a.m. and most likely to occur in apartments and apartment parking lots and streets and highways.

4. Aggravated assaults are most likely to occur between 11:00 p.m. and 1:00 a.m.

5. Rapes are most likely to occur between 1:00 a.m. and 3:00 a.m. and sixteen percent of rapes occur on public streets and highways.

6. Thirty-one percent of robberies occur on streets and highways.

Although the city was unable to provide precise data concerning the number of juveniles who commit crimes during the curfew hours, or the number of juvenile victims of crimes committed during the curfew, the city nonetheless provided sufficient data to demonstrate that the classification created by the ordinance "fits" the state's compelling interest.

Furthermore, we are convinced that this curfew ordinance also employs the least restrictive means of accomplishing its goals. The ordinance contains various "defenses" that allow affected minors to remain in public areas during curfew hours.

In the past, curfew ordinances have been held unconstitutional because of their broad general applications.

With the ordinance before us today, the city of Dallas has created a nocturnal juvenile curfew that satisfies strict scrutiny. By including the defenses to a violation of the ordinance, the city has enacted a narrowly drawn ordinance that allows the city to meet its stated goals while respecting the rights of the affected minors. As the city points out, a juvenile may move about freely in Dallas if accompanied by a parent or a guardian, or a person at least eighteen years of age who is authorized by a parent or guardian to have custody of the minor. If the juvenile is traveling interstate, returning from a school-sponsored function, a civic organization-sponsored function, or a religious function, or going home after work, the ordinance does not apply. If the juvenile is on an errand for his or her parent or guardian, the ordinance does not apply. If the juvenile is involved in an emergency, the ordinance does not apply. If the juvenile is on a sidewalk in front of his or her home *or* the home of a neighbor, the ordinance does not apply. Most notably, if the juvenile is exercising his or her First Amendment rights, the curfew ordinance does not apply.

With due respect to the able district court, we are convinced that upon examination its analysis collapses. It is true, of course, that the curfew ordinance would restrict some late-night activities of juveniles; if indeed it did not, then there would be no purpose in enacting it. But when balanced with the compelling interest sought to be addressed — protecting juveniles and preventing juvenile crime — the impositions are minor. The district court failed to observe that none of the activities it listed are restricted if the juvenile is accompanied by a parent or a guardian. Even if the child is unaccompanied by a parent or a guardian, we can presume that most events such as a "midnight basketball league" or a church youth group outing ordinarily would be organized, sponsored or supervised by an adult or an organization, and these are exceptions to the curfew. Although it is true that in some situations unaccompanied juveniles may be forced to attend early evening features of a movie or leave a play or concert before its conclusion, this imposition is ameliorated by several of the ordinance's defenses so that the juvenile is not deprived of actually attending such cultural and entertainment opportunities. Furthermore, a juvenile can take an "innocent stroll" and stare at the stars until 11:00 on week-nights and until 12:00 midnight on weekends; indeed, a juvenile may stare at the stars all night long from the front sidewalk of his or her home or the home of a neighbor. Thus, after carefully examining the juvenile curfew ordinance enacted by the city of Dallas, we conclude that it is narrowly tailored to address the city's compelling interest and any burden this ordinance places upon minors' constitutional rights will be minimal.

In addition to the claims presented by the minor plaintiffs, the parental plaintiffs argue that the curfew ordinance violates their fundamental right of privacy because it dictates the manner in which their children must be raised. Although we recognize that a parent's right to rear their children without undue governmental interference is a fundamental component of due process, we are convinced that this ordinance presents only a minimal intrusion into the parents' rights. In fact, the only aspect of parenting that this ordinance bears upon is the parents' right to allow the minor to remain in public places, unaccompanied by a parent or guardian or other authorized person, during the hours restricted by the curfew ordinance.

In this case, the parents have failed to convince us that the ordinance will impermissibly impinge on their rights as parents. The parents' only "evidence" to support their argument is the testimony of the mother of one of the plaintiffs that her daughter would soon be going to college, and the curfew ordinance — applying only between 11 p.m. and 6 a.m. — would somehow deprive her daughter of the opportunity to learn to manage her time and make decisions before going away to college. Certainly this testimony is insufficient to support the district court's finding that the ordinance unconstitutionally infringed the liberty and privacy interests of parents.

In conclusion, we find that the state has demonstrated that the curfew ordinance furthers a compelling state interest, *i.e.,* protecting juveniles from crime on the streets. We further conclude that the ordinance is narrowly tailored to achieve this compelling state interest. Accordingly, we hold that the nocturnal juvenile curfew ordinance enacted by the city of Dallas is constitutional.

The judgment of the district court is therefore REVERSED.

Holdings of *QUTB v. Bartlett:* In this case, the court held that, while age is not a "suspect class" the ordinance does impinge a fundamental right to move about freely in public, and, therefore, strict scrutiny applies. This means that there must be a compelling state interest and the law must be narrowly tailored. The ordinance furthers a compelling state interest (reduction of crimes by juveniles and protection juveniles from crime on the streets) and is narrowly tailored to achieve this interest, involving a minimal restriction on the rights of the youth and the parents.

Discussion Questions

What is the state's compelling interest for the curfew?

What are the exceptions that the curfew contained?

What exception(s) is/are the most important one(s) to make the curfew withstand strict scrutiny?

Nunez v. City of San Diego: In *Nunez v. City of San Diego*, the federal court was faced with a challenge to a curfew ordinance in San Diego, California. The ordinance made it unlawful for any minor under the age of 18 to "loiter, idle, wander, stroll or play upon" virtually any "unsupervised place" between the hours of 10 p.m. and daylight. The ordinance contained exceptions for a youth who was: accompanied by a parent, guardian or custodian; on an emergency errand directed by a parent or guardian; returning directly home from a meeting, entertainment or recreational activity of a local educational authority; and where the minor's presence is require employment or trade-related activities. There was not a "broad First Amendment" exception. Violations subjected the minor, parent, guardian or custodian to criminal liability. The city cited national crime statistics as well as some local statistics showing that recently there was a rise in juvenile crime during the curfew hours.

As you read *Nunez,* look for the following:

1. Identify the language in the San Diego ordinance that led to a different result for that in Dallas.

2. Compare the language about Equal Protection claims (treating people differently based on age) of the *Nunez* case to the *QUTB* case.

3. Examine the *Nunez* opinion to determine if the result would have been different if the ordinance left out the "loiter, idle, wander, stroll or play" language or used language that was less ambiguous.

Nunez v. City of San Diego
114 F.3d 935 (9th Cir. 1997)

WIGGINS, Circuit Judge.

Plaintiffs challenge the constitutionality of the City of San Diego's juvenile curfew ordinance. The district court granted summary judgment for the City, and plaintiffs appealed. We reverse.

THE ORDINANCE

The City of San Diego enacted its juvenile curfew ordinance in 1947. The ordinance reads as follows:

> It shall be unlawful for any minor under the age of eighteen (18) years, to loiter, idle, wander, stroll or play in or upon the public streets, highways, roads, alleys, parks, playgrounds, wharves, docks, or other public grounds, public places and public buildings, places of amusement and entertainment, vacant lots or other unsupervised places, between the hours of ten o'clock P.M. and daylight immediately following....

San Diego, Cal., Municipal Code Art. 8, § 58.01. The ordinance then provides that the curfew does not apply in four situations:

> (1) "when the minor is accompanied by his or her parents, guardian, or other adult person having the care and custody of the minor,"

> (2) "when the minor is upon an emergency errand directed by his or her parent or guardian or other adult person having the care and custody of the minor,"

(3) "when the minor is returning directly home from a meeting, entertainment or recreational activity directed, supervised or sponsored by the local educational authorities," or "when the presence of such minor in said place or places is connected with and required by some legitimate business, trade, profession or occupation in which said minor is lawfully engaged."

A minor violating § 58.01 commits a misdemeanor. Section 58.01.1 also creates criminal liability for the "parent, guardian or other adult person having the care and custody of a minor" who permits or allows the minor to violate the curfew ordinance. On April 25, 1994, the City adopted a resolution to enforce the curfew aggressively.

Plaintiffs are minors and parents of minors from San Diego. They brought an action under 42 U.S.C. § 1983 to challenge the ordinance's constitutionality on its face. Plaintiff minors allege, among other things, that the ordinance restricts them from many otherwise lawful activities after curfew hours, i.e., volunteering at a homeless shelter, attending concerts as a music critic, studying with other students, meeting with friends at their homes or in coffee houses, stopping at a restaurant to eat dinner after serving on the School District Board, auditioning for theater parts, attending ice hockey practice, practicing astronomy, and dancing at an under-21 dance club. Plaintiff parents allege that the ordinance impinges upon their ability to rear their children as they wish because they and their children would face misdemeanor liability under the curfew.

In this case, we find that the ordinance suffers constitutional deficiencies regardless of which of the two proffered interpretations of the basic prohibition is accepted. We conclude that no construction is "fairly possible that will contain the statute within constitutional grounds." As explained below, giving the ordinance's general prohibition a narrow construction renders it unconstitutionally vague. Under a broader construction, the ordinance does not survive strict scrutiny because it is not narrowly tailored to meet the City's compelling interests.

For the reasons explained below, we conclude that the plain language of the ordinance when read as a whole is vague. We reject the argument that the ordinance is saved by a narrowing construction of the phrase "loiter, wander, idle, stroll or play" made by the California courts because that construction itself does not survive constitutional scrutiny on vagueness grounds.

The phrase "loiter, wander, idle, stroll or play" uses imprecise terms. As a result, serious vagueness problems exist if "loiter, wander, idle, stroll or play" covers a narrower range of conduct than "presence," unless a sufficiently definite narrowing construction is given

We cannot accept as constitutionally definite the district court's construction of the ordinance. The district court concluded that "loiter, wander, idle, stroll or play" means "hanging out." The district court did not explain its meaning further, except to say that it "requires a degree of aimlessness." The problem with narrowing constructions such as "hanging out" and "aimless conduct" is that they are as inherently vague as the phrase "loiter, wander, idle, stroll or play" itself.

Examination of the ordinance's enumerated "exceptions" highlights the indefiniteness of the phrase "loiter, wander, idle, stroll or play." If the ordinance's general prohibition only proscribes "hanging out" or "aimlessness," then three of the ordinance's four enumerated exceptions are surplusage

Thus, examining California law makes it clear that the phrase "loiter, wander, idle, stroll or play" taken as a whole means something different than "presence," but what the relevant difference is remains unclear.

The narrow construction of the ordinance offered by the City is irreducibly subjective and renders most of the exceptions incoherent. Thus, we conclude that the phrase "loiter, wander, idle, stroll or play" is unconstitutionally vague.

Plaintiffs challenge the curfew ordinance under the Equal Protection Clause of the Fourteenth Amendment. The standard for reviewing the constitutionality of an ordinance depends on the right or classification involved.

The City and its amici contend that these are not fundamental rights for minors because minors are traditionally treated differently than adults. The City heavily relies on *Vernonia Sch. Dist. v. Acton* to show that "unemancipated minors lack some of the most fundamental rights of self-determination — including even the right of liberty in its narrow sense, i.e., the right to come and go at will." The City takes Vernonia's statement out of context. In the next sentence the Court explains that children "are subject, even as to their physical freedom, to the control of their parents or guardians." Because parental power is not subject to the constitutional constraints of state power, minors' lack of rights vis-a-vis parents does not necessarily show that they lack those rights vis-a-vis the state. The Court emphasized the school district's "custodial and tutelary responsibility for children," noting that constitutional rights are different in public schools than elsewhere. We decline to extend Vernonia to establish that the Constitution does not secure minors' fundamental right to free movement against the government acting without regard to the parents' wishes.

Although many federal courts have recognized that juvenile curfews implicate the fundamental rights of minors, the parties dispute whether strict scrutiny review is necessary. The Supreme Court teaches that rights are no less "fundamental" for minors than adults, but that the analysis of those rights may differ:

Constitutional rights do not mature and come into being magically only when one attains the state-defined age of majority. Minors, as well as adults, are protected by the Constitution and possess constitutional rights. The Court indeed, however, long has recognized that the State has somewhat broader authority to regulate the activities of children than of adults. It remains, then, to examine whether there is any significant state interest in [the effect of the statute] that is not present in the case of an adult.

Thus, minors' rights are not coextensive with the rights of adults because the state has a greater range of interests that justify the infringement of minors' rights.

The Supreme Court has articulated three specific factors that, when applicable, warrant differential analysis of the constitutional rights of minors and adults: (1) the peculiar vulnerability of children; (2) their inability to make critical decisions in an informed, mature manner; and (3) the importance of the parental role in child rearing.

Although the state may have a compelling interest in regulating minors differently than adults, we do not believe that this lesser degree of scrutiny is appropriate to review burdens on minors' fundamental rights. Thus, the district court erred in stating that minors' "circumscribed" liberty interest was not fundamental and could be subjected to intermediate scrutiny. The district court nevertheless correctly decided to apply strict scrutiny, despite its conclusion that a lower level of scrutiny was permissible.

Accordingly, we apply strict scrutiny to our review of the ordinance. In applying this standard, we are mindful that strict scrutiny in the context of minors may allow greater burdens on minors than would be permissible on adults as a result of the unique interests implicated in regulating minors.

The ostensible purposes of the ordinance identified by the City in its brief are to protect children from nighttime dangers, to reduce juvenile crime, and to involve parents in control of their children. At oral argument, the City admitted that its "compelling inter-est is, quite frankly, to reduce gang activity." As the City also admits, however, the ordi-nance is not limited to gang activities.

The City has a compelling interest in protecting the entire community from crime, including juvenile crime. The City's interest in protecting the safety and welfare of its mi-nors is also a compelling interest. The fact that much of the perceived danger stems from gang activity does not lessen the nature of the City's interest in protecting the safety and welfare of minors, although it may affect the analysis of whether the ordinance is nar-rowly tailored, as discussed below in Part II.B(2).

As other courts have recognized, *Bellotti* does not set forth reasons that always justify greater restrictions on minors than adults; rather, *Bellotti* sets forth factors for deter-mining whether the government has a greater justification for restricting minors than adults in the manner at issue. Our consideration of the *Bellotti* factors leads to the con-clusion that greater restrictions of minors may be justified because they have a greater vulnerability at night than do adults and because minors are not equally able as adults to make mature decisions regarding the safety of themselves and others. Some courts have reached the opposite conclusion. We agree with those courts that all citizens are vulner-able to crime at night and that minors' participation in many legitimate activities does not involve the kind of profound decisions of concern in *Bellotti*. Nonetheless, we find it un-exceptional for the City to conclude that minors are more susceptible to the dangers of the night and are generally less equipped to deal with danger that does arise. Thus, the City may have a compelling interest in placing greater restrictions on minors than adults to insure the minors' own safety.

In sum, we find that the City has a compelling interest in reducing juvenile crime and juvenile victimization. We analyze below whether the particular restrictions of the ordi-nance are narrowly tailored to meet that interest.

Plaintiffs offer two reasons why the ordinance is not narrowly tailored: (1) the record reflects little statistical support for the efficacy of the curfew; and (2) the exceptions are too narrow to protect minors' fundamental rights.

(a) Statistical Support for Curfew

The City offered several statistical reports to demonstrate that the juvenile curfew is a solution to rising juvenile crime and victimization.

The first piece of evidence is a Justice Department report on juvenile offenders and victims. It shows a rising juvenile crime rate in the nation as a whole but does not pro-vide information specific to San Diego. It also shows that juvenile crime peaks at 3 p.m. and again around 6 p.m. We accept the relevancy of the national crime statistics regard-ing the general increase of dangers to minors and others, but the national statistics do not conclusively show that the nocturnal juvenile curfew is a narrowly tailored solution.

Second, the City provided the local statistics regarding juvenile crime and victimiza-tion; our review of this evidence yields mixed results. The City's October 3, 1994, reso-lution to continue the aggressive enforcement policy stated that the violent crimes and juvenile activity had decreased during curfew hours from the previous year. In contrast, a San Diego Police Department report dated August 16, 1995, stated that violent crimes had decreased for the third year in a row and that total crime decreased for the sixth con-secutive year, thus weakening any link to the increased enforcement of the curfew that began in June 1994. The 1995 report also reveals that the percentage of juvenile victim-ization that occurred during curfew hours slightly increased in the year following the curfew initiative, that the decrease in overall victimization for adults was larger than for minors, and that only 15% of arrests for violent juvenile crimes occurred during curfew hours. The 1996 version of the Police Department's report better supports the City, revealing that from the first quarter of 1995 to 1996 the percentage of victimization that occurred during curfew hours dropped and showing a greater increase in arrests for violent crimes during curfew hours than during other hours.

Overall, the statistical evidence provides some, but not overwhelming, support for the proposition that a curfew will help reduce crime. The City makes little showing, however, that the nocturnal, juvenile curfew is a particularly effective means of achieving that reduction.

On the other hand, we reject the City's further justification that the ordinance has the additional beneficial deterrent effect of permitting police officers to get juveniles off the streets before crimes are committed. The Supreme Court has sharply critiqued this type of rationale as overinclusive, at least with respect to adults. Furthermore, the relatively light penalties imposed by the curfew are a small deterrent to crime when compared to the penalties for the actual crimes that the curfew ostensibly seeks to thwart.

(b) The Scope of the Exceptions

Clearly, San Diego could have enacted a narrower curfew ordinance that would pass constitutional muster. Its present ordinance is problematic because it does not provide exceptions for many legitimate activities, with or without parental permission. This is true even though minors may be uniquely vulnerable at night; the curfew's blanket coverage restricts participation in, and travel to or from, many legitimate recreational activities even those that may not expose their special vulnerability. In this regard, it is significant that San Diego rejected a proposal to tailor the ordinance more narrowly by adopting the broader exceptions used in the ordinance upheld in Qutb. The City's failure to provide adequate exceptions not only excessively burdens minors' right to free movement, but it also excessively burdens their right to free speech.

We therefore conclude that the City has not shown that the curfew is a close fit to the problem of juvenile crime and victimization because the curfew sweeps broadly, with few exceptions for otherwise legitimate activity. The broad sweep of the ordinance is particularly marked for an ordinance aimed, as the City admitted, at illegal gang activity. The district court in Waters eloquently explained the constitutional difficulty with a juvenile curfew lacking adequate exceptions:

We now explain our conclusion regarding plaintiff minors' fundamental First Amendment rights, which are incorporated against the states by the Fourteenth Amendment. Specifically, we address whether the ordinance's restrictions on legitimate exercise of minors' First Amendment rights makes the ordinance unconstitutionally overbroad.

Minors, like adults, have a fundamental right to freedom of expression. Expression includes speech and expressive conduct. Thus, a facial First Amendment challenge to an ordinance can be brought against regulation of "spoken words" or where a statute by its terms regulates the time, place and manner of expressive or communicative conduct.

The San Diego ordinance is a general regulation of conduct, not speech. It does not disproportionately burden those engaged in First Amendment activities more than it burdens other activities during curfew hours; the curfew applies to minors regardless of whether they seek to exercise their right to free expression. The ordinance does, however, restrict minors' ability to engage in many First Amendment activities during curfew hours.

San Diego's curfew ordinance restricts access to any and all public forums.

San Diego's broader restriction prohibits conduct that is a necessary precursor to most public expression—thus qualifying as conduct "commonly associated with" expression.

For First Amendment purposes, the physical and psychological well-being of minors is a compelling government interest. Thus, the ordinance must be narrowly tailored to achieve that interest. We hold the ordinance is not narrowly tailored because it does not sufficiently exempt legitimate First Amendment activities from the curfew. The City did not create a robust, or even minimal, First Amendment exception to permit minors to express themselves during curfew hours without the supervision of a parent or guardian, apparently preferring instead to have no First Amendment exception at all. This is not narrow tailoring. The ordinance is not a reasonable time, place, and manner restriction under the First Amendment.

Examination of the ordinance's burden on the fundamental rights of the minors' parents provides an independent basis for our conclusion that the ordinance, even if construed to avoid vagueness, is nonetheless unconstitutional. It violates the plaintiff parents' substantive due process rights.

The right to rear children without undue governmental interference is a fundamental component of due process. Substantive due process under the Fourteenth Amendment "forbids the government to infringe certain 'fundamental' liberty interests at all, no matter what process is provided, unless the infringement is narrowly tailored to serve a compelling government interest."

The custody, care, and nurture of a child reside first in his or her parents. Parental rights are not absolute, however, and are subject to reasonable regulation. The City's interest in the health, safety, and welfare of minors is compelling, as analyzed above.

The curfew is, quite simply, an exercise of sweeping state control irrespective of parents' wishes. Without proper justification, it violates upon the fundamental right to rear children without undue interference. The ordinance is not a permissible "supportive" law, but rather an undue, adverse interference by the state. The ordinance does not allow an adult to pre-approve even a specific activity after curfew hours unless a custodial adult actually accompanies the minor. Thus, parents cannot allow their children to function independently at night, which some parents may believe is part of the process of growing up. Accordingly, we find the ordinance to be an unconstitutional burden on parents' fundamental rights.

We reverse the judgment below because we hold that the ordinance is unconstitutional. When construed in a way that avoids unconstitutional vagueness, it is not narrowly tailored to minimize the burden on minors' fundamental constitutional rights. The district court shall enter judgment for plaintiffs.

REVERSED.

Holdings of *Nunez v. City of San Diego:* In this case, the court held that the phrase "loiter, wander, idle, stroll or play" is unconstitutionally vague and the definitions supplied by the lower court ("hanging out" and "aimless conduct") are as vague as the phrase itself. The court held that this vagueness is highlighted by the fact that most of the exceptions would be unnecessary if the phrase was as clear and limited as argued. The court also held that the rights of the minors are fundamental and require strict scrutiny and that the City has a compelling interest in reducing juvenile crime and victimization. The court found that there is some (but not overwhelming) evidence supporting the claim that the curfew ordinance will reduce crime. The court rejected the claim that the ordinance has a deterrence effect, because of the over-inclusiveness of the approach and due to the insignificant penalties imposed. The court held that the ordinance is not narrowly tailored because the exceptions do not cover many legitimate activities with or without parental permission and that the ordinance also restricts the rights of minors to engage in many First Amendment activities during curfew hours. Furthermore, the court held that the ordinance is also a broad, sweeping control that violates parents' fundamental rights to rear their children without undue governmental interference.

Discussion Questions

How are the statistics relied upon in *Nunez* any less relevant than those relied upon by *QUTB*?

Would this curfew have survived if they had a general First Amendment exception like there was present in *QUTB*?

What additional arguments did the parents advance in *Nunez* that were not advanced in *QUTB* to result in a different outcome for the parents' claim?

Cox v. Turley: In *Cox v. Turley,* the United States Court of Appeals for the Sixth Circuit was faced with a case where the father of a 16-year-old son who was arrested for a curfew violation claimed that his son's constitutional rights were violated when he was arrested, denied many due process rights, and was confined in an adult facility. The court held that his due process rights were violated and that confinement of a juvenile with adult criminal defendants constituted cruel and unusual punishment.

As you read *Cox v. Turley,* look for the following:

1. Observe the court's review of the historical aspects of juvenile courts and the impact that the *Gault* decision had on review of the claims of violations of rights by juveniles.

2. Consider whether the Court is holding that juveniles can never be confined with adults.

3. Consider whether or not the fact that the case was a "status offense" (a curfew violation) as opposed to a delinquent case (a violation of the criminal code) played any role in shaping the court's decision.

Cox v. Turley
506 F.2d 1347 (6th Cir. 1974)

Mcallister, Senior Circuit Judge.

This is an appeal from an order of the District Court dismissing plaintiff's complaint for injunctive and declaratory relief for defendants' alleged violation of plaintiff's rights under the Fourth Amendment, the Eighth Amendment, and the due process and equal protection clause of the Fourteenth Amendment of the Constitution of the United States.

The complaint was brought by Thomas Cox, on behalf of his 16-year-old son, Duane Cox, and on behalf of all other juveniles residing within the confines of Madison County, Kentucky; the parents of all juveniles so situated; all juveniles who will be within the confines of Madison County, and the parents of all juveniles so situated.

The District Court held that the plaintiff failed to carry his burden of proof that the class he represented was deprived of rights guaranteed by the Federal Constitution.

This is a juvenile case. The Juvenile Court is a comparatively new institution. It is surprising so little is known about it.

"A new generation of lawyers, judges, social workers, and other professionals has come into being since the juvenile court was founded."

"The stream of reform that culminated in creating the first state-wide juvenile court in Illinois on July 1, 1899, sprang from such apparently disparate headwaters as the activity of philanthropic associations on behalf of street urchins, waifs, and wayward and misdemeanant youngsters; the growth of laws preventing cruelty to children and rescuing the dependent and neglected ... Most would agree with Judge Julian Mack that a crucial element was lacking prior to the passage of the Act: "What we did not have was the conception that a child that broke the law was to be dealt with by the state as a wise parent would deal with a wayward child."

In the case of *In Re Gault*, Mr. Justice Fortas, speaking for the Court said:

"The juvenile Court movement began in this country at the end of the last century. From the juvenile court statute adopted in Illinois in 1899, the system has spread to every State in the Union, the District of Columbia, and Puerto Rico ... The early reformers were appalled by adult procedures and penalties, and by the fact that children could be given long prison sentences and mixed in jails with hardened criminals."

And, in the same case, Mr. Justice Stewart observed:

"In the last 70 years many dedicated men and women have devoted their professional lives to the enlightened task of bringing us out of the dark world of Charles Dickens in meeting our responsibilities to the child in our society."

In some jurisdictions where the police operate a detention home in cases where the child is unable to be turned over to his parents, police are entrusted with deciding whether or not the arrested child should be detained. Teeters and Reineman, *The Challenge of Delinquency; Causation, Treatment, and Prevention of Juvenile Delinquency* (New York; Prentice-Hall, 1950, p. 228).

"Most detention homes violate the very principles of mental hygiene which were violated in the child's own home—denial of love and emotional security, lack of meaningful activity, little opportunity to make successful choices, and so forth." Sherman R. Norman. 'The Detention Home,' *Annals of the American Academy of Political and Social Science*, CCXLI (January 1949) p. 161.

"Outright cruelty is not unknown in some of the country's detention centers, to say nothing of dismal, crowded quarters and a staff calloused in spirit by overwork and inadequate facilities. In the case of children detained in such an institution, who are charged but not yet adjudicated as delinquents, the mockery is deplorable enough. It is outrageous in the case of neglected and dependent children; yet such occurrences are not infrequent."

To return to the facts of the present cause, the case arises out of the following circumstances as alleged by appellant: Duane Cox, a boy 16 years old, was walking down a street in the town of Richmond in Madison County, Kentucky, on a summer evening, Saturday, August 12, 1972. He was doing nothing to attract attention and, apparently, was only visiting the town in the county in which his cousin lived, adjoining the one in which he lived with his parents. A police officer arrested the boy for violation of the curfew law, took him to the Madison County jail and lodged him there on the verbal telephoned orders of defendant, Robert Turley, a non-lawyer judge, in charge of such juvenile affairs, as is the established custom of the defendants. When the boy was taken to jail, he asked for the right to telephone his father, to tell him where he was, and of his need for help. This request of the boy was abruptly refused. The boy was then lodged with the jailer of the Madison County jail. There was no hearing of any kind before the boy was turned over to the jailer.

The police officer who arrested the boy did not notify the parents or release the boy with a written promise to appear at a specified time, as provided by the Kentucky Statutes. The boy was not taken before any judicial officer before his incarceration.

On the fifth day after the arrest and imprisonment Defendant Robert Turley, the non-lawyer judge, had the boy brought before him. There is no record of what was said, as the case comes before us only on the pleadings, briefs and Joint Appendix. All that appears is that when the boy came before the judge, he was ordered to have a hair-cut, to shave his beard, and to appear before him a week later, on August 25, 1972, to show that such action had been taken. The boy was then released to his father with a promise to return on the above-mentioned date. The order of the court was obviously unlawful and arbitrary.

After the boy had complied with this order, he was released to his father, pending juvenile court proceedings—about which nothing so far has been done.

The boy in this case was never arraigned. The boy was denied his federal constitutional rights by being deprived of his liberty without due process of law. He was simply arrested and taken to jail, placed in the hands of the turnkey, and then confined with the general prison population.

As to the observation that the boy was confined to a jail cell with no contact whatever with other offenders, either adult or juvenile, the record does not show the boy's confinement to a cell but rather imprisonment in an "adult jail facility." It is almost unthinkable that a boy would be locked in a cell in solitary confinement from Saturday night to Wednesday morning, incommunicado, for the offense of being out after curfew, and plaintiff makes no suggestion that such monstrous mistreatment was indulged in. If the boy was confined in "an adult jail facility," as contended by plaintiff, it may be that he was confined to a cell at night, as prisoners usually are. But prisoners in a prison or jail mingle with each other on various and numerous occasions, and it is this intermingling of juvenile and adult offenders that the law forcefully commands shall not be permitted by prison or jail authorities. Courts take judicial notice that a general prison population includes criminals of all types, young and old, dangerous, of every character. And the courts also particularly take judicial notice that it is not uncommon to find the indiscriminate mixing of hardened criminals, including sexual assaulters, with young offenders.

It is to be observed that in many of the jails in this Circuit—federal as well as state—judges have forbidden the police to imprison arrested juveniles with the general prison population because of the danger to them of association with hardened criminals and to protect them from sexual assaults.

In the accompanying opinion, it is observed that:

"No court, to my knowledge, has ever held that confinement of a juvenile in a county jail for the comparatively brief period of five days without the benefit of recreational or educational facilities, or psychological treatment programs, or books or reading materials, constituted cruel and unusual punishment."

As I see it, this is not the point or issue on which the disposition of this case depends. In the first place, the juvenile was held, without charge or arraignment, in the county jail contrary to the state law—and the county judge and police knew he was being held in violation of the state law; and the boy was further being held in the jail in derogation of his rights under the federal constitution.

To clarify the problem, the 'cruel and unusual punishment' in this case does not reside in the above-quoted language of the concurring opinion. Rather, it is the ever-present peril of dangerous assault upon both the body and mind of the boy that is one of the constituents of cruelty that comes from confining this young boy with the general prison population. It is well known that the younger the boy who is confined, the more immediate is the danger to him. All of the foregoing is well illustrated by reference to the Reader's Digest issue of November, 1973. That issue carried an account of an interview concerning child arrests that casts a baleful light on the problem before us. Donald Robinson was interviewing Milton G. Rector, President of the National Council on Crime and Delinquency. In answer to the question, "Can you teach a child a lesson by letting him stay in jail a couple of nights?" Mr. Rector answered:

"No child deserves that kind of lesson. Being in jail is a traumatizing experience for youngsters. Some are brutalized. Some hurt themselves. All are further alienated from their parents. Just recently, a case came across my desk of a 17-year-old college freshman, who was arrested because police found marijuana in his dormitory room. The boy's father let the police keep him in jail overnight. When he got there in the morning, the boy's nose was broken and both his eyes blackened—the result of a fight begun when older, tougher prisoners tried to gang-rape the younger boys." What To Do If Your Child Is Arrested, Reader's Digest, Nov. 1973, pp. 167–168.

No notice was given him or his parents of the cause of his arrest. There was no probable cause hearing. The due process clause requires that notice of the charge must be given to the accused at the earliest practicable time and, in any event, sufficiently in advance of scheduled court proceedings so that reasonable opportunity to prepare will be afforded, and it must "set forth the alleged misconduct with particularity." It is said by counsel for appellees that there was no need to charge the boy because he knew the reason for his arrest. It may be probable that the defendant in this case was perfectly aware of the offense with which he was charged. It appears that he consented to go to trial, but a trial of what did he consent to? He was arrested and held in custody under the process of the court. It was his right to be informed, and it was the duty of the government to inform him of the accusation against him. This is done by arraignment and requiring the defendant to plead.

A boy 16 years old is not to be slighted and his rights bandied about because of his youth by a lay judge who knows nothing of the treatment to be accorded citizens, due to his lack of experience and training in the rigorous discipline of the law. There is something rather offensive to moral decency in considering the police officer telephoning the judge that he had arrested the boy, and the judge's immediate consent that the boy be forthwith locked up in the jail, without the right to call his father—all in violation of the law. It is difficult to define the relationship between the judge, the police officer, and the turnkey, as anything else but a well-understood collusion and connivance, and avoidance of the law.

A boy 16 years old is not to be slighted and ignored by a court because of his youth, and he is not to be arrested, denied the right to call his father or counsel, imprisoned without a charge placed against him, and without even being arraigned, any more than a judge of this court is to be so treated for a trivial misdemeanor. Of course, an adult could recover his freedom by writ of habeas corpus, which right the child, in this case, does not, incongruously and incompatibly, have—because of the duty of the state to protect him during these tender years, in every way, protecting him against being imprisoned with the general prison population, placing him immediately in the custody of his parents until his case is called—none of which was observed in this case.

The action taken by the judge, police, and jail authorities in this case, in derogation of the constitutional rights of an American citizen, is not to be gently tolerated by this court, because of niceties of pleading.

The boy was deprived of his constitutional rights under the due process clause by reason of his confinement with the general jail population without a charge lodged against him, without being arraigned, and without being taken before any judicial officer, "at the earliest practicable time" as prescribed in the case of *In Re Gault*, and without being given any notice of his alleged offense. Moreover, the officer's refusal to permit the boy to make a telephone call to his parents when he was taken to jail, and the refusal of the arresting officer to notify the boy's parents, as commanded by the Kentucky statutes, together with his confinement with the general jail population without a probable cause hearing, constituted cruel and unusual punishment, in violation of the boy's rights under the Eighth Amendment to the Federal Constitution.

The ordinary man can well contemplate the state of mind of this boy, arrested by a police officer, taken to jail, refused the right to call his parents to tell them where he was, turned over to the turnkey to be incarcerated with the jail population, in which it is not uncommon to find the indiscriminate mixing of hardened criminals, including degenerates, with young offenders—for a period of five days, with no way of communicating with relatives or friends.

What Judge Feinberg said in *Sostre v. McGinnis*, is here applicable:

"What might once have been acceptable does not necessarily determine what is 'cruel and unusual' today ... In this Orwellian age, punishment that endangers sanity, no less than physical injury by the strap, is prohibited by the Constitution. Indeed, we have learned ... that true inhumanity seeks to destroy the psyche rather than merely the body."

As Dean Francis A. Allen, in his admirable book, 'The Borderland of Criminal Justice,' states on page 37:

"There is one proposition which, if generally understood, would contribute more to clear thinking on these matters than any other. It is not a new insight. Garafalo asserted: 'The mere deprivation of liberty, however benign the administration of the place of confinement, is undeniably punishment.'"

The worst and most illegal feature of all these proceedings is in lodging the child with the general population of the jail, without his ever seeing some official of the court.

Judge Orman W. Ketcham, Judge of the Juvenile Court of the District of Columbia, Member of the Executive Committee, Advisory Council of Judges, National Council on Crime and Delinquency, formerly with the Department of Justice, in a contribution to a brilliantly-edited symposium on the subject by Margaret K. Rosenheim, Professor of Social Service Administration, University of Chicago, Justice for the Child, says:

"Prohibition against Use of Jails. During adolescence a child is presumed to be most impressionable. Consequently, it has long been recognized that a child's close contact with an adult can serve either a good or a bad purpose depending on the proclivities of the adult. With this in mind, the state promises that no child will be imprisoned or placed in a jail or lockup lest the state abet the downfall of a child by confining him with adult offenders. It also promises that the child will not otherwise be brought into contact with adult criminals or commingled with vicious or immoral persons."

It is astonishing that, although the trivial violation of the rule of curfew was committed by a 16-year-old boy (and it is difficult to imagine a more trivial violation), he has been subjected to all the various violations of law by the authorities. When he finally appeared before the juvenile judge, after confinement in jail with the common criminal population from Saturday evening until the following Wednesday, he was told by the judge to have his hair cut and was then released to his father. But the release to his father was merely to continue the custody of the boy, still subject to the court for trial on the violation of the curfew. That was on Wednesday, August 16, 1972, but the charge of violation of the curfew is still pending on this trivial matter — nearly twenty months after his appearance before the judge. There appears no possible reason for the court's continuing such custody. To continue and keep continuing this custody for twenty months after what the boy has gone through, seems an inexplicable injustice. Both the Fourth Amendment and the Fifth Amendment were violated because there was no prompt determination of probable cause — a constitutional mandate that protects juveniles as well as adults. The fact that a juvenile who was arrested was not deprived of his freedom but was left in the custody of his mother did not remove him from the protection of the Fourth Amendment, and he was entitled to a hearing to determine if there was probable cause to hold him for trial. The right to be free of a seizure of one's person made without probable cause does not depend upon the character of the subsequent custody.

In discussing a holding by a District Court that once a plea of guilty is accepted by a court of competent jurisdiction, jeopardy immediately attached as a result of proceedings in the Juvenile Court, the United States Court of Appeals stated:

"The District Court relied on some early state cases … But those cases throw little light on the issue before us. They are traditional criminal proceedings, which are essentially accusatory, adversary and punitive. Consequently, they involve considerations which are not relevant to the non-criminal *parens patriae* proceedings of the Juvenile Court." *United States v. Dickerson*.

In commenting on the above, Judge Paul W. Alexander of the Common Pleas Court of Lucas County, Ohio, stated:

"These trenchant last words leave little more to be said. In our American culture, there are now four institutions, each charged with certain distinctive responsibilities in the upbringing of children in the way they should go. They are home, church, school and juvenile court, the latter said by Roscoe Pound to be the greatest forward step in Anglo-American jurisprudence since the Magna Charta. To deny the juvenile court a fair trial is to deny the child himself a fair trial. To deprive the court of its rightful status, to impair its potential effectiveness is to deprive a child of not merely constitutional rights but of many invaluable rights regarded as the birthright of every American child. It is like denying a sick child the right to a good hospital … Justice to a child must be more than due process of law and fair legal treatment. No abstract right can be as sacred as a human child."

There is provision in Kentucky Revised Statutes, 208.110(3) requiring the peace officer who has taken the child into custody to notify the parents and to release the child to his parents, "unless the nature of the offense or other circumstances are such as to indicate the necessity of keeping the child in secure custody, or unless other directions have been given by the court." No notification was given to the parents in this case. It must be conceded that the nature of his offense or of any other circumstances was not such as to indicate the necessity of keeping the child in secure custody. When taken to the jail, the child asked to be allowed to telephone his father, or to have someone telephone his father to tell him where he was and what had happened to him. This request was absolutely re-fused. In any case, a person arrested is allowed one telephone call to his family, or friends, or lawyer. The only excuse for not allowing the child to call his father when he was arrested must then be that other directions were given by the court. The willingness of the court to order confinement without having seen or heard from the boy and without having personally observed his conduct or his character, indicates to us that his order was not merely an isolated act, but instead the usual treatment given to all juveniles arrested for being out after curfew. Where a judge adopts the same treatment for all persons having committed a similar offense, however trivial, such treatment is summary and arbitrary and must be set aside.

It is emphasized by counsel for defendants that the boy was charged with violation of state statutes, and it is not within the jurisdiction of a federal court to pass upon the va-lidity of state statutes; but, in this case, the violation of the state statutes constituted a vi-olation of the boy's rights under the Federal Constitution.

We are of the opinion that the constitutional rights of plaintiff's son were violated, as heretofore set forth. By failing to arraign the boy and by keeping him in custody, deny-ing him any rights to communicate with his parents, and without releasing the boy to his parents in accordance with the Kentucky statutes, and by failing to give notice of the cause of his arrest within the earliest practicable time, he was deprived of his liberty in viola-tion of the Fourth and Fifth Amendments of the Federal Constitution.

The judgment of the District Court is set aside and the case remanded. On the hear-ing on remand, the District Court may take such evidence from either party as appears proper and make such findings as the court deems appropriate.

William E. Miller, Circuit Judge (concurring in the result).

The complaint in this action was filed as a class action seeking injunctive, declaratory and general relief, because of the defendants' alleged violation of plaintiff's rights under the Fourth Amendment, the Eighth Amendment and the equal protection and due process clauses of the Fourteenth Amendment to the Constitution of the United States.

It is thus clear that the complaint does not challenge the right of the State of Kentucky to prosecute Duane Cox on the curfew charge, nor does it seek to nullify or enjoin the pend-ing state court prosecution on such charge. Neither does the complaint in any manner seek a declaration that the state court proceeding against the juvenile for the alleged violation of Kentucky law is void.

Judge McAllister's opinion makes only passing reference to the use of non-lawyers as juvenile court judges, and I do not construe the opinion to hold that this practice is of-fensive to any requirement of the federal constitution. Nevertheless, it is clear that Judge McAllister's opinion, in rather sharp terms at least, adversely criticizes the practice with-out actually ruling that it is unconstitutional. On this point, since the opinions remands the case to the district court for appropriate findings, I construe it to mean that the issue of non-lawyer juvenile court judges is left open so that the district court on remand will be free to make an independent determination. However, I am not prepared at this time to express an opinion or to join in the implied criticism of the Kentucky practice, in ef-fect in at least certain areas of that state and in general use to a large extent throughout the United States.

It is, of course, well settled that a juvenile, like an adult, is entitled to a probable cause hearing before being arrested and detained on a criminal charge, preferably before in-carceration or at least within a reasonable time thereafter. While the facts alleged in the complaint would tend to indicate that the juvenile in this case was not accorded a probable cause hearing within a reasonable time, I am of the opinion that no definitive ruling should be made on this point until, on remand, the district court has conducted an evidentiary hearing to determine the circumstances under which the arrest was made and under which the plaintiff was held in confinement. The question of reasonableness should be determined on the basis of the individualized facts of each case. We will be in better position to evaluate the facts in regard to this aspect of the case after the district court has conducted an evidentiary hearing and made appropriate and detailed findings of fact and conclusions of law.

In my view, the opinion of Judge McAllister goes much too far in dealing with cruel and unusual punishment. The opinion may even be read to reflect an outright holding that a juvenile is subjected to cruel and unusual punishment in any case where he is confined in an adult jail facility. I do not agree with this conclusion. The exact nature and circumstances of the confinement of the juvenile in each case must be determined before a court would be in position to say that the juvenile had been subjected to cruel and unusual punishment. The mere fact of confinement in an adult jail facility, particularly in a small county jail like the one in Madison County, Kentucky, is not sufficient in and of itself to warrant a finding of cruel and unusual punishment. I do not agree that there is anything in the present record to justify the inference repetitively indicated in the opinion, that the juvenile was thrown in with the 'general prison population,' if there was such a population at the time in this small county jail. We certainly are not warranted in taking judicial notice of any particular condition in the Madison County, Kentucky, jail nor to conclude without proof that the juvenile in this case was required to be exposed to adult or hardened criminals. We simply do not know the conditions of the juvenile's confinement, and we should not express an opinion until the facts have been established. Most clearly the complaint does not depict the conditions of the youth's actual confinement in such lurid terms as does the Court's opinion.

If the opinion is to be taken at face value, it would hold that federal courts have the power, by construing the federal constitution, specifically the Eighth Amendment, to require states to install separate jail facilities or detention centers for juveniles throughout their entire systems. I do not believe that we have such authority or that the Eighth Amendment imposes any such requirement. The question of cruel and unusual punishment must be determined on a case by case consideration and on the basis of the actual nature and character of any given confinement. The opinion is replete with references to the horrors of confining juveniles with hardened adult offenders and criminals, even including a reference to a Reader's Digest article of November, 1973, but the difficulty is that these general citations have no legal or authoritative value whatever and as far as we know at the present time have no relevance to any conditions which prevailed in Madison County, Kentucky, or in connection with plaintiff's confinement.

The only specific reference in the complaint to cruel and unusual punishment is contained in paragraph #12, which reads as follows:

The Plaintiff Duane Cox is a 16-year-old child who was held in an adult jail facility. There are no medical facilities, recreational or educational facilities in the jail or evaluative programs available to the child. He was not provided physical or psychological treatment programs. Specifically, the Plaintiff Duane Cox was not provided adequate medical examinations or treatment, recreation activities or equipment, soap, towels, education, books, or reading material. In addition, no social services were provided to benefit the child or class member.

This paragraph in my view falls far short of establishing cruel and unusual punishment under the Eighth Amendment and it certainly falls far short of the exacerbated conditions of confinement painted with such a broad brush in the opinion of the Court.

As the complaint was dismissed by the district court on a motion to dismiss without an evidentiary hearing, that court had no occasion to make findings of fact as to the class action issue. On remand, this question will be open and the court should make appropriate findings to indicate whether the action is properly filed as a class action. Following his findings and conclusions, on remand, the district court should then proceed to indicate any relief to which the plaintiff is entitled individually or as the representative of a class, including any injunctive or declaratory relief, or any other form of relief under the general prayer.

Because I am persuaded that the complaint contained sufficient allegations to warrant an evidentiary hearing, I concur in the result reached in Judge McAllister's opinion.

Holdings of *Cox v. Turley*: The court held that certain Due Process rights are afforded to juveniles in juvenile delinquency court proceedings, including at the time of arrest and pre-hearing detention. The court further held that confinement of a juvenile with adult criminal defendants constitutes cruel and unusual punishment.

Discussion Questions

Why didn't the Plaintiff challenge the constitutionality of confinement at all for a curfew violation?

The initial judge ordered the youth to have a hair-cut and to shave his beard, and upon compliance with those orders, he was released to the custody of his parents. Does an adult criminal court have the right to make this a requirement for pretrial release of a defendant? If not, why would a juvenile judge have the right to impose such conditions for release?

In re Michael G.: In *In re Michael G.*, the California Supreme Court was faced with a challenge to a court's ability to sentence a status offender to confinement for contempt of court for repeated violations of the conditions of probation imposed by the court. The California statute prohibits secure confinement as a sentencing option for status offenders.

As you read *In re Michael G.*, look for the following:

1. Notice the fact that a federal act (The Juvenile Justice and Delinquency Prevention Act) is followed by most states concerning a prohibition of secure confinement for status offenders.

2. Observe the historical basis for recognizing the ability of the court to imprison an individual for contempt of court for willfully disobeying a court order.

In re Michael G.

44 Cal.3d 283, 747 P.2d 1152, 243 Cal.Rptr. 224, (1988)

ARGUELLES, Justice.

In this case we decide whether a minor made a ward of the court pursuant to Welfare and Institutions Code section 601, subdivision (b) as a result of his truancy, and later found in contempt of court for wilfully disobeying a juvenile court order to attend school, may be punished with confinement in a secure facility during nonschool hours, or whether sections 601, subdivision (b) and 207 prohibit such a disposition. Like the majority of other state courts which have addressed similar statutory schemes, we conclude that a juvenile court retains the authority, pursuant to its contempt power, to order the secure, nonschool-hours confinement of a contemptuous section 601 ward. At the same time, in order to harmonize the juvenile court's exercise of its contempt power with the legislative determination that status offenders, including truants, should not ordinarily be confined in secure facilities, we conclude—again following the lead of a number of out-of-state decisions—that before a juvenile court orders such incarceration pursuant to its contempt authority, it should make a number of specified findings establishing the necessity of such a course of action.

FACTS

Petitioner Michael G., a minor, was adjudged a ward of the Fresno County Superior Court, Juvenile Division, pursuant to section 601, subdivision (b)—truancy. As a condition of probation he was ordered, inter alia, to "attend school regularly and not be tardy or absent." Following numerous unexcused absences from school, the court ordered petitioner to show cause why he should not be held in contempt of court.

Hearings were held on November 26 and December 3, 1984, after which the juvenile court concluded petitioner wilfully disobeyed the order of the court to attend school regularly and not be tardy or absent. Rejecting petitioner's demurrer and alternative motion to dismiss, the court ordered petitioner be delivered to the custody of the Director of Institutions of the Fresno County Probation Department for confinement for a 48-hour period. The court also ordered petitioner be held out of sight and hearing of any section 602 wards and that the 48-hour period would commence on Friday at 6 p.m., and end at 6 p.m., the following Sunday.

However, the juvenile court thereafter ordered petitioner to deliver himself into custody some 11 days hence "[t]o afford the minor the opportunity to ask review by the appellate court." Indeed, the juvenile court "earnestly" asked petitioner's counsel to seek writ review, stating: "[a]nd if it is determined that contempt proceedings or sanctions cannot be imposed against a Section 601(b) ward and that the Court cannot enforce its orders, then I certainly think that it's high time that the Court got out of the truancy business, [and] the [L]egislature place the Court in the position where it will have some dignity again. Certainly nothing is to be gained by the courts sitting here and pronouncing meaningless orders." The matter was later stayed by the Court of Appeal for the Fifth Appellate District but upon reflection, that court vacated the stay and denied a petition for a writ of habeas corpus and/or prohibition. We then granted review.

DISCUSSION

In finding petitioner in contempt for violating a valid court order, the juvenile court exercised the traditional power inherent in judicial officials. The contempt power thus exists independent from legislative sanction although in this case the Legislature has specifically recognized that the juvenile court retains the ordinary contempt powers.

Although petitioner concedes that the juvenile court in general retains authority to hold wards who disobey its orders in contempt, he argues that, with respect to truants and other status offenders, the Legislature has specifically proscribed the incarceration of such juveniles even as a sanction for contempt. He relies on sections 601, subdivision (b) and 207. In response, the People argue (1) that the limitations of those sections are inapplicable to the contempt setting, and (2) that if the sections were intended to limit the contempt power, they could not constitutionally do so. As we shall explain, we find that there is no need to reach the constitutional question in this case because we conclude that the applicable statutes can and should be harmonized to both preserve the trial court's contempt authority and at the same time give recognition to the legislative policy reflected in sections 601, subdivision (b) and 207.

We begin with the actual language of those sections. While the language of the statutes clearly indicates that the Legislature has determined that no juvenile is to be detained in jail or juvenile hall "solely upon the ground that he or she is a person described in section 601," neither statute expressly indicates that it was intended to apply to the contempt setting.

The structure of section 207 itself provides some hint as to our Legislature's intent, however. In addition to generally proscribing the secure detention of status offenders, that section permits three exceptions. "Under the familiar rule of construction, *expressio unius est exclusio alterius,* where exceptions to a general rule are specified by statute, other exceptions are not to be implied or presumed. This rule, of course, is inapplicable where its operation would contradict a discernible and contrary legislative intent. Thus, subject to a "discernible and contrary legislative intent," it is possible the Legislature, by specifying three exceptions to the general ban against secure detention for status offenders without also excepting juvenile contemners from the general rule, intended the general rule to apply to contemners.

Given the fundamental nature of the contempt power (see discussion, ante), we should not presume the Legislature intended to override such long-established power "unless such intention is made clearly to appear either by express declaration or by necessary implication."

Viewing the statutory scheme as a whole, we thus conclude that while the legislative history demonstrates an intent to prohibit the juvenile court from relying on a ward's violation of a court order as a justification for elevating a section 601 ward to a delinquent, there is nothing in that history which specifically indicates that the Legislature intended to prohibit a juvenile court from enforcing obedience to a court order through a contempt sanction that does not alter the status of the ward. Moreover, the Legislature's failure to expressly mention section 213 in either section 601, subdivision (b) or 207, or to amend section 213 itself, provides some evidence that it did not intend the secure detention ban or the school hours limitation to affect the scope of the juvenile court's contempt powers.

Although we conclude the limitations as stated in sections 207 and 601, subdivision (b) were not intended to affect the juvenile court's power to punish a contemptuous section 601 ward with secure detention during nonschool hours, we need not ignore the Legislature's general intent to deinstitutionalize status offenders. "'[E]very statute should be construed with reference to the whole system of law of which it is a part so that all may be harmonized and have effect.'" Thus, although the Legislature's general prohibition on the secure detention during nonschool hours for section 601 wards does not apply to contemners, respect for the intent of our coequal branch of government demands that courts exercise caution when imposing such sanctions against contemptuous status offenders.

In mandating that courts exercise caution before ordering a status offender into secure custody for a contemptuous act, we do not paint on a wholly blank canvas. In 1974, Congress passed the Juvenile Justice and Delinquency Prevention Act (hereafter the Act) (42 U.S.C. §§ 5601–5639 (1976) & Supp. III 1979, as amended by Juvenile Justice Amendments of 1980, Pub.L. No. 96-509, 94 Stat. 2750), conditioning block grants to the states on compliance with the Act's requirement of the deinstitutionalization of status offenders. As a result, nearly every state in the union passed a statute similar to section 207.

Thus, many of our sister states have already confronted the problem of how juvenile courts can effectively deal with status offenders who continually disobey the court's orders if secure incarceration is not an available option. Most states have affirmed their courts' use of the contempt power to order the secure detention of contemptuous status offenders despite an expression of legislative intent generally banning such detention, although a minority of states have disapproved this practice.

Interest of D.L.D. is perhaps most illustrative. In that case, the Supreme Court of Wisconsin was faced with a minor declared a "child in need of protection or services" (i.e., a status offender) who was not following the court's previously ordered conditions of supervision. The trial court found the minor in contempt of court, ordered the minor to serve 20 days in secure detention, and the intermediate appellate court affirmed. The high court reasoned that although the Wisconsin Children's Code generally prohibited the secure incarceration of status offenders with some exceptions, the statutory limitation cannot operate to deprive the court of its inherent contempt powers to enforce its orders.

However, the Wisconsin Supreme Court then stated: "[t]his court recognizes that the power of contempt is an extraordinary one that should be used sparingly and with the utmost sensitivity. This caveat is especially true since the 1977 revisions to the Children's Code adopted the general policy of deinstitutionalizing status offenders. Accordingly, we determine that a status offender may be found in contempt and incarcerated, but with the following limitations: (1) the juvenile is given sufficient notice to comply with the order and understands its provisions; (2) the violation of the court order is egregious; (3) less restrictive alternatives were considered and found to be ineffective; and (4) special confinement conditions are arranged consistent with ... [the statutory provisions barring intermingling with delinquents]."

These four qualifications are sound and we hold California courts should adhere to them. Imposition of these qualifications on a juvenile court's contempt power achieves the twin goals of vindicating the inherent power of the courts while giving practical effect to the Legislature's express intent to deinstitutionalize status offenders in general. The necessity of the first requirement is self-evident; due process concerns would be implicated if the juvenile who lacked notice of the court's orders was held in contempt for violating those orders.

The requirement of an egregious violation ensures that secure incarceration will not become a commonplace sanction in contravention of the Legislature's intent to comply with the federal mandate to deinstitutionalize status offenders. The reservation of the nonschool hours, secure-detention sanction for the most severe cases will require the juvenile court to decide whether, based on the entire record, imposition of this harsh penalty is justified because no other sanction will suffice. Moreover, this requirement has the additional benefit of ensuring our juvenile courts will exercise this facet of their inherent contempt power to the least extent possible so as to give maximum effect to the Legislature's avowed intent to house status offenders in nonsecure surroundings.

The third requirement—consideration and rejection of less restrictive sanctions—is closely akin to the second requirement that the violation of the court's order be egregious since it too has its genesis in the idea that incarceration should be the exception, not the rule. While the court need not necessarily have attempted lesser penalties before imposing secure confinement, the record should indicate that lesser alternatives were considered by the juvenile court before ordering incarceration.

By requiring the juvenile court to memorialize its findings on the record, we again ensure the court is aware that, by ordering the secure confinement of a juvenile who has not committed a criminal offense, it is taking the extraordinary step of acting contrary to the wishes of the Legislature but is justified in doing so because it is convinced there is no other alternative which will adequately serve the purpose of the contempt citation.

Finally, the juvenile court ordering the incarceration of a status offender should also prohibit the minor from coming in contact with those minors confined due to their commission of a crime, i.e., *section 602* wards. Although other states also impose this requirement, we need only turn to section 207 for a clear expression of our own Legislature's intent on this subject. It thus seems manifest that incarcerated status offenders must be segregated so as to avoid contact with section 602 wards and others confined due to their criminal conduct.

We realize our decision permits the contemptuous status offender to suffer the major disadvantage heretofore reserved for section 602 wards: secure confinement during non-school hours. However, the nature of the confinement suffered by the contemptuous status offender differs in at least one substantial respect: he cannot come in contact with other section 602 wards who may be confined in the same facility. This limitation, as recognized by the juvenile court below, is important to ensure the status offender's problems, noncriminal at that time, are not exacerbated by mingling with delinquents. We thus avoid the unsavory situation whereby "the youngster whose only offense against society was that he could not get along with his parents, found himself cheek by jowl with the underage rapist, robber or heroin peddler."

CONCLUSION

Applying these standards here, we hold that although the juvenile court ensured petitioner had notice of and understood the court's orders, and properly ordered petitioner's confinement be arranged to prevent contact with section 602 wards, it made no express findings that petitioner's contumacious conduct was egregious or that less restrictive alternatives to incarceration were not feasible. In the present case, of course, the trial court was unaware it must make these specific findings before ordering confinement pursuant to its contempt authority. The judgment of the Court of Appeal is therefore reversed with directions to remand the cause to the trial court for further proceedings consistent with this opinion.

BROUSSARD, Justice, dissenting.

I dissent. The Legislature has made it clear that juvenile status offenders are not to be incarcerated. The majority hold that the status offender who disobeys a court order to attend school can be incarcerated, despite the fact that there is no statutory language, case law, or evidence of legislative intent to support such a conclusion. The majority ignore the Legislature's considered judgment that the harm which incarceration causes a status offender is too great to be permitted, even when the status offender fails to obey court orders. Instead the majority exalt the dignity of the court issuing the order over the best interest of the minor. Neither logic nor compassion can countenance such a result.

Welfare and Institutions Code section 601 provides for wardship proceedings for minors who are beyond the control of their parents or guardians, or who are truant. Minors declared wards of the court under this section are called status offenders, in contrast with minors made wards of the court and incarcerated under section 602 for violation of state or federal law. "A status offender might be defined as one whose only offense against society is doing something that would not be legally prohibited if done by an adult." A minor may be made a ward of the court under subdivision (a) of section 601 for persistent disobedience of his parents or guardians, and under subdivision (b) for truancy. Subdivision (b) concludes with these words: "[I]t is the intent of the Legislature that no minor who is adjudged a ward of the court pursuant solely to this subdivision shall be removed from the custody of the parent or guardian except during school hours."

Section 207, subdivision (a) provides, with exceptions no one argues are applicable here, that "[n]o minor shall be detained in any jail, lockup, juvenile hall, or other secure facility who is taken into custody solely upon the ground that he or she is a person described by Section 601 or adjudged to be such or made a ward of the juvenile court solely upon that ground...."

Sections 601, subdivision (b) and 207, subdivision (a) prohibit the jailing of truants or other status offenders. Nonetheless, the majority hold that a directive not to jail truants does not prohibit jailing habitual truants who are in contempt of a court order to go to school. I do not agree with this conclusion. It is perfectly clear from the history of the relevant statutes that the Legislature has determined that jailing a status offender for contempt of court is not a good idea, and that the Legislature meant to prohibit such incarceration.

The conclusion is unavoidable that the Legislature understands that in every county but the pilot program county, a section 601, subdivision (a) ward who disobeys a dispositional order cannot be held in a secure placement. If it were otherwise, there would be no need for the special authorization for secure placement contained in this pilot program. Further, the data collected on whether secure placement reduced crime by or on these wards in the pilot county would be meaningless if secure placement is already available through the contempt power of the court.

Legislative authority for jailing truants for contempt of a section 601 order simply does not exist. I also see no constitutional infirmity in a system which prohibits incarceration of habitual truants. Though a court has the inherent power to punish contempt, the Legislature may place reasonable limitations on this power. A statute that took away all contempt power from the court or fixed a "wholly inadequate" penalty for a class of contempts would be an unconstitutional invasion of the court's power. But as long as the courts retain the power to "vindicate their authority and maintain the dignity and respect due to them," the legislative regulation of the contempt power is considered within constitutional bounds.

The juvenile court can punish the repeat truant for contempt, staying within the bounds of the section 601 wardship, by imposing fines, compulsory service to the community, or detention in nonsecure facilities during school hours. Under present law, except in the pilot county, the juvenile court cannot incarcerate a minor made a ward of the court as a result of his truancy for willfully failing to obey the court's order to attend school. In holding otherwise, the majority reach too far.

Holdings of *In re Michael G.*: The court held that judges can sentence juvenile status offenders to secure confinement for contempt of court, even though secure confinement is not allowed as a sentencing option for status offenders. The court further held that, when a judge sentences a status offender to secure confinement, the judge must determine that there are no less restrictive options available and cannot place the minor with other juveniles who were adjudicated for offenses that constitute violation of the criminal law.

Discussion Questions

If judges were not allowed to confine minors who were adjudicated for committing a status offense for contempt of court, what could be done to a status offender who openly "thumbs their nose" at the court and refuses to comply with any conditions of probation?

What would happens if the state does not have any secure facility other than ones that house offenders of criminal laws?

Key Concepts: Delinquency Laws and Status Offenses

- Courts recognize a compelling state interest in controlling juvenile crime and protecting minors from being victims of crimes and, if statutes are properly tailored, special restrictions can be imposed on minors that could not be acceptably imposed on adults.

- Minors charged with status offenses should not be detained or kept in secured facilities with adult criminal offenders.

- Minors adjudicated to have committed a status offense can be subject to long term placement in a residential treatment facility.

Practical Questions: Delinquency Laws and Status Offenses

1. José Hernandez, a leader of the "Latin Kings" gang, comes to your office complaining that the local law enforcement authorities are cracking down on gang members by charging them with curfew ordinance violations. The city ordinance has a broad First Amendment exception similar to that contained in the *QUTB v. Bartlett* case. José proposes that all gang members wear T-shirts imprinted (front and back) with: "Vote for Immigration Reform!" Can the gang members successfully claim that the First Amendment exception applies to them and that the ordinance cannot be enforced against them?

2. Michael Newberry, president of the state filmmakers' association, comes to your office with his 16-year-old son, Michael, Jr. who wants to follow in his father's footsteps. The city has a curfew ordinance similar to that described in the *QUTB v. Bartlett* case. The father tells you that his son is already very experienced in making films. However, he believes that his son needs much more experience in filming at nighttime where there is lower lighting and differing light sources such as street lights. During the summer, he wants his son to be able to practice filming during the late night, early-morning hours. "He has my permission and support," says the father. "Can the city really hold my son back from his career by making him wait with honing this skill until he is older?" What do you tell him?

3. Samuel Johnson, a 14-year-old male, has been detained in a juvenile detention center after his arrest for a status offense of "ungovernability." The authorities claim that Sam is guilty of this offense because he is associating with "known gang members" and has carved a pitchfork (a gang symbol) ink tattoo on his arm. Authorities have asked the court to order Sam to be sent to a juvenile treatment center until he reaches the age of majority (18) in order to force him to stay out of the gang. Can the juvenile court judge place Sam in an out-of-home placement for four (4) years just because he is keeping bad company?

Simulation Exercise I

Characters: Attorney for the City of Cleveland, attorney for the Students for a Democratic Society (SDS), and the Judge.

Facts: The City of Cleveland has a curfew ordinance that applies to all youth under the age of 18. The ordinance prohibits any minor (defined as "anyone under the age of

18") from being in a public place between the hours of 9:00 p.m. and 7:00 a.m. Exceptions are listed including when the minor is in the company of his or her parents, when attending or travelling to or from an event sponsored by an educational authority or a church, or when on an "emergency errand" directed by a parent or guardian. The City of Cleveland has documented that the number of criminal charges against minors has dropped by 23% in the past 2 years that the ordinance has been in force.

A student group called Students for a Democratic Society (SDS) has strong political activism, especially in the cause of closing the Guantanamo Prison. The SDS has identified that the Republican National Committee (RNC) is holding their national convention in Cleveland and that the "Platform Committee" of the RNC will be meeting from 9:30 p.m. to 11:00 p.m. on July 20th. The group desires to stand outside of the Auditorium where the platform committee meets on July 20th from 9:00 p.m. until 11:30 p.m. with signs and t-shirts proclaiming "Close Guantanamo" to influence the platform committee to include this issue on the party's platform. The group has obtained a permit for the demonstration, but was warned by city officials that the curfew ordinance will be strictly enforced. The attorney for SDS has filed a motion for a temporary injunction prohibiting the enforcement of the curfew ordinance to them on July 20th and a hearing on the motion is scheduled.

Simulation: The exercise is to conduct oral arguments on the motion for a temporary injunction prohibiting the enforcement of the curfew ordinance against the SDS. The attorney for SDS will present an oral argument that the ordinance is unconstitutional either on its face or as applied to the SDS in this instance. The attorney for the City of Cleveland will argue that the ordinance is constitutional. The judge should be prepared to ask any questions necessary to arrive at a ruling, the attorneys shall be prepared to answer any questions posed to them, and the judge will enter an oral ruling on the motion specifying findings and reasons for the ruling.

Chapter III

Interrogation of Minors

Overview: Courts have been forced to analyze the admissibility of confessions of minors on many occasions. The difficult issue for the reviewing courts is whether or not minors should receive protections that would not be available to adults. Courts have long recognized that minors are particularly vulnerable when interrogated by authorities, especially when they have no adult to give them advice or support. While the age of majority (18) is the "cut-off" point for such analysis, court's frequently look at the particular age of the minor in an evaluation of the "totality of the circumstances" in determining whether the interrogation passed constitutional muster.

Haley v. Ohio: In *Haley v. Ohio* the U.S. Supreme Court was faced with a challenge to the admissibility of the confession of a 15-year-old boy to a murder. After 5 hours of questioning by police (5 officers were involved in shifts of 1 or 2 each), the youth was shown a copy of a confession by a co-defendant, at which point the youth confessed. There was some evidence that the youth was beaten at the police station by officers. No friend or lawyer was present during the questioning and the youth was not informed of his right to counsel. After the signed confession, the youth was placed in jail for days and held "incommunicado." During the interval, a lawyer tried to contact defendant twice but was refused, and the mother was not allowed to see her son. However, a newspaper photographer was allowed to see defendant and take his picture shortly after the confession.

As you read *Haley v. Ohio,* look for the following:

1. Consider what factors the court relied on to find that "… this was a confession wrung from a child by means which the law should not sanction."

2. Consider how the post-confession factors (being held incommunicado, as well as the lawyer and the mother being denied contact with the youth) have any effect on the confession itself.

3. Notice the words used by the Justices to describe the youth that may emphasize their feeling that this youth was extremely young.

4. Notice the words used by the Justices to describe the interrogation that was imposed on the youth in describing their finding that the police had a "callous attitude" towards his rights.

Haley v. Ohio
332 U.S. 596 (1948)

Mr. Justice DOUGLAS announced the judgment of the Court and an opinion in which Mr. Justice BLACK, Mr. Justice MURPHY, and Mr. Justice RUTLEDGE join.

Petitioner was convicted in an Ohio court of murder in the first degree and sentenced to life imprisonment. The Court of Appeals of Ohio sustained the judgment of conviction over the objection that the admission of petitioner's confession at the trial violated the Fourteenth Amendment of the Constitution.

A confectionery store was robbed near midnight on October 14, 1945, and William Karam, its owner, was shot. It was the prosecutor's theory, supported by some evidence which it is unnecessary for us to relate, that petitioner, a Negro boy age 15, and two others, Willie Lowder, age 16, and Al Parks, age 17, committed the crime, petitioner acting as a lookout. Five days later—around midnight October 19, 1945—petitioner was arrested at his home and taken to police headquarters.

There is some contrariety in the testimony as to what then transpired. There is evidence that he was beaten. He took the stand and so testified. His mother testified that the clothes he wore when arrested, which were exchanged two days later for clean ones she brought to the jail, were torn and blood-stained. She also testified that when she first saw him five days after his arrest he was bruised and skinned. The police testified to the contrary on this entire line of testimony. So we put to one side the controverted evidence. Taking only the undisputed testimony, we have the following sequence of events. Beginning shortly after midnight this 15-year-old lad was questioned by the police for about five hours. Five or six of the police questioned him in relays of one or two each. During this time no friend or counsel of the boy was present. Around 5 a.m.—after being shown alleged confessions of Lowder and Parks—the boy confessed. A confession was typed in question and answer form by the police. At no time was this boy advised of his right to counsel; but the written confession started off with the following statement: 'we want to inform you of your constitutional rights, the law gives you the right to make this statement or not as you see fit. It is made with the understanding that it may be used at a trial in court either for or against you or anyone else involved in this crime with you, of your own free will and accord, you are under no force or duress or compulsion and no promises are being made to you at this time whatsoever.

'Do you still desire to make this statement and tell the truth after having had the above clause read to you? A. Yes.'

He was put in jail about 6 or 6:30 a.m. on Saturday, the 20th, shortly after the confession was signed. Between then and Tuesday, the 23d, he was held incommunicado. A lawyer retained by his mother tried to see him twice but was refused admission by the police. His mother was not allowed to see him until Thursday, the 25th. But a newspaper photographer was allowed to see him and take his picture in the early morning hours of the 20th, right after he had confessed. He was not taken before a magistrate and formally charged with a crime until the 23d—three days after the confession was signed.

The trial court, after a preliminary hearing on the voluntary character of the confession, allowed it to be admitted in evidence over petitioner's objection that it violated his rights under the Fourteenth Amendment. The court instructed the jury to disregard the confession if it found that he did not make the confession voluntarily and of his free will.

We do not think the methods used in obtaining this confession can be squared with that due process of law which the Fourteenth Amendment commands.

What transpired would make us pause for careful inquiry if a mature man were involved. And when, as here, a mere child—an easy victim of the law—is before us, special care in scrutinizing the record must be used. Age 15 is a tender and difficult age for a boy of any race. He cannot be judged by the more exacting standards of maturity. That which would leave a man cold and unimpressed can overawe and overwhelm a lad in his early teens. This is the period of great instability which the crisis of adolescence produces.

A 15-year-old lad, questioned through the dead of night by relays of police, is a ready victim of the inquisition. Mature men possibly might stand the ordeal from midnight to 5 a.m. But we cannot believe that a lad of tender years is a match for the police in such a contest. He needs counsel and support if he is not to become the victim first of fear, then of panic. He needs someone on whom to lean lest the overpowering presence of the law, as he knows it, may not crush him. No friend stood at the side of this 15-year-old boy as the police, working in relays, questioned him hour after hour, from midnight until dawn. No lawyer stood guard to make sure that the police went so far and no farther, to see to it that they stopped short of the point where he became the victim of coercion. No counsel or friend was called during the critical hours of questioning. A photographer was admitted once this lad broke and confessed. But not even a gesture towards getting a lawyer for him was ever made.

This disregard of the standards of decency is underlined by the fact that he was kept incommunicado for over three days during which the lawyer retained to represent him twice tried to see him and twice was refused admission. A photographer was admitted at once; but his closest friend—his mother—was not allowed to see him for over five days after his arrest. It is said that these events are not germane to the present problem because they happened after the confession was made. But they show such a callous attitude of the police towards the safeguards which respect for ordinary standards of human relationships compels that we take with a grain of salt their present apologia that the five-hour grilling of this boy was conducted in a fair and dispassionate manner. When the police are so unmindful of these basic standards of conduct in their public dealings, their secret treatment of a 15-year-old boy behind closed doors in the dead of night becomes darkly suspicious.

The age of petitioner, the hours when he was grilled, the duration of his quizzing, the fact that he had no friend or counsel to advise him, the callous attitude of the police towards his rights combine to convince us that this was a confession wrung from a child by means which the law should not sanction. Neither man nor child can be allowed to stand condemned by methods which flout constitutional requirements of due process of law.

But we are told that this boy was advised of his constitutional rights before he signed the confession and that, knowing them, he nevertheless confessed. That assumes, however, that a boy of fifteen, without aid of counsel, would have a full appreciation of that advice and that on the facts of this record he had a freedom of choice. We cannot indulge those assumptions. Moreover, we cannot give any weight to recitals which merely formalize constitutional requirements. Formulas of respect for constitutional safeguards cannot prevail over the facts of life which contradict them. They may not become a cloak for inquisitorial practices and make an empty form of the due process of law for which free men fought and died to obtain.

The Fourteenth Amendment prohibits the police from using the private, secret custody of either man or child as a device for wringing confessions from them.

Reversed.

Mr. Justice FRANKFURTER, joining in reversal of judgment.

But whether a confession of a lad of fifteen is 'voluntary' and as such admissible, or 'coerced' and thus wanting in due process, is not a matter of mathematical determination. Essentially it invites psychological judgment—a psychological judgment that reflects deep, even if inarticulate, feelings of our society. Judges must divine that feeling as best they can from all the relevant evidence and light which they can bring to bear for a confident judgment of such an issue, and with every endeavor to detach themselves from their merely private views.

This brings me to the precise issue on the record before us. Suspecting a 15-year-old boy of complicity in murder resulting from attempted robbery, at about midnight the police took him from his home to police headquarters. There he was questioned for about five hours by at least five police officers who interrogated in relays of two or more. About five o'clock in the morning this procedure culminated in what the police regarded as a confession, whereupon it was formally reduced to writing. During the course of the interrogation the boy was not advised that he was not obliged to talk, that it was his right if he chose to say not a word, nor that he was entitled to have the benefit of counsel or the help of his family. Bearing upon the safeguards of these rights, the Chief of Police admitted that while he knew that the boy 'had a right to remain mute and not answer any questions' he did not know that it was the duty of the police to apprise him of that fact. Unquestionably, during this whole period he was held incommunicado. Only after the night-long questioning had resulted in disclosures satisfactory to the police and as such to be documented, was there read to the boy a clause giving the conventional formula about his constitutional right to make or withhold a statement and stating that if he makes it, he makes it of his 'own free will.' Do these uncontested fact justify a State court in finding that the boy's confession was 'voluntary,' or do the circumstances by their very nature preclude a finding that a deliberate and responsible choice was exercised by the boy in the confession that came at the end of five hours questioning?

The answer, as has already been intimated, depends on an evaluation of psychological factors, or, more accurately stated, upon the persuasive feeling of society regarding such psychological factors. Unfortunately, we cannot draw upon any formulated expression of the existence of such feeling. Nor are there available experts on such matters to guide the judicial judgment. Our Constitutional system makes it the Court's duty to interpret those feelings of society to which the Due Process Clause gives legal protection. Because of their inherent vagueness the tests by which we are to be guided are most unsatisfactory, but such as they are we must apply them.

Unhappily we have neither physical nor intellectual weights and measures by which judicial judgment can determine when pressures in securing a confession reach the coercive intensity that calls for the exclusion of a statement so secured. Of course, the police meant to exercise pressures upon Haley to make him talk. That was the very purpose of their procedure. In concluding that a statement is not voluntary which results from pressures such as were exerted in this case to make a lad of fifteen talk when the Constitution gave him the right to keep silent and when the situation was so contrived that appreciation of his rights and thereby the means of asserting them were effectively withheld from him by the police, I do not believe I express a merely personal bias against such a procedure. Such a finding, I believe, reflects those fundamental notions of fairness and justice in the determination of guilt or innocence which lie embedded in the feelings of the American people and are enshrined in the Due Process Clause of the Fourteenth Amendment. To remove the inducement to resort to such methods this Court has repeatedly denied use of the fruits of illicit methods.

Accordingly, I think Haley's confession should have been excluded and the conviction based upon it should not stand.

Mr. Justice BURTON, with whom The CHIEF JUSTICE, Mr. Justice REED and Mr. Justice JACKSON concur, dissenting.

The issue here is a narrow one of fact turning largely upon the credibility of witnesses whose testimony on material points is in direct conflict with that of other witnesses. The judgment rendered today by this Court does not hold that the procedure authorized by the State of Ohio to determine the admissibility of the confession of a person accused of a capital offense violates per se the Due Process Clause of the Fourteenth Amendment.

It holds merely that the application made of that procedure in this case amounted to a violation of due process under the Fourteenth Amendment in that, on this record, it amounted to a refusal by the trial court to exclude from the jury this particular confession which this Court is convinced was an involuntary confession.

The question in this case is the simple one—was the confession in fact voluntary? As in many other cases it is difficult, because of conflicting testimony, to determine this controlling fact. It may not be possible to become absolutely certain of it. Self-serving perjury, however, must not be the passkey to a mandatory exclusion of the confession from use as evidence. It is for the trial judge and the jury, under the safeguards of constitutional due process of criminal law, to apply even-handed justice to the determination of the factual issues. To do this, they need every available lawful aid to help them test the credibility of the conflicting testimony.

The evidence in the record includes ample evidence to support the action taken by the trial judge and jury against the accused if this Court chooses to believe that evidence and to disbelieve the conflicting evidence. Furthermore, that evidence, if so believed, is strong and specific enough greatly to offset conflicting inferences which otherwise might be suggested to this Court by the undisputed evidence.

We are not in a position, on the basis of mere suspicion, to hold the trial court in error and to conclude 'that this was a confession wrung from a child by means which the law should not sanction.' While coercion and intimidation in securing a confession should be unequivocally condemned and punished and their product invalidated, nevertheless such coercion should not be presumed to exist because of a mere suggestion or suspicion, in the face of contrary findings by the triers of fact.

In testing due process this Court must first make sure of its facts. Until a better way is found for testing credibility than by the examination of witnesses in open court, we must give trial courts and juries that wide discretion in this field to which a living record, as distinguished from a printed record, logically entitles them. In this living record there are many guideposts to the truth which are not in the printed record. Without seeing them ourselves, we will do well to give heed to those who have seen them.

Holdings of _Haley v. Ohio:_ In this case, the court held that a number of factors combined to require a suppression of the confession by the youth, including: the age of boy, the hours when he was questioned, the duration of his interrogation, the fact that he had no friend or counsel to advise him, and the "callous attitude of the police towards his rights."

Discussion Questions

Does the conflicted testimony about the defendant being beaten have any impact on the majority decision?

What are the various factors that lead to the finding that Haley was denied his constitutional rights by being the subject of "inquisitorial practices"?

Are some of those factors more dispositive than others?

———————

Gallegos v. Colorado: In _Gallegos v. Colorado,_ the Supreme Court was faced with a case similar to _Haley v. Ohio,_ with the exception that the youth was not subjected to a long period of interrogation. In _Gallegos,_ the youth was only 14 years old. Gallegos and another youth assaulted a man and robbed him of $13. Gallegos was arrested on January 1 and convicted of "assault to injure" on January 16th. On January 26th, the victim died and Gallegos was charged with murder in adult court. The day after his arrest, his mother was denied a request to visit the youth because the request came outside of public visiting hours.

As you read *Gallegos v. Colorado,* look for the following:

1. The Court relies on *Haley v. Ohio,* but distinguishes this case from *Haley.* Note what important factor cited by *Haley* was not present here and what other factors were present.

2. Note the difference in the language used by the court in *Gallegos* compared to *Haley* in describing the conduct of the police.

3. In reviewing this case, consider how important the very young age (14) of the defendant was in the Court's analysis.

Gallegos v. Colorado
370 U.S. 49 (1962)

Mr. Justice DOUGLAS delivered the opinion of the Court.

Petitioner, a child of 14, and another juvenile followed an elderly man to a hotel, got into his room on a ruse, assaulted him, overpowered him, stole $13 from his pockets, and fled. All this happened on December 20, 1958. Petitioner was picked up by the police on January 1, 1959, and immediately admitted the assault and robbery. At that time, however, the victim of the robbery was still alive, though hospitalized. He died on January 26, 1959, and forthwith an information charging first degree murder was returned against petitioner. A jury found him guilty, the crucial evidence introduced at the trial being a formal confession which he signed on January 7, 1959, after he had been held for five days during which time he saw no lawyer, parent or other friendly adult. The Supreme Court of Colorado affirmed the judgment of conviction.

After petitioner's arrest on January 1, the following events took place. His mother tried to see him on Friday, January 2, but permission was denied, the reason given being that visiting hours were from 7 p.m. to 8 p.m. on Monday and Thursday. From January 1 through January 7, petitioner was in Juvenile Hall, where he was kept in security, though he was allowed to eat with the other inmates. He was examined by the police in Juvenile Hall January 2, and made a confession which an officer recorded in longhand. On January 3, 1959, a complaint was filed against him in the Juvenile Court by the investigating detectives.

The State in its brief calls this preliminary procedure in Juvenile Hall being 'booked in.' As noted, petitioner signed a full and formal confession on January 7. The trial in the Juvenile Court took place January 16 on a petition dated January 13 containing a charge of 'assault to injure.' He was committed to the State Industrial School for an indeterminate period. Thereafter, as noted above, the victim of the robbery died and the murder trial was held.

The application of these principles involves close scrutiny of the facts of individual cases. The length of the questioning, the use of fear to break a suspect, the youth of the accused are illustrative of the circumstances on which cases of this kind turn.

The fact that petitioner was only 14 years old puts this case on the same footing as *Haley v. Ohio.* There was here no evidence of prolonged questioning. But the five-day detention—during which time the boy's mother unsuccessfully tried to see him and he was cut off from contact with any lawyer or adult advisor—gives the case an ominous cast. The prosecution says that the boy was advised of his right to counsel, but that he did not ask either for a lawyer or for his parents. But a 14-year-old boy, no matter how sophisticated, is unlikely to have any conception of what will confront him when he is made accessible only to the police. That is to say, we deal with a person who is not equal to the police in knowledge and understanding of the consequences of the questions and answers being recorded and who is unable to know how to protest his own interests or how to get the benefits of his constitutional rights.

The prosecution says that the youth and immaturity of the petitioner and the five-day detention are irrelevant, because the basic ingredients of the confession came tumbling out as soon as he was arrested. But if we took that position, it would, with all deference, be in callous disregard of this boy's constitutional rights. He cannot be compared with an adult in full possession of his senses and knowledgeable of the consequences of his admissions. He would have no way of knowing what the consequences of his confession were without advice as to his rights — from someone concerned with securing him those rights — and without the aid of more mature judgment as to the steps he should take in the predicament in which he found himself. A lawyer or an adult relative or friend could have given the petitioner the protection which his own immaturity could not. Adult advice would have put him on a less unequal footing with his interrogators. Without some adult protection against this inequality, a 14-year-old boy would not be able to know, let alone assert, such constitutional rights as he had. To allow this conviction to stand would, in effect, be to treat him as if he had no constitutional rights.

There is no guide to the decision of cases such as this, except the totality of circumstances that bear on the two factors we have mentioned. The youth of the petitioner, the long detention, the failure to send for his parents, the failure immediately to bring him before the judge of the Juvenile Court, the failure to see to it that he had the advice of a lawyer or a friend — all these combine to make us conclude that the formal confession on which this conviction may have rested was obtained in violation of due process.

Reversed.

Mr. Justice CLARK, with whom Mr. Justice HARLAN and Mr. Justice STEWART join, dissenting.

The Court sets aside the conviction here on due process grounds, finding that the formal confession made by petitioner on January 7 was obtained by 'secret inquisitorial processes' and other forms of compulsion. In so doing it turns its back on the spontaneous oral admissions made by petitioner at the time of arrest on January 1, as well as a detailed confession made the next day, all long before the formal confession was given five days later. Moreover, I find nothing in the record that suggests any 'secret inquisitorial processes' were used or any compulsion was exerted upon petitioner even during that longer period. With due deference I cannot see how the Court concludes from the record that petitioner was 'cut off from contact with any lawyer or adult advisor' and 'made accessible only to the police,' that there was a failure to bring him before the juvenile judge in the manner required in juvenile delinquency cases, or that Gallegos' case is in anywise on the same footing with *Haley v. Ohio,* or the other cases cited by the majority.

As I have noted, in light of these facts I cannot conclude that this confession was involuntary. *A fortiori,* I could not determine, as the Court must, that so clear a case of coercion was made out that three prior findings that the confession was voluntary — including one by the jury which was specifically instructed to consider each of the factors relied on by the majority — can be reversed.

Finally, I see no similarity in *Haley v. Ohio,* the last case cited by the Court. There a 15-year-old boy never before in trouble was questioned 'through the dead of night' by five to six policemen in relays of one or two each and then only was led to confess by being shown alleged statements of two confederates incriminating him. *Haley* does not indicate that youth alone is sufficient to render a juvenile's confession inadmissible. Here we do not have any of the factors which led to the comment: 'What transpired would make us pause for careful inquiry if a mature man were involved.'

I regret that without support from prior cases and on the basis of inference and conjecture not supported in the record the Court upsets this conviction.

Holding of *Gallegos v. Colorado:* In this case, the court held that the confession was not voluntary under the totality of circumstances, which included: the age of the youth, the long detention, the failure to send for his parents, the failure immediately to bring him before the judge of the Juvenile Court, and the failure to see to it that he had the advice of a lawyer or a friend. This holding was in spite of the fact that there was not the lengthy interrogation that was present in *Haley*.

Discussion Questions

What factors warranting a reversal that were present in *Haley* were also present in *Gallegos*?

What factors warranting a reversal that were present in *Haley* were NOT present in *Gallegos*?

Would the majority reverse and suppress ANY confession by a 14-year-old that did not have the benefit of counsel or parental advice?

Fare v. Michael C.: In *Fare v. Michael C.,* a "16½ years old" youth, was implicated in a murder. He was arrested and informed of his *Miranda* rights. When asked if he wanted to waive his right to an attorney, he asked for his probation officer (from a prior offense). Officers refused to call his probation officer, and asked again if he wanted an attorney. The defendant asked, "How I know you guys won't pull no police officer in and tell me he's an attorney?" Again, the officers refused to contact his probation officer and so the defendant agreed to talk to the officers without an attorney present. Defendant was convicted of murder in juvenile court.

As you read *Fare v. Michael C.,* look for the following:

1. Examine whether or not the requirement under *Haley* that a juvenile should have the benefit of "friend or counsel" has now been reduced to "counsel" under this decision.

2. Note the lack of discussion of involvement of Michael C's parent in the interrogation.

3. Try to analyze the impact of the slightly older age (differing from *Haley* and *Gallegos*) in this case on the outcome.

Fare v. Michael C.
442 U.S. 707 (1979)

Mr. Justice BLACKMUN delivered the opinion of the Court.

In *Miranda v. Arizona*, this Court established certain procedural safeguards designed to protect the rights of an accused, under the Fifth and Fourteenth Amendments, to be free from compelled self-incrimination during custodial interrogation. The Court specified, among other things, that if the accused indicates in any manner that he wishes to remain silent or to consult an attorney, interrogation must cease, and any statement obtained from him during interrogation thereafter may not be admitted against him at his trial.

In this case, the State of California, in the person of its acting chief probation officer, attacks the conclusion of the Supreme Court of California that a juvenile's request, made while undergoing custodial interrogation, to see his probation officer is per se an invocation of the juvenile's Fifth Amendment rights as pronounced in *Miranda*.

Respondent Michael C. was implicated in the murder of Robert Yeager. The murder occurred during a robbery of the victim's home on January 19, 1976. A small truck registered in the name of respondent's mother was identified as having been near the Yeager home at the time of the killing, and a young man answering respondent's description was seen by witnesses near the truck and near the home shortly before Yeager was murdered.

On the basis of this information, Van Nuys, Cal., police took respondent into custody at approximately 6:30 p.m. on February 4. Respondent then was 16? years old and on probation to the Juvenile Court. He had been on probation since the age of 12. Approximately one year earlier he had served a term in a youth corrections camp under the supervision of the Juvenile Court. He had a record of several previous offenses, including burglary of guns and purse snatching, stretching back over several years.

Upon respondent's arrival at the Van Nuys station house two police officers began to interrogate him. The officers and respondent were the only persons in the room during the interrogation. The conversation was tape-recorded. One of the officers initiated the interview by informing respondent that he had been brought in for questioning in relation to a murder. The officer fully advised respondent of his Miranda rights. The following exchange then occurred, as set out in the opinion of the California Supreme Court (emphasis added by that court):

"Q. ... Do you understand all of these rights as I have explained them to you?

"A. Yeah.

"Q. Okay, do you wish to give up your right to remain silent and talk to us about this murder?

"A. What murder? I don't know about no murder.

"Q. I'll explain to you which one it is if you want to talk to us about it.

"A. Yeah, I might talk to you.

"Q. Do you want to give up your right to have an attorney present here while we talk about it?

"A. Can I have my probation officer here?

"Q. Well I can't get a hold of your probation officer right now. You have the right to an attorney.

"A. How I know you guys won't pull no police officer in and tell me he's an attorney?

"Q. Huh?

"A. [How I know you guys won't pull no police officer in and tell me he's an attorney?]

"Q. Your probation officer is Mr. Christiansen.

"A. Yeah.

"Q. Well I'm not going to call Mr. Christiansen tonight. There's a good chance we can talk to him later, but I'm not going to call him right now. If you want to talk to us without an attorney present, you can. If you don't want to, you don't have to. But if you want to say something, you can, and if you don't want to say something you don't have to. That's your right. You understand that right?

"A. Yeah.

"Q. Okay, will you talk to us without an attorney present?

"A. Yeah I want to talk to you."

Respondent thereupon proceeded to answer questions put to him by the officers. He made statements and drew sketches that incriminated him in the Yeager murder.

Largely on the basis of respondent's incriminating statements, probation authorities filed a petition in Juvenile Court alleging that respondent had murdered Robert Yeager, and that respondent therefore should be adjudged a ward of the Juvenile Court. Respondent thereupon moved to suppress the statements and sketches he gave the police during the interrogation. He alleged that the statements had been obtained in violation of *Miranda* in that his request to see his probation officer at the outset of the questioning constituted an invocation of his Fifth Amendment right to remain silent, just as if he had requested the assistance of an attorney. Accordingly, respondent argued that since the interrogation did not cease until he had a chance to confer with his probation officer, the statements and sketches could not be admitted against him in the Juvenile Court proceedings.

We note at the outset that it is clear that the judgment of the California Supreme Court rests firmly on that court's interpretation of federal law. This Court, however, has not heretofore extended the per se aspects of the *Miranda* safeguards beyond the scope of the holding in the *Miranda* case itself. We therefore must examine the California court's decision to determine whether that court's conclusion so to extend *Miranda* is in harmony with *Miranda*'s underlying principles.

The rule the Court established in *Miranda* is clear. In order to be able to use statements obtained during custodial interrogation of the accused, the State must warn the accused prior to such questioning of his right to remain silent and of his right to have counsel, retained or appointed, present during interrogation. "Once [such] warnings have been given, the subsequent procedure is clear."

"If the individual indicates in any manner, at any time prior to or during questioning, that he wishes to remain silent, the interrogation must cease. At this point he has shown that he intends to exercise his Fifth Amendment privilege; any statement taken after the person invokes his privilege cannot be other than the product of compulsion, subtle or otherwise.... If the individual states that he wants an attorney, the interrogation must cease until an attorney is present. At that time, the individual must have an opportunity to confer with the attorney and to have him present during any subsequent questioning. If the individual cannot obtain an attorney and he indicates that he wants one before speaking to police, they must respect his decision to remain silent."

Any statements obtained during custodial interrogation conducted in violation of these rules may not be admitted against the accused, at least during the State's case in chief.

The California court in this case, however, significantly has extended this rule by providing that a request by a juvenile for his probation officer has the same effect as a request for an attorney. Based on the court's belief that the probation officer occupies a position as a trusted guardian figure in the minor's life that would make it normal for the minor to turn to the officer when apprehended by the police, and based as well on the state-law requirement that the officer represent the interest of the juvenile, the California decision found that consultation with a probation officer fulfilled the role for the juvenile that consultation with an attorney does in general, acting as a "'protective [device] … to dispel the compulsion inherent in custodial surroundings.'"

The rule in *Miranda*, however, was based on this Court's perception that the lawyer occupies a critical position in our legal system because of his unique ability to protect the Fifth Amendment rights of a client undergoing custodial interrogation. Because of this special ability of the lawyer to help the client preserve his Fifth Amendment rights once the client becomes enmeshed in the adversary process, the Court found that "the right to have counsel present at the interrogation is indispensable to the protection of the Fifth Amendment privilege under the system" established by the Court. Moreover, the lawyer's presence helps guard against overreaching by the police and ensures that any statements actually obtained are accurately transcribed for presentation into evidence.

The *per se* aspect of *Miranda* was thus based on the unique role the lawyer plays in the adversary system of criminal justice in this country. Whether it is a minor or an adult who stands accused, the lawyer is the one person to whom society as a whole looks as the protector of the legal rights of that person in his dealings with the police and the courts. For this reason, the Court fashioned in *Miranda* the rigid rule that an accused's request for an attorney is per se an invocation of his Fifth Amendment rights, requiring that all interrogation cease.

A probation officer is not in the same posture with regard to either the accused or the system of justice as a whole. Often he is not trained in the law, and so is not in a position to advise the accused as to his legal rights. Neither is he a trained advocate, skilled in the representation of the interests of his client before both police and courts. He does not assume the power to act on behalf of his client by virtue of his status as adviser, nor are the communications of the accused to the probation officer shielded by the lawyer-client privilege.

Moreover, the probation officer is the employee of the State which seeks to prosecute the alleged offender. He is a peace officer, and as such is allied, to a greater or lesser extent, with his fellow peace officers. He owes an obligation to the State, notwithstanding the obligation he may also owe the juvenile under his supervision. In most cases, the probation officer is duty bound to report wrongdoing by the juvenile when it comes to his attention, even if by communication from the juvenile himself. Indeed, when this case arose, the probation officer had the responsibility for filing the petition alleging wrongdoing by the juvenile and seeking to have him taken into the custody of the Juvenile Court. It was respondent's probation officer who filed the petition against him, and it is the acting chief of probation for the State of California, a probation officer, who is petitioner in this Court today.

Nor do we believe that a request by a juvenile to speak with his probation officer constitutes a per se request to remain silent. As indicated, since a probation officer does not fulfill the important role in protecting the rights of the accused juvenile that an attorney plays, we decline to find that the request for the probation officer is tantamount to the request for an attorney. And there is nothing inherent in the request for a probation officer that requires us to find that a juvenile's request to see one necessarily constitutes an expression of the juvenile's right to remain silent. As discussed below, courts may take into account such a request in evaluating whether a juvenile in fact had waived his Fifth Amendment rights before confessing. But in other circumstances such a request might well be consistent with a desire to speak with the police. In the absence of further evidence that the minor intended in the circumstances to invoke his Fifth Amendment rights by such a request, we decline to attach such overwhelming significance to this request.

We hold, therefore, that it was error to find that the request by respondent to speak with his probation officer per se constituted an invocation of respondent's Fifth Amendment right to be free from compelled self-incrimination. It therefore was also error to hold that because the police did not then cease interrogating respondent the statements he made during interrogation should have been suppressed.

Miranda further recognized that after the required warnings are given the accused, "[i]f the interrogation continues without the presence of an attorney and a statement is taken, a heavy burden rests on the government to demonstrate that the defendant knowingly and intelligently waived his privilege against self-incrimination and his right to retained or appointed counsel." that the question whether the accused waived his rights "is not one of form, but rather whether the defendant in fact knowingly and voluntarily waived the rights delineated in the *Miranda* case." Thus, the determination whether statements obtained during custodial interrogation are admissible against the accused is to be made upon an inquiry into the totality of the circumstances surrounding the interrogation, to ascertain whether the accused in fact knowingly and voluntarily decided to forgo his rights to remain silent and to have the assistance of counsel.

This totality-of-the-circumstances approach is adequate to determine whether there has been a waiver even where interrogation of juveniles is involved. We discern no persuasive reasons why any other approach is required where the question is whether a juvenile has waived his rights, as opposed to whether an adult has done so. The totality approach permits — indeed, it mandates — inquiry into all the circumstances surrounding the interrogation. This includes evaluation of the juvenile's age, experience, education, background, and intelligence, and into whether he has the capacity to understand the warnings given him, the nature of his Fifth Amendment rights, and the consequences of waiving those rights.

On these facts, we think it clear that respondent voluntarily and knowingly waived his Fifth Amendment rights.

We hold, in short, that the California Supreme Court erred in finding that a juvenile's request for his probation officer was a per se invocation of that juvenile's Fifth Amendment rights under *Miranda*. We conclude, rather, that whether the statements obtained during subsequent interrogation of a juvenile who has asked to see his probation officer, but who has not asked to consult an attorney or expressly asserted his right to remain silent, are admissible on the basis of waiver remains a question to be resolved on the totality of the circumstances surrounding the interrogation. On the basis of the record in this case, we hold that the Juvenile Court's findings that respondent voluntarily and knowingly waived his rights and consented to continued interrogation, and that the statements obtained from him were voluntary, were proper, and that the admission of those statements in the proceeding against respondent in Juvenile Court was correct.

The judgment of the Supreme Court of California is reversed, and the case is remanded for further proceedings not inconsistent with this opinion.

It is so ordered.

Mr. Justice MARSHALL, with whom Mr. Justice BRENNAN and Mr. Justice STEVENS join, dissenting.

As this Court has consistently recognized, the coerciveness of the custodial setting is of heightened concern where, as here, a juvenile is under investigation. In *Haley v. Ohio*, the plurality reasoned that because a 15½-year-old minor was particularly susceptible to overbearing interrogation tactics, the voluntariness of his confession could not "be judged by the more exacting standards of maturity." The Court reiterated this point in *Gallegos v. Colorado*, observing that a 14-year-old suspect could not "be compared with an adult in full possession of his senses and knowledgeable of the consequences of his admissions." The juvenile defendant, in the Court's view, required "the aid of more mature judgment as to the steps he should take in the predicament in which he found himself. A lawyer or an adult relative or friend could have given the petitioner the protection which his own immaturity could not."

And, in *In re Gault*, the Court admonished that "the greatest care must be taken to assure that [a minor's] admission was voluntary."

It is therefore critical in the present context that we construe *Miranda's* prophylactic requirements broadly to accomplish their intended purpose—"dispel[ling] the compulsion inherent in custodial surroundings." To effectuate this purpose, the Court must ensure that the "protective device" of legal counsel be readily available, and that any intimation of a desire to preclude questioning be scrupulously honored. Thus, I believe *Miranda* requires that interrogation cease whenever a juvenile requests an adult who is obligated to represent his interests. Such a request, in my judgment, constitutes both an attempt to obtain advice and a general invocation of the right to silence. For, as the California Supreme Court recognized, "'[i]t is fatuous to assume that a minor in custody will be in a position to call an attorney for assistance,'" or that he will trust the police to obtain a lawyer for him. A juvenile in these circumstances will likely turn to his parents, or another adult responsible for his welfare, as the only means of securing legal counsel. Moreover, a request for such adult assistance is surely inconsistent with a present desire to speak freely. Requiring a strict verbal formula to invoke the protections of *Miranda* would "protect the knowledgeable accused from stationhouse coercion while abandoning the young person who knows no more than to ask for the ... person he trusts."

Thus, given the role of probation officers under California law, a juvenile's request to see his officer may reflect a desire for precisely the kind of assistance *Miranda* guarantees an accused before he waives his Fifth Amendment rights. At the very least, such a request signals a desire to remain silent until contact with the officer is made. Because the Court's contrary determination withdraws the safeguards of Miranda from those most in need of protection, I respectfully dissent.

Mr. Justice POWELL, dissenting.

Although I agree with the Court that the Supreme Court of California misconstrued *Miranda v. Arizona*, I would not reverse the California court's judgment. This Court repeatedly has recognized that "the greatest care" must be taken to assure that an alleged confession of a juvenile was voluntary. Respondent was a young person, 16 years old at the time of his arrest and the subsequent prolonged interrogation at the stationhouse. Although respondent had had prior brushes with the law, and was under supervision by a probation officer, the taped transcript of his interrogation—as well as his testimony at the suppression hearing—demonstrates that he was immature, emotional, and uneducated, and therefore was likely to be vulnerable to the skillful, two-on-one, repetitive style of interrogation to which he was subjected.

When given *Miranda* warnings and asked whether he desired an attorney, respondent requested permission to "have my probation officer here," a request that was refused. After stating that respondent had been "going through problems," the officer observed that "many times the kids don't understand what is going on, and what they are supposed to do relative to police...." This view of the limited understanding of the average 16-year-old was borne out by respondent's question when, during interrogation, he was advised of his right to an attorney: "How I know you guys won't pull no police officer in and tell me he's an attorney?" It was during this part of the interrogation that the police had denied respondent's request to "have my probation officer here."

It is clear that the interrogating police did not exercise "the greatest care" to assure that respondent's "admission was voluntary." In the absence of counsel, and having refused to call the probation officer, they nevertheless engaged in protracted interrogation.

Although I view the case as close, I am not satisfied that this particular 16-year-old boy, in this particular situation, was subjected to a fair interrogation free from inherently coercive circumstances. For these reasons, I would affirm the judgment of the Supreme Court of California.

Holding of *Fare v. Michael C.:* In this case, the court held that a request for consultation with a probation officer is not the same as a request for an attorney nor is it the equivalent of exercising a right to remain silent. The Court, furthermore, held that the confession was voluntary under the "totality of the circumstances," including: the juvenile's age, experience, education, background, and intelligence, and whether he has the capacity to understand the warnings given him, the nature of his Fifth Amendment rights, and the consequences of waiving those rights.

Discussion Questions

Would Michael believe that, if the cops were unwilling to call his probation officer at night that they would be willing to call his lawyer?

Does the "totality of the circumstances" test proposed by the majority reduce the concern about the vulnerability of a minor by relegating it to just one of several factors?

Would the result have been different if he had asked for a parent rather than the probation officer?

Yarborough v. Alvarado: In *Yarborough v. Alvarado*, the Supreme Court was forced to decide whether or not the age of the defendant was relevant to the determination of whether or not the defendant was in custody so as to implicate the cautions required by *Miranda*. Alvarado (who was "five months short of his 18th birthday") and a co-defendant attempted a car-jacking, and the co-defendant shot and killed the victim. During the investigation, officers asked Alvarado's parents to bring him to the station for questioning. Alvarado's parents waited in the lobby while he was interviewed. The interview lasted about 2 hours and was recorded. Only Alvarado and one officer was present. Alvarado was not given a *Miranda* warning.

As you read *Yarborough v. Alvarado*, look for the following:

1. Examine the opinion (and the dissents) to determine how to define a "reasonable person" and whether or not this should mean "a reasonable person in the situation of the defendant."

2. Contrast the holding of this case making age of the defendant irrelevant to the determination of whether or not a defendant is "in custody" for *Miranda* purposes and the previous cases in this chapter that are entirely dependent on age.

3. Decide whether or not the "totality of the circumstances" test applied in the previous cases in this chapter are applicable after *Yarborough* or whether the *Yarborough* decision only applies to the custody determination under *Miranda*.

Yarborough v. Alvarado
541 U.S. 652 (2004)

Justice KENNEDY delivered the opinion of the Court.

Paul Soto and respondent Michael Alvarado attempted to steal a truck in the parking lot of a shopping mall in Santa Fe Springs, California. Soto and Alvarado were part of a larger group of teenagers at the mall that night. Soto decided to steal the truck, and Alvarado agreed to help. Soto pulled out a .357 Magnum and approached the driver, Francisco Castaneda, who was standing near the truck emptying trash into a dumpster. Soto demanded money and the ignition keys from Castaneda. Alvarado, then five months short of his 18th birthday, approached the passenger side door of the truck and crouched down. When Castaneda refused to comply with Soto's demands, Soto shot Castaneda, killing him. Alvarado then helped hide Soto's gun.

Los Angeles County Sheriff's detective Cheryl Comstock led the investigation into the circumstances of Castaneda's death. About a month after the shooting, Comstock left word at Alvarado's house and also contacted Alvarado's mother at work with the message that she wished to speak with Alvarado. Alvarado's parents brought him to the Pico Rivera Sheriff's Station to be interviewed around lunchtime. They waited in the lobby while Alvarado went with Comstock to be interviewed. Alvarado contends that his parents asked to be present during the interview but were rebuffed.

Comstock brought Alvarado to a small interview room and began interviewing him at about 12:30 p.m. The interview lasted about two hours, and was recorded by Comstock with Alvarado's knowledge. Only Comstock and Alvarado were present. Alvarado was not given a warning under *Miranda v. Arizona.*

When the interview was over, Comstock returned with Alvarado to the lobby of the sheriff's station where his parents were waiting. Alvarado's father drove him home.

A few months later, the State of California charged Soto and Alvarado with first-degree murder and attempted robbery. Citing *Miranda*, Alvarado moved to suppress his statements from the Comstock interview. The trial court denied the motion on the ground that the interview was noncustodial. Alvarado and Soto were tried together, and Alvarado testified in his own defense. He offered an innocent explanation for his conduct, testifying that he happened to be standing in the parking lot of the mall when a gun went off nearby. The government's cross-examination relied on Alvarado's statement to Comstock. Alvarado admitted having made some of the statements but denied others. When Alvarado denied particular statements, the prosecution countered by playing excerpts from the audio recording of the interview.

During cross-examination, Alvarado agreed that the interview with Comstock "was a pretty friendly conversation," that there was "sort of a free flow between [Alvarado] and Detective Comstock," and that Alvarado did not "feel coerced or threatened in any way" during the interview. The jury convicted Soto and Alvarado of first-degree murder and attempted robbery. The trial judge later reduced Alvarado's conviction to second-degree murder for his comparatively minor role in the offense. The judge sentenced Soto to life in prison and Alvarado to 15-years-to-life.

Miranda itself held that preinterrogation warnings are required in the context of custodial interrogations given "the compulsion inherent in custodial surroundings." The Court explained that "custodial interrogation" meant "questioning initiated by law enforcement officers after a person has been taken into custody or otherwise deprived of his freedom of action in any significant way."

Our more recent cases instruct that custody must be determined based on how a reasonable person in the suspect's situation would perceive his circumstances.

Finally, in *Thompson v. Keohane*, the Court offered the following description of the *Miranda* custody test:

> "Two discrete inquiries are essential to the determination: first, what were the circumstances surrounding the interrogation; and second, given those circumstances, would a reasonable person have felt he or she was not at liberty to terminate the interrogation and leave. Once the scene is set and the players' lines and actions are reconstructed, the court must apply an objective test to resolve the ultimate inquiry: was there a formal arrest or restraint on freedom of movement of the degree associated with a formal arrest."

We turn now to the case before us and ask if the state-court adjudication of the claim "involved an unreasonable application" of clearly established law when it concluded that Alvarado was not in custody.

Based on these principles, we conclude that the state court's application of our clearly established law was reasonable. Ignoring the deferential standard of § 2254(d)(1) for the moment, it can be said that fairminded jurists could disagree over whether Alvarado was in custody.

The Court of Appeals reached the opposite result by placing considerable reliance on Alvarado's age and inexperience with law enforcement. Our Court has not stated that a suspect's age or experience is relevant to the *Miranda* custody analysis, and counsel for Alvarado did not press the importance of either factor on direct appeal or in habeas proceedings. According to the Court of Appeals, however, our Court's emphasis on juvenile status in other contexts demanded consideration of Alvarado's age and inexperience here.

Our opinions applying the *Miranda* custody test have not mentioned the suspect's age, much less mandated its consideration. The only indications in the Court's opinions relevant to a suspect's experience with law enforcement have rejected reliance on such factors.

In concluding that there was "no principled reason" why such factors should not also apply to the *Miranda* custody inquiry, the Court of Appeals ignored the argument that the custody inquiry states an objective rule designed to give clear guidance to the police, while consideration of a suspect's individual characteristics — including his age — could be viewed as creating a subjective inquiry.

The state court considered the proper factors and reached a reasonable conclusion. The judgment of the Court of Appeals is

Reversed.

Justice O'CONNOR, concurring.

I join the opinion of the Court, but write separately to express an additional reason for reversal. There may be cases in which a suspect's age will be relevant to the "custody" inquiry under *Miranda v. Arizona.* In this case, however, Alvarado was almost 18 years old at the time of his interview. It is difficult to expect police to recognize that a suspect is a juvenile when he is so close to the age of majority. Even when police do know a suspect's age, it may be difficult for them to ascertain what bearing it has on the likelihood that the suspect would feel free to leave. That is especially true here; 17½-year-olds vary widely in their reactions to police questioning, and many can be expected to behave as adults. Given these difficulties, I agree that the state court's decision in this case cannot be called an unreasonable application of federal law simply because it failed explicitly to mention Alvarado's age.

Justice BREYER, with whom Justice STEVENS, Justice SOUTER, and Justice GINSBURG join, dissenting.

In my view, Michael Alvarado clearly was "in custody" when the police questioned him (without *Miranda* warnings) about the murder of Francisco Castaneda. To put the question in terms of federal law's well-established legal standards: Would a "reasonable person" in Alvarado's "position" have felt he was "at liberty to terminate the interrogation and leave"? A court must answer this question in light of "all of the circumstances surrounding the interrogation." And the obvious answer here is "no."

The law in this case asks judges to apply, not arcane or complex legal directives, but ordinary common sense. Would a reasonable person in Alvarado's position have felt free simply to get up and walk out of the small room in the station house at will during his 2-hour police interrogation? I ask the reader to put himself, or herself, in Alvarado's circumstances and then answer that question: Alvarado hears from his parents that he is needed for police questioning. His parents take him to the station. On arrival, a police officer separates him from his parents. His parents ask to come along, but the officer says they may not. Another officer says, "'What do we have here; we are going to question a suspect.'"

The police take Alvarado to a small interrogation room, away from the station's public area. A single officer begins to question him, making clear in the process that the police have evidence that he participated in an attempted carjacking connected with a murder. When he says that he never saw any shooting, the officer suggests that he is lying, while adding that she is "giving [him] the opportunity to tell the truth" and "tak[e] care of [him]self." Toward the end of the questioning, the officer gives him permission to take a bathroom or water break. After two hours, by which time he has admitted he was involved in the attempted theft, knew about the gun, and helped to hide it, the questioning ends.

What reasonable person in the circumstances—brought to a police station by his parents at police request, put in a small interrogation room, questioned for a solid two hours, and confronted with claims that there is strong evidence that he participated in a serious crime, could have thought to himself, "Well, anytime I want to leave I can just get up and walk out"? If the person harbored any doubts, would he still think he might be free to leave once he recalls that the police officer has just refused to let his parents remain with him during questioning? Would he still think that he, rather than the officer, controls the situation?

There is only one possible answer to these questions. A reasonable person would not have thought he was free simply to pick up and leave in the middle of the interrogation.

I believe the California courts were clearly wrong to hold the contrary, and the Ninth Circuit was right in concluding that those state courts unreasonably applied clearly established federal law.

The facts to which the majority points make clear what the police did not do, for example, come to Alvarado's house, tell him he was under arrest, handcuff him, place him in a locked cell, threaten him, or tell him explicitly that he was not free to leave. But what is important here is what the police did do—namely, have Alvarado's parents bring him to the station, put him with a single officer in a small room, keep his parents out, let him know that he was a suspect, and question him for two hours. These latter facts compel a single conclusion: A reasonable person in Alvarado's circumstances would not have felt free to terminate the interrogation and leave.

What about Alvarado's youth? The fact that Alvarado was 17 helps to show that he was unlikely to have felt free to ignore his parents' request to come to the station. And a 17-year-old is more likely than, say, a 35-year-old, to take a police officer's assertion of authority to keep parents outside the room as an assertion of authority to keep their child inside as well.

The majority suggests that the law might prevent a judge from taking account of the fact that Alvarado was 17. I can find nothing in the law that supports that conclusion. Our cases do instruct lower courts to apply a "reasonable person" standard. But the "reasonable person" standard does not require a court to pretend that Alvarado was a 35-year-old with aging parents whose middle-aged children do what their parents ask only out of respect. Nor does it say that a court should pretend that Alvarado was the statistically determined "average person"—a working, married, 35-year-old white female with a high school degree.

In this case, Alvarado's youth is an objective circumstance that was known to the police. It is not a special quality, but rather a widely shared characteristic that generates commonsense conclusions about behavior and perception. To focus on the circumstance of age in a case like this does not complicate the "in custody" inquiry. And to say that courts should ignore widely shared, objective characteristics, like age, on the ground that only a (large) minority of the population possesses them would produce absurd results, the present instance being a case in point. I am not surprised that the majority points to no case suggesting any such limitation.

As I have said, the law in this case is clear. This Court's cases establish that, even if the police do not tell a suspect he is under arrest, do not handcuff him, do not lock him in a cell, and do not threaten him, he may nonetheless reasonably believe he is not free to leave the place of questioning—and thus be in custody for *Miranda* purposes.

Common sense, and an understanding of the law's basic purpose in this area, are enough to make clear that Alvarado's age—an objective, widely shared characteristic about which the police plainly knew—is also relevant to the inquiry. Unless one is prepared to pretend that Alvarado is someone he is not, a middle-aged gentleman, well versed in police practices, it seems to me clear that the California courts made a serious mistake. I agree with the Ninth Circuit's similar conclusions. Consequently, I dissent.

Holdings of *Yarborough v. Alvarado*: In this case, the court held that the custody inquiry under *Miranda* states an objective rule designed to give clear guidance to the police. A consideration of a suspect's individual characteristics—including age—would create a subjective inquiry, which is not mandated by cases that have interpreted the *Miranda* decision.

Discussion Questions

Does the fact that Alvarado said the questioning was "pretty friendly," "was a sort of a free flow" and that he did not "feel coerced or threatened in any way" establish that a reasonable person would perceive that he was not in custody?

The majority opinion says "Our court has not stated that a suspect's age or experience is relevant to the Miranda custody analysis ..." Isn't that exactly what the court said in Haley, Gallegos, and Michael C.?

———————

J.D.B. v. North Carolina: In *J.D.B. v. North Carolina,* a "13-year-old, seventh grade student" was removed from class by a uniformed police officer and taken to a closed-door conference room and questioned for 30 to 45 minutes about several home break-ins. Two police officers and two school administrators were present during the questioning. No one contacted the youth's grandmother (who was his legal guardian) and J.D.B. was not given his *Miranda* warnings, nor was he given an opportunity to talk to his grandmother. Only after J.D.B. confessed to the break-ins was he told that he was free to refuse to answer the investigator's questions or that he was free to leave. At the investigator's request, J.D.B. wrote out a confession and, once the bell rang indicating the end of the school day, he was allowed to "catch the bus home." This case revisits the question raised in the *Alvarado* case of whether or not age is a factor in making the custody determination required by *Miranda.*

As you read *J.D.B. v. North Carolina,* look for the following:

1. Search for language either in the majority opinion or in the dissenting opinions distinguishing or overruling the *Yarborough v. Alvarado* decision.

2. Try to find any distinguishing factors (other than the especially young age of the defendant) that cause a different result than that reached in the *Yarborough v. Alvarado* decision.

3. Try to determine what factors other than age may be used in the Miranda custody analysis under this case.

J.D.B. v. North Carolina
564 U.S. 261 (2011)

Justice SOTOMAYOR delivered the opinion of the Court.

This case presents the question whether the age of a child subjected to police questioning is relevant to the custody analysis of *Miranda v. Arizona.* It is beyond dispute that children will often feel bound to submit to police questioning when an adult in the same circumstances would feel free to leave. Seeing no reason for police officers or courts to blind themselves to that commonsense reality, we hold that a child's age properly informs the Miranda custody analysis.

Petitioner J.D.B. was a 13-year-old, seventh-grade student attending class at Smith Middle School in Chapel Hill, North Carolina when he was removed from his classroom by a uniformed police officer, escorted to a closed-door conference room, and questioned by police for at least half an hour.

This was the second time that police questioned J.D.B. in the span of a week. Five days earlier, two home break-ins occurred, and various items were stolen. Police stopped and questioned J.D.B. after he was seen behind a residence in the neighborhood where the crimes occurred. That same day, police also spoke to J.D.B.'s grandmother—his legal guardian—as well as his aunt.

Police later learned that a digital camera matching the description of one of the stolen items had been found at J.D.B.'s middle school and seen in J.D.B.'s possession. Investigator DiCostanzo, the juvenile investigator with the local police force who had been assigned to the case, went to the school to question J.D.B. Upon arrival, DiCostanzo informed the uniformed police officer on detail to the school (a so-called school resource officer), the assistant principal, and an administrative intern that he was there to question J.D.B. about the break-ins. Although DiCostanzo asked the school administrators to verify J.D.B.'s date of birth, address, and parent contact information from school records, neither the police officers nor the school administrators contacted J.D.B.'s grandmother.

The uniformed officer interrupted J.D.B.'s afternoon social studies class, removed J.D.B. from the classroom, and escorted him to a school conference room. There, J.D.B. was met by DiCostanzo, the assistant principal, and the administrative intern. The door to the conference room was closed. With the two police officers and the two administrators present, J.D.B. was questioned for the next 30 to 45 minutes. Prior to the commencement of questioning, J.D.B. was given neither Miranda warnings nor the opportunity to speak to his grandmother. Nor was he informed that he was free to leave the room.

After learning of the prospect of juvenile detention, J.D.B. confessed that he and a friend were responsible for the break-ins. DiCostanzo only then informed J.D.B. that he could refuse to answer the investigator's questions and that he was free to leave. Asked whether he understood, J.D.B. nodded and provided further detail, including information about the location of the stolen items. Eventually J.D.B. wrote a statement, at DiCostanzo's request. When the bell rang indicating the end of the schoolday, J.D.B. was allowed to leave to catch the bus home.

Two juvenile petitions were filed against J.D.B., each alleging one count of breaking and entering and one count of larceny. J.D.B.'s public defender moved to suppress his statements and the evidence derived therefrom. After a suppression hearing at which DiCostanzo and J.D.B. testified, the trial court denied the motion, deciding that J.D.B. was not in custody at the time of the schoolhouse interrogation and that his statements were voluntary. As a result, J.D.B. entered a transcript of admission to all four counts, renewing his objection to the denial of his motion to suppress, and the court adjudicated J.D.B. delinquent.

The State and its amici contend that a child's age has no place in the custody analysis, no matter how young the child subjected to police questioning. We cannot agree. In some circumstances, a child's age "would have affected how a reasonable person" in the suspect's position "would perceive his or her freedom to leave." That is, a reasonable child subjected to police questioning will sometimes feel pressured to submit when a reasonable adult would feel free to go. We think it clear that courts can account for that reality without doing any damage to the objective nature of the custody analysis.

A child's age is far "more than a chronological fact." It is a fact that "generates commonsense conclusions about behavior and perception." Such conclusions apply broadly to children as a class. And, they are self-evident to anyone who was a child once himself, including any police officer or judge.

Time and again, this Court has drawn these commonsense conclusions for itself. We have observed that children "generally are less mature and responsible than adults;" that they "often lack the experience, perspective, and judgment to recognize and avoid choices that could be detrimental to them;" that they "are more vulnerable or susceptible to ... outside pressures" than adults. Addressing the specific context of police interrogation, we have observed that events that "would leave a man cold and unimpressed can overawe and overwhelm a lad in his early teens." Describing no one child in particular, these observations restate what "any parent knows"—indeed, what any person knows—about children generally.

In fact, in many cases involving juvenile suspects, the custody analysis would be nonsensical absent some consideration of the suspect's age. This case is a prime example. Were the court precluded from taking J.D.B.'s youth into account, it would be forced to evaluate the circumstances present here through the eyes of a reasonable person of average years. In other words, how would a reasonable adult understand his situation, after being removed from a seventh-grade social studies class by a uniformed school resource officer; being encouraged by his assistant principal to "do the right thing"; and being warned by a police investigator of the prospect of juvenile detention and separation from his guardian and primary caretaker? To describe such an inquiry is to demonstrate its absurdity. Neither officers nor courts can reasonably evaluate the effect of objective circumstances that, by their nature, are specific to children without accounting for the age of the child subjected to those circumstances.

A student—whose presence at school is compulsory and whose disobedience at school is cause for disciplinary action—is in a far different position than, say, a parent volunteer on school grounds to chaperone an event, or an adult from the community on school grounds to attend a basketball game. Without asking whether the person "questioned in school" is a "minor," the coercive effect of the schoolhouse setting is unknowable.

Reviewing the question de novo today, we hold that so long as the child's age was known to the officer at the time of police questioning, or would have been objectively apparent to a reasonable officer, its inclusion in the custody analysis is consistent with the objective nature of that test. This is not to say that a child's age will be a determinative, or even a significant, factor in every case. It is, however, a reality that courts cannot simply ignore.

And in any event, a child's age, when known or apparent, is hardly an obscure factor to assess. Though the State and the dissent worry about gradations among children of different ages, that concern cannot justify ignoring a child's age altogether. Just as police officers are competent to account for other objective circumstances that are a matter of degree such as the length of questioning or the number of officers present, so too are they competent to evaluate the effect of relative age. Indeed, they are competent to do so even though an interrogation room lacks the "reflective atmosphere of a [jury] deliberation room." The same is true of judges, including those whose childhoods have long since passed. In short, officers and judges need no imaginative powers, knowledge of developmental psychology, training in cognitive science, or expertise in social and cultural anthropology to account for a child's age. They simply need the common sense to know that a 7-year-old is not a 13-year-old and neither is an adult.

The question remains whether J.D.B. was in custody when police interrogated him. We remand for the state courts to address that question, this time taking account of all of the relevant circumstances of the interrogation, including J.D.B.'s age at the time. The judgment of the North Carolina Supreme Court is reversed, and the case is remanded for proceedings not inconsistent with this opinion.

It is so ordered.

Justice ALITO, with whom THE CHIEF JUSTICE, Justice SCALIA, and Justice THOMAS join, dissenting.

The Court's decision in this case may seem on first consideration to be modest and sensible, but in truth it is neither. It is fundamentally inconsistent with one of the main justifications for the *Miranda* rule: the perceived need for a clear rule that can be easily applied in all cases. And today's holding is not needed to protect the constitutional rights of minors who are questioned by the police.

Today's decision shifts the *Miranda* custody determination from a one-size-fits-all reasonable-person test into an inquiry that must account for at least one individualized characteristic—age—that is thought to correlate with susceptibility to coercive pressures. Age, however, is in no way the only personal characteristic that may correlate with pliability, and in future cases the Court will be forced to choose between two unpalatable alternatives. It may choose to limit today's decision by arbitrarily distinguishing a suspect's age from other personal characteristics—such as intelligence, education, occupation, or prior experience with law enforcement—that may also correlate with susceptibility to coercive pressures. Or, if the Court is unwilling to draw these arbitrary lines, it will be forced to effect a fundamental transformation of the *Miranda* custody test—from a clear, easily applied prophylactic rule into a highly fact-intensive standard resembling the voluntariness test that the *Miranda* Court found to be unsatisfactory.

For at least three reasons, there is no need to go down this road. First, many minors subjected to police interrogation are near the age of majority, and for these suspects the one-size-fits-all *Miranda* custody rule may not be a bad fit. Second, many of the difficulties in applying the *Miranda* custody rule to minors arise because of the unique circumstances present when the police conduct interrogations at school. The Miranda custody rule has always taken into account the setting in which questioning occurs, and accounting for the school setting in such cases will address many of these problems. Third, in cases like the one now before us, where the suspect is especially young, courts applying the constitutional voluntariness standard can take special care to ensure that incriminating statements were not obtained through coercion.

Safeguarding the constitutional rights of minors does not require the extreme makeover of *Miranda* that today's decision may portend.

Indeed, it has always been the case under *Miranda* that the unusually meek or compliant are subject to the same fixed rules, including the same custody requirement, as those who are unusually resistant to police pressure.

That is undoubtedly why this Court's *Miranda* cases have never before mentioned "the suspect's age" or any other individualized consideration in applying the custody standard. And unless the *Miranda* custody rule is now to be radically transformed into one that takes into account the wide range of individual characteristics that are relevant in determining whether a confession is voluntary, the Court must shoulder the burden of explaining why age is different from these other personal characteristics.

Why, for example, is age different from intelligence? Suppose that an officer, upon going to a school to question a student, is told by the principal that the student has an I.Q. of 75 and is in a special-education class. Are those facts more or less important than the student's age in determining whether he or she "felt . . . at liberty to terminate the interrogation and leave"? An I.Q. score, like age, is more than just a number. And an individual's intelligence can also yield "conclusions" similar to those "we have drawn ourselves" in cases far afield of *Miranda*.

How about the suspect's cultural background? Suppose the police learn (or should have learned, see ante, at 11) that a suspect they wish to question is a recent immigrant from a country in which dire consequences often befall any person who dares to attempt to cut short any meeting with the police. Is this really less relevant than the fact that a suspect is a month or so away from his 18th birthday?

The defendant's education is another personal characteristic that may generate "conclusions about behavior and perception." Under today's decision, why should police officers and courts "blind themselves," to the fact that a suspect has "only a fifth-grade education"? Alternatively, what if the police know or should know that the suspect is "a college-educated man with law school training"? How are these individual considerations meaningfully different from age in their "relationship to a reasonable person's understanding of his freedom of action"? The Court proclaims that "[a] child's age … is different," but the basis for this ipse dixit is dubious.

I have little doubt that today's decision will soon be cited by defendants—and perhaps by prosecutors as well—for the proposition that all manner of other individual characteristics should be treated like age and taken into account in the *Miranda* custody calculus. Indeed, there are already lower court decisions that take this approach.

The Court holds that age must be taken into account when it "was known to the officer at the time of the interview," or when it "would have been objectively apparent" to a reasonable officer. The first half of this test overturns the rule that the "initial determination of custody" does not depend on the "subjective views harbored by … interrogating officers." The second half will generate time-consuming satellite litigation over a reasonable officer's perceptions. When, as here, the interrogation takes place in school, the inquiry may be relatively simple. But not all police questioning of minors takes place in schools. In many cases, courts will presumably have to make findings as to whether a particular suspect had a sufficiently youthful look to alert a reasonable officer to the possibility that the suspect was under 18, or whether a reasonable officer would have recognized that a suspect's I.D. was a fake. The inquiry will be both "time-consuming and disruptive" for the police and the courts. It will also be made all the more complicated by the fact that a suspect's dress and manner will often be different when the issue is litigated in court than it was at the time of the interrogation.

Even after courts clear this initial hurdle, further problems will likely emerge as judges attempt to put themselves in the shoes of the average 16-year-old, or 15-year-old, or 13-year-old, as the case may be. Consider, for example, a 60-year-old judge attempting to make a custody determination through the eyes of a hypothetical, average 15-year-old. Forty-five years of personal experience and societal change separate this judge from the days when he or she was 15 years old.

Take a fairly typical case in which today's holding may make a difference. A 16½-year-old moves to suppress incriminating statements made prior to the administration of *Miranda* warnings. The circumstances are such that, if the defendant were at least 18, the court would not find that he or she was in custody, but the defendant argues that a reasonable 16½-year-old would view the situation differently. The judge will not have the luxury of merely saying: "It is common sense that a 16½-year-old is not an 18-year-old. Motion granted." Rather, the judge will be required to determine whether the differences between a typical 16½-year-old and a typical 18-year-old with respect to susceptibility to the pressures of interrogation are sufficient to change the outcome of the custody determination. Today's opinion contains not a word of actual guidance as to how judges are supposed to go about making that determination.

Finally, in cases like the one now before us, where the suspect is much younger than the typical juvenile defendant, courts should be instructed to take particular care to ensure that incriminating statements were not obtained involuntarily. The voluntariness inquiry is flexible and accommodating by nature, and the Court's precedents already make clear that "special care" must be exercised in applying the voluntariness test where the confession of a "mere child" is at issue. If *Miranda*'s rigid, one-size-fits-all standards fail to account for the unique needs of juveniles, the response should be to rigorously apply the constitutional rule against coercion to ensure that the rights of minors are protected. There is no need to run *Miranda* off the rails.

Under today's new, "reality"-based approach to the doctrine, perhaps these and other principles of our *Miranda* jurisprudence will, like the custody standard, now be ripe for modification. Then, bit by bit, *Miranda* will lose the clarity and ease of application that has long been viewed as one of its chief justifications. I respectfully dissent.

Holding of *J.D.B. v. North Carolina*: In this case, the court held that a child's age may affect how a reasonable person' in the suspect's position would perceive his or her freedom to leave, and that courts can account for that reality under the *Miranda* custody analysis.

Discussion Questions

Is this decision based on the "in custody" standard or on the presumption that no questioning should ever occur to a young child without a parent or attorney present?

If the authorities would have called the youth's grandmother (legal guardian) or aunt (with whom they had previously talked) and had her/them present, would the result have been different?

Does the majority make age one factor in the analysis or dispositive of the analysis?

State v. Pearson: In *State v. Pearson*, the Iowa Supreme Court was faced with a nuance of the *Miranda* custody analysis addressed in *Yarborough* and *J.D.B.* Jesse Pearson, ("seven months shy of his eighteenth birthday") from a residential treatment center robbed an elderly, mentally challenged man in the man's home, beating him bloody with a cast iron frying pan. When apprehended by the police, officers contacted Pearson's mother by phone and she gave them permission to question her son. Pearson refused to waive his *Miranda* rights and refused to answer any questions until he was returned to the residential center and spoke with his lawyer. The next morning, Pearson's social worker visited Pearson in the residential treatment center without his attorney present and asked him "Did you actually do what everybody's saying you did?" Pearson confessed. The woman to whom he confessed had been his social worker for 8 years, was an employee of the state, but did not talk to Pearson at the request of the police.

As you read *State v. Pearson*, look for the following:

1. Examine the language used by the court to describe the age of the defendant in discussing this case.

2. The defendant was involuntarily placed in a facility of the state and Pearson was questioned by an employee of the state. Look for the ways that the Court discounts the impact of these facts on their decision.

3. Think of other state employees that the state could use to circumvent a youth's request for a lawyer before answering any questions.

State v. Pearson

804 N.W.2d 260 (Iowa 2011)

WATERMAN, Justice.

This case presents our first opportunity to address the impact of a defendant's underage status on the *Miranda* custody analysis in light of *J.D.B. v. North Carolina*. Our analysis turns on the specific circumstances of this interview: a confession received by a familiar social worker conducting the juvenile's status assessment at his youth home—without the coercive pressure of an unfamiliar police officer interrogating him at the station to solve a crime.

Defendant, Jesse Pearson, a seventeen-year-old runaway from the Bremwood Residential Treatment Center in Waverly, robbed an elderly, mentally disabled man in the victim's Waterloo home and beat him bloody with a cast iron frying pan. When apprehended later that day by the Waterloo police, Pearson refused to waive his *Miranda* rights and said he would not talk before he returned to Bremwood and spoke with his lawyer. The next morning, however, he promptly confessed to his social worker, Marie Mahler, without his attorney present. The district court ruled Mahler's interview was not a custodial interrogation implicating *Miranda* safeguards and denied Pearson's motion to suppress this confession. A Black Hawk County jury convicted him of first-degree robbery, willful injury, and going armed with intent.

We conclude Mahler's interview of Pearson was not a custodial interrogation for *Miranda* purposes and that his confession to her was voluntary and admissible.

Pearson had known Mahler for nearly eight years, since she was assigned his caseworker when he was age eleven after he was adjudicated a child in need of assistance (CINA). Mahler is a social worker employed by the Department of Human Services (DHS) in Buchanan County. As Pearson's caseworker, Mahler oversaw his juvenile proceedings and monitored his education, peer interactions, health, and general welfare. In July 2009, Pearson, seven months shy of his eighteenth birthday, resided at Bremwood by court order. Bremwood is a youth home, not a prison, jail, or juvenile detention facility. Bremwood provides a "home like" atmosphere to juveniles needing an intensive rehabilitative environment. At Bremwood, Pearson lived in a cottage with a kitchen, bathroom, living area, and bedroom. Despite these amenities, Pearson and D.S., another Bremwood resident, ran away.

They turned up the morning of July 14 at the door of the Waterloo home of Peter Weiss, a sixty-nine-year-old, mentally challenged man who lived alone. Weiss recognized D.S. from the neighborhood and let them enter when they asked to use his phone and bathroom. Once inside, Pearson began going through Weiss's drawers, over the protests of the elderly resident. Matters escalated when Pearson took a cast iron frying pan from the stove and hit Weiss over the head with it repeatedly. Pearson's blows left a clump of Weiss's hair on the kitchen floor and broke the iron handle off the pan. Weiss was knocked down with a fractured skull and multiple scalp lacerations that bled profusely. The teenagers ran out the door.

Weiss was able to call 9-1-1, and the operator kept him on the line as an ambulance and police were dispatched. Neighbors who spotted the teens hiding in bushes placed another call to police. Pearson was apprehended with Weiss's blood on his shirt and taken to the Waterloo police station. Officer Robert Michael reached Pearson's mother by phone, and she gave permission for the police to interview her son. Pearson was already a juvenile delinquent experienced in police procedures. Officer Michael read Pearson his *Miranda* rights, including that he had the right to remain silent, that if he chose to talk, anything he said would or could be used against him, and that he had a right to an attorney. Pearson responded by refusing to sign a form waiving his *Miranda* rights and by stating that he was not going to talk until he returned to Bremwood and spoke with his attorney. Pearson already had a public defender assigned to represent him on pending juvenile charges in Buchanan County. Later that afternoon, Bremwood staff picked Pearson up at the Waterloo police station and drove with him back to the youth home. His victim spent the night in the hospital with fifteen staples in his scalp to close his head wounds.

Bremwood staff moved Pearson to a different room called Trinity Cottage, but he was not locked in it. Trinity is windowless and positioned where staff can observe the doorway. Staff relocated Pearson there because he had run away and faced new charges. On July 15, Mahler arrived at 8 a.m. to meet with Pearson. She had already been told by Pearson's mother and Bremwood staff that Pearson had run away and been involved in an assault on an older man. Mahler also had spoken with a public defender assigned to Pearson's juvenile case who told her he would tell Pearson "not to talk to the officers or anybody about the incident." This defense counsel, however, did not tell Mahler to refrain from talking with Pearson. Mahler did not speak with the Waterloo police at this time.

As Pearson's CINA caseworker, Mahler needed to interview him to reassess his status after he had run away from Bremwood and been arrested. She was concerned Bremwood would evict him. She did not interview Pearson at the request of the Waterloo police, but rather, as his social worker.

Pearson was sleeping when Mahler arrived the morning after he assaulted Weiss, and staff awakened him. She met with him in Trinity Cottage and kept the door open so the staff could intervene if he became aggressive. Mahler first asked Pearson how he was doing, and he said, "I'm okay." Then she asked him, "Did you actually do what everybody's saying you did?" He said, "What did I do?" Mahler responded, "Did you actually hit an old man?" Without any further prompting, Pearson confessed: "Yeah. So? I hit him over the head with a frying pan." After making this admission, Pearson told Mahler his lawyer "told him to shut up" and that he had not answered questions from the police. Mahler asked no further questions about the assault at that time and spent the next hour talking with Pearson about why he had run away from Bremwood and where matters would go from there.

Mahler filed a report on her caseworker interview with the Buchanan County authorities handling Pearson's previously pending CINA and juvenile proceedings. Her report noted Pearson's "cocky" attitude and lack of remorse. She did not submit a report to the Black Hawk County Attorney or Waterloo police investigating the Weiss assault and robbery. Mahler was surprised to learn that the Waterloo police arrested Pearson the afternoon of July 15 and took him to jail. Days later, Officer Michael asked Mahler to provide a statement. She assumed information from her report to Buchanan County authorities had reached Michael's attention. Mahler refused to give the police a statement until her superiors at DHS in Des Moines authorized her to do so. Mahler also spoke with Pearson on August 7 when she asked him what the victim's injuries had been. Pearson told her the victim had fourteen to fifteen staples in his head and a fractured skull. Mahler again noted Pearson showed no remorse. On September 4, Pearson told Mahler that D.S. told him to hit the victim, so he did. Pearson admitted they were trying to get clothes from Weiss's home.

Pearson was charged in Black Hawk County with robbery in the first degree, willful injury, and going armed with intent. Pearson moved to transfer the case to juvenile court. The district court noted his "extended history of involvement with the juvenile court, primarily in Buchanan County," and "that the predominant delinquent history of the Defendant involves assault." Pearson had repeatedly assaulted his mother beginning at age eight and had assaulted police officers. The district court found "no evidence of any reasonable prospects for rehabilitation" and that Pearson "is a significant threat to the community." Accordingly, his motion to transfer was denied and the case proceeded in district court.

Pearson's trial counsel filed a motion to suppress his July 15 confession to Mahler. The district court denied the motion, concluding "the *Miranda* warning was not required because there was neither custody nor interrogation of the defendant." The district court found "the record is devoid of any threats, deceit, or other improper promises which were made to Pearson prior to his making admissions." The district court concluded Pearson's statements "were made willingly and voluntarily and satisfy due process rights."

The motion to suppress did not address the admissions Pearson made to Mahler on August 7 and September 4. Mahler testified at the jury trial regarding Pearson's confession and subsequent admissions. Weiss and D.S. both testified at trial that Pearson beat Weiss with the frying pan. Other witnesses established that DNA testing confirmed Weiss's blood was on the shirt worn by Pearson when he was arrested the day of the assault. Weiss's blood was not found on the clothing worn by D.S.

The jury convicted Pearson on all three counts.

We exercise our discretion on further review in this case to decide a single issue: whether the district court erred by denying Pearson's motion to suppress his July 15 confession to Mahler.

The dispositive issue in this case is whether Mahler's July 15 interview of Pearson at Bremwood without his lawyer present was a custodial interrogation under *Miranda*. The day before, Pearson unequivocally invoked his right to remain silent and his right to counsel and expressly declined Officer Michael's invitation to waive his *Miranda* rights, ending his interrogation at the Waterloo police station before it began.

We begin with an overview of *Miranda* to guide our determination whether Mahler's interview falls within the "types of situations" that implicate its requirements.

The Supreme Court in *J.D.B. v. North Carolina* recently reviewed the concerns that motivated adoption of the *Miranda* safeguards and emphasized one of the evils to be avoided is coerced, false confessions from an innocent juvenile:

> Indeed, the pressure of custodial interrogation is so immense that it "can induce a frighteningly high percentage of people to confess to crimes they never committed." That risk is all the more troubling—and recent studies suggest, all the more acute—when the subject of custodial interrogation is a juvenile.

Importantly, the *J.D.B.* Court reiterated that, because the *Miranda* safeguards "protect the individual against the coercive nature of custodial interrogation, they are required 'only where there has been such a restriction on a person's freedom as to render him in custody.'"

Against this backdrop, we apply the factors for determining whether Mahler's July 15 interview of Pearson was a "custodial interrogation" under *Miranda*. We conclude the circumstances of this confession lack the coercive pressure of a custodial interrogation. Accordingly, his July 15 confession is admissible.

Our analysis begins with the scene of the confession—Trinity Cottage at Bremwood—and the players, the underage suspect and his social worker employed by the state. We will next review the players' lines and actions to see if this interview had the characteristics of a formal arrest to constitute a custodial interrogation for purposes of *Miranda*.

1. *The scene.* The Waterloo police had released Pearson from their custody, and Bremwood staff drove him from the police station back to the Bremwood campus in Waverly the afternoon of July 14. Bremwood was Pearson's place of residence. It is not a detention or lockdown facility. Rather, it provides a "home like" environment. Because he had run away and had charges pending, Pearson was moved into Trinity Cottage, an unlocked, windowless room where he could be closely observed by staff. He was not handcuffed or summoned by Mahler for questioning in another room. Rather, she interviewed him in his room with the door open. The scene of their interview is not a factor tending to establish custody.

2. *The players.* Pearson was nearly seventeen and one-half years old by mid-July. Because he was a minor, we will begin with the age analysis mandated by *J.D.B.* The concern is that underage suspects may be more vulnerable than adults to the coercive pressure of a police interrogation.

J.D.B. involved a thirteen-year-old seventh grader suspected of residential burglaries. The *J.D.B.* Court requires consideration of the suspect's age when it is known or objectively apparent to a reasonable officer at the time of questioning.

The *J.D.B.* Court itself recognized age is an insignificant factor when the defendant is a teenager close to the age of majority. Pearson was just seven months shy of his eighteenth birthday at the time of his confession. Every parent and adult who works with teenagers can appreciate the difference between a 13-year-old and a 17-year-old. We are not dealing with a frightened seventh grader accused of furtive thefts. Pearson brazenly beat an elderly man in the victim's own kitchen. He had a prior history of assaulting adults, including his mother and police. He had no difficulty invoking his *Miranda* rights at the Waterloo police station after his apprehension in this case. It is relevant, although not determinative, to the age/custody analysis that the district court denied Pearson's motion to transfer this case to juvenile court based in part on the court's determination that there were no "reasonable prospects for rehabilitating the child if the juvenile court retain[ed] jurisdiction." His age does not support a finding of custody.

We next consider Mahler's status as a social worker. Pearson relies on *Deases*, where we recognized "the mere fact that the state official conducting the interrogation" is not a law enforcement officer "should not insulate the State from the requirements of *Miranda* where these safeguards would otherwise apply."

Pearson's case is more like *State v. Trigon, Inc.*, in which we held that *Miranda* did not apply to an IOSHA inspector's office-interview of a corporation's president regarding a workplace fatality. We noted the IOSHA inspector was investigating "whether the fatality resulted from a lapse in safety procedures and devices that would put other employees at risk of injury unless abated." The inspector "had no weapon, no badge, and no authority to arrest" and "was [not] mounting a criminal investigation." The same is true for Mahler. She was not a law enforcement officer, parole officer, or probation officer.

Mahler's nearly 8-year history as Pearson's caseworker cuts against a finding of custody.

Mahler and Officer Michael had different roles that did not intersect until days after Pearson's confession. Michael was the Waterloo police officer investigating criminal charges against Pearson in the Weiss incident. Mahler's purpose for interviewing Pearson was to perform a status assessment for his pending CINA and juvenile proceedings in Buchanan County. There is nothing in the record indicating Mahler was an agent for law enforcement. Michael did not ask Mahler to interview Pearson; they spoke for the first time days after Pearson's July 15 confession. She refused to give Michael her statement until authorized to do so by her DHS supervisor.

We therefore conclude Mahler was not an agent or stalking horse for the Waterloo police; she had her own reasons, as Pearson's caseworker, to interview him. Mahler's status as a DHS caseworker operating independently from the Waterloo police reinforces our conclusion that her interview of Pearson was not a custodial interrogation.

3. *The players' lines and actions.* Mahler immediately confronted Pearson with evidence of his guilt. This factor supports a finding of a custodial interrogation. Her first words to him after he was awakened asked how he was doing, and when he said, "I'm okay," she said, "Did you actually do what everybody's saying you did?" He responded, "What did I do?" Mahler then asked, "Did you actually hit an old man?" Pearson's next line was his confession, "Yeah. So? I hit him over the head with a frying pan."

Similarly, we conclude that Mahler did not convert her status assessment into a custodial interrogation by asking Pearson at the outset what he had done. Mahler did not wear him down through a lengthy interrogation; Pearson freely admitted what he did to the victim at the very outset of their discussions. Pearson knew the day before he could refuse to answer the questions of the Waterloo police; we see no reason he did not feel equally at liberty to decline to answer Mahler's questions.

The district court correctly found that "[t]he record is devoid of any threats, deceit, or other improper promises which were made to Pearson prior to his making admissions" and that Pearson's statements "were made willingly and voluntarily."

This case is lacking the "essential ingredients of a 'police-dominated atmosphere' and compulsion" that implicate the concerns underlying *Miranda*. Pearson was not handcuffed or physically restrained; the door to his room was left open. He confessed without any lengthy or aggressive or hostile questioning from Mahler, and the brevity of Mahler's interview preceding his confession belies a finding of compulsion. Mahler noted Pearson was "cocky" and remorseless, not intimidated or frightened.

Based on our own de novo review of the totality of the circumstances, we reach the same conclusion as the district court and court of appeals: Pearson objectively would not have felt he was under arrest or restrained to a degree associated with formal arrest when he confessed. Accordingly, we hold Mahler's July 15 interview was not a custodial interrogation for *Miranda* purposes and that Pearson's confession was voluntary and admissible.

We affirm the decision of the court of appeals and affirm Pearson's district court convictions and sentence for first-degree robbery and willful injury.

Holdings of *State v. Pearson:* In this case, the court held that, Pearson's confession was not a custodial interrogation for *Miranda* purposes and his confession was voluntary and admissible. The court based the decision on a number of factors, including: (1) The residential facility was not a detention or lockdown facility. (2) Pearson was not handcuffed or summoned by Mahler for questioning in another room. Rather, she interviewed him in his room with the door open. (3) Pearson was just seven months shy of his eighteenth birthday at the time of his confession. (4) The social worker was not an agent for the police. (5) There was no lengthy interrogation.

Discussion Questions

Is it important that Pearson was "seven months shy of his eighteenth birthday"?

Of what relevance is the fact that Pearson was "already a juvenile delinquent experienced in police procedures" and "already had a public defender assigned to represent him on pending juvenile charges"?

The court says that the social worker "did not interview Pearson at the request of the Waterloo police, but rather, as his social worker"? Would it have made a difference if she did so at the request of the police?

Aren't the facts that Pearson is in "state custody" (in a placement facility) and questioned by a state employee (a DHS worker) enough to trigger Miranda?

Key Concepts: Interrogation of Minors

- Minors are treated differently than adults when determining whether or not the confession was voluntary. Courts generally look at the totality of the circumstances in determining whether or not a minor's confession was voluntary.

- Age is an important factor in determining whether or not an interrogation of a minor is coercive and the courts appear to apply a different standard for very young suspects and those suspects that are approaching the age of majority.

- Minors should be offered the benefit of a lawyer and the advice of a parent, guardian or adult friend before being interrogated. Some statutes actually require that parents be contacted before any interrogation of minors below a specified age can begin.

- Age must be considered in determining whether or not the youth was in custody so as to make the *Miranda* requirements applicable.

Practical Questions: Interrogation of Minors

1. Your client, Michael, is age 13 and is charged with being an accessory to a robbery. His co-defendant (James) is age 17 and was charged earlier with the underlying robbery. Within hours of the crime, police came to James' home and found both youths present. James' mother was present and consented to the questioning of him. Police officers called Michael's mother who, over the phone, consented to the questioning. James and Michael were taken to separate rooms at James' home, questioned for about two hours, and both confessed. James' attorney filed a motion to suppress his confession, but the court overruled the motion, finding that the confession was not a "custodial" interrogation under *Miranda*. What arguments would you make to support a different result for Michael?

2. You are appointed to represent 15-year-old Steven Jones who is accused of second degree arson. His mother, Sharon, called police to report that she believed that her son set fire to the family's garage. The police asked Sharon to bring Steven to the police station, which she did. At the police stations, officers asked Sharon to sign a "victim's complaint" against her son so that they could formally charge him. After Sharon signed the victim's complaint, she also signed a form authorizing officers to question her son. During the 3-hour interrogation, Sharon was present and several times ordered Steven to answer the officer's questions. At one point, Steven asked if he could leave. The officers said nothing, but Sharon said, "You are staying right here until you tell them the truth." Finally, Steven confessed to setting the fire. Explain on which factors you will rely to support a motion to suppress the confession.

Simulation Exercise II

Characters: Prosecuting attorney, defense attorney, and Judge.

Facts: Sarah Richards, a 15-year-old passenger in a stolen car driven by a 25-year-old male, was taken to the police station at 11:00 p.m. Police immediately notified Sarah that they suspected that she had been working as a prostitute. Officers asked Sarah how her parents could be located. Afraid of her parent's reaction to the charges, Sarah refused to give the police any contact information for her parents. Officers did nothing more to locate her parents. Officers placed her in a small interview room that was six feet by six feet in size, with only a small table and two folding chairs. The room was cold, and Sarah was wearing only a tank top and shorts. She was left in the interview room alone until 6:00 a.m.

A video of the interview room showed Sarah shivering and crying throughout the time that she was left alone in the interview room. At 6:00 a.m., a police officer entered the room, read Sarah her *Miranda* rights and asked her to sign a waiver of those rights, which she did. Sarah initially denied being involved in prostitution, but said she had been hitchhiking and was picked up by the older male. The officer kept telling Sarah he knew better, but Sarah stuck to her story. At 8:30 a.m., Sarah finally said that she had been acting as a prostitute that evening. She was charged with prostitution, a felony.

Sarah was given a court-appointed attorney, who promptly filed a motion to suppress Sarah's confession, and an oral hearing on the motion has been scheduled.

Simulation: The exercise is to conduct oral arguments on the motion to suppress the confession. The attorney for Sarah will present an oral argument that Sarah's confession is inadmissible. The prosecuting attorney will argue that the confession was knowingly and voluntarily made and, as such, is admissible. The judge should be prepared to ask any questions necessary to arrive at a ruling, the attorneys shall be prepared to answer any questions posed to them, and the judge will enter an oral ruling on the motion specifying findings and reasons for the ruling.

Chapter IV

Searches of Minors

Overview: Because minors usually live at home, courts have often been forced to analyze the admissibility of evidence against a minor that was obtained as a result of a search pursuant to the consent of the parent. Courts have long recognized that minors have rights protected by the Fourth Amendment. However, courts have also recognized that parents have a duty to supervise their children (especially in the parent's home), and, as a result, parents may be able to consent to searches of rooms in their home. Problems arise when a parent consents but the youth objects, when the search applies to containers rather than a room itself, as well as when the offspring is living with the parent after adulthood.

Wimberly v. State: In *Wimberly v. State,* the Alabama Appeals Court was faced with a challenge to the admissibility of a box of 9mm shells found in the bedroom of Wimberly who was accused of murder. Wimberly was 17 years old and lived in the home of his mother. The mother signed a written consent allowing the police to search Wimberly's bedroom. Wimberly's attorney moved to suppress the evidence on the grounds that Wimberly did not consent to the search of his own bedroom and that the consent provided by his mother was not sufficient as applied to Wimberly.

As you read *Wimberly v. State,* look for the following:

1. Consider why the court does not accept the analogy that a consent of a youth's bedroom by a parent is similar to the consent to search an apartment by a landlord.

2. Consider whether or not, if Wimberly would have been paying rent to his mother for the use of the bedroom, the result would have been different.

3. Look at the language of the court to determine whether or not the fact that Wimberly is a minor is dispositive of the issue of consent by the parent or whether or not the same would be true if Wimberly had been an adult.

Wimberly v. State
934 So.2d 411 (Ala. Crim. App. 2005)

The appellant, Shaber Chamond Wimberly, was convicted of two counts of capital murder for murdering Mary Spivey during the course of a robbery and a burglary. The jury recommended, by a vote of 10 to 2, that Wimberly be sentenced to death. The circuit court sentenced Wimberly to death.

The State's evidence tended to show the following. On June 24, 1997, Ray Spivey discovered the body of his mother, Mary Spivey, lying on the floor of her house near Columbia. Spivey had been shot in the face. The autopsy revealed that Spivey died from a gunshot wound to her left eye that entered her brain and fractured her skull. The back door of Spivey's house had been pried open, the house ransacked, and numerous items taken from the house and from a convenience store operated by Spivey that was connected to her house. Spivey's green minivan was also taken and the cash register from the convenience store was missing.

In the early morning hours of June 24, 1997, Houston County Deputy Sheriff Jeff Carlisle saw a green minivan hit a curb and lose a hubcap. Carlisle followed the minivan to return the hubcap. When the minivan stopped, another car, a Chevrolet, also stopped. Wimberly was driving the minivan and Junior Pruitt was driving the Chevrolet. After he gave Wimberly the hubcap, he allowed them to leave.

Junior Pruitt testified that Wimberly had awakened him in the early morning on June 24, 1997, and asked him to follow him in his car so that he could return the minivan that he was driving to his aunt. He said that after the minivan was stopped by Deputy Carlisle and they were allowed to proceed, he and Wimberly drove their vehicles to a deserted area, and Wimberly poured gasoline on the minivan and set it on fire. Pruitt took Wimberly to an area adjacent to Spivey's store where Wimberly's vehicle was stuck in a ditch. He said that at the time Wimberly was carrying a large sum of money.

A.D. Dawsey testified that he saw Wimberly and Evester Tharp, Wimberly's codefendant, in a green minivan on the day of the murder. He said that he saw Tharp burning bags and checks. Dawsey said that Wimberly telephoned him later in the day and told him to go to Wimberly's house and get Wimberly's sister. Dawsey said that Wimberly's sister retrieved a pistol from the attic and gave it to him to dispose of. He said that he buried the pistol in a ditch. The gun was never recovered, but a box of 9 mm ammunition was seized from Wimberly's bedroom.

Johnny Frank Coleman testified that he had seen Wimberly with a silver-plated 9 mm pistol on the day of the murder. He said that Wimberly was with Tharp and that he loaned them his car and when they returned it it was covered in mud.

Houston County Deputy Sheriff Sgt. Gary Lindsey testified that on the morning of June 24, 1997, he was dispatched to an area near Spivey's house where he discovered a green minivan that was registered to Spivey. The van had been burned.

The record shows that Wimberly was born on September 6, 1979, and that he murdered Mary Spivey on June 24, 1997. Wimberly was 17 years old when he committed the murder. The United States Supreme Court recently in *Roper v. Simmons,* held that it was a violation of the Eighth and Fourteenth Amendments to impose a death sentence on an offender who was under the age of 18 at the time the crime was committed.

Wimberly raises several arguments concerning the penalty phase of his capital trial. However, because Wimberly's death sentence is due to be set aside based on *Roper v. Simmons*, any questions concerning the penalty phase are moot and will not be discussed in this opinion.

Wimberly argues that the circuit court erred in denying his motion to suppress the evidence seized as a result of the search of his bedroom at his mother's house.

At the suppression hearing, Deputy Richard St. John of the Houston County Sheriff's Department testified that he went to the home of Patricia Wade, Wimberly's mother, on June 24, 1997. He said that Wimberly lived in a room in his mother's house. St. John testified, and the signed consent form was introduced as State's Exhibit 5, that Wade signed a consent to search form. He further testified that she was not threatened or coerced to sign the form. St. John discovered ammunition for a 9 mm pistol in Wimberly's room.

Wimberly argued at trial and now on appeal that his mother could not legally give her consent to search his bedroom. He analogizes the situation to one arising out of a landlord/tenant relationship and says that a landlord cannot give a valid consent to search a tenant's lodgings.

However, this Court has held that a parent's rights are superior to that of a child.

"""If a son or daughter, whether or not still a minor, is residing in the home of the parents, generally it is within the authority of the father or mother to consent to a police search of that home which will be effective against the offspring. This is unquestionably so as to areas of common usage, and is also true of the bedroom of the son or daughter when a parent has ready access for purposes of cleaning it or when because of the minority of the offspring the parent is still exercising parental authority. Because in the latter circumstances the parent's rights are "superior to the rights of children who live in the house," a parent's consent would prevail even if the child were present and objecting and even if the child had taken special measures in an effort to ensure he had exclusive use of the area searched.'"

Here, Wimberly was 17 years old and was living in his mother's house. It is uncontested that Wade consented to the search of her entire house. Wade's rights as a parent were superior to Wimberly's rights, and Wade could legally give her consent to search Wimberly's bedroom. The circuit court correctly denied the motion to suppress the evidence seized as result of the search.

AFFIRMED AS TO CONVICTION; REMANDED WITH INSTRUCTIONS AS TO SENTENCE.

Holdings of *Wimberly v. State:* The court held that, in the case of a youth residing in the home of an adult, the parent's rights are "superior to the rights of children who live in the house," and that the parent has the legal right to consent to the search of the child's bedroom.

Discussion Questions

Why did the court reject the argument of the youth that his bedroom should be treated just like that in a landlord/tenant relationship?

In determining whose rights are superior, the parent's or the child's, relative to the consent to search, what did the Court decide? WHY?

Wouldn't it have been easier just to rule that BOTH the child and the parent had the authority to give consent to search?

———————

In re Scott K.: In *In re Scott K.,* the California Supreme Court was faced with a challenge to the admissibility of marijuana found in a locked tool box in a youth's bedroom. The youth was 17 years old and lived with his parents. The father had given the police consent to search the youth's bedroom where they found a locked toolbox. The police told the youth that the father had consented to their breaking open the locked toolbox if the youth didn't give them a key. As a result, the police were provided a key that unlocked the toolbox containing the marijuana. The youth's attorney moved to suppress the marijuana, arguing that the parent may have the right to consent to the search of the youth's bedroom located in the parent's house, but not the right to open a locked box owned by the youth.

As you read *In re Scott K.,* look for the following:

1. Consider how the court differentiates between the rights of a parent vs. the rights of a child and the rights of the child vs. the rights of the state.

2. Consider whether or not the *Wimberly v. State* court would take the same approach in analyzing the motion to suppress.

3. Think about why the Court would differentiate between the parent's right to consent to the search of the bedroom and the parent's right to consent to the search of the locked toolbox.

4. Consider whether or not the fact that the toolbox was locked is essential to the holding of the court.

In re Scott K.

595 P.2d 105 (Cal. 1979)

NEWMAN, Justice.

A 17-year-old defendant appeals from an order declaring him a juvenile court ward and placing him on probation. The order was based on the court's finding that defendant unlawfully possessed marijuana for purpose of sale in violation of section 11359 of the Health and Safety Code. The question is whether a warrantless, parent-approved, police search of defendant's personal property was permissible.

Defendant's mother found marijuana in his desk drawer. She gave it to an off-duty police officer who lived in the neighborhood and told him that conversations with other parents led her to believe that her son might be selling marijuana. A week later that officer's report was given to Narcotics Officer Schian for follow-up. He telephoned the father to advise that he was about to arrest defendant. The conversation was as follows:

"In substance, I advised the father that I was in charge of the follow-up investigation of the marijuana that his wife had turned over to the police officer; that an arrest would result from this situation, arrest of the son; that I intended to come out and arrest his son if his son was home, and then I received the information that he was working on his motorcycle in the garage.

"And I asked him, 'Is it all right with you then that I go to the garage and arrest your boy there and do you wish to join us out there then, or what shall we do to make it easy on maybe the rest of the family?'

"And he indicated, 'Why don't you just come on inside after you have arrested him?'"

Without warrant, Schian and other officers went to the garage. Schian arrested defendant and took him to the house, where the father gave permission to search defendant's bedroom. The search disclosed a locked toolbox. The father told Schian that he had no key and that it was defendant's box. When asked about the key, defendant replied he had lost it. Schian said, "Your father already told me I could break the toolbox open if I couldn't find a key, but it's not in my interest to destroy the lock. Let me see the keys you have in your pocket." Defendant gave Schian his keys, one of which opened the box. Inside were nine baggies of marijuana.

The court nonetheless denied a motion to suppress as evidence the marijuana found in the toolbox. The court reasoned that, because the father owned the house and had a duty to control his son's activities, he could permit the search at any time, whether or not his son was present or under arrest.

The People contend that a father has authority to inspect the belongings of a minor child to promote the child's health and welfare; also, that in consenting to the search this father was "merely using the police as an instrumentality to assist him in complying with his parental duty."

The formulation of issues in both the trial court's ruling and the People's argument seems misleading. Is not an important distinction obscured — the distinction between the parent-child relation and a constitutionally prescribed relation between people and government? A minor's interest in both those relations is identifiable even when, as here, his or her assertion of privacy rights against the government appears to conflict with parental authority. The primary issue in this case involves the minor's rights regarding his government.

By no means are the rights of juveniles coextensive with those of adults. Minors' rights are often legitimately curtailed when the restriction serves a state's interest in promoting the health and growth of children. In juvenile court proceedings, rights may not be asserted if they might disrupt unique features of the proceedings; for example, jury trial is not required. Search and seizure laws, however, hardly seem disruptive or otherwise inconsistent with the state's interest in child welfare. It is established that minors have a liberty interest that entitles them to due process whenever a state initiates action to deprive them of liberty. Enforcement of search and seizure protections helps ensure that the factfinding process conforms with standards of due process.

Justice should not be compromised by well-intentioned aims to correct transgressing youths, and the rehabilitative value of treating juveniles with fairness must not be underrated. Among sister states the extension of Fourth Amendment protections to minors is widespread.

The minor here contends that, because the toolbox was his own property, warrantless police search violated both his right to privacy and his right to be free from unreasonable search and seizure. He was age 17, old enough to assert his rights. When the police asked him for the key he did not consent to the search; instead the father gave consent.

Though the record discloses some discord in the parent-child relation, no evidence suggests that the discord concerned control of the box. The facts rather support the son's claim that the box was his own.

The People argue that, because a parent is responsible for minor children and may himself inspect their property, police search of that property when pursuant to parental consent is reasonable and accordingly constitutional. Implicit is the notion that the father here could effectively waive his son's right to be secure in the son's effects. We reject that view.

Our final question is whether the toolbox search was reasonable because the father's consent qualified under the third-party-consent exception to warrant requirements. A warrantless search is reasonable when consent is granted by one who has a protectible interest in the property. Valid consent may come from the sole owner of property or from "a third party who possessed common authority over or other sufficient relationship to the premises or effects sought to be inspected."

The trial court here held that the father's authority was based on the combined circumstance of his ownership of the home and his duty to control his son. Yet neither fact shows the requisite link between the father's interest and the property inspected. Common authority over personal property may not be implied from the father's proprietary interest in the premises. Neither may it be premised on the nature of the parent-child relation.

Parents may have a protectible interest in property belonging to children, but that fact may not be assumed. When a warrantless search is challenged the People must show that it was reasonable. Here the People did not establish that the consenting parent had a sufficient interest under search and seizure law. The father claimed no interest in the box or its contents. He acknowledged that the son was owner, and the son did not consent to the search. Because those facts were known to the police there was no justification either for their relying on the father's consent to conduct the search or for their failure to seek the warrant required by law.

The trial court's order is reversed.

CLARK, Justice, dissenting.

Scott's right under the California Constitution to be free from unreasonable searches and seizures was not violated when his father and mother enlisted police assistance in discharging their parental responsibilities and consented to the search of Scott's toolbox. But his parents' right to care for, discipline and control their minor children a liberty interest protected by the due process clause of the Fourteenth Amendment to the United States Constitution is violated by the decision reached by this court's majority today.

Admittedly, minors as well as adults possess constitutional rights. However, as the majority concede, the rights of minors are by no means coextensive with those of adults. In particular, the right to be free from unreasonable searches and seizures does not extend as far when a minor is involved.

By bringing Scott's possession and possible sale of marijuana to the attention of the authorities, and by cooperating with them in the investigation of these offenses, Scott's parents certainly did not jeopardize his health or safety, nor did their actions "have a potential for significant social burdens." Quite the contrary. However, the majority's decision very likely will have such deleterious effects by diminishing the authority of parents to discipline and control their children.

The judgment should be affirmed.

RICHARDSON, Justice, dissenting.

I concur in part and respectfully dissent in part. On the one hand, parents, in my view, have both the right and the responsibility to preserve the lawful nature of activities in their home. Both generally, as law-abiding citizens, and particularly, as model-setting parents, their obligation, assuredly, is to control and eliminate any criminal activity in the home. Children in a home setting are more than tenants at will of the rooms which they occupy, and a parent is more than a landlord. On the other hand, a minor child no less than an adult retains substantial Fourth Amendment rights, but I do not view these as absolute or unconditional in a home environment.

How may we reconcile the seemingly conflicting interests and obligations? The Fourth Amendment proscription against "Unreasonable" searches and seizures provides the key. I would hold that a minor child living in a home situation is not powerless before an unrestricted exploratory police search even though undertaken with parental consent. However, both the child's Fourth Amendment and privacy rights are not unrestricted. Bearing in mind the dual relationships involved herein, namely, the minor-citizen versus the officer-state invoking Fourth Amendment rights, and the private parent-child familial relationship, I would adopt the following principles. A parent may validly consent, over the objection of his dependent minor child living in the family home, to a police search of the premises and possessions used or owned by the child on the premises, if reasonable grounds (not necessarily amounting to probable cause) support a belief that the place or thing searched will yield criminal evidence. In this situation I would not elevate a child's Fourth Amendment or privacy rights above a parent's right to maintain a lawful, stable home environment free from criminal activity. The minor has no "reasonable expectation of privacy" in these limited circumstances where the police act reasonably in good faith reliance on the parents' consent.

The evidence here clearly supports the instant search. Scott's parents had already discovered marijuana in his room. Their own discussions with other parents established the substantial possibility that Scott was trafficking in the substance. On that basis, they initiated contact with the police. After further independent investigation, the authorities became convinced there was probable cause for Scott's arrest. Detective Schian, one of the arresting officers, testified he told the parents that a search of Scott's bedroom was the best way to prove or disprove Scott's involvement. This was reasonable. The parents had a legitimate purpose in seeking to ferret out the existence of any criminal activity conducted in any part of their home. Their responsibility to themselves, and as parents of Scott and of any other children in the family required that they do so. Parents in certain situations have a right to be suspicious, and to act reasonably in accordance with those suspicions. They do not help their children if they do otherwise. A locked container controlled solely by the suspect minor and found in his room would, of course, be one of the most logical places for concealment of contraband or criminal evidence.

Under the foregoing conditions, I would not recognize a child's right of "sanctuary" vis-a-vis the responsible parent. I therefore conclude that the search was proper, and that the judgment should be affirmed.

Holdings of *In re Scott K.*: In this case, the court articulated a distinction between the parent-child relation and the relation between people and government. Because the father claimed no interest in the box or its contents, there was no justification either for police relying on the father's consent to conduct the search or for their failure to seek a search warrant as required by law.

Discussion Questions

What facts in this case lead to the different outcome from the *Wimberly* case?

What rights are balanced by the majority opinion: Child vs. Parent, Child vs. State, or Parent vs. State?

Why doesn't the parent-homeowner in this case have the right to give consent to the search just like in the *Wimberly* case?

***In re D.C.*:** In *In re D.C.*, the California Appeals Court was faced with a challenge to the admissibility of stolen goods found in a minor's bedroom during a search of the apartment he shared with his mother and older brother. While the minor's mother consented to a search of the entire apartment, the youth objected and attempted to block the officers' entry, but relented when his mother told him to "get out of the way."

As you read *In re D.C.*, look for the following:

1. Consider whether or not the result would be different if the older brother (an adult) had been the one to resist entry into his bedroom.

2. Consider whether or not this decision is consistent with both *Wimberly* and *Scott K.* or if this case departs from either one of those decisions.

In re D.C.

115 Cal. Rptr.3d 837 (Cal. App. 2011)

Appellant D.C., a minor, was continued as a ward of the court after police found stolen goods in his bedroom during a search of the apartment he shared with his mother and older brother. Police originally went to the apartment to conduct a probation search relating to the older brother, suspecting he might have been involved in local crimes. As they arrived, the officers obtained consent from appellant's mother to search the entire apartment. Appellant objected and attempted to block the officers' entry, but he relented when his mother told him to "get out of the way."

Appellant contends evidence of the stolen goods should have been suppressed because (1) his mother did not have the authority to consent to a search of his bedroom and (2) his objection to the officers' entry to the apartment precluded a consensual search. While the arguments appellant raises might have prevailed were he an adult, we conclude his mother, as the parent of a minor child, had the authority to consent to a search of his bedroom and to override any objection he raised to the search of her apartment.

As appellant argues, it has been held, outside the parent-child context, that adults sharing a residence but maintaining separate bedrooms do not have the apparent authority to consent to the search of one another's bedrooms, at least when officers have no other information about their living arrangements.

California courts, however, have come to a different conclusion when an adult child maintains a bedroom in the home of his or her parents. In *People v. Daniels*, the court held that the search of an adult child's bedroom in his parents' home made with the consent of a parent is reasonable "absent circumstances establishing the son has been given exclusive control over the bedroom." The court reasoned that "[p]arents with whom a son is living, on premises owned by them, do not ipso facto relinquish exclusive control over that portion thereof used by the son. To the contrary, the mere fact the son is permitted to use a particular bedroom, as such, does not confer upon him exclusive control thereof. His occupancy is subservient to the control of his parents. He may be excluded from the premises by them at any time."

When the child is a minor, there is an even stronger case for apparent authority in a parent to consent to the search of the child's bedroom. Unlike the parents of adult children, the parents of minor children have legal rights and obligations that both permit and, in essence, require them to exercise common authority over their child's bedroom. Parents have the "right to direct and control the activities of a minor child.... 'The liberty interest ... of parents in the care, custody, and control of their children ... is perhaps the oldest of the fundamental liberty interests....'" Conversely, parents have affirmative legal duties toward their minor children.

Under *Matlock,* "common authority" over a residence is found if there is "mutual use of the property by persons generally having joint access or control for most purposes, so that it is reasonable to recognize that any of the co-inhabitants has the right to permit the inspection in his own right...." Given the legal rights and obligations of parents toward their minor children, common authority over the child's bedroom is inherent in the parental role. Carrying out their duty of supervision and control requires a parent to have the ability to monitor their child's activities whenever the parent deems it appropriate, even when the child is in a bedroom nominally regarded as private. Proper exercise of parental duties therefore demands that the parent have "joint access or control" of a minor child's bedroom. This is true regardless of whether the parent finds it necessary to exercise that privilege frequently. Further, given the parental duty of control and supervision, it is reasonable "to recognize that [the parent] has the right to permit the inspection in his own right...." In the absence of evidence suggesting a parent has abdicated this role toward his or her child, police officers may reasonably conclude that a parent can validly consent to the search of a minor child's bedroom.

While there is very little evidence in the record regarding the relationship between appellant and his mother, what little information we have suggests his mother not only had apparent authority to consent to the search of his room, but actual authority as well. It is notable that when appellant's mother told him to let the officers pass, he moved aside, acknowledging his mother's superior authority. Thereafter, appellant did not attempt to intervene to prevent the search of his room, implicitly recognizing his mother's control over the entire premises.

Defendant also argues a parent cannot waive the Fourth Amendment rights of a child, citing *In re Scott K.,* in which the Supreme Court ruled invalid a father's consent to the police search of his minor son's toolbox. The entire area of law governed by *Matlock,* however, concerns just this subject—the waiver by one occupant of the Fourth Amendment warrant requirement that would otherwise apply to a search of premises jointly occupied. Concerning the issue relevant here, a parent's authority to consent to a search of a child's room, as opposed to a closed container within the room, *Scott K.* is consistent with our decision. The Supreme Court did not question the validity of the father's consent to the search of his son's room, but only the father's consent regarding the closed container belonging to his son. Because a person's authority to consent to the search of closed containers within a residence is evaluated separately from the authority to consent to a search of the residence itself, the ruling of *Scott K.* regarding the toolbox has no bearing on the issue here.

Appellant also contends the police could not validly search his bedroom because he objected to their entry into the apartment.

Appellant argues the officers' failure to honor his objection to their entry constituted a violation of his constitutional rights, noting minors are entitled to the protections of the Constitution and, in particular, the search and seizure provisions of the Fourth Amendment. While there is no question minors are entitled to the protection of the Fourth Amendment, adults and minors are not necessarily entitled to the same degree of constitutional protection. To fulfill their duty of supervision, parents must be empowered to authorize police to search the family home, even over the objection of their minor children. While a minor child's Fourth Amendment rights may be narrower in these circumstances than those of an adult cohabiting with another, the difference is not great; police will still be required to obtain the consent of a person with common authority over the home—the parent—before the requirement of a search warrant is excused.

The judgment of the trial court is affirmed.

Holdings of *In re D.C.*: In this case, the court held that, in order to fulfill their duty of supervision, parents are empowered to authorize police to search the family home, even over the objection of their minor children.

Discussion Questions

What facts in this case lead to the different outcome from previous cases?

Would the result be different if the youth locked the bedroom door and the parents did not have a key?

What would have happened if the youth would have continued to stay in front of the door and refuse the court entry?

Key Concepts: Searches of Minors

- While minors enjoy Fourth Amendment protections, those protections are not the equivalent of the rights enjoyed by adults.

- Minors who live in a home owned by their parents are subject to waiver of their Fourth Amendment rights by the parent, as least as to the search of the room itself within that home.

- Some courts have held that even an adult person living in the home of a parent, may be subject to waiver of their Fourth Amendment rights by the parent for a search of rooms in the family home.

- Search of personal property or containers located within the confines of a home owned by a parent may not be subject to a waiver of the minor's Fourth Amendment rights by the parent if the minor can establish exclusive dominion or control over the property.

Practical Questions: Searches of Minors

1. Joseph Anderson, a 17-year-old male, comes to your office asking you to represent him on possession of marijuana and drug paraphernalia charges in juvenile court. Joseph graduated from high school early, and is employed full-time as a computer repair technician. Joseph lives at a duplex owned by his mother and pays her $850 per month rent, although they have no written lease agreement. Joseph's mother lives in the other half of the duplex. Both units have separate entrances. Joseph's mother has a key to the front door of the half of the duplex where Joseph lives, but Joseph says that they have an agreement that his mother will not enter his half of the duplex without prior permission from Joseph. The mother has never entered Joseph's portion of the duplex without his permission in the past. Last week, police came to Joseph's residence when he was at work. Joseph's mother consented to the police search of Joseph's half of the duplex, and she used her key to let the police into the unit. Police found ½ ounce of marijuana and a bong in Joseph's bedroom. Explain what you think will happen if you file a motion to suppress in Joseph's case.

2. William Anderson, a 16-year-old, was at a local public park with his mother, Sophia, when police approached him and asked him if he would consent to a search of his person. William refused. After Sophia identified herself as William's mother, police asked her if she would consent to a "search of William's person." Sophia gave consent to the search and, with great resistance from William, officers removed a wallet from his pocket. In the wallet was a nude photograph of William's 15-year-old girlfriend. William was charged with possession of child pornography. You have been appointed to represent William on the charge. Explain what you think will happen if you file a motion to suppress in William's case.

Simulation Exercise III

Characters: Prosecuting attorney, defense attorney, and Judge.

Facts: 17-year-old Michael Johnson was walking in the shopping mall during his summer break from school when he was confronted by a police officer with Michael's mother at his side. "There he is. That's Michael," said Michael's mother. "I just bet he is the one who stole my gold necklace last week. He probably has it in his pocket right now." The police officer asked Michael to give consent to search his pockets, and Michael refused. The police officer asked Michael's mother if Michael was a minor (and the mother said "yes") and asked if Michael lived with her (and the mother again said "yes"). Finally, the officer asked Michael's mother if she would give her consent to the search of Michael (and the mother again said "yes"). The officer then proceeded to search Michael and found a gold woman's necklace in his pocket. Michael was charged with 1st degree theft, a felony.

A waiver hearing was scheduled to determine whether or not Michael's case should be transferred to adult court. Prior to the waiver hearing, Michael's attorney filed a motion to suppress the necklace, and the prosecuting attorney resisted the motion. Both attorneys conceded that there was not probable cause for the search, but the state claimed that the mother's consent made the search "consensual."

Simulation: The exercise is for both attorneys to conduct oral arguments on the motion to suppress the evidence, focusing on whether or not Michael's mother's consent was effective to make an otherwise illegal search consensual. The judge should be prepared to ask any questions necessary to arrive at a ruling, the attorneys shall be prepared to answer any questions posed to them, and the judge will enter an oral ruling on the motion specifying findings and reasons for the ruling.

Chapter V

Students' Rights at School

A. Searches of Students' Persons

Overview: Minors spend half of their waking day in school. Since public schools are creatures of the state, their searches of students are covered by the Fourth Amendment. The results of a school search often lead to charges in juvenile or adult court. Unlike law enforcement officers, teachers and school administrators are given the responsibility of ensuring that schools provide a safe and learning environment for students. As a result, the courts have been forced to decide how far the Fourth Amendment should be applied in a public school setting. In addition, schools often have a police officer present at the school (called a "school liaison officer") who frequently assumes the responsibilities of searches of students and, as such, the courts are forced to decide whether the scope of the Fourth Amendment rights that are commonly applied to police officers also apply in the school setting by school liaison officers.

New Jersey v. T.L.O.: In *New Jersey v. T.L.O.,* the United States Supreme Court was forced to decide whether or not the Fourth Amendment applied to searches of students by school officials and, if applicable, how far the Fourth Amendment protections should be extended. In this case, a 14-year-old student was accused of smoking cigarettes in the school bathroom. When the student denied smoking, the Assistant Vice-Principal searched the student's purse. He found cigarettes, but also saw rolling papers. He believed that the presence of rolling papers indicated the use of marijuana, and he therefore conducted a full search of the student's purse. The full search resulting in finding a small amount of marijuana, a pipe, a number of empty plastic bags, a substantial quantity of money in one-dollar bills, an index card that appeared to be a list of students who owed the student money, and two letters that implicated the student in marijuana dealing. The police were called and the student was charged with a delinquent act. Her attorney filed a motion to suppress the evidence uncovered in the search of the student's purse.

As you read *New Jersey v. T.L.O.,* look for the following:

1. Notice how easily the court determines that the Fourth Amendment applies to students in a school setting, but how difficult the application of the limits of those rights are for the court.

2. Consider what responsibilities of school officials require a more flexible approach to the application of the Fourth Amendment in public school settings.

3. Look at the standard to justify a search that is established by the *T.L.O.* court and consider whether such a standard is easier for schools to apply than the traditional (probable cause) approach.

New Jersey v. T.L.O.

469 U.S. 325 (1985)

Justice WHITE delivered the opinion of the Court.

We granted certiorari in this case to examine the appropriateness of the exclusionary rule as a remedy for searches carried out in violation of the Fourth Amendment by public school authorities. Our consideration of the proper application of the Fourth Amendment to the public schools, however, has led us to conclude that the search that gave rise to the case now before us did not violate the Fourth Amendment. Accordingly, we here address only the questions of the proper standard for assessing the legality of searches conducted by public school officials and the application of that standard to the facts of this case.

On March 7, 1980, a teacher at Piscataway High School in Middlesex County, N.J., discovered two girls smoking in a lavatory. One of the two girls was the respondent T.L.O., who at that time was a 14-year-old high school freshman. Because smoking in the lavatory was a violation of a school rule, the teacher took the two girls to the Principal's office, where they met with Assistant Vice Principal Theodore Choplick. In response to questioning by Mr. Choplick, T.L.O.'s companion admitted that she had violated the rule. T.L.O., however, denied that she had been smoking in the lavatory and claimed that she did not smoke at all.

Mr. Choplick asked T.L.O. to come into his private office and demanded to see her purse. Opening the purse, he found a pack of cigarettes, which he removed from the purse and held before T.L.O. as he accused her of having lied to him. As he reached into the purse for the cigarettes, Mr. Choplick also noticed a package of cigarette rolling papers. In his experience, possession of rolling papers by high school students was closely associated with the use of marihuana. Suspecting that a closer examination of the purse might yield further evidence of drug use, Mr. Choplick proceeded to search the purse thoroughly. The search revealed a small amount of marihuana, a pipe, a number of empty plastic bags, a substantial quantity of money in one-dollar bills, an index card that appeared to be a list of students who owed T.L.O. money, and two letters that implicated T.L.O. in marihuana dealing.

Mr. Choplick notified T.L.O.'s mother and the police, and turned the evidence of drug dealing over to the police. At the request of the police, T.L.O.'s mother took her daughter to police headquarters, where T.L.O. confessed that she had been selling marihuana at the high school. On the basis of the confession and the evidence seized by Mr. Choplick, the State brought delinquency charges against T.L.O. in the Juvenile and Domestic Relations Court of Middlesex County. Contending that Mr. Choplick's search of her purse violated the Fourth Amendment, T.L.O. moved to suppress the evidence found in her purse as well as her confession, which, she argued, was tainted by the allegedly unlawful search.

Although we originally granted certiorari to decide the issue of the appropriate remedy in juvenile court proceedings for unlawful school searches, our doubts regarding the wisdom of deciding that question in isolation from the broader question of what limits, if any, the Fourth Amendment places on the activities of school authorities prompted us to order reargument on that question. Having heard argument on the legality of the search of T.L.O.'s purse, we are satisfied that the search did not violate the Fourth Amendment.

In determining whether the search at issue in this case violated the Fourth Amendment, we are faced initially with the question whether that Amendment's prohibition on unreasonable searches and seizures applies to searches conducted by public school officials. We hold that it does.

These two propositions—that the Fourth Amendment applies to the States through the Fourteenth Amendment, and that the actions of public school officials are subject to the limits placed on state action by the Fourteenth Amendment—might appear sufficient to answer the suggestion that the Fourth Amendment does not proscribe unreasonable searches by school officials. On reargument, however, the State of New Jersey has argued that the history of the Fourth Amendment indicates that the Amendment was intended to regulate only searches and seizures carried out by law enforcement officers; accordingly, although public school officials are concededly state agents for purposes of the Fourteenth Amendment, the Fourth Amendment creates no rights enforceable against them.

It may well be true that the evil toward which the Fourth Amendment was primarily directed was the resurrection of the pre-Revolutionary practice of using general warrants or "writs of assistance" to authorize searches for contraband by officers of the Crown. But this Court has never limited the Amendment's prohibition on unreasonable searches and seizures to operations conducted by the police. Rather, the Court has long spoken of the Fourth Amendment's strictures as restraints imposed upon "governmental action"— that is, "upon the activities of sovereign authority."

Notwithstanding the general applicability of the Fourth Amendment to the activities of civil authorities, a few courts have concluded that school officials are exempt from the dictates of the Fourth Amendment by virtue of the special nature of their authority over schoolchildren. Teachers and school administrators, it is said, act in loco parentis in their dealings with students: their authority is that of the parent, not the State, and is therefore not subject to the limits of the Fourth Amendment.

Such reasoning is in tension with contemporary reality and the teachings of this Court. We have held school officials subject to the commands of the First Amendment. If school authorities are state actors for purposes of the constitutional guarantees of freedom of expression and due process, it is difficult to understand why they should be deemed to be exercising parental rather than public authority when conducting searches of their students. In carrying out searches and other disciplinary functions pursuant to such policies, school officials act as representatives of the State, not merely as surrogates for the parents, and they cannot claim the parents' immunity from the strictures of the Fourth Amendment.

To hold that the Fourth Amendment applies to searches conducted by school authorities is only to begin the inquiry into the standards governing such searches. Although the underlying command of the Fourth Amendment is always that searches and seizures be reasonable, what is reasonable depends on the context within which a search takes place. The determination of the standard of reasonableness governing any specific class of searches requires "balancing the need to search against the invasion which the search entails." On one side of the balance are arrayed the individual's legitimate expectations of privacy and personal security; on the other, the government's need for effective methods to deal with breaches of public order.

Although this Court may take notice of the difficulty of maintaining discipline in the public schools today, the situation is not so dire that students in the schools may claim no legitimate expectations of privacy. We have recently recognized that the need to maintain order in a prison is such that prisoners retain no legitimate expectations of privacy in their cells, but it goes almost without saying that "[t]he prisoner and the schoolchild stand in wholly different circumstances, separated by the harsh facts of criminal conviction and incarceration." We are not yet ready to hold that the schools and the prisons need be equated for purposes of the Fourth Amendment.

Nor does the State's suggestion that children have no legitimate need to bring personal property into the schools seem well anchored in reality. Students at a minimum must bring to school not only the supplies needed for their studies, but also keys, money, and the necessaries of personal hygiene and grooming. In addition, students may carry on their persons or in purses or wallets such nondisruptive yet highly personal items as photographs, letters, and diaries. Finally, students may have perfectly legitimate reasons to carry with them articles of property needed in connection with extracurricular or recreational activities. In short, schoolchildren may find it necessary to carry with them a variety of legitimate, noncontraband items, and there is no reason to conclude that they have necessarily waived all rights to privacy in such items merely by bringing them onto school grounds.

How, then, should we strike the balance between the schoolchild's legitimate expectations of privacy and the school's equally legitimate need to maintain an environment in which learning can take place? It is evident that the school setting requires some easing of the restrictions to which searches by public authorities are ordinarily subject. The warrant requirement, in particular, is unsuited to the school environment: requiring a teacher to obtain a warrant before searching a child suspected of an infraction of school rules (or of the criminal law) would unduly interfere with the maintenance of the swift and informal disciplinary procedures needed in the schools. Just as we have in other cases dispensed with the warrant requirement when "the burden of obtaining a warrant is likely to frustrate the governmental purpose behind the search," we hold today that school officials need not obtain a warrant before searching a student who is under their authority.

The school setting also requires some modification of the level of suspicion of illicit activity needed to justify a search. Ordinarily, a search—even one that may permissibly be carried out without a warrant—must be based upon "probable cause" to believe that a violation of the law has occurred.

We join the majority of courts that have examined this issue in concluding that the accommodation of the privacy interests of schoolchildren with the substantial need of teachers and administrators for freedom to maintain order in the schools does not require strict adherence to the requirement that searches be based on probable cause to believe that the subject of the search has violated or is violating the law. Rather, the legality of a search of a student should depend simply on the reasonableness, under all the circumstances, of the search. Determining the reasonableness of any search involves a twofold inquiry: first, one must consider "whether the ... action was justified at its inception," second, one must determine whether the search as actually conducted "was reasonably related in scope to the circumstances which justified the interference in the first place". Under ordinary circumstances, a search of a student by a teacher or other school official will be "justified at its inception" when there are reasonable grounds for suspecting that the search will turn up evidence that the student has violated or is violating either the law or the rules of the school. Such a search will be permissible in its scope when the measures adopted are reasonably related to the objectives of the search and not excessively intrusive in light of the age and sex of the student and the nature of the infraction.

This standard will, we trust, neither unduly burden the efforts of school authorities to maintain order in their schools nor authorize unrestrained intrusions upon the privacy of schoolchildren. By focusing attention on the question of reasonableness, the standard will spare teachers and school administrators the necessity of schooling themselves in the niceties of probable cause and permit them to regulate their conduct according to the dictates of reason and common sense. At the same time, the reasonableness standard should ensure that the interests of students will be invaded no more than is necessary to achieve the legitimate end of preserving order in the schools.

There remains the question of the legality of the search in this case. We recognize that the "reasonable grounds" standard applied by the New Jersey Supreme Court in its consideration of this question is not substantially different from the standard that we have adopted today. Nonetheless, we believe that the New Jersey court's application of that standard to strike down the search of T.L.O.'s purse reflects a somewhat crabbed notion of reasonableness. Our review of the facts surrounding the search leads us to conclude that the search was in no sense unreasonable for Fourth Amendment purposes.

The incident that gave rise to this case actually involved two separate searches, with the first—the search for cigarettes—providing the suspicion that gave rise to the second the search for marihuana. Although it is the fruits of the second search that are at issue here, the validity of the search for marihuana must depend on the reasonableness of the initial search for cigarettes, as there would have been no reason to suspect that T.L.O. possessed marihuana had the first search not taken place. Accordingly, it is to the search for cigarettes that we first turn our attention.

The relevance of T.L.O.'s possession of cigarettes to the question whether she had been smoking and to the credibility of her denial that she smoked supplied the necessary "nexus" between the item searched for and the infraction under investigation. Thus, if Mr. Choplick in fact had a reasonable suspicion that T.L.O. had cigarettes in her purse, the search was justified despite the fact that the cigarettes, if found, would constitute "mere evidence" of a violation.

Because the hypothesis that T.L.O. was carrying cigarettes in her purse was itself not unreasonable, it is irrelevant that other hypotheses were also consistent with the teacher's accusation. Accordingly, it cannot be said that Mr. Choplick acted unreasonably when he examined T.L.O.'s purse to see if it contained cigarettes.

Our conclusion that Mr. Choplick's decision to open T.L.O.'s purse was reasonable brings us to the question of the further search for marihuana once the pack of cigarettes was located. The suspicion upon which the search for marihuana was founded was provided when Mr. Choplick observed a package of rolling papers in the purse as he removed the pack of cigarettes. Although T.L.O. does not dispute the reasonableness of Mr. Choplick's belief that the rolling papers indicated the presence of marihuana, she does contend that the scope of the search Mr. Choplick conducted exceeded permissible bounds when he seized and read certain letters that implicated T.L.O. in drug dealing. This argument, too, is unpersuasive. The discovery of the rolling papers concededly gave rise to a reasonable suspicion that T.L.O. was carrying marihuana as well as cigarettes in her purse. This suspicion justified further exploration of T.L.O.'s purse, which turned up more evidence of drug-related activities: a pipe, a number of plastic bags of the type commonly used to store marihuana, a small quantity of marihuana, and a fairly substantial amount of money. Under these circumstances, it was not unreasonable to extend the search to a separate zippered compartment of the purse; and when a search of that compartment revealed an index card containing a list of "people who owe me money" as well as two letters, the inference that T.L.O. was involved in marihuana trafficking was substantial enough to justify Mr. Choplick in examining the letters to determine whether they contained any further evidence. In short, we cannot conclude that the search for marihuana was unreasonable in any respect.

Because the search resulting in the discovery of the evidence of marihuana dealing by T.L.O. was reasonable, the New Jersey Supreme Court's decision to exclude that evidence from T.L.O.'s juvenile delinquency proceedings on Fourth Amendment grounds was erroneous. Accordingly, the judgment of the Supreme Court of New Jersey is

Reversed.

Justice POWELL, with whom Justice O'CONNOR joins, concurring.

I agree with the Court's decision, and generally with its opinion. I would place greater emphasis, however, on the special characteristics of elementary and secondary schools that make it unnecessary to afford students the same constitutional protections granted adults and juveniles in a nonschool setting.

In any realistic sense, students within the school environment have a lesser expectation of privacy than members of the population generally. They spend the school hours in close association with each other, both in the classroom and during recreation periods. The students in a particular class often know each other and their teachers quite well. Of necessity, teachers have a degree of familiarity with, and authority over, their students that is unparalleled except perhaps in the relationship between parent and child. It is simply unrealistic to think that students have the same subjective expectation of privacy as the population generally. But for purposes of deciding this case, I can assume that children in school—no less than adults—have privacy interests that society is prepared to recognize as legitimate.

The special relationship between teacher and student also distinguishes the setting within which schoolchildren operate. Law enforcement officers function as adversaries of criminal suspects. These officers have the responsibility to investigate criminal activity, to locate and arrest those who violate our laws, and to facilitate the charging and bringing of such persons to trial. Rarely does this type of adversarial relationship exist between school authorities and pupils. Instead, there is a commonality of interests between teachers and their pupils. The attitude of the typical teacher is one of personal responsibility for the student's welfare as well as for his education.

The primary duty of school officials and teachers, as the Court states, is the education and training of young people. A State has a compelling interest in assuring that the schools meet this responsibility. Without first establishing discipline and maintaining order, teachers cannot begin to educate their students. And apart from education, the school has the obligation to protect pupils from mistreatment by other children, and also to protect teachers themselves from violence by the few students whose conduct in recent years has prompted national concern. For me, it would be unreasonable and at odds with history to argue that the full panoply of constitutional rules applies with the same force and effect in the schoolhouse as it does in the enforcement of criminal laws.

In sum, although I join the Court's opinion and its holding, my emphasis is somewhat different.

Justice BLACKMUN, concurring in the judgment.

I join the judgment of the Court and agree with much that is said in its opinion. I write separately, however, because I believe the Court omits a crucial step in its analysis of whether a school search must be based upon probable-cause.

The Court's implication that the balancing test is the rule rather than the exception is troubling for me because it is unnecessary in this case. The elementary and secondary school setting presents a special need for flexibility justifying a departure from the balance struck by the Framers. As Justice POWELL notes, "[w]ithout first establishing discipline and maintaining order, teachers cannot begin to educate their students." Maintaining order in the classroom can be a difficult task. A single teacher often must watch over a large number of students, and, as any parent knows, children at certain ages are inclined to test the outer boundaries of acceptable conduct and to imitate the misbehavior of a peer if that misbehavior is not dealt with quickly. Every adult remembers from his own schooldays the havoc a water pistol or peashooter can wreak until it is taken away. Thus, the Court has recognized that "[e]vents calling for discipline are frequent occurrences and sometimes require immediate, effective action." Indeed, because drug use and possession of weapons have become increasingly common among young people, an immediate response frequently is required not just to maintain an environment conducive to learning, but to protect the very safety of students and school personnel.

Such immediate action obviously would not be possible if a teacher were required to secure a warrant before searching a student. Nor would it be possible if a teacher could not conduct a necessary search until the teacher thought there was probable cause for the search. A teacher has neither the training nor the day-to-day experience in the complexities of probable cause that a law enforcement officer possesses, and is ill-equipped to make a quick judgment about the existence of probable cause. The time required for a teacher to ask the questions or make the observations that are necessary to turn reasonable grounds into probable cause is time during which the teacher, and other students, are diverted from the essential task of education. A teacher's focus is, and should be, on teaching and helping students, rather than on developing evidence against a particular troublemaker.

The special need for an immediate response to behavior that threatens either the safety of schoolchildren and teachers or the educational process itself justifies the Court in excepting school searches from the warrant and probable-cause requirement, and in applying a standard determined by balancing the relevant interests. I agree with the standard the Court has announced, and with its application of the standard to the facts of this case. I therefore concur in its judgment.

Justice BRENNAN, with whom Justice MARSHALL joins, concurring in part and dissenting in part.

I fully agree with Part II of the Court's opinion. Teachers, like all other government officials, must conform their conduct to the Fourth Amendment's protections of personal privacy and personal security.

I do not, however, otherwise join the Court's opinion. Today's decision sanctions school officials to conduct full-scale searches on a "reasonableness" standard whose only definite content is that it is not the same test as the "probable cause" standard found in the text of the Fourth Amendment. In adopting this unclear, unprecedented, and unnecessary departure from generally applicable Fourth Amendment standards, the Court carves out a broad exception to standards that this Court has developed over years of considering Fourth Amendment problems. Its decision is supported neither by precedent nor even by a fair application of the "balancing test" it proclaims in this very opinion.

I agree that schoolteachers or principals, when not acting as agents of law enforcement authorities, generally may conduct a search of their students' belongings without first obtaining a warrant. To agree with the Court on this point is to say that school searches may justifiably be held to that extent to constitute an exception to the Fourth Amendment's warrant requirement. Such an exception, however, is not to be justified, as the Court apparently holds, by assessing net social value through application of an unguided "balancing test" in which "the individual's legitimate expectations of privacy and personal security" are weighed against "the government's need for effective methods to deal with breaches of public order." The Warrant Clause is something more than an exhortation to this Court to maximize social welfare as we see fit. It requires that the authorities must obtain a warrant before conducting a full-scale search. The undifferentiated governmental interest in law enforcement is insufficient to justify an exception to the warrant requirement. Rather, some special governmental interest beyond the need merely to apprehend lawbreakers is necessary to justify a categorical exception to the warrant requirement. For the most part, special governmental needs sufficient to override the warrant requirement flow from "exigency"—that is, from the press of time that makes obtaining a warrant either impossible or hopelessly infeasible. Only after finding an extraordinary governmental interest of this kind do we—or ought we—engage in a balancing test to determine if a warrant should nonetheless be required.

In this case, such extraordinary governmental interests do exist and are sufficient to justify an exception to the warrant requirement. Students are necessarily confined for most of the schoolday in close proximity to each other and to the school staff. I agree with the Court that we can take judicial notice of the serious problems of drugs and violence that plague our schools. As Justice BLACKMUN notes, teachers must not merely "maintain an environment conducive to learning" among children who "are inclined to test the outer boundaries of acceptable conduct," but must also "protect the very safety of students and school personnel." A teacher or principal could neither carry out essential teaching functions nor adequately protect students' safety if required to wait for a warrant before conducting a necessary search.

I emphatically disagree with the Court's decision to cast aside the constitutional probable-cause standard when assessing the constitutional validity of a schoolhouse search. The Court's decision jettisons the probable-cause standard—the only standard that finds support in the text of the Fourth Amendment—on the basis of its Rorschach-like "balancing test." Use of such a "balancing test" to determine the standard for evaluating the validity of a full-scale search represents a sizable innovation in Fourth Amendment analysis. This innovation finds support neither in precedent nor policy and portends a dangerous weakening of the purpose of the Fourth Amendment to protect the privacy and security of our citizens.

As compared with the relative ease with which teachers can apply the probable-cause standard, the amorphous "reasonableness under all the circumstances" standard freshly coined by the Court today will likely spawn increased litigation and greater uncertainty among teachers and administrators. Of course, as this Court should know, an essential purpose of developing and articulating legal norms is to enable individuals to conform their conduct to those norms. A school system conscientiously attempting to obey the Fourth Amendment's dictates under a probable-cause standard could, for example, consult decisions and other legal materials and prepare a booklet expounding the rough outlines of the concept. Such a booklet could be distributed to teachers to provide them with guidance as to when a search may be lawfully conducted. I cannot but believe that the same school system faced with interpreting what is permitted under the Court's new "reasonableness" standard would be hopelessly adrift as to when a search may be permissible.

Applying the constitutional probable-cause standard to the facts of this case, I would find that Mr. Choplick's search violated T.L.O.'s Fourth Amendment rights.

On my view of the case, we need not decide whether the initial search conducted by Mr. Choplick—the search for evidence of the smoking violation that was completed when Mr. Choplick found the pack of cigarettes — was valid. For Mr. Choplick at that point did not have probable cause to continue to rummage through T.L.O.'s purse. Mr. Choplick's suspicion of marihuana possession at this time was based solely on the presence of the package of cigarette papers. The mere presence without more of such a staple item of commerce is insufficient to warrant a person of reasonable caution in inferring both that T.L.O. had violated the law by possessing marihuana and that evidence of that violation would be found in her purse. Just as a police officer could not obtain a warrant to search a home based solely on his claim that he had seen a package of cigarette papers in that home, Mr. Choplick was not entitled to search possibly the most private possessions of T.L.O. based on the mere presence of a package of cigarette papers. Therefore, the fruits of this illegal search must be excluded and the judgment of the New Jersey Supreme Court affirmed.

Justice STEVENS, with whom Justice MARSHALL joins, and with whom Justice BRENNAN joins as to Part I, concurring in part and dissenting in part.

The search of a young woman's purse by a school administrator is a serious invasion of her legitimate expectations of privacy. A purse "is a common repository for one's personal effects and therefore is inevitably associated with the expectation of privacy." Although such expectations must sometimes yield to the legitimate requirements of government, in assessing the constitutionality of a warrantless search, our decision must be guided by the language of the Fourth Amendment: "The right of the people to be secure in their persons, houses, papers and effects, against unreasonable searches and seizures, shall not be violated...." In order to evaluate the reasonableness of such searches, "it is necessary 'first to focus upon the governmental interest which allegedly justifies official intrusion upon the constitutionally protected interests of the private citizen,' for there is 'no ready test for determining reasonableness other than by balancing the need to search [or seize] against the invasion which the search [or seizure] entails.'"

The "limited search for weapons" in *Terry* was justified by the "immediate interest of the police officer in taking steps to assure himself that the person with whom he is dealing is not armed with a weapon that could unexpectedly and fatally be used against him." When viewed from the institutional perspective, "the substantial need of teachers and administrators for freedom to maintain order in the schools," (majority opinion), is no less acute. Violent, unlawful, or seriously disruptive conduct is fundamentally inconsistent with the principal function of teaching institutions which is to educate young people and prepare them for citizenship. When such conduct occurs amidst a sizable group of impressionable young people, it creates an explosive atmosphere that requires a prompt and effective response.

Thus, warrantless searches of students by school administrators are reasonable when undertaken for those purposes. But the majority's statement of the standard for evaluating the reasonableness of such searches is not suitably adapted to that end. The majority holds that "a search of a student by a teacher or other school official will be 'justified at its inception' when there are reasonable grounds for suspecting that the search will turn up evidence that the student has violated or is violating either the law or the rules of the school." This standard will permit teachers and school administrators to search students when they suspect that the search will reveal evidence of even the most trivial school regulation or precatory guideline for student behavior. The Court's standard for deciding whether a search is justified "at its inception" treats all violations of the rules of the school as though they were fungible. For the Court, a search for curlers and sunglasses in order to enforce the school dress code is apparently just as important as a search for evidence of heroin addiction or violent gang activity.

The Court's standard for evaluating the "scope" of reasonable school searches is obviously designed to prohibit physically intrusive searches of students by persons of the opposite sex for relatively minor offenses. The Court's effort to establish a standard that is, at once, clear enough to allow searches to be upheld in nearly every case, and flexible enough to prohibit obviously unreasonable intrusions of young adults' privacy only creates uncertainty in the extent of its resolve to prohibit the latter. Moreover, the majority's application of its standard in this case—to permit a male administrator to rummage through the purse of a female high school student in order to obtain evidence that she was smoking in a bathroom—raises grave doubts in my mind whether its effort will be effective. Unlike the Court, I believe the nature of the suspected infraction is a matter of first importance in deciding whether any invasion of privacy is permissible.

In the view of the state court, there is a quite obvious and material difference between a search for evidence relating to violent or disruptive activity, and a search for evidence of a smoking rule violation. This distinction does not imply that a no-smoking rule is a matter of minor importance. Rather, like a rule that prohibits a student from being tardy, its occasional violation in a context that poses no threat of disrupting school order and discipline offers no reason to believe that an immediate search is necessary to avoid unlawful conduct, violence, or a serious impairment of the educational process.

Like the New Jersey Supreme Court, I would view this case differently if the Assistant Vice Principal had reason to believe T.L.O.'s purse contained evidence of criminal activity, or of an activity that would seriously disrupt school discipline. There was, however, absolutely no basis for any such assumption—not even a "hunch."

In this case, Mr. Choplick overreacted to what appeared to be nothing more than a minor infraction—a rule prohibiting smoking in the bathroom of the freshmen's and sophomores' building. It is, of course, true that he actually found evidence of serious wrongdoing by T.L.O., but no one claims that the prior search may be justified by his unexpected discovery. As far as the smoking infraction is concerned, the search for cigarettes merely tended to corroborate a teacher's eyewitness account of T.L.O.'s violation of a minor regulation designed to channel student smoking behavior into designated locations. Because this conduct was neither unlawful nor significantly disruptive of school order or the educational process, the invasion of privacy associated with the forcible opening of T.L.O.'s purse was entirely unjustified at its inception.

A review of the sampling of school search cases relied on by the Court demonstrates how different this case is from those in which there was indeed a valid justification for intruding on a student's privacy. In most of them the student was suspected of a criminal violation; in the remainder either violence or substantial disruption of school order or the integrity of the academic process was at stake. Few involved matters as trivial as the no-smoking rule violated by T.L.O. The rule the Court adopts today is so open-ended that it may make the Fourth Amendment virtually meaningless in the school context. Although I agree that school administrators must have broad latitude to maintain order and discipline in our classrooms, that authority is not unlimited.

The schoolroom is the first opportunity most citizens have to experience the power of government. Through it passes every citizen and public official, from schoolteachers to policemen and prison guards. The values they learn there, they take with them in life. One of our most cherished ideals is the one contained in the Fourth Amendment: that the government may not intrude on the personal privacy of its citizens without a warrant or compelling circumstance. The Court's decision today is a curious moral for the Nation's youth. Although the search of T.L.O.'s purse does not trouble today's majority, I submit that we are not dealing with "matters relatively trivial to the welfare of the Nation. There are village tyrants as well as village Hampdens, but none who acts under color of law is beyond reach of the Constitution."

I respectfully dissent.

Holdings of *New Jersey v. T.L.O.:* This case is considered the "seminal" case relative to the search of students in public schools. In *T.L.O.,* the court held that, while the Fourth Amendment does apply to students in school, the application of those rights are different in such a setting due to the responsibilities of school officials to provide a safe, learning environment for students. The court held that a warrant is not required for a search of a student by school officials, and furthermore that probable cause is not required. Instead, the court held that the search is justified if, from the inception, there were reasonable grounds to suspect that the search would yield evidence of violations of the law or of school rules.

Discussion Questions

How does the majority conclude that the 4th Amendment applies to school authorities and not just to law enforcement?

The majority opinion finds that (1) the 4th Amendment applies to the states through the 14th Amendment and (2) that the actions of school authorities are subject to the limits of the 14th Amendment. So, how does the majority conclude that the search in this case did not violate the constitution?

Explain the "reasonableness" standard created by the majority for school searches.

––––––––––

State v. Angelia D.B.: In *State v. Angelia D.B.,* the Wisconsin Supreme Court was faced with a challenge to the admissibility of a knife found on a student at school. Another student had reported seeing a knife in Angelia's backpack and also indicated that she may have a gun in her possession. A police officer, who also served as a school liaison officer, patted down Angelia and searched her backpack, locker and jacket, finding nothing. The officer lifted up the bottom of her shirt to reveal her waistband, where he observed two inches of a brown knife handle tucked in her waistband by her right hip. The nine-inch knife was locked in an open position, resulting in her arrest. The State filed a juvenile delinquency petition charging her with carrying a concealed weapon. Angelia's attorney moved to suppress the use of the knife as evidence based on the Fourth Amendment.

As you read *State v. Angelia D.B.,* look for the following:

1. Consider what role the police officer (school liaison officer) played in the school setting.

2. Consider whether or not the same result would apply to evidence or the violation of a school rule that did not pose a danger to other students.

3. Look at the language of the *T.L.O.* court that reserved this issue (searches by police officers at school in conjunction with school officials) and whether or not one would anticipate how the *T.L.O.* court would have ruled in this case.

State v. Angelia D.B.

211 Wis.2d 140 (Wisc. 1997)

Angelia D.B. was charged with carrying a concealed weapon, after a school liaison police officer found a nine-inch knife hidden in her clothing. The Circuit Court for Winnebago County, Judge Robert A. Haase, suppressed the knife and all derivative evidence obtained from Angelia D.B., because it concluded that the search violated her state and federal constitutional rights to be free from unreasonable searches and seizures. The state appealed these orders, and the court of appeals certified two questions for our review.

First, in determining the reasonableness of a search conducted in a public school by a police officer in conjunction with school authorities, is the proper Fourth Amendment standard the less stringent "reasonable grounds" standard set forth in *New Jersey v. T.L.O.*, or the general standard of "probable cause"? Second, was the search conducted by the police school liaison officer in the instant case reasonable under the circumstances? We hold that the *T.L.O.* reasonable grounds standard applies to a search conducted on school grounds by a police officer at the request of, and in conjunction with, school authorities. Because the search of Angelia D.B. was reasonable under this standard to insure the safety of the students and school officials, we reverse the orders of the circuit court and remand for further proceedings.

On October 12, 1995, a Neenah High School student informed the assistant principal, David Rouse, that he had observed a knife in another student's backpack earlier that day. The informant also indicated that the other student might have access to a gun. Rouse called Officer Dan Dringoli, a City of Neenah police officer and school liaison officer on duty at Neenah High School at the time. After arriving at Rouse's office, Dringoli interviewed the informant, who repeated what he had observed and identified the other student by her first name, Angelia. When Rouse checked the computer and determined Angelia's last name, the student said he believed her to be the person. Dringoli then went to Angelia D.B.'s classroom with Dean of Students Mark Duerwaechter, who entered the classroom and escorted Angelia D.B. to the hallway outside.

Dringoli identified himself and informed Angelia D.B. that they had received information that she may be carrying a knife or gun. While in the hallway, Dringoli conducted a brief pat down search of her jacket and pants and had Angelia D.B. search her backpack while he observed. No weapons were discovered. Angelia D.B. then accompanied Dringoli back to his office, where another police officer, Corporal Radtke, was present. Before returning to Dringoli's office, Duerwaechter searched Angelia D.B.'s locker as authorized by school policy, but did not discover any weapons.

After Angelia D.B. denied that she possessed any weapons, Dringoli informed her that he was going to check her further. Angelia D.B. first removed her jacket for Dringoli to search. When he did not find a weapon in her jacket, Dringoli lifted up the bottom of her shirt to reveal her waistband. Dringoli then observed two inches of a brown knife handle tucked in her waistband by her right hip. After Dringoli removed the nine-inch knife, which was locked in an open position, Dringoli informed Angelia D.B. that she was under arrest and advised her of her Miranda rights.

The State filed a juvenile delinquency petition charging Angelia D.B. with carrying a concealed weapon. Seeking to suppress the use of the knife as evidence, Angelia D.B. argued to the circuit court that Officer Dringoli's search of her person, specifically his lifting of her shirt, was highly intrusive and required a showing of probable cause. Because the search was based solely on the informant's allegation without further corroboration,

Angelia D.B. further asserted that Dringoli's search was not supported by probable cause. The circuit court granted Angelia D.B.'s motions to suppress the knife and all derivative evidence, ruling that the search of her person was unreasonable under all the circumstances. The State appealed. The court of appeals certified this appeal for our review on July 17, 1996.

In this case, we are asked to determine the appropriate Fourth Amendment standard of reasonableness for a search of a student on school grounds by a police officer at the request of, and in conjunction with, school authorities. Specifically, the question is whether such a search is governed by the reasonable grounds standard set forth in *T.L.O.* or the general standard of probable cause.

The *T.L.O.* Court recognized that the Fourth Amendment's prohibition against unreasonable searches and seizures applied to searches conducted by public school officials as well as by police officers. The Court, however, dispensed with the warrant and probable cause requirements in the public school context when the search was conducted by school authorities.

In balancing the student's legitimate expectation of privacy and the school's need to maintain a safe and proper educational environment, the Court concluded that teachers and school officials do not need a warrant or probable cause before searching a student who is under their authority. "Rather, the legality of a search of a student should depend simply on the reasonableness, under all the circumstances, of the search." To determine the reasonableness of a search of a student, the Court established the following twofold inquiry: first, the action must be "justified at its inception"; and second, the search, as actually conducted, must be "reasonably related in scope to the circumstances which justified the interference in the first place."

Applying this test, the *T.L.O.* Court held that the search of the student's purse was reasonable, given that a teacher had reported seeing the student smoking in the lavatory in violation of school rules and that the student denied doing so. The Court, however, limited its holding to searches carried out by school authorities, noting that "[t]his case does not present the question of the appropriate standard for assessing the legality of searches conducted by school officials in conjunction with or at the behest of law enforcement agencies, and we express no opinion on that question."

Because the Court in *T.L.O.* expressly reserved judgment on this question, lower courts since *T.L.O.* have applied different standards to searches conducted by law enforcement officials in conjunction with school officials, depending on the extent of police involvement. In situations where school officials initiate the search or police involvement is minimal, most courts have held the reasonable grounds standard to apply.

The reasonable grounds standard has also been applied in cases involving school police or liaison officers acting on their own authority.

Notably, the probable cause standard is consistently applied where outside police officers initiate a search or where school officials act at the behest of law enforcement agencies.

We agree that there are inherent differences between the roles of police officers and school officials which make the reasonable grounds standard inapplicable to searches conducted by police officers acting independently of school officials. A police investigation that includes the search of a public school student, when the search is initiated by police and conducted by police, usually lacks the "commonality of interests" existing between teachers and students. But when school officials, who are responsible for the welfare and education of all of the students within the campus, initiate an investigation and conduct it on school grounds in conjunction with police, the school has brought the police into the school-student relationship.

In this case, in contrast, the investigation was initiated at the request of school officials. The investigation continued in conjunction with school officials. Further, Angelia D.B. was suspected of possessing a dangerous weapon within a public high school. Unlike a dangerous weapon located within a residence, a dangerous weapon within a school setting poses a significant and imminent threat of danger to school staff and to the other students compelled to be there.

In Wisconsin, school attendance is compulsory, with certain exceptions, until age 18. School officials not only educate students who are compelled to attend school, but they have a responsibility to protect those students and their teachers from behavior that threatens their safety and the integrity of the learning process. With the growing incidence of violence and dangerous weapons in schools, this task has become increasingly difficult. As a result, many school officials have sought the assistance of school liaison officers in enforcing rules and maintaining order in public schools.

That is the nature of the case before us. Officer Dringoli was on duty as a school liaison officer for Neenah High School. He became involved in this investigation only after school officials requested his assistance and, throughout the course of the investigation, he acted in conjunction with school officials on school grounds. Although the record is not clear as to Dringoli's specific duties, we may reasonably infer that where a law enforcement official has an office in the school, one of the official's responsibilities as a school liaison officer is to assist school officials in maintaining a safe and proper educational environment. Because the report of a knife on school premises posed an imminent threat of danger to students and teachers, it is reasonable to conclude that Dringoli conducted the search of Angelia D.B. in conjunction with school officials and in furtherance of the school's objective to maintain a safe and proper educational environment.

Were we to conclude otherwise, our decision might serve to encourage teachers and school officials, who generally are untrained in proper pat down procedures or in neutralizing dangerous weapons, to conduct a search of a student suspected of carrying a dangerous weapon on school grounds without the assistance of a school liaison officer or other law enforcement official. While the *T.L.O.* Court adopted the less stringent reasonable grounds standard in part because of the need of teachers to "maintain swift and informal disciplinary procedures," it could be hazardous to discourage school officials from requesting the assistance of available trained police resources. Even in *Terry*, the Court recognized that it would be unreasonable to require that police officers take unnecessary risks in the performance of their duties. The proper standard for the constitutional reasonableness of searches conducted on public school grounds by school officials, or by police working at the request of and in conjunction with school officials, should not promote unreasonable risk-taking.

Teachers and school officials are trained to educate children and to provide a proper learning environment. Law enforcement officials, on the other hand, receive specialized training on how best to disarm individuals without subjecting themselves or others to danger. When faced with a potentially dangerous situation beyond their expertise and training, school officials must be allowed "a certain degree of flexibility" to seek the assistance of trained law enforcement officials without losing the protections afforded by the reasonable grounds standard. We therefore find it permissible for school officials who have a reasonable suspicion that a student may be in possession of a dangerous weapon on school grounds to request the assistance of a school liaison officer or other law enforcement officials in conducting a further investigation.

Although *T.L.O.* did not address this question, we conclude that an application of the *T.L.O.* reasonable grounds standard, and not probable cause, to a search conducted by a school liaison officer at the request of and in conjunction with school officials of a student reasonably suspected of carrying a dangerous weapon on school grounds is consistent with both the special needs of public schools recognized in *T.L.O.* and with decisions by courts in other jurisdictions.

The case before us involved two separate searches conducted by Officer Dringoli. The initial search was a quick pat down of Angelia D.B.'s coat and pants. Due to the nature of the allegations by the eyewitness student-informant, Angelia D.B. concedes that this search was reasonable. At issue in this case, however, is whether the second search, a more thorough search of Angelia D.B.'s coat and person within Dringoli's office, was reasonable. Weighing the gravity of a knife within the school concealed on a student's person, and the state's substantial interest in maintaining a safe and proper educational environment against the student's legitimate expectation of privacy, we find the search here reasonable.

In reaching this conclusion, we apply the two-prong test of *T.L.O.* First, the search must be reasonable at its inception; and second, the search as actually conducted must be reasonably related in scope to the circumstances justifying the interference in the first instance.

In applying this test, Dringoli must have had reasonable grounds to suspect that Angelia D.B. possessed a knife in violation of the law or school rules for his search of her to be justified at its inception. Dringoli conducted the search of Angelia D.B. after being informed that a student had observed her in possession of a knife. Under these circumstances, Dringoli had reasonable grounds to suspect that Angelia D.B. possessed a knife. The search was justified at its inception.

Next, we consider whether the scope of the search was reasonable. "[A] search will be permissible in its scope when the measures adopted are reasonably related to the objectives of the search and are not excessively intrusive in light of the age and sex of the student and the nature of the infraction."

As part of the investigation of the student informant's allegations, Dringoli initially conducted a brief pat down search of Angelia D.B.'s pants and jacket in the hallway. The Dean of Students, Mark Duerwaechter was present. Dringoli then asked the student to search her own backpack. After these efforts disclosed no weapon, Dringoli requested that Angelia D.B. accompany him back to his office. Duerwaechter conducted a locker search, but found no weapon. Entering the office, Dringoli, in the presence of Corporal Radtke, informed Angelia D.B. that he was going to conduct a more thorough search. Dringoli first searched her coat and then lifted up the bottom of her shirt to expose her waistband. After Dringoli observed a knife tucked into Angelia D.B's waistband and then removed it from her person, the search stopped.

Throughout this investigation, Officer Dringoli was searching for a knife that a student reportedly observed in Angelia D.B.'s possession earlier that day. Angelia D.B. does not allege, nor does the record indicate, that Dringoli was searching for anything but the knife that the informant claimed to be in her possession. Further, Dringoli limited his search only to areas where Angelia D.B. could reasonably conceal a weapon. We, therefore, find that the measures employed by Dringoli were reasonably related to the objective of determining whether Angelia D.B. had a knife in her possession on school grounds.

We also conclude that the search was not excessively intrusive in light of Angelia D.B's age and gender, and the nature of the infraction. Angelia D.B. is female and was almost sixteen years old at the time of the search. She was suspected of possessing a dangerous weapon within a public school. Because Dringoli lifted her shirt only high enough to observe Angelia D.B.'s waistline, this search was a relatively minor intrusion when compared to the nature of the infraction — possession of a dangerous weapon on school grounds.

Since we conclude that Dringoli's search was reasonable under the circumstances, we hold that the circuit court erred in suppressing the knife and all derivative evidence. Accordingly, the orders of the circuit court are reversed and the case is remanded to the circuit court for further proceedings.

The orders of the circuit court are reversed and cause remanded.

Holdings of *State v. Angelia D.B.*: In this case, the court held that, when faced with a potentially dangerous situation beyond their expertise and training, school officials must be allowed to seek the assistance of trained law enforcement officials without losing the protections afforded by the reasonable grounds standard. The court, therefore, held that it is permissible for school officials who have a reasonable suspicion that a student may be in possession of a dangerous weapon on school grounds to request the assistance of a school liaison officer or other law enforcement officials in conducting a further investigation.

Discussion Questions

Are there different rules if the search is done by a liaison officer at a school as opposed to any other police officer at the school?

Are there different rules if the police officer is acting at the request of the school authorities as opposed to law enforcement's own initiative?

Can a police officer who has information not quite to the level of probable cause just wait until the youth is at school, then report their suspicion to the school authorities to obtain the lower threshold permitted by *TLO*?

Key Concepts: Searches of Students in School

- While students enjoy Fourth Amendment protections in a school setting, those protections are not the same as would apply elsewhere.
- School officials do not need a warrant to search a student.
- School officials do not need probable cause to search a student, but only need reasonable grounds to suspect that the search would yield evidence of violations of the law or of school rules.
- Searches of students in a school setting by police officers working in conjunction with school authorities are permissible on the same standards as those searches conducted by school authorities, at least when it comes to the suspicion of the presence of a dangerous weapon.

Practical Questions: Searches of Students' Persons

1. When school officials arrived on Monday morning, there was a message on the school's voicemail from an unknown caller saying: "A student at your school will come with a gun today. Look out." The school principal immediately called the police. Police arrived and the school and lined up all 600 students and searched them all. No weapons of any sort were found, although a number of students were found with drugs on their person and were charged and arrested. Your client, Susan, was found to have 3 loose pre-

scription pills (Adderall) in her pocket, and she did not have a prescription for them. She was charged with Illegal Possession of a Prescription Drug. What arguments can you make to support your motion to suppress?

2. Robin Johnson, the principal of East High School, says that she has observed over her career that a vast majority of students who regularly listen to Bob Marley music are drug users. Can Ms. Johnson use her experience and knowledge to provide the "reasonable suspicion" required by the *T.L.O.* case to search students who wear Bob Marley T-Shirts or who are found to be listening to his music in school?

B. Strip Searches of Students

Overview: One of the most intrusive forms of search is a strip search. Most of the key cases evaluating the rights of students to be free from this extreme form of search are in the context of § 1983 civil actions. However, these cases are applicable to potential motions to suppress the results of such searches in criminal or delinquency cases because they define the constitutional protections afforded to students in such cases.

Doe v. Renfrow: In *Doe v. Renfrow,* the federal court was faced with a § 1983 civil lawsuit concerning a strip search of a female student after a "sniffer dog" alerted that the student had drugs on her person. All students at Highland Junior High School in Highland, Indiana were subjected to a "sniffer dog" inspection. Every single student was sniffed, inspected, and examined at least once by a dog and a joint school-police team, and students who were singled out by the dog, were examined. Four junior high students (all girls) were removed from their classes, stripped nude, and interrogated. Not one of them was found to possess any illicit material. Although the canine response raised suspicion toward 50 students, only 15 were found to possess contraband. Parties brought a civil action for damages for violation of their 4th Amendment rights.

As you read *Doe v. Renfrow,* look for the following:

1. Consider what importance the age of the girl (13) subjected to the strip search had on the ultimate decision of the court.

2. Consider whether or not this court would ever find a strip search (which the court describes as "not only unlawful but outrageous") by school officials to be justified or legal.

Doe v. Renfrow
631 F.2d 91 (7th Cir. 1980)

In May 1979, plaintiff Diane Doe, a student at Highland Junior High School in Highland, Indiana, and four other students filed a civil rights complaint under 28 U.S.C. ss 1343(3) and 1343(4). The gravamen of the complaint was that plaintiff and others were illegally sniffed by police dogs during school hours and pocket-searched if a dog alerted to them in order to determine whether they possessed controlled substances and contraband. As part of the drug investigation, plaintiff alleged that she and three other students "were compelled to remove their clothing and submit to visual inspection by defendants' agents."

The complaint also charged that 2,780 students at Highland High School were subject to the canine sniffing and that 17 of them thereafter "were summarily suspended, expelled, or compelled to withdraw from attendance at school." According to plaintiff, defendants' practice was "unsupported by particularized facts, reasonable suspicion or probable cause to believe that any of the persons" subject to the canine drug investigation would possess controlled substances. Alleging that defendants' acts violated the Fourth and Fourteenth Amendments in particular, Diane Doe sought $50,000 in actual damages and an equal amount in punitive damages, as well as declaratory and injunctive relief.

A hearing was held on June 7, 1979, with respect to various motions of the parties. On August 30, 1979, Judge Sharp dismissed the action on the merits as to the Highland police chief and dog trainer Patricia Little because they did not participate in the strip search. He granted defendant school officials summary judgment on the issue of monetary damages for the body search of Diane Doe. However, he held that she was entitled to declaratory relief upon the court's finding that the nude body search was made without a finding of reasonable cause and in violation of her Fourth Amendment rights. The judgment denied all other aspects of her prayer for declaratory relief, denied her motion for a permanent injunction and denied class certification.

For the reasons given in Judge Sharp's scholarly opinion, which we adopt as our own, the judgment is affirmed except with respect to the portion of the decision that the defendant school officials are immune from liability arising out of the nude search because they had a "good faith" defense as articulated in *Wood v. Strickland*. The *Wood* case found that school officials who act "in good-faith fulfillment of their responsibilities and within the bounds of reason under all the circumstances" and "not in ignorance or disregard of settled indisputable principles of law" are immune from liability. The district court in the instant case added that it "will not charge school officials with 'predicting the future course of constitutional law.'" No one can quarrel with these propositions but we do take exception to the application of these sterling principles to the facts of this case.

It does not require a constitutional scholar to conclude that a nude search of a 13-year-old child is an invasion of constitutional rights of some magnitude. More than that: it is a violation of any known principle of human decency. Apart from any constitutional readings and rulings, simple common sense would indicate that the conduct of the school officials in permitting such a nude search was not only unlawful but outrageous under "settled indisputable principles of law."

Wood v. Strickland accords immunity to school officials who act in good faith and within the bounds of reason. We suggest as strongly as possible that the conduct herein described exceeded the "bounds of reason" by two and a half country miles. It is not enough for us to declare that the little girl involved was indeed deprived of her constitutional and basic human rights. We must also permit her to seek damages from those who caused this humiliation and did indeed act as though students "shed at the schoolhouse door rights guaranteed by ... any ... constitutional provision".

We return the matter to the trial court for a determination of damages stemming from the body search. The decision is otherwise affirmed, costs to be borne equally by the respective parties.

Holdings of *Doe v. Renfrow*: The court held that a nude search of a 13-year-old child is an invasion of constitutional rights of some magnitude and, as such, is a "violation of any known principle of human decency." The court also held that simple common sense would indicate that the conduct of the school officials in permitting such a nude search was not only unlawful but outrageous.

Discussion Questions

Did the age of the girls strip searched (13) have an impact on the decision?

Would the result have been any different if the child strip-searched were younger (say, 8) or older (say, 17)?

Cornfield by Lewis v. Consol. High Sch. Dist. No. 230: In *Cornfield by Lewis v. Consol. High Sch. Dist. No. 230,* the federal court was faced with a § 1983 civil lawsuit concerning a strip search of a student by school officials. Brian Cornfield, a 16-year-old student enrolled in a behavioral disorder program, was suspected of having "crotched" drugs at school. Among other reasons, school officials' suspicions were based upon their belief that he seemed to have an unusual bulge in his crotch area. As a result of their suspicions, school officials telephoned the minor's mother to seek consent for a search. She refused. School officials, nevertheless, proceeded with the search. They escorted Cornfield to the boys' locker room to conduct a strip search. After making certain that no one else was present in the locker room, they locked the door. One official stood about fifteen feet from Cornfield, and the other stood on the opposite side, approximately ten to twelve feet away, while they had him remove his street clothes and put on a gym uniform. The officials visually inspected his naked body and physically inspected his clothes. Neither man performed a body cavity search. They found no evidence of drugs or any other contraband.

As you read *Cornfield by Lewis v. Consol. High Sch. Dist. No. 230,* look for the following:

1. Consider what impact age has on both the ability to consent to a strip search as well as the extent of intrusion caused by the strip search.

2. Examine that steps that the school authorities took in this case to attempt to minimize the intrusion caused by the strip search, and what other steps, in any, could have been employed to further reduce the extent of intrusion.

3. Look at the language of the court to determine whether or not the fact that the student was in a behavioral disorder program had any impact on the court's decision.

Cornfield by Lewis v. Consol. High Sch. Dist. No. 230
991 F.2d 1316 (7th Cir. 1993)

Brian Cornfield was enrolled in a behavioral disorder program at Carl Sandburg High School. Kathy Stacy, a teacher's aide in that program, found him outside the school building in violation of school rules on March 7, 1991. When she reported the infraction to Richard Spencer, Cornfield's teacher, and Dean Richard Frye, Stacy also alerted them to her suspicion that Cornfield appeared "too well-endowed." Another teacher, Joyce Lawler, and teacher's aide Lori Walsh corroborated Stacy's observation of an unusual bulge in Cornfield's crotch area. Neither defendant took any action at that time. The following day Cornfield was boarding the bus home when Spencer and Frye took him aside. Spencer himself had observed the unusual bulge in the crotch area of Cornfield's sweatpants. Believing the 16-year-old Cornfield was "crotching" drugs, Spencer and Frye asked him to accompany them to Frye's office to investigate further. When confronted with their suspicion, Cornfield grew agitated and began yelling obscenities. At Cornfield's request, Frye telephoned the minor's mother Janet Lewis to seek consent for a search. She refused.

Spencer and Frye nevertheless proceeded with the search. Believing a pat down to be excessively intrusive and ineffective at detecting drugs, they escorted Cornfield to the boys' locker room to conduct a strip search. After making certain that no one else was present in the locker room, they locked the door. Spencer then stood about fifteen feet from Cornfield, and Frye was standing on the opposite side, approximately ten to twelve feet away, while they had him remove his street clothes and put on a gym uniform. Spencer and Frye visually inspected his naked body and physically inspected his clothes. Neither man performed a body cavity search. They found no evidence of drugs or any other contraband. Afterwards the school bus was recalled, and it took Cornfield home.

Alleging that the search violated his Fourth, Fifth, and Fourteenth Amendment rights, Cornfield brought an action under 42 U.S.C. § 1983 against Consolidated High School District No. 230 ("District 230"), the parent organization of Carl Sandburg High School, and against Spencer and Frye in their professional and individual capacities.

The first question we address on review is whether the strip search of Cornfield was consistent with the Fourth Amendment. The Supreme Court established in *New Jersey v. T.L.O.* that reconciling the privacy interests of children with the needs of schools to maintain order does not require strict adherence to a probable cause standard for Fourth Amendment purposes.

To strike a balance, the Supreme Court fashioned a two-prong test for evaluating whether a search of a student is constitutional. First, the search must be "justified at its inception." Second, the search must be permissible in scope.

Therefore, whether a search is "reasonable" in the constitutional sense will vary according to the context of the search. In this regard, a couple of points should be immediately apparent. A nude search of a student by an administrator or teacher of the opposite sex would obviously violate this standard. Moreover, a highly intrusive search in response to a minor infraction would similarly not comport with the sliding scale advocated by the Supreme Court in *T.L.O.* To elaborate, "[a] search of a child's person or of a closed purse or other bag carried on her person, no less than a similar search carried out on an adult, is undoubtedly a severe violation of subjective expectations of privacy." Accordingly, "[s]ubjecting a student to a nude search is more than just the mild inconvenience of a pocket search, rather it is an intrusion into an individual's basic justifiable expectation of privacy." "It does not require a constitutional scholar to conclude that a nude search of a 13-year-old child is an invasion of constitutional rights of some magnitude. More than that: it is a violation of any known principle of human decency." Therefore, as the intrusiveness of the search of a student intensifies, so too does the standard of Fourth Amendment reasonableness. What may constitute reasonable suspicion for a search of a locker or even a pocket or pocketbook may fall well short of reasonableness for a nude search.

Thus, this flexible standard allows a school administrator or court to weigh the interest of a school in maintaining order against the substantial privacy interests of students in their bodies. In this regard, no one would seriously dispute that a nude search of a child is traumatic. The actual impact of a strip search will, of course, vary with the individual child, which is difficult to predict, and with the child's age, which is not. Although the Supreme Court in *T.L.O.* identified age as one of the factors used to evaluate the reasonableness of a search, it did not elaborate how age mattered. Whether the child is seven or seventeen is nonetheless relevant. First, the likelihood that a child is engaging in independent criminal activity will tend to increase with the age of the child. Second, a child's capacity to meaningfully consent to the strip search decision will depend on the child's age.

Since the ages of seven and fourteen are regarded as important transition periods in child development, they also can serve as useful guideposts for us here. In fact, these same age divisions correspond neatly with assumptions long employed in criminal law. At common law children under the age of seven were considered to be without criminal capacity. Children over the age of fourteen were treated as having the same criminal capacity as adults. And children between the ages of seven and fourteen were presumed to be incapable of committing crimes, although this presumption was rebuttable. In other words, adolescents are generally presumed to be as capable of independent criminal activity as adults. By contrast, elementary school children are far less likely to engage independently in criminal activity, including concealing contraband in private areas. Accordingly, adolescents will generally have the same capacity as adults to understand the issues involved in a strip search, including deciding whether to consent. Because of the presumption regarding elementary school children, we would naturally be much more circumspect about their ability to comprehend the impact of a strip search, or to consent to one. In sum, the legitimate expectations of privacy that students in school may claim are not monolithic.

Whether the search of Cornfield comports with the two-prong *T.L.O.* standard requires careful scrutiny of the circumstances surrounding the search. One fact is not in dispute: Cornfield was in a behavioral disorder program at the high school. In this regard, Cornfield contends that his problems are exclusively behavioral, which would be too thin a reed to support reasonable suspicion for a strip search: The fact that students in such a program exhibit inconsistent behavior and that drug users behave erratically does not lead inevitably to a conclusion that a student in a behavioral disorder program is a drug user. Spencer and Frye, however, have attested to a number of other independent factors to support the reasonableness of their suspicions of drug possession by Cornfield.

Spencer, one of Cornfield's teachers, had more direct contact with the appellant than Frye and alleged in his affidavit several incidents on which to ground of his suspicions. According to Spencer, Cornfield once stated that prior to December of 1990 he was dealing drugs and that in February 1991, he would test positive for marijuana. Spencer also believed that Cornfield did not successfully complete a drug rehabilitation program in December of 1990. And on January 29, 1991, Cornfield was found in possession of a live bullet at school. The remaining incidents giving rise to Spencer's suspicion occurred at some unspecified time prior to the date of the strip search: Cornfield's bus driver had reported the smell of marijuana from where Cornfield was sitting on the bus, one student reported having observed Cornfield smoking marijuana on one occasion on the bus, another student had advised Spencer of Cornfield's possession of drugs while on school grounds, Cornfield himself had related to Spencer that he was constantly thinking about drugs, and teacher's aide Kathy Stacy had informed Spencer that Cornfield claimed he had "crotched" drugs during a police raid at his mother's house. Spencer also attested to the fact that he had the opportunity to view Cornfield throughout the year; and March 7, 1991 was the first time he had observed the unusual bulge in Cornfield's crotch area.

According to Frye's affidavit, Spencer shared with Frye any information or incidents involving Cornfield. In addition, Palos Park police officer William Jackson communicated to Carl Sandburg's Head Dean Sutor that on October 24, 1990 he had received information that Cornfield was selling marijuana to other students. Head Dean Sutor conveyed this to Frye. Cornfield also acknowledged at some point to Sutor, in the presence of Kathy Stacy, that he failed a urine analysis for cocaine. Sutor advised Spencer and Frye of this as well.

Cornfield argues that Spencer and Frye could not reasonably have formed any manner of belief that he possessed drugs. Except for a couple of these incidents that he either has acknowledged or could not refute, Cornfield maintains the remainder never occurred. Specifically, he denies that he ever crotched drugs, that he smoked marijuana on the bus, that he brought marijuana onto school grounds, that he stated he would test positive for marijuana, that he had failed a cocaine test, and that he acknowledged to Spencer or anyone else he constantly thought about drugs. Furthermore, Cornfield's mother asserts in her affidavit that Cornfield left the drug rehab program because he was found "inappropriate." The program concluded that he had attention deficit disorder, not a drug problem. His mother also contends that he was not even on the bus the day the driver smelled marijuana.

In denying that any of these incidents occurred, Cornfield is effectively arguing that it would be unreasonable to form a suspicion on the stated grounds. That is, neither Spencer nor Frye could have received a significant portion of the information on which they relied because those events never occurred. According to Cornfield's affidavits, the only undisputed facts prior to the events leading up to the strip search were Officer Jackson's report, a single tip by another student, and Cornfield's possession of a live bullet. He contends that these three incidents, along with the perceptions of Spencer and Frye on the day of the strip search, are not sufficient to create a reasonable suspicion. However, several teachers and aides corroborated their suspicion of an unusual bulge in Cornfield's crotch area. More importantly, some of the statements on which Spencer and Frye apparently relied were from third parties, not Cornfield. Cornfield has not established that these statements, even if untrue, were not made or that Spencer and Frye could not reasonably believe them to be true.

To overcome the district court's grant of summary judgment, Cornfield would need to establish a genuine issue of material fact. Because we are faced with a number of incidents that allegedly served as a foundation for reasonable suspicion, whether individual incidents actually occurred is material only if the total number of undisputed or uncontroverted facts are not sufficient to form a reasonable suspicion. Thus, while we assume for purposes of summary judgment that Spencer and Frye did not rely on direct statements from Cornfield that Cornfield denies having made, they nonetheless considered more than the three wholly uncontested factors to form their suspicion.

Cornfield's case does differ from other student search cases in that Spencer and Frye based their decision on evidence or events that had occurred over some period of time. This aspect of the case evokes some concern because school teachers and administrators can marshal negative incidents and perceptions while discounting any contrary evidence that may accumulate over the course of a number of months, or longer. As the facts of this case stand, however, Spencer and Frye relied on a number of relatively recent incidents reported by various teachers and aides as well as their personal observations, the cumulative effect of which is sufficient to create a reasonable suspicion that Cornfield was crotching drugs.

The second prong of our inquiry concerns whether the search was permissible in scope. On the one hand, the 16-year-old Cornfield was of an age at which children are extremely self-conscious about their bodies; thus, the potential impact of a strip search was substantial. However, given Spencer and Frye's suspicion that Cornfield was crotching drugs, their conclusion that a strip search was the least intrusive way to confirm or deny their suspicions was not unreasonable. As administered, two male school personnel performed the search and did so in the privacy of the boys' locker room. Cornfield contends that other students could have seen him although he does not say that anyone actually did. As Cornfield changed, Spencer and Frye observed from a certain distance away to ensure

Cornfield could not conceal any drugs or other contraband he was suspected of carrying. In addition, Spencer and Frye did not physically touch him or subject him to a body cavity search, nor did they have him suffer the indignity of standing naked before them but allowed him to put on a gym uniform while they searched his street clothes. Finally, the fact that Spencer and Frye found no drugs or other contraband does not allow us to conclude retrospectively that the search was unreasonable in scope.

Cornfield, who bears the burden of establishing the particularized right, points to our decision in *Doe v. Renfrow* as proof of the unconstitutionality of strip searches of students. Actually, our sharp condemnation of the conduct of the school officials in that case stemmed from the fact that the strip search of Doe was executed without any individualized suspicion and without reasonable cause. *Renfrow*'s requirement of reasonable cause for searching students is in fact consistent with the standard subsequently enunciated in *T.L.O.* In addition, we have found defendants' conduct to be reasonable under the circumstances. Because Cornfield has not succeeded in placing the actions taken by Spencer and Frye outside a "clearly established" constitutional norm, they are entitled to qualified immunity.

For the foregoing reasons, the decision of the district court is Affirmed.

Holdings of *Cornfield by Lewis v. Consol. High Sch. Dist. No. 230:* In this case, the court held that the search in question was "reasonable." As the intrusiveness of the search of a student intensifies, so too does the standard of Fourth Amendment reasonableness. A nude search of a student by an administrator or teacher of the opposite sex would be unreasonable, as would a highly intrusive search, in response to a minor infraction.

Discussion Questions

One of the pieces of "evidence" that the school authorities used to support their reasonable suspicion was a call from the police relating that they suspected him of selling drugs at school. Isn't this a case of the police (who don't have probable cause) using the school authorities to search for them at a lower standard?

Since all of the background "reasons" of the authorities to have a "reasonable suspicion" of Cornfield will continue to be present, can the school authorities continue to rely on those reasons to continue to search him almost every day?

———————

Safford Unified Sch. Dist. No. 1 v. Redding: In *Safford Unified Sch. Dist. No. 1 v. Redding,* the United States Supreme Court was faced with a § 1983 civil lawsuit concerning a strip search of a student by school officials. A school official came into 13-year-old Savana Redding's math class and asked Savana to go to his office, where Savana was accused of giving the pills to other students, which Savana denied. Savana agreed to a search, and her backpack was searched, which revealed nothing improper. Savana was taken to the school nurse's office to search her clothes for pills, where she was asked to remove her jacket, socks, and shoes, leaving her in stretch pants and a T-shirt (both without pockets), which she was then asked to remove. Finally, Savana was told to pull her bra out and to the side and shake it, and to pull out the elastic on her underpants, thus exposing her breasts and pelvic area to some degree. No pills were found.

As you read *Safford Unified Sch. Dist. No. 1 v. Redding,* look for the following:

1. Consider why the court seems to differentiate between prescription drugs and "street drugs."

2. Consider whether or not allegations of possession of a dangerous weapon would lead to a different result in this case.

3. Look at the language of the court to determine whether or not the court indicates that a strip search would ever be authorized.

Safford Unified Sch. Dist. No. 1 v. Redding
557 U.S. 364 (2009)

Justice SOUTER delivered the opinion of the Court.

The issue here is whether a 13-year-old student's Fourth Amendment right was violated when she was subjected to a search of her bra and underpants by school officials acting on reasonable suspicion that she had brought forbidden prescription and over-the-counter drugs to school. Because there were no reasons to suspect the drugs presented a danger or were concealed in her underwear, we hold that the search did violate the Constitution, but because there is reason to question the clarity with which the right was established, the official who ordered the unconstitutional search is entitled to qualified immunity from liability.

The events immediately prior to the search in question began in 13-year-old Savana Redding's math class at Safford Middle School one October day in 2003. The assistant principal of the school, Kerry Wilson, came into the room and asked Savana to go to his office. There, he showed her a day planner, unzipped and open flat on his desk, in which there were several knives, lighters, a permanent marker, and a cigarette. Wilson asked Savana whether the planner was hers; she said it was, but that a few days before she had lent it to her friend, Marissa Glines. Savana stated that none of the items in the planner belonged to her.

Wilson then showed Savana four white prescription-strength ibuprofen 400-mg pills, and one over-the-counter blue naproxen 200-mg pill, all used for pain and inflammation but banned under school rules without advance permission. He asked Savana if she knew anything about the pills. Savana answered that she did not. Wilson then told Savana that he had received a report that she was giving these pills to fellow students; Savana denied it and agreed to let Wilson search her belongings. Helen Romero, an administrative assistant, came into the office, and together with Wilson they searched Savana's backpack, finding nothing.

At that point, Wilson instructed Romero to take Savana to the school nurse's office to search her clothes for pills. Romero and the nurse, Peggy Schwallier, asked Savana to remove her jacket, socks, and shoes, leaving her in stretch pants and a T-shirt (both without pockets), which she was then asked to remove. Finally, Savana was told to pull her bra out and to the side and shake it, and to pull out the elastic on her underpants, thus exposing her breasts and pelvic area to some degree. No pills were found.

Savana's mother filed suit against Safford Unified School District # 1, Wilson, Romero, and Schwallier for conducting a strip search in violation of Savana's Fourth Amendment rights. The individuals (hereinafter petitioners) moved for summary judgment, raising a defense of qualified immunity. The District Court for the District of Arizona granted the motion on the ground that there was no Fourth Amendment violation, and a panel of the Ninth Circuit affirmed.

A closely divided Circuit sitting en banc, however, reversed. Following the two-step protocol for evaluating claims of qualified immunity, the Ninth Circuit held that the strip search was unjustified under the Fourth Amendment test for searches of children by school officials set out in *New Jersey v. T.L.O.* The Circuit then applied the test for qualified immunity, and found that Savana's right was clearly established at the time of the search: "'[t]hese notions of personal privacy are "clearly established" in that they inhere in all of us, particularly middle school teenagers, and are inherent in the privacy component of the Fourth Amendment's proscription against unreasonable searches.'" The upshot was reversal of summary judgment as to Wilson, while affirming the judgments in favor of Schwallier, the school nurse, and Romero, the administrative assistant, since they had not acted as independent decisionmakers.

We granted certiorari, and now affirm in part, reverse in part, and remand.

In *T.L.O.*, we recognized that the school setting "requires some modification of the level of suspicion of illicit activity needed to justify a search," and held that for searches by school officials "a careful balancing of governmental and private interests suggests that the public interest is best served by a Fourth Amendment standard of reasonableness that stops short of probable cause." We have thus applied a standard of reasonable suspicion to determine the legality of a school administrator's search of a student, and have held that a school search "will be permissible in its scope when the measures adopted are reasonably related to the objectives of the search and not excessively intrusive in light of the age and sex of the student and the nature of the infraction."

Perhaps the best that can be said generally about the required knowledge component of probable cause for a law enforcement officer's evidence search is that it raise a "fair probability," or a "substantial chance," of discovering evidence of criminal activity. The lesser standard for school searches could as readily be described as a moderate chance of finding evidence of wrongdoing.

In this case, the school's policies strictly prohibit the nonmedical use, possession, or sale of any drug on school grounds, including "'[a]ny prescription or over-the-counter drug, except those for which permission to use in school has been granted pursuant to Board policy.'" A week before Savana was searched, another student, Jordan Romero (no relation of the school's administrative assistant), told the principal and Assistant Principal Wilson that "certain students were bringing drugs and weapons on campus," and that he had been sick after taking some pills that "he got from a classmate." On the morning of October 8, the same boy handed Wilson a white pill that he said Marissa Glines had given him. He told Wilson that students were planning to take the pills at lunch.

Wilson learned from Peggy Schwallier, the school nurse, that the pill was Ibuprofen 400 mg, available only by prescription. Wilson then called Marissa out of class. Outside the classroom, Marissa's teacher handed Wilson the day planner, found within Marissa's reach, containing various contraband items. Wilson escorted Marissa back to his office.

In the presence of Helen Romero, Wilson requested Marissa to turn out her pockets and open her wallet. Marissa produced a blue pill, several white ones, and a razor blade. Wilson asked where the blue pill came from, and Marissa answered, "'I guess it slipped in when she gave me the IBU 400s.'" When Wilson asked whom she meant, Marissa replied, "'Savana Redding.'" Wilson then enquired about the day planner and its contents; Marissa denied knowing anything about them. Wilson did not ask Marissa any followup questions to determine whether there was any likelihood that Savana presently had pills: neither asking when Marissa received the pills from Savana nor where Savana might be hiding them.

Schwallier did not immediately recognize the blue pill, but information provided through a poison control hotline indicated that the pill was a 200-mg dose of an anti-inflammatory drug, generically called naproxen, available over the counter. At Wilson's direction, Marissa was then subjected to a search of her bra and underpants by Romero and Schwallier, as Savana was later on. The search revealed no additional pills.

It was at this juncture that Wilson called Savana into his office and showed her the day planner. Their conversation established that Savana and Marissa were on friendly terms: while she denied knowledge of the contraband, Savana admitted that the day planner was hers and that she had lent it to Marissa. Wilson had other reports of their friendship from staff members, who had identified Savana and Marissa as part of an unusually rowdy group at the school's opening dance in August, during which alcohol and cigarettes were found in the girls' bathroom. Wilson had reason to connect the girls with this contraband, for Wilson knew that Jordan Romero had told the principal that before the dance, he had been at a party at Savana's house where alcohol was served. Marissa's statement that the pills came from Savana was thus sufficiently plausible to warrant suspicion that Savana was involved in pill distribution.

This suspicion of Wilson's was enough to justify a search of Savana's backpack and outer clothing. If a student is reasonably suspected of giving out contraband pills, she is reasonably suspected of carrying them on her person and in the carryall that has become an item of student uniform in most places today. If Wilson's reasonable suspicion of pill distribution were not understood to support searches of outer clothes and backpack, it would not justify any search worth making. And the look into Savana's bag, in her presence and in the relative privacy of Wilson's office, was not excessively intrusive, any more than Romero's subsequent search of her outer clothing.

Here it is that the parties part company, with Savana's claim that extending the search at Wilson's behest to the point of making her pull out her underwear was constitutionally unreasonable. The exact label for this final step in the intrusion is not important, though strip search is a fair way to speak of it. Romero and Schwallier directed Savana to remove her clothes down to her underwear, and then "pull out" her bra and the elastic band on her underpants. Although Romero and Schwallier stated that they did not see anything when Savana followed their instructions, we would not define strip search and its Fourth Amendment consequences in a way that would guarantee litigation about who was looking and how much was seen. The very fact of Savana's pulling her underwear away from her body in the presence of the two officials who were able to see her necessarily exposed her breasts and pelvic area to some degree, and both subjective and reasonable societal expectations of personal privacy support the treatment of such a search as categorically distinct, requiring distinct elements of justification on the part of school authorities for going beyond a search of outer clothing and belongings.

Savana's subjective expectation of privacy against such a search is inherent in her account of it as embarrassing, frightening, and humiliating. The reasonableness of her expectation (required by the Fourth Amendment standard) is indicated by the consistent experiences of other young people similarly searched, whose adolescent vulnerability intensifies the patent intrusiveness of the exposure. The common reaction of these adolescents simply registers the obviously different meaning of a search exposing the body from the experience of nakedness or near undress in other school circumstances. Changing for gym is getting ready for play; exposing for a search is responding to an accusation reserved for suspected wrongdoers and fairly understood as so degrading that a number of communities have decided that strip searches in schools are never reasonable and have banned them no matter what the facts may be.

The indignity of the search does not, of course, outlaw it, but it does implicate the rule of reasonableness as stated in *T.L.O.*, that "the search as actually conducted [be] reasonably related in scope to the circumstances which justified the interference in the first place." The scope will be permissible, that is, when it is "not excessively intrusive in light of the age and sex of the student and the nature of the infraction."

Here, the content of the suspicion failed to match the degree of intrusion. Wilson knew beforehand that the pills were prescription-strength ibuprofen and over-the-counter naproxen, common pain relievers equivalent to two Advil, or one Aleve. He must have been aware of the nature and limited threat of the specific drugs he was searching for, and while just about anything can be taken in quantities that will do real harm, Wilson had no reason to suspect that large amounts of the drugs were being passed around, or that individual students were receiving great numbers of pills.

Nor could Wilson have suspected that Savana was hiding common painkillers in her underwear. Petitioners suggest, as a truth universally acknowledged, that "students ... hid[e] contraband in or under their clothing," and cite a smattering of cases of students with contraband in their underwear. But when the categorically extreme intrusiveness of a search down to the body of an adolescent requires some justification in suspected facts, general background possibilities fall short; a reasonable search that extensive calls for suspicion that it will pay off. But nondangerous school contraband does not raise the specter of stashes in intimate places, and there is no evidence in the record of any general practice among Safford Middle School students of hiding that sort of thing in underwear; neither Jordan nor Marissa suggested to Wilson that Savana was doing that, and the preceding search of Marissa that Wilson ordered yielded nothing. Wilson never even determined when Marissa had received the pills from Savana; if it had been a few days before, that would weigh heavily against any reasonable conclusion that Savana presently had the pills on her person, much less in her underwear.

In sum, what was missing from the suspected facts that pointed to Savana was any indication of danger to the students from the power of the drugs or their quantity, and any reason to suppose that Savana was carrying pills in her underwear. We think that the combination of these deficiencies was fatal to finding the search reasonable.

In so holding, we mean to cast no ill reflection on the assistant principal, for the record raises no doubt that his motive throughout was to eliminate drugs from his school and protect students from what Jordan Romero had gone through. Parents are known to overreact to protect their children from danger, and a school official with responsibility for safety may tend to do the same. The difference is that the Fourth Amendment places limits on the official, even with the high degree of deference that courts must pay to the educator's professional judgment.

We do mean, though, to make it clear that the *T.L.O.* concern to limit a school search to reasonable scope requires the support of reasonable suspicion of danger or of resort to underwear for hiding evidence of wrongdoing before a search can reasonably make the quantum leap from outer clothes and backpacks to exposure of intimate parts. The meaning of such a search, and the degradation its subject may reasonably feel, place a search that intrusive in a category of its own demanding its own specific suspicions.

A school official searching a student is "entitled to qualified immunity where clearly established law does not show that the search violated the Fourth Amendment."

T.L.O. directed school officials to limit the intrusiveness of a search, "in light of the age and sex of the student and the nature of the infraction," and as we have just said at some length, the intrusiveness of the strip search here cannot be seen as justifiably related to the circumstances. But we realize that the lower courts have reached divergent conclusions regarding how the *T.L.O.* standard applies to such searches.

We think these differences of opinion from our own are substantial enough to require immunity for the school officials in this case.

The strip search of Savana Redding was unreasonable and a violation of the Fourth Amendment, but petitioners Wilson, Romero, and Schwallier are nevertheless protected from liability through qualified immunity. Our conclusions here do not resolve, however, the question of the liability of petitioner Safford Unified School District # 1, a claim the Ninth Circuit did not address. The judgment of the Ninth Circuit is therefore affirmed in part and reversed in part, and this case is remanded for consideration of the Monell claim.

It is so ordered.

Justice STEVENS, with whom Justice GINSBURG joins, concurring in part and dissenting in part.

In *New Jersey v. T.L.O.*, the Court established a two-step inquiry for determining the reasonableness of a school official's decision to search a student.

Nothing the Court decides today alters this basic framework. It simply applies *T.L.O.* to declare unconstitutional a strip search of a 13-year-old honors student that was based on a groundless suspicion that she might be hiding medicine in her underwear. This is, in essence, a case in which clearly established law meets clearly outrageous conduct. I have long believed that "'[i]t does not require a constitutional scholar to conclude that a nude search of a 13-year-old child is an invasion of constitutional rights of some magnitude.'" The strip search of Savana Redding in this case was both more intrusive and less justified than the search of the student's purse in *T.L.O.* Therefore, while I join Parts I–III of the Court's opinion, I disagree with its decision to extend qualified immunity to the school official who authorized this unconstitutional search.

The Court of Appeals properly rejected the school official's qualified immunity defense, and I would affirm that court's judgment in its entirety.

Justice GINSBURG, concurring in part and dissenting in part.

I agree with the Court that Assistant Principal Wilson's subjection of 13-year-old Savana Redding to a humiliating stripdown search violated the Fourth Amendment. But I also agree with Justice Stevens, that our opinion in *New Jersey v. T.L.O.*, "clearly established" the law governing this case.

In contrast to *T.L.O.*, where a teacher discovered a student smoking in the lavatory, and where the search was confined to the student's purse, the search of Redding involved her body and rested on the bare accusation of another student whose reliability the Assistant Principal had no reason to trust. The Court's opinion in *T.L.O.* plainly stated the controlling Fourth Amendment law: A search ordered by a school official, even if "justified at its inception," crosses the constitutional boundary if it becomes "excessively intrusive in light of the age and sex of the student and the nature of the infraction."

Justice THOMAS, concurring in the judgment in part and dissenting in part.

I agree with the Court that the judgment against the school officials with respect to qualified immunity should be reversed. Unlike the majority, however, I would hold that the search of Savana Redding did not violate the Fourth Amendment. The majority imposes a vague and amorphous standard on school administrators. It also grants judges sweeping authority to second-guess the measures that these officials take to maintain discipline in their schools and ensure the health and safety of the students in their charge. This deep intrusion into the administration of public schools exemplifies why the Court should return to the common-law doctrine of in loco parentis under which "the judiciary was reluctant to interfere in the routine business of school administration, allowing schools and teachers to set and enforce rules and to maintain order." But even under the prevailing Fourth Amendment test established by *New Jersey v. T.L.O.*, all petitioners, including the school district, are entitled to judgment as a matter of law in their favor.

For nearly 25 years this Court has understood that "[m]aintaining order in the classroom has never been easy, but in more recent years, school disorder has often taken particularly ugly forms: drug use and violent crime in the schools have become major social problems." In schools, "[e]vents calling for discipline are frequent occurrences and sometimes require immediate, effective action."

For this reason, school officials retain broad authority to protect students and preserve "order and a proper educational environment" under the Fourth Amendment. This authority requires that school officials be able to engage in the "close supervision of schoolchildren, as well as ... enforc[e] rules against conduct that would be perfectly permissible if undertaken by an adult." Seeking to reconcile the Fourth Amendment with this unique public school setting, the Court in *T.L.O.* held that a school search is "reasonable" if it is "'justified at its inception'" and "'reasonably related in scope to the circumstances which justified the interference in the first place.'" The search under review easily meets this standard.

Here, petitioners had reasonable grounds to suspect that Redding was in possession of prescription and nonprescription drugs in violation of the school's prohibition of the "non-medical use, possession, or sale of a drug" on school property or at school events. As an initial matter, school officials were aware that a few years earlier, a student had become "seriously ill" and "spent several days in intensive care" after ingesting prescription medication obtained from a classmate. Fourth Amendment searches do not occur in a vacuum; rather, context must inform the judicial inquiry. In this instance, the suspicion of drug possession arose at a middle school that had "a history of problems with students using and distributing prohibited and illegal substances on campus."

The school's substance-abuse problems had not abated by the 2003–2004 school year, which is when the challenged search of Redding took place. School officials had found alcohol and cigarettes in the girls' bathroom during the first school dance of the year and noticed that a group of students including Redding and Marissa Glines smelled of alcohol. Several weeks later, another student, Jordan Romero, reported that Redding had hosted a party before the dance where she served whiskey, vodka, and tequila ... Romero had provided this report to school officials as a result of a meeting his mother scheduled with the officials after Romero "bec[a]me violent" and "sick to his stomach" one night and admitted that "he had taken some pills that he had got[ten] from a classmate." At that meeting, Romero admitted that "certain students were bringing drugs and weapons on campus." One week later, Romero handed the assistant principal a white pill that he said he had received from Glines. He reported "that a group of students [were] planning on taking the pills at lunch."

School officials justifiably took quick action in light of the lunchtime deadline. The assistant principal took the pill to the school nurse who identified it as prescription-strength 400-mg Ibuprofen. A subsequent search of Glines and her belongings produced a razor blade, a Naproxen 200-mg pill, and several Ibuprofen 400-mg pills. When asked, Glines claimed that she had received the pills from Redding. A search of Redding's planner, which Glines had borrowed, then uncovered "several knives, several lighters, a cigarette, and a permanent marker." Thus, as the majority acknowledges, the totality of relevant circumstances justified a search of Redding for pills.

The remaining question is whether the search was reasonable in scope. Under *T.L.O.*, "a search will be permissible in its scope when the measures adopted are reasonably related to the objectives of the search and not excessively intrusive in light of the age and sex of the student and the nature of the infraction." The majority concludes that the school officials' search of Redding's underwear was not "'reasonably related in scope to the circumstances which justified the interference in the first place,'" notwithstanding the officials' reasonable suspicion that Redding "was involved in pill distribution." According to the majority, to be reasonable, this school search required a showing of "danger to the students from the power of the drugs or their quantity" or a "reason to suppose that [Redding] was carrying pills in her underwear." Each of these additional requirements is an unjustifiable departure from bedrock Fourth Amendment law in the school setting, where this Court has heretofore read the Fourth Amendment to grant considerable leeway to school officials. Because the school officials searched in a location where the pills could have been hidden, the search was reasonable in scope under *T.L.O.*

The majority finds that "subjective and reasonable societal expectations of personal privacy support ... treat[ing]" this type of search, which it labels a "strip search," as "categorically distinct, requiring distinct elements of justification on the part of school authorities for going beyond a search of clothing and belongings." Thus, in the majority's view, although the school officials had reasonable suspicion to believe that Redding had the pills on her person, they needed some greater level of particularized suspicion to conduct this "strip search." There is no support for this contortion of the Fourth Amendment.

The Court has generally held that the reasonableness of a search's scope depends only on whether it is limited to the area that is capable of concealing the object of the search.

The analysis of whether the scope of the search here was permissible under that standard is straightforward. Indeed, the majority does not dispute that "general background possibilities" establish that students conceal "contraband in their underwear." It acknowledges that school officials had reasonable suspicion to look in Redding's backpack and outer clothing because if "Wilson's reasonable suspicion of pill distribution were not understood to support searches of outer clothes and backpack, it would not justify any search worth making." The majority nevertheless concludes that proceeding any further with the search was unreasonable. But there is no support for this conclusion. The reasonable suspicion that Redding possessed the pills for distribution purposes did not dissipate simply because the search of her backpack turned up nothing. It was eminently reasonable to conclude that the backpack was empty because Redding was secreting the pills in a place she thought no one would look.

Redding would not have been the first person to conceal pills in her undergarments. Nor will she be the last after today's decision, which announces the safest place to secrete contraband in school.

The majority compounds its error by reading the "nature of the infraction" aspect of the *T.L.O.* test as a license to limit searches based on a judge's assessment of a particular school policy. According to the majority, the scope of the search was impermissible because the school official "must have been aware of the nature and limited threat of the specific drugs he was searching for" and because he "had no reason to suspect that large amounts of the drugs were being passed around, or that individual students were receiving great numbers of pills." Thus, in order to locate a rationale for finding a Fourth Amendment violation in this case, the majority retreats from its observation that the school's firm no-drug policy "makes sense, and there is no basis to claim that the search was unreasonable owing to some defect or shortcoming of the rule it was aimed at enforcing."

Even accepting the majority's assurances that it is not attacking the rule's reasonableness, it certainly is attacking the rule's importance. This approach directly conflicts with *T.L.O.* in which the Court was "unwilling to adopt a standard under which the legality of a search is dependent upon a judge's evaluation of the relative importance of school rules." Indeed, the Court in *T.L.O.* expressly rejected the proposition that the majority seemingly endorses — that "some rules regarding student conduct are by nature too 'trivial' to justify a search based upon reasonable suspicion."

The majority's decision in this regard also departs from another basic principle of the Fourth Amendment: that law enforcement officials can enforce with the same vigor all rules and regulations irrespective of the perceived importance of any of those rules. The Fourth Amendment rule for searches is the same: Police officers are entitled to search regardless of the perceived triviality of the underlying law.

The majority has placed school officials in this "impossible spot" by questioning whether possession of Ibuprofen and Naproxen causes a severe enough threat to warrant investigation. Had the suspected infraction involved a street drug, the majority implies that it would have approved the scope of the search. In effect, then, the majority has replaced a school rule that draws no distinction among drugs with a new one that does. As a result, a full search of a student's person for prohibited drugs will be permitted only if the Court agrees that the drug in question was sufficiently dangerous. Such a test is unworkable and unsound. School officials cannot be expected to halt searches based on the possibility that a court might later find that the particular infraction at issue is not severe enough to warrant an intrusive investigation.

Judges are not qualified to second-guess the best manner for maintaining quiet and order in the school environment. It is a mistake for judges to assume the responsibility for deciding which school rules are important enough to allow for invasive searches and which rules are not.

Even if this Court were authorized to second-guess the importance of school rules, the Court's assessment of the importance of this district's policy is flawed. It is a crime to possess or use prescription-strength Ibuprofen without a prescription. By prohibiting unauthorized prescription drugs on school grounds — and conducting a search to ensure students abide by that prohibition — the school rule here was consistent with a routine provision of the state criminal code. It hardly seems unreasonable for school officials to enforce a rule that, in effect, proscribes conduct that amounts to a crime.

Moreover, school districts have valid reasons for punishing the unauthorized possession of prescription drugs on school property as severely as the possession of street drugs; "[t]eenage abuse of over-the-counter and prescription drugs poses an increasingly alarming national crisis." As one study noted, "more young people ages 12–17 abuse prescription drugs than any illicit drug except marijuana — more than cocaine, heroin, and methamphetamine combined." And according to a 2005 survey of teens, "nearly one in five (19 percent or 4.5 million) admit abusing prescription drugs in their lifetime."

Admittedly, the Ibuprofen and Naproxen at issue in this case are not the prescription painkillers at the forefront of the prescription-drug-abuse problem. But they are not without their own dangers. As nonsteroidal anti-inflammatory drugs (NSAIDs), they pose a risk of death from overdose. Moreover, the side-effects caused by the use of NSAIDs can be magnified if they are taken in combination with other drugs.

In determining whether the search's scope was reasonable under the Fourth Amendment, it is therefore irrelevant whether officials suspected Redding of possessing prescription-strength Ibuprofen, nonprescription-strength Naproxen, or some harder street drug. Safford prohibited its possession on school property. Reasonable suspicion that Redding was in possession of drugs in violation of these policies, therefore, justified a search extending to any area where small pills could be concealed. The search did not violate the Fourth Amendment.

By declaring the search unreasonable in this case, the majority has "'surrender[ed] control of the American public school system to public school students'" by invalidating school policies that treat all drugs equally and by second-guessing swift disciplinary decisions made by school officials. The Court's interference in these matters of great concern to teachers, parents, and students illustrates why the most constitutionally sound approach to the question of applying the Fourth Amendment in local public schools would in fact be the complete restoration of the common-law doctrine of in loco parentis.

If the common-law view that parents delegate to teachers their authority to discipline and maintain order were to be applied in this case, the search of Redding would stand. There can be no doubt that a parent would have had the authority to conduct the search at issue in this case. Parents have "immunity from the strictures of the Fourth Amendment" when it comes to searches of a child or that child's belongings.

As acknowledged by this Court, this principle is based on the "societal understanding of superior and inferior" with respect to the "parent and child" relationship. In light of this relationship, the Court has indicated that a parent can authorize a third-party search of a child by consenting to such a search, even if the child denies his consent. Certainly, a search by the parent himself is no different, regardless of whether or not a child would prefer to be left alone.

In the end, the task of implementing and amending public school policies is beyond this Court's function. Parents, teachers, school administrators, local politicians, and state officials are all better suited than judges to determine the appropriate limits on searches conducted by school officials. Preservation of order, discipline, and safety in public schools is simply not the domain of the Constitution. And, common sense is not a judicial monopoly or a Constitutional imperative.

"[T]he nationwide drug epidemic makes the war against drugs a pressing concern in every school." And yet the Court has limited the authority of school officials to conduct searches for the drugs that the officials believe pose a serious safety risk to their students. By doing so, the majority has confirmed that a return to the doctrine of in loco parentis is required to keep the judiciary from essentially seizing control of public schools. By deciding that it is better equipped to decide what behavior should be permitted in schools, the Court has undercut student safety and undermined the authority of school administrators and local officials. Even more troubling, it has done so in a case in which the underlying response by school administrators was reasonable and justified. I cannot join this regrettable decision. I, therefore, respectfully dissent from the Court's determination that this search violated the Fourth Amendment.

Holdings of *Safford Unified Sch. Dist. No. 1 v. Redding:* In this case, the court held that, because there were no reasons to suspect the drugs presented a danger or were concealed in her underwear, the search was constitutionally prohibited. The suspicion of school authorities was enough to justify a search of the student's backpack and outer clothing. However, the content of the suspicion failed to match the degree of intrusion caused by a strip search. What was missing from the suspected facts that pointed to Savana was any indication of danger to the students from the power of the drugs or their quantity, and any reason to suppose that Savana was carrying pills in her underwear.

Discussion Questions

How does the majority conclude that a strip search is treated differently than a search of the outer clothes or a backpack?

Does the majority require probable cause, a warrant, or something more to allow a strip search by school authorities?

Key Concepts: Strip Searches of Students

- As the intrusiveness of the search of a student intensifies, so too does the standard of Fourth Amendment reasonableness. Since a "strip search" is an extremely intrusive type of search, the level of suspicion required to support such is search is much higher than would be required for most other searches.

- The age of the student impacts both the student's ability to consent to a search as well as the amount of intrusiveness experienced by the student subject to a strip search.

- Safety issues, including weapons and dangerous drugs, have a greater likelihood of supporting a strip search than mere rules violations or other criminal act.

Practical Questions: Strip Searches of Students

1. Jonathan Wilson, a 17-year-old high school senior, is a D+ student. Most teachers and administrators at the school believe Jonathan will not graduate. Jonathan received grades of 100% in his last two math tests (a course that he had been failing). Students use laptops for exams. After one exam, a student reported that he saw Jonathan place a flash-drive in the laptop computer during the exam (which is prohibited) and using the data from the flash-dive to complete the exam. The principal, Mr. Smith, grabbed Jonathan as he exited the room from taking an exam and took him to Smith's office. The math teacher reported that the exam just taken by Jonathan was, once again, perfect. Smith had Jonathan empty his pockets, and no flash-drive was found. Can Smith follow the strip-search procedure used in the *Cornfield* case with Jonathan?

2. East High School has been plagued with gang activity including members of the Gangster Disciples Gang threatening other students with physical violence. Mary Peters, East High School Principal, has received training from the local police department that initiation into the Gangster Disciples Gang involves a two-step process: First, the initiate is required to have a "Fork" tattooed on his buttocks and, then, within 2 days of the tattooing, must "take down" an unsuspecting student. "Taking down" involves attacking an unsuspecting nonmember and inflicting such physical violence as to require at least 2 days of hospitalization. In the past year, at least 5 students have been subjected to such an unprovoked attack. Three students have advised Mary that an identified 17-year-old student began the initiation last night by receiving the tattoo and will attack another student in the next 2 days. Principal Smith contacted the identified student's teachers from

the morning classes and both have indicated that the student seems to be uncomfortable sitting in the desk that day. Can principal Smith have two of the male gym teachers escort the student to the locker room in private and ask him to expose his buttocks so that it can be determined if the student has begun initiation into the Gangster Disciples Gang?

C. Backpacks and Cellphones in School

Overview: In *T.L.O.*, the court set forth a two-part test to determine the limitations on school officials for the search of a student. Courts have been forced to determine the limits of what constitutes the "inception" of the search as well as a "reasonable suspicion" to justify a search. Today, students often carry backpacks where virtually all of their personal effects are contained as well as cellphones which have become virtual computers. These two sources comprise regular sources of cases testing the application of the rules set forth in *T.L.O.*

DesRoches v. Caprio: In *DesRoches v. Caprio,* the federal court was faced with a § 1983 civil lawsuit concerning a search of a student's backpack by school officials. Because a student's tennis shoes were stolen from a classroom, the dean of students decided to search the personal belongings of all 19 students in the class. Everyone except DesRoches "consented" to a search (refusal to consent could result in a suspension). Nothing was found in the personal belongings of the other 18 students, so DesRoches was taken to the office and requested again to allow a search of his backpack. When he still refused, DesRoches was immediately suspended for 10 days. The court was faced with the issue of whether or not the "reasonable suspicion" requirement of *T.L.O.* can be supplied by the process of elimination: everyone else voluntarily agreeing to a search and nothing being found.

As you read *DesRoches v. Caprio,* look for the following:

1. Consider why the court needed to determine when the "inception" of the search occurred.

2. Consider whether the mere fact that DesRoches was the only one refusing to give consent would provide the needed "reasonable suspicion" to authorize a search or whether the lack of finding the shoes in the possession of any of the other students is crucial.

3. Look for anything that DesRoches did that would provide reasonable suspicion that he was guilty other than his exercise of his constitutional rights.

DesRoches v. Caprio
156 F.3d 571 (4th Cir. 1998)

MURNAGHAN, Circuit Judge:

Appellants, Principal Michael Caprio, Superintendent Roy Nichols, Jr., and the City of Norfolk School Board, appeal the judgment of the district court finding a violation of the Fourth Amendment arising from the suspension of Appellee, James DesRoches, Jr. (DesRoches), following his refusal to consent to a search of his backpack by school officials investigating a missing pair of tennis shoes. Because we believe the proposed search was reasonable under the circumstances, we reverse.

On May 2, 1997, James DesRoches was a ninth-grade student at Granby High School, a public high school in Norfolk, Virginia. On that day, he attended his fourth period art class, which met for half an hour before and after lunch. During the first half of class, one of the nineteen students in the class, Shamra Hursey (Hursey), placed her girls' tennis shoes on top of her desk. While the students went to lunch, Hursey left her shoes unattended in the classroom.

During lunch, the art classroom was unlocked, and the teacher remained in the classroom. For a "very short" portion of the time, however, the teacher was in a closet in the classroom cutting paper. The teacher could not see out of the closet into the classroom, but she stated that while she was in the classroom she never saw any students whom she did not know. One student in the classroom during the lunch period, however, testified that a student who was not enrolled in the fourth period art class was in the classroom during lunch. A few other students who were enrolled in the class returned to the classroom for a few minutes during lunch.

Upon Hursey's return from class, she noticed her shoes were missing. DesRoches and others assisted Hursey in looking for the shoes. When the shoes were not found, Hursey reported the shoes as stolen to the school's Dean of Students, James Lee, whose responsibilities include attending to matters of school security. Lee was aware that a ring had been reported missing in the same class the day before.

Upon arriving at the classroom, Lee spoke in the hallway with the class's teacher, Ms. Ratliffe, who informed him that, to her knowledge, only three students had remained in the classroom during lunch. When interviewed, those students informed Lee that Hursey had placed the shoes on her desk before the lunch period and that they were unaware of what might have happened to the shoes during lunch.

From his talks with these people, it was Lee's understanding that there had been students in the art classroom at all times during lunch, that the teacher knew all these students, that none of the students had been left alone in the classroom, and that the teacher was in the classroom at all times. It is also clear from the record that, although a student testified at trial to (1) seeing DesRoches in the cafeteria or courtyard during the lunch break; (2) seeing DesRoches with his backpack during lunch; and (3) whether DesRoches returned to the classroom after Shamra, no one told Lee anything about this at or before the time of the search.

On the basis of what he had learned during his investigation, Lee determined that it was necessary to conduct a search of the personal belongings of all nineteen students in the class. He announced his intention to search, asking whether anyone objected. At that point, DesRoches and another student raised their hands. When Lee reminded them that school policy authorized a ten-day suspension for a student's refusal to consent, the other student provided his consent but DesRoches continued to refuse. Lee told DesRoches "that he could just sit there and [they] would talk about it later," and then proceeded to search the bags and backpacks of the consenting students. Because those searches were unfruitful, Lee escorted DesRoches to the principal's office where the school's principal, Michael Caprio, renewed Lee's request to search DesRoches's backpack. When DesRoches refused, Caprio allowed him to call his parents in the unrealized hope that they would convince him to change his mind. DesRoches was then suspended for ten days, commencing immediately.

On May 8, 1997, DesRoches filed this action by his father and next friend, pursuant to 42 U.S.C. § 1983, seeking injunctive relief, monetary damages, and attorneys fees, on the grounds that the school officials had violated his rights under the First, Fourth, and Fourteenth Amendments to the United States Constitution.

The sole issue presented on appeal is whether the district court erred in concluding that the proposed search of DesRoches was unreasonable under the Fourth Amendment.

Appellants answer that question in the affirmative, arguing that Lee's demand to search DesRoches was reasonable under the circumstances.

The Supreme Court laid the ground rules for suspicion-based school searches in *T.L.O.* There, the Court held that the constitutionality of school searches based on individualized suspicion would be evaluated by the two-pronged reasonableness standard first announced in *Terry v. Ohio.* Pursuant to that standard, the reasonableness of a search is determined by considering first "whether the … action was justified at its inception," and second, "whether the search as actually conducted was reasonably related in scope to the circumstances which justified the interference in the first place.'"

T.L.O. did not hold that individualized suspicion is an essential element of reasonableness for all school searches. The Court found it unnecessary to address that issue since any requirement of individualized suspicion was easily satisfied by the facts presented in that case. Nevertheless, the Court cautioned that, as in other contexts, a search conducted in the absence of individualized suspicion would be reasonable only in a narrow class of cases, "where the privacy interests implicated by a search are minimal and where 'other safeguards' are available 'to assure that the individual's reasonable expectation of privacy is not subject to the discretion of the official in the field.'"

In the case at bar, the district court properly analyzed the reasonableness of the school's actions in light of the above principles. The district court recognized that, in some situations, a group of students may be so small that the entire group may be searched without violating the individualized suspicion requirement ("sufficient probability, not certainty, is the touchstone of reasonableness under the Fourth Amendment"). Then the court searched for individualized suspicion. After concluding that the proposed search was not based on individualized suspicion, the court analyzed the case according to the "special needs" inquiry laid out in *Vernonia, Chandler,* and other cases in which the government has offered a compelling government interest as justification for a suspicionless search. The court concluded that the circumstances facing school officials at the time of the search — theft of personal property not posing a risk of imminent harm to students or school personnel — were insufficient to justify the substantial invasion of privacy that would occasion the proposed search.

The Supreme Court has held that the existence of Fourth Amendment protections depends on whether the individual has a legitimate expectation of privacy in the thing or place to be searched. Like members of the public generally, schoolchildren enjoy a legitimate expectation of privacy in their persons and effects. Therefore, in the present case, there is no question but that DesRoches enjoyed a legitimate expectation of privacy in his backpack so as to trigger the protections of the Fourth Amendment.

The next question, then, is whether the proposed search of the backpack was reasonable under the circumstances. Consistent with our discussion above, we begin by determining whether the search was supported by individualized suspicion. Our analysis of that question is guided by *T.L.O.* There, the Court explained that the first step in the reasonableness inquiry is to determine whether the search was "justified at its inception," which requires us to determine whether there were "reasonable grounds for suspecting that the search will turn up evidence that the student has violated or is violating either the law or the rules of the school."

In the present case, where consent to search was requested and the individual was later punished for refusing consent, we are faced with the threshold issue of what constitutes the "inception" of the search. Not surprisingly, the parties offer competing views of the matter. DesRoches argues that the inception of the search occurred when school officials first announced their intention to search the class. He maintains, therefore, that the reasonableness of the school's actions must be judged by the circumstances known to school officials prior to their search of the first student. Appellants, on the other hand, argue that the inception of the search occurred not at the moment DesRoches was threatened with suspension, but at the moment he was actually suspended for refusing to consent. Therefore, while Appellants concede that individualized suspicion was lacking with respect to DesRoches when the search was first announced to the class, they maintain that such suspicion had arisen by the time DesRoches was punished for refusing to consent to the search.

The district court agreed with DesRoches. In the court's opinion, "allowing [DesRoches] to be searched after the fruitless search of the consenting students compromises the principle that a search's reasonableness must be judged at its inception."

We respectfully disagree. Underlying the district court's reasoning is the premise that school officials conducted but one search of nineteen students, such that the reasonableness of the school's actions must be judged in the aggregate. We believe that premise is flawed, since school officials conducted not one but nineteen individual searches, each of which must be independently assessed for its reasonableness. Therefore, whether any given search was justified at its inception must be adjudged according to the circumstances existing at the moment that particular search began, rather than, as the district court believed, the circumstances existing when the first student in the class was searched.

DesRoches argues that the inception of the search, as directed against him, occurred when school officials threatened him with suspension after he refused their request to search his backpack, because at that point he was required to choose between the proposed search and the possibility of suspension. We believe that argument misses the mark. For DesRoches to maintain a Fourth Amendment claim, there must have been an infringement on a protected Fourth Amendment interest. While we agree, of course, that *actual* suspension for refusal to consent constitutes such an infringement when the proposed search is unreasonable, we cannot agree that the Fourth Amendment is implicated merely by a demand to search coupled with threats of punishment, where the threats are unsuccessful in bringing about the individual's consent.

DesRoches contends that his punishment became final when he refused, for the second time, to consent to the requested search, after being warned that his refusal to do so would result in a ten-day suspension. He argues, in essence, that his punishment was automatically imposed when he refused to provide his consent. Yet, the facts do not support such a contention. Far from automatically punishing DesRoches for refusing to consent, school officials told DesRoches "that he could just sit there, and [they] would talk about it later." In fact, following the threat of suspension, DesRoches was provided with at least two more opportunities to consent to the search before his suspension was actually imposed.

In light of the discussion thus far, it is apparent that the inception of the school's actions with respect to DesRoches occurred not when the search was first announced to the class, nor when DesRoches was threatened the first or second time with suspension, but when DesRoches was actually punished for refusing to provide his consent. So viewing the inception of the search, we agree with Appellants that, while school officials initially lacked individualized suspicion with respect to DesRoches, they developed such suspicion by virtue of their unsuccessful search of the classroom and the other eighteen students. As the facts demonstrate, those who remained in the classroom during lunch informed school officials that, to the best of their knowledge, only one student from outside the art class had entered the classroom during lunch. Therefore, once the classroom and the other eighteen students had been searched, school officials had certainly developed individualized suspicion with respect to DesRoches and the unnamed non-classmember, not by way of any particular information suggesting that one of those two was the thief, but simply by the process of elimination. We therefore cannot fault school officials for renewing their request to search once individualized suspicion had arisen, or for suspending DesRoches when he refused to consent to the search.

In summary, we hold that the proposed search of DesRoches's backpack was reasonable under the Fourth Amendment. The judgment of the district court is, therefore,

REVERSED.

Holdings of *DesRoches v. Caprio:* In this case, the court held that, once the classroom and the other eighteen students had been searched, school officials had developed individualized suspicion with respect to DesRoches not by way of any particular information suggesting that he was the thief, but simply by the process of elimination.

Discussion Questions

Under the court's reasoning, isn't it likely that innocent students would consent to the search and so, once everyone else consents and is found to be innocent, every guilty party is liable to be searched?

What if 2 or 3 students refused the search, would that be individualized enough to search those 2 or 3?

Klump v. Nazareth Area School Dist.: In *Klump v. Nazareth Area School Dist.*, the federal court was faced with a § 1983 civil lawsuit concerning the seizure of, search into and use of a cellphone of a student by school officials. A teacher confiscated Christopher Klump's cell phone when it fell out of his pocket and came to rest on his leg during school hours, in violation of a school policy prohibiting the use or display of a cell phone during school. Subsequently, the teacher and Assistant Principal called nine other students listed in Christopher's phone number directory to determine whether they, too, were violating the school's cell phone policy. They also accessed Christopher's text messages and voice mail, and held a conversation with Christopher's younger brother by using the cell phone's America Online Instant Messaging feature, without identifying themselves as being anyone other than Christopher.

As you read *Klump v. Nazareth Area School Dist.*, look for the following:

1. Look for any justification provided by the school district to justify its ban on cell-phones in order to seize a student's phone.
2. Consider what, if anything, school authorities are permitted to do with a seized cell phone.

Klump v. Nazareth Area School Dist.
425 F.Supp.2d 622 (E.D. Penn. 2006)

The events giving rise to plaintiffs' First Amended Complaint occurred on March 17, 2004. At that time, plaintiff Christopher Klump was a student at Nazareth Area High School.

The high school has a policy which permits students to carry, but not use or display cell phones during school hours. On March 17, 2004 Christopher's cell phone fell out of his pocket and came to rest on his leg. Upon seeing Christopher's cell phone, Shawn Kimberly Kocher, a teacher at the high school, enforced the school policy prohibiting use or display of cell phones by confiscating the phone. These events occurred at approximately 10:15 a.m.

Subsequently, Ms. Kocher, along with Assistant Principal Margaret Grube, began making phone calls with Christopher's cell phone. Ms. Kocher and Ms. Grube called nine other Nazareth Area High School students listed in Christopher's phone number directory to determine whether they, too, were violating the school's cell phone policy.

Next, defendants Kocher and Grube accessed Christopher's text messages and voice mail. Finally, defendants Kocher and Grube held an America Online Instant Messaging conversation with Mr. Klump's younger brother without identifying themselves as being anyone other than the primary user of the cell phone, Christopher Klump.

On March 22, 2004, Christopher Klump's parents, plaintiffs Toby Klump and Leigh Klump, met with Ms. Kocher, Ms. Grube, and Assistant Superintendent Diane Dautrich regarding the events of March 17. During that meeting, Ms. Grube told Mr. and Mrs. Klump that while she was in possession of their son's phone, Christopher received a text message from his girlfriend requesting that he get her a "f* * *in' tampon". The term "tampon", Ms. Grube later averred, is a reference to a large marijuana cigarette and prompted her subsequent use of the phone to investigate possible drug use at the school.

In Count VI, plaintiffs assert a violation of Christopher Klump's Fourth Amendment rights by defendants Grube and Kocher. Plaintiffs aver that by accessing Christopher's phone number directory, voice mail, and text messages, and subsequently using the phone to call individuals listed in the directory, defendants Grube and Kocher violated Christopher's Fourth Amendment right to be free from unreasonable searches and seizures. In addition, plaintiffs assert that defendants are liable for damages pursuant to 42 U.S.C. §1983.

Defendants aver that plaintiffs cannot prevail on their Fourth Amendment claim because the search was justified at its inception and was reasonable in scope. Finally, defendants argue that defendants Grube and Kocher are entitled to qualified immunity from section 1983 claims unless plaintiffs can prove that these defendants violated a clearly-established constitutional right and that a reasonable person in the same position would have known that their conduct violated a constitutional right.

Although students are protected by the Fourth Amendment, the probable cause requirement does not apply to students at school. The Supreme Court has held that a student search must nevertheless satisfy the reasonableness requirement of the Fourth Amendment. In the context of searches conducted by school officials, this means that the search must be justified at its inception and reasonable in scope. To be justified at its inception, there must be "reasonable grounds for believing that the search will turn up evidence that the student has violated or is violating either the law or the rules of the school."

Here, defendant Kocher was justified in seizing the cell phone, as plaintiff Christopher Klump had violated the school's policy prohibiting use or display of cell phones during school hours. In calling other students, however, defendants Grube and Kocher were conducting a search to find evidence of other students' misconduct, which they may not do under the standard articulated above. They had no reason to suspect at the outset that such a search would reveal that Christopher Klump himself was violating another school policy; rather, they hoped to utilize his phone as a tool to catch other students' violations.

Further, we must accept plaintiffs' allegation that the school officials did not see the allegedly drug-related text message until after they initiated the search of Christopher's cell phone. Accordingly, based upon the averments of the Complaint, which we must accept as true at this stage, there was no justification for the school officials to search Christopher's phone for evidence of drug activity.

Moreover, the law in this area is not as unsettled as defendants suggest. It is clear, based on the case law cited by defendants, that students have a Fourth Amendment right to be free from unreasonable searches and seizures by school officials. Although the meaning of "unreasonable searches and seizures" is different in the school context than elsewhere, it is nonetheless evident that there must be some basis for initiating a search. A reasonable person could not believe otherwise. Accordingly, we deny defendants' motion to dismiss Count VI against defendants Grube and Kocher on the basis of qualified immunity.

Holdings of *Klump v. Nazareth Area School Dist.*: The court held that school officials were justified in seizing the cell phone, as the student had violated the school's policy prohibiting use or display of cell phones during school hours. In calling other students, however, school officials were unlawfully conducting a search to find evidence of other students' misconduct. They had no reason to suspect at the outset that such a search would reveal that Klump himself was violating another school policy; rather, they hoped to utilize his phone as a tool to catch other students' violations. School officials did not see the allegedly drug-related text message until after they initiated the search of Christopher's cell phone, and there was no justification for the school officials to search Christopher's phone for evidence of drug activity.

Discussion Questions

Would the holding be different if the phone were seized because someone said they overheard Klump make a drug deal on the phone?

If the school authorities had the right to seize the phone, why didn't they have the right to use it?

Key Concepts: Backpacks and Cellphones in School

- Students retain a Fourth Amendment right of privacy to the contents of their backpacks and cellphones in school.
- The "reasonable suspicion" that is necessary to support a search of a backpack or cellphone must be present at the inception of the search itself, but information obtained from other valid (or consensual) searches prior to the search of the particular backpack or cellphone may provide the necessary information to support create such a reasonable suspicion for that particular search.
- The fact that school authorities have the authority to seize a cellphone does not mean that they also have the authority to use or search the contents of the phone.

Practical Questions: Backpacks and Cellphones in School

1. You are contacted by the principal of Summerset High School for a legal opinion. The principal says that drugs are rampant at the school, with at least two overdoses at school occurring per week. He tells you that he would like to implement a new policy to catch the students who are dealing drugs in school: All students will be asked for permission to search their backpacks upon entry to school property every day so that a search for drugs can be conducted. Any student who refuses to consent, is immediately sus-

pended for ten days (2 school weeks). Of course, since this procedure will occur every day, the student will need to go through the same process when his suspension is completed. "Can we make is so that a student dealing drugs can never come back on school property by this daily search?" he asks. What is your advice?

2. The principal has a second option/proposal: At the daily request for search of all students, anyone refusing the search is taken to the office to wait for further action. In the office, the student is reminded that he will be suspended for 10 days if he refuses the search. If a student still refuses, the backpack will be searched without his consent. "It is obvious at that point that he is hiding drugs," he tells you. "Why would he take a suspension if he has nothing to hide? Doesn't that create enough suspicion for me to search his backpack?" What do you tell him?

D. School Lockers

Overview: School lockers create a special concern for the courts when applying Fourth Amendment principles. A search of a student's locker is less intrusive than the search of a student's person, and lockers have special circumstances that affect the student's expectation of privacy. First, lockers usually have locks on them, sometimes providing the student with exclusive access to the locker. Second, the locker itself is usually owned by the school, not the student. Finally, schools often have written policies attempting to define the student's expectation of privacy in the lockers.

State v. Jones: In *State v. Jones,* the Iowa Supreme Court was faced with a motion to suppress based on the search of a jacket found in a student's locker. The school had an annual clean-up day (which was announced in advance) where students were required to open their locker and go through the contents in the presence of school officials. Jones, along with a number of other students, didn't show up on the day designated by school authorities. Later, school officials went to the lockers of those students who were not available for the pre-arranged clean-out procedure. Authorities opened Jones' locker and found only a blue jacket hanging in the locker. In checking the pockets of the jacket, they found a small bag of marijuana. Jones was charged with possession of a controlled substance.

As you read *State v. Jones,* look for the following:

1. Consider the "interest" of the school authorities in seeing the contents of the locker and whether or not those same interests were present in searching the jacket itself when they found it hanging in the locker.

2. Consider whether the ruling would have been any different if Jones had shown up when the initial pre-arranged procedure was scheduled and the same events had happened.

State v. Jones
666 N.W.2d 142 (Iowa 2003)

In this appeal, we consider a number of issues arising from the search of a high school student's locker in light of the state and federal constitutional prohibitions against unreasonable search and seizure. After considering the search conducted in light of the balance between the student's privacy interest and the interest of the school in maintaining a proper educational environment, we conclude that the search was permissible and the district court erred in suppressing evidence obtained in the course of the search.

On December 20, 2001, teachers and administrators at Muscatine High School attempted to complete an annual pre-winter break cleanout of the lockers assigned to each student at the school. The students were asked three to four days before the cleanout to report to their locker at an assigned time to open it so a faculty member could observe its contents. The general purpose of the cleanout was to ensure the health and safety of the students and staff and to help maintain the school's supplies. Accordingly, faculty assigned to examine the lockers kept an eye out for overdue library books, excessive trash, and misplaced food items. They also watched for items of a more nefarious nature, including weapons and controlled substances. The cleanout functioned as expected for approximately 1400 of the 1700 students at the school. However, a sizeable minority — including the appellee, Marzel Jones — did not report for the cleanout at their designated time.

The next day, two building aides went around to the lockers that had not been checked the day before. Acting pursuant to rules and regulations adopted by the school board, the aides opened each locker to inspect its contents. The aides did not know the names of the students assigned to the lockers they were inspecting. One of the lockers they opened contained only one item: a blue, nylon coat, which hung from one of the two hooks in the locker. Apparently curious about its ownership and concerned that it might hold trash, supplies, or contraband, one of the aides manipulated the coat and discovered a small bag of what appeared to be marijuana in an outside pocket. The aides then returned the coat to the locker and contacted the school's principal.

After crosschecking the locker number with records kept by the administration, the principal determined the locker in which the suspected marijuana was found belonged to Jones. The principal and aides then went to Jones' classroom and escorted him to his locker. Jones was asked to open the locker and, after doing so, was further asked if anything in the locker "would cause any educational or legal difficulties for him." Jones replied in the negative. The principal then removed the coat from the locker. Jones grabbed the coat, struck the principal across the arms, broke free from him, and ran away. The principal gave chase and, after three attempts, captured and held Jones until the police arrived. The police retrieved the bag and determined that it held marijuana.

Jones was later charged with possession of a controlled substance in violation of Iowa Code section 124.401(5) (2001). He subsequently filed a motion to suppress the evidence — the marijuana — obtained during the search of his locker. He claimed that the search violated his right to be free from unreasonable search and seizure pursuant to the Fourth Amendment of the United States Constitution and article I, section 8 of the Iowa Constitution. The lone witness at the suppression hearing was the principal of the high school, who testified about school policy relating to search and seizure and the events of December 20 and 21. The district court granted the motion to suppress. It found that the school officials did not have reasonable grounds for searching Jones' coat pocket. The State filed a motion requesting the judge reconsider and alter his decision. The motion was denied. The State then sought discretionary review, which we granted.

As we have recognized on numerous occasions in the past, "the Fourth Amendment exists to protect the right of the people to be free from unreasonable searches and seizures by government officials."

Although students maintain their constitutional rights within the school setting, the United States Supreme Court has acknowledged this setting "requires some easing of the restrictions to which searches by public authorities are ordinarily subject." The Court has provided specific commentary on this "easing of the restrictions" in three cases.

In the first case, *New Jersey v. T.L.O.,* the Court articulated several baseline principles related to the search of a student in the school setting. However, *T.L.O.* focused on the search of a specific student whose property was searched based on some measure of individualized suspicion of her conduct. In two subsequent cases, the Court considered the propriety of searches conducted in the absence of individualized suspicion of a particular student. In these cases, the search of the students was premised on generalized concerns about drug use prevention in light of the effect of the presence of drugs on the educational environment as a whole.

We believe the locker search conducted by the school officials in this case is most closely analogized to the broad searches conducted in *Acton* and *Earls.* Although this search eventually focused on Jones' locker, the process leading to that point was random and carried out with the purpose of protecting the health and safety of the whole student body to preserve a proper educational environment. Although *T.L.O., Acton,* and *Earls* each provide helpful insight on search and seizure in schools, it is the sum of their holdings, crystallized in the Court's opinion in *Earls,* from which our analysis must launch. Under the *Earls* analysis, we must consider three factors: (1) "the nature of the privacy interest allegedly compromised" by the search, (2) "the character of the intrusion imposed by the [search] [p]olicy," and (3) "the nature and immediacy of the [school's] concerns and the efficacy of the [search] [p]olicy in meeting them."

We turn now to our analysis of this appeal under the *Earls* factors.

In assessing the nature of the privacy interest in this case, it is imperative to remember this controversy arose within the school context "where the State is responsible for maintaining discipline, health, and safety." This reality has led the Court to acknowledge that "[s]ecuring order in the school environment sometimes requires that students be subjected to greater controls than those appropriate for adults." Although this may be the case, we do not believe it can be said that students have no expectation of privacy in a school setting, particularly in a location such as a locker.

In *T.L.O.,* the Court observed:

> Students at a minimum must bring to school not only the supplies needed for their studies, but also keys, money, and the necessaries of personal hygiene and grooming. In addition, students may carry on their persons or in purses or wallets such nondisruptive yet highly personal items as photographs, letters, and diaries. Finally, students may have perfectly legitimate reasons to carry with them articles of property needed in connection with extracurricular or recreational activities. In short, schoolchildren may find it necessary to carry with them a variety of legitimate, noncontraband items, and there is no reason to conclude that they have necessarily waived all rights to privacy in such items merely by bringing them onto school grounds.

However, the Court specifically avoided answering the question of whether a student "has a legitimate expectation of privacy in lockers, desks, or other school property provided for the storage of school supplies." Likely due in part to the absence of an authoritative statement on this issue, various courts considering it have produced a divergence of opinion. Some courts have concluded that there is no expectation of privacy in a student locker, particularly in situations in which there exists a school or state regulation specifically disclaiming any privacy right. Other courts have concluded that a student does have a legitimate expectation of privacy in the contents of a school locker, even if a school or state regulation exists. In this case, both Muscatine school district policy and state law clearly contemplate and regulate searches of school lockers. Nevertheless, we believe Jones maintained a legitimate expectation of privacy in the contents of his locker.

T.L.O. involved the search of a student's purse, but a student's locker presents a similar island of privacy in an otherwise public school. Numerous permissible items of a private nature are secreted away within a locker on a daily basis with the expectation that those items will remain private. In fact, Muscatine's school policy effectively presumes this to be the case and protects this interest: in those situations in which the school seeks to search a locker, the school's rules contemplate the presence of the student or at least a "waiver" of the student's opportunity to be present and supervising the search. Moreover, the school rules and state law related to search and seizure in schools are premised on a presumption of privacy; such legislation would likely be unnecessary if no expectation of privacy existed in the first place. Each of these factors indicates a broad societal recognition of a legitimate expectation of privacy in a school locker. Accordingly, we conclude that a student such as Jones has a measure of privacy in the contents of his locker.

We must next "consider the character of the intrusion imposed by the [search] [p]olicy." The district court concluded the actions of the school officials were overly intrusive in light of what the court perceived to be unreasonable grounds to search Jones' particular locker. However, we believe the locker search was not overly intrusive, especially in light of the underlying governmental interest and broader purpose of the search.

The locker cleanout was premised on the need to maintain a proper educational environment, which school officials had determined was undermined by violations of school rules and potential violations of the law. Most students cooperated in the school's efforts to check the lockers for such violations. Although there was no indication that students on the day of the original cleanout had the contents of their lockers searched, the students were also present and supervised by a teacher who was responsible for observing the contents of the locker and ensuring the cleanout functioned as planned. Moreover, the teacher supervisors surely could have communicated with a student present at the locker about its contents and taken further steps if the situation warranted.

The search on the second day came under different circumstances. The advantage of carrying out the cooperative cleanout and inspection of the previous day had passed. Students who had been advised that they were to report to their lockers for a cleanout had failed to do so, and caused the school to switch to an alternative method to ensure the cleanout was achieved. On entering Jones' locker, the only item in sight was the blue coat. The school officials believed that trash, supplies, or other items could be in the coat pockets, and did not have the advantage of turning to Jones to ask him about its contents, as they likely could have done the day before. For this reason, they decided to make a cursory check of the coat for such items. Although they found the bag of marijuana, they just as well could have found a banana peel. The scope of the search was supported by the underlying purpose of the search.

While it is possible that there would have been alternative ways to check the coat's contents, constitutional search and seizure provisions do not require the least intrusive action possible. Instead, they require a measure of "reasonableness, under all the circumstances." Under this standard, we conclude the search of the contents of Jones' locker was not overly intrusive.

The education of the students of the State of Iowa is a profound responsibility vested, ultimately, in the capable hands of local teachers, administrators, and school boards. What may be a daunting task to begin with is only made more difficult by the presence of various distractions ranging from excessive trash and missing supplies to—potentially—more troublesome items, such as controlled substances or weapons. These developments serve as the backdrop against which the conduct of school officials must be considered, especially as it relates to their duty to educate students while also protecting them from numerous threats to that mission.

The principal of the school testified that the annual winter break locker cleanout was conducted by the school to prevent violations of both school rules related to the accumulation of trash and school supplies and the sharing of lockers and the law related to possession of controlled substances and weapons. School officials were aware that students tended to accumulate excessive trash and supplies in their lockers and sometimes shared the lockers against school policy. Moreover, they knew that if controlled substances or weapons were present in the school, either type of item would present a threat to the school environment that they were responsible for maintaining.

To counteract the problems caused by these items, the school presented reasonable notice to the student body and attempted to check the lockers with student assistance. Some students, including Jones, did not follow this procedure and left the school with little choice of methods by which it could carry out what it considered to be a legitimate method by which school rules could be maintained. Although the school did not have individualized suspicion of rule or law violations before the locker cleanout operation, constitutional search and seizure provisions include no irreducible requirement that such suspicion exist. Moreover, it would be contrary to the mission of our educational system to force schools to wait for problems to grow worse before allowing steps to be taken to prevent those problems. Given the public school context in which this controversy arose and the present realities of public education, we conclude that the search conducted by school officials was proper.

Although students are not stripped of constitutional protections in the school context, those protections must be balanced against the necessity of maintaining a controlled and disciplined environment in which the education of all students can be achieved. Thus, while students maintain a legitimate expectation of privacy in the contents of their school locker, that privacy may be impinged upon for reasonable activities by the school in furtherance of its duty to maintain a proper educational environment. The search of Jones' locker was permissible in light of these principles, and the district court's grant of a motion to suppress evidence obtained during the search was in error. For that reason, we reverse the decision of the district court and remand for further proceedings consistent with this opinion.

REVERSED AND REMANDED.

Holdings of *State v. Jones:* The court held that the locker search was not overly intrusive, especially in light of the underlying governmental interest and broader purpose of the search. Although the school did not have individualized suspicion of rule or law violations before the locker cleanout operation, constitutional search and seizure provisions include no irreducible requirement that such suspicion exist.

Discussion Questions

Doesn't the claim that the annual "Locker Cleanout" was in part to make sure there were not "violations of school rules and potential violations of the law" just mean that they would make a blanket search for drugs and weapons?

Then, where is the individualized suspicion?

In re Patrick Y.: In *In re Patrick Y.,* a school security officer received information from a source he could not recall that "there were drugs and or weapons in the middle school area of the school." In response, the principal authorized a search of all lockers in the middle school area. Inside Patrick's locker, authorities found a bookbag, which they also searched. Inside the bookbag were the two contraband items—a folding knife with a 2½ inch blade and a pager. Patrick was charged with having a deadly weapon on school property, and moved to suppress the evidence recovered from his locker.

As you read *In re: Patrick Y.,* look for the following:

1. Consider why the court does not seem to take into account the published policy of the school for locker searches in determining whether or not Patrick had a reasonable expectation of privacy to the locker.

2. Consider whether school authorities need any suspicion at all to search student lockers in this jurisdiction.

In re Patrick Y.

358 Md. 50 (2000)

WILNER, Judge.

The District Court of Maryland, sitting as the juvenile court in Montgomery County, found petitioner to be a delinquent child by reason of his having had a deadly weapon and a pager in his possession while on public school property. He admitted possession of the two items and complains only that they were unlawfully obtained by the State and, for that reason, should have been suppressed. The trial court rejected his contention that the seizure of the items violated his Fourth Amendment rights, and the Court of Special Appeals affirmed. We agree and shall affirm the judgment of the appellate court.

Petitioner was an eighth grade student at the Mark Twain School in Montgomery County. The school is a public middle and senior high school that, at its Rockville campus, serves approximately 245 children with significant social, emotional, learning, and behavioral difficulties. The school publishes a set of "Policies Regarding Student Behavior," a copy of which was given to petitioner and his parent and was signed by them. The document states that the school is "committed to maintain a safe environment for students and staff," and advises:

> "Mark Twain subscribes to Montgomery County Public Schools' Search and Seizure policy, which provides that the principal or the administration's designee may conduct a search of a student or of the student's locker if there is probable cause to believe that the student has in his/her possession an item, the possession of which constitutes a criminal offense under the laws of the State of Maryland. These items include weapons, drugs or drug paraphernalia, alcohol, beepers and electronic signalling devices."

At approximately 10:40 on the morning of May 23, 1997, the school security officer, Patrick Rooney, received information from a source he could not recall that "there were drugs and or weapons in the middle school area of the school." Mr. Rooney alerted the principal, who authorized a search of all lockers in the middle school area. The record indicates that the search was conducted by Mr. Rooney and one other person but does not reveal how the search was conducted. We do not know how many lockers were searched, other than that the search did not extend beyond the middle school area, or how the search was conducted. No evidence was produced of whether the lockers were even locked or, if locked, whether the school had a master key or a list of the combinations that would open combination locks, although a fair inference can be drawn from the apparent ease with which the search was conducted that the school had ready access to the lockers. As petitioner was not informed in advance of the intent to search his locker and was not present when his locker was opened, it is clear that the locker was opened without his assistance or permission.

Inside petitioner's locker, Mr. Rooney found a bookbag, which he also searched. Inside the bookbag were the two contraband items — a folding knife with a 2½ inch blade and a pager — both of which, as noted, are expressly forbidden on school property. Petitioner, it appears, was in some other, unrelated difficulty at the time of the search. He had threatened to leave the school building without permission and was being restrained on that account when he was confronted with the knife and the pager, which he admitted were his. The issue raised by petitioner is whether the Fourth Amendment was violated "by a search of Petitioner's locker, based solely upon a vague and unsubstantiated rumor, 'that there were drugs and or weapons in the middle school area.'"

Petitioner asserts that (1) he had a legitimate expectation of privacy in his locker, (2) whatever may be the Constitutional standard for conducting locker searches, the published school policy required probable cause, which was lacking, (3) the school officials did not have even a "reasonable suspicion," that there was any contraband in his locker, and (4) by opening his bookbag, the search exceeded any permissible scope that might have justified opening the locker. Relying principally on *Vernonia School District v. Acton*, the State contends that general reasonableness, not probable cause, is the appropriate standard to apply and that, under that standard, the search of petitioner's locker and bookbag was justified. It urges that petitioner had, at best, only a limited privacy interest in his school locker, that the search of the locker was a minimal intrusion, that school safety constitutes a compelling governmental interest, that the locker search was an "efficacious" means of satisfying that interest, and that, on balance, the minimal intrusion of the locker search was outweighed by the compelling interest in school safety.

As noted, the issue raised in the petition for certiorari was limited to whether the search of petitioner's locker violated the Fourth Amendment. That statement of the issue does not include any complaint about the search of the bookbag or, indeed, whether petitioner was entitled to relief solely because the locker search violated the published Montgomery County School Policy. Because it was not raised in the petition, we shall not consider the search of the bookbag. The published school policy needs to be addressed, not as an independent basis for suppression, but in the Fourth Amendment context of its effect on petitioner's reasonable expectation of privacy in the locker.

Two Supreme Court cases have come to dominate the current debate over locker searches in the public schools — *Acton*, and *New Jersey v. T.L.O* — although neither of them dealt with a locker search. T.L.O., the earlier of the two cases, involved the search of a student's purse.

On the merits, the Court first determined, as a threshold matter, that the Fourth Amendment does apply to searches conducted by public school officials. Largely because of the compulsory school attendance laws, public school officials, unlike their counterparts in private school, do not stand in loco parentis in their dealings with students and therefore do not have the exemption from Fourth Amendment requirements enjoyed by the parents. They do not merely exercise authority delegated to them by the students' parents, but act in furtherance of mandated educational and disciplinary policies.

Proceeding from that premise, the Court then recognized that students were entitled to bring to school "a variety of legitimate, noncontraband items," that there was "no reason to conclude that they have necessarily waived all rights to privacy in such items merely by bringing them onto school grounds," and that, as a result, the search of a child's person or of a closed purse or bag carried on the person was "a severe violation of subjective expectations of privacy." Against that right of privacy, however, the "substantial interest of teachers and administrators in maintaining discipline in the classroom and on school grounds" had to be balanced. In that regard, the Court took note that, in recent years, the maintenance of order in the schools, which had never been easy, had "often taken particularly ugly forms: drug use and violent crime in the schools have become major social problems." It acknowledged that, even in schools spared the most serious problems, "the preservation of order and a proper educational environment requires close supervision of schoolchildren, as well as the enforcement of rules against conduct that would be perfectly permissible if undertaken by an adult." That imperative requires "a certain degree of flexibility in school disciplinary procedures."

In striking the balance, the Court concluded that the warrant requirement of the Fourth Amendment was unsuited to the school environment and that the generally applicable probable cause standard was unnecessary. Rather, it held, "the legality of a search of a student should depend simply on the reasonableness, under all the circumstances, of the search." That, in turn, required a two-part inquiry: whether the action was justified at its inception, and whether the search, as conducted, was reasonably related in scope to the circumstances that justified the interference in the first place.

Acton, which was decided 10 years after *T.L.O.*, involved a different kind of search— random urinalysis for students involved in inter-scholastic athletics. The Vernonia school district, legitimately concerned over an increasing incidence of drug abuse on the part of students, which had led to a significant escalation in discipline problems, especially among student athletes, adopted a policy of requiring all students intending to engage in inter-scholastic athletics, and the parents of those students, to sign a written consent to the random drug testing of the students through urinalysis. Special efforts were made to assure both reasonable privacy in obtaining the specimens and confidentiality and reliability of the test results. Acton and his parents refused to consent to the procedure and when, as a result, Acton was not permitted to play football for his school team, he and his parents sued for declaratory and injunctive relief, claiming that the policy violated his rights under the Fourth and Fourteenth Amendments.

The Court began by observing that the ultimate measure of the Constitutionality of a governmental search is reasonableness—balancing its intrusion on the individual's Fourth Amendment interests against its promotion of legitimate governmental interests. Although a search conducted by law enforcement persons normally requires a warrant, issuable only upon a demonstration of probable cause, neither a warrant nor the probable cause standard are required where special needs make them impracticable. In *T.L.O.*, the Court concluded that the warrant requirement and the probable cause standard were not required in the student search setting—that adherence to a probable cause standard would undercut the need of school officials for freedom to maintain order. The *Acton* Court held that, although the search in T.L.O. was based on individualized suspicion of wrongdoing, that too was not an "irreducible requirement" of the Fourth Amendment.

Turning then to the first aspect of the question—the degree of intrusion on a legitimate expectation of privacy—the Court confirmed earlier holdings that students in a public school setting, while not shedding their Constitutional rights at the schoolhouse gate, nonetheless have a lesser expectation of privacy than do adults. Simply as unemancipated minors, they lack "some of the most fundamental rights of self-determination." Although public school officials do not stand entirely in loco parentis with respect to the students, they do exercise a "custodial and tutelary" authority that permits "a degree of supervision and control that could not be exercised over free adults" and that cannot be ignored in conducting a "reasonableness" inquiry. Reflecting on the target group at issue, the Court held that legitimate privacy interests were even less with regard to student athletes, who are required to dress and undress in locker rooms not noted for their privacy, and who, in other ways as well, have a reduced expectation of privacy. The degree of intrusion manifested by the drug testing program on that reduced expectation, the Court held, was not significant in light of the procedures used in its implementation.

Addressing then the "nature and immediacy of the governmental concern," the Court noted the "compelling" need to deter drug use by schoolchildren. Indeed, it recognized that the effects of a drug-infested school extend beyond those using the drugs and impact as well on the entire student body and faculty by disrupting the educational process. That general concern was heightened in the particular case both by the special vulnerability of student athletes to harm when either on drugs themselves or in contact with other athletes on drugs and by the significant increase in disciplinary problems actually experienced in the Vernonia schools that was attributed to drug use. Rejecting Acton's suggestion that a less intrusive alternative was possible—testing only on suspicion of drug use—the Court observed that it had "repeatedly refused to declare that only the 'least intrusive' search practicable can be reasonable under the Fourth Amendment." The net holding was that "when the government acts as guardian and tutor the relevant question is whether the search is one that a reasonable guardian and tutor might undertake," and in *Acton*, the answer was in the affirmative.

Petitioner regards *T.L.O.* as the more relevant case, requiring some individualized suspicion as a necessary predicate for a locker search. He seems to view *Acton* as limited to student athletes and their lesser expectation of privacy, noting the Court's reference to their "communal undress," the fact that inter-scholastic athletics was a voluntary endeavor, and the further fact that, in *Acton*, most of the parents approved the drug-testing policy. We do not regard *Acton* as being so limited.

Both *T.L.O.* and *Acton* instruct us as to the analytical process that should be followed. First, we must determine whether, and to what extent, petitioner had a legitimate expectation of privacy in his locker. Although that is ultimately a legal issue, it depends on the facts.

In the absence of such a clear policy, and especially when there is a contrary policy purporting to limit the ability of the school authorities to conduct a search, courts have concluded that students do have some legitimate privacy interest, even if a limited one.

As noted, the only factual evidence in this record bearing on whether petitioner may have had a legitimate expectation of privacy was the school policy statement that he and his parent signed which, in sharp distinction to the kinds of statements evident in the above-cited cases, purports to limit the right of school officials to search lockers to situations in which the official has "probable cause" to believe that the student has in his/her possession an item that is contraband under the criminal law of the State. On its face, and without regard to the broader legal context, that document, published by the local school authorities, could serve as a basis for an expectation that lockers will not otherwise be searched. That local policy cannot be considered in a vacuum, however. There is a statute enacted by the General Assembly, supplemented by a by-law adopted by the State

Board of Education, that defines and controls the authority of school officials to search public school lockers, and it is that State policy that determines whether, and to what extent, petitioner had any reasonable expectation of privacy in the locker assigned to him.

The plain words of the statute and by-law establish a State policy distinguishing between the search of students and the search of lockers. In conformance with the requirements of *T.L.O.*, the search of a student requires a reasonable belief on the part of the school official that the student has contraband in his or her possession. School lockers, on the other hand, are not regarded as the personal property of the student. They are classified as school property, part of the "plant of the school and its appurtenances," and, no doubt because of that, school officials are permitted to search the lockers as they could any other school property. No probable cause is required; nor is any reasonable suspicion required.

This policy is deliberate and has a long history.

By both statute and State Board of Education by-law, school lockers are treated as school property and are subject to search by designated school officials in the same manner as other school property. It is not within the power of a local school board or superintendent, or any subordinate official, to establish and enforce a policy that provides otherwise.

The Montgomery County policy statement upon which petitioner relies is obviously inconsistent with the governing State law. It imposes probable cause to believe that the student is in possession of an item, the possession of which constitutes a criminal offense as the standard necessary to justify a search of both students and lockers, which, under State law, is not the test for either. Accordingly, that local policy is invalid and nugatory and cannot serve as a basis for a student to have a reasonable expectation of privacy in the locker provided by the school.

As petitioner could have no reasonable expectation of privacy in the school locker, the search of it by the school security officer, upon direction of the principal, did not violate any Fourth Amendment right of petitioner.

Because we conclude that, in light of § 7-308 and the State Board of Education by-law, petitioner had no reasonable expectation of privacy in the locker temporarily assigned to him, we need not consider, if he had such an expectation, what the nature of it would be and whether the governmental interest in conducting the search and the limited nature and extent of the intrusion manifested by the search would nonetheless suffice to justify the search.

JUDGMENT AFFIRMED, WITH COSTS.

BELL, Chief Judge, dissenting:

The majority holds that a knife and a pager, recovered as the result of a search of the petitioner's school locker, were properly admitted into evidence during the petitioner's delinquency proceedings. When the search occurred, the petitioner was an eighth grade student at the Mark Twain School in Montgomery County and, as such, subject to that school's "Policies Regarding Student Behavior," a copy of which he and his parent had received and signed for. In addition to stating the school's commitment "to maintain[ing] a safe environment for students and staff," the policy this document announces on the search of school lockers is as follows:

"Mark Twain subscribes to Montgomery County Public Schools' Search and Seizure policy, which provides that the principal or the administration's designee may conduct a search of a student or of the student's locker if there is probable cause to believe that the student has in his/her possession an item, the possession of which constitutes a criminal offense under the laws of the State of Maryland. These items include weapons, drugs or drug paraphernalia, alcohol, beepers and electronic signalling devices."

Not surprisingly, the petitioner relied heavily on this policy in arguing that the evidence against him should be suppressed.

As hard as the majority tries, it has not persuasively explained why the issue that we took this case to decide—whether the search of petitioner's school locker violated the Fourth Amendment—has not been presented. To be sure, it cannot be gainsaid that the petitioner had an expectation of privacy. Not only was there a school policy granting a level of privacy, but it was communicated in the student policies, and given to the petitioner and his parent, both of whom were required to sign it in acknowledgment of receipt. Thus, the critical issue is whether the petitioner could legitimately rely on the policy, and whether the policy could give rise to an expectation of privacy.

The test of a valid privacy expectation is whether a subjective expectation of privacy existed that society would recognize as reasonable. Generally, Fourth Amendment protections are based on the petitioner's legitimate expectation of privacy in light of the relevant circumstances. Whether, in a given circumstance, a petitioner's expectation of privacy is legitimate and reasonable is determined by "balancing the need to search against the invasion which the search entails." The totality of the circumstances, including the nature of the thing alleged to be the basis of the expectation, the actions of the petitioner and of the school, all inform that determination.

Cases on searches of a student's person teach that "reasonableness of the circumstances" is the correct standard.

The school policy is thus the standard against which to judge whether the petitioner's expectation of privacy was reasonable in light of the circumstances.

The State statute exists, to be sure, but it is by no means as clear as the majority says it is, nor is the local school policy obviously inconsistent with that statute. It also is quite clear that there has been utterly no compliance with the statutory requirement of prior notification, a circumstance which, by itself, would seem to call for suppression of the search fruits and reversal of the delinquency judgment.

Section 7-308(b) clearly conditions a school official's right to search a student's locker on the student having been given prior notification. In the case sub judice, previous notice of an absolute right to search was never given; indeed, the notice that was given was that the exact opposite situation applied. Therefore, I would hold that this is a sufficient basis on which to hold that the school had no right to search, even if the State statute is controlling. Invoking the right post hoc not only is unfair under the circumstances, but it violates expressly what is unambiguously the language of the statute and thus the intent of the Legislature. The majority argues that, because the school's announced policy was invalid, compliance with the State statute is excused. That cannot be correct. As my mother put it to me years ago, "two wrongs do not make a right."

Holdings of *In re Patrick Y.*: The court held that, while the search of a student requires a reasonable belief on the part of the school official that the student has contraband in his or her possession, school lockers, on the other hand, are not regarded as the personal property of the student. They are classified as school property, part of the 'plant of the school and its appurtenances,' and, because of that, school officials are permitted to search the lockers as they could any other school property. No probable cause is required; nor is any reasonable suspicion required.

Discussion Questions

Doesn't the school's "Policies Regarding Student Behavior" create a higher standard that set forth in *TLO* by requiring probable Cause? Doesn't that raise the level of expectation of privacy?

Why doesn't the school policy (which Patrick and his parents signed) take precedent over the state statute and the state board of education rules when it comes to Expectation of Privacy?

Key Concepts: School Lockers

- Different jurisdictions take different positions concerning the need for suspicion to justify the search of school lockers by school authorities.
- Searches of lockers are less intrusive than searches of a student's person or backpacks.
- Some jurisdictions hold that students have to reasonable expectation of privacy when it comes to lockers owned by the school itself.

Practical Questions: School Lockers

1. The Director of the Department of Education held a statewide summit meeting with all superintendents and principals in the state. At the summit, there was a discussion of the "standards" that must be met to search a student's backpack or purse, specifically referring to the "reasonable suspicion" standards imposed by *T.L.O.* The Director advised the attendees that, if they did not believe that they had a reasonable suspicion to search a backpack or purse, they should just follow the student until the student put the backpack or purse in his or her locker and then search the locker. "We don't need any suspicion to search a locker, so just wait until it is there and then take it." The principal of the high school in your city comes to you and asks if this is correct. "Can I do that?" he asks. What do you tell him?

2. You are representing a youth whose locker was searched and marijuana was found. School officials had no suspicion whatsoever implicating any improper conduct by your client. Your client tells you that she was initially approached by the guidance counsellor who told her that they were taking her to the office to ask her some questions. He told her that, if she didn't want her backpack searched, she had better not bring it with her. "Just stick it in your locker," he told her. As soon as she did so, officials took the backpack from the locker, searched it, found the marijuana and called police. You find out that this guidance counsellor has routinely done this to other students, encouraging them to place items he wanted to search in their lockers. What will you argue in the motion to suppress the marijuana? What do you predict will happen on your motion?

E. Video Cameras in Schools

Overview: Video cameras in schools pose unique problems for the courts. First, they don't discriminate, but record everything. That means there is no individual suspicion that is applicable, but, rather, only general safety and learning concerns. Second, depending on where the cameras are located, the videotaping may amount to a "strip search," which is one of the most invasive of searches possible.

Courts who have addressed this issue have struggled to find a way to apply the *T.L.O.* standards to the use of video cameras in schools.

Brannum v. Overton County School Board: In *Brannum v. Overton County School Board,* the federal court was faced with a § 1983 civil lawsuit concerning the videotaping of students in various states of undress in a locker room of a school. The school received complaints from a visiting school of a video camera in the girls' locker room. School officials viewed the images in a school official's office by remote access. According to the school official, the videotapes of the 10 to 14-year-old girls contained "nothing more than images of a few bras and panties." School employees removed the locker room cameras later that day. The system was accessed ninety-eight different times in the course of about 3 months, including through internet service providers located in at least 3 different cities in several states. Forty-three students filed a § 1983 action against the school system and school employees.

As you read *Brannum v. Overton County School Board,* look for the following:

1. Consider what concerns of the schools support the use of video cameras by school authorities

2. Consider whether the use of video cameras in more "public" areas of the school, such as hallways and classrooms, would have survived the challenges raised in this case.

3. Look for anything that could justify the installation of video cameras in the bathrooms or locker rooms of schools.

Brannum v. Overton County School Board

516 F.3d 489 (6th Cir. 2008)

RYAN, Circuit Judge.

Thirty-four Tennessee middle school students sued various officials of the Overton County, Tennessee, public school system under 42 U.S.C. § 1983 and others, alleging that the defendant school authorities violated the students' constitutional right to privacy by installing and operating video surveillance equipment in the boys' and girls' locker rooms in Livingston Middle School (LMS), and by viewing and retaining the recorded images.

The defendant Overton County school board members, the director of schools, the LMS principal, and the assistant principal, moved for summary judgment claiming qualified immunity. The district court denied their motions and they now appeal.

We conclude that the district court correctly denied summary judgment to the school officials, who are not entitled to claim the defense of qualified immunity, and incorrectly denied summary judgment to the defendant board members and the Director of Schools, who are immune.

In an effort to improve security at LMS, the Overton County School Board approved the installation of video surveillance equipment throughout the school building. The school board engaged the education technology firm, Edutech, Inc., to install cameras and monitoring equipment.

After several meetings, Assistant Principal Jolley and an Edutech representative decided to install the cameras throughout the school in areas facing the exterior doors, in hallways leading to exterior doors, and in the boys' and girls' locker rooms. The cameras were installed and were operational by July 2002.

The images captured by the cameras were transmitted to a computer terminal in Jolley's office where they were displayed and were stored on the computer's hard drive. Jolley testified that, in September 2002, he discovered that the locker room cameras were videotaping areas in which students routinely dressed for athletic activities. He said that he immediately notified Principal Beatty of the situation and suggested that the placement of the cameras be changed. But, the cameras were not removed nor were their locations changed for the remainder of the fall semester.

In addition to Jolley receiving the images on his computer, they were also accessible via remote internet connection. Any person with access to the software username, password, and Internet Protocol (IP) address could access the stored images. Neither Jolley nor anyone else had ever changed the system password or username from its default setting. The record indicates that the system was accessed ninety-eight different times between July 12, 2002, and January 10, 2003, including through internet service providers located in Rock Hill, South Carolina; Clarksville, Tennessee; and Gainsboro, Tennessee.

During a girls' basketball game at LMS on January 9, 2003, visiting team members from Allons Elementary School noticed the camera in the girls' locker room and brought this to the attention of their coach, Kathy Carr. Carr questioned Principal Beatty, who assured Carr that the camera was not activated. In fact, the camera was activated and had recorded images of the Allons team members in their undergarments when they changed their clothes. After the game, Carr reported the camera incident to the Allons school principal, who contacted Defendant Needham later that evening. Needham immediately accessed the security system from his home and viewed the recorded images. The following morning, January 10, Needham, Beatty, and two other officials viewed the images in Needham's office by remote access. Needham later stated that in his opinion, the videotapes of the 10 to 14-year-old girls contained "nothing more than images of a few bras and panties." School employees removed the locker room cameras later that day.

From July 2002 to January 2003, when the cameras were operational, a number of children from Overton County Schools and schools from the surrounding counties used the LMS locker rooms for athletic events and were videotape recorded while changing their clothes.

Congress enacted 42 U.S.C. § 1983 to permit an injured person to recover in federal court against defendants who violate a plaintiff's federal statutory or constitutional rights while acting under color of state law. There is no dispute in this case that the defendant school officials were acting under color of state law when they authorized the installation and operation of the security cameras at LMS. However, public officials are entitled to be dismissed from a lawsuit on qualified immunity grounds if they can show that they did not violate any of the plaintiff's federal statutory or constitutional rights that were "clearly established" at the time of the alleged misconduct and of which the defendants could reasonably be expected to have been aware.

The students argue that their constitutionally protected right to privacy encompasses the right not to be videotaped while dressing and undressing in school athletic locker rooms—a place specifically designated by the school authorities for such intimate, personal activity. The plaintiffs also argue that the basis of their privacy right resides in the Due Process Clause of the Fourteenth Amendment as well as in the Fourth Amendment as made applicable to the states through incorporation into the Fourteenth Amendment. We conclude that the privacy right involved here is one protected by the Fourth Amendment's guarantee against unreasonable searches, and that in this case, the defendants violated the students' rights under the amendment.

The Fourth Amendment to the United States Constitution provides that the federal government shall not violate "[t]he right of the people to be secure in their persons, houses, papers, and effects, against unreasonable searches and seizures...." The Supreme Court has held that the Fourth Amendment applies in the public school context to protect students from unconstitutional searches conducted by school officials.

Neither the Supreme Court nor this court has ever addressed the applicability of video surveillance to the Fourth Amendment's proscription against unreasonable searches.

We recognize, of course, that this is not a case of "naked bodies" being viewed by the surveillance cameras, but rather underwear clad teen and pre-teen boys and girls. However, the difference is one of degree, rather than of kind.

A search—and there can be no dispute that videotaping students in a school locker room is a search under the Fourth Amendment—is "permissible in its scope when the measures adopted are reasonably related to the objectives of the search and not excessively intrusive in light of the age and sex of the student and the nature of the infraction." It is a matter of balancing the scope and the manner in which the search is conducted in light of the students' reasonable expectations of privacy, the nature of the intrusion, and the severity of the school officials' need in enacting such policies, including particularly, any history of injurious behavior that could reasonably suggest the need for the challenged intrusion.

To meet the requirements imposed by the Constitution, the method chosen by the defendants to improve school building security in this case need not have been the only method available or even the one this court might have chosen; it is necessary, however, that the method chosen was, in the circumstances, justifiably intrusive in light of the purpose of the policy being carried out.

The Fourth Amendment does not protect all expectations of privacy; only those that society recognizes as reasonable and legitimate. The Supreme Court has acknowledged that generally, students have a less robust expectation of privacy than is afforded the general population. Indeed, this expectation may be even less for student athletes in locker rooms, which the Court has previously observed are places "not notable for the privacy they afford."

This does not mean, however, that a student's expectation of privacy in his or her school locker room is nonexistent. In fact, we have stated before that even in locker rooms, students retain "a significant privacy interest in their unclothed bodies." Unlike the situation in Vernonia, where the students and their parents were well aware that participation in school sports was conditioned on the students submitting to the drug testing policies, neither the students nor their parents in this case were aware of the video surveillance in the locker rooms, to say nothing of the videotaping. Further, while the Court in Vernonia pointed out the lower level of privacy typically associated with school locker rooms, we are satisfied that students using the LMS locker rooms could reasonably expect that no one, especially the school administrators, would videotape them, without their knowledge, in various states of undress while they changed their clothes for an athletic activity.

Video surveillance is inherently intrusive. As one authority has put it, a video camera "sees all, and forgets nothing."

In this case, the scope of the search consisted of the video recording and image storage of the children while changing their clothes. In *Vernonia*, procedural safeguards were put into place to protect the students' privacy, but in this case, the school officials wholly failed to institute any policies designed to protect the privacy of the students and did not even advise the students or their parents that students were being videotaped. Likewise, as the female students in *Beard* were inspected while in their undergarments, the students here were also observed in their undergarments while they were in the school locker rooms. We believe that the scope of the secret surveillance in this case, like the strip search in *Beard*, significantly invaded the students' reasonable expectations of privacy.

In determining whether a search is excessive in its scope, "the nature and immediacy of the governmental concern" that prompted the search is considered. Of course, a valid purpose does not necessarily validate the means employed to achieve it. In order to satisfy the constitutional requirements, the means employed must be congruent to the end sought.

In this case, the defendants were prompted to install video surveillance cameras by a concern that school safety measures should be enhanced. It is indisputable that the operation of the video cameras intruded upon the students' privacy; the question is whether, given the purpose for which the cameras were operating, the intrusion was reasonable. One measure of reasonableness is the congruence or incongruence of the policy to be served (student safety), and the means adopted to serve it. Surveillance of school hallways and other areas in which students mingle in the normal course of student life is one thing; camera surveillance of students dressing and undressing in the locker room—a place specifically set aside to offer privacy—is quite another. The two do not stand on equal footing.

Stated differently, the surveillance methodology employed, in particular the installation and operation of the cameras in the locker rooms, in order to be reasonable in its scope, must be congruent to the need for such a search in order to serve the policy goal of school safety and security. There is nothing whatsoever in this record to indicate that the defendants entertained any concerns about student safety or security in the locker rooms that would reasonably justify the installation of the cameras to record all the activities there. The defendants do not claim that any misconduct occurred in these areas in the past or that the plan to install the surveillance equipment in the school locker rooms was adopted because of any reasonable suspicion of wrongful activity or injurious behavior in the future. Indeed, the record suggests that the school board members and Director Needham were not even aware that cameras were positioned to monitor activities in the locker rooms.

While at a hypothetical level there might exist a heightened concern for student safety in the "privacy" of student locker rooms, that does not render any and all means of detection and deterrence reasonable. As the commonly understood expectation for privacy increases, the range and nature of permissible government intrusion decreases.

Given the universal understanding among middle school age children in this country that a school locker room is a place of heightened privacy, we believe placing cameras in such a way so as to view the children dressing and undressing in a locker room is incongruent to any demonstrated necessity, and wholly disproportionate to the claimed policy goal of assuring increased school security, especially when there is no history of any threat to security in the locker rooms.

We are satisfied that both the students' expectation of privacy and the character of the intrusion are greater in this case than those at issue in *Vernonia* and *T.L.O.* We conclude that the locker room videotaping was a search, unreasonable in its scope, and violated the students' Fourth Amendment privacy rights.

Our conclusion that the students' constitutional rights were violated does not end the inquiry, however. Under the qualified immunity doctrine, public officials cannot be held liable for violating a person's constitutional rights unless the right was clearly established at the time of the alleged improper conduct.

The "pass" does not extend, however, to violating a constitutional right that is "clearly established" and of which the violator is, or ought to have been, aware.

Some personal liberties are so fundamental to human dignity as to need no specific explication in our Constitution in order to ensure their protection against government invasion. Surreptitiously videotaping the plaintiffs in various states of undress is plainly among them. Stated differently, and more specifically, a person of ordinary common sense, to say nothing of professional school administrators, would know without need for specific instruction from a federal court, that teenagers have an inherent personal dignity, a sense of decency and self-respect, and a sensitivity about their bodily privacy that are at the core of their personal liberty and that are grossly offended by their being surreptitiously videotaped while changing their clothes in a school locker room. These notions of personal privacy are "clearly established" in that they inhere in all of us, particularly middle school teenagers, and are inherent in the privacy component of the Fourth Amendment's proscription against unreasonable searches. But even if that were not self-evident, the cases we have discussed would lead a reasonable school administrator to conclude that the students' constitutionally protected privacy right not to be surreptitiously videotaped while changing their clothes is judicially clearly established.

We therefore conclude that the plaintiffs have adequately alleged a Fourth Amendment violation of their constitutional right to privacy because the students had a reasonable expectation of privacy and the invasion of the students' privacy in this case was not justified by the school's need to assure security. We further conclude that this constitutional violation is actionable because this particular right was clearly established at the time of the videotaping, such that a reasonable person who knew or ought to have known of the videotaping would be aware that what he or she was doing violated the Fourth Amendment. Therefore, the school officials directly involved in the decision to install the cameras and responsible for determining their locations, that is, defendants Beatty and Jolley, are not entitled to qualified immunity.

Accordingly, we AFFIRM the district court's judgment denying qualified immunity to the defendants Melinda Beatty and Robert Jolley. We REVERSE the denial of summary judgment as to the defendant school board members and William Needham because they are entitled to claim qualified immunity, and REMAND the case for further proceedings.

Holdings of *Brannum v. Overton County School Board:* The court held that video surveillance is inherently intrusive. The court held further that surveillance of school hallways and other areas in which students mingle in the normal course of student life is one thing; camera surveillance of students dressing and undressing in the locker room—a place specifically set aside to offer privacy—is quite another.

Discussion Questions

Is camera surveillance in the hallways a search subject to the limits of the Fourth Amendment?

Could the school have placed cameras in the locker rooms if they had established a history of drug use and assaults in the locker rooms?

Key Concepts: Video Cameras in School

- Videotaping in areas where the students enjoy a heightened sense of privacy (such as locker rooms or bathrooms) is inherently intrusive and, as such, require a high level of safety concerns to justify such an extreme intrusion.

- Videotaping of students in areas where the students do not enjoy a higher expectation of privacy (such as hallways and classrooms) has a lower level of intrusiveness on the privacy of the students and, as such, does not require as great of interest by school authorities in order to justify such surveillance.

Practical Questions: Video Cameras in Schools

1. You have been appointed to represent James Michaelson who is charged with possession of cocaine with the intent to deliver at his local high school. James was in the toilet stall of the boys' bathroom when a school video camera captured him dividing up cocaine into "bindles." When the school principal viewed the video "live," he promptly went to the boys' bathroom, grabbed your client, seized his cocaine and called the police. Should the evidence be suppressed as being a violation of James' 4th Amendment rights?

2. School officials believed that students were slipping into a maintenance closet at the high school for sexual encounters. In order to discourage the practice, school officials placed a video camera in the closet and announced to all students that a camera was operated in the closet. In spite of this warning, one student slipped into the closet to "smoke a joint." As a result of the video recording, the student was charged with possession of a controlled substance on school property, a felony. Is the evidence admissible?

F. Sniffer Dogs in Schools

Overview: Courts are in disagreement as to the constitutionality of the use of "sniffer dogs" in public schools. Some courts find that the use of a sniffer dog is not a search, while others find that the use of a sniffer dog is a minimal intrusion. Finally, some courts find that use of a sniffer dog is a search for Fourth Amendment purposes and apply *T.L.O.* to require an individualized suspicion before employing the dog on school children.

Jones v. Latexo Indep. School Dist.: In *Jones v. Latexo Indep. School Dist.,* the federal court was faced with a § 1983 civil lawsuit concerning a search of a students and their vehicles after a sniffer dog signaled them and their vehicles as having drugs present. As a result of this subsequent search, six students (3 of whom were siblings) were suspended from school for possession of "drug paraphernalia" on campus in violation of school regulations. These students brought a § 1983 action against the school district claiming that the use of a sniffer dog violated their 4th Amendment rights.

As you read *Jones v. Latexo Indep. School Dist.,* look for the following:

1. Consider what factors cause the court to find that the use of a sniffer dog is a search for 4th Amendment purposes.

2. Consider what factors were considered that caused the use of the dog to be found to be intrusive and what factors were considered that led to the conclusion that the intrusion was minimal.

3. Consider the impact of the application of the *T.L.O.* analysis to the use of sniffer dogs.

Jones v. Latexo Indep. School Dist.

499 F.Supp. 223 (E.D. Texas 1980)

MEMORANDUM OPINION

JUSTICE, Chief Judge.

On April 11, 1980, the student body at the school operated by the Latexo Independent School District was subjected to the super-sensitive nose of "Merko", a dog trained to detect the odor of marijuana and other narcotics, as well as various other substances. Those students designated by Merko to be emanating such odors were subsequently searched by school authorities. Merko also sniffed the students' automobiles, which were parked in the school parking lot, in an effort to detect the odor of contraband. Vehicles singled out by the dog were thoroughly searched. As a result of this procedure, six students were suspended from school for possession of "drug paraphernalia" on campus in violation of school regulations.

Plaintiffs in this action are three of the suspended students, all siblings, and their parent. They challenge the school's actions, demanding injunctive and declaratory relief, and likewise damages under 42 U.S.C. s 1983. Their complaint, originally filed on July 9, 1980, and amended on August 18, 1980, alleges that the sniffing carried out by Merko and the resulting searches violated their fourth amendment rights. The plaintiffs also allege that their suspension from school on the basis of evidence obtained through such procedures, and without constitutionally-mandated due process of law, violated the fourteenth amendment.

On April 11th, Merko and Ms. Lounsberry appeared at the Latexo school to conduct their first inspection of the campus. Along with Superintendent Acker and a teacher, Ms. Dunn, they moved from classroom to classroom where the students sat at their desks. While the students remained seated, Merko, accompanied by his handler, walked up and down the aisles in the room sniffing each child in turn before departing. If Merko detected a target odor (contraband of some description) emerging from any student, he "alerted" (signaled) his handler, who informed Mr. Acker of the suspect's identity after the dog left the classroom. The dog then proceeded to the student parking lot where it employed its sensitive nostrils to locate additional illicit smells.

Two of the plaintiff students, Scott and Michael Jones, were singled out by Merko during the class-by-class hunt for contraband. They, like all other students so selected by the dog, were removed from class and told to empty their pockets. A cigarette lighter was taken from Scott. The search of Michael's pockets revealed a hair clip which appeared to be burnt and a bottle of "Sinex" nasal spray. The vehicles driven to school by Scott and Michael were also picked out by Merko and searched. Items identified by Kim Lounsberry as "roaches" (the tag ends of marijuana cigarettes) were found in both vehicles. A plastic box identified by Ms. Lounsberry as a case for carrying "joints" (marijuana cigarettes) was also found in the vehicle Scott had brought to school.

Following the vehicle searches, Superintendent Acker summoned plaintiff Michele Jones from class. Merko had previously sniffed Michele during his tour of the classrooms without "alerting" on her. When Michele arrived at the parking lot, her purse was searched. A small piece of metal tubing and a hemostat, identified by Ms. Lounsberry as "drug paraphernalia", were found and taken from her at that time.

Superintendent Acker informed the three Jones children that they had been found in possession of drug paraphernalia and other contraband in violation of school rules. He gave them an opportunity to rebut the charges orally. Following a brief discussion during which all three children denied that the items seized had been used in connection with drugs, they were suspended from school for a period of three days and sent home.

Pursuant to school policy, three points for each day missed due to suspension were deducted from the course grades of each student for the final quarter of the school year. As a result of the nine point penalty imposed on Scott Jones, it became mathematically impossible for him to pass American History, a required course, before he took the final examination. Faced with the inevitability of failure, this high school senior declined to take his final examination in American History and in two other courses he was enrolled in. As a result, Scott failed to graduate with his classmates in June. The other two Jones children were able to pass all their courses despite the grade penalty resulting from their suspension.

Merko and his handler paid several subsequent surprise visits to the Latexo school during which the procedure described above was generally repeated. On June 23, 1980, the Latexo School Board voted to rehire SAI and its canine detection service for the 1980–81 school year beginning on September 2, 1980.

The blanket inspection carried out by the "sniffer dog" and the resulting searches of selected students and private vehicles constituted state action cognizable under 42 U.S.C. s 1983. School boards, no less than other state entities, are subject to the commands of the fourteenth amendment, and are amenable to suit. While the doctrine of in loco parentis places the school teacher or employee in the role of a parent for some purposes, that doctrine cannot transcend constitutional rights. Thus, the individual defendants implementing School Board policy, like the School District itself, are legally accountable for any constitutional violations they might have committed in the performance of their public duties.

The School Board's concern over the problem of drug abuse in the Latexo Independent School District was most appropriate. Narcotics and other dangerous drugs have no place in our public schools. In the hands of children, the use of such substances may cause serious physical or psychological harm.

In carrying out their responsibility to maintain the health and safety of public school students within a productive learning environment, the independent school districts of the State of Texas have broad discretion to enact rules and regulations governing student conduct while school is in session.

Even if the School Board's rules were entirely valid, the defendants would not be permitted to violate constitutional standards in attempting to enforce them. Students, like all other "persons" under our Constitution, have fundamental rights which must be respected by state authorities. Those basic liberties, embodied in the Bill of Rights, have been extended to the states by the fourteenth amendment. If the dog's sniffing of the students and their property was an unreasonable search under the Fourth Amendment, a constitutional violation has occurred and the victims are entitled to redress.

In deciding whether the inspection by Merko, the "sniffer dog", violated the fourth amendment rights of plaintiffs, a twofold test is required. First, it must be determined whether a search of constitutional dimension actually occurred. If it is found that a search occurred, the second issue is whether or not the search was reasonable.

The dog's inspection was virtually equivalent to a physical entry into the students' pockets and personal possessions. In effect, he perceived what the students had secreted and communicated that information to his handler. By way of analogy, if the police approached citizens on the street with a portable x-ray machine to discern what they were carrying in their pockets, purses, and briefcases, surely such a procedure would be a search under the fourth amendment. Yet that was precisely the way in which Merko was employed. Like an x-ray machine, his superhuman sense of smell invaded the students' outer garments and detected the presence of items they were expecting to keep private. All citizens have a reasonable expectation that their privacy will not be intruded upon by electronic surveillance, x-ray machines, or sniffing dogs at the whim of the state. The use of the "sniffer dog" in the Latexo school was thus a search under the fourth amendment.

The designation of the sniffing conducted by Merko as a search does not end the constitutional inquiry, for the fourth amendment prohibits only those searches which are "unreasonable". The constitutional validity of any search depends upon the outcome of a balancing test between the competing interests of public need for the search on one hand and the individual's right to personal security on the other. The implementation of this test requires the court to examine the totality of circumstances surrounding the search at issue. Relevant factors to be considered include the scope of intrusion, the manner of intrusion, the justification for the search, and the place where it is conducted.

The degree of intrusion committed by Merko's sniffing the students and their property was somewhat less extensive than that stemming from a physical search. No laying on of hands was contemplated during the procedure until the dog had completed his tour of each classroom. In that respect, the intrusion more closely resembled electronic bugging or x-rays, which convey private information without a discernible physical intrusion. Moreover, since Merko only signalled his trainer if contraband was detected, this type of search was more limited in nature than other surveillance methods which pick up private information, both incriminating and non-incriminating, in an indiscriminate manner.

On the other hand, the use of an animal such as Merko to conduct a search may offend the sensibilities of those targeted for inspection more seriously than would an electronic gadget. Merko, a German Shepherd, is a large animal who had been trained as an attack dog. Testimony by the school's principal, Mr. Emmons, indicated that the dog "slobbered" on one child in the course of a search. The dog's trainer acknowledged that Merko might physically touch a child during a search if the dog became overly excited. Such a tool of surveillance could prove both intimidating and frightening, particularly to the children, some as young as kindergarten age, enrolled at Latexo. Hence, the degree of intrusion caused by the search was significant, far greater than that which the Fifth Circuit has found unacceptable in the "beeper" cases.

Defendants particularly emphasize that the student body was warned by Superintendent Acker that Merko would be conducting surprise inspections of the school prior to the search conducted on April 11th. They suggest that such a disclosure greatly diminished any expectation of privacy plaintiffs might have held prior to that time. But the mere announcement by officials that individual rights are about to be infringed upon cannot justify the subsequent infringement. Again through the medium of comparison, if the Government announced that all telephone lines would henceforth be tapped, it is apparent that, nevertheless, the public would not lose its expectation of privacy in using the telephone.

The search at the Latexo school cannot be analogized to passenger searches at airports, where citizens are warned that they will be subject to search should they choose to board a plane. In such circumstances, the individual is free to avoid the search by refraining from air travel. But the students at the Latexo school had no means of avoiding the impending searches, after they were announced, had they wished to do so. School attendance is compelled by law, and no students were permitted to leave their classrooms before Merko commenced sniffing. The search was mandatory for all. Thus, the reasonable expectation of students to be free from such an intrusion survived all warnings by school officials that such searches were to take place.

A principal factor in evaluating the reasonableness of this particular search is its sweeping, undifferentiated, and indiscriminate scope. The fourth amendment was designed, in large part, to prevent wholesale intrusions upon the personal security of our citizens. Although the probable cause standard embodied in the Constitution may be relaxed somewhat when limited intrusions are involved, some "specific and articulable facts which, taken together with rational inferences from those facts, reasonably warrant ... intrusion" on an individual by the state must be demonstrated.

This demand for specificity in the information upon which police action is predicated is the central teaching of this Court's Fourth Amendment jurisprudence.

The defendants in this case ignored the need to ascertain individualized suspicion prior to intruding upon the privacy rights of the students at Latexo. There was not a shred of evidence at the time of the sniff-search on April 11th that any of the student-plaintiffs were in possession of drugs or any other contraband on school grounds. It was, instead, the purpose of the search itself to ferret out such evidence in order to justify a more extensive search of selected students and property. But the ultimate fruits of a search, however bountiful, cannot justify the intrusion after the fact. Just as the police could not lawfully bring Merko into a restaurant, football stadium, or shopping center to sniff-search citizens indiscriminately for hidden drugs, the school officials exceeded the bounds of reasonableness in using Merko to inspect virtually the entire Latexo student body without any facts to raise a reasonable suspicion regarding specific individuals.

The sniff-search of plaintiffs' vehicles, isolated from the search of the plaintiffs themselves, also exceeded the bounds of reasonableness. Under school regulations, students had no access to their vehicles while school was in session. Thus, the school's legitimate interest in what students had left in their vehicles was minimal at best. The search was conducted in a blanket, indiscriminate manner without individualized suspicion of any kind. The capabilities of the dog, in penetrating the closed doors of the vehicles in a manner far beyond the range of human senses, resembled those of an x-ray machine or bugging device. While the extent of personal intrusion was somewhat less serious than in the dog's sniffing each individual student, the combination of other factors place the vehicle searches on the wrong side of the constitutional line.

As mentioned above, the determination of reasonableness in each case must be made on an ad hoc basis. To date, five courts of appeals have approved searches by "sniffer dogs" in circumstances which contrast sharply with those presented by the case at bar. None of those cases support the reasonableness of defendant's indiscriminate search of the students at Latexo.

Despite the apparent unreasonableness of defendants' blanket sniff-search at the Latexo school, defendants make an additional argument which merits attention. Under the in loco parentis doctrine, school teachers and administrators have specific responsibility for the health, safety, and conduct of students during school hours which gives them authority to impose discipline and maintain order. Defendants suggest that the sniff-search was necessarily reasonable since it was carried out in the exercise of that power and in furtherance of valid school regulations.

It is certainly true that the standards for a search in the public school context are considerably more lax than they are in the community at large. Courts have generally approved searches conducted in schools on the basis of "reasonable cause to believe" that contraband would be found, rather than requiring that the stricter standard of probable cause be met. Moreover, a warrant may not be required for such a search in many cases when the school is pursuing its legitimate interest in maintaining a safe environment conducive to the learning process.

But the doctrine of in loco parentis does not render the fourth amendment completely inapplicable to school searches, nor does it strip students attending school of their constitutional rights. State-operated schools may not operate as enclaves of totalitarianism where students are searched at the caprice of school officials. Thus, while the unique role of education in our society is a factor to be taken into account in assessing the reasonableness of this search, it does not necessarily outweigh all other factors. Some articulable facts which focus suspicion on specific students must be demonstrated before any school search can be carried out. That requirement was not met prior to the sniff-search conducted at Latexo.

Defendants' indiscriminate search of plaintiffs and other students was not rendered constitutionally permissible because it took place on the campus of a public school. The sniff-search conducted on April 11th was unreasonable under the fourth amendment, and since the search was carried out under color of state law, the constitutional rights of plaintiffs have been violated under the fourth amendment. Unless some other justification can be found to validate the subsequent searches of plaintiffs and their vehicles, those searches violated the fourth amendment as well.

There is no doubt that the physical searches of plaintiffs and their vehicles on April 11th resulted chiefly from the constitutionally deficient sniff-search. Except for the unreasonable employment of Merko's olfactory talents, the particularized suspicion needed to compel students to undergo such treatment would not have existed. Defendants suggest, as an alternative rationale, that all the plaintiffs consented to be searched. If consent were given, the requirement that reasonable suspicion or another quantum of proof be satisfied in advance would be excused.

To render such a search valid, consent must be freely and voluntarily offered. Voluntariness is a question of fact to be decided on the basis of the totality of circumstances. Coercion, either express or implied, vitiates apparent consent. If state officials give any affirmative indication that an individual must agree to be searched, that, in itself, would establish the involuntariness of a subsequent search.

The search of plaintiffs at the Latexo school cannot be characterized as consensual under these standards. The targets of the search were children with limited experience in a threatening situation. Insubordination is a disciplinary offense under school rules. Accustomed to receiving orders and obeying instructions from school officials, they were incapable of exercising unconstrained free will when asked to empty their pockets and open their vehicles to be searched. Moreover, plaintiffs were told repeatedly that if they refused to cooperate with the search, their mother would be called and a warrant procured from the police if necessary. These threats aggravated the coercive atmosphere in which the searches were conducted.

A consideration of all relevant facts makes it evident that the plaintiffs did not freely and voluntarily consent to be searched. Since the fruits of the illegal sniff-search, the sole source of evidence placing the plaintiffs under reasonable suspicion, could also not be used as a justification, the physical searches of plaintiffs and their vehicles were unreasonable under the fourth amendment.

Having obtained evidence against the plaintiffs by means of an unconstitutional search, the defendants could not use that evidence as a justification for imposing punishment. Although criminal proceedings were never instituted against the students, the fourth amendment protects citizens against unreasonable invasions of privacy by government officials in the civil area as well. In determining the existence of a fourth amendment violation and effectuating an appropriate response, courts must not be misled by the legal classification of the proceeding in which the violation occurred.

The primary vehicle for enforcing the strictures of the fourth amendment in our legal system is the "exclusionary rule," which prevents the use of unconstitutionally obtained evidence by the government in subsequent proceedings. While the exclusionary rule is most often employed in criminal cases, it has been resorted to on numerous occasions to redress fourth amendment violations in a variety of civil contexts as well.

The plaintiff-students suffered a penalty as a result of the illegal searches carried out by defendants. Although the punishment imposed was non-criminal in nature, it was, nonetheless, a deprivation rather than merely the restitution of monies wrongfully retained, as in Janis. Moreover, the school officials who suspended the plaintiffs on the basis of the unlawfully obtained evidence were the very same individuals who planned and implemented the searches. Excluding the use of such evidence from school disciplinary proceedings will directly and effectively deter unconstitutional conduct by these officials, in the manner contemplated by the Supreme Court in Mapp.

The failure to apply a corollary of the exclusionary rule in this context would leave school officials free to trench upon the constitutional rights of students in their charge without meaningful restraint or fear of adverse consequences.

An illegal search is no less consequential under the fourth amendment because it is carried out by the Latexo School Board rather than by the Department of Justice. Such unwarranted invasions of personal privacy as are reflected in the record of this case can be effectively deterred only through a variant of the exclusionary rule. Applying such a standard here, the items seized as a result of the unconstitutional searches of plaintiffs and their property could not be used as grounds for subjecting these students to disciplinary measures. Since there was no evidence that plaintiffs had violated school rules other than the fruits of those searches, their suspension from school and accompanying loss of grade points were unconstitutional.

A preliminary injunction will issue. Defendants shall be enjoined from denying Scott Jones an opportunity to make up the three final examinations he did not take in May and from failing to make available instructional materials and other assistance to him in preparation for those examinations. Defendants shall also be enjoined from reducing Scott Jones' grades for the three days of school Scott missed during his suspension in April. If his test scores, when averaged in with his other grades from the 1979–1980 school year, exceed those necessary for passing all required courses under school regulations, the school officials will be enjoined to award a high school diploma to him.

Defendants shall further be enjoined from using "sniffer dogs" to search the person or property of plaintiffs Michele or Michael Jones in the absence of reasonable cause to believe that those particular individuals are in possession of contraband in violation of school rules.

An order will be entered in accordance with this memorandum opinion.

Holdings of *Jones v. Latexo Indep. School Dist.*: The court held that the use of the "sniffer dog" in the Latexo school was a search under the Fourth Amendment. The mere announcement by officials that individual rights are about to be infringed upon cannot justify the subsequent infringement. Because school attendance is compelled by law, and no students were permitted to leave their classrooms before Merko commenced sniffing, the search was mandatory for all and not consensual. Some articulable facts which focus suspicion on specific students must be demonstrated before any school search can be carried out. That requirement was not met prior to the sniff-search conducted at Latexo.

Discussion Questions

If the school authorities had enough suspicion to search a particular student, can that allow them to use the dog to sniff out that student's car in the school parking lot?

This court held that the illegal search could not be used for disciplinary action. Could it be used for a suppression motion in criminal or delinquency court?

———————

Doe v. Renfrow: In *Doe v. Renfrow,* the federal court was faced with a § 1983 civil lawsuit concerning use of sniffer dogs on students and, when the dogs alerted on a student or car, a full-scale search. The schools did not have an "individualized suspicion" until the sniffer dogs alerted to a particular student or car.

As you read *Doe v. Renfrow,* look for the following:

1. Consider whether the mere fact that the court finds that the use of a sniffer dog is not a search makes *T.L.O.* inapplicable.

2. Consider whether or not the alerting of a sniffer dog can provide the reasonable, individualized suspicion to support the second search as required by *T.L.O.*

Doe v. Renfrow
631 F.2d 91 (7th Cir. 1980)

In May 1979, plaintiff Diane Doe, a student at Highland Junior High School in Highland, Indiana, and four other students filed a civil rights complaint under 28 U.S.C. §§ 1343(3) and 1343(4). The gravamen of the complaint was that plaintiff and others were illegally sniffed by police dogs during school hours and pocket-searched if a dog alerted to them in order to determine whether they possessed controlled substances and contraband. As part of the drug investigation, plaintiff alleged that she and three other students "were compelled to remove their clothing and submit to visual inspection by defendants' agents."

The complaint also charged that 2,780 students at Highland High School were subject to the canine sniffing and that 17 of them thereafter "were summarily suspended, expelled, or compelled to withdraw from attendance at school." According to plaintiff, defendants' practice was "unsupported by particularized facts, reasonable suspicion or probable cause to believe that any of the persons" subject to the canine drug investigation would possess controlled substances.

A hearing was held on June 7, 1979, with respect to various motions of the parties. On August 30, 1979, Judge Sharp dismissed the action on the merits as to the Highland police chief and dog trainer Patricia Little because they did not participate in the strip search. He granted defendant school officials summary judgment on the issue of monetary damages for the body search of Diane Doe. However, he held that she was entitled to declaratory relief upon the court's finding that the nude body search was made without a finding of reasonable cause and in violation of her Fourth Amendment rights. The judgment denied all other aspects of her prayer for declaratory relief, denied her motion for a permanent injunction and denied class certification.

For the reasons given in Judge Sharp's scholarly opinion, which we adopt as our own, the judgment is affirmed except with respect to the portion of the decision that the defendant school officials are immune from liability arising out of the nude search because they had a "good faith" defense as articulated in *Wood v. Strickland*.

We return the matter to the trial court for a determination of damages stemming from the body search. The decision is otherwise affirmed, costs to be borne equally by the respective parties.

SWYGERT, Circuit Judge, dissenting from the order denying the petition for rehearing.

I am deeply troubled by this court's holding that the dragnet inspection of the entire student body of the Highland Senior and Junior High Schools by trained police dogs and their dog-handlers did not constitute a search under the Fourth Amendment. No doctrine of in loco parentis or diminished constitutional rights for children in a public school setting excuses this alarming invasion by police and school authorities of the constitutional rights of thousands of innocent children. Any attempt by the district court or this court to portray the events of March 23, 1979 as only a deviation in degree from the normal school day is grossly misplaced. In my view, those events were a deviation in kind and constituted a danger not only to the psychological well-being of the children but to the fundamental concepts of our Bill of Rights.

Although a number of incidents involving alcohol, drugs, or related paraphernalia had been reported to school authorities, no more than twenty-one out of 2,780 students had been involved. School authorities had to concede that, in general, conditions at the Highland schools were at least average and could well have been better than at most other schools. At the time of the raid, they possessed no specific information as to particular drugs or contraband, transactions or events, or drug suppliers or abusers. Nevertheless, over a period of weeks a scheme was developed and executed that implicated all 2,780 students and subjected all to a humiliating search by police dogs.

The raids began at 8:45 A.M. on March 23, 1979. The searchers were divided into teams consisting of at least one dog, one dog handler, one school administrator or teacher, and one or two uniformed police officers. Fourteen dogs were on hand. For the duration of the raid, all schoolhouse doors were either locked or tightly guarded by police and school officials. All students were detained in their first period classrooms; any late arrivers or visitors were led to and detained in a room set aside for that purpose. No student was allowed to leave his or her classroom, and if any claimed to need to use the lavatory facilities, school or police authorities escorted and watched over them.

Every student was instructed to place his belongings in view and his hands on his desk. Girls placed their purses on the floor between their feet. The teams of searchers moved from room to room, and from desk to desk. Every single student was sniffed, inspected, and examined at least once by a dog and a joint school-police team. The extraordinary atmosphere at the school was supplemented still further when representatives of the press and other news media, invited in by school authorities, entered the schoolhouses and classrooms during the raid and observed the searches while in progress.

The raid lasted about three hours. After the sniffing and examination of 2,780 students, the searchers found fifteen high school students—and no junior high students—in possession of illicit materials. School and police authorities removed five high school students—three girls and two boys—from their classrooms and subjected them to personal interrogations and thorough, but not nude, searches. None was found to be in possession of any contraband. Three or four junior high students were similarly treated and cleared. Four junior high students—all girls—were removed from their classes, stripped nude, and interrogated. Not one of them was found to possess any illicit material.

The district judge held in an opinion adopted by a panel of this court that "the presence of the dog and its trainer within the classroom, also at the request and supervision of the school officials, was only an aide to that official's observation of students.... (T)he sniffing of a trained narcotic detecting canine is not a search." I strongly disagree. In my view, the circumstances of March 23 can hardly be likened to the observations of a school administrator, sniffing the air about him as he goes about his business. Here there was evidence that the trained dogs ran their noses along pupils' legs, actually touching the bodies of the students.

The cases cited by the district court as holding that sniffing dogs do not constitute a search are totally inapposite because in those cases the dogs were sniffing inanimate and unattended objects rather than people. Here the intrusive probings by the dogs were in no sense mere observation of "'physical characteristics ... constantly exposed to the public, ... (but) constituted the type of 'severe, though brief, intrusion upon cherished personal security' that is subject to constitutional scrutiny." We need not speculate afar about the psychological trauma suffered by the students during this mass search. The accusing finger of the police may well remain for a lifetime upon these young, impressionable minds.

Had a warrant properly been sought, I am convinced that none could have issued consistent with the Fourth Amendment. The police and school officials neither possessed nor attempted to gain specific information about any particular student. There was also no information as to any particular drug or contraband transaction or event. Thus, all 2,780 students were under suspicion, and there was no known crime.

A search under these conditions is unconstitutional under either a reasonable suspicion or a probable cause standard. I cannot consider this a "school" case because the mass search was planned and executed with extensive police involvement rather than solely by school personnel. But even considered in the context of "school" cases, there was no reasonable suspicion here to justify the mass search. Nor was the constitutional violation abrogated by the fact that the police did not plan any arrests. The Fourth Amendment protects against unreasonable searches because of "the right of the people to be secure in their persons" whether or not an arrest would necessarily follow.

Violations of a person's "cherished personal security," whether engaged in by violent antisocial elements of our society or by overzealous, insensitive police, must be equally condemned. Both should be dealt with in accordance with legal consequences that foster deterrence.

FAIRCHILD, Chief Judge, dissenting.

I voted for rehearing en banc and surely join in Judge Swygert's concern whether the dogs were used in a manner which itself without further individual intervention invaded protected privacy rights. I further question whether the record demonstrates that the responses of the dogs were sufficiently reliable indicators of the presence of contraband to constitute probable cause justifying the individual searches. After all, it appears that although the canine response raised suspicion toward 50 students, only 15 were found to possess contraband. As to plaintiff Doe, I gather that she probably caused the dog to respond to her because she had been playing that morning with her own dog which was in heat.

Holdings of *Doe v. Renfrow*: The court held the inspection of the entire student body of the Highland Senior and Junior High Schools by trained police dogs and their dog-handlers did not constitute a search under the Fourth Amendment.

Discussion Questions

How does this court come to the exact opposite opinion than the *Jones/Latexo* court?

Does this court hold that sniffer dogs are never an intrusion and can always be used?

––––––––––

Horton v. Goose Creek Indep. Sch. Dist.: In *Horton v. Goose Creek Indep. Sch. Dist.:* the federal court was faced with a § 1983 civil lawsuit concerning the use of sniffer dogs in a public school. If the dogs "alerted" the presence of drugs on a student, the student was searched. If the dog alerted the presence of drugs in a car or locker, the locker or car was searched. The students claimed that the use of sniffer dogs on the students, their lockers and their cars violated their Fourth Amendment rights.

As you read *Horton v. Goose Creek Indep. Sch. Dist.*, look for the following:

1. Consider why the court differentiated between the sniffing of cars and lockers and the sniffing of persons.

2. Consider how accurate the dogs need to be in order to justify a search of a car or locker based on the dog alerting to the presence of drugs.

Horton v. Goose Creek Indep. Sch. Dist.
690 F.2d 470 (5th Cir. 1982)

This case presents a question of first impression in this circuit: as a matter of constitutional law, can a school district, acting in good faith in an effort to deal with a serious drug and alcohol problem, subject students, their lockers, and their automobiles to the exploratory sniffing of dogs trained to detect certain contraband? We must consider the special circumstances peculiar to the public school environment, the duty of school officials to protect the minors in their care, the growing problem of drug and alcohol abuse in the schools, the students' interest in the integrity of their persons and effects, and the importance of demonstrating to the young that constitutional guarantees are not only lofty theories but do in practice control our government. Bearing in mind all these considerations, we hold that the dogs' sniffing of cars and lockers does not constitute a search within the purview of the fourth amendment. We hold further that the dogs' sniffing of the childrens' persons does constitute a search within the purview of the fourth amendment, and that in a school setting, individualized reasonable suspicion is required in order for the sniffing to be constitutional.

The named plaintiffs, Robby Horton, Heather Horton, and Sandra Sanchez, brought this action by their next friend, Robert Horton, seeking to represent all students enrolled in the Goose Creek Consolidated Independent School District (GCISD) in a challenge under 42 U.S.C. § 1983 to the defendant school district's canine drug detection program.

The defendant, GCISD, adopted the challenged program in response to a growing drug and alcohol abuse problem in the schools. It contracted with a security services firm, Securities Associates International, Inc. (SAI), that provides dogs (generally Doberman pinschers and German shepherds) trained to alert their handlers to the presence of any one of approximately sixty different substances, including alcohol and drugs, both over-the-counter and controlled. The defendant conducted assemblies in the elementary schools to acquaint the children with the dogs and informed students in the junior and senior high schools of the program. On a random and unannounced basis, the dogs are taken to the various schools in the district, where they sniff students' lockers and automobiles. They also go into the classrooms, on leashes, to sniff the students themselves. During their "playtime" at the schools, the dogs are sometimes taken off their leashes. When a dog alerts the handler to the odor of an illicit substance on a student's person, after the sweep of the class is completed and the dog and handler have departed, a school official discreetly asks the student to leave the class and go to the administrator's office, where he is subjected to a search of pockets, purse, and outer garments. When a dog alerts his handler to an automobile, the student driver is asked to open the doors and the trunk. If he refuses, the school notifies the parents. When a dog alerts his handler to a locker, the school searches the locker without the consent of the student to whom it is assigned. If the student is found to possess substances that violate school policy, he may agree to seek outside counseling; otherwise the administrator may recommend to the superintendent that the student be suspended. Second-time violators do not have the option of counseling.

The named plaintiffs were all subjected to the sniffing of the canine drug detectors. Two of them, Robby Horton and Sandra Sanchez, triggered alerts. School officials questioned Sandra, took her purse, and searched it without her consent. They found a small bottle of perfume, which they returned to her. Robby was asked to empty his pockets, which he did. When nothing incriminating was found, the school officials searched his socks and lower pants legs but again found no contraband.

The plaintiffs brought this action, alleging a violation of the fourth amendment prohibition of unreasonable searches and seizures and a violation of the fourteenth amendment prohibition of deprivations of liberty and property without due process. On a motion for class certification and cross-motions for summary judgment, the district court denied certification and held that the sniffing, although it is a search, is not unreasonable. Further, it held that reasonable cause is the standard for searches of students and their property by school officials acting in loco parentis, and the alert of the dogs provides reasonable cause for searches of lockers and cars as well as for searches of the pockets, purses, and outer garments of students. Finally, the district court held that the program does not violate the due process clause, because it subjects the students to minimal intrusion, humiliation, and fear. The plaintiffs appeal both on the merits and on the question of class certification.

The problem presented in this case is the convergence of two troubling questions. First, is the sniff of a drug-detecting dog a "search" within the purview of the fourth amendment? Second, to what extent does the fourth amendment protect students against searches by school administrators seeking to maintain a safe environment conducive to education? On each question, we find an abundance of precedent but scant guidance.

Frequent use of drug-detecting dogs by law enforcement officials has led to a great number of cases challenging the admissibility of the fruits of a canine sniff. From these cases, one proposition is clear and universally accepted: if the police have some basis for suspecting an individual of possessing contraband, they may, consonant with the fourth amendment, use a drug-detecting dog to sniff checked luggage, shipped packages, storage lockers, trailers, or cars. While the rationales of these cases are not the same, the majority view is that the sniffing of objects by a dog is not a search. Only the Ninth Circuit has held that the sniffing of objects is a search, though it may at times be reasonable.

The decision to characterize an action as a search is in essence a conclusion about whether the fourth amendment applies at all. If an activity is not a search or seizure (assuming the activity does not violate some other constitutional or statutory provision), then the government enjoys a virtual carte blanche to do as it pleases. The activity is "excluded from judicial control and the command of reasonableness." We must analyze the question of whether dog sniffing is a search in terms of whether the sniffing offends reasonable expectations of privacy, and must look at the degree of intrusiveness of the challenged action to determine whether it is the type of activity that can be tolerated in a free society.

The courts have in effect adopted a doctrine of "public smell" analogous to the exclusion from fourth amendment coverage of things exposed to the public "view." The courts have reasoned that if a police officer, positioned in a place where he has a right to be, is conscious of an odor, say, of marijuana, no search has occurred; the aroma emanating from the property or person is considered exposed to the public "view" and, therefore, unprotected. From this proposition the courts have concluded that the sniffing of a dog is "no different," or that the dog's olfactory sense merely "enhances" that of the police officer in the same way that a flashlight enhances the officer's sight.

We find Goldstein to be controlling on the question of whether the dogs' sniffing of student lockers in public hallways and automobiles parked on public parking lots was a search. The sniffs occurred while the objects were unattended and positioned in public view. Had the principal of the school wandered past the lockers and smelled the pungent aroma of marijuana wafting through the corridors, it would be difficult to contend that a search had occurred. Goldstein stands for the proposition that the use of the dogs' nose to ferret out the scent from inanimate objects in public places is not treated any differently. We hold accordingly that the sniffs of the lockers and cars did not constitute a search and therefore we need make no inquiry into the reasonableness of the sniffing of the lockers and automobiles.

The use of the dogs to sniff the students, however, presents an entirely different problem. After all, the fourth amendment "protects people, not places."

The students' persons certainly are not the subject of lowered expectations of privacy. On the contrary, society recognizes the interest in the integrity of one's person, and the fourth amendment applies with its fullest vigor against any intrusion on the human body. In fact, the Supreme Court has suggested that all governmental intrusions upon personal security are governed by the fourth amendment:

In our view the sounder course is to recognize that the Fourth Amendment governs all intrusions by agents of the public upon personal security, and to make the scope of the particular intrusion, in light of all the exigencies of the case, a central element in the analysis of reasonableness. This seems preferable to an approach which attributes too much significance to an overly technical definition of "search," and which turns in part upon a judge-made hierarchy of legislative enactments in the criminal sphere.

The commentators agree that "the intensive smelling of people, even if done by dogs, (is) indecent and demeaning." Most persons in our society deliberately attempt not to expose the odors emanating from their bodies to public smell. In contrast, where the Supreme Court has upheld limited investigations of body characteristics not justified by individualized suspicion, it has done so on the grounds that the particular characteristic was routinely exhibited to the public. Intentional close proximity sniffing of the person is offensive whether the sniffer be canine or human. One can imagine the embarrassment which a young adolescent, already self-conscious about his or her body, might experience when a dog, being handled by a representative of the school administration, enters the classroom specifically for the purpose of sniffing the air around his or her person.

We need only look at the record in this case to see how a dog's sniffing technique — i.e., sniffing around each child, putting his nose on the child and scratching and manifesting other signs of excitement in the case of an alert — is intrusive. The SAI representative explained that Doberman pinschers and German shepherds were used precisely because of the image maintained by the large dogs. Plaintiff, Heather Horton, described what happened when the dog entered the classrooms:

> Well, we were in the middle of a major French exam and the dog came in and
> walked up and down the aisles and stopped at every desk and sniffed on each side
> all around the people, the feet, the parts where you keep your books under the desk.

Ms. Horton went on to express her fear of the large dogs. The SAI representative testified that the dogs put their noses "up against" the persons they are investigating.

On the basis of our examination of the record which indicates the degree of personal intrusiveness involved in this type of activity, we hold that sniffing by dogs of the students' persons in the manner involved in this case is a search within the purview of the fourth amendment. We need not decide today whether the use of dogs to sniff people in some other manner, e.g., at some distance, is a search.

Our decision that the sniffing is a search does not, however, compel the conclusion that it is constitutionally impermissible. The fourth amendment does not prohibit all searches; it only restricts the government to "reasonable" searches.

A dog's sniff of a person, particularly where the dogs actually touch the person as they do in the GCISD program, may be analogous to the warrantless "stop and frisk" upheld by the Supreme Court on the basis of a suspicion that fell short of probable cause.

Because the sniffing in this case occurred in a school environment, we need not address the question whether the sniffing of a person in a non-school setting is sufficiently intrusive to require the full panoply of fourth amendment protections — probable cause and a warrant — or whether such sniffing is less intrusive, requiring only reasonable suspicion. We leave that question for another day.

The courts have encountered substantial difficulty in accommodating the fourth amendment to the special situation presented by the public schools, where school officials have both a right and a duty to provide a safe environment conducive to education. At one time, it was not uncommon for a court to view the school official who searched a student as acting under authority derived from the parent and therefore as a private party not subject to the constraints of the fourth amendment. As courts in most recent cases have decided, we think it beyond question that the school official, employed and paid by the state and supervising children who are, for the most part, compelled to attend, is an agent of the government and is constrained by the fourth amendment. The Supreme Court's application to school officials of other constitutional restraints applicable only to state action compels that result.

But the decision that school officials are governed by the fourth amendment does not dictate a holding that their activity in this case was unconstitutional. The basic concern of the fourth amendment is reasonableness, and reasonableness depends on the circumstances. Often the ordinary requirements of the fourth amendment are modified to deal with special situations. The public school presents special circumstances that demand similar accommodations of the usual fourth amendment requirements. When society requires large groups of students, too young to be considered capable of mature restraint in their use of illegal substances or dangerous instrumentalities, it assumes a duty to protect them from dangers posed by anti-social activities—their own and those of other students—and to provide them with an environment in which education is possible. To fulfill that duty, teachers and school administrators must have broad supervisory and disciplinary powers. At the same time, though, we must protect the fourth amendment rights of students. Indeed, constitutional rights in the schools take on a special importance.

When the school official acts in furtherance of his duty to maintain a safe environment conducive to education, the usual accommodation is to require that the school official have "reasonable cause" for his action. Although the standard is less stringent than that applicable to law enforcement officers, it requires more of the school official than good faith or minimal restraint. The Constitution does not permit good intentions to justify objectively outrageous intrusions on student privacy. Thus, though we do not question the good faith of the GCISD officials in their attempt to eradicate a serious and menacing drug and alcohol abuse problem, we cannot approve the program on that basis; we must examine its objective reasonableness.

The intrusion on dignity and personal security that goes with the type of canine inspection of the student's person involved in this case cannot be justified by the need to prevent abuse of drugs and alcohol when there is no individualized suspicion, and we hold it unconstitutional.

The plaintiffs urge that, even if the initial sniffing of the cars and lockers by the dogs is permissible, the dogs' reactions do not give the defendant a sufficiently strong basis for suspicion to justify a further search. The district court stated that the "generalized perception of a problem of drug and alcohol abuse" along with the positive reaction of the dog give the school sufficient cause to believe that the student occupant or driver has violated school policy to justify opening the locker or car and searching it. The court did not, however, make any finding on the reliability of the dogs, and there was no evidence in the record to support such a finding. In fact, although the representative of SAI asserted that the dogs were quite reliable, he admitted that there were no comprehensive records kept of those incidents when the dogs reacted positively in the absence of contraband. On this record, then, we cannot say whether the reaction of the dogs provided adequate cause for more intrusive searches, and summary judgment is inappropriate. We remand to the district court for development of the record on that point. The standard enunciated by the district court, however, was proper: GCISD need not show that the dogs are infallible or even that they are reliable enough to give the defendant probable cause; instead, the dogs must be reasonably reliable. It will not, however, be enough to show that the dogs are reasonably reliable in indicating the presence or recent presence of contraband. If the reaction is to justify a search, it must give rise to reasonable suspicion that the search will produce something—i.e., reasonable suspicion that contraband is currently present. If the school does have reasonable cause to suspect the presence of contraband, the ease with which it can be destroyed or moved presents an exigent circumstance that excuses the warrant requirement.

The plaintiffs also argue that the use of the dogs violates their rights under the fourteenth amendment, by depriving them of a liberty interest without due process. The question remains whether the presence of a dog on campus, and the practice of occasionally allowing him to play on campus unrestrained by a leash but supervised by the handler, constitute a violation of the due process clause.

The dogs trained and provided by SAI are large animals — usually German shepherds and Doberman pinschers, and occasionally Labradors — breeds selected because the animals are often sold to police forces who, according to the testimony of the SAI representative, use these dogs to maintain an image of strength and ferocity. The individual animals, however, are selected on the basis of their docility, and SAI has never received a complaint about the dogs' injuring anyone in any way. The defendant goes to considerable pains to educate the younger students, who are more likely to be frightened, by introducing the dogs at assemblies and demonstrating their friendliness. Furthermore, there is nothing in the record to indicate that those students who do not wish to join in the play with the dogs cannot avoid them.

We recognize that large dogs, particularly those breeds that are sometimes used as attack dogs, often engender an irrational fear, and we do question the wisdom of permitting them to roam parts of the campus unleashed. But, as long as the dogs are carefully selected for their nonaggressive character, and the handlers supervise them during their playtime, we do not think that the minimal "harassment" arising from their mere presence on campus rises to the level of a constitutional violation.

We conclude that the use of dogs in dragnet sniff-searches of the students of GCISD is unconstitutional, but that the use of the dogs in similar dragnet sniffing of lockers and cars is not, and we direct the district court to grant relief by appropriate declaration and injunction. Although the use of the dogs in dragnet sniffing of lockers and cars is permissible, we must remand to the district court for the case to proceed to trial on the reliability of the dogs' reactions as the basis for further searches.

AFFIRMED in part, REVERSED in part, and REMANDED.

Holdings of *Horton v. Goose Creek Indep. Sch. Dist.*: The court held that that the dogs' sniffing of cars and lockers does not constitute a search within the purview of the Fourth Amendment. The court held further that the dogs' sniffing of the children's persons does constitute a search within the purview of the Fourth Amendment, and that in a school setting, individualized reasonable suspicion is required in order for the sniffing to be constitutional.

Discussion Questions

How is use of a sniffer dog NOT a search when it is applied to lockers and cars, but IS a search when applied to a person?

How accurate does the sniffer dog have to constitute an individualized reasonable suspicion so as to justify a follow-up search as?

Key Concepts: Sniffer Dogs in Schools

- Some courts believe that the "sniffing" of students by a dog constitutes a search require applications of Fourth Amendment protections. Other courts believe that such sniffing by dogs does not constitute a search and, as such, the Fourth Amendment is not implicated by the use of sniffer dogs in schools.

- Some court differentiate between the use of sniffer dogs on the students persons from the use of such a procedure on lockers, cars and other personal effects, finding the use of such dogs on persons is more intrusive than their use on property.

- The way that a particular court analyses the intrusiveness of the use of sniffer dogs controls whether or not the T.L.O. standards requiring an individualized suspicion will be applied.

Practical Questions: Sniffer Dogs in Schools

1. Parents of a middle-school student come to your office concerned about a new school policy implemented to deal with a growing drug problem at the school. They tell you that, at random, students will be subjected to a "sniff" by a trained German Shephard. Students are not allowed to "opt out" of the procedure. Their child is terrified of dogs, having been mauled by a pit bull two years ago. They show you a letter from the youth's psychiatrist saying that the procedure would be "devastating" to the child and could cause long-lasting psychological trauma to him. What legal arguments would you make to the school to prevent the policy from being applied to this child?

2. You are representing a student in juvenile delinquency court who has been charged with possession of marijuana at school. He was searched as a result of the "indication" by a sniffer dog, and, during the search, one-half ounce of marijuana was found in a baggie in the student's pocket. What facts to you want to know about the dogs used in the search to determine whether or not your client has a chance of suppressing the evidence?

G. Police & Resource Officers at School

Overview: As we learned earlier, courts have held that school officials wishing to search a student are not held to the same standards as are police officers. A warrant is not required and only a reasonable suspicion is necessary (rather than probable cause) to justify a search by school authorities. Now that many schools have police officers in residence at the school (often called "school resource officers" or SROs), the courts are forced to decide which standards are applicable when the search is performed by a police officer assigned to a school: the higher standard of probable cause and a warrant, or the lower standard applied to school authorities.

State v. Heirtzler: In *State v. Heirtzler,* the New Hampshire Supreme Court was forced to decide what standards apply to a search by school authorities when the search by school authorities is at the behest of a school resource (police) officer. In this case, the school resource officer conceded that a "silent understanding" existed between him and school officials that passing information to the school when he could not act was a technique used to gather evidence otherwise inaccessible to him "due to constitutional restraints." In such a case, a student was searched by school officials when he was suspected of passing drugs in school, but the officer did not believe he had enough evidence to meet the constitutional requirements justifying a search by him. The officer passed the matter on to school authorities, who searched the student and found LSD. The student was charged with possession and distribution of a controlled substance. The student filed a motion to suppress the evidence obtained claiming that the search by school authorities violated his Fourth Amendment rights.

As you read *State v. Heirtzler,* look for the following:

1. Consider whether or not the result would have been different if the school authorities would have searched Heirtzler when they observed him passing a tin foil packet to another student rather than first passing the case on to the school resource officer.

2. Compare the traditional roles of school authorities and of law enforcement and consider how those roles justify different rules for searches for the two groups.

State v. Heirtzler

147 N.H. 344 (2002)

The defendant, Joseph Heirtzler, was charged with possession and distribution of a controlled drug. The State appeals an order of the Superior Court (*Coffey,* J.) granting his motion to suppress evidence obtained as a result of an interrogation and search conducted by a school official. We affirm.

The record supports the following facts. Londonderry Police Officer Michael Bennette was assigned as the school resource officer for Londonderry High School (school). One reason for Bennette's assignment was the Londonderry Police Department's (department) perception that the school was investigating criminal matters, which should have been reported to and handled by the department. As the school resource officer, Bennette remained under the direct control and supervision of the department, and his job essentially was to investigate criminal activity on school grounds. The department's policy was to investigate reports of criminal activity at the school in the same manner as other criminal complaints.

Prior to assuming his assignment at the school, Bennette met with school officials to discuss the parameters of his job. He made clear that cases were to be reported and prosecuted, not "whitewashed" by school officials. Bennette told school officials to contact him when cases involved criminal activity or required criminal investigation. They agreed, but asserted that administrative and disciplinary matters involving students fell within the sole authority and control of the school. According to Bennette, the school principal was keenly aware of the difference between administrative duties and law enforcement within the school.

Because of the number of searches conducted at the school under its search policy, Bennette could not handle the investigation of every potential criminal matter. The school, therefore, agreed to investigate the less serious potential criminal matters, including searches. Indeed, at the suppression hearing, assistant principal James O'Neill testified as follows:

Q: But I guess when Officer Bennett [*sic*] and you worked out what the parameters of his job ...

A: Yes.

Q: ... this would be acceptable to the school, because you had to agree to let him come, right?

A: Let him come into the building? Yes.

Q: So part of that agreement was a lot of those potential criminal matters you would handle, and some of the more serious criminal matters they would handle?

A: That's fair.

Bennette's testimony regarding this agreement was as follows:

Q: Drug investigation. Do you recall me asking you: "Is it fair to say that, in your mind at least, you delegated some of the responsibility of investigating these cases to the school administration?" Your answer is, "Yeah," right?

A: Yes.

This delegation of responsibility, according to Bennette, would occur at his direction after he assessed the information brought to his attention to determine "what level it [rose] to." Bennette stated at his deposition that if the safety level and threat were high, such as in cases involving a report that a student possessed a knife or gun, he would conduct the investigation and any necessary search. If the information involved drugs, however, he would pass it along to school officials for action. Essentially, if Bennette lacked probable cause to pursue a less serious criminal matter and perhaps make an arrest, he would deem it a school issue and turn the information over to school officials. Once he turned the information over, he had no further involvement unless the school requested it. He testified, however, that when officials seized contraband from a student they would contact him.

Bennette conceded that a "silent understanding" existed between him and school officials that passing information to the school when he could not act was a technique used to gather evidence otherwise inaccessible to him due to constitutional restraints. At his deposition, Bennette stated:

Q: I mean, isn't it fair to say that it is a technique that is used that when you have some information, but it is not enough under the existing case law to permit you to do a search, that one of the techniques you would have utilized, or did utilize was to pass it on to the school, because you know they don't need all the probable cause that you need in order to act?

A: I know that, and I know that going in, the first day of school. And [school officials] know it themselves too....

Q: But isn't it fair to say that there is sort of a silent understanding that when you pass on this type of information....

A: Well, I think we both know, you know and I know it, and so does the school administration....

At the time of his arrest for possession and distribution of a controlled drug, the defendant was a student at the school. During science class, his teacher observed him pass what appeared to be a folded piece of tinfoil to another student. The student removed something from the tinfoil, put it in a piece of cellophane and passed the folded tinfoil back to the defendant. After class ended, the teacher contacted Bennette and told him what she had observed. Bennette testified that although he may have had articulable suspicion to investigate further, he ultimately decided that he did not have enough information to warrant further investigation. Instead, Bennette passed the information to O'Neill for action.

After receiving the information from Bennette, O'Neill told him that the matter was a school administrative issue. O'Neill testified that although the situation could involve drugs or illegal substances, since it did not involve criminal activity of a more serious nature, it was the school's administrative duty to act upon the information. O'Neill and another assistant principal, Robert Shaps, called the defendant to the office, questioned him and asked if they could search him. The defendant complied with the search request and a piece of paper wrapped in tinfoil was found in his cigarette pack. After further questioning, the defendant stated that the piece of paper might be LSD. Once the search produced the potential presence of an illegal drug, O'Neill contacted Bennette and turned the matter over to him.

In his motion to suppress, the defendant argued that O'Neill and Shaps were acting as agents of the police and thus their interrogation and search had to conform with the procedural safeguards afforded criminal suspects when the State acts. Alternatively, the defendant argued that even if O'Neill and Shaps were not acting as agents of the State, they lacked reasonable grounds to interrogate and search him.

A warrantless search or seizure is presumptively illegal and the prosecution has the burden of establishing that it falls within a recognized exception to the warrant requirement. The acquisition of evidence by an individual acting as an agent of the police must be reviewed by the same constitutional standards that govern law enforcement officials. This "agency rule" prevents the police from having a private individual conduct a search or seizure that would be unlawful if performed by the police themselves. Because we uphold the trial court's suppression order under the State Constitution, we need not undertake a separate federal constitutional analysis and look to federal caselaw for guidance only.

An agency relationship requires "proof of some affirmative action by a police officer or other governmental official that preceded the interrogation [of the defendant, which] can reasonably be seen to have induced the third party to conduct the interrogation that took place."

Whether formal or informal, the agreement must "evince an understanding that the third party will be acting on the government's behalf or for the government's benefit."

The fundamental concern of the agency rule is to curb unconstitutional activity by government; it is meant to prevent the government from circumventing the rights of a defendant by securing private parties to do what it cannot. Although the existence of an agreement or a request forms the crux of our agency analysis, these two "varieties" of government action are not intended to narrow a trial court's consideration of all the factual circumstances surrounding an alleged agency relationship.

We begin by examining the scope of school officials' administrative duties. School officials are "responsible for administration and discipline within the school and must regularly conduct inquiries concerning both violations of school rules and violations of law." Their administrative duties, however, do not include enforcing the law or investigating criminal matters. School officials are not law enforcement officers and they should not be charged with knowing the intricacies of constitutional criminal procedure.

Because they are not law enforcement officers, when school officials search for contraband in order to foster a safe and healthy educational environment, they are afforded greater flexibility than if a law enforcement officer performed the same search. If school officials agree to take on the mantle of criminal investigation and enforcement, however, they assume an understanding of constitutional criminal law equal to that of a law enforcement officer. In such circumstances, even if school officials *claim* their actions fall within the ambit of their administrative authority, they should be charged with abiding by the constitutional protections required in criminal investigations. In sum, the role of school officials is to foster a safe and healthy educational environment. In order to do so, it is necessary that they be afforded some flexibility to swiftly resolve potential problems affecting this environment. However, enforcing the law or investigating criminal matters is outside the scope of a school official's administrative authority.

The presence of law enforcement personnel within schools requires school officials to establish a working relationship with them. It is here that school officials should be vigilant not to assume responsibilities beyond the scope of their administrative authority. Constitutional rights, which remain intact as students pass through the schoolhouse door, must be protected against school officials who inadvertently assume the role of law enforcement. Examining the relationship between school officials and law enforcement personnel within the school is a fact-intensive inquiry.

The record supports the trial court's conclusion that a prior agreement existed between the department and school officials for purposes of establishing that an agency relationship existed. Bennette testified that he delegated the responsibility of investigating less serious, potential criminal matters — drug cases — to school officials, and O'Neill confirmed that this was a "fair" characterization of the arrangement between the school and the department. Thus, while Bennette was responsible for investigating more serious crimes, such as possession of a dangerous weapon, the school accepted responsibility for investigating less serious ones. Bennette also conceded that a "silent understanding" existed between him and school officials that passing information to the school when he could not act was a technique used to gather evidence otherwise inaccessible to him due to constitutional restraints. The school, by "a mere wink or nod" or something more concrete, agreed to investigate certain potential criminal matters on the State's behalf or for its benefit.

Recognizing that the trier of fact is in the best position to assess the relationship between law enforcement and school officials under an agency analysis, we conclude that the record also supports the trial court's finding that Bennette's actions induced the school officials to conduct the interrogation and search of the defendant. Accordingly, we find no error with the trial court's order granting the defendant's motion to suppress.

Affirmed.

Holdings of *State v. Heirtzler*: The court held that, when school officials agree to take on the mantle of criminal investigation and enforcement, they will be held to the standard for justification of searches of a student equal to that of a law enforcement officer.

Discussion Questions

Is the fact that there was a "wink and nod" agreement or "silent understanding" between the school authorities and the SRO controlling here?

If the SRO and school authorities just would have said, "No, we did not have any kind of agreement like that" would the result have been different?

State v. D.S.: In *State v. D.S.*, the Florida Appellate Court was faced with a student search by school officials in the presence of a police officer assigned to the school. When school officials suspected a student of distributing drugs in school, they escorted the student to the assistant principal's office. When they entered the office, a Dade County Public School Police Officer was sitting at the assistant principal's desk doing paperwork. The officer continued his work as the assistant principal told the juvenile that she believed that he possessed contraband and told the juvenile to empty his pockets on a table. A baggie of marijuana was produced, and the officer was asked to arrest the student, who later filed a motion to suppress the evidence when he was charged in juvenile court with possession of marijuana in a public school.

As you read *State v. D.S.*, look for the following:

1. Consider whether or not the court would have ruled differently if it was established that this was a "setup" — the officer was intentionally at the assistant principal's desk to be available if a search was conducted.

2. Look for anything in the opinion that shows who employed the police officer and to whom the police officer directly reported.

State v. D.S.

685 So.2d 41 (Fla. App. 1997)

The State appeals the trial court's order granting a juvenile's motion to suppress. For the following reasons, we reverse the order granting the motion to suppress.

After Karen Robinson (hereinafter "Robinson"), an Assistant Principal of a Middle School, received separate reports from four students that D.S., a juvenile and student at the school, had offered to sell drugs that he had with him, Robinson explained the situation to Alberto Carvalho (hereinafter "Carvalho"), a second Assistant Principal. Thereafter, both Assistant Principals escorted D.S. to Robinson's office. When they entered the office, a Dade County Public School Police Officer was sitting at Robinson's desk doing paperwork. He continued his work as Robinson told the juvenile that she believed that he possessed contraband and told the juvenile to empty his pockets on a table. *After* D.S. placed a plastic bag with marijuana on the table, Robinson asked the school police officer to come forward. Robinson informed the school police officer that the juvenile had possessed marijuana, which violated public school rules.

The next day, the State filed a Petition for Delinquency against D.S., charging him with possession of marijuana in a public middle school. The juvenile denied the charge and moved to suppress the marijuana, arguing that the school search required probable cause because a school police officer was present in the room where the search was conducted. On February 21, 1996, the trial court granted the motion to suppress, finding that Robinson had a reasonable belief that the juvenile possessed drugs, but that the search required probable cause because a police officer was present, and that the search was not supported by probable cause. The State appeals this order.

In granting the motion to suppress, the trial court erred for three significant reasons, any one of which, considered alone, would require reversal.

First, the trial court ruled that the fact that the search was conducted in the presence of a school board police officer required probable cause to justify the search.

However, the fact that the school police officer was coincidentally inside Robinson's office doing paper work does not mean that he directed, participated, or acquiesced in the search. In other words, it was error for the trial court to require probable cause to support the search because the officer did not participate in the search.

Second, the appropriate requirement that should have been applied herein, is *reasonable suspicion,* the standard applicable to school officials.

The majority of decisions filed after the *T.L.O.* opinion, which deal with police officers in school settings, have been summarized by the Illinois Supreme Court:

> Where school officials initiate the search or police involvement is minimal, most courts have held that the reasonable suspicion test obtains. The same is true in cases involving school police or liaison officers acting on their own authority. However, where outside police officers initiate a search, or where school officials

act at the behest of law enforcement agencies, the probable cause standard has been applied.

People v. Dilworth. We adopt the above language from *Dilworth* and hold that school board police officers, who participate in searches initiated by school officials, or who act on their own authority, need only *reasonable suspicion* to justify a search.

We specifically hold that a search conducted by a *school* police officer only requires *reasonable suspicion* in order to legally support the search, as distinguished from the probable cause that is usually required to support a search conducted, away from the school property, by an *outside* police officer who is employed by a municipal or county governmental entity unrelated to the school district or its employees and officials. Consequently, even if the school police officer had directed, participated, or acquiesced in the search herein, only *reasonable suspicion,* rather than probable cause, would have been required to justify the search herein, since the *school* police officer is a school official who is employed by the district School Board.

Third, and finally, we find that the record in this case contains more than ample *probable cause,* if such a standard were to be required herein, to support the legality of the search that took place in this case.

Accordingly, and for each of the reasons discussed above, the trial court was in error in suppressing the evidence. This cause is remanded with directions to deny the defendant's motion to suppress and for further proceedings consistent herewith.

Reversed and remanded with directions.

Holdings of *State v. D.S.:* The court held that a search conducted by a school police officer only requires reasonable suspicion in order to legally support the search, as distinguished from the probable cause that is usually required to support a search conducted, away from the school property, by an outside police officer who is employed by a municipal or county governmental entity unrelated to the school district or its employees and officials. The court held that this would be true even if the school police officer had directed, participated, or acquiesced in the search "since the school police officer is a school official who is employed by the district School Board."

Discussion Questions

Does this court hold that any search by an SRO automatically only requires the "reasonable suspicion" standard of *T.L.O.?*

Why does this court make a distinction between a SCHOOL police officer and an OUTSIDE police officer? Is there really a difference? Does the constitution make such a differentiation?

Patman v. State: In *Patman v. State,* the Georgia appellate court was faced with a case where an officer of the local police department who was working a special detail at Clarke Central High School was alerted by the school secretary that a student (Patman) came to school smelling of marijuana. The officer ultimately searched the student and found eight individually wrapped packages of marijuana. The student was charged with possession of marijuana with the intent to distribute. The student filed a motion to suppress the evidence arguing that the search violated his Fourth Amendment rights.

As you read *Patman v. State,* look for the following:

1. Consider why the court summarily held that a search by a law enforcement officer assigned to a school must meet the traditional standards of the Fourth Amendment (requiring probable cause) rather than the more relaxed standards imposed on school authorities.

2. Consider whether the mere fact that the police officer was an employee of the police department rather than the school was dispositive of the court's decision in this case.

Patman v. State

244 Ga. App. 833 (2000)

Following a bench trial, high school student Travarous Patman was found guilty of possession of marijuana with intent to distribute. In his sole enumeration of error on appeal, Patman contends the trial court erred in failing to suppress the evidence of the marijuana, asserting that the police officer lacked authority to search him. Patman's claim of error lacks merit, and we affirm.

The record demonstrates that on March 12, 1998, Officer Dale Pope of the Athens-Clarke County Police Department was working a special detail at Clarke Central High School. At 10:00 a.m., Mildred Huff, the school secretary, told Pope that high school student Patman, who had arrived late to school, smelled of marijuana.

Pope followed Patman down a hallway and stopped him. After he stopped Patman, Pope smelled "a strong odor of marijuana." For safety purposes, Pope frisked Patman to check for weapons, and he felt several packages that he described as "little stamp bags" in Patman's jacket pocket. Because Pope knew that such bags were used to package marijuana and because Patman smelled of marijuana, Pope believed Patman had marijuana in his pocket. Pope then asked Patman what was in his pocket, and he responded, "Pope, come on and let me slide." Pope, who viewed Patman's statement as a confession, reached into Patman's pocket and removed eight individually wrapped bags of marijuana.

Prior to trial, Patman moved to suppress the marijuana evidence, arguing that the search that yielded the drugs "was conducted without probable cause, and without a reasonable, articulable suspicion that [Patman] was either armed or dangerous, and without [Patman's] consent." The trial court denied the motion, and Patman was convicted.

Although students are not stripped of their constitutional rights upon entering school, a student does not enjoy the same degree of privacy while on school property that he would enjoy elsewhere. A student's interest in privacy must be balanced against "the substantial interest of teachers and administrators in maintaining discipline in the classroom and on school grounds." Such discipline is necessary to provide students with a safe and secure school environment. Accordingly, the Fourth Amendment permits school officials to search students based upon circumstances which do not rise to the level of probable cause. The legality of a search of a student depends simply on the reasonableness, under all the circumstances, of the search. In Georgia, school officials may search "subject only to the most minimal restraints necessary to insure that students are not whimsically stripped of personal privacy and subjected to petty tyranny."

If Patman had been searched by a school official, there is no question that the search would be considered reasonable under the circumstances. Patman smelled of marijuana, which gave rise to suspicion that he had recently smoked marijuana. Moreover, when Pope asked Patman what was in his pocket, Patman's request to "let [him] slide," was, if not a confession, at the very least incriminating. However, Patman was not searched by a school official, but by a police officer. Unlike a school official, a police officer must have probable cause to search a suspect.

Nevertheless, we agree that the trial court did not err in denying Patman's motion to suppress. The odor of marijuana is one factor that may be considered in determining whether, under the totality of the circumstances, an officer had probable cause to institute a search. In this case, the totality of the circumstances gave rise to probable cause. As noted previously, Pope smelled marijuana on Patman, which gave rise to reasonable suspicion that he had recently smoked marijuana. Pope then patted Patman and felt what he believed to be packages of marijuana in Patman's pocket. When he asked Patman what was in the pocket, Patman's request to "let [him] slide" suggested that he had something incriminating in his pocket. Taken together, the circumstances establish probable cause to search Patman, and the trial court did not err in denying his motion to suppress.

Judgment affirmed.

Holdings of *Patman v. State:* The court held that, unlike a school official, a police officer must have probable cause to search a suspect. However, in this case, the court found that the police officer did have probable cause for the search.

Discussion Questions

Does this court hold that ANY search by a police officer at a school requires probable cause?

The court here finds that probable cause existed. If this were an adult on the street, would that also be true or did the court accept a "lower level" of probable cause to support the search because it was at school?

Cason v. Cook: In *Cason v. Cook,* the federal court was faced with a § 1983 civil lawsuit concerning a search of her person and her possessions by school officials with the assistance of a school resource officer. In this case, the officer was a police officer who had been assigned to North High School as a liaison officer pursuant to an established police liaison program between the Des Moines Police Department and the school district. The liaison program was funded jointly by the police department and the school district. The officer did not wear a police uniform and drove an unmarked automobile. The liaison officer was instructed to cooperate with the school officials. Students suspected of several thefts were taken out of class, questioned and searched by a school official who had asked the liaison officer to join her in the process. The bulk of the interaction was conducted by the school official with the officer merely present. Each of the girls was suspended from school and after meeting with Ms. Jones no further action was taken.

As you read *Cason v. Cook,* look for the following:

1. Consider what impact the connection between the school and the local police department has on the outcome of this case.

2. Consider whether or not the result would be different if the liaison officer rather than the school official had played the primary role in the investigation.

3. Look for any clues of what would have to occur for a search of a student by a school official working in conjunction with law enforcement personnel to rise to a level where the standard applicable to law enforcement would be required.

Cason v. Cook

810 F.2d 188 (8th Cir. 1987)

Shy Cason appeals from the district court's grant of a directed verdict in favor of the appellees. Shy brought this action pursuant to 42 U.S.C. section 1983 alleging that her constitutional rights to due process and to be free from unreasonable search and seizure were violated when she was removed from her high school classroom, questioned, and both her person and possessions were searched by the appellees Cook and Jones. The district court directed a verdict at the close of all the evidence after determining that there was no constitutional violation of the appellant's rights. We affirm.

Viewing the evidence in the light most favorable to Shy, the stipulated facts and the record evidence show that on May 17, 1983, Shy was a student at North High School in Des Moines, Iowa. At approximately 12:20 p.m. on that date, a student approached the appellee Connie Cook, the vice-principal of North High School, and told her that her locker had been broken into and that she was missing a pair of sweatpants and a duffle bag. She also reported that a friend was missing a pair of sweatpants. At approximately 12:40 p.m., another student approached Ms. Cook and reported that her wallet and coin purse had been taken from her gym locker. The student reported that the wallet contained $65 along with several credit cards. Ms. Cook recorded a detailed description of the missing items.

Standing with Ms. Cook when these reports were made was the appellee Wanda Jones, a police officer who had been assigned to North High School as a liaison officer pursuant to an established police liaison program between the Des Moines Police Department and the school district. The liaison program is funded jointly by the police department and the school district. The officer does not wear a police uniform and drives an unmarked automobile. The liaison officer is instructed to cooperate with the school officials.

After receiving the reports of stolen items, Ms. Cook decided to investigate the alleged thefts and asked Ms. Jones if she would accompany her to the locker room. Ms. Cook interviewed several students in the locker room and was supplied with the names of four students who had been seen in the locker area around the time of the thefts: Shy Cason, Jerrie Harvey, Monica Harvey and Tabatha Prather. These four students did not have permission to be in the locker area at this time nor were they assigned to the gym class of the prior period. Ms. Cook also recalled having seen Shy, Jerrie and Monica together in the lobby just prior to receiving the reports of the thefts.

Ms. Cook and Ms. Jones then proceeded to the office where Ms. Cook checked the schedules of the four students. Ms. Cook again asked Ms. Jones to accompany her as she interviewed each of the students. Jerrie was removed from her classroom by Ms. Cook and was taken into an empty classroom where she was questioned. Ms. Jones did not participate in this questioning and in fact, remained in the hallway during this time period. Shy and Monica were then removed from their classroom and taken into an empty restroom. Shy testified that Monica remained outside and that she was taken into the restroom and that Ms. Cook locked the door. Ms. Jones was also inside the locked restroom but again did not participate in any questioning of Shy.

Ms. Cook informed Shy why she was being questioned and allowed Shy an opportunity to respond. After Shy admitted being in the locker room but denied having any of the missing items, Ms. Cook told Shy that she was going to search her purse. Ms. Cook then took Shy's purse and dumped the contents onto a shelf in the restroom. In Shy's purse was a coin purse that matched exactly the description of the missing coin purse. After this purse was found, Shy testified that Ms. Jones conducted a pat-down search of Shy from her shoulders to her toes while Shy was made to stand against the wall with her hands up and legs spread.

Monica and Shy were then taken to the office area and on the way, Shy was asked by Ms. Cook to open her locker and a search of the locker was conducted by Ms. Cook. At the office, Monica and Shy were placed in separate rooms with Ms. Jones remaining with Monica while Ms. Cook continued to question Shy. Ms. Jones did not participate in the questioning of either Shy or Monica at this point. It was learned that Shy and Jerrie were in fact involved with the thefts and Jerrie was summoned to come to the office. Ms. Jones did participate in a joint interview with Shy and Jerrie and when the two girls could not agree on the events that had transpired in the locker room, Ms. Jones presented each girl with a juvenile appearance card. Juvenile appearance cards are utilized by the police liaison program whenever possible in lieu of an arrest. The card required each of the girls and their parents to report to Ms. Jones' office at the police station on May 19, 1983.

Shy's mother was not made aware of the events of this day until she arrived to pick up Shy after school. No attempt was made to contact Shy's mother prior to any questioning or the search of Shy and her possessions. While at school, Shy was not informed of a right to remain silent or of a right to counsel. Both Shy and her mother signed a waiver and consent form before they visited with Ms. Jones at her office on the 19th. Each of the girls was suspended from school and after meeting with Ms. Jones no further action was taken.

This is the precise question that is presented to this court by the case at bar: Whether the reasonableness standard should apply when a school official acts in conjunction with a police liaison officer. The district court found that the reasonableness standard was the correct standard and that the appellee Cook had met this standard and thus there was no violation of the appellant's constitutional rights. We agree.

There is no evidence to support the proposition that the activities were at *the behest of* a law enforcement agency. The uncontradicted evidence showed that Ms. Cook, the school official, conducted the investigation of the thefts that had been reported to her. Ms. Jones' involvement was limited to a pat-down search conducted after a coin purse matching the description of the one stolen was found and to briefly interviewing Shy and Jerrie and presenting juvenile appearance cards to the girls. At most, then, this case represents a police officer working *in conjunction with* school officials.

The imposition of a probable cause warrant requirement based on the limited involvement of Ms. Jones would not serve the interest of preserving swift and informal disciplinary procedures in schools. Ms. Jones did not conduct any of the initial interviews of the students and participated in a pat-down search only after evidence was discovered. Ms. Cook, on the other hand, made the initial determination to investigate the reported thefts and conducted the investigation. This school official procured the names of four students who had been seen in the locker room area at an unscheduled time and without permission. Ms. Cook also recalled having personally observed these same students together in the hall just prior to receiving the reports of the thefts. The students were removed from their classrooms by Ms. Cook and each was provided with an explanation as to the reason for their removal and was provided with an opportunity to respond prior to any search.

It was Ms. Cook who conducted the search of Shy's purse which led to the discovery of the coin purse. It was only after this discovery that Ms. Jones conducted a limited pat-down search of Shy. The only other involvement of the police liaison officer occurred when the students were unable to agree on the events that had transpired in the locker room. This involvement was limited to some questioning and the issuance of juvenile appearance cards.

It is clear that the correct standard to apply under the circumstances presented in this case is the standard enunciated by the Court in *T.L.O.*: Whether the search was reasonable under all of the circumstances. Based on the foregoing discussion of the facts, the initial search of the appellant's purse was based on a reasonable suspicion that Shy Cason had been involved in a violation of school rules and of the criminal law. The subsequent pat-down search was made when this suspicion was increased due to the finding of physical evidence in the appellant's possession. In addition, the scope of the search was reasonable. The theft victim had reported $65 as missing along with her wallet. Due to the nature of this missing item, patting down the appellant was not "excessively intrusive in light of the age and sex of the student and the nature of the infraction."

We do not hold that a search of a student by a school official working in conjunction with law enforcement personnel could never rise to a constitutional violation, but only that under the record as presented to the court, no such violation occurred here. The district court did not err in granting a directed verdict at the close of all the evidence.

Accordingly, the order of the district court is affirmed.

Holdings of *Cason v. Cook*: The court held that there is no evidence to support the proposition that the activities were at *the behest of* a law enforcement agency. At most, this case represents a police officer working *in conjunction with* school officials. The court held that, under such circumstances, the Fourth Amendment standards applicable to school authorities (reasonable suspicion) are applicable.

Discussion Questions

How important is it to the outcome of the case that "The Liaison program is jointly funded by the police department and the school district. The officer does not wear a police uniform and drives an unmarked automobile. The liaison officer is instructed to cooperate with school officials."?

Would the outcome have been different if the officer had participated in the investigation and the questioning?

Doesn't the mere presence of the police officer have some effect on the situation?

Key Concepts: Police & Resource Officers at School

- *T.L.O.* reserved the issue of what standards (reasonable suspicion vs. probable cause) would apply to a search of a student conducted by school officials who were working at the behest of or in conjunction with law enforcement.

- Because of the presence of law enforcement officers in schools, courts have struggled with the issue of what standards should be applied to justify a search of a student in a school setting by law enforcement officers assigned to schools or to school officials conducting a search of a student in the presence of or at the request of law enforcement officials assigned to the school.

- Courts addressing this issue have examined many factors, including the funding of the school resource officer (SRO) position, the relationship between the SRO and school officials, as well as the role of the SRO in the particular search.

• Courts are more apt to apply the higher standards for justifying a search of a student when it appears that there is either an explicit or implicit understanding that the relationship between the SRO and school authorities is intentionally used to avoid the higher standard imposed on law enforcement.

Practical Questions: Police & Resource Officers at School

1. You have been asked by a local school board to draft a policy and procedures agreement with the local police force for providing school resource officers from the police force to be present at the middle and high schools during all school hours.

What policies and procedures should be considered relative to the roles of school officials and the school resource officers relative to the rights and duties concerning searches of students?

2. You represent a student who has been charged with possession of a controlled substance at a school with the intent to deliver. You discover that a uniformed police officer (called a "school resource officer") is assigned full-time at the school, although his salary is paid 100% by the local police force. That officer maintains his own office at the school. On the day of the incident, officials were told by 3 students that they had seen your client selling drugs in the school bathroom that day. The school officials reported the information (without identifying the names of the reporting students) to the school resource officer who asked school officials to remove your client from his class and bring him to the officer's office. School officials removed your client from class, took him to the officer's office and left. The officer searched your client, found three bindles of heroin and immediately arrested him. What standard of proof was needed to support the officer's search of your client?

Simulation Exercise IV

Characters: Jimmie Metcalf (school age youth) and the attorney.

Facts: Jimmie Metcalf is sent to your office by his parents for legal advice. He tells you that he attends a public school where he has a reputation as a "stoner." You ask him if the reputation is deserved, and he smiles and says, "Well, yeah." He tells you that he normally wears his hair in "dreads," wears almost exclusively Bob Marley T-Shirts, and has a NORML [National Organization for the Reform of Marijuana Laws] bumper sticker on his car and on all of his notebooks. He says that the principal, Mr. Turnbill, has notified him that they will search his backpack and his pockets at school next Thursday, which is April 20th. He was told that the school resource office (on assignment from the local police department) will be present during the search. He asks, "Can they do that just because it's me and its 4-20?"

Simulation: The exercise is to interview Jimmie asking any other questions to provide any additional information needed to answer his questions. Once the attorney has enough information to answer Jimmie's questions, the attorney shall give Jimmie advice, recommendations and predictions of what will happen.

H. Drug Testing in School

Overview: In *T.L.O.*, the court required an individualized reasonable suspicion to justify a search of a student by school authorities. As a result of the proliferation of the use and trafficking of drugs in schools, some schools have attempted to address this problem by requiring various forms of drug testing. Courts have always held that a drug test by the government is a "search" and, as such courts have been asked to determine whether or not there must be an "individualized" approach for the requirement of drug testing or whether or not "blanket" drug testing can be required. Furthermore, courts have had to decide what provisions of a drug-testing program are necessary to minimize the intrusion of such procedure.

Vernonia School District 475 v. Acton: In *Vernonia School District 475 v. Acton,* the Supreme Court was faced with a civil lawsuit asking the court to declare the drug-testing policy of the School district imposed on athletes in the schools as unconstitutional. The school district provided evidence that drug usage had increased among its students, that the school's athletes were the "leaders" in the school drug culture, and that athletes were at significantly enhanced risk for injury if using drugs. The school's policy imposed substantial procedural safeguards to provide privacy to a student submitting to a urine test and for the protection of the information gleaned from the tests.

As you read *Vernonia School District 475 v. Acton,* look for the following:

1. Consider what factors considered by the court to justify the drug tests are unique to imposing the testing requirement on only athletes as opposed to the student body as a whole.

2. Consider what procedural protections of the Vernonia School District were essential to successfully minimize the intrusion on the students involved.

3. Look for anything in the school's policies that impose additional (and perhaps unnecessary) intrusions on the privacy interests of the students.

Vernonia School District 475 v. Acton
515 U.S. 646 (1995)

Justice SCALIA delivered the opinion of the Court.

The Student Athlete Drug Policy adopted by School District 47J in the town of Vernonia, Oregon, authorizes random urinalysis drug testing of students who participate in the District's school athletics programs. We granted certiorari to decide whether this violates the Fourth and Fourteenth Amendments to the United States Constitution.

Petitioner Vernonia School District 47J (District) operates one high school and three grade schools in the logging community of Vernonia, Oregon. As elsewhere in small-town America, school sports play a prominent role in the town's life, and student athletes are admired in their schools and in the community.

Drugs had not been a major problem in Vernonia schools. In the mid-to-late 1980s, however, teachers and administrators observed a sharp increase in drug use. Students began to speak out about their attraction to the drug culture, and to boast that there was nothing the school could do about it. Along with more drugs came more disciplinary problems. Between 1988 and 1989 the number of disciplinary referrals in Vernonia schools rose to more than twice the number reported in the early 1980s, and several students were suspended. Students became increasingly rude during class; outbursts of profane language became common.

Not only were student athletes included among the drug users but, as the District Court found, athletes were the leaders of the drug culture. This caused the District's administrators particular concern, since drug use increases the risk of sports-related injury.

Expert testimony at the trial confirmed the deleterious effects of drugs on motivation, memory, judgment, reaction, coordination, and performance. The high school football and wrestling coach witnessed a severe sternum injury suffered by a wrestler, and various omissions of safety procedures and misexecutions by football players, all attributable in his belief to the effects of drug use.

Initially, the District responded to the drug problem by offering special classes, speakers, and presentations designed to deter drug use. It even brought in a specially trained dog to detect drugs, but the drug problem persisted.

At that point, District officials began considering a drug-testing program. They held a parent "input night" to discuss the proposed Student Athlete Drug Policy (Policy), and the parents in attendance gave their unanimous approval. The school board approved the Policy for implementation in the fall of 1989. Its expressed purpose is to prevent student athletes from using drugs, to protect their health and safety, and to provide drug users with assistance programs.

The Policy applies to all students participating in interscholastic athletics. Students wishing to play sports must sign a form consenting to the testing and must obtain the written consent of their parents. Athletes are tested at the beginning of the season for their sport. In addition, once each week of the season the names of the athletes are placed in a "pool" from which a student, with the supervision of two adults, blindly draws the names of 10% of the athletes for random testing. Those selected are notified and tested that same day, if possible.

The student to be tested completes a specimen control form which bears an assigned number. Prescription medications that the student is taking must be identified by providing a copy of the prescription or a doctor's authorization. The student then enters an empty locker room accompanied by an adult monitor of the same sex. Each boy selected produces a sample at a urinal, remaining fully clothed with his back to the monitor, who stands approximately 12 to 15 feet behind the student. Monitors may (though do not always) watch the student while he produces the sample, and they listen for normal sounds of urination. Girls produce samples in an enclosed bathroom stall, so that they can be heard but not observed. After the sample is produced, it is given to the monitor, who checks it for temperature and tampering and then transfers it to a vial.

The samples are sent to an independent laboratory, which routinely tests them for amphetamines, cocaine, and marijuana. Other drugs, such as LSD, may be screened at the request of the District, but the identity of a particular student does not determine which drugs will be tested. The laboratory's procedures are 99.94% accurate. The District follows strict procedures regarding the chain of custody and access to test results. The laboratory does not know the identity of the students whose samples it tests. It is authorized to mail written test reports only to the superintendent and to provide test results to District personnel by telephone only after the requesting official recites a code confirming his authority. Only the superintendent, principals, vice-principals, and athletic directors have access to test results, and the results are not kept for more than one year.

If a sample tests positive, a second test is administered as soon as possible to confirm the result. If the second test is negative, no further action is taken. If the second test is positive, the athlete's parents are notified, and the school principal convenes a meeting with the student and his parents, at which the student is given the option of (1) participating for six weeks in an assistance program that includes weekly urinalysis, or (2) suffering suspension from athletics for the remainder of the current season and the next athletic season. The student is then retested prior to the start of the next athletic season for which he or she is eligible. The Policy states that a second offense results in automatic imposition of option (2); a third offense in suspension for the remainder of the current season and the next two athletic seasons.

In the fall of 1991, respondent James Acton, then a seventh grader, signed up to play football at one of the District's grade schools. He was denied participation, however, because he and his parents refused to sign the testing consent forms. The Actons filed suit, seeking declaratory and injunctive relief from enforcement of the Policy on the grounds that it violated the Fourth and Fourteenth Amendments to the United States Constitution and Article I, §9, of the Oregon Constitution.

Traditionally at common law, and still today, unemancipated minors lack some of the most fundamental rights of self-determination — including even the right of liberty in its narrow sense, i.e., the right to come and go at will. They are subject, even as to their physical freedom, to the control of their parents or guardians. When parents place minor children in private schools for their education, the teachers and administrators of those schools stand in loco parentis over the children entrusted to them. In fact, the tutor or schoolmaster is the very prototype of that status.

In *T.L.O.* we rejected the notion that public schools, like private schools, exercise only parental power over their students, which of course is not subject to constitutional constraints. Such a view of things, we said, "is not entirely 'consonant with compulsory education laws,'" and is inconsistent with our prior decisions treating school officials as state actors for purposes of the Due Process and Free Speech Clauses. But while denying that the State's power over schoolchildren is formally no more than the delegated power of their parents, *T.L.O.* did not deny, but indeed emphasized, that the nature of that power is custodial and tutelary, permitting a degree of supervision and control that could not be exercised over free adults. Thus, while children assuredly do not "shed their constitutional rights ... at the schoolhouse gate," the nature of those rights is what is appropriate for children in school.

Fourth Amendment rights, no less than First and Fourteenth Amendment rights, are different in public schools than elsewhere; the "reasonableness" inquiry cannot disregard the schools' custodial and tutelary responsibility for children.

Legitimate privacy expectations are even less with regard to student athletes. School sports are not for the bashful. They require "suiting up" before each practice or event, and showering and changing afterwards. Public school locker rooms, the usual sites for these activities, are not notable for the privacy they afford. The locker rooms in Vernonia are typical: No individual dressing rooms are provided; shower heads are lined up along a wall, unseparated by any sort of partition or curtain; not even all the toilet stalls have doors.

There is an additional respect in which school athletes have a reduced expectation of privacy. By choosing to "go out for the team," they voluntarily subject themselves to a degree of regulation even higher than that imposed on students generally. In Vernonia's public schools, they must submit to a preseason physical exam (James testified that his included the giving of a urine sample), they must acquire adequate insurance coverage or sign an insurance waiver, maintain a minimum grade point average, and comply with any "rules of conduct, dress, training hours and related matters as may be established for each sport by the head coach and athletic director with the principal's approval." Somewhat like adults who choose to participate in a "closely regulated industry," students who voluntarily participate in school athletics have reason to expect intrusions upon normal rights and privileges, including privacy.

Having considered the scope of the legitimate expectation of privacy at issue here, we turn next to the character of the intrusion that is complained of. We recognized in Skinner that collecting the samples for urinalysis intrudes upon "an excretory function traditionally shielded by great privacy." We noted, however, that the degree of intrusion depends upon the manner in which production of the urine sample is monitored. Under the District's Policy, male students produce samples at a urinal along a wall. They remain fully clothed and are only observed from behind, if at all. Female students produce samples in an enclosed stall, with a female monitor standing outside listening only for sounds of tampering. These conditions are nearly identical to those typically encountered in public restrooms, which men, women, and especially schoolchildren use daily. Under such conditions, the privacy interests compromised by the process of obtaining the urine sample are in our view negligible.

The other privacy-invasive aspect of urinalysis is, of course, the information it discloses concerning the state of the subject's body, and the materials he has ingested. In this regard it is significant that the tests at issue here look only for drugs, and not for whether the student is, for example, epileptic, pregnant, or diabetic. Moreover, the drugs for which the samples are screened are standard, and do not vary according to the identity of the student. And finally, the results of the tests are disclosed only to a limited class of school personnel who have a need to know; and they are not turned over to law enforcement authorities or used for any internal disciplinary function.

Respondents argue, however, that the District's Policy is in fact more intrusive than this suggests, because it requires the students, if they are to avoid sanctions for a falsely positive test, to identify in advance prescription medications they are taking. We agree that this raises some cause for concern.

The General Authorization Form that respondents refused to sign, which refusal was the basis for James's exclusion from the sports program, said only (in relevant part): "I ... authorize the Vernonia School District to conduct a test on a urine specimen which I provide to test for drugs and/or alcohol use. I also authorize the release of information concerning the results of such a test to the Vernonia School District and to the parents and/or guardians of the student." While the practice of the District seems to have been to have a school official take medication information from the student at the time of the test, that practice is not set forth in, or required by, the Policy, which says simply: "Student athletes who ... are or have been taking prescription medication must provide verification (either by a copy of the prescription or by doctor's authorization) prior to being tested." It may well be that, if and when James was selected for random testing at a time that he was taking medication, the School District would have permitted him to provide the requested information in a confidential manner—for example, in a sealed envelope delivered to the testing lab. Nothing in the Policy contradicts that, and when respondents choose, in effect, to challenge the Policy on its face, we will not assume the worst. Accordingly, we reach the same conclusion as in Skinner: that the invasion of privacy was not significant.

Finally, we turn to consider the nature and immediacy of the governmental concern at issue here, and the efficacy of this means for meeting it.

That the nature of the concern is important—indeed, perhaps compelling—can hardly be doubted. School years are the time when the physical, psychological, and addictive effects of drugs are most severe. "Maturing nervous systems are more critically impaired by intoxicants than mature ones are; childhood losses in learning are lifelong and profound"; "children grow chemically dependent more quickly than adults, and their record of recovery is depressingly poor." And of course the effects of a drug-infested school are visited not just upon the users, but upon the entire student body and faculty, as the educational process is disrupted. In the present case, moreover, the necessity for the State to act is magnified by the fact that this evil is being visited not just upon individuals at large, but upon children for whom it has undertaken a special responsibility of care and direction. Finally, it must not be lost sight of that this program is directed more narrowly to drug use by school athletes, where the risk of immediate physical harm to the drug user or those with whom he is playing his sport is particularly high. Apart from psychological effects, which include impairment of judgment, slow reaction time, and a lessening of the perception of pain, the particular drugs screened by the District's Policy have been demonstrated to pose substantial physical risks to athletes.

As to the efficacy of this means for addressing the problem: It seems to us self-evident that a drug problem largely fueled by the "role model" effect of athletes' drug use, and of particular danger to athletes, is effectively addressed by making sure that athletes do not use drugs.

Taking into account all the factors we have considered above—the decreased expectation of privacy, the relative unobtrusiveness of the search, and the severity of the need met by the search—we conclude Vernonia's Policy is reasonable and hence constitutional.

We caution against the assumption that suspicionless drug testing will readily pass constitutional muster in other contexts. The most significant element in this case is the first we discussed: that the Policy was undertaken in furtherance of the government's responsibilities, under a public school system, as guardian and tutor of children entrusted to its care.

We may note that the primary guardians of Vernonia's schoolchildren appear to agree. The record shows no objection to this districtwide program by any parents other than the couple before us here—even though, as we have described, a public meeting was held to obtain parents' views. We find insufficient basis to contradict the judgment of Vernonia's parents, its school board, and the District Court, as to what was reasonably in the interest of these children under the circumstances.

The Ninth Circuit held that Vernonia's Policy not only violated the Fourth Amendment, but also, by reason of that violation, contravened Article I, § 9, of the Oregon Constitution. Our conclusion that the former holding was in error means that the latter holding rested on a flawed premise. We therefore vacate the judgment, and remand the case to the Court of Appeals for further proceedings consistent with this opinion.

It is so ordered.

Justice GINSBURG, concurring.

The Court constantly observes that the School District's drug-testing policy applies only to students who voluntarily participate in interscholastic athletics. Correspondingly, the most severe sanction allowed under the District's policy is suspension from extracurricular athletic programs. I comprehend the Court's opinion as reserving the question whether the District, on no more than the showing made here, constitutionally could impose routine drug testing not only on those seeking to engage with others in team sports, but on all students required to attend school.

Justice O'CONNOR, with whom Justice STEVENS and Justice SOUTER join, dissenting.

The population of our Nation's public schools, grades 7 through 12, numbers around 18 million. By the reasoning of today's decision, the millions of these students who participate in interscholastic sports, an overwhelming majority of whom have given school officials no reason whatsoever to suspect they use drugs at school, are open to an intrusive bodily search.

In justifying this result, the Court dispenses with a requirement of individualized suspicion on considered policy grounds. First, it explains that precisely because every student athlete is being tested, there is no concern that school officials might act arbitrarily in choosing whom to test. Second, a broad-based search regime, the Court reasons, dilutes the accusatory nature of the search. In making these policy arguments, of course, the Court sidesteps powerful, countervailing privacy concerns. Blanket searches, because they can involve "thousands or millions" of searches, "pos[e] a greater threat to liberty" than do suspicion-based ones, which "affec[t] one person at a time." Searches based on individualized suspicion also afford potential targets considerable control over whether they will, in fact, be searched because a person can avoid such a search by not acting in an objectively suspicious way. And given that the surest way to avoid acting suspiciously is to avoid the underlying wrongdoing, the costs of such a regime, one would think, are minimal.

But whether a blanket search is "better," than a regime based on individualized suspicion is not a debate in which we should engage. In my view, it is not open to judges or government officials to decide on policy grounds which is better and which is worse. For most of our constitutional history, mass, suspicionless searches have been generally considered per se unreasonable within the meaning of the Fourth Amendment. And we have allowed exceptions in recent years only where it has been clear that a suspicion-based regime would be ineffectual. Because that is not the case here, I dissent.

The view that mass, suspicionless searches, however evenhanded, are generally unreasonable remains inviolate in the criminal law enforcement context.

Thus, it remains the law that the police cannot, say, subject to drug testing every person entering or leaving a certain drug-ridden neighborhood in order to find evidence of crime. And this is true even though it is hard to think of a more compelling government interest than the need to fight the scourge of drugs on our streets and in our neighborhoods. Nor could it be otherwise, for if being evenhanded were enough to justify evaluating a search regime under an open-ended balancing test, the Warrant Clause, which presupposes that there is some category of searches for which individualized suspicion is nonnegotiable ... would be a dead letter.

One searches today's majority opinion in vain for recognition that history and precedent establish that individualized suspicion is "usually required" under the Fourth Amendment (regardless of whether a warrant and probable cause are also required) and that, in the area of intrusive personal searches, the only recognized exception is for situations in which a suspicion-based scheme would be likely ineffectual. Far from acknowledging anything special about individualized suspicion, the Court treats a suspicion-based regime as if it were just any run-of-the-mill, less intrusive alternative—that is, an alternative that officials may bypass if the lesser intrusion, in their reasonable estimation, is outweighed by policy concerns unrelated to practicability.

The great irony of this case is that most (though not all) of the evidence the District introduced to justify its suspicionless drug testing program consisted of first- or second-hand stories of particular, identifiable students acting in ways that plainly gave rise to reasonable suspicion of in-school drug use—and thus that would have justified a drug-related search under our *T.L.O.* decision. Small groups of students, for example, were observed by a teacher "passing joints back and forth" across the street at a restaurant before school and during school hours. Another group was caught skipping school and using drugs at one of the students' houses. Several students actually admitted their drug use to school officials (some of them being caught with marijuana pipes). One student presented himself to his teacher as "clearly obviously inebriated" and had to be sent home. Still another was observed dancing and singing at the top of his voice in the back of the classroom; when the teacher asked what was going on, he replied, "Well, I'm just high on life." To take a final example, on a certain road trip, the school wrestling coach smelled marijuana smoke in a motel room occupied by four wrestlers, an observation that (after some questioning) would probably have given him reasonable suspicion to test one or all of them.

In light of all this evidence of drug use by particular students, there is a substantial basis for concluding that a vigorous regime of suspicion-based testing (for which the District appears already to have rules in place) would have gone a long way toward solving Vernonia's school drug problem while preserving the Fourth Amendment rights of James Acton and others like him.

I recognize that a suspicion-based scheme, even where reasonably effective in controlling in-school drug use, may not be as effective as a mass, suspicionless testing regime. In one sense, that is obviously true — just as it is obviously true that suspicion-based law enforcement is not as effective as mass, suspicionless enforcement might be. "But there is nothing new in the realization" that Fourth Amendment protections come with a price.

The principal counterargument to all this, central to the Court's opinion, is that the Fourth Amendment is more lenient with respect to school searches. That is no doubt correct, for, as the Court explains schools have traditionally had special guardian-like responsibilities for children that necessitate a degree of constitutional leeway. This principle explains the considerable Fourth Amendment leeway we gave school officials in *T.L.O.* In that case, we held that children at school do not enjoy two of the Fourth Amendment's traditional categorical protections against unreasonable searches and seizures: the warrant requirement and the probable cause requirement.

The instant case, however, asks whether the Fourth Amendment is even more lenient than that, i.e., whether it is so lenient that students may be deprived of the Fourth Amendment's only remaining, and most basic, categorical protection: its strong preference for an individualized suspicion requirement, with its accompanying antipathy toward personally intrusive, blanket searches of mostly innocent people.

By contrast, intrusive, blanket searches of schoolchildren, most of whom are innocent, for evidence of serious wrongdoing are not part of any traditional school function of which I am aware. Indeed, many schools, like many parents, prefer to trust their children unless given reason to do otherwise. As James Acton's father said on the witness stand, "[suspicionless testing] sends a message to children that are trying to be responsible citizens ... that they have to prove that they're innocent..., and I think that kind of sets a bad tone for citizenship."

On this record, then, it seems to me that the far more reasonable choice would have been to focus on the class of students found to have violated published school rules against severe disruption in class and around campus — disruption that had a strong nexus to drug use, as the District established at trial. Such a choice would share two of the virtues of a suspicion-based regime: testing dramatically fewer students, tens as against hundreds, and giving students control, through their behavior, over the likelihood that they would be tested. Moreover, there would be a reduced concern for the accusatory nature of the search, because the Court's feared "badge of shame," would already exist, due to the antecedent accusation and finding of severe disruption.

Holdings of *Vernonia School District 475 v. Acton:* The court held that, based on a number of factors—the decreased expectation of privacy, the relative unobtrusiveness of the search, and the severity of the need met by the search—Vernonia's Policy is reasonable and constitutional. The court further found that students going out for sports have a decreased expectation of privacy, and that this decision should not be viewed supporting the assumption that "suspicionless drug testing will readily pass constitutional muster in other contexts."

Discussion Questions

Would the result for the majority have been different if positive drug tests were turned over to law enforcement?

How does this opinion differ from the *T.L.O.* case?

Would random drug testing be permissible under the majority opinion if applied to ALL students rather than just student athletes?

Board of Ed. of Independent Sch. Dist. v. Earls: In *Board of Ed. of Independent Sch. Dist. v. Earls,* the United States Supreme Court was faced with a § 1983 civil lawsuit alleging that the school district's drug-testing policy was unconstitutional. The drug-testing required all students who participate in competitive extracurricular activities to submit to drug testing. Under the Policy, students were required to take a drug test before participating in an extracurricular activity, were required to submit to random drug testing while participating in that activity, and were required agree to be tested at any time upon reasonable suspicion. The test results were not turned over to any law enforcement authority, nor would the test results lead to the imposition of discipline or have any academic consequence. Lindsay Earls was a member of the show choir, the marching band, the Academic Team, and the National Honor Society. The other plaintiff, Daniel James, sought to participate in the Academic Team.

As you read *Board of Ed. of Independent Sch. Dist. v. Earls,* look for the following:

1. Consider whether or not the school district identified any reason to single out students participating in extra-curricular activities for the drug-testing policy.

2. Look for anything in the record supporting the idea that drug usage in the Tecumseh schools was reaching levels warranting action by the schools authorities.

Board of Ed. of Independent Sch. Dist. v. Earls
536 U.S. 822 (2002)

Justice THOMAS delivered the opinion of the Court.

The Student Activities Drug Testing Policy implemented by the Board of Education of Independent School District No. 92 of Pottawatomie County (School District) requires all students who participate in competitive extracurricular activities to submit to drug testing. Because this Policy reasonably serves the School District's important interest in detecting and preventing drug use among its students, we hold that it is constitutional.

The city of Tecumseh, Oklahoma, is a rural community located approximately 40 miles southeast of Oklahoma City. The School District administers all Tecumseh public schools.

In the fall of 1998, the School District adopted the Student Activities Drug Testing Policy (Policy), which requires all middle and high school students to consent to drug testing in order to participate in any extracurricular activity. In practice, the Policy has been applied only to competitive extracurricular activities sanctioned by the Oklahoma Secondary Schools Activities Association, such as the Academic Team, Future Farmers of America, Future Homemakers of America, band, choir, pom-pom, cheerleading, and athletics. Under the Policy, students are required to take a drug test before participating in an extracurricular activity, must submit to random drug testing while participating in that activity, and must agree to be tested at any time upon reasonable suspicion. The urinalysis tests are designed to detect only the use of illegal drugs, including amphetamines, marijuana, cocaine, opiates, and barbiturates, not medical conditions or the presence of authorized prescription medications.

At the time of their suit, both respondents attended Tecumseh High School. Respondent Lindsay Earls was a member of the show choir, the marching band, the Academic Team, and the National Honor Society. Respondent Daniel James sought to participate in the Academic Team. Together with their parents, Earls and James brought a Rev. Stat. § 1979, 42 U.S.C. § 1983, action against the School District, challenging the Policy both on its face and as applied to their participation in extracurricular activities. They alleged that the Policy violates the Fourth Amendment as incorporated by the Fourteenth Amendment and requested injunctive and declarative relief. They also argued that the School District failed to identify a special need for testing students who participate in extracurricular activities, and that the "Drug Testing Policy neither addresses a proven problem nor promises to bring any benefit to students or the school."

Given that the School District's Policy is not in any way related to the conduct of criminal investigations, respondents do not contend that the School District requires probable cause before testing students for drug use. Respondents instead argue that drug testing must be based at least on some level of individualized suspicion. It is true that we generally determine the reasonableness of a search by balancing the nature of the intrusion on the individual's privacy against the promotion of legitimate governmental interests. But we have long held that "the Fourth Amendment imposes no irreducible requirement of [individualized] suspicion."

We first consider the nature of the privacy interest allegedly compromised by the drug testing.

Respondents argue that because children participating in nonathletic extracurricular activities are not subject to regular physicals and communal undress, they have a stronger expectation of privacy than the athletes tested in *Vernonia*. This distinction, however, was not essential to our decision in *Vernonia*, which depended primarily upon the school's custodial responsibility and authority.

In any event, students who participate in competitive extracurricular activities voluntarily subject themselves to many of the same intrusions on their privacy as do athletes. Some of these clubs and activities require occasional off-campus travel and communal undress. All of them have their own rules and requirements for participating students that do not apply to the student body as a whole.

Next, we consider the character of the intrusion imposed by the Policy.

Under the Policy, a faculty monitor waits outside the closed restroom stall for the student to produce a sample and must "listen for the normal sounds of urination in order to guard against tampered specimens and to insure an accurate chain of custody." The monitor then pours the sample into two bottles that are sealed and placed into a mailing pouch along with a consent form signed by the student. This procedure is virtually identical to that reviewed in *Vernonia*, except that it additionally protects privacy by allowing male students to produce their samples behind a closed stall. Given that we considered the method of collection in *Vernonia* a "negligible" intrusion, the method here is even less problematic.

In addition, the Policy clearly requires that the test results be kept in confidential files separate from a student's other educational records and released to school personnel only on a "need to know" basis.

Moreover, the test results are not turned over to any law enforcement authority. Nor do the test results here lead to the imposition of discipline or have any academic consequences. Rather, the only consequence of a failed drug test is to limit the student's privilege of participating in extracurricular activities. Indeed, a student may test positive for drugs twice and still be allowed to participate in extracurricular activities. After the first positive test, the school contacts the student's parent or guardian for a meeting. The student may continue to participate in the activity if within five days of the meeting the student shows proof of receiving drug counseling and submits to a second drug test in two weeks. For the second positive test, the student is suspended from participation in all extracurricular activities for 14 days, must complete four hours of substance abuse counseling, and must submit to monthly drug tests. Only after a third positive test will the student be suspended from participating in any extracurricular activity for the remainder of the school year, or 88 school days, whichever is longer.

Given the minimally intrusive nature of the sample collection and the limited uses to which the test results are put, we conclude that the invasion of students' privacy is not significant.

Finally, this Court must consider the nature and immediacy of the government's concerns and the efficacy of the Policy in meeting them. This Court has already articulated in detail the importance of the governmental concern in preventing drug use by schoolchildren. The drug abuse problem among our Nation's youth has hardly abated since *Vernonia* was decided in 1995. In fact, evidence suggests that it has only grown worse. As in *Vernonia*, "the necessity for the State to act is magnified by the fact that this evil is being visited not just upon individuals at large, but upon children for whom it has undertaken a special responsibility of care and direction." The health and safety risks identified in *Vernonia* apply with equal force to Tecumseh's children. Indeed, the nationwide drug epidemic makes the war against drugs a pressing concern in every school.

Given the nationwide epidemic of drug use, and the evidence of increased drug use in Tecumseh schools, it was entirely reasonable for the School District to enact this particular drug testing policy.

Finally, we find that testing students who participate in extracurricular activities is a reasonably effective means of addressing the School District's legitimate concerns in preventing, deterring, and detecting drug use. While in *Vernonia* there might have been a closer fit between the testing of athletes and the trial court's finding that the drug problem was "fueled by the 'role model' effect of athletes' drug use," such a finding was not essential to the holding. *Vernonia* did not require the school to test the group of students most likely to use drugs, but rather considered the constitutionality of the program in the context of the public school's custodial responsibilities. Evaluating the Policy in this context, we conclude that the drug testing of Tecumseh students who participate in extracurricular activities effectively serves the School District's interest in protecting the safety and health of its students.

Within the limits of the Fourth Amendment, local school boards must assess the desirability of drug testing schoolchildren. In upholding the constitutionality of the Policy, we express no opinion as to its wisdom. Rather, we hold only that Tecumseh's Policy is a reasonable means of furthering the School District's important interest in preventing and deterring drug use among its schoolchildren. Accordingly, we reverse the judgment of the Court of Appeals.

It is so ordered.

Justice BREYER, concurring.

I agree with the Court that *Vernonia School Dist. 47J v. Acton,* governs this case and requires reversal of the Tenth Circuit's decision. The school's drug testing program addresses a serious national problem by focusing upon demand, avoiding the use of criminal or disciplinary sanctions, and relying upon professional counseling and treatment. In my view, this program does not violate the Fourth Amendment's prohibition of "unreasonable searches and seizures." I reach this conclusion primarily for the reasons given by the Court, but I would emphasize several underlying considerations, which I understand to be consistent with the Court's opinion.

In respect to the school's need for the drug testing program, I would emphasize the following: First, the drug problem in our Nation's schools is serious in terms of size, the kinds of drugs being used, and the consequences of that use both for our children and the rest of us.

Second, the government's emphasis upon supply side interdiction apparently has not reduced teenage use in recent years.

Third, public school systems must find effective ways to deal with this problem. Today's public expects its schools not simply to teach the fundamentals, but "to shoulder the burden of feeding students breakfast and lunch, offering before and after school child care services, and providing medical and psychological services," all in a school environment that is safe and encourages learning. The law itself recognizes these responsibilities with the phrase in loco parentis—a phrase that draws its legal force primarily from the needs of younger students (who here are necessarily grouped together with older high school students) and which reflects, not that a child or adolescent lacks an interest in privacy, but that a child's or adolescent's school-related privacy interest, when compared to the privacy interests of an adult, has different dimensions. A public school system that fails adequately to carry out its responsibilities may well see parents send their children to private or parochial school instead—with help from the State.

Fourth, the program at issue here seeks to discourage demand for drugs by changing the school's environment in order to combat the single most important factor leading schoolchildren to take drugs, namely, peer pressure. It offers the adolescent a nonthreatening reason to decline his friend's drug-use invitations, namely, that he intends to play baseball, participate in debate, join the band, or engage in any one of half a dozen useful, interesting, and important activities.

In respect to the privacy-related burden that the drug testing program imposes upon students, I would emphasize the following: First, not everyone would agree with this Court's characterization of the privacy-related significance of urine sampling as " 'negligible.' " Some find the procedure no more intrusive than a routine medical examination, but others are seriously embarrassed by the need to provide a urine sample with someone listening "outside the closed restroom stall." When trying to resolve this kind of close question involving the interpretation of constitutional values, I believe it important that the school board provided an opportunity for the airing of these differences at public meetings designed to give the entire community "the opportunity to be able to participate" in developing the drug policy. The board used this democratic, participatory process to uncover and to resolve differences, giving weight to the fact that the process, in this instance, revealed little, if any, objection to the proposed testing program.

Second, the testing program avoids subjecting the entire school to testing. And it preserves an option for a conscientious objector. He can refuse testing while paying a price (nonparticipation) that is serious, but less severe than expulsion from the school.

Third, a contrary reading of the Constitution, as requiring "individualized suspicion" in this public school context, could well lead schools to push the boundaries of "individualized suspicion" to its outer limits, using subjective criteria that may "unfairly target members of unpopular groups," or leave those whose behavior is slightly abnormal stigmatized in the minds of others. If so, direct application of the Fourth Amendment's prohibition against "unreasonable searches and seizures" will further that Amendment's liberty-protecting objectives at least to the same extent as application of the mediating "individualized suspicion" test, where, as here, the testing program is neither criminal nor disciplinary in nature.

I cannot know whether the school's drug testing program will work. But, in my view, the Constitution does not prohibit the effort. Emphasizing the considerations I have mentioned, along with others to which the Court refers, I conclude that the school's drug testing program, constitutionally speaking, is not "unreasonable." And I join the Court's opinion.

Justice GINSBURG, with whom Justice STEVENS, JUSTICE O'CONNOR, and Justice SOUTER join, dissenting.

Seven years ago, in *Vernonia School Dist. 47J v. Acton,* this Court determined that a school district's policy of randomly testing the urine of its student athletes for illicit drugs did not violate the Fourth Amendment. In so ruling, the Court emphasized that drug use "increase[d] the risk of sports-related injury" and that Vernonia's athletes were the "leaders" of an aggressive local "drug culture" that had reached "'epidemic proportions.'" Today, the Court relies upon *Vernonia* to permit a school district with a drug problem its superintendent repeatedly described as "not ... major," ..., to test the urine of an academic team member solely by reason of her participation in a nonathletic, competitive extracurricular activity-participation associated with neither special dangers from, nor particular predilections for, drug use.

The particular testing program upheld today is not reasonable; it is capricious, even perverse: Petitioners' policy targets for testing a student population least likely to be at risk from illicit drugs and their damaging effects. I therefore dissent.

This case presents circumstances dispositively different from those of *Vernonia*.

Vernonia cannot be read to endorse invasive and suspicionless drug testing of all students upon any evidence of drug use, solely because drugs jeopardize the life and health of those who use them. Many children, like many adults, engage in dangerous activities on their own time; that the children are enrolled in school scarcely allows government to monitor all such activities. Had the *Vernonia* Court agreed that public school attendance, in and of itself, permitted the State to test each student's blood or urine for drugs, the opinion in *Vernonia* could have saved many words.

The second commonality to which the Court points is the voluntary character of both interscholastic athletics and other competitive extracurricular activities. "By choosing to 'go out for the team,' [school athletes] voluntarily subject themselves to a degree of regulation even higher than that imposed on students generally." Comparably, the Court today observes, "students who participate in competitive extracurricular activities voluntarily subject themselves to" additional rules not applicable to other students.

While extracurricular activities are "voluntary" in the sense that they are not required for graduation, they are part of the school's educational program; for that reason, the petitioner (hereinafter School District) is justified in expending public resources to make them available. Participation in such activities is a key component of school life, essential in reality for students applying to college, and, for all participants, a significant contributor to the breadth and quality of the educational experience. Students "volunteer" for extracurricular pursuits in the same way they might volunteer for honors classes: They subject themselves to additional requirements, but they do so in order to take full advantage of the education offered them.

Enrollment in a public school, and election to participate in school activities beyond the bare minimum that the curriculum requires, are indeed factors relevant to reasonableness, but they do not on their own justify intrusive, suspicionless searches. Vernonia, accordingly, did not rest upon these factors; instead, the Court performed what today's majority aptly describes as a "fact-specific balancing." Balancing of that order, applied to the facts now before the Court, should yield a result other than the one the Court announces today.

In this case, however, Lindsay Earls and her parents allege that the School District handled personal information collected under the policy carelessly, with little regard for its confidentiality. Information about students' prescription drug use, they assert, was routinely viewed by Lindsay's choir teacher, who left files containing the information unlocked and unsealed, where others, including students, could see them; and test results were given out to all activity sponsors whether or not they had a clear "need to know."

Finally, the "nature and immediacy of the governmental concern," faced by the Vernonia School District dwarfed that confronting Tecumseh administrators. Vernonia initiated its drug testing policy in response to an alarming situation: "[A] large segment of the student body, particularly those involved in interscholastic athletics, was in a state of rebellion ... fueled by alcohol and drug abuse as well as the student[s'] misperceptions about the drug culture." Tecumseh, by contrast, repeatedly reported to the Federal Government during the period leading up to the adoption of the policy that "types of drugs [other than alcohol and tobacco] including controlled dangerous substances, are present [in the schools] but have not identified themselves as major problems at this time."

Not only did the Vernonia and Tecumseh districts confront drug problems of distinctly different magnitudes, they also chose different solutions: Vernonia limited its policy to athletes; Tecumseh indiscriminately subjected to testing all participants in competitive extracurricular activities. Urging that "the safety interest furthered by drug testing is undoubtedly substantial for all children, athletes and nonathletes alike," ..., the Court cuts out an element essential to the *Vernonia* judgment.

The Vernonia district, in sum, had two good reasons for testing athletes: Sports team members faced special health risks and they "were the leaders of the drug culture." No similar reason, and no other tenable justification, explains Tecumseh's decision to target for testing all participants in every competitive extracurricular activity.

Nationwide, students who participate in extracurricular activities are significantly less likely to develop substance abuse problems than are their less-involved peers. Even if students might be deterred from drug use in order to preserve their extracurricular eligibility, it is at least as likely that other students might forgo their extracurricular involvement in order to avoid detection of their drug use. Tecumseh's policy thus falls short doubly if deterrence is its aim: It invades the privacy of students who need deterrence least, and risks steering students at greatest risk for substance abuse away from extracurricular involvement that potentially may palliate drug problems.

To summarize, this case resembles *Vernonia* only in that the School Districts in both cases conditioned engagement in activities outside the obligatory curriculum on random subjection to urinalysis. The defining characteristics of the two programs, however, are entirely dissimilar. The Vernonia district sought to test a subpopulation of students distinguished by their reduced expectation of privacy, their special susceptibility to drug-related injury, and their heavy involvement with drug use. The Tecumseh district seeks to test a much larger population associated with none of these factors. It does so, moreover, without carefully safeguarding student confidentiality and without regard to the program's untoward effects. A program so sweeping is not sheltered by *Vernonia*; its unreasonable reach renders it impermissible under the Fourth Amendment.

For the reasons stated, I would affirm the judgment of the Tenth Circuit declaring the testing policy at issue unconstitutional.

Holdings of *Board of Ed. of Independent Sch. Dist. v. Earls*: The court held that the school's policies on drug testing were reasonable in that they only applied to students who voluntarily participated in extra-curricular activities, that the epidemic of drug abuse justified the actions of the school district in addressing the problem, and that, given the minimally intrusive nature of the sample collection and the limited uses to which the test results are put, the invasion of students' privacy was not significant.

Discussion Questions

How does the majority deal with the "lesser expectation of privacy" for athletes that is now being extended to groups such as the academic team?

The majority says that the activities of athletes (like the locker room) create a lower expectation of privacy for them and that the claim of athletes serving as "role models" for the rest of the school were not determinative factors in *Vernonia* (even though cited as support in the *Vernonia* decision). What other factors, if any, relied on in *Vernonia* were present in this case?

Can a school take disciplinary action against a student who tests positive for drugs under this decision?

Would a positive drug test in this case supply enough reasonable suspicion to search a student's purse or pockets?

Key Concepts: Drug Testing in School

- The courts still recognize that a drug-test of students is a search of the student and appear to still hold that a "blanket" drug-testing requirement of all students would be unconstitutional because it is not based upon any individualized suspicion as required by *T.L.O.*

- One of the factors that appear to be dispositive in finding that a school's drug-testing policy is constitutional is when the policy is only applied to students who "elect" to participate in activities not required in the regular curriculum of the school.

- In order to avoid constitutional conflict, schools imposing drug-testing programs must have procedures in place to protect the privacy of the students during the testing procedure as well as to protect the information gleaned from the test.

Practical Questions: Drug Testing in School

1. You are the attorney for your local school district. Like most other schools, the use of drugs among high school students in the district is reaching "epidemic proportions." However, the school district has limited funds to apply to a drug testing policy. The school principal tells you that he would like to implement a policy of "voluntary" random drug testing. At the end of every school day, he proposes that 10 students selected at random be asked to submit to providing a urine sample for a "drug screen." The principal says that anyone refusing a test will have his or her belongings searched. "My experience tells me that any student who refuses the test is hiding something, so a refusal gives me enough suspicion to support the search, right?" he asks. What is your answer?

2. Local prosecutors have used the "possession of a controlled substance" statute to support charges against anyone who tests positive for controlled substances. Pursuant to the school's drug control policy, your client, a member of the high school debate team, was required to submit to random drug testing to stay on the team. He tested positive for marijuana, and school authorities promptly turned over the drug test results to the local prosecutor who charged your client with possession of a controlled substance. What arguments will you make to support your motion to suppress the test results?

Chapter VI

The Course of a Juvenile Delinquency Case

Overview: Juvenile delinquency courts have historically been treated very differently than adult criminal courts. In fact, even the language used is different. In juvenile delinquency courts, the trial is deemed an "adjudicatory hearing" and rather than being convicted, the juvenile is "adjudicated" to be a delinquent. Also, the sentencing hearing is called a "dispositional hearing" and rather than calling it a sentence, it is called a "disposition." The course of progression of a juvenile delinquency case is much different than that of a criminal case, and there are many decision points as an individual case progresses that can greatly affect the ultimate outcome in the case. This portion of the text is designed to provide a general overview of the progression of a juvenile delinquency case. Later in this chapter, a greater discussion of these steps will be explored.

Intake and Diversion: When a youth is accused of committing a delinquent act, the first decisions are often made by the law enforcement authority charged with enforcement of the laws. Law enforcement must determine whether or not to refer the youth's case for system involvement and whether or not to take the youth into custody. If the matter is referred by law enforcement to the juvenile authorities, the juvenile court officers or juvenile court probation officers must determine whether or proceed to (1) dismiss the matter; (2) proceed informally in an informal or diversion program; or (3) file formal charges for the youth. If the juvenile officials decide to proceed informally, no formal charges are filed with the court. Normally, an "informal probation" occurs (or the youth is required to complete a diversion program specific to the acts alleged) and, once completed, no formal charges are filed. If the youth does not successfully complete the conditions, the juvenile authorities may continue the informal procedure or simply file formal charges.

Detention of the Youth: If a youth is detained in a detention (secure) facility, the youth is entitled to a *detention hearing* before the court to determine whether the detention can continue or if the youth can be released to the parents or to another appropriate place (which may include foster care or a residential facility) while the formal process continues. In most states, the youth is entitled to a *detention review hearing* at various times and stages of the proceedings.

Formal Charges in Juvenile Court: If the juvenile authorities decide to file formal charges against the youth, the prosecuting attorney files formal charges in a charging document of some sort (often called a *delinquency petition).* This formal charging document begins the court proceedings. The first court proceeding is an *arraignment* or an *initial appearance* where the youth is provided a lawyer, presented with the charging document, and advised of the youth's rights.

Waiving Jurisdiction to Adult Court: A prosecutor who believes that a youth who is subject to juvenile court jurisdiction should be prosecuted in adult criminal court rather than juvenile court, may file a *motion to waive jurisdiction* and the youth will then be given a *waiver hearing.* Normally, the sole issue at a waiver hearing is to determine whether or not the juvenile court should waive its jurisdiction of the youth (and the case) and transfer the case to the adult criminal court. If the court grants the motion, the case is transferred to adult criminal court. If the court denies the motion, the case will remain in juvenile court.

Adjudication as a Delinquent: The guilt or innocence of the youth is determined at an *adjudicatory hearing.* This hearing is the equivalent of a trial in adult criminal court. Rather than find the youth "guilty", the judge "adjudicates" the youth to be a "delinquent." If the court determines that the state has failed to meet its burden of proof in establishing that the youth committed the delinquent act, the case is dismissed and closed.

Disposing of the Case: If the youth has been adjudicated as a delinquent, the court must determine what to do in response to the adjudication. The youth is then given a *dispositional hearing.* The dispositional hearing is the equivalent of a sentencing hearing in adult criminal court. The juvenile court judge has many options for dealing with the youth ranging from probation to commitment of the youth to a secure facility.

Chapter VII

Pre-Adjudication Detention

Overview: When a minor is accused of committing a delinquent act, there is the possibility that the youth will be "detained" pending trial. A juvenile court judge may order the youth to be "placed" or "detained" either as a temporary placement prior to a dispositional order or as a longer term placement as part of the dispositional order. A "placement" is when the youth is ordered to be placed in an out-of-home placement such as foster care, a shelter facility or a group home. These facilities are not locked facilities. A more restrictive placement is when the court orders the youth to be "detained" in a detention facility. Detention facilities are "secure" facilities, meaning that the doors are locked and are the equivalent of an adult jail. Bail is not generally available for minors in juvenile court, and, as a result, youth are provided with timely reviews of detention orders prior to the entry of a dispositional order. Courts can even detain minors simply to prevent them from committing further delinquent acts during the pendency of the delinquency action.

L.O.W. v. District Court: While the *Gault* decision guaranteed some constitutional rights to minors who were the subject of juvenile delinquency proceedings, the Supreme Court has not clearly indicated whether or not a minor has a constitutional right to bail pending adjudication. Unlike most other states, Colorado provides bail in juvenile delinquency cases. However, in this particular case, the youth was denied bail to obtain his pretrial release. In *Lowe v. District Court,* the Colorado Supreme Court was faced with an Eighth Amendment challenge to bail for a minor in a juvenile delinquency proceeding.

As you read *L.O.W. v. District Court,* look for the following:

1. Look for the reasons that this court found that a denial of bail for minors in a juvenile delinquency court is "fundamentally fair."

2. Consider what "adverse impact" this court found could occur if bail were granted in pre-adjudication proceedings.

3. Consider what "benefits" this court found could be anticipated if bail were granted in pre-adjudication proceedings.

L.O.W. v. District Court
623 P.2d 1253 (Colo. 1981)

Petitioner L. O. W., a child, was charged in a delinquency petition in Arapahoe County District Court with acts which would have constituted second-degree burglary, a class three felony, if the child had been an adult. At a detention hearing on October 23, 1980, the district court heard testimony from the investigating police officer and reviewed both a counselor's report and the petitioner's court history. The evidence disclosed that the petitioner twice had been adjudicated a delinquent child and was the subject of a reserved ruling in another case. He had previously failed to appear for a jury trial and revocation hearing in Arapahoe County and had missed a court appearance in Jefferson County. At the time of the detention hearing L. O. W. was on probation for carrying a concealed weapon. Delinquency petitions based on serious charges were pending against him in Denver and Jefferson Counties. He was also subject to probation revocation proceedings based on the allegations in this case.

The district court found that probable cause existed to believe that the petitioner had committed an act of delinquency and that it was in the best interests of the child and the community for him to remain in detention at the Arapahoe Youth Center. The trial court denied the petitioner's request that bond be set in a reasonable amount.

The petitioner contends that the trial court's refusal to set bond contravenes U.S.Const., Amend. VIII and Colo.Const., Art. II, Sec. 20 prohibiting excessive bail. We conclude that a child does not have an absolute constitutional or statutory right to bail pending adjudication of the charges filed against him in juvenile court. Because the respondent district court's findings in this case justified detention of L. O. W. without bail, we discharge the Rule.

The Eighth Amendment to the United States Constitution provides that "(e)xcessive bail shall not be required...." Beginning with the Judiciary Act of 1789, federal law has provided that, in all but capital cases, a person accused of a crime has an absolute right to be admitted to bail. The United States Supreme Court has interpreted the Eighth Amendment to require that bail be set because the "... traditional right to freedom before conviction permits the unhampered preparation of a defense and serves to prevent the infliction of punishment prior to conviction.... Unless this right to bail is preserved, the presumption of innocence, secured only after centuries of struggle, would lose its meaning."

Section 20 of Article II of the Colorado Constitution is identical to the Eighth Amendment. In addition, Section 19 of Article II of the Colorado Constitution provides that: "All persons shall be bailable by sufficient sureties except for capital offenses, when the proof is evident or the presumption great."

We have interpreted Section 19 to confer an absolute right to bail in all except capital cases. The purpose of bail is to ensure the defendant's presence at trial and not to punish him before he has been convicted.

Rights provided to adult defendants in criminal proceedings, however, have not been made uniformly available to juveniles because the protective purposes of juvenile proceedings preponderate over their punitive function. Although early decisions held that "the juvenile is not entitled to bail, to indictment by grand jury, to a public trial or to trial by jury," the "applicable due process standard in juvenile proceedings, as (since) developed by *Gault* and *Winship* is fundamental fairness."

The general thrust of these Supreme Court decisions has been to accommodate the goals and philosophies of the juvenile system within the due process framework of fundamental fairness.

We have held that the fundamental fairness standard obligates trial courts to comply with statutory and constitutional speedy trial requirements in juvenile as well as adult proceedings; that the standard of proof beyond a reasonable doubt which governs adult probation revocation proceedings also governs juvenile probation revocation proceedings; and that the rule authorizing an adult defendant in a criminal proceeding to challenge for cause a prospective juror employed by a law enforcement agency is equally applicable to juvenile delinquency proceedings. However, Sections 19 and 20 of Article II of the Colorado Constitution have not heretofore been applied to juvenile pre-adjudication proceedings.

To determine whether a juvenile has a constitutional right to bail, we first must inquire whether consistently with fundamental fairness "the juvenile court's assumed ability to function in a unique manner," justifies withholding from juveniles the constitutional right to bail. We must weigh the adverse impact of bail on informal pre-adjudication juvenile proceedings against the benefits to be anticipated from a right to bail.

The use of bail in adult criminal proceedings has been criticized, particularly because it disadvantages indigent defendants. Observing that "to superimpose a provision for bail in the Juvenile Court would cause unexplored difficulties for most juveniles, particularly those who are indigent," the California Supreme Court declined to decide whether juveniles have a constitutional right to bail. Instead the court ruled that the state's juvenile court law, which does not require that bond be posted, establishes an adequate system for the pre-hearing release of juveniles. Few children are financially independent and their parents may be unwilling or unable to post bail. At the same time, commercial surety may be unavailable because minors' contracts are voidable. If children are detained too frequently, a right to bail will not remedy the practice. It is more likely that, were it recognized, a right to bail would become a substitute for other, more appropriate forms of release.

Virtually every court which has considered the issue has found that juvenile code safeguards obviate the need for a right to bail in juvenile pre-adjudication proceedings. The American Bar Association's Juvenile Justice Standards Relating to Interim Status, recommend that "the use of bail bonds in any form as an alternative interim status should be prohibited." *Section 4.7 at 24.* See also President's Commission on Law Enforcement and the Administration of Justice, Task Force Report: Juvenile Delinquency and Youth Crime at 36 (1967).

The United States Court of Appeals for the Ninth Circuit, refusing to overturn Oregon's statutory ban on bail for juveniles, noted that Oregon had enacted an elaborate statutory scheme governing pre-adjudication detention and called the statutory detention hearing a "critical stage" in the juvenile proceeding. Unlike bail setting proceedings, informal detention hearings afford a judge an opportunity to consider the child's needs and welfare. In some instances, the court may consider substitute care for the child if the parent is unwilling to have the child return home or the child does not wish to remain at home pending an adjudication hearing.

Bail does not necessarily result in a juvenile's release from detention. When a juvenile's bail is not posted, the setting of bail alone does not effectuate the presumption of innocence, aid the child's preparation of a defense, or assure the child's presence at future court proceedings. The presumption of innocence and the child's participation in preparation of his defense may, however, be effectuated by curtailing the use of pre-adjudication detention. And while monetary bail may, in some cases, provide an additional assurance of appearance if a child's inadequate ties to the community or record of past failures to appear militate against a personal recognizance bond, it is within the trial court's discretion to set bond for a child in such cases.

If the policy expressed in section 19-2-103(3)(a)(I) of the Children's Code disapproving the use of detention except in cases satisfying the demanding statutory standards is implemented, the need for bail will be minimized in juvenile proceedings. We therefore hold that there is no unqualified constitutional right to bail for a juvenile under the United

States and Colorado Constitutions. However, a trial court may detain a juvenile without bail only after giving due weight to a presumption that a juvenile should be released pending a dispositional hearing except in narrowly defined circumstances where the state establishes that detention is necessary to protect the child from imminent harm or to protect others in the community from serious bodily harm which the child is likely to inflict.

The trial court in this case applied the Children's Code standards for detention: "... it would be contrary to the welfare of the child or of the community to release the child from detention." These standards were first published in the "Standard Juvenile Court Act" in 1959 by the National Probation and Parole Association (predecessor of the National Council on Crime and Delinquency). The "Standard Juvenile Court Act" permitted detention if the child's "immediate welfare" or "the protection of the community requires that he be detained."

The standards for juvenile detention recommended recently by the American Bar Association are more precise:

"3.1 Restraints on the freedom of accused juveniles pending trial and disposition are generally contrary to public policy. The preferred course in each case should be unconditional release.

3.2 The imposition of interim control or detention on an accused juvenile may be considered for the purposes of:

A. Protecting the jurisdiction and process of the courts;

B. Reducing the likelihood that the juvenile may inflict serious bodily harm on others during the interim period; or

C. Protecting the accused juvenile from imminent bodily harm upon his or her request.

3.3 The interim control or detention should not be imposed on an accused juvenile:

A. To punish, treat, or rehabilitate the juvenile;

B. To allow parents to avoid their legal responsibilities;

C. To satisfy demands by a victim, the police, or the community;

D. To permit more convenient administrative access to the juvenile;

E. To facilitate further interrogation or investigation; or

F. Due to a lack of a more appropriate facility or status alternative.

4.2 The state should bear the burden at every stage of the proceedings of persuading the relevant decision maker with clear and convincing evidence that restraints on an accused juvenile's liberty are necessary, and that no less intrusive alternative will suffice.

4.3 Whenever a decision is made at any stage of the proceedings to adopt an interim measure other than unconditional release, the decision maker should concurrently state in writing or on the record the specificity of evidence relied upon for that conclusion, and the authorized purpose or purposes that justify that action."

American Bar Association, Juvenile Justice Standards Relating to Interim Status, supra at 50.

The transcript of the trial court's ruling includes specific findings that L. O. W. had avoided the jurisdiction and process of the court in the past and had been in possession of a deadly weapon. The court's findings and conclusions indicate that it gave due weight to the presumption that the petitioner should be released pending the dispositional hearing but found that there was a factual basis for detaining L. O. W. in order to protect others in the community from serious bodily harm which he was likely to inflict. The trial court's findings here were sufficient to detain the child without bail.

One issue remains to be resolved. Colorado is one of a handful of states which by statute provide for bail in juvenile court proceedings.

Our opinion here should not be construed to negate the availability of bail to juveniles in appropriate situations. For example, bail may be appropriate if a juvenile is subject to detention solely because of danger that he will not appear for adjudication. In such situations bail should be considered as a viable, if not constitutionally mandated, alternative to detention. We recognize that the option of setting monetary bail in a juvenile proceeding does not preclude a trial court from considering conditions of release which will be in the child's best interests.

The trial judge here did not have a statutory or constitutional mandate to grant bail pending the juvenile delinquency adjudication. The court's reasons for detaining the petitioner justify denial of bail.

Rule discharged

Holdings of *L.O.W. v. District Court:* The court held that there is no statutory or constitutional requirement that minors be granted bail pending a juvenile delinquency adjudication.

Discussion Questions

What makes juvenile courts so unique compared to adult criminal courts to justify a refusal to grant bail to minors?

If there is a presumption of innocence in juvenile delinquency court, why can a minor be held in a secure facility without bail before a determination of guilt is established?

How can the court seriously say that the minor might benefit from the lack of availability of bail?

Schall v. Martin: In *Schall v. Martin,* the United States Supreme Court was faced with a challenge to statutory language that permitted "preventive detention" of juveniles charged with serious charges. Juveniles who were charged with serious charges were allowed to be held in detention or custody to protect the public from further dangerous acts of the youth prior to a fact-finding hearing. The statutory scheme included procedural protections prior to a fact-finding hearing in order to assure that the detention was short in duration and that the youth was afforded certain rights before being held pre-adjudication.

As you read *Schall v. Martin,* look for the following:

1. Look for the various procedural protections built into the preventive detention statute to convince the court that the statute is acceptable.

2. Consider what leads the court to conclude that preventative detention was not being used as punishment.

3. Consider how the court concludes that juveniles are always under some form of custody.

Schall v. Martin

467 U.S. 253 (1984)

Justice REHNQUIST delivered the opinion of the Court.

Section 320.5(3)(b) of the New York Family Court Act authorizes pretrial detention of an accused juvenile delinquent based on a finding that there is a "serious risk" that the child "may before the return date commit an act which if committed by an adult would constitute a crime." Appellees brought suit on behalf of a class of all juveniles detained pursuant to that provision. We conclude that preventive detention under the FCA serves a legitimate state objective, and that the procedural protections afforded pretrial detainees by the New York statute satisfy the requirements of the Due Process Clause of the Fourteenth Amendment to the United States Constitution.

Appellee Gregory Martin was arrested on December 13, 1977, and charged with first-degree robbery, second-degree assault, and criminal possession of a weapon based on an incident in which he, with two others, allegedly hit a youth on the head with a loaded gun and stole his jacket and sneakers. Martin had possession of the gun when he was arrested. He was 14 years old at the time and, therefore, came within the jurisdiction of New York's Family Court. The incident occurred at 11:30 at night, and Martin lied to the police about where and with whom he lived. He was consequently detained overnight.

A petition of delinquency was filed, and Martin made his "initial appearance" in Family Court on December 14th, accompanied by his grandmother. The Family Court Judge, citing the possession of the loaded weapon, the false address given to the police, and the lateness of the hour, as evidencing a lack of supervision, ordered Martin detained under § 320.5(3)(b). A probable cause hearing was held five days later, on December 19th, and probable cause was found to exist for all the crimes charged. At the factfinding hearing held December 27–29, Martin was found guilty on the robbery and criminal possession charges. He was adjudicated a delinquent and placed on two years' probation. He had been detained pursuant to § 320.5(3)(b), between the initial appearance and the completion of the factfinding hearing, for a total of 15 days.

Appellees Luis Rosario and Kenneth Morgan, both age 14, were also ordered detained pending their factfinding hearings. Rosario was charged with attempted first-degree robbery and second-degree assault for an incident in which he, with four others, allegedly tried to rob two men, putting a gun to the head of one of them and beating both about the head with sticks. At the time of his initial appearance, on March 15, 1978, Rosario had another delinquency petition pending for knifing a student, and two prior petitions had been adjusted. Probable cause was found on March 21. On April 11, Rosario was released to his father, and the case was terminated without adjustment on September 25, 1978.

Kenneth Morgan was charged with attempted robbery and attempted grand larceny for an incident in which he and another boy allegedly tried to steal money from a 14-year-old girl and her brother by threatening to blow their heads off and grabbing them to search their pockets. Morgan, like Rosario, was on release status on another petition (for robbery and criminal possession of stolen property) at the time of his initial appearance on March 27, 1978. He had been arrested four previous times, and his mother refused to come to court because he had been in trouble so often she did not want him home. A probable-cause hearing was set for March 30, but was continued until April 4, when it was combined with a factfinding hearing. Morgan was found guilty of harassment and petit larceny and was ordered placed with the Department of Social Services for 18 months. He was detained a total of eight days between his initial appearance and the factfinding hearing.

There is no doubt that the Due Process Clause is applicable in juvenile proceedings. "The problem," we have stressed, "is to ascertain the precise impact of the due process requirement upon such proceedings." We have held that certain basic constitutional protections enjoyed by adults accused of crimes also apply to juveniles. But the Constitution does not mandate elimination of all differences in the treatment of juveniles. The State has "a parens patriae interest in preserving and promoting the welfare of the child," which makes a juvenile proceeding fundamentally different from an adult criminal trial. We have tried, therefore, to strike a balance—to respect the "informality" and "flexibility" that characterize juvenile proceedings, and yet to ensure that such proceedings comport with the "fundamental fairness" demanded by the Due Process Clause.

The statutory provision at issue in these cases, § 320.5(3)(b), permits a brief pretrial detention based on a finding of a "serious risk" that an arrested juvenile may commit a crime before his return date. The question before us is whether preventive detention of juveniles pursuant to § 320.5(3)(b) is compatible with the "fundamental fairness" required by due process. Two separate inquiries are necessary to answer this question. First, does preventive detention under the New York statute serve a legitimate state objective? And, second, are the procedural safeguards contained in the FCA adequate to authorize the pretrial detention of at least some juveniles charged with crimes?

The "legitimate and compelling state interest" in protecting the community from crime cannot be doubted. The harm suffered by the victim of a crime is not dependent upon the age of the perpetrator. And the harm to society generally may even be greater in this context given the high rate of recidivism among juveniles.

The juvenile's countervailing interest in freedom from institutional restraints, even for the brief time involved here, is undoubtedly substantial as well. But that interest must be qualified by the recognition that juveniles, unlike adults, are always in some form of custody. Children, by definition, are not assumed to have the capacity to take care of themselves. They are assumed to be subject to the control of their parents, and if parental control falters, the State must play its part as parens patriae. In this respect, the juvenile's liberty interest may, in appropriate circumstances, be subordinated to the State's "parens patriae interest in preserving and promoting the welfare of the child."

The substantiality and legitimacy of the state interests underlying this statute are confirmed by the widespread use and judicial acceptance of preventive detention for juveniles. Every State, as well as the United States in the District of Columbia, permits preventive detention of juveniles accused of crime. A number of model juvenile justice Acts also contain provisions permitting preventive detention. And the courts of eight States, including the New York Court of Appeals, have upheld their statutes with specific reference to protecting the juvenile and the community from harmful pretrial conduct, including pretrial crime.

There is no indication in the statute itself that preventive detention is used or intended as a punishment. First of all, the detention is strictly limited in time. If a juvenile is detained at his initial appearance and has denied the charges against him, he is entitled to a probable-cause hearing to be held not more than three days after the conclusion of the initial appearance or four days after the filing of the petition, whichever is sooner. If the Family Court judge finds probable cause, he must also determine whether continued detention is necessary pursuant to § 320.5(3)(b).

Detained juveniles are also entitled to an expedited factfinding hearing. If the juvenile is charged with one of a limited number of designated felonies, the factfinding hearing must be scheduled to commence not more than 14 days after the conclusion of the initial appearance. If the juvenile is charged with a lesser offense, then the factfinding hearing must be held not more than three days after the initial appearance. In the latter case, since the times for the probable-cause hearing and the factfinding hearing coincide, the two hearings are merged.

Thus, the maximum possible detention under § 320.5(3)(b) of a youth accused of a serious crime, assuming a 3-day extension of the factfinding hearing for good cause shown, is 17 days. The maximum detention for less serious crimes, again assuming a 3-day extension for good cause shown, is six days. These time frames seem suited to the limited purpose of providing the youth with a controlled environment and separating him from improper influences pending the speedy disposition of his case.

The conditions of confinement also appear to reflect the regulatory purposes relied upon by the State. When a juvenile is remanded after his initial appearance, he cannot, absent exceptional circumstances, be sent to a prison or lockup where he would be exposed to adult criminals. Instead, the child is screened by an "assessment unit" of the Department of Juvenile Justice. The assessment unit places the child in either nonsecure or secure detention. Nonsecure detention involves an open facility in the community, a sort of "halfway house," without locks, bars, or security officers where the child receives schooling and counseling and has access to recreational facilities.

Secure detention is more restrictive, but it is still consistent with the regulatory and parens patriae objectives relied upon by the State. Children are assigned to separate dorms based on age, size, and behavior. They wear street clothes provided by the institution and partake in educational and recreational programs and counseling sessions run by trained social workers. Misbehavior is punished by confinement to one's room. We cannot conclude from this record that the controlled environment briefly imposed by the State on juveniles in secure pretrial detention "is imposed for the purpose of punishment" rather than as "an incident of some other legitimate governmental purpose."

Pretrial detention need not be considered punitive merely because a juvenile is subsequently discharged subject to conditions or put on probation. In fact, such actions reinforce the original finding that close supervision of the juvenile is required. Lenient but supervised disposition is in keeping with the Act's purpose to promote the welfare and development of the child.

Even when a case is terminated prior to fact finding, it does not follow that the decision to detain the juvenile pursuant to § 320.5(3)(b) amounted to a due process violation. A delinquency petition may be dismissed for any number of reasons collateral to its merits, such as the failure of a witness to testify. The Family Court judge cannot be expected to anticipate such developments at the initial hearing. He makes his decision based on the information available to him at that time, and the propriety of the decision must be judged in that light. Consequently, the final disposition of a case is "largely irrelevant" to the legality of a pretrial detention.

It may be, of course, that in some circumstances detention of a juvenile would not pass constitutional muster. But the validity of those detentions must be determined on a case-by-case basis.

Given the legitimacy of the State's interest in preventive detention, and the nonpunitive nature of that detention, the remaining question is whether the procedures afforded juveniles detained prior to fact-finding provide sufficient protection against erroneous and unnecessary deprivations of liberty.

In many respects, the FCA provides far more predetention protection for juveniles than we found to be constitutionally required for a probable-cause determination for adults in Gerstein. The initial appearance is informal, but the accused juvenile is given full notice of the charges against him and a complete stenographic record is kept of the hearing. The juvenile appears accompanied by his parent or guardian. He is first informed of his rights, including the right to remain silent and the right to be represented by counsel chosen by him or by a law guardian assigned by the court. The initial appearance may be adjourned for no longer than 72 hours or until the next court day, whichever is sooner, to enable an appointed law guardian or other counsel to appear before the court. When his counsel is present, the juvenile is informed of the charges against him and furnished with a copy of the delinquency petition. A representative from the presentment agency appears in support of the petition.

The nonhearsay allegations in the delinquency petition and supporting depositions must establish probable cause to believe the juvenile committed the offense. Although the Family Court judge is not required to make a finding of probable cause at the initial appearance, the youth may challenge the sufficiency of the petition on that ground. Thus, the juvenile may oppose any recommended detention by arguing that there is not probable cause to believe he committed the offense or offenses with which he is charged. If the petition is not dismissed, the juvenile is given an opportunity to admit or deny the charges.

At the conclusion of the initial appearance, the presentment agency makes a recommendation regarding detention. A probation officer reports on the juvenile's record, including other prior and current Family Court and probation contacts, as well as relevant information concerning home life, school attendance, and any special medical or developmental problems. He concludes by offering his agency's recommendation on detention. Opposing counsel, the juvenile's parents, and the juvenile himself may all speak on his behalf and challenge any information or recommendation. If the judge does decide to detain the juvenile under § 320.5(3)(b), he must state on the record the facts and reasons for the detention.

As noted, a detained juvenile is entitled to a formal, adversarial probable-cause hearing within three days of his initial appearance, with one 3-day extension possible for good cause shown. The burden at this hearing is on the presentment agency to call witnesses and offer evidence in support of the charges. Testimony is under oath and subject to cross-examination. The accused juvenile may call witnesses and offer evidence in his own behalf. If the court finds probable cause, the court must again decide whether continued detention is necessary under § 320.5(3)(b). Again, the facts and reasons for the detention must be stated on the record.

In sum, notice, a hearing, and a statement of facts and reasons are given prior to any detention under § 320.5(3)(b). A formal probable-cause hearing is then held within a short while thereafter, if the factfinding hearing is not itself scheduled within three days. These flexible procedures have been found constitutionally adequate under the Fourth Amendment, and under the Due Process Clause.

The dissent would apparently have us strike down New York's preventive detention statute on two grounds: first, because the preventive detention of juveniles constitutes poor public policy, with the balance of harms outweighing any positive benefits either to society or to the juveniles themselves, and, second, because the statute could have been better drafted to improve the quality of the decisionmaking process. But it is worth recalling that we are neither a legislature charged with formulating public policy nor an American Bar Association committee charged with drafting a model statute. The question before us today is solely whether the preventive detention system chosen by the State of New York and applied by the New York Family Court comports with constitutional standards. Given the regulatory purpose for the detention and the procedural protections that precede its imposition, we conclude that § 320.5(3)(b) of the New York FCA is not invalid under the Due Process Clause of the Fourteenth Amendment.

The judgment of the Court of Appeals is

Reversed.

Justice MARSHALL, with whom Justice BRENNAN and Justice STEVENS join, dissenting.

The Court today holds that preventive detention of a juvenile pursuant to § 320.5(3)(b) does not violate the Due Process Clause. Two rulings are essential to the Court's decision: that the provision promotes legitimate government objectives important enough to justify the abridgment of the detained juveniles' liberty interests; and that the provision incorporates procedural safeguards sufficient to prevent unnecessary or arbitrary impairment of constitutionally protected rights. Because I disagree with both of those rulings, I dissent.

The first step in the process that leads to detention under § 320.5(3)(b) is known as "probation intake." A juvenile may arrive at intake by one of three routes: he may be brought there directly by an arresting officer; he may be detained for a brief period after his arrest and then taken to intake; he may be released upon arrest and directed to appear at a designated time. The heart of the intake procedure is a 10- to 40-minute interview of the juvenile, the arresting officer, and sometimes the juvenile's parent or guardian. The objectives of the probation officer conducting the interview are to determine the nature of the offense the child may have committed and to obtain some background information on him.

On the basis of the information derived from the interview and from an examination of the juvenile's record, the probation officer decides whether the case should be disposed of informally ("adjusted") or whether it should be referred to the Family Court. If the latter, the officer makes an additional recommendation regarding whether the juvenile should be detained. "There do not appear to be any governing criteria which must be followed by the probation officer in choosing between proposing detention and parole...."

The actual decision whether to detain a juvenile under § 320.5(3)(b) is made by a Family Court judge at what is called an "initial appearance"—a brief hearing resembling an arraignment. The information on which the judge makes his determination is very limited. He has before him a "petition for delinquency" prepared by a state agency, charging the juvenile with an offense, accompanied with one or more affidavits attesting to the juvenile's involvement. Ordinarily the judge has in addition the written report and recommendation of the probation officer. However, the probation officer who prepared the report rarely attends the hearing. Nor is the complainant likely to appear. Consequently, "[o]ften there is no one present with personal knowledge of what happened."

In the typical case, the judge appoints counsel for the juvenile at the time his case is called. Thus, the lawyer has no opportunity to make an independent inquiry into the juvenile's background or character, and has only a few minutes to prepare arguments on the child's behalf. The judge ordinarily does not interview the juvenile, id., at 708, makes no inquiry into the truth of allegations in the petition, id., at 702, and does not determine whether there is probable cause to believe the juvenile committed the offense. The typical hearing lasts between 5 and 15 minutes, and the judge renders his decision immediately afterward.

Neither the statute nor any other body of rules guides the efforts of the judge to determine whether a given juvenile is likely to commit a crime before his trial. In making detention decisions, "each judge must rely on his own subjective judgment, based on the limited information available to him at court intake and whatever personal standards he himself has developed in exercising his discretionary authority under the statute." Family Court judges are not provided information regarding the behavior of juveniles over whose cases they have presided, so a judge has no way of refining the standards he employs in making detention decisions.

To comport with "fundamental fairness," § 320.5(3)(b) must satisfy two requirements. First, it must advance goals commensurate with the burdens it imposes on constitutionally protected interests. Second, it must not punish the juveniles to whom it applies.

The majority only grudgingly and incompletely acknowledges the applicability of the first of these tests, but its grip on the cases before us is undeniable. It is manifest that § 320.5(3)(b) impinges upon fundamental rights. If the "liberty" protected by the Due Process Clause means anything, it means freedom from physical restraint. Only a very important government interest can justify deprivation of liberty in this basic sense.

The majority seeks to evade the force of this principle by discounting the impact on a child of incarceration pursuant to § 320.5(3)(b). The curtailment of liberty consequent upon detention of a juvenile, the majority contends, is mitigated by the fact that "juveniles, unlike adults, are always in some form of custody." In any event, the majority argues, the conditions of confinement associated with "secure detention" under § 320.5(3)(b) are not unduly burdensome. These contentions enable the majority to suggest that § 320.5(3)(b) need only advance a "legitimate state objective" to satisfy the strictures of the Due Process Clause.

The majority's arguments do not survive scrutiny. Its characterization of preventive detention as merely a transfer of custody from a parent or guardian to the State is difficult to take seriously. Surely there is a qualitative difference between imprisonment and the condition of being subject to the supervision and control of an adult who has one's best interests at heart. And the majority's depiction of the nature of confinement under § 320.5(3)(b) is insupportable on this record. As noted above, the District Court found that secure detention entails incarceration in a facility closely resembling a jail and that pretrial detainees are sometimes mixed with juveniles who have been found to be delinquent.

In short, fairly viewed, pretrial detention of a juvenile pursuant to § 320.5(3)(b) gives rise to injuries comparable to those associated with imprisonment of an adult. In both situations, the detainee suffers stigmatization and severe limitation of his freedom of movement. Indeed, the impressionability of juveniles may make the experience of incarceration more injurious to them than to adults; all too quickly juveniles subjected to preventive detention come to see society at large as hostile and oppressive and to regard themselves as irremediably "delinquent." Such serious injuries to presumptively innocent persons — encompassing the curtailment of their constitutional rights to liberty — can be justified only by a weighty public interest that is substantially advanced by the statute.

To state the case more precisely, two circumstances in combination render § 320.5(3)(b) invalid in toto: in the large majority of cases in which the provision is invoked, its asserted objectives are either not advanced at all or are only minimally promoted; and, as the provision is written and administered by the state courts, the cases in which its asserted ends are significantly advanced cannot practicably be distinguished from the cases in which they are not.

Both of the courts below concluded that only occasionally and accidentally does pretrial detention of a juvenile under § 320.5(3)(b) prevent the commission of a crime. Three subsidiary findings undergird that conclusion. First, Family Court judges are incapable of determining which of the juveniles who appear before them would commit offenses before their trials if left at large and which would not.

Second, § 320.5(3)(b) is not limited to classes of juveniles whose past conduct suggests that they are substantially more likely than average juveniles to misbehave in the immediate future. The provision authorizes the detention of persons arrested for trivial offenses21 and persons without any prior contacts with juvenile court. Even a finding that there is probable cause to believe a juvenile committed the offense with which he was charged is not a prerequisite to his detention.

Third, the courts below concluded that circumstances surrounding most of the cases in which § 320.5(3)(b) has been invoked strongly suggest that the detainee would not have committed a crime during the period before his trial if he had been released. In a significant proportion of the cases, the juvenile had been released after his arrest and had not committed any reported crimes while at large, see supra, at 2422; it is not apparent why a juvenile would be more likely to misbehave between his initial appearance and his trial than between his arrest and initial appearance. Even more telling is the fact that "the vast majority" of persons detained under § 320.5(3)(b) are released either before or immediately after their trials. The inference is powerful that most detainees, when examined more carefully than at their initial appearances, are deemed insufficiently dangerous to warrant further incarceration.

In summary, application of the litmus test the Court recently has used to identify punitive sanctions supports the finding of the lower courts that preventive detention under § 320.5(3)(b) constitutes punishment. Because punishment of juveniles before adjudication of their guilt violates the Due Process Clause, the provision cannot stand.

A review of the hearings that resulted in the detention of the juveniles included in the sample of 34 cases reveals the majority's depiction of the decisionmaking process to be hopelessly idealized. For example, the operative portion of the initial appearance of Tyrone Parson, the three-card monte player, consisted of the following:

"COURT OFFICER: Will you identify yourself.

"TYRONE PARSON: Tyrone Parson, Age 15.

"THE COURT: Miss Brown, how many times has Tyrone been known to the Court?

"MISS BROWN: Seven times.

"THE COURT: Remand the respondent."

This kind of parody of reasoned decisionmaking would be less likely to occur if judges were given more specific and mandatory instructions regarding the information they should consider and the manner in which they should assess it.

The concerns that powered these decisions are strongly implicated by New York's preventive-detention scheme. The effect of the lack of procedural safeguards constraining detention decisions under § 320.5(3)(b) is that the liberty of a juvenile arrested even for a petty crime is dependent upon the "caprice" of a Family Court judge. The absence of meaningful guidelines creates opportunities for judges to use illegitimate criteria when deciding whether juveniles should be incarcerated pending their trials — for example, to detain children for the express purpose of punishing them. Even the judges who strive conscientiously to apply the law have little choice but to assess juveniles' dangerousness on the basis of whatever standards they deem appropriate. The resultant variation in detention decisions gives rise to a level of inequality in the deprivation of a fundamental right too great to be countenanced under the Constitution.

The majority acknowledges—indeed, founds much of its argument upon—the principle that a State has both the power and the responsibility to protect the interests of the children within its jurisdiction. Yet the majority today upholds a statute whose net impact on the juveniles who come within its purview is overwhelmingly detrimental. Most persons detained under the provision reap no benefit and suffer serious injuries thereby. The welfare of only a minority of the detainees is even arguably enhanced. The inequity of this regime, combined with the arbitrariness with which it is administered, is bound to disillusion its victims regarding the virtues of our system of criminal justice. I can see—and the majority has pointed to—no public purpose advanced by the statute sufficient to justify the harm it works.

I respectfully dissent.

Holdings of *Schall v. Martin:* The court held that the state has a "legitimate and compelling state interest" in protecting the community from crime. The Court also found that there was no evidence that preventive detention was being used as punishment, and that the procedures afforded juveniles detained provided sufficient protection against erroneous and unnecessary deprivations of liberty to survive a challenge on Due Process grounds.

Discussion Questions

Does the fact that some of the youth detained in these cases were ultimately either given probation or had the charges dismissed have any impact on the claim of the risk or re-offense if released?

Would the court have ruled any differently in this case if these were adult criminal cases?

———

Alfredo A. v. Superior Court of Los Angeles County: In *Alfredo A. v. Superior Court of Los Angeles County,* the California Supreme Court was faced with a Fourth Amendment challenge to California's guarantee that a minor charged with juvenile delinquency must have a judicial determination of probable cause within 72 hours of detention. The rule established by the United States Supreme Court for adults was that a judicial determination of probable cause must occur for adults within 48 hours of a warrantless arrest.

As you read *Alfredo A. v. Superior Court of Los Angeles County,* look for the following:

1. Look for the various procedural protections built into the California Juvenile Delinquency statute.

2. Consider why the majority opinion believes that the "promptness" requirement for judicial review of pre-trial detention is defined differently for minors than for adults.

Alfredo A. v. Superior Court of Los Angeles County
6 Cal.4th 1212, 865 P.2d 56 (1994)

LUCAS, Chief Justice.

In *Gerstein v. Pugh,* the United States Supreme Court held that the Fourth Amendment requires a prompt judicial determination of "probable cause to believe the suspect has committed a crime" as a prerequisite to an extended pretrial detention following a warrantless arrest. The court stopped short of mandating a specific timetable for making a "prompt" determination of probable cause. In *County of Riverside v. McLaughlin*, the high court sought to further define the "promptness" requirement for making the probable cause determination mandated in *Gerstein*. The court held that, "Taking into account the competing interests articulated in *Gerstein*, we believe that a jurisdiction that provides judicial determinations of probable cause within 48 hours of arrest will, as a general matter, comply with the promptness requirement of *Gerstein*."

Neither *Gerstein* nor *McLaughlin* was a juvenile detention case. In contrast, the United States Supreme Court's decision in *Schall v. Martin* did directly address the constitutional parameters of a key provision of New York State's *juvenile* pretrial detention statute. *Schall* was decided nine years after *Gerstein* but seven years prior to *McLaughlin*. *Schall*, and other decisions of the high court, make it abundantly clear that Fourth Amendment and related due process claims pertaining to the pretrial detention of juveniles following warrantless arrests for criminal activity cannot be viewed in the same light as similar challenges to adult detentions. This is so because, in the words of the Supreme Court, juvenile proceedings are "fundamentally different" from adult criminal proceedings, requiring that a "balance" be struck between the "informality" and "flexibility" that must of necessity inhere in juvenile proceedings, and the further requirement that those proceedings comport with the juvenile's constitutional rights, and the " 'fundamental fairness' demanded by the Due Process Clause."

In July of 1991, the Los Angeles County Juvenile Court, after consultation with county counsel, adopted the "official position" that *McLaughlin*'s strict 48-hour rule does not apply in *juvenile* detention proceedings. We granted review in this case to determine whether that position passes constitutional muster, or whether *McLaughlin*'s 48-hour rule strictly applies to the pretrial detention of adults and juveniles alike following warrantless arrest for criminal activity.

It is beyond dispute that *Gerstein*'s constitutional requirement of a *prompt* judicial determination of probable cause for the extended pretrial detention of any person arrested without a warrant applies to juveniles as well as adults. However, for reasons to be explained, and having considered the comprehensive analysis the court invoked in *Schall* to scrutinize the constitutionality of the juvenile detention provisions there at issue, we have concluded that the high court did not intend that the strict 48-hour rule subsequently announced in *McLaughlin*—a ruling handed down in a case involving the pretrial detention of *adults*— should automatically apply in the juvenile detention setting. To conclude otherwise we would have to ignore the fundamental differences between adult and juvenile proceedings recognized in all of the high court's cases that have specifically addressed juvenile detention issues.

As will be explained, California's juvenile detention statutes basically afford juvenile detainees who have been arrested without a warrant a formal, adversarial "detention hearing" within 72 hours of a warrantless arrest, which proceeding incorporates the "probable cause" determination mandated under *Gerstein*. The relevant statutes also prescribe various other procedures designed to ensure that an arrested juvenile will be released, in accordance with well-established and codified policies, at the earliest possible time following arrest, preferably to the custody of a parent or legal guardian. Given the fundamental difference in purpose and procedure between the treatment of adult and juvenile detainees, we have further concluded that *juvenile* detainees are constitutionally entitled to a judicial "probable cause" determination within 72 hours of arrest, consistent with the integrated provisions of our juvenile detention statutory scheme.

I. FACTS AND PROCEDURAL HISTORY

On July 24, 1991, petitioner Alfredo A., a minor, was taken into custody without a warrant pursuant on suspicion of having possessed cocaine base for sale on that date.

On July 25, 1991, petitioner sought his immediate release by filing a petition for a writ of habeas corpus in the Court of Appeal for the Second Appellate District. He based his challenge to his postarrest detention on the holding in *McLaughlin*, alleging that he was a juvenile who had been arrested without a warrant the previous day for commission of a criminal offense, and that: "Pursuant to the Fourth Amendment to the United States Constitution, petitioner is entitled to a judicial determination of probable cause for his continued detention within 48 hours of his arrest. No such judicial determination has been made, and no determination will be made within the 48-hour period. This is because the Los Angeles County Superior Court, Juvenile Court, has adopted as its 'official position' that a juvenile is not entitled to such a prompt probable cause determination."

Several weeks prior to petitioner's arrest, the Presiding Judge of the Los Angeles County Juvenile Court sent a memorandum to all juvenile court judges, commissioners, and referees, indicating that county counsel had furnished the juvenile court with an opinion concluding that *McLaughlin*'s 48-hour rule does not apply in juvenile court proceedings. County counsel based that determination on the reasoning of *Schall*, in which a New York juvenile "preventive detention" statute was found facially valid under the due process clause of the Fourteenth Amendment. The presiding judge and supervising judges thereafter unanimously agreed to adopt county counsel's position as the Los Angeles County Juvenile Court's "official position."

By an order to show cause filed the following day, the Court of Appeal determined to treat the petition for a writ of habeas corpus as a petition for a writ of mandate, and directed respondent Los Angeles County Superior Court to show cause why a peremptory writ of mandate should not issue ordering that judicial probable cause determinations for the extended postarrest detention of juveniles be made within 48 hours of their arrest.

On that same day, July 26, 1991, a wardship petition was filed in the juvenile court alleging petitioner came within the provisions of section 602 by having violated Health and Safety Code on July 24, 1991. However, when petitioner appeared in court on the next "judicial day" (July 29, 1991), no detention report was provided to the juvenile court in preparation for the detention hearing, and petitioner was ordered immediately released. He thereafter waived the statutory time limitations for arraignment.

In the mandamus proceeding, petitioner acknowledged that his release after spending five days in custody rendered the petition moot as to him. The Court of Appeal nonetheless determined to hear and decide petitioner's systemic challenge to the juvenile court's "official position," concluding that similar claims had proved "capable of repetition, yet evading review" because "review usually takes longer than the [challenged] temporary detention...."

In its opinion, the Court of Appeal reviewed the relevant provisions of the Welfare and Institutions Code governing pretrial detention of juvenile arrestees. After determining that the juvenile detention issue in this case must be evaluated in light of the constitutional analysis conducted in *Schall*, the court concluded that California's statutory postarrest juvenile detention scheme withstands constitutional scrutiny, reasoning that: "[The] statutes provide procedural safeguards that accommodate the individual's right to liberty and the state's duty to control crime. They reflect the balance that must be struck between the informality and flexibility of juvenile proceedings even as they comport with the fundamental fairness required by due process. The statutory scheme protects a minor's right to freedom, consistent with the state interest in protecting the minor and society." Implicit in these conclusions was the court's rejection of petitioner's claim that *McLaughlin*'s strict 48-hour rule applies to juvenile as well as adult postarrest detention proceedings.

II. DISCUSSION

Relevant Statutory Provisions

In order to meaningfully examine and apply the controlling constitutional principles and case law, we need a brief overview of the relevant statutory provisions that govern juvenile detentions following warrantless arrests in California.

Under our juvenile criminal justice system, a peace officer can take a minor into temporary custody for violating a federal or state law, or a local ordinance. When a minor is arrested and detained on suspicion of having committed a crime, the minor is not formally "charged" with the crime in the sense that adult arrestees are criminally prosecuted. Rather, a determination is made whether to commence wardship proceedings with the filing of a petition by the prosecuting attorney pursuant to section 602.

Various official functions must be performed at the time of the juvenile's arrest, and within the initial 24- to 48-hour period following the arrest—all patently designed to ensure that the detained minor is afforded every reasonable opportunity for his or her immediate release, preferably to a parent or guardian.

Hence, the arresting officer may release the minor outright, deliver him or her to a public or private shelter facility in contract with the city or county to provide shelter care, counseling, or diversion services to such minors, or release the minor on his or her written promise to appear before a county juvenile probation officer, or to a parent, guardian, or other responsible relative, who may also be required to execute a written promise to appear along with the minor. If the arresting officer elects instead to deliver custody of the minor directly to the county probation officer, the officer must prepare a concise, written statement of the probable cause for taking the minor into temporary custody, to be furnished along with custody of the minor to the juvenile probation officer within 24 hours of the initial detention following the arrest.

The policy underlying this choice of dispositions provided for in section 626 is expressly set forth in the statute: "In determining which disposition of the minor to make, *the officer shall prefer the alternative which least restricts the minor's freedom of movement,* provided that alternative is compatible with the best interests of the minor and the community."

When custody of the minor is transferred to a probation officer at a juvenile hall or any other place of confinement, the detaining officer is further required to "take immediate steps to notify the minor's parent, guardian, or responsible relative that such minor is in custody and the place where he is being held."

Section 628 requires the juvenile probation officer to "immediately investigate the circumstances of the minor and the facts surrounding his being taken into custody," and further requires the officer to "immediately release the minor to the custody of his parent, guardian, or responsible relative unless one or more … [specified] conditions exist.…"

Like the arresting officer, the county juvenile probation officer is empowered with discretion at the intake-investigatory stage to "adjust the situation which brings the minor within the jurisdiction [or probable jurisdiction] of the court" by "delineat[ing] specific programs of supervision for the minor," or referring the case to another agency, arranging for informal supervision, or requesting the district attorney to prepare a wardship petition for filing.

A minor taken into custody must be released within 48 hours, excluding "nonjudicial days," unless a wardship petition is filed within that initial 48-hour period. If a section 602 petition is filed, the minor must be afforded a formal, adversarial "detention hearing" in juvenile court "as soon as possible but in any event [no later than] the expiration of the next judicial day after a petition to declare the minor a ward ... has been filed"—i.e., 48 to 72 hours after arrest (excluding "nonjudicial days").

If the offense for which the minor is taken into custody is "a misdemeanor that does not involve violence, the threat of violence, or possession or use of a weapon, and if the minor is not currently on probation or parole," then the minor must be released within 48 hours after having been taken into custody (again, excluding "nonjudicial days") unless a wardship petition is filed *and* "the minor has been ordered detained by a judge or referee of the juvenile court pursuant to Section 635" within that initial 48-hour period.

Most significantly, when a minor is detained on suspicion of criminal activity, in contrast to an adult detained under similar circumstances, the inquiry into the propriety of the extended detention is much broader in scope than a determination, in the strict Fourth Amendment sense, of whether "factual" probable cause exists to believe the minor committed the crime for which he was taken into custody. Section 628 lists seven "conditions," one or more of which must be found to exist in order to warrant detaining the minor and scheduling a detention hearing within 72 hours of his or her arrest (again, excluding "nonjudicial" days). These conditions include whether:

(1) The minor is in need of proper and effective parental care or control and has no parent, guardian, or responsible relative; or has no parent, guardian, or responsible relative willing to exercise or capable of exercising such care or control; or has no parent, guardian, or responsible relative actually exercising such care or control.

(2) The minor is destitute or is not provided with the necessities of life or is not provided with a home or suitable place of abode.

(3) The minor is provided with a home which is an unfit place for him by reason of neglect, cruelty, depravity or physical abuse of either of his parents, or of his guardian or other person in whose custody or care he is.

(4) Continued detention of the minor is a matter of immediate and urgent necessity for the protection of the minor or reasonably necessary for the protection of the person or property of another.

(5) The minor is likely to flee the jurisdiction of the court.

(6) The minor has violated an order of the juvenile court.

(7) The minor is physically dangerous to the public because of a mental or physical deficiency, disorder or abnormality.

Section 635 sets forth the factors to be considered by the juvenile court at the detention hearing, and the standard the court must apply, in evaluating the probation officer's findings pursuant to section 628 and determining whether to continue the minor's detention or order his or her release from custody. The section provides:

The court will examine such minor, his parent, guardian, or other person having relevant knowledge, hear such relevant evidence as the minor, his parent or guardian or their counsel desires to present, and, unless it appears that such minor has violated an order of the juvenile court or has escaped from the commitment of the juvenile court or that it is a matter of immediate and urgent necessity for the protection of such minor or reasonably necessary for the protection of the person or property of another that he be detained or that such minor is likely to flee to avoid the jurisdiction of the court, the court shall make its order releasing such minor from custody. The circumstances and gravity of the alleged offense may be considered, in conjunction with other factors, to determine whether it is a matter of immediate and urgent necessity for the protection of the minor or reasonably necessary for the protection of the person or property of another that the minor be detained.

The minor and his or her parent or guardian have the right to be represented by counsel at every stage of the detention proceedings. If the minor or the parent or guardian is indigent or cannot otherwise afford an attorney, counsel will be appointed by the court. In any case in which it appears to the court that there is a conflict of interest between a parent or guardian and the minor, separate counsel may be appointed for the minor and the parent or guardian.

As is evident from the foregoing summary of the relevant statutory provisions, the determination whether to detain a *minor* following a warrantless arrest for criminal activity is a complex one, requiring consideration of various factors personal to the minor and his family situation, and the application of several important statutory presumptions favoring the minor's early release to a parent, guardian or responsible relative, or, if extended detention is warranted, selection of the detention alternative most "compatible with the best interests of the minor ...," and "which least restricts the minor's freedom of movement." These presumptions, and the policies they implement, are unique to juvenile detention proceedings and are *not* implicated when a judicial determination is made whether factual probable cause exists to extend the detention of an adult arrestee.

We emphasize that we do not today suggest a juvenile arrestee facing postarrest detention has no Fourth Amendment liberty interest in a prompt determination of the legal cause for his or her extended detention. The Fourth Amendment principles at the core of the holding in *Gerstein*, apply to juveniles as well as adults. The high court expressly reaffirmed as much eight years ago in *Schall*. Indeed, although the court in *Schall* twice characterized its earlier holding in *Gerstein* to be "that a judicial determination of probable cause is a prerequisite to any extended restraint on the liberty of an *adult* accused of crime," we think that such characterization cannot, in reason or fairness, be understood as an attempt by the court to limit the fundamental principles announced in *Gerstein* solely to adult detentions. The court subsequently made it clear in *Schall* that children have a protected liberty interest in "freedom from institutional restraints."

California's postarrest juvenile detention statutes are plainly designed to protect the arrested minor's Fourth Amendment rights. The arresting officer must, within 24 hours of the arrest, prepare a written summary of the probable cause for taking the minor into temporary custody. In contrast to adult criminal proceedings, the statutory presumptions *require* "immediate release" of the minor to the custody of his or her parents or legal guardian unless specific factors warranting extended detention are found to exist. Even when such factors supportive of further detention are found to exist, the juvenile arrestee must nonetheless be released within 48 hours unless a wardship petition is filed within that initial 48-hour period. And, if a wardship petition is filed, a formal, adversarial detention hearing, which incorporates a probable cause determination, and at which counsel is provided for both the minor and his parents or guardian, must be conducted "as soon as possible but in any event [no later than] the expiration of the next judicial day after a petition to declare the minor a ward ... has been filed" (i.e., no later than 72 hours after arrest, excluding "nonjudicial days"). At that detention hearing, the juvenile court will consider "[t]he circumstances and gravity of the alleged offense" in determining whether extended pretrial detention is warranted under all the facts and circumstances.

In light of the foregoing, we therefore conclude that the United States Supreme Court's adoption of the strict 48-hour rule in *McLaughlin* was neither foreseen nor intended by that court to be rigidly operable in juvenile postarrest detention proceedings. Given the fundamental differences between juvenile and adult detention proceedings recognized in a long line of that court's decisions, we will not infer otherwise, absent an express and definitive ruling from the high court to the contrary.

As has been shown, our Legislature, in its wisdom, has enacted a comprehensive statutory scheme governing postarrest juvenile detention that is designed to implement specific policies and procedures deemed to be in the juvenile detainees' best interests, while balancing their fundamental constitutional rights against the well-recognized need for "informality" and "flexibility" in juvenile criminal justice systems. Our juvenile courts, of course, are duty bound to comply with both constitutional and statutory requirements. Having examined the integrated components of California's juvenile detention statutes, we conclude that the Constitution, as interpreted by the United States Supreme Court's pertinent decisions reviewed herein, requires no more than that *juvenile* arrestees be afforded a judicial determination of "probable cause" for any postarrest detention extending beyond the 72-hour period immediately following a warrantless arrest.

In light of these conclusions, it follows that the formal detention hearing provided for in section 632, subdivision (a), may also serve to fulfill the constitutional requirement when the court at such a hearing, *where it is held within 72 hours of the juvenile's arrest*, makes a determination that sufficient probable cause exists for the extended postarrest detention of the juvenile. Consistent with our analysis and conclusions herein, if the 72-hour period immediately following arrest includes one or more "nonjudicial days," such that the juvenile court is unable or unwilling to provide a full statutory detention hearing within that period, then the Constitution independently requires that the juvenile be afforded a separate, timely judicial determination of probable cause for any extended period of detention beyond the 72 hours following arrest.

III. CONCLUSION

The judgment of the Court of Appeal is affirmed.

ARABIAN, Justice, concurring and dissenting.

I concur in the lead opinion in-so-far as it requires prompt probable cause determinations for juveniles within 72 hours of warrantless arrest. I respectfully dissent, however, from the due process analysis by which the lead opinion reaches this conclusion. Petitioner does not dispute his postarrest detention on that basis; nor does he raise such a challenge to any provision of the juvenile court law governing wardship detentions in general. Rather, he asserts that, like any adult in comparable circumstances, a detained minor is entitled to a probable cause determination of suspected criminal activity within 48 hours of a warrantless arrest as mandated by the United States Supreme Court's decision in *McLaughlin*. As framed by petitioner, the only issue before us is whether the rule of *McLaughlin* applies to juveniles. Accordingly, we are constrained to refract his contentions solely through a Fourth Amendment prism, for that is the limited nature of the constitutional claim. The specificity of the question demands an equally precise answer, not the due process circuity submitted in the lead opinion.

While I agree with Justice Mosk that we should pursue a Fourth Amendment tack in resolving this case, I conclude that for juvenile detainees a probable cause determination within 72 hours satisfies the constitutional mandate of "promptness." I am unpersuaded *McLaughlin*, is dispositive or controlling here. Factually, that case involved only adults. In assessing the protections afforded minors, the United States Supreme Court has consciously "refrained ... from taking the easy way with a flat holding that all rights constitutionally assured for the adult accused are to be imposed on the state juvenile proceeding." Thus, I do not construe the holding in *McLaughlin* to extend perforce to juveniles simply because it does not expressly restrict its scope to adults. In my view, the issue warrants an independent examination, bearing in mind both the general nature of the Fourth Amendment guaranty with its rubric of reasonableness and the particularized concerns of the juvenile justice system.

Since any official detention can adversely affect a minor as critically and undeniably as it does an adult, juveniles do have a protectible liberty interest with respect to such restraint, even though they are generally subject to greater restriction of their freedom by virtue of their minority. Moreover, while juveniles do not ipso facto possess the same constitutional rights as adults, it is now a settled proposition that the "promptness" requirement of *Gerstein v. Pugh,* embraces all warrantless detentions regardless of the detainee's age. The question remains, however, to quantify the mandate of *Gerstein* for juveniles as the United States Supreme Court has done for adults in *McLaughlin*. Although we lack a direct answer, decisions of the high court provide some useful contours to the analytical framework.

In general, the juvenile context is highly relevant in determining whether and to what extent a particular constitutional principle applies to minors. Depending upon the interest at stake, this circumstance may dictate that juveniles have rights coextensive with adults, may debar them entirely, or may necessitate some modification of rights.

Regardless of its ultimate conclusion in these cases, the Supreme Court has continually emphasized in its analyses the need to maintain a measure of flexibility to accommodate the special attention with which our society still endeavors to treat youthful offenders. I believe this concern to maximize individualized response is particularly relevant to the question of probable cause determinations because the detention of juveniles implicates additional considerations related to their minority. It also segues with the explicit premise of the Fourth Amendment, which proscribes only "unreasonable" seizures.

These collateral matters do not necessarily preclude probable cause determinations within a shorter period; indeed, as both Justice Mosk and Justice George argue in their dissents, every effort should be made to minimize the period of detention at this juncture in the adjudicatory process. Nevertheless, they provide a rational basis on which to premise some latitude beyond the 48-hour limit delineated in *McLaughlin*. Moreover, even with respect to adult detentions, the Supreme Court has reiterated that "probable cause determinations must be prompt—not immediate" to maintain a necessary measure of "'flexibility' and 'experimentation'" within each state's criminal justice system. These latter considerations are all the more significant in the juvenile justice system, which seeks to provide intervention and rehabilitation, not simply punishment.

I therefore conclude that under the Fourth Amendment the circumstances of a juvenile differ sufficiently from those of an adult that the "promptness" requirement of *Gerstein v.*

Pugh is satisfied if a juvenile detainee is provided a probable cause determination within 72 hours following a warrantless arrest with no extension of time for nonjudicial days.

MOSK, Justice, dissenting.

The Fourth Amendment to the United States Constitution—one of the core provisions of the Bill of Rights—declares: "The right of the people to be secure in their persons, houses, papers and effects, against unreasonable searches and seizures, shall not be violated, and no warrants shall issue, but upon probable cause, supported by oath or affirmation, and particularly describing the place to be searched, and the persons or things to be seized."

In *Gerstein v. Pugh,* the United States Supreme Court held that the Fourth Amendment mandates, as a prerequisite to extended restraint of liberty, a prompt judicial determination that there is probable cause to believe that a person has in fact committed a criminal offense following a warrantless arrest based on suspicion thereof.

In *McLaughlin,* the court defined "promptness" under *Gerstein* as generally within 48 hours of the warrantless arrest.

Thus, under the Fourth Amendment as construed by *Gerstein* and *McLaughlin,* a law-abiding person wrongfully arrested without a warrant is guaranteed his freedom within about 48 hours.

Today, a majority of this court refuse to honor that guaranty when the person in question happens to be a juvenile.

I cannot join in such a breach of our constitutional obligation.

The question before the court is bipartite. Is *Gerstein's* promptness requirement applicable to juveniles? If so, does *McLaughlin's* definition of "promptness" operate in this setting?

A

In *Gerstein,* the United States Supreme Court held that the Fourth Amendment mandates a prompt judicial probable cause determination as a prerequisite to extended restraint of liberty following a warrantless arrest.

In reaching this conclusion, the *Gerstein* court sought to reconcile or at least accommodate an individual's Fourth Amendment rights and the state's legitimate interest in law enforcement.

The *Gerstein* court also made plain that this prompt judicial probable cause determination does not require the "full panoply of adversary safeguards" of "counsel, confrontation, cross-examination, and compulsory process...." Rather, "a nonadversary proceeding [based] on hearsay and written testimony" is sufficient. "The sole issue is whether there is probable cause for detaining the arrested person pending further proceedings. This issue can be determined reliably without an adversary hearing. The standard is the same as that for arrest. That standard—probable cause to believe the suspect has committed a crime—traditionally has been decided by a magistrate in a nonadversary proceeding on hearsay and written testimony...." The court noted: "Because the standards [for arrest and detention] are identical, ordinarily there is no need for further investigation before the probable cause determination can be made."

The *Gerstein* court "recognize[d] that state systems of criminal procedure vary widely. There is no single preferred pretrial procedure, and the nature of the probable cause determination usually will be shaped to accord with a State's pretrial procedure viewed as a whole." But it declared: "Whatever procedure a State may adopt, it must provide a fair and reliable determination of probable cause as a condition for any significant pretrial restraint of liberty, and this determination must be made by a judicial officer ... promptly after arrest" when the arrest itself is made without a warrant.

B

In *McLaughlin,* the United States Supreme Court undertook to define "promptness" under *Gerstein.* The facts there are similar to those here. The *McLaughlin* court adhered to, and indeed reaffirmed, the holding of *Gerstein* that the Fourth Amendment mandates a prompt judicial probable cause determination as a prerequisite to extended restraint of liberty following a warrantless arrest.

The *McLaughlin* court also remained faithful to *Gerstein's* view that "promptness" must be measured in terms of the time that is required for the state "to take the administrative steps incident to arrest." In its own words: "Under *Gerstein,* jurisdictions may choose to combine probable cause determinations with other pretrial proceedings, so long as they do so promptly. This necessarily means that only certain proceedings are candidates for combination. Only those proceedings that arise very early in the pretrial process — such as bail hearings and arraignments — may be chosen." The reason is plain. To allow "promptness" to be defined reference to other "steps" that a state might desire to "take" beyond those "incident to arrest" — for example, the holding of a preliminary examination — would render the requirement nugatory. A federal constitutional mandate that is designed to constrain the states cannot be dependent on the individual policy choices that any given state might happen to make.

All the same, the *McLaughlin* court recognized that the bare mandate of a "prompt" judicial probable cause determination had proved inadequate. It stated: "Unfortunately, as lower court decisions applying *Gerstein* have demonstrated, it is not enough to say that probable cause determinations must be 'prompt.' This vague standard simply has not provided sufficient guidance. Instead, it has led to a flurry of systemic challenges to city and county practices, putting federal judges in the role of making legislative judgments and overseeing local jailhouse operations."

The *McLaughlin* court declined to hold that a judicial probable cause determination is "prompt" only if it is provided *immediately* after the state has "take[n] the administrative steps incident to arrest." It stated: "Taking into account the competing interests articulated in *Gerstein,* we believe that a jurisdiction that provides judicial determinations of probable cause within 48 hours of arrest will, as a general matter, comply with the promptness requirement of *Gerstein.* For this reason, such jurisdictions will be immune from systemic challenges."

The *McLaughlin* court then added: "This is not to say that the probable cause determination in a particular case passes constitutional muster simply because it is provided within 48 hours. Such a hearing may nonetheless violate *Gerstein* if the arrested individual can prove that his or her probable cause determination was delayed unreasonably." But "[w]here an arrested individual does not receive a probable cause determination within 48 hours, the calculus changes. In such a case, the arrested individual does not bear the burden of proving an unreasonable delay. Rather, the burden shifts to the government to demonstrate the existence of a bona fide emergency or other extraordinary circumstance. The fact that in a particular case it may take longer than 48 hours to consolidate pretrial proceedings does not qualify as an extraordinary circumstance. Nor, for that matter, do intervening weekends. A jurisdiction that chooses to offer combined proceedings must do so as soon as is reasonably feasible, but in no event later than 48 hours after arrest."

IV

As stated above, the question before this court is whether *Gerstein's* promptness requirement is applicable to juveniles and, if so, whether *McLaughlin's* definition of "promptness" operates in this setting.

A

The first issue is the applicability of *Gerstein's* promptness requirement to juveniles.

Gerstein declares, both expressly and impliedly, from beginning to end, that the Fourth Amendment's protection extends to "persons" or "individuals." It does not purport to limit the constitutional guaranty to adults or even to qualify its benefit to juveniles.

I find no reason within *Gerstein's* four corners to cabin its conclusion. The *Gerstein* court did not itself choose to restrict the scope of the requirement that it established. I decline to do what it did not.

Neither do I discern outside *Gerstein* any ground to delimit its holding.

It was firmly established almost a decade before *Gerstein* was handed down that "the Bill of Rights is [not] for adults alone."

Indeed, this court itself has expressly held that among the rights of the United States Constitution to which juveniles are entitled "is the guarantee of freedom from unreasonable searches and seizures contained in the Fourth Amendment...." To be sure, the particular commands and prohibitions of the Fourth Amendment may vary in some respects for adults and juveniles. The basic criterion of the constitutional provision is, of course, "reasonableness."

Whatever differentiation may be justified in some areas for adults and juveniles under the Fourth Amendment is not justified here. In *McLaughlin,* the court predicated *Gerstein's* promptness requirement on the proposition that "[a] State has no legitimate interest in detaining for extended periods individuals who have been arrested without probable cause." This applies to *all* individuals—whether or not they have attained the age of majority. When probable cause is lacking, detention is unsupported as a matter of law. That proposition does not depend on how old the detainee is. The presence of youth does not make up for the absence of probable cause.

I recognize that the state, as *parens patriae,* may have a legitimate interest in detaining a juvenile for criminal activity prior to trial. That interest, however, is not served by holding *Gerstein's* promptness requirement inapplicable. Without question, an adult arrested without probable cause must be released as soon as reasonably possible. The reason: grounds for detention are lacking. So too, a juvenile arrested without probable cause must be released as soon as reasonably possible. The reason is the same. Absent probable cause, the state's exercise of its power to preserve and promote the welfare of the child is without support. For juveniles as for adults, *Gerstein's* promptness requirement operates to conserve and allocate resources by limiting the class of detainees to those who are properly subject to detention. Of course, the state, as *parens patriae,* may have a legitimate interest in detaining a juvenile for reasons *unrelated to criminal activity.* But no such interest is implicated here.

I also recognize that, in detaining a juvenile for criminal activity prior to trial, the state may use means and/or facilities different from those it uses for adults. That fact, however, is not determinative. It simply cannot be said that the restraint of liberty imposed on a juvenile is somehow less significant, in and of itself, than that imposed on an adult. Indeed, "[p]retrial detention is an onerous experience, *especially for juveniles...."*

Moreover, it appears that since *Gerstein* was decided, all reported decisions that have considered the question to resolution have held or stated, expressly or impliedly, that *Gerstein* is applicable to *all* "persons" or "individuals," juveniles as well as adults.

Therefore, I conclude that *Gerstein's* promptness requirement is indeed applicable to juveniles.

B

The second issue is whether *McLaughlin's* definition of "promptness" operates in the juvenile setting.

McLaughlin declares, both expressly and impliedly, from beginning to end, that its definition of "promptness" extends to "probable cause determinations" generally. It does not purport to limit its scope to adults or even to qualify its meaning for juveniles.

I do not see in *McLaughlin* itself any basis to restrict its definition of "promptness" against juveniles. Quite the contrary. The reasoning of the *McLaughlin* court is premised on an assessment that the "undefined" promptness requirement of *Gerstein* is simply too "vague" a "standard." That assessment holds as true for juvenile proceedings relating to minors as for criminal actions involving adults. Perhaps truer. For if "it is not enough to say that probable cause determinations must be 'prompt'" for criminal actions, which are governed by a procedural law that is relatively well defined, a fortiori it is not nearly enough for juvenile proceedings, which are guided by norms of another sort. Similarly, if the "undefined" promptness requirement has already "led to a flurry of systemic challenges to city and county practices [in criminal actions], putting federal judges in the role of making legislative judgments and overseeing local jailhouse operations," it will surely lead to like challenges in juvenile proceedings — of which the present is, apparently, only the first — involving the state judiciary as well as the federal in matters that belong largely to the other branches of government.

Neither do I discover any support outside *McLaughlin* to condition its definition of "promptness" against juveniles. As stated, juveniles as well as adults are entitled to the protections of the Fourth Amendment. As also stated, the basic criterion of the constitutional provision is "reasonableness." The definition articulated by the *McLaughlin* court serves to give content to this test. No reason appears to deny its benefit to juveniles. Unquestionably, "it is not enough to say that probable cause determinations must be 'prompt'" when the state acts as enforcer of the criminal law for the sake of the community generally. The same is true when the state acts as *parens patriae* for the benefit of the child. The word "prompt" is no less "vague" in the latter situation than in the former. As noted, under the Fourth Amendment as construed by *Gerstein* and *McLaughlin,* a law-abiding person wrongfully arrested without a warrant is guaranteed his freedom within about 48 hours. It would be unreasonable to hold that when the person in question happens to be a juvenile, the guaranty is illusory.

Therefore, I conclude that *McLaughlin's* definition of "promptness" does in fact operate in the juvenile setting.

C

In conducting my analysis, I have not overlooked *Schall v. Martin,* which was decided nine years after *Gerstein* and seven years before *McLaughlin.*

In *Schall,* the United States Supreme Court held that a section of the New York Family Court Act was not invalid under the due process clause of the Fourteenth Amendment. The provision in question authorized court-ordered "preventive detention" of a juvenile accused of delinquency, i.e., pretrial detention based on a judicial finding that there is a "serious risk" that the juvenile "'may before the return date commit an act which if committed by an adult would constitute a crime.'" The court expressly noted that the propriety of detention *based on a warrantless arrest* was "not at issue": the sole question concerned "*judicially ordered* detention."

In scrutinizing the New York statutory scheme, the *Schall* court asked whether the authorization of court-ordered preventive detention was compatible with "fundamental fairness" under the Fourteenth Amendment's due process clause. It identified two subsidiary inquiries. First, did court-ordered preventive detention under the statutory provision serve a legitimate state objective? Second, were the procedural safeguards contained therein adequate against erroneous and unnecessary restraints of liberty?

At the outset, the *Schall* court observed: "There is no doubt that the Due Process Clause is applicable in juvenile proceedings. 'The problem ... is to ascertain the precise impact of the due process requirement upon such proceedings.'" It went on: "[C]ertain basic constitutional protections enjoyed by adults accused of crimes also apply to juveniles. But the Constitution does not mandate elimination of all differences in the treatment of juveniles. The State has 'a *parens patriae* interest in preserving and promoting the welfare of the child,' which makes a juvenile proceeding fundamentally different from an adult criminal trial." In view thereof, it had "tried ... to strike a balance—to respect the 'informality' and 'flexibility' that characterize juvenile proceedings, and yet to ensure that such proceedings comport with the 'fundamental fairness' demanded by the Due Process Clause."

The *Schall* court concluded that the New York statutory scheme with its authorization of court-ordered preventive detention was indeed compatible with "fundamental fairness" under the Fourteenth Amendment's due process clause. It did so because it answered each of the two subsidiary inquiries in the affirmative.

After even brief consideration, it becomes plain that *Schall* does not affect the conclusion that *Gerstein*'s promptness requirement is indeed applicable to juveniles and that *McLaughlin*'s definition of "promptness" does in fact operate in this setting.

"It is axiomatic," of course, "that cases are not authority for propositions not considered."

To begin with, *Schall* is based on the Fourteenth Amendment's due process clause. *Gerstein* and *McLaughlin,* by contrast, rest on the Fourth Amendment. Indeed, the *Schall* court effectively declared that its reach did not extend to the Fourth Amendment question presented here when it expressly noted that it was solely concerned with "*judicially ordered* detention." Moreover, the *Schall* court referred only to formal, adversarial probable cause hearings, and not the informal, nonadversarial judicial probable cause determinations discussed in *Gerstein* and *McLaughlin.* Lastly, and perhaps most important, the *Schall* court dealt with a situation in which the juvenile was already detained pursuant to court order—unlike the situation here, where he was not.

To be sure, at one point in its opinion the *Schall* court stated: "In *Gerstein*..., we held that a judicial determination of probable cause is a prerequisite to any extended restraint on the liberty of an *adult* accused of crime." And at another point: "In many respects, the [New York statutory scheme] provides far more predetention protection for juveniles than we found to be constitutionally required for a probable-cause determination for *adults* in *Gerstein.*"

The *Schall* court's dicta, isolated and irrelevant as they are, cannot reasonably be read as an after-the-fact attempt to limit *Gerstein* to adults, but must be viewed merely as a reflection of the general factual context out of which *Gerstein* arose. Indeed, it appears that no reported decision — with the singular exception of the opinion of the Court of Appeal below — has construed these words to impose such a limitation. This is certainly true of *McLaughlin*. In that case, the court could easily have used this language, which was cited by the parties and amici curiae therein, to limit *Gerstein* to adults. Conspicuously, it did not do so.

It can perhaps be argued that there is tension between *Schall* and *McLaughlin*. The former implies that a formal, adversarial probable cause hearing within at most nine days of the warrantless arrest of a juvenile who is already in court-ordered preventive detention suffices for the Fourteenth Amendment's due process clause. By contrast, the latter holds that a judicial probable cause determination, albeit informal and nonadversarial, is required by the Fourth Amendment generally within 48 hours of a warrantless arrest.

Any such tension, however, must necessarily be resolved in favor of the later-decided *McLaughlin* and against the earlier-decided *Schall*. By its terms, the *Schall* implication depends on *Gerstein*'s "undefined" promptness requirement and *Gerstein*'s consequent approval of a delay of five days between a warrantless arrest and a formal, adversarial probable cause hearing. The *McLaughlin* holding, however, expressly defines "promptness" as generally within 48 hours and thereby withdraws approval of a 5-day delay. Therefore, the *Schall* implication simply does not survive the *McLaughlin* holding.

In conducting my analysis, I have also not overlooked *Flores*. In *Flores*, the United States Supreme Court rejected a constitutional challenge, based solely on the due process clause of the Fifth Amendment, to an Immigration and Naturalization Service regulation governing the detention of allegedly deportable alien juveniles.

Since a case, like *Schall*, is not authority for a proposition it *did not* consider, a fortiori, a case, like *Flores*, cannot be authority for a proposition it *could not have* considered.

V

The lead opinion is much taken with *Schall*. Too much so. The lead opinion implies that *Schall* is "authoritative" on the Fourth Amendment standards governing the detention of juveniles. But at most, it is such only as to *court-ordered* preventive detention. Detention of that sort, however, is *not* what is involved here. The lead opinion attempts to avoid the limited scope of *Schall*. But it trips on the opinion's very words: the propriety of detention *based on a warrantless arrest* was "not at issue"; the sole question concerned "*judicially ordered* detention."

The lead opinion also implies that *Schall* requires examination of "all the procedural components" of the juvenile court law because *Schall* itself examined "all the procedural components" of the New York Family Court Act. That is not so. *Schall*'s consideration of the New York statute was dictated solely by the fact that, in that case, the statute had been challenged as invalid under the due process clause of the Fourteenth Amendment. The juvenile court law is not challenged here at all.

Lastly, the lead opinion assumes that the "authority" of *Schall* is unaffected by *McLaughlin*. But, as explained, in part relevant here the earlier-decided *Schall* does not even survive the later-decided *McLaughlin*.

Even if the lead opinion's premise is sound, its conclusion is simply incorrect. Whenever the state predicates detention on criminal activity — in whatever proceeding, under whatever role, or for whatever objective — probable cause is crucial for Fourth Amendment purposes. And whenever probable cause is crucial, *Gerstein*'s promptness requirement, as defined by *McLaughlin*, is applicable. A prompt judicial probable cause determination generally within 48 hours of a juvenile's warrantless arrest — a determination that may be informal and nonadversarial — is altogether consistent with the juvenile court law, the goals of which include the expeditious resolution of issues in a relatively open and cooperative setting.

I recognize that under the juvenile court law, the state may detain a juvenile for reasons *unrelated to criminal activity* — although only in a separate nonsecure facility segregated from those suspected of crime — as when the minor appears in public suffering from a sickness or injury that requires care. In such a situation, *Gerstein* and *McLaughlin* are not implicated by their very terms. But such a situation does not obtain here.

In a word, when the state detains a person for criminal activity, it must establish probable cause. It is now settled that "[a] State has *no legitimate interest* in detaining ... individuals who have been arrested without probable cause" generally beyond 48 hours. It is inconceivable that a "legitimate interest" could somehow spring into being when the individual in question turns out to be a juvenile.

The lead opinion also suggests that *Gerstein*'s promptness requirement, at least as defined by *McLaughlin*, is inapplicable to juveniles because their interest in freedom from restraint of liberty under the Fourth Amendment is assertedly less substantial than that of adults. But as stated, the basic criterion of the constitutional provision is "reasonableness." Extended restraint for a criminal offense in the absence of probable cause is no more reasonable for juveniles than adults. Arguably less so. In California at least, adults generally have the right to release on bail. Juveniles do not. "[D]etaining ... individuals who have been arrested without probable cause" beyond 48 hours is presumptively unreasonable. It is unexplained how the individual's status as a juvenile can change the rule.

Most prominently, I believe, the lead opinion suggests that *Gerstein*'s promptness requirement, at least as defined by *McLaughlin*, is inapplicable to juveniles because the juvenile court law assertedly has more "procedural safeguards" than the criminal law. The short answer is that none of these "protections" even purports to be an equivalent for a prompt judicial probable cause determination. Indeed, the provisions cited by the lead opinion generally relate to the disposition of the detained juvenile within the juvenile system. *They do not primarily concern whether the juvenile ought to have been detained within the system in the first place.* That is the function of a prompt judicial probable cause determination. The cited "procedural safeguards" "protect" the juvenile who has been arrested without probable cause in much the same way as prison health and safety regulations "protect" an inmate who has been wrongfully convicted. They are too little, too late. In brief, they simply do not guarantee that a law-abiding juvenile wrongfully arrested without a warrant will regain his freedom within about 48 hours.

I acknowledge that in certain instances the probation officer appears obligated to investigate the question of probable cause. But, by definition, the prompt judicial probable cause determination mandated by the Fourth Amendment as construed by *Gerstein* and *McLaughlin* must be made by a *judicial* officer. Obviously, the probation officer is not such. He has responsibility to law enforcement, seeing that he is possessed of the "powers and authority conferred by law upon peace officers...." The probation officer's "responsibility to law enforcement is inconsistent with the constitutional role of a neutral and detached magistrate."

What the lead opinion may mean to suggest in alluding to the "procedural safeguards" of the juvenile court law is that, in *Gerstein*'s words, "existing procedures ... satisfy the requirement of the Fourth Amendment." If it does, it is wrong. As stated, the cited "protections" simply do not guarantee that a law-abiding juvenile wrongfully arrested without a warrant will regain his freedom within about 48 hours.

The lead opinion next suggests that *Gerstein*'s promptness requirement, at least as defined by *McLaughlin*, is inapplicable to juveniles because it is assertedly incompatible with the "'informality' and 'flexibility' that characterize juvenile proceedings...."

Plainly, the "informality" and "flexibility" of juvenile proceedings — both in American jurisdictions generally and in California specifically — are designed to make the process *more expeditious* than that of criminal actions, *not less.* The review by the lead opinion proves the point as to the juvenile court law. Thus, if any colorable attack could be mounted against *McLaughlin*'s definition of "promptness," it would be that it is *too long, not too short.*

Further, it is evident that a prompt judicial probable cause determination generally within 48 hours of a juvenile's warrantless arrest — like similar determinations routinely and quickly made on application for an arrest warrant — can readily be accommodated. I note that in a case such as this, the arresting officer must presently prepare a "concise written statement of ... probable cause" "without necessary delay" — and specifically within 24 hours if the criminal offense in question is a misdemeanor. I also note, in words from *Gerstein*, that "[b]ecause the standards [for arrest and detention] are identical, ordinarily there is no need for further investigation before the [judicial] probable cause determination can be made." Evidently, a longer "period of detention" is not required for the state "to take the administrative steps incident to arrest" for a juvenile than for an adult. Indeed, at oral argument on rehearing, counsel for respondent effectively conceded the point: a judicial probable cause determination, he admitted, is "not ... difficult" to make.

It may also be true, as the lead opinion asserts, that the so-called "factual probable cause determination is but one component of the broader inquiry...." But this "component" is the first to be decided both in time and in logic.

To repeat: "A state has *no legitimate interest* in detaining ... individuals who have been arrested without probable cause" generally beyond 48 hours whether or not such individuals have attained the age of majority. Surely, the state may have a "legitimate interest" in continuing to detain juveniles who have been arrested without probable cause beyond 48 hours when there exists a supported basis for doing so separate and independent from the unsupported suspicion of criminal activity, as for example the presence of sickness or injury that requires care. In such cases, the state may continue to detain without implicating *Gerstein* and *McLaughlin.*

The foregoing assessment of the feasibility of a prompt judicial probable cause determination generally within 48 hours of a juvenile's warrantless arrest is confirmed by experience. Petitioner represents, without dispute, that a number of the state's largest counties, including San Diego, Orange, Santa Clara, Sacramento, San Francisco, Fresno, and San Mateo, are successfully providing determinations of this kind. At oral argument on rehearing, counsel for respondent conceded that Los Angeles is doing the same, at least for most juveniles.

One thing remains to be said. And it is important. The lead opinion's reasoning does not express the views of a majority of this court. As a result, its analysis "lacks authority as precedent" and hence cannot bind. Therefore, its mischief is limited to this case and to this case alone.

VI

For the reasons stated, I conclude that *Gerstein*'s promptness requirement is indeed applicable to juveniles and that *McLaughlin*'s definition of "promptness" does in fact operate in this setting.

From this conclusion, it follows that petitioner's systemic Fourth Amendment challenge to the superior court's "official position" that *Gerstein*'s promptness requirement, at least as defined by *McLaughlin*, is not applicable to juveniles is successful.

I would therefore reverse the judgment of the Court of Appeal with directions to cause issuance of a peremptory writ of mandate compelling the superior court to comply with *Gerstein*'s promptness requirement as defined by *McLaughlin* with regard to juveniles as well as adults.

Accordingly, I dissent.

GEORGE, Justice, dissenting.

I previously have expressed my view that generally worded constitutional and statutory provisions typically do *not* lend themselves to application through fixed, mechanical rules established by judicial decree. The United States Supreme Court has spoken in the present context, however, holding in *McLaughlin,* that a state's criminal statutory scheme does not comply with the Fourth Amendment unless it provides that a "person" (without differentiation between adults and juveniles), arrested and detained without a warrant, will be afforded a judicial determination of probable cause within 48 hours of arrest. That federal constitutional rule is now settled and, of course, binding upon this court.

Although, as the lead opinion recognizes, the procedures constitutionally mandated in juvenile proceedings need not mirror in all respects the procedures required in adult criminal proceedings, I agree with Justice Mosk's conclusion that the People have not identified any state interest that would justify incarcerating a juvenile, detained solely because law enforcement authorities believe he or she has committed a crime, for a period of time (before according the juvenile an impartial judicial determination of probable cause) longer than the time the state could detain an adult under similar circumstances. Indeed, in this context, I believe the need for a very prompt judicial determination of probable cause may be a more crucial factor in assessing the "reasonableness" of the "seizure" of a juvenile than of an adult, because the consequences of even a relatively brief, wrongful incarceration are likely to be more detrimental and long-lasting to an innocent, vulnerable child than to an innocent adult. In my view, the lead opinion's conclusion to the contrary is not supported either by *Schall* or the very recent decision in *Flores,* because neither case purported to address the propriety of an extended detention of a juvenile who could be released to the custody of his or her family but has been detained solely because he or she is suspected of committing a crime.

Holdings of *Alfredo A. v. Superior Court of Los Angeles County:* The majority opinion held that juveniles charged with committing a delinquent act are not entitled to all of the due process protections afforded to adults in criminal proceedings. The majority opinion held that a 72-hour requirement for holding a juvenile without a judicial determination of probable cause was reasonable in spite of the fact that the U.S. Supreme Court interpreted the Constitution to require a judicial review within 48-hours for adult criminal defendants.

Discussion Questions

Why would it take more time for authorities to provide a hearing for a juvenile detained on a warrantless "arrest" than is required for an adult arrested for an alleged criminal violation?

How does the fact that there is a strong presumption that youth should be placed with their parents in a juvenile delinquency proceeding affect the reasonableness of delay in providing the youth an early probable cause determination?

Why does the court find that it is not reasonable to hold the state to providing a detention hearing when, in fact, many of the large counties in the state already do so?

Key Concepts: Pre-Adjudication (Pretrial) Detention

- The United States Constitutional right to reasonable bail is not applicable to juvenile delinquency proceedings, and, as a result, most states do not provide bail for a youth detained for an alleged delinquent act.

- Preventive detention is constitutionally acceptable for juvenile offenders.

- While the United States Constitution requires that a minor held in detention prior to adjudication must promptly be given the opportunity for a judicial determination of probable cause (a detention hearing), the definition of "prompt" may be different (longer) than in adult criminal cases.

Chapter VIII

Waiver to Adult Court

Overview: Adult criminal systems and juvenile delinquency systems have traditionally been entirely separate from each other. When a minor commits an act that would be a crime if the youth were an adult, the juvenile delinquency court traditionally had exclusive jurisdiction of the offense. Every state has created exceptions where older youth committing very serious crimes could be subject to the jurisdiction of the adult criminal court. Most states provide that, at a certain age, the prosecution may ask the court to "waive jurisdiction" of a youth, and, if the motion is granted, the juvenile court gives up its exclusive jurisdiction of the case, transferring the case to the adult criminal court. Before waiver is granted, a hearing must be held on the motion to waive jurisdiction. This hearing is commonly called a "waiver hearing." Once the "crack down on crime" movement began, states began adding more ways for minors to be subject to adult criminal court jurisdiction. Over half of all states have statutory exclusions that allow a criminal case to be filed directly in adult court when the crime is one that is enumerated in the statute and the youth is of a certain minimum age. Approximately one-third of states allow the prosecutor to exercise his discretion to file cases in adult criminal court when the crime is one that is enumerated in the statute and the youth is of a certain minimum age.

Kent v. U.S.: In *Kent v. U.S.,* the United States Supreme Court was asked to determine whether or not a waiver-of-jurisdiction hearing is such a critically important action to warrant the implication of Due Process rights for a juvenile and, if so, what rights are applicable to a waiver hearing. The order waiving jurisdiction in *Kent* was made without any hearing or any specific findings in support of the order. In adult court, the jury found Kent not guilty by reason of insanity on the counts alleging rape. On the six counts of housebreaking and robbery, the jury found that petitioner was guilty. Kent was sentenced to serve five to 15 years on each count as to which he was found guilty, or a total of 30 to 90 years in prison.

As you read *Kent v. U.S.,* look for the following:

1. Consider why the court determined that a waiver hearing was a "critically important" step in the prosecution of a juvenile.

2. Look for what specific rights are afforded to a youth before a waiver to adult court can be ordered as well as what rights are not guaranteed under *Kent.*

3. Look for the reasons that the court found that youth in the District of Columbia had the "worst of both worlds" concerning waiver from juvenile to adult court.

Kent v. U.S.
383 U.S. 541 (1966)

Mr. Justice FORTAS delivered the opinion of the Court.

This case is here on certiorari to the United States Court of Appeals for the District of Columbia Circuit. The facts and the contentions of counsel raise a number of disturbing questions concerning the administration by the police and the Juvenile Court authorities of the District of Columbia laws relating to juveniles. Apart from raising questions as to the adequacy of custodial and treatment facilities and policies, some of which are not within judicial competence, the case presents important challenges to the procedure of the police and Juvenile Court officials upon apprehension of a juvenile suspected of serious offenses. Because we conclude that the Juvenile Court's order waiving jurisdiction of petitioner was entered without compliance with required procedures, we remand the case to the trial court.

Morris A. Kent, Jr., first came under the authority of the Juvenile Court of the District of Columbia in 1959. He was then aged 14. He was apprehended as a result of several housebreakings and an attempted purse snatching. He was placed on probation, in the custody of his mother who had been separated from her husband since Kent was two years old. Juvenile Court officials interviewed Kent from time to time during the probation period and accumulated a 'Social Service' file.

On September 2, 1961, an intruder entered the apartment of a woman in the District of Columbia. He took her wallet. He raped her. The police found in the apartment latent fingerprints. They were developed and processed. They matched the fingerprints of Morris Kent, taken when he was 14 years old and under the jurisdiction of the Juvenile Court. At about 3 p.m. on September 5, 1961, Kent was taken into custody by the police. Kent was then 16 and therefore subject to the 'exclusive jurisdiction' of the Juvenile Court. He was still on probation to that court as a result of the 1959 proceedings.

Upon being apprehended, Kent was taken to police headquarters where he was interrogated by police officers. It appears that he admitted his involvement in the offense which led to his apprehension and volunteered information as to similar offenses involving housebreaking, robbery, and rape. His interrogation proceeded from about 3 p.m. to 10 p.m. the same evening.

Sometime after 10 p.m. petitioner was taken to the Receiving Home for Children. The next morning he was released to the police for further interrogation at police headquarters, which lasted until 5 p.m.

The record does not show when his mother became aware that the boy was in custody but shortly after 2 p.m. on September 6, 1961, the day following petitioner's apprehension, she retained counsel.

Counsel, together with petitioner's mother, promptly conferred with the Social Service Director of the Juvenile Court. In a brief interview, they discussed the possibility that the Juvenile Court might waive jurisdiction and remit Kent to trial by the District Court. Counsel made known his intention to oppose waiver.

Petitioner was detained at the Receiving Home for almost a week. There was no arraignment during this time, no determination by a judicial officer of probable cause for petitioner's apprehension.

During this period of detention and interrogation, petitioner's counsel arranged for examination of petitioner by two psychiatrists and a psychologist. He thereafter filed with the Juvenile Court a motion for a hearing on the question of waiver of Juvenile Court jurisdiction, together with an affidavit of a psychiatrist certifying that petitioner 'is a victim of severe psychopathology' and recommending hospitalization for psychiatric observation. Petitioner's counsel, in support of his motion to the effect that the Juvenile Court should retain jurisdiction of petitioner, offered to prove that if petitioner were given adequate treatment in a hospital under the aegis of the Juvenile Court, he would be a suitable subject for rehabilitation.

At the same time, petitioner's counsel moved that the Juvenile Court should give him access to the Social Service file relating to petitioner which had been accumulated by the staff of the Juvenile Court during petitioner's probation period, and which would be available to the Juvenile Court judge in considering the question whether it should retain or waive jurisdiction. Petitioner's counsel represented that access to this file was essential to his providing petitioner with effective assistance of counsel.

The Juvenile Court judge did not rule on these motions. He held no hearing. He did not confer with petitioner or petitioner's parents or petitioner's counsel. He entered an order reciting that after 'full investigation, I do hereby waive' jurisdiction of petitioner and directing that he be 'held for trial for (the alleged) offenses under the regular procedure of the U.S. District Court for the District of Columbia.' He made no findings. He did not recite any reason for the waiver. He made no reference to the motions filed by petitioner's counsel. We must assume that he denied, *sub silentio*, the motions for a hearing, the recommendation for hospitalization for psychiatric observation, the request for access to the Social Service file, and the offer to prove that petitioner was a fit subject for rehabilitation under the Juvenile Court's jurisdiction.

Presumably, prior to entry of his order, the Juvenile Court judge received and considered recommendations of the Juvenile Court staff, the Social Service file relating to petitioner, and a report dated September 8, 1961 (three days following petitioner's apprehension), submitted to him by the Juvenile Probation Section. The Social Service file and the September 8 report were later sent to the District Court and it appears that both of them referred to petitioner's mental condition. The September 8 report spoke of 'a rapid deterioration of (petitioner's) personality structure and the possibility of mental illness.' As stated, neither this report nor the Social Service file was made available to petitioner's counsel.

Meanwhile, on September 25, 1961, shortly after the Juvenile Court order waiving its jurisdiction, petitioner was indicted by a grand jury of the United States District Court for the District of Columbia. The indictment contained eight counts alleging two instances of housebreaking, robbery, and rape, and one of housebreaking and robbery.

On March 7, 1963, the District Court held a hearing on petitioner's motion to determine his competency to stand trial. The court determined that petitioner was competent. At trial, petitioner's defense was wholly directed toward proving that he was not criminally responsible because 'his unlawful act was the product of mental disease or mental defect.' Extensive evidence, including expert testimony, was presented to support this defense. The jury found as to the counts alleging rape that petitioner was 'not guilty by reason of insanity.' Under District of Columbia law, this made it mandatory that petitioner be transferred to St. Elizabeth's Hospital, a mental institution, until his sanity is restored. On the six counts of housebreaking and robbery, the jury found that petitioner was guilty.

Kent was sentenced to serve five to 15 years on each count as to which he was found guilty, or a total of 30 to 90 years in prison. The District Court ordered that the time to be spent at St. Elizabeth's on the mandatory commitment after the insanity acquittal be counted as part of the 30- to 90-year sentence.

It is to petitioner's arguments as to the infirmity of the proceedings by which the Juvenile Court waived its otherwise exclusive jurisdiction that we address our attention. Petitioner attacks the waiver of jurisdiction on a number of statutory and constitutional grounds. He contends that the waiver is defective because no hearing was held; because no findings were made by the Juvenile Court; because the Juvenile Court stated no reasons for waiver; and because counsel was denied access to the Social Service file which presumably was considered by the Juvenile Court in determining to waive jurisdiction.

We agree that the order of the Juvenile Court waiving its jurisdiction and transferring petitioner for trial in the United States District Court for the District of Columbia was invalid.

We agree with the Court of Appeals that the statute contemplates that the Juvenile Court should have considerable latitude within which to determine whether it should retain jurisdiction over a child or—subject to the statutory delimitation—should waive jurisdiction. But this latitude is not complete.

We do not consider whether, on the merits, Kent should have been transferred; but there is no place in our system of law for reaching a result of such tremendous consequences without ceremony—without hearing, without effective assistance of counsel, without a statement of reasons. It is inconceivable that a court of justice dealing with adults, with respect to a similar issue, would proceed in this manner. It would be extraordinary if society's special concern for children, as reflected in the District of Columbia's Juvenile Court Act, permitted this procedure. We hold that it does not.

The theory of the District's Juvenile Court Act, like that of other jurisdictions, is rooted in social welfare philosophy rather than in the *corpus juris*. Its proceedings are designated as civil rather than criminal. The Juvenile Court is theoretically engaged in determining the needs of the child and of society rather than adjudicating criminal conduct. The objectives are to provide measures of guidance and rehabilitation for the child and protection for society, not to fix criminal responsibility, guilt and punishment. The State is *parens patriae* rather than prosecuting attorney and judge. But the admonition to function in a 'parental' relationship is not an invitation to procedural arbitrariness.

While there can be no doubt of the original laudable purpose of juvenile courts, studies and critiques in recent years raise serious questions as to whether actual performance measures well enough against theoretical purpose to make tolerable the immunity of the process from the reach of constitutional guaranties applicable to adults. There is much evidence that some juvenile courts, including that of the District of Columbia, lack the personnel, facilities and techniques to perform adequately as representatives of the State in a *parens patriae* capacity, at least with respect to children charged with law violation. There is evidence, in fact, that there may be grounds for concern that the child receives the worst of both worlds: that he gets neither the protections accorded to adults nor the solicitous care and regenerative treatment postulated for children.

This concern, however, does not induce us in this case to accept the invitation to rule that constitutional guaranties which would be applicable to adults charged with the serious offenses for which Kent was tried must be applied in juvenile court proceedings concerned with allegations of law violation.

It is clear beyond dispute that the waiver of jurisdiction is a 'critically important' action determining vitally important statutory rights of the juvenile.

The net, therefore, is that petitioner—then a boy of 16—was by statute entitled to certain procedures and benefits as a consequence of his statutory right to the 'exclusive' jurisdiction of the Juvenile Court. In these circumstances, considering particularly that decision as to waiver of jurisdiction and transfer of the matter to the District Court was potentially as important to petitioner as the difference between five years' confinement and a death sentence, we conclude that, as a condition to a valid waiver order, petitioner as entitled to a hearing, including access by his counsel to the social records and probation or similar reports which presumably are considered by the court, and to a statement of reasons for the Juvenile Court's decision. We believe that this result is required by the statute read in the context of constitutional principles relating to due process and the assistance of counsel.

We are of the opinion that the Court of Appeals misconceived the basic issue and the underlying values in this case. It did note, as another panel of the same court did a few months later in Black and Watkins, that the determination of whether to transfer a child from the statutory structure of the Juvenile Court to the criminal processes of the District Court is 'critically important.' We hold that it is, indeed, a 'critically important' proceeding.

Meaningful review requires that the reviewing court should review. It should not be remitted to assumptions. It must have before it a statement of the reasons motivating the waiver including, of course, a statement of the relevant facts. It may not 'assume' that there are adequate reasons, nor may it merely assume that 'full investigation' has been made. Accordingly, we hold that it is incumbent upon the Juvenile Court to accompany its waiver order with a statement of the reasons or considerations therefor. We do not read the statute as requiring that this statement must be formal or that it should necessarily include conventional findings of fact. But the statement should be sufficient to demonstrate that the statutory requirement of 'full investigation' has been met; and that the question has received the careful consideration of the Juvenile Court; and it must set forth the basis for the order with sufficient specificity to permit meaningful review.

Correspondingly, we conclude that an opportunity for a hearing which may be informal, must be given the child prior to entry of a waiver order. Under Black, the child is entitled to counsel in connection with a waiver proceeding, and under Watkins, counsel is entitled to see the child's social records. These rights are meaningless—an illusion, a mockery—unless counsel is given an opportunity to function.

The right to representation by counsel is not a formality. It is not a grudging gesture to a ritualistic requirement. It is of the essence of justice. Appointment of counsel without affording an opportunity for hearing on a 'critically important' decision is tantamount to denial of counsel. There is no justification for the failure of the Juvenile Court to rule on the motion for hearing filed by petitioner's counsel, and it was error to fail to grant a hearing.

We do not mean by this to indicate that the hearing to be held must conform with all of the requirements of a criminal trial or even of the usual administrative hearing; but we do hold that the hearing must measure up to the essentials of due process and fair treatment.

With respect to access by the child's counsel to the social records of the child, we deem it obvious that since these are to be considered by the Juvenile Court in making its decision to waive, they must be made available to the child's counsel.

If a decision on waiver is 'critically important' it is equally of 'critical importance' that the material submitted to the judge—which is protected by the statute only against 'indiscriminate' inspection—be subjected, within reasonable limits having regard to the theory of the Juvenile Court Act, to examination, criticism and refutation. While the Juvenile Court judge may, of course, receive ex parte analyses and recommendations from his staff, he may not, for purposes of a decision on waiver, receive and rely upon secret information, whether emanating from his staff or otherwise. The Juvenile Court is governed in this respect by the established principles which control courts and quasi-judicial agencies of the Government.

For the reasons stated, we conclude that the Court of Appeals and the District Court erred in sustaining the validity of the waiver by the Juvenile Court.

Ordinarily we would reverse the Court of Appeals and direct the District Court to remand the case to the Juvenile Court for a new determination of waiver. If on remand the decision were against waiver, the indictment in the District Court would be dismissed. However, petitioner has now passed the age of 21 and the Juvenile Court can no longer exercise jurisdiction over him. In view of the unavailability of a redetermination of the waiver question by the Juvenile Court, it is urged by petitioner that the conviction should be vacated and the indictment dismissed. In the circumstances of this case, and in light of the remedy which the Court of Appeals fashioned in Black, supra, we do not consider it appropriate to grant this drastic relief. Accordingly, we vacate the order of the Court of Appeals and the judgment of the District Court and remand the case to the District Court for a hearing de novo on waiver, consistent with this opinion. If that court finds that waiver was inappropriate, petitioner's conviction must be vacated. If, however, it finds that the waiver order was proper when originally made, the District Court may proceed, after consideration of such motions as counsel may make and such further proceedings, if any, as may be warranted, to enter an appropriate judgment.

Reversed and remanded.

Holdings of *Kent v. U.S.*: The court held that an opportunity for a hearing must be afforded a juvenile before the juvenile can be waived to adult court. Such hearing may be informal and must be given to the youth prior to entry of a waiver order. It is not required that the waiver hearing conform with all of the requirements of a criminal trial or even an administrative hearing; but the hearing must measure up to the essentials of due process and fair treatment, including the right to counsel and the right to examine the evidence used against the juvenile.

Discussion Questions

What Due Process rights are applied by the *Kent* decision to waiver hearings?

What Due Process rights may not apply to waiver hearings?

———————

Manduley v. Superior Court: In *Manduley v. Superior Court,* the California Supreme Court was faced with state statute that allowed the prosecutor, rather than the court, to decide whether a minor accused of committing a crime should be treated as an adult and subjected to the criminal court system. A group of youth alleged that the statute violated their constitutional rights.

As you read *Manduley v. Superior Court,* look for the following:

1. Observe how the court addresses the Separation of Powers issue.

2. Consider how the court addresses the Due Process issue.

3. Consider how the court addresses the Equal Protection issue.

Manduley v. Superior Court

27 Cal.4th 537, 117 Cal.Rptr.2d 168, 41 P.3d 3 (2002)

George, C.J.

Proposition 21, titled the Gang Violence and Juvenile Crime Prevention Act of 1998 and approved by the voters at the March 7, 2000, Primary Election (Proposition 21), made a number of changes to laws applicable to minors accused of committing criminal offenses. As relevant here, the initiative measure broadened the circumstances in which prosecutors are authorized to file charges against minors 14 years of age and older in the criminal division of the superior court, rather than in the juvenile division of that court. Welfare and Institutions Code section 707, subdivision (d) (section 707(d)), confers upon prosecutors the discretion to bring specified charges against certain minors directly in criminal court, without a prior adjudication by the juvenile court that the minor is unfit for a disposition under the juvenile court law.

Petitioners are eight minors accused of committing various felony offenses. As authorized by section 707(d), the People filed charges against petitioners directly in criminal court. Petitioners demurred to the complaint, contending that section 707(d) is unconstitutional on several grounds.

In considering the validity of the Court of Appeal's decision, we emphasize that this court is not confronted with any question regarding the wisdom of authorizing the prosecutor, rather than the court, to decide whether a minor accused of committing a crime should be treated as an adult and subjected to the criminal court system. In the present case, rather, we must decide whether section 707(d) satisfies minimum constitutional requirements; we are not called upon to resolve the competing public policies implicated by the measure, considered by the electorate when it voted upon Proposition 21, and discussed at length by numerous amici curiae who have filed briefs in support of petitioners or the People. As we shall explain, we conclude that a prosecutor's decision to file charges against a minor in criminal court pursuant to section 707(d) is well within the established charging authority of the executive branch. Our prior decisions instruct that the prosecutor's exercise of such charging discretion, before any judicial proceeding is commenced, does not usurp an exclusively judicial power, even though the prosecutor's decision effectively can preclude the court from selecting a particular sentencing alternative. Accordingly, we disagree with the Court of Appeal's conclusion that section 707(d) is unconstitutional under the separation of powers doctrine.

Because the Court of Appeal held that the statute violates the separation of powers doctrine, the appellate court did not resolve the other constitutional challenges to section 707(d) raised by petitioners in that court. In order to prevent continued uncertainty regarding the status of numerous proceedings involving accusations of criminal conduct committed by minors, we shall resolve those remaining issues in the present case. As discussed below, we have reached the following conclusions with regard to these questions: (1) the absence of a provision requiring that a judicial fitness hearing take place before a minor can be charged in criminal court pursuant to section 707(d) does not deprive petitioners of due process of law; (2) prosecutorial discretion to file charges against some minors in criminal court does not violate the equal protection clause; and (3) Proposition 21 does not violate the single-subject rule, set forth in article II, section 8, subdivision (d), of the California Constitution, applicable to initiative measures.

I

By a single felony complaint filed in the superior court, the People charged petitioners with eight felonies: four counts of assault with a deadly weapon by means of force likely to produce great bodily injury against four victims, two counts of willful infliction of injury upon an elder under circumstances likely to result in great bodily harm or death, and two counts of robbery. The complaint alleged that these crimes were committed because of the victims' race, color, religion, nationality, country of origin, ancestry, gender, disability, or sexual orientation, and while petitioners acted in concert, and that some of the petitioners personally inflicted great bodily injury upon the victims. Finally, the complaint alleged that four petitioners were 16 years of age or older at the time they committed the offenses, and that the remaining four petitioners were 14 years of age or older at the time they committed the offenses.

Petitioners demurred to the complaint, contending that section 707(d) is unconstitutional on a number of grounds. First, petitioners claimed that section 707(d) violates the separation of powers doctrine by vesting in the district attorney the discretion whether to file specified charges against minors 14 years of age and older in either the juvenile division or the criminal division of the superior court. Petitioners further contended that section 707(d) deprives them of due process of law because the statute does not provide for any hearing to determine whether they are fit for a disposition under the juvenile court law. Petitioners also claimed that section 707(d) violates their right to uniform operation of the laws and equal protection of the laws, because it permits two classes of minors charged with the same crime to be treated differently at the discretion of the prosecutor. Furthermore, petitioners asserted that placing minors in prison with adult offenders violates the constitutional prohibitions against cruel and unusual punishment. Finally, petitioners contended that Proposition 21 violates the single-subject rule because it addresses at least three assertedly distinct, unrelated subjects: (1) the juvenile justice system, (2) criminal gang activity, and (3) sentencing provisions unrelated to juveniles or gang activity.

II

We begin our analysis of petitioners' challenge to section 707(d) by reviewing relevant provisions of the juvenile court law and then describing the pertinent changes effected by Proposition 21.

The law apart from the provisions of Proposition 21 provides that except as otherwise specified by statute, any individual less than 18 years of age who violates the criminal law comes within the jurisdiction of the juvenile court, which may adjudge such an individual a ward of the court. A minor accused of a crime is subject to the juvenile court system, rather than the criminal court system, unless the minor is determined to be unfit for treatment under the juvenile court law or is accused of certain serious crimes. For example, when a petition is filed alleging that a minor 16 years of age or older has violated the criminal law and should be adjudged a ward of the juvenile court, the minor generally is subject to the juvenile court law unless the court concludes, upon the motion of the prosecutor and after an investigation and report by a probation officer, that the minor would not be amenable to the care, treatment, and training program available through the facilities of the juvenile court. In assessing the minor's fitness for treatment under the juvenile court law, the court considers the minor's degree of criminal sophistication, whether the minor can be rehabilitated prior to the expiration of the juvenile court's jurisdiction, the minor's previous delinquent history, the success of previous attempts by the juvenile court to rehabilitate the minor, and the circumstances and gravity of the alleged offense.

A minor 14 years of age or older who is alleged to have committed one of the serious crimes specified — such as murder, robbery, or assault with a firearm — is presumed not to be a fit and proper subject for treatment under the juvenile court law. At the juvenile court hearing to determine the question of fitness for treatment, a minor accused of such a crime has the burden of rebutting this presumption of unfitness by a preponderance of the evidence. If a minor is declared not to be a fit and proper subject for treatment under the juvenile court law in accordance with the foregoing statutes, the district attorney may file an accusatory pleading against the minor in a court of criminal jurisdiction, and the case then proceeds according to the laws applicable to a criminal proceeding.

Before the passage of Proposition 21, certain minors who were 16 years of age or older at the time they committed specified crimes were required to be prosecuted in a court of criminal jurisdiction — without any requirement of a determination by the juvenile court that the minor was unfit for treatment under the juvenile court law. Section 602, former subdivision (b), provided that an individual at least 16 years of age, who previously had been declared a ward of the court for having committed a felony after the age of 14 years, "shall be prosecuted in a court of criminal jurisdiction if he or she is alleged to have committed" any of several enumerated serious offenses, such as first degree murder where the minor personally killed the victim, certain violent sex offenses, and aggravated forms of kidnapping. When such a prosecution lawfully was initiated in a court of criminal jurisdiction, the individual would be subject to the same sentence as an adult convicted of the identical offense, subject to specified exceptions.

Former section 1732.6 of the Welfare and Institutions Code provided that in a criminal proceeding against a minor, the court retained discretion to sentence the minor to the California Youth Authority (Youth Authority), unless the minor (1) was convicted of a violent or serious felony, and (2) received a sentence of life imprisonment, an indeterminate period up to life imprisonment, or a determinate period of years such that the maximum number of years of potential confinement could require incarceration of the minor beyond the age of 25 years. In addition, under no circumstances could a minor less than 16 years of age be housed in any facility under the jurisdiction of the Department of Corrections.

Proposition 21 revised the juvenile court law to broaden the circumstances in which minors 14 years of age and older can be prosecuted in the criminal division of the superior court, rather than in juvenile court. Section 707(d), as amended by the initiative, authorizes specified charges against certain minors to be filed directly in a court of criminal jurisdiction, without a judicial determination of unfitness under the juvenile court law. The statute sets forth three situations in which the prosecutor may choose to file an accusatory pleading against a minor in either juvenile court or criminal court: (1) a minor 16 years of age or older is accused of committing one of the violent or serious offenses enumerated; (2) a minor 14 years of age or older is accused of committing certain serious offenses under specified circumstances; and (3) a minor 16 years of age or older is accused of committing specified offenses, and the minor previously has been adjudged a ward of the court because of the commission of any felony offense when he or she was 14 years of age or older.

Where the prosecutor files an accusatory pleading directly in a court of criminal jurisdiction pursuant to section 707(d), at the preliminary hearing the magistrate must determine whether "reasonable cause exists to believe that the minor comes within the provisions of" the statute e.g., reasonable cause to believe that a minor at least 16 years of age has committed an offense enumerated, or that a minor at least 14 years of age has committed such an offense under the circumstances set forth. If such reasonable cause is not established, the case must be transferred to the juvenile court.

Section 602, subdivision (b), which specifies circumstances in which a minor must be prosecuted in a court of criminal jurisdiction, also was amended by Proposition 21. The revised statute decreases the juvenile's minimum age for such mandatory criminal prosecutions from 16 years to 14 years and alters in some respects the list of crimes for which a criminal prosecution is required.

In addition, Proposition 21 amended section 1732.6 to broaden the circumstances in which a minor shall not be committed to the Youth Authority. For example, a commitment to the Youth Authority is prohibited where a minor in a criminal action is convicted of an offense described in section 707(d)(1), (2), or (3) and the additional circumstances enumerated in those subdivisions are found true by the trier of fact. As was provided prior to the passage of Proposition 21, however, minors less than 16 years of age shall not be housed in any facility under the jurisdiction of the Department of Corrections.

Among the changes effected by Proposition 21, petitioners challenge only the aspect of section 707(d) that confers upon the prosecutor the discretion to file certain charges against specified minors directly in criminal court, without any judicial determination that the minor is unfit for a juvenile court disposition. We proceed to consider petitioners' various constitutional claims that section 707(d) is invalid.

III

Petitioners first contend that section 707(d) violates the separation of powers doctrine by vesting in the prosecutor the authority to make a decision—whether to initiate a proceeding in criminal court or juvenile court—that ultimately dictates whether minors charged with certain offenses, upon conviction, shall be sentenced under the criminal law or receive a disposition under the juvenile court law. The exercise of such authority by the executive branch, petitioners contend, invades the exclusive power of the judiciary to determine the appropriate sentence for individuals who commit criminal offenses. Petitioners' contention is based upon article III, section 3, of the California Constitution, which states: "The powers of state government are legislative, executive, and judicial. Persons charged with the exercise of one power may not exercise either of the others except as permitted by this Constitution."

The majority of the Court of Appeal agreed with petitioners that section 707(d) violates the separation of powers doctrine. The majority reasoned that resolution of this question depends upon whether the district attorney's choice between filing a petition in juvenile court or an accusatory pleading in criminal court is a charging decision properly allocated to the executive branch, or instead is a sentencing decision properly allocated to the judicial branch. According to the majority, "the fundamental nature of the decision given to district attorneys under section 707(d) is a decision that the adult sentencing scheme rather than the juvenile court dispositional scheme must be imposed if the juvenile is found guilty of the charged offenses." Section 707(d), the majority held, confers upon the prosecutor "the power to preemptively veto a court's sentencing discretion" and therefore violates separation of powers principles.

The dissent in the Court of Appeal, on the other hand, stated that prosecutors traditionally have possessed great discretion, largely unsupervised by the judiciary, to determine what charges to file against an individual, or whether to file charges at all. The dissent observed that a prosecutor's decision pursuant to section 707(d) whether to file charges in juvenile or criminal court is made before charges have been filed; therefore, the prosecutor exercises no veto over any judicial decision made after the proceeding is commenced. Because, in the dissent's view, the Legislature (or the voters through the initiative power) could abolish the juvenile justice system completely, or deny access to that system to juveniles of a certain age charged with certain crimes, the dissent concluded that section 707(d) properly could "take a more moderate approach" and delegate to the executive branch the discretion to determine where to file — in juvenile court or criminal court — charges against juveniles of a certain age accused of particular crimes. In this court, the People adopt a position similar to that reflected in the dissent in the Court of Appeal.

We believe that the majority of the Court of Appeal adopted an unduly restrictive view of the scope of the executive power traditionally vested in prosecutors to decide what charges shall be alleged, and against whom charges shall be brought. This broad power to charge crimes extends to selecting the forum, among those designated by statute, in which charges shall be filed. Contrary to the majority of the Court of Appeal, the circumstance that such a charging decision may affect the sentencing alternatives available to the court does not establish that the court's power improperly has been usurped by the prosecutor.

"'[S]ubject to the constitutional prohibition against cruel and unusual punishment, the power to define crimes and fix penalties is vested exclusively in the legislative branch.'

Petitioners contend that the legislative branch unconstitutionally has conferred upon the executive branch (that is, the prosecutor) an exclusively judicial function of choosing the appropriate dispositions for certain minors convicted of specified crimes. Several decisions of this court have addressed similar claims. As we shall explain, these decisions establish that the separation of powers doctrine prohibits the legislative branch from granting prosecutors the authority, *after* charges have been filed, to control the legislatively specified sentencing choices available to a court. A statute conferring upon prosecutors the discretion to make certain decisions *before* the filing of charges, on the other hand, is not invalid simply because the prosecutor's exercise of such charging discretion necessarily affects the dispositional options available to the court. Rather, such a result generally is merely incidental to the exercise of the executive function — the traditional power of the prosecutor to charge crimes. Because section 707(d) does not confer upon the prosecutor any authority to interfere with the court's choice of legislatively specified sentencing alternatives after an action has been commenced pursuant to that statute, we conclude that section 707(d) does not violate the separation of powers doctrine.

The prosecutor's discretionary charging decision pursuant to section 707(d), which thus can limit the dispositional alternatives available to the court, is no different from the numerous prefiling decisions made by prosecutors (e.g., whether to charge a wobbler as a felony, or whether to charge a particular defendant with assault, assault with a deadly weapon, or another form of aggravated assault, or whether to charge manslaughter or murder, or whether to allege facts that would preclude probation eligibility that limit the dispositions available to the court after charges have been filed. Conferring such authority upon the prosecutor does not limit the judicial power, after charges have been filed, to choose among the dispositional alternatives specified by the legislative branch. The voters, through the enactment of Proposition 21, have determined that the judiciary shall not make the determination regarding a minor's fitness for a juvenile disposition where the prosecutor initiates a criminal action pursuant to section 707(d).

IV

Petitioners further challenge section 707(d) on the ground that it deprives them of due process of law as guaranteed by the federal and California Constitutions. According to petitioners, a minor accused of criminal conduct possesses a statutory right to be subject to the jurisdiction of the juvenile court. Before a prosecutor may deprive a minor of that right by filing an action in criminal court pursuant to section 707(d), petitioners contend, the minor is entitled to a hearing to determine, pursuant to established criteria, whether he or she is amenable for a juvenile court disposition. Because section 707(d) neither provides for such a hearing nor sets forth criteria guiding the prosecutor's exercise of discretion, petitioners claim that the statute violates minimum constitutional standards of procedural fairness.

The premise of petitioners' claim is false, however, because minors who commit crimes under the circumstances set forth in section 707(d) do not possess any statutory right to be subject to the jurisdiction of the juvenile court. Although the juvenile court has jurisdiction over minors accused of most crimes, under the statutory provisions adopted by the enactment of Proposition 21, the criminal court also has jurisdiction over those minors who come within the scope of section 707(d), when the prosecutor files charges in that court. (§ 707(d)(4).) In these circumstances, when governing statutes provide that the juvenile court and the criminal court have concurrent jurisdiction, minors who come within the scope of section 707(d) do not possess any right to be placed under the jurisdiction of the juvenile court before the prosecutor initiates a proceeding accusing them of a crime. Thus, the asserted interest that petitioners seek to protect through a judicial hearing does not exist.

In sum, under the circumstances of the present case, petitioners do not possess any right to be subject to the jurisdiction of the juvenile court. As we have concluded, the legislative branch properly can delegate to the prosecutor — who traditionally has been entrusted with the charging decision — discretion whether to file charges against a minor directly in criminal court, and the Legislature also can eliminate a minor's statutory right to a judicial fitness hearing. Therefore, a prosecutor's decision pursuant to section 707(d) to file charges in criminal court does not implicate any protected interest of petitioners that gives rise to the requirements of procedural due process.

V

Petitioners next challenge section 707(d) on the ground that it violates their right to the equal protection of the laws, because the statute permits identically situated minors to be subject to different laws and disparate treatment at the discretion of the prosecutor. Petitioners assert that minors of the same age and charged with the same crime under the circumstances enumerated in section 707(d) are subject either to the juvenile court law or to the criminal justice system, based solely upon a prosecutorial decision that is unguided by any statutory standards. According to petitioners, the creation of two classes of minors pursuant to section 707(d) implicates fundamental liberty interests, and the disparity in treatment of minors falling within the scope of the statute is neither justified by a compelling state interest nor rationally related to a legitimate interest. Therefore, they contend, section 707(d) is unconstitutional on its face. We conclude that petitioners' equal protection claim lacks merit.

As petitioners implicitly concede, all minors who meet the criteria enumerated in section 707(d) equally are subject to the prosecutor's discretion whether to file charges in criminal court. Any unequal treatment of such minors who commit the same crime under similar circumstances results solely from the decisions of individual prosecutors whether to file against particular minors a petition in juvenile court or instead an accusatory pleading in criminal court. Although, as petitioners assert, a prosecutor's decision in this regard can result in important consequences to the accused minor, so does a decision by a prosecutor to initiate criminal charges against *any* individual, including an adult. Claims of unequal treatment by prosecutors in selecting particular classes of individuals for prosecution are evaluated according to ordinary equal protection standards. These standards require the defendant to show that he or she has been singled out deliberately for prosecution on the basis of some invidious criterion, and that the prosecution would not have been pursued except for the discriminatory purpose of the prosecuting authorities. "[A]n invidious purpose for prosecution is one that is arbitrary and thus unjustified because it bears no rational relationship to legitimate law enforcement interests...."

Section 707(d) contains no overtly discriminatory classification. In their challenge to section 707(d), petitioners do not contend that the district attorney filed charges against them in criminal court on the basis of some invidious criterion or for a discriminatory purpose, or that section 707(d) has had any discriminatory effect. Petitioners instead contend that section 707(d) *might* result in invidious discrimination because it contains no standards guiding the prosecutor's discretion whether to file charges in criminal court. Similarly, several amici curiae8 assert that historical data regarding racial disparities in the juvenile justice system suggest that section 707(d) *likely* will exacerbate such inequities. Such speculation is insufficient to establish a violation of the equal protection clause.

Thus, petitioners cannot establish a violation of their right to the equal protection of the laws by showing that other minors in circumstances similar to those of petitioners can be prosecuted under the juvenile court law. Section 707(d) limits the prosecutor's discretion to file charges in criminal court to minors of a specified age who commit enumerated crimes under certain circumstances, and at the preliminary hearing the magistrate must find reasonable cause to believe that the minor has committed such a crime under those circumstances. In addition, the prosecutor's decision is subject to constitutional constraints against invidious discrimination and against vindictive or retaliatory prosecution. Therefore, contrary to petitioners' contention, the prosecutor's decision is not unfettered or entirely without standards. The prosecutor's discretion to select those statutorily eligible cases in which to seek a criminal disposition against a minor—based upon permissible factors such as the circumstances of the crime, the background of the minor, or a desire to show leniency, for example—does not violate the equal protection clause.

In light of prior case authority considering prosecutorial charging discretion, discussed above, we conclude that section 707(d) does not deprive petitioners of the equal protection (or the uniform operation) of the laws.

The judgment of the Court of Appeal is reversed.

Holdings of *Manduley v. Superior Court:* The court held that the statute was not unconstitutional.

Discussion Questions

If Due Process is not implicated because a minor does not have any statutory right to be subject to juvenile court jurisdiction, how does the minor have any due process rights in juvenile court?

Is there any type of control over a prosecutor who exercises his discretionary power to charge minors in adult criminal court in a discriminatory manner?

State v. Aalim: In *State v. Aalim*, the Ohio Supreme Court was faced with a statute that required mandatory transfer from juvenile court to adult criminal court for older minors charged with enumerated serious crimes.

As you read *State v. Aalim*, look for the following:

1. Observe the role of "fundamental fairness" in the majority decision.

2. Consider how the court treats mandatory transfer of jurisdiction to adult court differently than the discretionary transfer by a prosecutor.

State v. Aalim

___ Ohio St.3d ___, ___ N.E.2d ___ (2016);
[Slip Opinion No. 2016-Ohio-8278]

LANZINGER, J.

In this case we are asked whether certain provisions of the Revised Code that make transfer of juveniles to adult court mandatory in specific circumstances violate constitutional due-process and equal-protection provisions. We hold that mandatory transfer of juveniles without providing for the protection of a discretionary determination by the juvenile court judge violates juveniles' right to due process.

I. CASE BACKGROUND

In December 2013, a complaint was filed in the Juvenile Division of the Montgomery County Court of Common Pleas, alleging that appellant, Matthew I. Aalim, engaged in conduct that would be considered aggravated robbery if committed by an adult. The complaint also contained a firearm specification. Appellee, the state of Ohio, filed a motion to transfer Aalim, requesting that the juvenile court relinquish jurisdiction and transfer him to the general division of the common pleas court to be tried as an adult pursuant to R.C. 2152.10(A)(2)(b) and 2152.12(A)(1)(b), which provide for mandatory transfer of juveniles to adult court in certain circumstances.

After conducting a hearing, the juvenile court found that Aalim was 16 years old at the time of the alleged offense and that there was probable cause to believe that he committed the conduct alleged in the complaint, including the firearm specification. The juvenile court automatically transferred the case to the general division of the common pleas court as the statute required. An indictment was issued charging Aalim with two counts of aggravated robbery with accompanying firearm specifications.

Aalim filed a motion to dismiss the indictment and transfer his case back to juvenile court, arguing that mandatory transfer of juveniles pursuant to R.C. 2152.10(A)(2)(b) and 2152.12(A)(1)(b) violates their rights to due process and equal protection as well as the prohibition against cruel and unusual punishments under both the United States and Ohio Constitutions. The trial court overruled the motion, and Aalim entered pleas of no contest to the two counts of aggravated robbery. The court accepted the pleas, dismissed the firearm specifications consistently with a plea agreement that the parties had reached, and sentenced Aalim to concurrent prison terms of four years on each count.

II. LEGAL ANALYSIS

R.C. 2152.10(A) sets forth which juvenile cases are subject to mandatory transfer and provides:

(A) A child who is alleged to be a delinquent child is eligible for mandatory transfer and shall be transferred as provided in section 2152.12 of the Revised Code in any of the following circumstances:

(1) The child is charged with a category one offense and either of the following apply:

(a) The child was sixteen years of age or older at the time of the act charged.

(b) The child was fourteen or fifteen years of age at the time of the act charged and previously was adjudicated a delinquent child for committing an act that is a category one or category two offense and was committed to the legal custody of the department of youth services upon the basis of that adjudication.

(2) The child is charged with a category two offense, other than a violation of section 2905.01 of the Revised Code, the child was sixteen years of age or older at the time of the commission of the act charged, and either or both of the following apply:

(a) The child previously was adjudicated a delinquent child for committing an act that is a category one or a category two offense and was committed to the legal custody of the department of youth services on the basis of that adjudication.

(b) The child is alleged to have had a firearm on or about the child's person or under the child's control while committing the act charged and to have displayed the firearm, brandished the firearm, indicated possession of the firearm, or used the firearm to facilitate the commission of the act charged.

Aggravated robbery is a category-two offense, and Aalim was 16 years old at the time the offense was committed. Because he was also charged with a firearm specification, automatic transfer was required. A juvenile court must transfer automatically under these circumstances if "there is probable cause to believe that the child committed the act charged."

The juvenile courts "occupy a unique place in our legal system." The juvenile court system is a legislative creation based on promoting social welfare and eschewing traditional, objective criminal standards and retributive notions of justice. "Since its origin, the juvenile justice system has emphasized individual assessment, the best interest of the child, treatment, and rehabilitation, with a goal of reintegrating juveniles back into society." "[T]he General Assembly has adhered to the core tenets of the juvenile system even as it has made substantive changes to the Juvenile Code in a get-tough response to increasing juvenile caseloads, recidivism, and the realization that the harms suffered by victims are not dependent upon the age of the perpetrator."

A common thread underlying the analysis in our juvenile cases is the recognition "that a juvenile could 'receive[ ] the worst of both worlds' in the juvenile court system by being provided 'neither the protections accorded to adults nor the solicitous care and regenerative treatment postulated for children.'" In recognition of juveniles' need for procedural protections, our decisions have acknowledged that "numerous constitutional safeguards normally reserved for criminal prosecutions are equally applicable to juvenile delinquency proceedings."

1. Juveniles are entitled to fundamental fairness

We have accordingly observed, "Because of the state's stake in the rehabilitation of the juvenile offender and the theoretically paternal role that the state continues to play in juvenile justice, a balanced approach is necessary to preserve the special nature of the juvenile process while protecting procedural fairness."

We have recently discussed the concept of fundamental fairness in juvenile proceedings in holding that automatic, lifelong registration and notification requirements on juvenile sex offenders tried within the juvenile system violates due process. In *C.P.*, we emphasized that the discretion of the juvenile judge is an "essential element of the juvenile process." We accordingly held that fundamental fairness requires that the juvenile court judge decide the appropriateness of any adult penalty for juvenile acts. Of particular importance to this case, we explained that fundamental fairness may require additional procedural protections for juveniles:

> [F]undamental fairness is not a one-way street that allows only for an easing of due process requirements for juveniles; instead, fundamental fairness may require, as it does in this case, additional procedural safeguards for juveniles in order to meet the juvenile system's goals of rehabilitation and reintegration into society.

Aalim argues that we should apply the principles of our previous juvenile cases to hold that he is entitled to be treated as a juvenile under the jurisdiction of the juvenile court and should receive an amenability hearing before any transfer to the general division of common pleas court. He asserts that juvenile court judges are in the best position to evaluate each juvenile's suitability for juvenile or adult court, that fundamental fairness requires that juveniles have the opportunity to demonstrate a capacity to change and suitability to juvenile court, and that an amenability hearing is accordingly necessary before juveniles are transferred. We agree.

2. The special status of juveniles

The legislative decision to create a juvenile court system, along with our cases addressing due-process protections for juveniles, have made clear that Ohio juveniles have been given a special status. This special status accords with recent United States Supreme Court decisions indicating that even when they are tried as adults, juveniles receive special consideration.

In this line of cases, the Supreme Court has established that youth is a mitigating factor for purposes of sentencing. While those cases featured Eighth Amendment claims, the court has clearly stated that "children are constitutionally different from adults for purposes of sentencing," The court has explained three significant differences between juveniles and adults:

> First, children have a "'lack of maturity and an underdeveloped sense of responsibility,'" leading to recklessness, impulsivity, and heedless risk-taking. Second, children "are more vulnerable ... to negative influences and outside pressures," including from their family and peers; they have limited "contro[l] over their own environment" and lack the ability to extricate themselves from horrific, crime-producing settings. And third, a child's character is not as "well formed" as an adult's; his traits are "less fixed" and his actions less likely to be "evidence of irretrievabl[e] deprav[ity]."

We have acknowledged these federal principles in our own recent holdings with respect to Ohio law.

For purposes of delinquency proceedings, the General Assembly has chosen to treat every person under the age of 18 as a child until transfer has occurred. R.C. 2152.02(C).

All 16- and 17-year-olds accordingly fall under the definition of "child" and are afforded the constitutional protections that all children until their transfer has been completed. Their age should not be treated as the sole decisive factor in determining whether they are transferred for criminal prosecution, and it is therefore a logical step for us to hold that *all* children, regardless of age, must have individual consideration at amenability hearings before being transferred from the protections of juvenile court to adult court upon a finding of probable cause for certain offenses.

We now recognize that because children are constitutionally required to be treated differently from adults for purposes of sentencing, juvenile procedures themselves also must account for the differences in children versus adults. The mandatory-transfer statutes preclude a juvenile court judge from taking any individual circumstances into account before automatically sending a child who is 16 or older to adult court. This one-size-fits-all approach runs counter to the aims and goals of the juvenile system, and even those who would be amenable to the juvenile system are sent to adult court. Juvenile court judges must be allowed the discretion that the General Assembly permits for other children. They should be able to distinguish between those children who should be treated as adults and those who should not. Cognizant of our statement in *C.P.* that fundamental fairness may require additional procedural safeguards for juveniles in order to meet the juvenile system's goals of rehabilitation and reintegration into society, we hold that the right to due process under the Ohio Constitution requires that all children have the right to an amenability hearing before transfer to adult court and that the mandatory transfer statutes violate the right to due process as guaranteed by Article I, Section 16 of the Ohio Constitution.

Given the special status of children, we are unconvinced by the state's argument that the only process due in these circumstances is codified in the mandatory-transfer statutes as a special measure created for certain specified circumstances. The existence of a juvenile court system and the principles set forth in our previous cases dictate that children are fundamentally different from adults. All children are entitled to fundamental fairness in the procedures by which they may be transferred out of juvenile court for criminal prosecution, and an amenability hearing like the one required in the discretionary-transfer provisions of the Revised Code is required to satisfy that fundamental fairness.

3. Discretionary transfer

The General Assembly has provided for discretionary transfer of children aged 14 or older when there is probable cause to believe the child committed the charged act, the child is not amenable to care or rehabilitation within the juvenile system, and the safety of the community may require that the child be subject to adult sanctions. Before transferring, the juvenile court must "order an investigation into the child's social history, education, family situation, and any other factor bearing on whether the child is amenable to juvenile rehabilitation, including a mental examination of the child." R.C. 2152.12(C). R.C. 2152.12(B) further provides:

> In making its decision under this division, the court shall consider whether the applicable factors under division (D) of this section indicating that the case should be transferred outweigh the applicable factors under division (E) of this section indicating that the case should not be transferred. The record shall indicate the specific factors that were applicable and that the court weighed.

R.C. 2152.12(D) and (E) enumerate nonexhaustive factors in favor of and against transfer, respectively, for the juvenile court to consider. These factors include the emotional, physical, and psychological maturity of the child; the child's previous experiences in the juvenile system; the harm suffered by the victim; whether the child was the principal actor in the conduct charged; and whether the child was under any negative influence or coercion at the time of the conduct charged.

The discretionary-transfer process satisfies fundamental fairness under the Ohio Constitution. It takes into account the fact that children are constitutionally different from adults for purposes of an eventual sentencing after findings of guilt. Its factors account for the differences between children and adults noted by the *Miller* court: children's lack of maturity, their vulnerability to negative influences and outside pressures, and their more malleable character that makes their actions less likely to be evidence of irretrievable depravity. In doing so, the discretionary-transfer process ensures that only those children who are not amenable to dispositions in juvenile court will be transferred. Thus, while we hold that the mandatory-transfer statutes violate juveniles' right to due process as guaranteed under the Ohio Constitution, transfer of juveniles amenable to adult court may still occur via the discretionary-transfer process set forth in R.C. 2152.10(B) and 2152.12(B) through (E).

III. CONCLUSION

We hold that the mandatory transfer of juveniles to the general division of common pleas court violates juveniles' right to due process as guaranteed by Article I, Section 16 of the Ohio Constitution. We also hold that the discretionary transfer of juveniles 14 years old or older to the general division of common pleas court pursuant to the process set forth in R.C. 2152.10(B) and 2152.12(B) through (E) satisfies due process as guaranteed by Article I, Section 16 of the Ohio Constitution.

We accordingly reverse the judgment of the Second District Court of Appeals and remand the cause to the juvenile court for an amenability hearing pursuant to R.C. 2152.10 and 2152.12.

Judgment reversed and cause remanded.

KENNEDY, J., concurring in part and dissenting in part.

I agree with the majority that the discretionary-bindover process under R.C. 2152.10(B) and 2152.12(B) through (E) does not offend due process as guaranteed by Article I, Section 16 of the Ohio Constitution. I part with the majority, however, in its determination that Article I, Section 16 provides a unique protection that R.C. 2152.10(A), which sets forth the mandatory-bindover process, violates on its face.

The majority relies on the due-process standard of "fundamental fairness." Due process is a flexible concept; however, at its core, it requires an opportunity to be heard when the government seeks to infringe on a protected liberty or property right.

Fundamental fairness is a "unique doctrine [that] is not appropriately applied in every case but only in those instances when the interests involved are especially compelling." "It is appropriately applied in those rare cases where not to do so will subject the defendant to oppression, harassment, or egregious deprivation." The majority holds that the current mandatory-bindover procedure violates fundamental fairness. I disagree.

The majority takes this unique, statutorily created court system and bootstraps onto it "fundamental fairness" requirements that are not required by statute or by the explicit text or history of the Ohio Constitution. This is unsound. The majority reaches its conclusion by relying on past juvenile cases regarding the right to counsel; automatic, lifetime sex-offender registration and notification requirements; and sentencing juvenile offenders to life without the possibility of parole for nonhomicide offenses. However, these decisions are distinguishable because they relied on specific constitutional guarantees like the right to counsel contained in the Sixth Amendment applied to juvenile proceedings through the Due Process Clause and the prohibition against cruel and unusual punishments contained in the Eighth Amendment rather than the broad and "'"opaque"'" principle of "fundamental Fairness."

"It is undisputed that the General Assembly is ' "the ultimate arbiter of public policy" ' and the only branch of government charged with fulfilling that role." By declaring that juvenile courts are constitutionally required to provide an amenability hearing to those juveniles that the General Assembly has mandated are to be bound over after a probable-cause determination, the majority has unmoored due process from the precedents that have ensured that the judicial branch does not abuse the guarantee by imposing its policy views on the General Assembly under the rubric of alleged "fundamental fairness."

The majority, however, now uses Article I, Section 16 of the Ohio Constitution as a tool to rewrite the balance the General Assembly struck between ensuring that dangerous juvenile offenders receive punishment commensurate with their crimes and allowing other juvenile offenders the opportunity for rehabilitation and reintegration. By elevating a juvenile's statutory right to an amenability hearing under R.C. 2152.10 and 2152.12 to a constitutional right mandated by Article I, Section 16, the majority will allow this court to invalidate any statutory or procedural rule that four members of this court believe is unfair. Therefore, while I concur in the majority's holding that the discretionary-bindover procedure is constitutional, I must dissent from the majority's holding that the mandatory-bindover procedure violates Article I, Section 16 of the Ohio Constitution.

FRENCH, J., dissenting.

I respectfully dissent.

While asserting no basis—other than mere permissibility—for holding that the Ohio Constitution affords juveniles greater due-process protections regarding transfer than the United States Constitution provides, and without considering whether the federal Due Process Clause guarantees juveniles an individualized amenability hearing, the majority concludes that Ohio's mandatory transfer provisions—R.C. 2152.10(A)(2)(b) and 2152.12(A)(1)(b)—violate Article I, Section 16 of the Ohio Constitution. I disagree with the majority's cavalier decision to create greater protections under the Ohio Constitution, absent compelling reasons to do so. And on the merits, I disagree with the majority's conclusion that Ohio's statutory mandatory-transfer provisions are unconstitutional.

Appellant, Matthew I. Aalim, raises a facial due-process challenge to Ohio's mandatory-transfer procedures. In 1969, the General Assembly enacted a statutory scheme by which a juvenile court could remove certain juveniles from its authority and transfer them to adult court for criminal prosecution. The current scheme provides for two types of transfer: mandatory and discretionary. Discretionary transfer affords juvenile court judges discretion to transfer to adult court juveniles who do not appear amenable to care or rehabilitation within the juvenile system and who appear to be a threat to public safety. "An amenability hearing helps determine whether a juvenile who is eligible for discretionary [transfer] will be transferred to adult court." Mandatory transfer, on the other hand, removes judicial discretion and requires transfer in certain circumstances, based on the juvenile's age and offense. A juvenile who qualifies for mandatory transfer is not statutorily entitled to an amenability determination, but the juvenile is entitled to a hearing at which the juvenile court must determine before transferring the juvenile for criminal prosecution that the juvenile was 16 or 17 years old at the time of the charged conduct and that there is probable cause to believe that the juvenile committed that conduct. Here, we consider the statutory provisions regarding mandatory transfer.

Aalim, as a 16-year-old alleged to be delinquent as a result of a category-two offense committed with a firearm, fell within the category of juveniles subject to mandatory transfer. R.C. 2152.10(A)(2)(b). R.C. 2152.12(A)(1)(b)(ii) required the juvenile court to transfer Aalim to adult court upon a finding of probable cause to believe that he committed the charged offense.

Aalim argues that Ohio's mandatory-transfer provisions are unconstitutional because due process requires an amenability hearing — giving the juvenile the opportunity to demonstrate a capacity for change — before a juvenile court judge may transfer *any* juvenile to adult court. To succeed on his due-process challenge, Aalim must prove beyond a reasonable doubt that Ohio's mandatory-transfer provisions are clearly incompatible with constitutional due process. To do so, he must overcome a strong presumption that the provisions are constitutional.

In my view, Aalim does not satisfy that heavy burden.

The phrase "due process" "expresses the requirement of 'fundamental fairness,'" and applying the Due Process Clause is "an uncertain enterprise which must discover what 'fundamental fairness' consists of in a particular situation." But the Due Process Clause guarantees more than fair process; it also provides heightened protection against governmental interference with certain fundamental rights and liberty interests. "So-called 'substantive due process' prevents the government from engaging in conduct that 'shocks the conscience'... or interferes with rights 'implicit in the concept of ordered liberty' ..." Substantive due process bars "certain arbitrary, wrongful government actions 'regardless of the fairness of the procedures used to implement them.'" Procedural due process, on the other hand, requires the government to implement any action that deprives a person of life, liberty or property in a fair manner, even if the governmental action survives substantive due-process scrutiny.

Ohio's mandatory-transfer provisions do not offend either substantive or procedural due process.

Substantive due process protects only "fundamental rights and liberties which are, objectively, 'deeply rooted in this Nation's history and tradition'... and 'implicit in the concept of ordered liberty,' such that 'neither liberty nor justice would exist if they were sacrificed.'" Protected rights and liberties include the specific freedoms guaranteed by the Bill of Rights as well as such "deeply rooted" rights as the right to marry, the right to have children, and the right to bodily integrity. The United States Supreme Court has expressed reluctance to expand the concept of substantive due process.

It is evident from the history and evolution of juvenile proceedings in this country, as well as courts' consistent rejection of claims of fundamental rights to juvenile proceedings, that there is no fundamental right deeply rooted in the nation's history to juvenile court proceedings or to an amenability hearing. Juvenile courts are legislative creations rooted in social-welfare philosophy. The first juvenile court was not established in this country until 1899, and it was not until 1937 that the Ohio General Assembly conferred exclusive jurisdiction over minors upon Ohio's juvenile courts.

Criminal common law did not differentiate between adults and juveniles who had reached the age of criminal responsibility — seven at common law. A juvenile offender who was over the age of criminal responsibility "was arrested, put into prison, indicted by the grand jury, tried by a petit jury, under all the forms and technicalities of our criminal law, with the aim of ascertaining whether it had done the specific act—nothing else—and if it had, then of visiting the punishment of the state upon it." It was only the advent of juvenile statutes and juvenile courts that advanced the age of criminal responsibility and created different procedures for juvenile adjudication.

This court has repeatedly held that any right to juvenile proceedings is purely statutory. And other state and federal courts have similarly rejected the idea of a fundamental constitutional right to juvenile status or juvenile proceedings. Because there is no deeply rooted, fundamental right to juvenile court proceedings, Ohio's mandatory-transfer provisions do not violate substantive due process.

Aalim's claim fares no better under procedural due process. To demonstrate a procedural-due-process violation, a plaintiff must first show that the state deprived him or her of a protected interest in life, liberty or property. Protected liberty interests may arise from the Due Process Clause itself or the laws of the states. In a procedural-due-process claim, the deprivation of a constitutionally protected interest in life, liberty or property is not itself unconstitutional; what is unconstitutional is the deprivation of that interest without due process of law. Before depriving a person of a protected interest, the state must afford the person some type of hearing unless the governmental interest involved justifies delaying the hearing.

There is "no doubt" that the Due Process Clause applies in juvenile proceedings. But there is also no doubt that the Due Process Clause itself does not give rise to an interest in juvenile proceedings because the right to juvenile proceedings is purely statutory.

To be sure, a juvenile facing a delinquency adjudication in juvenile court is entitled to certain basic constitutional rights enjoyed by adults accused of a crime. These include the right to counsel, the privilege against self-incrimination, the right to confront and cross-examine witnesses, the right to use of the beyond-a-reasonable-doubt standard of proof, and the right to be free from double jeopardy. As a result of *Gault* and its progeny, "juveniles secured more of the rights afforded to adults."

The majority opinion states:

> A common thread underlying the analysis in our juvenile cases is the recognition "that a juvenile could 'receive the worst of both worlds' in the juvenile court system by being provided 'neither the protections accorded to adults nor the solicitous care and regenerative treatment postulated for children.'"

But when a juvenile is tried as an adult, the case does not implicate the "worst of both worlds" concern.

In *Kent*, the Supreme Court expressed concern that juvenile courts were not measuring up to their laudable purpose of "provid[ing] measures of guidance and rehabilitation for the child and protection for society, not to fix criminal responsibility, guilt and punishment." The concern that a juvenile could receive "the worst of both worlds" in the juvenile court system stemmed from juvenile courts discarding procedural safeguards available to adults in a criminal prosecution. A juvenile like Aalim who is tried in adult court, however, receives all the rights and protections afforded to juvenile offenders in juvenile court, and then some. An adult criminal court protects a juvenile's rights; it does not diminish them.

But even if we were to conclude that mandatory transfer to adult court does deprive a juvenile of a liberty interest, I would nevertheless also conclude that the process and substance of that transfer provide appropriate, predeprivation procedural protections.

Because the legislature has exclusive authority to provide for treatment as a juvenile, it "may restrict or qualify that right as it sees fit, as long as no arbitrary or discriminatory classification is involved." A juvenile who qualifies for mandatory transfer has the right to a pretransfer hearing at which the state must prove not only that the juvenile falls within the statutory classifications for mandatory transfer but also that probable cause exists to believe that the juvenile committed the charged offense. At that hearing, the juvenile has an unwaivable right to counsel, the right to remain silent, the right to present evidence, the right to cross-examine witnesses, and the right to notice of the charges against him or her. In my view, these protections give the juvenile adequate due process prior to a transfer to adult court. Aalim apparently agrees, because he does not even argue that any procedural due process was lacking with respect to the juvenile court's probable-cause hearing.

The majority cites this court's prior recognition that juveniles have a "special status" under Ohio law and that children are constitutionally different from adults for purposes of sentencing in support of its holdings that statutory transfer provisions must account for the differences in children versus adults and that a juvenile court judge must have discretion to determine which children should be treated as adults and which children should not. But while a majority of this court may prefer to afford juvenile court judges discretion to determine, in all instances, whether a juvenile offender should be treated as an alleged delinquent in juvenile court or as a criminal defendant in adult court, that is an issue for the General Assembly. The Due Process Clause does not invest this court with the power to sit as a super-legislature to second-guess the General Assembly's policy choices.

The majority also cites a line of recent Eighth Amendment decisions of the United States Supreme Court that establishes that children are constitutionally different from adults for purposes of sentencing and that youth is a mitigating factor. Fair enough. But the case before us now is not about the propriety of the punishment Aalim may receive. It can't be—Aalim concedes that he may receive a shorter term of confinement in adult court than he would in juvenile court. So the majority's reliance on the federal decisions concerning the Eighth Amendment implications for juvenile sentences is wholly misplaced here.

I agree with the majority that "[a]ll children are entitled to fundamental fairness in the procedures by which they may be transferred out of juvenile court for criminal prosecution." In my view, however, the concept of fundamental fairness does not preclude mandatory transfer. Fundamental fairness and the requirements of procedural due process are met when, after a probable-cause hearing, the juvenile court determines that the juvenile qualifies for mandatory transfer pursuant to duly enacted statutory prerequisites and that there is probable cause to believe that the juvenile committed the charged offense. The procedures set out in the mandatory-transfer provisions and in the Juvenile Rules provide the requisite process and afford the juvenile fundamental fairness. I therefore conclude that R.C. 2152.10(A)(2)(b) and 2152.12(A)(1)(b) do not violate the rights to due process guaranteed by either the United States or Ohio Constitution.

Because I conclude that Ohio's mandatory-transfer provisions do not violate due process, I briefly consider—but ultimately reject—Aalim's argument that they violate equal protection under the Fourteenth Amendment to the United States Constitution and Article I, Section 2 of the Ohio Constitution. The standards for determining whether a statute violates equal protection are "essentially the same under the state and federal Constitutions."

A statute that does not implicate a fundamental right or a suspect classification does not violate equal protection if it is rationally related to a legitimate government interest.

As stated in my due-process analysis, the mandatory-transfer provisions do not abridge fundamental rights. Nor do they involve a suspect classification; age is not a suspect classification for purposes of equal protection.

Aalim argues that Ohio's mandatory-transfer provisions irrationally treat children who are 16 or 17 when they commit a category-two offense with a firearm and are subject to mandatory transfer differently from children who are 14 or 15 and who are subject to discretionary transfer. Aalim states that "no ground can be conceived to justify" those age-based distinctions. I disagree.

We grant substantial deference to the General Assembly when conducting an equal-protection, rational-basis review. "'[A] legislative choice ... may be based on rational speculation unsupported by evidence or empirical data,'" and the state is not obligated to produce evidence to sustain the rationality of a legislative classification,

The mandatory-transfer provisions are "part of Ohio's response to rising juvenile crime" and "one of the hallmarks of [the General Assembly's] 'get tough' approach." I agree with those Ohio appellate courts that have concluded that the General Assembly's decision to single-out older juvenile offenders—who are "potentially more streetwise, hardened, dangerous, and violent"—is rationally related to the legitimate governmental interests in protecting society and reducing violent crimes. I therefore conclude that the mandatory-transfer provisions do not violate equal-protection principles under either the United States or the Ohio Constitution.

For these reasons, I respectfully dissent.

Holdings of *State v. Aalim*: The court held that the mandatory transfer of juveniles to adult criminal court violated the youth's Due Process rights under the Ohio Constitution. The court further held that the discretionary transfer of juveniles aged 14 and over satisfied the Due Process clause of the Ohio Constitution.

Discussion Questions

Under this opinion, could the legislature lower the age of jurisdiction for juvenile court to 14, requiring cases of all youth aged 14 or older to be filed directly in adult court?

Does "fundamental fairness" require some kind of hearing in all cases before a youth's case can be moved to adult criminal court?

Key Concepts: Waiver to Adult Court

- A waiver hearing is a "critically important" proceeding, triggering at least some due process protections for a juvenile.
- A waiver hearing must contain the essentials of due process and fair treatment, including the right to counsel and the right to examine the evidence used to support the waiver of jurisdiction.
- States have created various statutory schemes allowing cases of older juveniles involved in enumerated serious offenses to be automatically filed in adult court.
- Some states have also created statutory schemes allowing prosecutors discretion to file cases of older juveniles involved in enumerated serious offenses in adult court

Practical Questions: Waiver to Adult Court

1. You have been appointed to represent Samuel Jones in adult court on a charge of simple assault. Sam is 16 years old. A statute holds that once a youth has been waived to adult

court on a juvenile delinquency case, all further offenses by the youth are automatically under the jurisdiction of adult court. Sam had previously been "waived to adult court" on a drug charge, he successfully completed probation, and that case has been closed for over a year. Is the statute automatically giving adult court jurisdiction where there has been a previous waiver valid? Doesn't Due Process require that a hearing be held on the waiver issue?

2. You are representing a 17-year-old youth in a delinquency proceeding. The state has filed a Motion to Waive Jurisdiction to Adult Court. The motion recites no facts, but simply states that "due to the age of the defendant, the juvenile court is unable to provide appropriate services." Does this notice comply with Due Process?

Chapter IX

Constitutional Minimums for Adjudicatory Hearings

Overview: Historically, juveniles were given very few of the rights that have been given to adults because advocates believed that juvenile courts were not adversarial in nature and that the purpose was not punishment but rehabilitation. Juvenile delinquency courts were believed to take an almost paternalistic approach. However, as the nature of juvenile delinquency courts evolved, they became more and more adversarial and punitive. A complete reworking of the rights of juveniles in juvenile delinquency courts was begun by the seminal case of *In re Gault*. Courts have now been faced with claims that the constitutional requirements in the Bill of Rights applied to juveniles as well as adults. The result is that the courts have been forced to determine what due process rights are applicable to juveniles in delinquency courts and which rights should not be extended to juveniles.

In re Gault: In *In re Gault*, the United States Supreme Court was faced with a case where the juvenile, 15-year-old Gerald Gault, was accused of participating in making obscene phone calls to a neighbor lady with another youth. Gerald was not given proper notice, and the proceedings were very informal without the complainant even appearing. Gault was not given an attorney, and ultimately was sentenced to the state Industrial School until he was age twenty-one (a maximum of six years). If Gerald had been over 18, he would not have been subject to Juvenile Court proceedings, and in adult court, for the particular offense involved, the maximum punishment would have been a fine of $5 to $50, or imprisonment in jail for not more than two months. In this case, the Court ruled: "Under our Constitution, the condition of being a boy does not justify a kangaroo court." The Court then determined what minimal due process protections were guaranteed for juveniles in juvenile delinquency courts.

As you read *In re Gault*, look for the following:

1. Observe the historical role noted by the Court in terms of the traditional function and purposes of juvenile delinquency courts.

2. Consider whether the Court is finding that juvenile delinquency courts are not living up to the traditional views of the purpose and function of those courts.

3. Consider what fundamental rights accorded to adults in criminal courts have not been specifically extended to juveniles by *Gault*.

In re Gault

387 U.S. 1, (1967)

Mr. Justice FORTAS delivered the opinion of the Court.

On Monday, June 8, 1964, at about 10 a.m., Gerald Francis Gault and a friend, Ronald Lewis, were taken into custody by the Sheriff of Gila County. Gerald was then still subject to a six months' probation order which had been entered on February 25, 1964, as a result of his having been in the company of another boy who had stolen a wallet from a lady's purse. The police action on June 8 was taken as the result of a verbal complaint by a neighbor of the boys, Mrs. Cook, about a telephone call made to her in which the caller or callers made lewd or indecent remarks. It will suffice for purposes of this opinion to say that the remarks or questions put to her were of the irritatingly offensive, adolescent, sex variety.

At the time Gerald was picked up, his mother and father were both at work. No notice that Gerald was being taken into custody was left at the home. No other steps were taken to advise them that their son had, in effect, been arrested. Gerald was taken to the Children's Detention Home. When his mother arrived home at about 6 o'clock, Gerald was not there. Gerald's older brother was sent to look for him at the trailer home of the Lewis family. He apparently learned then that Gerald was in custody. He so informed his mother. The two of them went to the Detention Home. The deputy probation officer, Flagg, who was also superintendent of the Detention Home, told Mrs. Gault 'why Jerry was there' and said that a hearing would be held in Juvenile Court at 3 o'clock the following day, June 9.

Officer Flagg filed a petition with the court on the hearing day, June 9, 1964. It was not served on the Gaults. Indeed, none of them saw this petition until the habeas corpus hearing on August 17, 1964. The petition was entirely formal. It made no reference to any factual basis for the judicial action which it initiated. It recited only that 'said minor is under the age of eighteen years, and is in need of the protection of this Honorable Court; (and that) said minor is a delinquent minor.' It prayed for a hearing and an order regarding 'the care and custody of said minor.' Officer Flagg executed a formal affidavit in support of the petition.

On June 9, Gerald, his mother, his older brother, and Probation Officers Flagg and Henderson appeared before the Juvenile Judge in chambers. Gerald's father was not there. He was at work out of the city. Mrs. Cook, the complainant, was not there. No one was sworn at this hearing. No transcript or recording was made. No memorandum or record of the substance of the proceedings was prepared. Our information about the proceedings and the subsequent hearing on June 15, derives entirely from the testimony of the Juvenile Court Judge, Mr. and Mrs. Gault and Officer Flagg at the habeas corpus proceeding conducted two months later. From this, it appears that at the June 9 hearing Gerald was questioned by the judge about the telephone call. There was conflict as to what he said. His mother recalled that Gerald said he only dialed Mrs. Cook's number and handed the telephone to his friend, Ronald. Officer Flagg recalled that Gerald had admitted making the lewd remarks. Judge McGhee testified that Gerald 'admitted making one of these (lewd) statements.' At the conclusion of the hearing, the judge said he would 'think about it.' Gerald was taken back to the Detention Home. He was not sent to his own home with his parents. On June 11 or 12, after having been detained since June 8, Gerald was released and driven home. There is no explanation in the record as to why he was kept in the Detention Home or why he was released. At 5 p.m. on the day of Gerald's release, Mrs. Gault received a note signed by Officer Flagg. It was on plain paper, not letterhead. Its entire text was as follows:

'Mrs. Gault:

'Judge McGHEE has set Monday June 15, 1964 at 11:00 A.M. as the date and time for further Hearings on Gerald's delinquency

'/s/ Flagg'

At the appointed time on Monday, June 15, Gerald, his father and mother, Ronald Lewis and his father, and Officers Flagg and Henderson were present before Judge McGhee.

Witnesses at the habeas corpus proceeding differed in their recollections of Gerald's testimony at the June 15 hearing. Mr. and Mrs. Gault recalled that Gerald again testified that he had only dialed the number and that the other boy had made the remarks. Officer Flagg agreed that at this hearing Gerald did not admit making the lewd remarks. But Judge McGhee recalled that 'there was some admission again of some of the lewd statements. He-he didn't admit any of the more serious lewd statements.' Again, the complainant, Mrs. Cook, was not present. Mrs. Gault asked that Mrs. Cook be present 'so she could see which boy that done the talking, the dirty talking over the phone.' The Juvenile Judge said 'she didn't have to be present at that hearing.' The judge did not speak to Mrs. Cook or communicate with her at any time. Probation Officer Flagg had talked to her once—over the telephone on June 9.

At this June 15 hearing a 'referral report' made by the probation officers was filed with the court, although not disclosed to Gerald or his parents. This listed the charge as 'Lewd Phone Calls.' At the conclusion of the hearing, the judge committed Gerald as a juvenile delinquent to the State Industrial School 'for the period of his minority (that is, until 21), unless sooner discharged by due process of law.' An order to that effect was entered. It recites that 'after a full hearing and due deliberation the Court finds that said minor is a delinquent child, and that said minor is of the age of 15 years.'

At the habeas corpus hearing on August 17, Judge McGhee was vigorously cross-examined as to the basis for his actions. He testified that he had taken into account the fact that Gerald was on probation.

Asked about the basis for his conclusion that Gerald was 'habitually involved in immoral matters,' the judge testified, somewhat vaguely, that two years earlier, on July 2, 1962, a 'referral' was made concerning Gerald, 'where the boy had stolen a baseball glove from another boy and lied to the Police Department about it.' The judge said there was 'no hearing,' and 'no accusation' relating to this incident, 'because of lack of material foundation.' But it seems to have remained in his mind as a relevant factor. The judge also testified that Gerald had admitted making other nuisance phone calls in the past which, as the judge recalled the boy's testimony, were 'silly calls, or funny calls, or something like that.'

The Supreme Court of Arizona held that due process of law is requisite to the constitutional validity of proceedings in which a court reaches the conclusion that a juvenile has been at fault, has engaged in conduct prohibited by law, or has otherwise misbehaved with the consequence that he is committed to an institution in which his freedom is curtailed. This conclusion is in accord with the decisions of a number of courts under both federal and state constitutions.

This Court has not heretofore decided the precise question. Accordingly, while these cases relate only to restricted aspects of the subject, they unmistakably indicate that, whatever may be their precise impact, neither the Fourteenth Amendment nor the Bill of Rights is for adults alone.

We do not in this opinion consider the impact of these constitutional provisions upon the totality of the relationship of the juvenile and the state. We do not even consider the entire process relating to juvenile 'delinquents.' For example, we are not here concerned with the procedures or constitutional rights applicable to the pre-judicial stages of the juvenile process, nor do we direct our attention to the post-adjudicative or dispositional process. We consider only the problems presented to us by this case. These relate to the proceedings by which a determination is made as to whether a juvenile is a 'delinquent' as a result of alleged misconduct on his part, with the consequence that he may be committed to a state institution. As to these proceedings, there appears to be little current dissent from the proposition that the Due Process Clause has a role to play. The problem is to ascertain the precise impact of the due process requirement upon such proceedings.

From the inception of the juvenile court system, wide differences have been tolerated-indeed insisted upon-between the procedural rights accorded to adults and those of juveniles. In practically all jurisdictions, there are rights granted to adults which are withheld from juveniles. In addition to the specific problems involved in the present case, for example, it has been held that the juvenile is not entitled to bail, to indictment by grand jury, to a public trial or to trial by jury. It is frequent practice that rules governing the arrest and interrogation of adults by the police are not observed in the case of juveniles.

The history and theory underlying this development are well-known, but a recapitulation is necessary for purposes of this opinion. The Juvenile Court movement began in this country at the end of the last century. From the juvenile court statute adopted in Illinois in 1899, the system has spread to every State in the Union, the District of Columbia, and Puerto Rico. The constitutionality of juvenile court laws has been sustained in over 40 jurisdictions against a variety of attacks.

It is claimed that juveniles obtain benefits from the special procedures applicable to them which more than offset the disadvantages of denial of the substance of normal due process. As we shall discuss, the observance of due process standards, intelligently and not ruthlessly administered, will not compel the States to abandon or displace any of the substantive benefits of the juvenile process. But it is important, we think, that the claimed benefits of the juvenile process should be candidly appraised.

Certainly, these figures and the high crime rates among juveniles to which we have referred could not lead us to conclude that the absence of constitutional protections reduces crime, or that the juvenile system, functioning free of constitutional inhibitions as it has largely done, is effective to reduce crime or rehabilitate offenders. We do not mean by this to denigrate the juvenile court process or to suggest that there are not aspects of the juvenile system relating to offenders which are valuable.

While due process requirements will, in some instances, introduce a degree of order and regularity to Juvenile Court proceedings to determine delinquency, and in contested cases will introduce some elements of the adversary system, nothing will require that the conception of the kindly juvenile judge be replaced by its opposite, nor do we here rule upon the question whether ordinary due process requirements must be observed with respect to hearings to determine the disposition of the delinquent child.

Ultimately, however, we confront the reality of that portion of the Juvenile Court process with which we deal in this case. A boy is charged with misconduct. The boy is committed to an institution where he may be restrained of liberty for years. It is of no constitutional consequence—and of limited practical meaning—that the institution to which he is committed is called an Industrial School. The fact of the matter is that, however euphemistic the title, a 'receiving home' or an 'industrial school' for juveniles is an institution of confinement in which the child is incarcerated for a greater or lesser time. His world becomes 'a building with whitewashed walls, regimented routine and institutional hours ...' Instead of mother and father and sisters and brothers and friends and classmates, his world is peopled by guards, custodians, state employees, and 'delinquents' confined with him for anything from waywardness to rape and homicide.

In view of this, it would be extraordinary if our Constitution did not require the procedural regularity and the exercise of care implied in the phrase 'due process.' Under our

Constitution, the condition of being a boy does not justify a kangaroo court. The essential difference between Gerald's case and a normal criminal case is that safeguards available to adults were discarded in Gerald's case. The summary procedure as well as the long commitment was possible because Gerald was 15 years of age instead of over 18.

If Gerald had been over 18, he would not have been subject to Juvenile Court proceedings. For the particular offense immediately involved, the maximum punishment would have been a fine of $5 to $50, or imprisonment in jail for not more than two months. Instead, he was committed to custody for a maximum of six years. If he had been over 18 and had committed an offense to which such a sentence might apply, he would have been entitled to substantial rights under the Constitution of the United States as well as under Arizona's laws and constitution. The United States Constitution would guarantee him rights and protections with respect to arrest, search, and seizure, and pretrial interrogation. It would assure him of specific notice of the charges and adequate time to decide his course of action and to prepare his defense. He would be entitled to clear advice that he could be represented by counsel, and, at least if a felony were involved, the State would be required to provide counsel if his parents were unable to afford it. If the court acted on the basis of his confession, careful procedures would be required to assure its voluntariness. If the case went to trial, confrontation and opportunity for cross-examination would be guaranteed. So wide a gulf between the State's treatment of the adult and of the child requires a bridge sturdier than mere verbiage, and reasons more persuasive than cliche can provide. As Wheeler and Cottrell have put it, 'The rhetoric of the juvenile court movement has developed without any necessarily close correspondence to the realities of court and institutional routines.'

We now turn to the specific issues which are presented to us in the present case.

NOTICE OF CHARGES

Appellants allege that the Arizona Juvenile Code is unconstitutional or alternatively that the proceedings before the Juvenile Court were constitutionally defective because of failure to provide adequate notice of the hearings. No notice was given to Gerald's parents when he was taken into custody on Monday, June 8. On that night, when Mrs. Gault went to the Detention Home, she was orally informed that there would be a hearing the next afternoon and was told the reason why Gerald was in custody. The only written notice Gerald's parents received at any time was a note on plain paper from Officer Flagg delivered on Thursday or Friday, June 11 or 12, to the effect that the judge had set Monday, June 15, 'for further Hearings on Gerald's delinquency.'

A 'petition' was filed with the court on June 9 by Officer Flagg, reciting only that he was informed and believed that 'said minor is a delinquent minor and that it is necessary that some order be made by the Honorable Court for said minor's welfare.'

We cannot agree with the court's conclusion that adequate notice was given in this case. Notice, to comply with due process requirements, must be given sufficiently in advance of scheduled court proceedings so that reasonable opportunity to prepare will be afforded, and it must 'set forth the alleged misconduct with particularity.' It is obvious, as we have discussed above, that no purpose of shielding the child from the public stigma of knowledge of his having been taken into custody and scheduled for hearing is served by the procedure approved by the court below. The 'initial hearing' in the present case was a hearing on the merits. Notice at that time is not timely; and even if there were a conceivable purpose served by the deferral proposed by the court below, it would have to yield to the requirements that the child and his parents or guardian be notified, in writing, of the specific charge or factual allegations to be considered at the hearing, and that such written notice be given at the earliest practicable time, and in any event sufficiently in advance of the hearing to permit preparation. Due process of law requires notice of the sort we have described—that is, notice which would be deemed constitutionally adequate in a civil or criminal proceeding. It does not allow a hearing to be held in which a youth's freedom and his parents' right to his custody are at stake without giving them timely notice, in advance of the hearing, of the specific issues that they must meet. Nor, in the circumstances of this case, can it reasonably be said that the requirement of notice was waived.

RIGHT TO COUNSEL

Probation officers, in the Arizona scheme, are also arresting officers. They initiate proceedings and file petitions which they verify, as here, alleging the delinquency of the child; and they testify, as here, against the child. And here the probation officer was also superintendent of the Detention Home. The probation officer cannot act as counsel for the child. His role in the adjudicatory hearing, by statute and in fact, is as arresting officer and witness against the child. Nor can the judge represent the child. There is no material difference in this respect between adult and juvenile proceedings of the sort here involved. In adult proceedings, this contention has been foreclosed by decisions of this Court. A proceeding where the issue is whether the child will be found to be 'delinquent' and subjected to the loss of his liberty for years is comparable in seriousness to a felony prosecution. The juvenile needs the assistance of counsel to cope with problems of law, to make skilled inquiry into the facts, to insist upon regularity of the proceedings, and to ascertain whether he has a defense and to prepare and submit it. The child 'requires the guiding hand of counsel at every step in the proceedings against him.' Just as in *Kent v. United States*, we indicated our agreement with the United States Court of Appeals for the District of Columbia Circuit that the assistance of counsel is essential for purposes of waiver proceedings, so we hold now that it is equally essential for the determination of delinquency, carrying with it the awesome prospect of incarceration in a state institution until the juvenile reaches the age of 21.

During the last decade, court decisions, experts, and legislatures have demonstrated increasing recognition of this view. In at least one-third of the States, statutes now provide for the right of representation by retained counsel in juvenile delinquency proceedings, notice of the right, or assignment of counsel, or a combination of these. In other States, court rules have similar provisions.

We conclude that the Due Process Clause of the Fourteenth Amendment requires that in respect of proceedings to determine delinquency which may result in commitment to an institution in which the juvenile's freedom is curtailed, the child and his parents must be notified of the child's right to be represented by counsel retained by them, or if they are unable to afford counsel, that counsel will be appointed to represent the child.

At the habeas corpus proceeding, Mrs. Gault testified that she knew that she could have appeared with counsel at the juvenile hearing. This knowledge is not a waiver of the right to counsel which she and her juvenile son had, as we have defined it. They had a right expressly to be advised that they might retain counsel and to be confronted with the need for specific consideration of whether they did or did not choose to waive the right. If they were unable to afford to employ counsel, they were entitled in view of the seriousness of the charge and the potential commitment, to appointed counsel, unless they chose waiver. Mrs. Gault's knowledge that she could employ counsel was not an 'intentional relinquishment or abandonment' of a fully known right.

CONFRONTATION, SELF-INCRIMINATION, CROSS-EXAMINATION

Our first question, then, is whether Gerald's admission was improperly obtained and relied on as the basis of decision, in conflict with the Federal Constitution. For this purpose, it is necessary briefly to recall the relevant facts.

Mrs. Cook, the complainant, and the recipient of the alleged telephone call, was not called as a witness. Gerald's mother asked the Juvenile Court Judge why Mrs. Cook was not present and the judge replied that 'she didn't have to be present.' So far as appears, Mrs. Cook was spoken to only once, by Officer Flagg, and this was by telephone. The judge did not speak with her on any occasion. Gerald had been questioned by the probation officer after having been taken into custody. The exact circumstances of this questioning do not appear but any admissions Gerald may have made at this time do not appear in the record. Gerald was also questioned by the Juvenile Court Judge at each of the two hearings. The judge testified in the habeas corpus proceeding that Gerald admitted making 'some of the lewd statements ... (but not) any of the more serious lewd statements.' There was conflict and uncertainty among the witnesses at the habeas corpus proceeding—the Juvenile Court Judge, Mr. and Mrs. Gault, and the probation officer—as to what Gerald did or did not admit.

We shall assume that Gerald made admissions of the sort described by the Juvenile Court Judge, as quoted above. Neither Gerald nor his parents were advised that he did not have to testify or make a statement, or that an incriminating statement might result in his commitment as a 'delinquent.'

It would be entirely unrealistic to carve out of the Fifth Amendment all statements by juveniles on the ground that these cannot lead to 'criminal' involvement. In the first place, juvenile proceedings to determine 'delinquency,' which may lead to commitment to a state institution, must be regarded as 'criminal' for purposes of the privilege against self-incrimination. To hold otherwise would be to disregard substance because of the feeble enticement of the 'civil' label-of-convenience which has been attached to juvenile proceedings. Indeed, in over half of the States, there is not even assurance that the juvenile will be kept in separate institutions, apart from adult 'criminals.' In those States juveniles may be placed in or transferred to adult penal institutions after having been found 'delinquent' by a juvenile court. For this purpose, at least, commitment is a deprivation of liberty. It is incarceration against one's will, whether it is called 'criminal' or 'civil.' And our Constitution guarantees that no person shall be 'compelled' to be a witness against himself when he is threatened with deprivation of his liberty—a command which this Court has broadly applied and generously implemented in accordance with the teaching of the history of the privilege and its great office in mankind's battle for freedom.

In addition, apart from the equivalence for this purpose of exposure to commitment as a juvenile delinquent and exposure to imprisonment as an adult offender, the fact of the matter is that there is little or no assurance in Arizona, as in most if not all of the States, that a juvenile apprehended and interrogated by the police or even by the Juvenile Court itself will remain outside of the reach of adult courts as a consequence of the offense for which he has been taken into custody. In Arizona, as in other States, provision is made for Juvenile Courts to relinquish or waive jurisdiction to the ordinary criminal courts. In the present case, when Gerald Gault was interrogated concerning violation of a section of the Arizona Criminal Code, it could not be certain that the Juvenile Court Judge would decide to 'suspend' criminal prosecution in court for adults by proceeding to an adjudication in Juvenile Court.

It is also urged, as the Supreme Court of Arizona here asserted, that the juvenile and presumably his parents should not be advised of the juvenile's right to silence because confession is good for the child as the commencement of the assumed therapy of the juvenile court process, and he should be encouraged to assume an attitude of trust and confidence toward the officials of the juvenile process. This proposition has been subjected to widespread challenge on the basis of current reappraisals of the rhetoric and realities of the handling of juvenile offenders.

In fact, evidence is accumulating that confessions by juveniles do not aid in 'individualized treatment,' as the court below put it, and that compelling the child to answer questions, without warning or advice as to his right to remain silent, does not serve this or any other good purpose.

Further, authoritative opinion has cast formidable doubt upon the reliability and trustworthiness of 'confessions' by children.

We conclude that the constitutional privilege against self-incrimination is applicable in the case of juveniles as it is with respect to adults. We appreciate that special problems may arise with respect to waiver of the privilege by or on behalf of children, and that there may well be some differences in technique—but not in principle—depending upon the age of the child and the presence and competence of parents. The participation of counsel will, of course, assist the police, Juvenile Courts and appellate tribunals in administering the privilege. If counsel was not present for some permissible reason when an admission was obtained, the greatest care must be taken to assure that the admission was voluntary, in the sense not only that it was not coerced or suggested, but also that it was not the product of ignorance of rights or of adolescent fantasy, fright or despair.

The 'confession' of Gerald Gault was first obtained by Officer Flagg, out of the presence of Gerald's parents, without counsel and without advising him of his right to silence, as far as appears. The judgment of the Juvenile Court was stated by the judge to be based on Gerald's admissions in court. Neither 'admission' was reduced to writing, and, to say the least, the process by which the 'admissions,' were obtained and received must be characterized as lacking the certainty and order which are required of proceedings of such formidable consequences. Apart from the 'admission,' there was nothing upon which a judgment or finding might be based. There was no sworn testimony. Mrs. Cook, the complainant, was not present. The Arizona Supreme Court held that 'sworn testimony must be required of all witnesses including police officers, probation officers and others who are part of or officially related to the juvenile court structure.' We hold that this is not enough. No reason is suggested or appears for a different rule in respect of sworn testimony in juvenile courts than in adult tribunals. Absent a valid confession adequate to support the determination of the Juvenile Court, confrontation and sworn testimony by witnesses available for cross-examination were essential for a finding of 'delinquency' and an order committing Gerald to a state institution for a maximum of six years.

For the reasons stated, the judgment of the Supreme Court of Arizona is reversed and the cause remanded for further proceedings not inconsistent with this opinion. It is so ordered.

Judgment reversed and cause remanded with directions.

Mr. Justice BLACK, concurring.

The juvenile court laws of Arizona and other States, as the Court points out, are the result of plans promoted by humane and forward-looking people to provide a system of courts, procedures, and sanctions deemed to be less harmful and more lenient to children than to adults. For this reason such state laws generally provide less formal and less public methods for the trial of children. In line with this policy, both courts and legislators have shrunk back from labeling these laws as 'criminal' and have preferred to call them 'civil.' This, in part, was to prevent the full application to juvenile court cases of the Bill of Rights safeguards, including notice as provided in the Sixth Amendment, the right to counsel guaranteed by the Sixth, the right against self-incrimination guaranteed by the Fifth, and the right to confrontation guaranteed by the Sixth. The Court here holds, however, that these four Bill of Rights safeguards apply to protect a juvenile accused in a juvenile court on a charge under which he can be imprisoned for a term of years. This holding strikes a well-nigh fatal blow to much that is unique about the juvenile courts in the Nation.

The juvenile court planners envisaged a system that would practically immunize juveniles from 'punishment' for 'crimes' in an effort to save them from youthful indiscretions and stigmas due to criminal charges or convictions. I agree with the Court, however, that this exalted ideal has failed of achievement since the beginning of the system. Indeed, the state laws from the first one on contained provisions, written in emphatic terms, for arresting and charging juveniles with violations of state criminal laws, as well as for taking juveniles by force of law away from their parents and turning them over to different individuals or groups or for confinement within some state school or institution for a number of years. The latter occurred in this case. Young Gault was arrested and detained on a charge of violating an Arizona penal law by using vile and offensive language to a lady on the telephone. If an adult, he could only have been fined or imprisoned for two months for his conduct. As a juvenile, however, he was put through a more or less secret, informal hearing by the court, after which he was ordered, or more realistically, 'sentenced,' to confinement in Arizona's Industrial School until he reaches 21 years of age. Thus, in a juvenile system designed to lighten or avoid punishment for criminality, he was ordered by the State to six years' confinement in what is in all but name a penitentiary or jail.

Where a person, infant or adult, can be seized by the State, charged, and convicted for violating a state criminal law, and then ordered by the State to be confined for six years, I think the Constitution requires that he be tried in accordance with the guarantees of all the provisions of the Bill of Rights made applicable to the States by the Fourteenth Amendment. Undoubtedly this would be true of an adult defendant, and it would be a plain denial of equal protection of the laws—an invidious discrimination—to hold that others subject to heavier punishments could, because they are children, be denied these same constitutional safeguards. I consequently agree with the Court that the Arizona law as applied here denied to the parents and their son the right of notice, right to counsel, right against self-incrimination, and right to confront the witnesses against young Gault. Appellants are entitled to these rights, not because 'fairness, impartiality and orderliness—in short, the essentials of due process'—require them and not because they are 'the procedural rules which have been fashioned from the generality of due process,' but because they are specifically and unequivocally granted by provisions of the Fifth and Sixth Amendments which the Fourteenth Amendment makes applicable to the States.

Mr. Justice HARLAN, concurring in part and dissenting in part.

Each of the 50 States has created a system of juvenile or family courts, in which distinctive rules are employed and special consequences imposed. The jurisdiction of these courts commonly extends both to cases which the States have withdrawn from the ordinary processes of criminal justice, and to cases which involve acts that, if performed by an adult, would not be penalized as criminal. Such courts are denominated civil, not criminal, and are characteristically said not to administer criminal penalties. One consequence of these systems, at least as Arizona construes its own, is that certain of the rights guaranteed to criminal defendants by the Constitution are withheld from juveniles. This case brings before this Court for the first time the question of what limitations the Constitution places upon the operation of such tribunals. For reasons which follow, I have concluded that the Court has gone too far in some respects, and fallen short in others, in assessing the procedural requirements demanded by the Fourteenth Amendment.

The proper issue here is, however, not whether the State may constitutionally treat juvenile offenders through a system of specialized courts, but whether the proceedings in Arizona's juvenile courts include procedural guarantees which satisfy the requirements of the Fourteenth Amendment.

No more evidence of the importance of the public interests at stake here is required than that furnished by the opinion of the Court; it indicates that 'some 601,000 children under 18, or 2% of all children between 10 and 17, came before juvenile courts' in 1965, and that 'about one-fifth of all arrests for serious crimes' in 1965 were of juveniles. The Court adds that the rate of juvenile crime is steadily rising. All this, as the Court suggests, indicates the importance of these due process issues, but it mirrors no less vividly that state authorities are confronted by formidable and immediate problems involving the most fundamental social values. The state legislatures have determined that the most hopeful solution for these problems is to be found in specialized courts, organized under their own rules and imposing distinctive consequences. The terms and limitations of these systems are not identical, nor are the procedural arrangements which they include, but the States are uniform in their insistence that the ordinary processes of criminal justice are inappropriate, and that relatively informal proceedings, dedicated to premises and purposes only imperfectly reflected in the criminal law, are instead necessary.

Measured by these criteria, only three procedural requirements should, in my opinion, now be deemed required of state juvenile courts by the Due Process Clause of the Fourteenth Amendment: first, timely notice must be provided to parents and children of the nature and terms of any juvenile court proceeding in which a determination affecting their rights or interests may be made; second, unequivocal and timely notice must be given that counsel may appear in any such proceeding in behalf of the child and its parents, and that in cases in which the child may be confined in an institution, counsel may, in circumstances of indigency, be appointed for them; and third, the court must maintain a written record, or its equivalent, adequate to permit effective review on appeal or in collateral proceedings.

The question remains whether certain additional requirements, among them the privilege against self-incrimination, confrontation, and cross-examination, must now, as the Court holds, also be imposed. I share in part the views expressed in my Brother WHITE'S concurring opinion, but believe that there are other, and more deep-seated, reasons to defer, at least for the present, the imposition of such requirements.

Finally, I turn to assess the validity of this juvenile court proceeding under the criteria discussed in this opinion. Measured by them, the judgment below must, in my opinion, fall. Gerald Gault and his parents were not provided adequate notice of the terms and purposes of the proceedings in which he was adjudged delinquent; they were not advised of their rights to be represented by counsel; and no record in any form was maintained of the proceedings. It follows, for the reasons given in this opinion, that Gerald Gault was deprived of his liberty without due process of law, and I therefore concur in the judgment of the Court.

Mr. Justice STEWART, dissenting.

The Court today uses an obscure Arizona case as a vehicle to impose upon thousands of juvenile courts throughout the Nation restrictions that the Constitution made applicable to adversary criminal trials. I believe the Court's decision is wholly unsound as a matter of constitutional law, and sadly unwise as a matter of judicial policy.

Juvenile proceedings are not criminal trials. They are not civil trials. They are simply not adversary proceedings. Whether treating with a delinquent child, a neglected child, a defective child, or a dependent child, a juvenile proceeding's whole purpose and mission is the very opposite of the mission and purpose of a prosecution in a criminal court. The object of the one is correction of a condition. The object of the other is conviction and punishment for a criminal act.

In the last 70 years many dedicated men and women have devoted their professional lives to the enlightened task of bringing us out of the dark world of Charles Dickens in meeting our responsibilities to the child in our society. The result has been the creation in this century of a system of juvenile and family courts in each of the 50 States. There can be no denying that in many areas the performance of these agencies has fallen disappointingly short of the hopes and dreams of the courageous pioneers who first conceived them. For a variety of reasons, the reality has sometimes not even approached the ideal, and much remains to be accomplished in the administration of public juvenile and family agencies—in personnel, in planning, in financing, perhaps in the formulation of wholly new approaches.

The inflexible restrictions that the Constitution so wisely made applicable to adversary criminal trials have no inevitable place in the proceedings of those public social agencies known as juvenile or family courts. And to impose the Court's long catalog of requirements upon juvenile proceedings in every area of the country is to invite a long step backwards into the nineteenth century. In that era there were no juvenile proceedings, and a child was tried in a conventional criminal court will all the trappings of a conventional criminal trial. So it was that a 12-year-old boy named James Guild was tried in New Jersey for killing Catharine Beakes. A jury found him guilty of murder, and he was sentenced to death by hanging. The sentence was executed. It was all very constitutional.

A State in all its dealings must, of course, accord every person due process of law. And due process may require that some of the same restrictions which the Constitution has placed upon criminal trials must be imposed upon juvenile proceedings. For example, I suppose that all would agree that a brutally coerced confession could not constitutionally be considered in a juvenile court hearing. But it surely does not follow that the testimonial privilege against self-incrimination is applicable in all juvenile proceedings. Similarly, due process clearly requires timely notice of the purpose and scope of any proceedings affecting the relationship of parent and child. But it certainly does not follow that notice of a juvenile hearing must be framed with all the technical niceties of a criminal indictment.

I would dismiss the appeal.

Holdings of *In re: Gault*: The court held that certain Due Process rights are afforded to juveniles in juvenile delinquency court proceedings, including: (1) *Notice of Charges:* Notice must be given sufficiently in advance of scheduled court proceedings so that reasonable opportunity to prepare will be afforded, and it must set forth the alleged misconduct with particularity. (2) *Right to Counsel:* In respect of proceedings to determine delinquency which may result in commitment to an institution, the child and his parents must be notified of the child's right to be represented by counsel retained by them, or if they are unable to afford counsel, that counsel will be appointed to represent the child. (3) *Confrontation, Self-Incrimination, Cross-Examination:* The constitutional privilege against self-incrimination is applicable in the case of juveniles as it is with respect to adults. Also, absent a valid plea, confrontation and sworn testimony by witnesses available for cross-examination are essential for a finding of delinquency.

Discussion Questions

What does *Gault* require for state procedures to comply with Due Process in the following areas:

1. Notice of Charges.
2. Right to Counsel.
3. Right to Confrontation.
4. Right Against Self-Incrimination.
5. Cross-Examination of Witnesses.

Are there any other rights given to juveniles in delinquency proceedings by the *Gault* decision?

A. Right to Counsel

Overview: Once the *Gault* decision made it clear that juveniles charged with a delinquency case were entitled to an attorney, the question has arisen as to whether or not the juvenile or the youth's parent can waive that right. Different states have approached this question in different ways: some by court decisions and some by statutes. In either event, several approaches have been taken. Some courts have held that the minor can waive the right to counsel so long as the youth is advised of his rights and has the knowledge, maturity and intelligence to make an informed decision about waiving the right to counsel. Other courts have held that, under no circumstances can the youth waive the right to counsel without the benefit of counsel in making that decision.

In re Manuel R.: In *In re Manuel R.,* the Connecticut Supreme Court was forced to decide whether or not a juvenile had properly waived his right to counsel in a juvenile dispositional matter, where he was ordered to be placed in a secure facility (training school) for two years. The youth was encouraged by his mother to waive the right to counsel, and agreed to the waiver on the record.

As you read *Manuel R.,* look for the following:

1. Consider whether or not the mother's self-interest influenced her more than her son's best interests in assisting the youth in waiving his right to counsel.
2. Look for any evidence in the record showing that the youth did not fully appreciate his right to counsel and the impact that such a decision would have on the outcome of the case.

In re Manuel R.

207 Conn. 725, 543 A.2d 719 (1988)

The right to legal representation is guaranteed by statute to any child charged with delinquency. The question in this case is whether, and under what circumstances, that right to counsel can be waived by the child. The respondent, Manuel R., appeals from the disposition of the Superior Court committing him to the department of children and youth services (DCYS) for placement at Long Lane School. We find error and remand for a new dispositional hearing.

I

The record discloses the following chronology of events: On January 5, 1987, Manuel was placed on probation by the Superior Court for a period of one year on a burglary charge. The court ordered Manuel, as a condition of his probation, to attend high school and to adhere to its rules and regulations. Approximately four months later, William B. Carlos, a probation officer, filed a petition alleging that Manuel was a delinquent child because he had violated the terms of the court's probation order. Specifically, the petition charged that Manuel, then fifteen years old, had skipped school and, while in attendance, had brought a radio with him in violation of school rules. An application for Manuel's detention during the delinquency proceeding was filed at the same time.

A hearing on the application for detention was held on April 22, 1987. According to the transcript of this hearing, the probation department sought to detain Manuel not on the basis of his alleged probation violations but rather because he had allegedly committed a third degree assault on his mother. The court declined to place Manuel in the only then available group home and instead continued the detention review hearing until the following week to allow a further exploration of residential placement possibilities. At this hearing, and at all subsequent detention and adjudicatory hearings, Manuel was represented by Attorney George Oleyer of the office of the public defender.

At the follow-up hearing on April 29, 1987, Manuel was remanded to detention by the trial court, *Barnett, J.,* on the understanding that he could be transferred to a local residential facility if an opening became available. At the close of the hearing, Manuel's mother, Carmen R., stated that, while she had confidence in Manuel and hoped that the detention would help him, she was "not going to keep letting him pull me down 'cuz I still have a life to lead, too. And he fails to realize that I'm punished for every time he does something."

The adjudicative phase of the proceeding took place two weeks later. After a colloquy following Manuel's admission that he had violated the terms of his probation, the trial court, *Barnett, J.,* accepted the plea of admission and adjudicated Manuel a delinquent child. The alleged assault, having previously been nolled by the state, did not enter into this adjudication. The case was then continued for disposition and Manuel was released into the custody of his mother on the promise that he would abide by the terms of a "contract" with his mother that had been prepared by the probation department.

Manuel next appeared before the Superior Court, so far as the record discloses, on August 17, 1987, at proceedings that, although docketed as relating to the entry of pleas on new charges, quickly evolved into a disposition of the previously adjudicated probation violations. These are the proceedings whose validity is presently at issue in this appeal.

According to the docket sheet for juvenile matters on August 17, 1987, Manuel was scheduled to appear at 10:30 a.m. for the sole purpose of entering pleas on three new charges unrelated to this appeal. Before commencing the plea hearing, the trial court, *McGrath, J.,* summoned Attorney Oleyer to the courtroom, having been told by the probation officer that Oleyer represented Manuel. Oleyer appeared on the scene within a few moments and asked the court, "Can we pass this? I haven't seen him. I didn't know [Manuel and his mother] were here." Manuel's mother objected to a continuance in the following manner: "Excuse me, but I don't want—I don't want—if I have to go without an attorney I'll go without an attorney because Mr. Oleyer's going to force this thing into where Manuel's going back home and Manuel's going to do the same thing again. I'm going to miss more time from work and I'm going to lose my job, and I'm not going for it. If I have to represent my son I'll represent him."

In order to allow for further consultation between the parties, the trial court called a five minute recess. Upon its expiration, the hearing resumed when all parties, except Oleyer, reentered the courtroom. Thereafter the following exchange took place:

"Mrs. [R]: I don't want Mr. Oleyer for my son's attorney.

"The Court: Well, we have nobody else here.

"Mrs. [R]: Well, I'll represent him myself then. He tells me—he tells us five minutes then he goes out there and he's calling everybody else into the office sitting there with him. I mean, I have to go to work 'cuz I got other kids I gotta support."

The trial court then moved ahead with the plea hearing by informing Manuel of three new charges against him: larceny in the sixth degree, harassment and possession of illegal fireworks. Having described the charges, the court expressed its reluctance to proceed any further without representation for Manuel, to which Mrs. R. responded: "Yeah, but Mr. Oleyer—he thinks that he's gonna come in here and sit here and have Manuel sent home again today, or whatever, and just keep sending him back and forth, back and forth."

Before Mrs. R. could complete her objections to a continuance on the entry of the pleas, Elizabeth Gleason, the state's advocate, brought to the court's attention, for the first time, Manuel's outstanding adjudication of delinquency and asked the court to enter a disposition in accordance with the recommendation of the probation officer, "which the state strongly supports." Mrs. R. then commented that if Manuel were sent home again and "he goes and gets in trouble again then I gotta miss work again." The probation officer informed the court that three residential facilities had rejected Manuel and that the only option was placement at the state training school (Long Lane). In answer to the trial court's question, "Is this for disposition today?" the probation officer replied, "Well, yes, I was going to ask that it go for disposition because of problems in the home." After again being told that Manuel had already been adjudicated delinquent for probation violations, the trial court initiated the following discussion between all present:

The Court: Okay. You want to get rid of those other two files [the probation violations] that he has against him?

Mrs. [R]: Yes, sir.

The Court: All right, and you're waiving on behalf of your son the attorney that would be sitting here? That's Mr. Oleyer because he was involved in these files.

Mrs. [R]: Yes, sir.

Mr. Carlos [the probation officer]: Your Honor, would you like me to get another attorney?

The Court: No. The mother has indicated that she doesn't want it—it's for disposition—a replacement. And its recommendation by you is to place him in Mead Hall until other placement is found?

Mr. Carlos: Oh, well, no, your Honor. My recommendation today is Long Lane. That's why I was concerned about him not being represented.

The Court: Do you understand what that recommendation is?

Mrs. [R]: Yes, I do.

The Court: And you still don't want him to be represented?

Mrs. [R]: Yes.

Mr. Carlos: I've also explained it to the youngster, your Honor. He might have different feelings about it. But I did explain to him what I was recommending.

Mrs. [R]: Do you want an attorney?

The Respondent [Manuel]: No.

The Court: You don't?

Mrs. [R]: You sure?

The Respondent: (Nods no.)

The Court: You understand that the recommendation is for you to be committed to Long Lane?

The Respondent: Yes.

The court thereafter ordered Manuel committed to the custody of the DCYS for a period of two years with placement at Long Lane. We conclude that the record in this case fails to establish that Manuel knowingly and voluntarily waived the assistance of counsel during the dispositional stage of his delinquency proceeding. Accordingly, we find error and remand for a new hearing.

II

Any child in Connecticut is guaranteed the right to assistance of counsel in the defense of a delinquency petition by virtue of General Statutes § 46b-135(a), which provides that, "[a]t the commencement of any proceeding" involving his or her delinquency, a child "shall have the right to counsel" and, if necessary because of indigency, the state shall incur the cost. Under Connecticut law, a delinquency proceeding is bifurcated into adjudicatory and dispositional phases. The express language of § 46b-135(a) is without limitation and therefore encompasses both phases of the proceeding. This statutory right to counsel comports with governing constitutional requirements. *In re Gault*, 387 U.S. 1, 87 S.Ct. 1428, 18 L.Ed.2d 527 (1967) (establishing a due process right to counsel at the adjudicatory stage of delinquency proceedings).

The sole issue in this case, then, is whether a valid waiver of the respondent's right to counsel took place during the dispositional hearing. The respondent makes a two-fold attack on the validity of the waiver, claiming (1) that a child's right to counsel during a delinquency proceeding is nonwaivable as a matter of law, and (2) that, even if the right to counsel is waivable, the record in this case fails to establish a knowing and voluntary relinquishment of legal representation. While we disagree with the first of these claims, we agree with the second. We conclude that, in the circumstances of this case, the child did not effectively waive his right to counsel and that his mother, given her primary concern for a speedy resolution of the case, had such a conflict of interest that she lacked authority to do so on his behalf.

A

The respondent first urges us to adopt a per se rule declaring that children under the age of sixteen are legally incompetent to waive the assistance of counsel under any circumstance. In support of this claim, the respondent cites empirical research that suggests a definite correlation between youth and lack of comprehension of constitutional rights. This research has special relevance, according to the respondent, because in Connecticut the only persons who are subject to the delinquency jurisdiction of the Superior Court are below the age of sixteen. In light of empirical findings that persons of such tender years are, as a class, prone to misunderstanding legal rights, the respondent argues that a per se rule is justified.

We are not persuaded, however, that a per se rule based on the age of the child is an appropriate response to the admittedly delicate issue of juveniles' waiver of rights. The empirical evidence to date suggests that age, by itself, is not a reliable touchstone for determining a juvenile's capacity to exercise fundamental rights. A major study concluded that "age itself is quite limited in its effectiveness as a guide for weighing decisions about juveniles' understanding." It is true that, for all children below the age of fourteen, the available evidence suggests that comprehension of legal rights is elusive. With regard to children between the ages of fourteen and sixteen, however, general intelligence level, as well as socioeconomic status and prior court experience, become increasingly significant factors in a child's ability to grasp and exercise legal rights. The empirical literature therefore fails definitively to identify age as a surrogate for incapacity for children below the age of sixteen.

Furthermore, a per se rule of nonwaivability might actually frustrate a principal goal of juvenile law of encouraging children to accept responsibility for their transgressions and take an active role in their rehabilitation. Juvenile law embodies goals of control and treatment that are often difficult to reconcile. On the one hand, protecting society from disruptive and dangerous children often requires that courts control and incarcerate children in prison-like institutions. On the other hand, nurturing children into productive and responsible adults requires that persistent efforts be made toward individualized treatment and rehabilitation. Without minimizing the significance of this inevitable tension, we are persuaded that allowing a child to make an informed and deliberate choice about legal representation, if properly supervised by the trial court, can advance both the goal of control and that of treatment.

In juvenile proceedings, counsel for the child plays an important role in ensuring the reliability of adjudications underlying disposition and in developing alternative placement plans thereafter. To mandate the presence of counsel, however, might serve to reduce the child's own sense of involvement and might enhance his perception of his own role as merely that of spectator. The difficulty of engaging children meaningfully in their own cases has been recognized as a major challenge: "Courtroom deliberations often make the delinquent highly aware of his own irrelevance and inability to affect the course of the proceeding. Many decisions are reached, for example, without consulting the youth and in ways that suggest his complete incompetence to determine his own future." For those concerned with intervening successfully in the lives of troubled young persons, there is an increasing awareness that the procedures followed by the court can have a lasting impact on the child's development. In light of these principles, we believe that the waiver of counsel decision, *in itself,* can be a significant rehabilitative moment for the child. We accordingly reject the respondent's invitation to impose a per se rule of incompetency on all children.

B

We now turn to the central question of this appeal: what standards are to guide the trial court in its determination of whether to find that a child has validly waived his or her right to counsel. As the present proceedings poignantly demonstrate, those standards must take into account the possibility of a conflict of interest when a parent or guardian advocates a waiver on behalf of the child.

We begin our analysis with a reiteration of the standards for the waiver of counsel by adult defendants. A valid waiver is defined, in accordance with the well known test that a proper waiver of counsel must be intelligent and voluntary and that its basis, having been "clearly determined" by the trial court, should appear on the record.

In like fashion, Practice Book §961 mandates a "thorough inquiry" into specific factors about which the court must be "satisfied" before the accused "shall be permitted" to forego counsel. In particular, §961 establishes four criteria for an effective waiver: (1) clear advisement of the right to counsel; (2) possession of sufficient intelligence and capacity to appreciate the consequences of self-representation; (3) comprehension of the charges and proceeding, the permissible punishment exposure and any additional facts essential to a broad understanding of the case; and (4) awareness of the dangers and disadvantages of self-representation.

We conclude that these constitutional and procedural guidelines apply with equal, if not greater, force in the context of a delinquency proceeding. It is now commonly recognized that courts should take "special care" in scrutinizing a purported confession or waiver by a child. As the United States Supreme Court acknowledged in *In re Gault*, "special problems may arise with respect to waiver of the privilege by or on behalf of children and ... there may well be some differences in technique — but not in principle — depending upon the age of the child and the presence and competence of parents."

These judicial pronouncements embody the common sense notion that the validity of a child's waiver of counsel depends upon furnishing the child full information not only about the child's own legal rights but also about the overall nature of the proceeding against him or her. The need for broad-gauged advice is underscored by recent empirical studies demonstrating that significant numbers of children erroneously believe that lawyers are responsible for deciding issues of guilt and punishment, that defense lawyers will not advocate the interests of a juvenile who admits to the violation and that defense lawyers have a duty to report to the court any evidence of the juvenile client's culpability. Only a full colloquy between the court and the child can avoid such misperceptions and provide a solid basis for the intelligent exercise or waiver of the right to counsel. Only a full colloquy will permit the court to make an accurate determination of whether a child who professes to wish to proceed pro se, without counsel, has the developmental and cognitive ability to undertake a realistic assessment of the consequences of such an action. For all these reasons, our general policy of indulging every presumption against the waiver of fundamental rights has special application in the context of juvenile waiver.

The fact that, at juvenile proceedings, a child is often accompanied by a parent or guardian does not diminish judicial responsibility for a searching inquiry into the validity of a potential waiver of the right to counsel. At a minimum, the presence of a lay parent or guardian, with no training in law, is no guarantee that a child will be fully informed or meaningfully represented. Moreover, as judicial and scholarly authorities attest, parents may, for their own reasons, exert pressure on children to confess to alleged offenses and to waive the assistance of counsel.

The potential for undue parental influence is greatly increased in the event of a specific conflict of interest between parent and child. Such a potential conflict may arise, for example, when the parent bears fiscal responsibility for the cost of retained counsel; or acts as the complaining witness in the delinquency petition; or harbors anger and resentment about the child's misbehavior. Recognizing the possibility of such conflicts of interest between parent and child, Practice Book § 1045(2)(b) expressly provides that the court "shall appoint … counsel for the child, whether a request is made or not … if in the opinion of the court the interests of the child and his parents conflict…." Similarly, once a conflict of interest becomes apparent, the court may not permit a parent to waive counsel for a child.

Applying these standards for the validity of a child's waiver of the right to counsel to the facts of this case, we conclude that the record fails to establish that Manuel knowingly and voluntarily waived his right to legal representation at his dispositional hearing. The record manifests minimal participation by Manuel himself and substantial deference to the conflicting interests of his mother in immediate disposition of the charges against her son. Our statute and § 961 of our rules of practice require more of the court.

The first of the four inquiries that a court must make, under § 961, before it accepts a waiver of the right to counsel, is whether the defendant, in this case the child, has been advised of his right to counsel. Concededly, that advice was given to the respondent in this case.

The second inquiry that § 961 requires concerns the child's intelligence and capacity to appreciate the consequence of the decision to represent himself. On this question, the trial court record is sparse at best. The court made no effort to address the respondent directly to determine whether he possessed the qualities described by the rule. In fact, the transcript reveals that Manuel uttered only five words throughout the hearing: the answer "Yes" or "No" on five separate occasions. Of these five monosyllabic answers, two were in response to the questions whether he understood his right to counsel and his right to remain silent and three were in response to the following questions from the bench: (1) "Do you want an attorney?"; (2) "You don't?"; and (3) "You understand you are going up to Long Lane for a period of time?"

To compensate for the lack of direct inquiry into the respondent's intellectual capacity to represent himself, the state argues that an eight page predispositional report prepared by the probation officer adequately apprised the trial court of the respondent's capacity to proceed pro se. We are not persuaded. The record does not show whether the trial court had the opportunity to read the report. Indeed, the fact that the proceeding began as a plea hearing, but was transformed in midstream into a dispositional hearing upon the joint suggestion of the probation officer and the state advocate, makes it doubtful that the court would have fully considered this detailed report before it made its disposition. We note in addition that the trial court did not preside over the detention and adjudicatory phases of this case and therefore had no prior opportunity on this record to observe the respondent and form a judgment about his mental capacity. Finally, even if the trial court did evaluate the report, the record contains no indication that its contents were determinative. Accordingly, the record falls short of "*affirmatively* show[ing] that [the respondent] was literate, competent and understanding, and that he voluntarily exercised his informed free will."

The third requirement of § 961 is that the court satisfy itself that the child comprehends the "charges and proceedings, the range of permissible punishments, and any additional facts essential to a broad understanding of the case." The record in this regard raises the contrary inference, that the respondent did *not* understand the proceeding or the range of potential dispositions. According to the probation officer, when told that Long Lane was the proposed disposition, the respondent said he had "different feelings about it." Only moments later, however, the respondent purported to waive the presence of the one person whose responsibility it was to augment and investigate the state's recommendation. This curious juxtaposition suggests an incomplete understanding of the possibility that there might be dispositional alternatives other than those recommended by the probation officer.

Finally, it is apparent that the respondent was not "made aware of the dangers and disadvantages of self-representation" as required by the fourth element of § 961. Counsel can perform a variety of useful functions during the dispositional phase of a delinquency proceeding. In particular, the child might be informed that a primary obligation of defense counsel is to augment and investigate the placement recommendation of the state so that the ultimate disposition is tailored to the child's individual needs. Additionally, counsel can exercise the rights of confrontation and cross-examination; subpoena witnesses, ensure adherence to procedural regularity and assist the child and the family in securing important state services. On the record before us, there was no effort whatsoever to inform the respondent and his mother of the risks of self-representation.

In its totality, this record manifests a canvass that fails to comport with well established rules concerning waiver of the right to counsel. Without a compliance with Practice Book § 961, and in the absence of other evidence sufficient to establish the respondent's knowing and voluntary waiver of his statutory right to counsel, it was error to order his commitment to the department of children and youth services with placement at the state training school.

There is error, the judgment is set aside and the case is remanded to the trial court for a new dispositional hearing.

Holdings of *In re Manuel R.*: The court held that the child's right to counsel in a delinquency proceeding is not unwaivable as a matter of law. The court further held that the youth in this case did not knowingly and voluntarily waive his right to counsel at his dispositional hearing. The ruling of the lower court was reversed.

Discussion Questions

What role could (or should) the attorney initially appointed to represent the youth have taken in this case?

The court held that a "per se rule" prohibiting a minor from waiving his right to counsel "might actually frustrate a principal goal of juvenile law of encouraging children to accept responsibility for their transgressions and take an active role in their rehabilitation." Doesn't that argument actually support allowance of a guilty plea rather than a waiver of counsel?

Does this court's refusal to adopt the "per se rule" of unwaivability of right to counsel show that the court is still believing that the role of juvenile court is to provide "treatment" for the youth? If so, does that really apply when the court is sentencing the youth to confinement for several years?

What four criteria must be established for a valid waiver of a juvenile's right to counsel?

D.R. v. Commonwealth: In *D.R. v. Commonwealth,* the Kentucky Appeals Court was forced to decide whether or not a juvenile's plea was valid when he pled guilty to a charge without having had an attorney appointed for him.

As you read *D.R. v. Commonwealth* look for the following:

1. Consider what record was missing (other than the lack of an attorney) that was necessary to establish that the plea was knowing and voluntary.

2. Look for any evidence in the opinion to establish whether this court is applying a constitutional right rather than a mere statutory right.

D.R. v. Commonwealth

64 S.W.3d 292 (Ky. App. 2001)

D.R., a minor child, brings this appeal from a September 22, 2000 judgment of the Lincoln Circuit Court. We reverse and remand.

Appellant's mother filed a beyond control petition in juvenile court against appellant. Appellant initially appeared *pro se* before the Lincoln District Court on January 14, 1999. On that day, he entered an admission of guilt. In response to his guilty plea, he was placed on probation for a period of one year, until January 14, 2000. On January 13, 2000, the district court determined appellant violated terms of his probation and ordered extension of probation through January 14, 2001. The court also ordered fourteen days' detention with four to serve, and the balance probated. Subsequently, appellant was accused of again violating terms of probation. On March 9, 2000, the court ordered thirty days' detention, probated upon the condition appellant follow terms of the existing probation order. An appeal ensued to the Lincoln Circuit Court. The circuit court set aside the thirty days of detention but affirmed the district court upon all other grounds. The Court of Appeals granted discretionary review on December 27, 2000. We now turn to appellant's arguments upon review.

Appellant contends that his January 14, 1999 admission of guilt was not made knowingly and intelligently. Specifically, he claims that the requirements of *Boykin v. Alabama*, 395 U.S. 238, 89 S.Ct. 1709, 23 L.Ed.2d 274 (1969) were not met, and that he was not afforded counsel. We shall address these issues separately.

In determining the validity of guilty pleas in criminal cases, the plea must represent a voluntary and intelligent choice among the alternative course[s] of action open to the defendant. The United States Supreme Court has held that both federal and state courts must satisfy themselves that guilty pleas are voluntarily and intelligently made by competent defendants. Since pleading guilty involves the waiver of several constitutional rights, including the privilege against compulsory self-incrimination, the right to trial by jury, and the right to confront one's accusers, a waiver of these rights cannot be presumed from a silent record. The court must question the accused to determine that he has a full understanding of what the plea connotes and of its consequences, and this determination should become part of the record. The validity of a guilty plea must be determined not from specific key words uttered at the time the plea was taken, but from considering the totality of circumstances surrounding the plea. These circumstances include the accused's demeanor, background and experience, and whether the record reveals that the plea was voluntarily made.

To determine the validity of appellant's admission of guilt, we shall initially review the dialogue between appellant and the district court:

THE COURT: [D.R.], before we start, let me advise you of your rights. First of all, you have the right to remain silent. If you give up that right, anything you say can be used against you. You also have the right to have an attorney at these proceedings. So, similar to adult rights to have an attorney, it's your right, not—

it doesn't belong to your parents, they can't waive it for you. If you can't afford an attorney or they can't afford an attorney for you, I will appoint a public defender to represent you, but I may require some of it to be paid back to the public defender program. So, I need to know whether you want an attorney to represent you in this matter?

[D.R.]: No, sir.

THE COURT: You don't?

[D.R.]: No, sir.

THE COURT: Okay. The charge laid against you is that you are beyond control of your parents. The complaint talks about not obeying household rules, asking permission before you leave home, doing your school work. Apparently, you've been expelled?

[D.R.]: Yeah.

THE COURT: Is that for the rest of the year?

[D.R.]: Yes, sir.

THE COURT: Says you were caught with marijuana. Did you have charges filed against you for that?

[D.R.]: No. They just expelled me free [sic] for the school year.

THE COURT: Okay. Also some violence and stuff at home apparently between you and INAUDIBLE, some problems. It notes that you are improving, but your mother believes you still need a little help. The family needs a little help. What can you tell me about this?

[D.R.]: Well, I was violent and I was a little bit out of control, but I don't think I was that much out of control. Enough to get it filed.

THE COURT: What about this thing about attacking your mother, laying your hands on her, whatever all that means? Did you do that INAUDIBLE [sic]

[D.R.]: I didn't attack her. She was hitting me and stuff and I grabbed her arms so she would quit.

THE COURT: Had you been anywhere being treated for these crimes? In a hospital or anything for treatment?

[D.R.]: Yeah. They put me in INAUDIBLE in Danville.

THE COURT: How long ago was that?

[D.R.]: It was in October.

THE COURT: Of last year?

[D.R.]: Yeah.

THE COURT: How long were you there?

[D.R.]: A week and three days.

THE COURT: Okay. I need to know whether you want to plead guilty or not guilty to being out of control with your parents?

[D.R.]: Guilty.

From the above, it is clear that appellant was not informed of the consequences of an admission of guilt. Specifically, he was not informed of constitutional rights waived by admitting guilt or of the range of possible punishments. In short, appellant was not informed of a single consequence of his decision to enter an admission of guilt. Appellant was a 15-year-old child who had no previous experience with the court system. Upon the totality of circumstances, we are convinced that appellant's admission of guilt was not made knowingly and intelligently.

Next, appellant asserts that KRS 610.060(1)(a) mandates appointment of counsel.

[W]e construe subsection (a) as mandating the district court to initially appoint the child counsel; after appointment and consultation with counsel, the child then may waive the right to counsel under subsection (e). Simply stated, we think a child may waive the right to counsel *only if* that child has first been appointed, and consulted with, counsel concerning the waiver.

In the case *sub judice,* the record indicates that appellant waived counsel without first being appointed counsel. We believe such waiver ineffectual and contrary to KRS 610.060(1).

For the foregoing reasons, the judgment of the Lincoln Circuit Court is reversed, and this cause is remanded for proceedings consistent with this opinion.

Holdings of *D.R. v. Commonwealth:* The court held that a child may waive the right to counsel *only if* that child has first been appointed, and consulted with, counsel concerning the waiver.

Discussion Questions

Should a minor ever be allowed to waive their right to counsel?

Is the decision of this court prohibiting an uncounseled waiver or counsel based on a statute or on the Constitution?

Key Concepts: Right to Counsel

- The *Gault* decision held that the Due Process Clause of the Fourteenth Amendment requires that, in respect of proceedings to determine delinquency which may result in commitment to an institution in which the juvenile's freedom is curtailed, the child and his parents must be notified of the child's right to be represented by counsel retained by them, or if they are unable to afford counsel, that counsel will be appointed to represent the child.

- For those states that allow a minor to waive her or his right to counsel, courts require strong proof that the waiver was voluntary and knowing.

- Some states have held that a minor cannot waive his or her right without the benefit of counsel in making the decision to waive that right.

B. Competency to Stand Trial

Overview: The seminal case of *In re Gault* established certain rights for minors in juvenile courts but never mentioned the requirement of competency to stand trial. The prohibition of subjecting an accused to a trial when the accused is incompetent is a bedrock requirement in the adult criminal system, and, in the adult system, courts have recognized a presumption of competence. Almost all states that have been faced with the competence issue in juvenile courts have held that juveniles have such a right. Only one state appears to find that the right is not applicable to juvenile delinquency cases. *See, G.J.I. v. State,* 778 P.2d 485 (Okla. Crim. App. 1989). Courts have still had to struggle with whether or not a presumption of competency exists in juvenile court and with a method for determining competency for a minor.

In the Interest of S.H.: In *In the Interest of S.H.,* the Georgia Appeals Court was faced with a 12-year-old boy with a full scale IQ of 40 and the mental age of a 6-year-old who was convicted of a sexual assault of a 6-year-old. The court was forced to determine if the youth had a due process right to only be subjected to an adjudicatory hearing if he was competent to stand trial.

As you read *In the Interest of S.H.,* look for the following:

1. Observe the historical role noted by the Court in terms of the traditional function and purposes of juvenile delinquency courts.

2. Consider whether the Court has provided any guidance to how competency should be determined for a youth.

In the Interest of S.H.

20 Ga. App. 569, 469 S.E.2d 810 (Ga. App. 1996)

A petition alleging delinquency was filed in juvenile court accusing S.H., age 12, with aggravated sodomy. A hearing was held pursuant to OCGA § 15-11-33(a), and the juvenile court found that S.H. had committed the act. Because the offense would have been a crime if committed by an adult, the court adjudicated S.H. delinquent. The court also found that S.H. was incompetent. S.H. appeals the juvenile court's decision to hold the adjudicatory hearing despite his incompetence.

The record shows that S.H.'s mental age at the time of the offense was that of a six-year-old child, with an I.Q. of 40. His court-appointed guardian ad litem testified that S.H. did not know the difference between right or wrong, and a court-ordered evaluation of S.H. noted that he was "not a good historian for detail."

S.H.'s court-appointed counsel moved to have S.H. declared incompetent to stand trial. Although the court determined that S.H. was in fact incompetent, it nevertheless denied the motion. The court reasoned that because "Georgia law does not provide a statutory framework in order to protect juveniles [sic] rights not to be tried in a delinquency proceeding while they are incompetent," as a juvenile, S.H. was not entitled to be competent during the adjudicative proceedings.

The evidence presented at the adjudicatory proceeding was conflicting. The victim's 5-year-old sister witnessed the alleged incident and testified that S.H. removed his own clothing, pulled down her brother's pants, made her brother lie on his back, and got on top for just a minute until her big brother arrived. She testified that the victim said nothing, but made a giggling noise. The victim reportedly told his mother that S.H. got on top of him and placed his penis in the victim's mouth and then attempted to anally sodomize him. The mother admitted that a physician informed her that the victim had not been penetrated. The victim's babysitter, the first person the victim talked to after the incident, gave a statement to police indicating that the victim told her only about the act involving anal sodomy. Neither the victim nor S.H. testified. S.H. presented no defense.

The court subsequently adjudicated S.H. guilty of the act alleged beyond a reasonable doubt. At the hearing, the court stated that there was no evidence that S.H. actually committed anal sodomy. It also found that the delinquent behavior occurred due to a lack of adult supervision. The court observed that S.H. "is not a mean or violent child but is recreating events that have occurred to him and he does not realize the wrong of his actions." The court ordered S.H. jointly committed to the Department of Children & Youth Services ("DCYS"), and the Department of Human Resources permitted him to be released into his mother's custody pending placement and recommended that he not be placed in a detention environment. However, the court stated that "at every turn" the DCYS "recklessly disregarded" its direction by detaining S.H., ceasing his mental health counseling, and failing to consult with S.H.'s guardian ad litem regarding his treatment plan.

S.H. argues that the juvenile court violated his due process rights by adjudicating him delinquent and depriving him of his liberty when he was not competent to understand the nature of the proceedings or assist in his own defense. We agree.

The stated purpose of the Juvenile Court Code is to assist, protect, and restore children whose well-being is threatened as secure law-abiding members of society, and the Code must be liberally construed to that end. To promote this commendable purpose, the General Assembly created a comprehensive civil forum for treating and protecting juveniles, "replete with distinctions between criminal matters and matters concerning juveniles alleged delinquent." These differences, which emphasize treatment and rehabilitation, spare the child some of the collateral consequences of a criminal conviction. As is evident in this case, however, the consequences do not always differ. Both juvenile and criminal proceedings may result in a significant loss of liberty.

It follows that constitutional considerations must necessarily transcend even the most admirable legislative purposes. "'[T]he juvenile charged with "delinquency" is entitled *by right* to have the court apply those common law jurisprudential principles which experience and reason have shown are necessary to give the accused the essence of a fair trial.'" (Emphasis in original.) Without question, these include the right to adequate notice of the charges, appointment of counsel, the constitutional privilege against self-incrimination, and the right to confront opposing witnesses.

We believe the cornerstone of these substantive rights is competence to understand the nature of the charges and assist in a defense. A want of competence renders the other rights meaningless. "It has long been accepted that a person whose mental condition is such that he lacks the capacity to understand the nature and object of the proceedings against him, to consult with counsel, and to assist in preparing his defense may not be subjected to a trial." Principles of fundamental fairness require that this right be afforded in juvenile proceedings.

The conflicting evidence presented in this case and the minimal proof supporting the aggravating factors underscore the gravity of the competence requirement. The court itself made a finding at the close of the evidence that S.H.'s counsel had "no defense due to the lack of his client's ability to assist him." Thus, all the other procedural rights afforded S.H. in this proceeding could not guarantee him the "essence of a fair trial" when his incompetence prevented him from mounting any defense. Notwithstanding the State's assertion to the contrary, there is a vast qualitative difference between being a minor and being incompetent to stand trial when it comes to the abilities to understand the nature and object of the proceedings, comprehend one's own position in relation to the proceedings, and assist in one's own defense. We caution, however, that our holding does not create a bright-line rule that a juvenile's mental age is determinative of his incompetence. We focus solely on the foregoing abilities and question whether the goals of the Juvenile Court Code can be achieved when children lacking them are subjected to the consequences of an adjudicatory proceeding. Accordingly, we reverse and remand for proceedings consistent with this opinion.

Judgment reversed and case remanded.

Holdings of *In the Interest of S.H.*: The court held that Due Process requires that a minor in juvenile court who is not competent cannot be subjected to an adjudicatory hearing. The court also held that their holding "does not create a bright-line rule that a juvenile's mental age is determinative of his incompetence."

Discussion Questions

What facts in the *S.H.* case caused the court to question the competency of the youth involved, beyond mental age?

Can a minor be so young that he/she is incompetent as a matter of law?

In re Williams: In *In re Williams* the Ohio Appellate Court was faced with a competency issue for a minor in a juvenile delinquency proceeding where two experts filed conflicting reports relative to the competency issue. Both experts agreed that the 15-year-old charged had the intellectual abilities of a 6-year-old and a full scale IQ of only 40. However, the experts disagreed as to whether or not the youth was competent to stand trial.

As you read *In re Williams,* look for the following:

1. Examine the reports of the two experts and on what their opinions were based.

2. Consider whether the Court is finding that, as a matter of law, this youth was incompetent to stand trial.

In re Williams
16 Ohio App.3d 237, 687 N.E.2d 507 (Ohio App. 2 Dist. 1997)

Frederick N. Young, Presiding Judge.

This appeal arises from an action in the Montgomery County Court of Common Pleas, Juvenile Division. Nicholas Williams, a moderately retarded 15-year-old juvenile, informed his therapist that he had engaged in a brief sexual relationship with a 9-year-old girl the previous summer, while he was a runaway. A complaint charging Nicholas with two counts of statutory rape, an aggravated felony of the first degree was filed on November 2, 1996, and a detention hearing was held the same day.

One week after the initial hearing, Nicholas's attorney filed a motion for mental evaluation. Nicholas was evaluated by Dr. Laura Fugimura, the court psychologist, and Dr. Mark Williams, an independent psychologist, for the purpose of determining his competency to stand trial. Both doctors filed psychological evaluation reports with the court. The reports documented Nicholas's history of physical abuse at the hands of his mother, physical and sexual abuse by other family members, and his own past victimization of other children. His social history report revealed that Nicholas had attended outpatient sex specific counseling and that he was placed in a foster home soon after the alleged rape occurred. While Nicholas apparently ran away from his foster home on the first night he was there, he later came to enjoy living with his foster parents who, according to Nicholas, express affection and caring in a manner that he has never before experienced. After examining him, both doctors determined that Nicholas has the intellectual abilities of a 6-year-old, but disagreed as to his competency to stand trial. Dr. Fujimura found that, although Nicholas "did not seem to understand the functions of a Judge, jury, or witness," he had an adequate understanding of the role of the attorneys and the circumstances surrounding the charges to be competent for trial. Dr. Williams, on the other hand, concluded that Nicholas was incompetent to stand trial.

Magistrate Cunningham found Nicholas to be competent to stand trial in an entry captioned "Delinquency Magistrate's Order of Continuance." The plea and dispositional hearing was held on February 13, 1996, before Magistrate Cunningham. At the hearing, Nicholas Williams admitted to one count of rape. Before accepting the plea, Magistrate Cunningham explained each of Nicholas's relevant rights and, after each one, asked whether he understood the right. Nicholas responded "yes" to every question. Nicholas also answered "yes" when the magistrate asked him whether the allegations in the complaint were true. Without any further exchanges with Nicholas, the magistrate accepted the admission and proceeded to disposition.

The guardian *ad litem*, Gordon Taylor, indicated that his primary concern was that Nicholas receive treatment. Wayne Gilkison, the probation officer, emphasized Nicholas's need for treatment, but stated that the probation department had been unsuccessful in finding placement for him. He stated that there would be no services available to Nicholas if he were returned to the community and recommended that Nicholas be committed because of the high risk that he would re-offend. Nicholas's attorney asserted that Gordon Taylor had been able to locate "two institutions or treatment facilities willing and ready to take Nicholas with his I.Q. and his sex-specific needs." One of the facilities was Fairfield Academy in Thornville, Ohio, which would have provided placement for Nicholas at a cost of $225 per day, for a period of between eighteen and twenty-four months. According to Nicholas's attorney, the other facility, which is located in Parma, Ohio, was ready to assess Nicholas for placement. The guardian *ad litem* qualified these assertions, noting that Nicholas's acceptance into Fairfield Academy was contingent on a satisfactory interview. He also stated that while he was unaware whether the Parma facility had or would formally accept Nicholas, it was his understanding that acceptance was dependent on assurances of funding and, possibly, an interview with Nicholas.

The magistrate responded that she did not believe that sufficient funding was available for Nicholas to receive $225 per day treatment. The guardian *ad litem* urged the magistrate to consider attempting to find funding through the Interagency Clinical Assessment Team (ICAT) before imposing a sentence. However, the magistrate concluded that a continuance would cause "unnecessary delay." The magistrate also denied Nicholas's attorney's oral motion requesting that an ICAT assessment be completed to determine whether funding could be found for the placement of Nicholas in a sex-offender facility. Finally, the magistrate announced that she was committing Nicholas to the Ohio Department of Youth Services for a period of one year, and ordering that he receive sex-specific counseling and treatment while in detention.

The magistrate's decision and judge's order of adjudication and disposition, filed on February 20, 1996, committed Nicholas "to the Department of Youth Services for care and rehabilitation" for a term of at least one year and not more than six years. The decision made no express mention of sex-specific counseling. Included with the decision was the judge's order stating only that "[t]he above Magistrate's Decision is hereby adopted as an Order of this Court." Nicholas Williams filed a timely notice of appeal and asserts five assignments of error.

The United States Supreme Court and the Supreme Court of Ohio have held that fundamental notions of due process demand that a criminal defendant who is not legally competent may not be tried or convicted of a crime. Because an incompetent defendant may not be convicted of a crime, a court's decision regarding the competency of an individual to stand trial will always be outcome-determinative in the most fundamental sense. Thus, if error occurred in the competency proceedings such that the magistrate's conclusion that Nicholas was competent to stand trial cannot be relied upon, the decision must be reversed.

Although Nicholas is not a criminal defendant, this court has held that "the right not to be tried while incompetent" is as fundamental in juvenile proceedings as it is in criminal trials of adults. The constitutional test under the Fourteenth Amendment for competency to stand trial is "whether [the defendant] has sufficient present ability to consult with his lawyer with a reasonable degree of rational understanding—and whether he has a rational as well as factual understanding of the proceedings against him." Under Ohio's codification of this standard, a defendant is presumed to be competent unless it is demonstrated by a preponderance of the evidence that "because of his present mental condition he is incapable of understanding the nature and objective of the proceedings against him or of presently assisting in his defense." While Juv.R. 32(A)(4) provides that the court may order a mental examination where competency is in issue, no statutory standard has been enacted to guide competency determinations in juvenile proceedings. This court, however, has determined that the standard enunciated in R.C. 2945.37(A) governs competency evaluations of juveniles, so long as it is applied in light of juvenile rather than adult norms. Thus, we review the magistrate's determination of competency in order to determine whether there was sufficient credible evidence upon which she could find that Nicholas was capable of understanding the nature and objective of the proceedings against him and of assisting in his own defense.

In addition to the psychological reports prepared by Dr. Williams and Dr. Fujimura, the magistrate heard the testimony of both doctors at the competency hearing. Dr. Williams testified that he conducted a two and one-half hour interview with Nicholas at the detention center. He stated that his understanding, gleaned from previous reports on Nicholas, that Nicholas has significant cognitive limitations was quickly confirmed. Nicholas was unable to give his date of birth, was unable to spell his own middle name, and was unclear on when and for how long he had been incarcerated. When asked about the two pending rape charges, Nicholas recounted that he had become involved with a 9-year-old girl during a time when he was living on the streets. Nicholas stated that he had been offered a place to stay for the weekend in the house of a family that had several adoptive placements. Nicholas stated that during his stay, he was approached by the girl, who invited him up to her bedroom, disrobed, and asked him to have sex with her. He told Dr. Williams that this situation arose twice over the weekend and that he complied with the girl's requests both times. Dr. Williams testified that Nicholas expressed no guilt or remorse regarding these encounters, but that Nicholas indicated that he knew that his behavior was "wrong." Nicholas also revealed that when he was twelve years old an adult relative of his had sexually abused and threatened him.

Dr. Williams further testified that he administered two psychological tests on Nicholas. The first, the Weschler Intelligence Skill for children, revealed that Nicholas's cognitive functioning and reading skills were so low that the standard tests normally administered to adolescents could not be employed. The test revealed that Nicholas has a full scale I.Q. of 40, and that 99.9 percent of other children in his age group would have shown a higher level of cognitive functioning. For the second test, the doctor administered the "house-tree-person" test. Nicholas drew the test's eponymous figures and Dr. Williams used the drawings to make inferences concerning Nicholas's psychological development. According to Dr. Williams, Nicholas's drawings revealed, among other things, the following: a low level of psychosexual maturity; poor social emotional development; feelings of social isolation, inadequacy, emptiness, and futility; and a strong desire for acceptance and approval.

With respect to competency, Dr. Williams opined that Nicholas was not mentally competent to stand trial. In support of this conclusion, Dr. Williams stated that Nicholas, while aware of the facts, would not be able to assist in his own defense, would likely have only a nominal understanding of the roles of the attorneys and the judge, but no real appreciation of their functions or relationship in the courtroom, and did not sufficiently understand the consequences of the offense with which he was charged. Dr. Williams expressed the belief that Nicholas had only a superficial understanding of the events and people involved and could not appreciate the significance of his acts to the young girl involved.

Dr. Laura Fujimura testified for the state. Dr. Fujimura stated that she also conducted an interview of Nicholas Williams for the purpose of determining whether he was competent to stand trial. Dr. Fujimura testified that she administered the Weschler Individual Achievement Test, the "house-tree-person" test, and the Georgia Court Competency Test to Nicholas. Like Dr. Williams, she testified that her administration of the Weschler test revealed that Nicholas was functioning at a kindergarten level. She testified that the Georgia Court Competency Test is an oral test that is designed to aid in ascertaining an individual's understanding of courtroom procedures and personnel, and to assess his ability to explain the circumstances surrounding the charges. The administration of the test produces a point total on a range up to one hundred, with a score of seventy points or more indicating competency. Dr. Fujimura testified that Nicholas received a score of eighty points. She stated that Nicholas was able to answer most of the questions, especially those involving the circumstances leading up to the rape charges. He was "weaker," however, regarding courtroom procedures and personnel, and Dr. Fujimura stated that he was "not certain of the role of the judge or the jury."

Regarding the circumstances surrounding the alleged offense, Dr. Fujimura testified that Nicholas told her that he had initially been approached by the girl and that she asked him to have sex with her. The doctor testified that Nicholas stated that he knew that his conduct was wrong, but that he has uncontrollable urges to touch others in a sexual manner. She expressed the opinion that Nicholas was competent to stand trial. She explained that her opinion was based largely on Nicholas's ability to answer the questions of the Georgia Competency Test.

Appellant argues that the standard employed by the magistrate in her determination that Nicholas was legally competent was unclear because it was not articulated in the order containing her conclusion. He argues that, moreover, Dr. Fujimura's conclusion of competency is tainted by her apparent reliance on the incorrect legal standards. Dr. Fujimura focused largely on Nicholas's ability to determine whether his actions were morally right or wrong, his ability to state the circumstances leading up to his arrest, and the likelihood that he would reoffend. As Dr. Fujimura stated at the competency hearing:

"The bottom line is Nicholas was able to answer those questions, given his limitations, and he indicated to me that he does not always act out on his urges because he sometimes fears he is going to get caught, which indicates to me that this is not an individual who just indiscriminately acts on his urges because he doesn't know what he is doing, or doesn't know what the consequences are. He indicated to me that if he believed he's going to get caught then he somehow makes himself stop, but that is very difficult for him to do so.

"He was able to explain the circumstances leading up to his pending charges, and I do believe that he would be able to cooperate with his attorney, and I believe that he is competent to stand trial."

Dr. Fujimura's "bottom line" does not answer the question posed by a competency hearing—whether the accused is capable of understanding the nature and objective of the proceedings against him and of assisting in his own defense. Rather, although the doctor may have stated the proper legal standard in her testimony and her report, her conclusion seems to be influenced primarily by her evaluation of Nicholas's legal *sanity* and her own conception of moral culpability. As appellant points out, a defendant's ability to determine right from wrong is an appropriate inquiry in the legal determination of sanity, not competency. Likewise, the risk that the defendant will continue to offend if released is wholly irrelevant to the issue of his competency to stand trial.

While Dr. Fujimura's conclusions appear to have been tainted by considerations of Nicholas's moral responsibility for his behavior, rather than simply his mental competency to stand trial, Dr. Williams's conclusion may have been unduly influenced by his opposition to the state's decision to pursue statutory rape charges against Nicholas. Dr. Williams's report concluded the following, in pertinent part:

"2. While Nicholas' inappropriate sexual behavior, resulting in current and past rape charges, is self-admitted and undenied, felony level charges of the severity of rape are deemed to be unwarranted.

"3. Given his consistently and severely deficient levels of mental functioning and moral judgment, the prosecution and conviction of rape charges are excessive and unjustified."

These conclusions suggest a preoccupation with matters beyond the scope of Dr. Williams's role of evaluating Nicholas's competency to stand trial. Attached to Dr. Williams's report is a letter from Dr. Williams dated January 24, 1996. The letter reads as follows:

"At the request from Mr. Wayne Gilkison, probation officer for Nicholas D. Williams (DOB: 12/10/79), this letter is written as a supplement to my recently submitted psychological evaluation report on this youth. Mr. Gilkison informed me that the court required a more explicit conclusion as to Nicholas' competency to stand trial on the delinquency charges of rape he now faces.

"Please know that the third point listed in my original report was intended to address this issue. Inasmuch as the Court requires a more explicit statement I must conclude, based on findings contained in my original report, that Nicholas is *not*, in my expert opinion, competent to stand trial on these charges." (Emphasis *sic*.)

While pursuing the rape charges against Nicholas may well have been "excessive and unjustified," Dr. Williams's reliance on that conclusion is troubling. We believe that the reports and testimony of both expert witnesses in this case were irreparably muddled with incorrect standards of law and inappropriate judgments pertaining to moral responsibility. In light of these deficiencies in the evidence, the magistrate could not have made a reliable competency finding based on the expert testimony and the reports that would satisfy Nicholas's substantive and procedural due process rights. Accordingly, Nicholas's fundamental right not to be tried or convicted of an offense while incompetent has not been adequately protected.

Of course, where the evidence presented by both sides is suspect, the allocation of the burden of proof will often become the dispositive issue. The United States Supreme Court has held that a state may, as Ohio does, presume competence and place the burden on the defendant to prove his incompetence by a preponderance of the evidence without violating due process. Thus, if both experts are unreliable because of their apparent confusion of the appropriate standard with notions of moral culpability, the presumption of competence should stand firm. However, the United States Supreme Court's recent decision striking down as violative of due process an Oklahoma statute's requirement that the defendant prove incompetence by clear and convincing evidence may counsel against a cavalier reliance on R.C. 2945.37(A)'s presumption of competency. In *Cooper*, the unanimous court explained the rationale supporting its conclusion in *Medina* as follows:

> "Our conclusion that the presumption of competence offends no recognized principle of fundamental fairness rested in part on the fact that the procedural rule affects the outcome only in a narrow class of cases where the evidence is in equipoise; that is, where the evidence that a defendant is competent is just as strong as the evidence that he is incompetent."

In the case *sub judice,* we cannot say that there was presented an equipoise of evidence such that the presumption of competence should be left undisturbed. Rather, when the testimony and reports of the experts are pruned of their opinions on Nicholas's ability to distinguish "right" from "wrong" and on whether prosecution was "excessive" or "unwarranted," the remaining evidence seems to point toward the conclusion that Nicholas was not competent to stand trial. Nicholas has, according to Dr. Williams's report, a full scale I.Q. of 40 and both parties agree that he has, at least in many respects, the mind of a 6-year-old. Such indications of low intellectual ability as I.Q. and mental age may be crucial factors in a competency determination. Furthermore, Dr. Fujimura herself testified that Nicholas had difficulty understanding the roles of the judge and jury, and her psychological report revealed that he was afraid that if he told his defense attorney the facts surrounding his arrest he would "get sent up to jail for the rest of [his] life." It is difficult to reconcile these findings with Dr. Fujimura's conclusion that Nicholas was capable of assisting his attorney in his own defense.

Moreover, on cross-examination, Nicholas's trial attorney questioned Dr. Fujimura about whether she believed that Nicholas understood that the reason supporting the charges of statutory rape was not simply that he had engaged in sex acts with the girl, but that the girl was only nine years old at the time. The doctor responded that Nicholas "may not have been aware … of the details," but that he understood "enough about the situation that he did not say to me that rape means you load up cans of soup into the grocery cart and reel it out the door." This, of course, is not an adequate understanding of the nature of the charge to support a finding of competency. In a statutory rape prosecution, it is the "details" that make the case. In fact, Nicholas's statements that are included in Dr. Fujimura's report reveal that Nicholas may equate the term "rape" with any sexual intercourse, and did not appreciate the significance of the girl's age — the "detail" that made his alleged acts criminal.

The evidence appears to establish a prima facie case that Nicholas did not understand the nature of the proceedings against him or was incapable of assisting in his own defense, and, accordingly, the presumption of competence may not, by itself, defeat Nicholas's claim of incompetency. In light of the apparent confusion over the appropriate legal standard at issue, the substantial evidence of incompetence, and the lack of competent and credible evidence tending to show competency, we believe that the magistrate erred in finding Nicholas competent to stand trial on the basis of the competency hearing and the experts' reports. Accordingly, the first assignment of error is sustained, and we reverse the magistrate's finding and remand this case for a competency hearing in which the appropriate legal standard is clearly applied.

Accordingly, the magistrate's finding, and the court's presumed adoption thereof, that Nicholas Williams was competent to stand trial is reversed and the cause is remanded for a new hearing on the issue of competency. All findings subsequent to and predicated on the competency determination regarding Nicholas's delinquency and commitment to the Department of Youth Services are vacated.

Judgment accordingly.

GRADY, Judge, concurring:

I am completely in accord with Judge Young's well-reasoned opinion. I write separately only to point out that the magistrate's decision appears to have been affected by considerations of the cost involved in securing the treatment for Nicholas that a finding of incompetency would require. If so, that is wholly improper. *R.C. 2945.38* sets out the procedures required in that event. If costs must be paid by the committing authority, it may look to other agencies to share in that cost, but it cannot reject the alternatives provided because of the costs involved.

Holdings of *In re: Williams:* The court held that the competency requirement for a youth subjected to juvenile delinquency proceeds is so fundamental that all of the other Due Process rights are meaningless if the youth is incompetent to stand trial. The court also held that there is a presumption of competence, but that the youth can overcome that presumption by establishing that he (1) does not understand the nature of the proceedings against him or (2) was incapable of assisting in his own defense.

Discussion Questions

What issues does the court say that are posed by the competency hearing?

What issues or questions were relied upon by Dr. Fujimura that were not appropriate on the competency issue?

The court ruled that, "The evidence appears to establish a prima facie case that Nicholas did not understand the nature of the proceedings against him or was incapable of assisting in his own defense, and, accordingly, the presumption of competence may not, by itself, defeat Nicholas's claim of incompetency." With that finding, why did the court order a new competency hearing rather than just ruling that the youth was not competent?

Matter of W.A.F.: In *Matter of W.A.F.,* the D.C. Appellate Court was faced with the issue of whether or not the adult standard for competency (as set forth in the United States Supreme Court decision in *Dusky*) applies to juvenile delinquency proceedings.

As you read *Matter of W.A.F.,* look for the following:

1. Observe the historical role noted by the trial Court in support of his denial of the youth with a competency hearing.

2. Observe what happens to the youth in D.C. if the youth is determined to be incompetent to stand trial.

Matter of W.A.F.

573 A.2d 1264 (D.C.App. 1990)

Rogers, Chief Judge:

Appellant, W.A.F., a mildly retarded youth, appeals from an adjudication of delinquency on the ground that his due process rights were violated when the trial judge refused to apply the adult standard for determining his competency to stand trial, as set forth in *Dusky v. United States,* 362 U.S. 402, 80 S.Ct. 788, 4 L.Ed.2d 824 (1960). Appellant further contends that, because he is not competent to stand trial under this standard and not subject to alternative civil commitment proceedings, he must be released under *Jackson v. Indiana,* 406 U.S. 715, 738, 92 S.Ct. 1845, 1858, 32 L.Ed.2d 435 (1972). *See Thomas v. United States,* 418 A.2d 122 (D.C.1980). We agree that the trial judge erred in failing to apply the *Dusky* standard and accordingly reverse the judgment and remand the case for further proceedings.

I

Appellant was arrested three times in short succession and charged as a juvenile delinquent with distribution and possession with intent to distribute a controlled substance (phencyclidine on marijuana and cocaine). His counsel filed a motion seeking a determination of appellant's incompetency under *Dusky, supra,* and his release under *Jackson v. Indiana.* Following an evidentiary hearing, the trial judge found that appellant was competent to stand trial because he was not incompetent within the meaning of D.C.Code § 16-2315(c)(1) (1989), and the juvenile statutory scheme did not contemplate any other competency exception to delinquency proceedings. Based on stipulated facts, the judge found that appellant was a delinquent and committed him to the care and supervision of the District of Columbia Department of Human Services, with placement in a group home and continued attendance at a private special education school in Virginia.

II

Under *Dusky,* the accused must have "… sufficient present ability to consult with his lawyer with a reasonable degree of rational understanding [and have] a rational as well as factual understanding of the proceedings against him." The trial judge rejected appellant's claim that this standard applied in juvenile delinquency proceedings, ruling instead that D.C.Code § 16-2315(c)(1) defined the standard for incompetency in delinquency proceedings. Thus, under § 16-2315(c)(1), in the trial judge's view, juvenile delinquency proceedings may be suspended due to incompetency *only* if the respondent is incapable of participating in his defense "by reason of mental illness or at least moderate mental retardation." The judge's conception of § 16-2315(c)(1)'s role in the juvenile delinquency statutory scheme was based on his view that the standard for juvenile incompetency was intended to be identical to the standard for commitment of mentally retarded juveniles. This symmetry was attractive to the judge because a juvenile offender would receive treatment either as a result of a juvenile delinquency disposition or through a facility for the mentally retarded, and, thus there would be no possibility of a child being found incompetent to stand trial, but not subject to civil commitment and therefore released. The trial judge viewed this interpretation to be most consistent with the principles underlying the juvenile court system which, unlike the focus in adult criminal proceedings on the imposition of punishment, are designed to provide treatment and rehabilitation for juvenile offenders.

Notwithstanding the laudable efforts of the trial judge to assure that appellant would not fall through the cracks of the statutory scheme, we conclude that the denial of appellant's motion for a *Dusky* incompetency determination founders on the failure to appreciate the constitutional limits of the statutory scheme.

In *Pate v. Robinson*, 383 U.S. 375, 86 S.Ct. 836, 15 L.Ed.2d 815 (1966), the Supreme Court held that the failure to observe procedures adequate to protect a defendant's right not to be tried or convicted while incompetent to stand trial is a deprivation of due process. This court acknowledged in *In re C.W.M., supra,* that, as a matter of course, a person subject to a juvenile delinquency proceeding has the constitutional right to due process, which includes numerous procedural safeguards accorded adult offenders. Noting, however, that the Supreme Court has repeatedly declined to hold that a juvenile delinquency proceeding must conform to all the requirements of an adult criminal trial, the court recognized that the question remains whether "fundamental fairness" requires that certain requirements of adult criminal proceedings apply to juvenile delinquency proceedings. In *C.W.M.,* the court concluded that the insanity defense, prohibited in juvenile delinquency proceedings under D.C.Code § 16-2315(d), did not serve a function essential to fundamental fairness that could not otherwise be performed adequately in the juvenile system and, hence, proceedings pursuant to D.C.Code § 16-2315(d) were fundamentally fair. Since the right not to be tried while incompetent is a due process right, the *Dusky* type competency standard would be applicable to juvenile delinquency proceedings unless the juvenile system adequately protects that right. We conclude that the incompetency standard in section 16-2315(c)(1), together with other procedures in the juvenile system, does not do so.

In an adult criminal prosecution, the purpose of an inquiry into an accused's competency is twofold: first, to assure that the accused understands the nature of the proceedings against him and is able to consult with his lawyer in order to prepare a defense, recognizing that a proper defense is essential to the accuracy of the guilt determination process, and, second, "to prevent the infliction of punishment upon a person so lacking in mental capacity as to be unable to understand the nature and purpose of the punishment," A finding of incompetency results in the commitment of a defendant for care and treatment, and for observation and examination, in order to evaluate the possibility of a defendant regaining his competency. If the defendant regains competency, the prosecution can be resumed, but if it appears that the accused will not become competent in the reasonably foreseeable future, the criminal proceedings must be dismissed and civil commitment proceedings may be commenced pursuant to D.C.Code § 21-541 (1989). Since the standard of incompetency to stand trial does not mirror the standard for civil commitment, a criminal defendant could be found incompetent to stand trial and also not be subject to civil commitment, and, therefore, would be entitled to be released.

The first function served by the adult competency requirement and the *Dusky* standard is to assure that the person charged with violating the law is able to prepare a defense, in order to increase the accuracy of the factual and guilt determinations. No less a need exists for a youth in juvenile delinquency proceedings. The condition precedent for the court's ordering of a rehabilitative disposition in a juvenile delinquency proceeding is a factual determination that the juvenile has violated a provision of the criminal law. Even if all parties to a juvenile delinquency proceeding share the goal of finding a disposition in the child's best interests, and the proceedings may be less adversarial than adult prosecution, such proceedings clearly present an opportunity for factual disputes. Differing views of what is in the child's best interests may arise from these disputes as to the underlying facts. In addition, a disposition may well not be in the best interests of a child if it rests on an erroneous or unreliable factfinding determination. While counsel as well as a guardian ad litem are available to juvenile delinquents, as they were to appellant, both are limited in their ability to prepare a defense by the juvenile's knowledge, understanding, and ability to reconstruct and communicate the facts. For this reason, the legislature has given the juvenile an unqualified right to be present at "a factfinding hearing" in delinquency proceedings. Consequently, we find no inconsistency between the goals of the juvenile justice system, as reflected in our statutory scheme, and the basic principle that the accuracy of the factfinding determination — and the accused's own minimal contribution thereto — is part of the fundamental fairness inherent in due process.

Accordingly, we hold that the determination of mental competency of a juvenile is one of those instances where the procedure followed in adult criminal prosecutions must be applied to juvenile delinquency proceedings. The right not to be tried or convicted while incompetent is a fundamental right of a juvenile in juvenile delinquency proceedings, and we read our statute accordingly.

Appellant further contends that the record demonstrates that he is incompetent under the *Dusky* standard, there being no evidence to the contrary. Therefore, he argues because the government is foreclosed by his established and unchanging status as mildly retarded from civilly committing him under section 16-2315(c), he is entitled to release. Although we recognize that some courts have held on appeal that a juvenile appellant is incompetent to stand trial, we do not find occasion to do so here, and we remand the case to the trial judge, who, now applying the correct standard, can determine appellant's competency to stand trial and the nature of any other relief to which he may be entitled.

Accordingly, the judgment is reversed and the case remanded for proceedings not inconsistent with this opinion.

So ordered.

FARRELL, Associate Judge, concurring:

Although the issue is not free from doubt, I agree with the court that the standard of competency set forth in *Dusky v. United States* applies in juvenile delinquency proceedings. The issue is not without doubt because the Supreme Court has implied that the effect upon liberty of conviction as an adult may be different from the effect of a delinquency adjudication, inasmuch as "juveniles, unlike adults, are always in some form of custody...." Nevertheless, our decisions have emphasized that it is a "criminal statute [that gives] rise to the [delinquency] proceeding and that a determination of guilt or innocence ends its fact-finding aspects." Thus, it would take stronger indications than I can find by the Supreme Court to persuade me that *In re Gault* does not require the juvenile to be able to understand the proceedings against him and minimally assist in his own defense. Indeed, I am not convinced that a constitutional ruling is necessary on this point. By statute, an accused in a delinquency proceeding has an unqualified right to be present at a factfinding hearing. To hold *Dusky's* standard of competency inapplicable would be to say that the legislature meant this right to be strictly formal or symbolic, an implausible idea.

I understand Judge Wertheim's concern that juveniles alleged to be delinquent not fall between the cracks—be incompetent to stand trial yet not committable, though possibly dangerous. The concern may be somewhat overstated, however. There are alternative procedures, *viz.*, CINS (children in need of supervision) and neglect proceedings, which can lead to custodial treatment of juveniles who have committed antisocial and criminal acts. The court's opinion rightly does not suggest whether *Dusky* would apply to either of those proceedings; as to them the analysis might be very different. Indeed, I am disturbed by the apparent acquiescence of everyone below in the view that if W.A.F. cannot be dealt with as a delinquent, he cannot be treated (in custody) at all. If the allegations of the petition are true, W.A.F. appears to have been—at the time of filing—a neglected child "without proper parental care or *control*," though through no fault of his mother: his mental retardation made him the more or less unwitting instrument of drug dealers.

Since I agree with the court that, whether as a statutory or constitutional matter, the *Dusky* test applies to delinquency proceedings, I join its opinion and the result.

Holdings of *Matter of W.A.F.*: The court held: (1) the determination of mental competency of a juvenile is one of those instances where the procedure followed in adult criminal prosecutions must be applied to juvenile delinquency proceedings; and (2) the right not to be tried or convicted while incompetent is a fundamental right of a juvenile in juvenile delinquency proceedings,

Discussion Questions

What does *Matter of W.A.F.* require for a finding of incompetency in juvenile delinquency proceedings?

Key Concepts: Competency to Stand Trial

- In the *Gault* decision, the Supreme Court granted certain due process rights to youth accused of having committed a delinquent act, and most courts have held that the requirement that a minor is competent is fundamental to the existence of all of the other Due Process rights granted by *Gault*.

- Competence to stand trial requires that a youth understands the nature of the proceedings against him and was capable of assisting in his own defense.

- Most states apply a rebuttable presumption of competence in juvenile delinquency cases.

- States differ as to whether or not they employ the same standards of competency for adult criminal and juvenile delinquency proceedings.

C. Right to a Speedy Trial

Overview: The *Gault* decision said nothing about whether the Constitutional right to a speedy trial is applicable to juveniles in delinquency hearings. The United States Supreme Court has still not ruled on the applicability of that right in such proceedings. In about two-thirds of the states, there are deadlines for holding adjudication hearings in delinquency cases, with about half of the states doing so by court rule or legislation. Some states have extended the constitutional right to delinquency proceedings by court decisions. Other states have refused to find a constitutional right to a speedy trial in such cases and, as a result, have allowed a more flexible approach to apply the right through enforcement of the rules or statutes imposing time deadlines.

In the Interest of T.K.: In *In the Interest of T.K.*, the Kansas Supreme Court was asked to determine whether or not the constitutional right to a Speedy Trial was applicable to juvenile delinquency cases, or if that "right" is only a "procedural rule," requiring a less strict application of the right.

As you read *In the Interest of T.K.*, look for the following:

1. Consider why the court determined that the Kansas statute did not amount to an acknowledgement of a constitutional right to a speedy trial.

2. Look for the factors that would make noncompliance with statutory timelines fatal for a prosecution.

In the Interest of T.K.

11 Kan.App.2d 632 (1987)

This is an appeal from the decision of the district court affirming the finding by a district magistrate court that T.K. was a juvenile offender. Also appealed is the district court's denial of T.K.'s motion to dismiss on the basis that de novo review was not held in a timely manner.

T.K.'s adjudication as a juvenile offender arose out of two separate incidents at his home in Grant County. In the first incident on March 25, 1985, the testimony indicated that T.K.'s mother called him for school early one morning. When T.K. did not respond, his mother went to his room and called again. T.K. rebuffed his mother by telling her he would not get up for school until noon. Shortly afterward, T.K.'s mother once against attempted to rouse him, at which time T.K. leaped from his bed and went into his closet. The mother testified she knew T.K. had his shotgun in the closet and she heard him click the action on the gun as if he were loading a shell. T.K.'s mother then went back upstairs. She testified she decided not to push him any further because she was afraid of what he would do.

The second incident occurred some four months later, on July 30, 1985, and involved T.K.'s father. T.K.'s father testified that he entered their rural residence one day and was informed by his wife that she and T.K. had been arguing. T.K.'s father confronted T.K. for the purpose of discussing this incident, which ultimately led to a wrestling match between father and son on the floor of the family dining room. The upshot was that T.K.'s father ordered T.K. to leave the house. T.K. complied and was followed outside by his father. T.K. then picked up a partially burned Christmas tree stump and came running toward the house with it. T.K.'s father testified that as T.K. was approaching the house he was uttering threats and warning his father that he could not be stopped from entering the house. Testimony also indicated that T.K. had the stump raised above his head and appeared to be in a mood to try to use it. T.K.'s father stepped back and let T.K. enter the house. Shortly thereafter, law enforcement authorities arrived and took T.K. into custody.

A detention hearing was held on the following day, July 31, 1985. The magistrate judge ordered T.K. detained and further ordered that a predisposition investigation occur. Detention was reviewed by the magistrate judge on September 9, 1985, and T.K. was further ordered held until the adjudication hearing.

On September 12, 1985, an adjudication hearing was held before the magistrate judge, which resulted in a finding that T.K. had committed two separate assaults based on the incidents on March 25 and July 30, 1985. T.K. was adjudicated a juvenile offender and placed in the temporary care and custody of SRS.

The next day, September 13, 1985, T.K.'s attorney filed a notice of appeal with the district court for a de novo review of the magistrate judge's decision. On October 25, 1985, T.K.'s attorney filed a motion to dismiss for failure to hold the de novo hearing within 30 days of the appeal under K.S.A. 38-1683(a). Nothing further occurred in the case until February 5, 1986, when the district judge sent a letter to the parties affirming the adjudication of T.K. as a juvenile offender, affirming the disposition, and denying the motion to dismiss. A journal entry to that effect was filed March 5, 1986.

As his first issue on appeal, T.K. contends the district judge erred in denying his motion to dismiss for failure to provide a timely de novo hearing on his appeal from the order entered by the magistrate judge. Appeals in juvenile offender cases are generally governed by K.S.A. 38-1681 *et seq.* At issue here is the interpretation to be given K.S.A. 38-1683(a), which provides: "An appeal from an order entered by a district magistrate judge shall be to a district judge. The appeal shall be heard *de novo* within 30 days from the date the notice of appeal was filed."

In this case, the notice of appeal from the order entered by the magistrate judge was filed on September 13, 1985, and there was no ruling by the district judge until either February 5 or March 5, 1986, depending on whether the judge's letter or the journal entry of the hearing on the latter date is used as the final decision point. Apparently the district judge conducted his review by listening to the audio tapes of the adjudication hearing conducted by the magistrate judge.

The parties are in conflict as to the effect of this procedural violation. T.K. takes the position that the 30-day hearing requirement either creates a statutory right to a speedy trial, or codifies the constitutional right to a speedy trial equivalent of the speedy trial rights that are enjoyed by a criminal defendant. He therefore argues that failure to hold a timely review hearing requires dismissal of the charges.

This precise issue has not previously received appellate consideration in Kansas. However, in the case of *Findlay v. State*, the juvenile involved made a similar argument that he was constitutionally entitled to a jury trial. On that occasion our Supreme Court soundly rejected the proposition that district court proceedings in juvenile offender cases are essentially criminal trials. The *Findlay* court took particular notice of the portions of K.S.A. 38-1601 which provided:

"'K.S.A.... 38-1601 through 38-1685 shall be known and may be cited as the Kansas juvenile offenders code and shall be liberally construed to the end that each juvenile coming within its provisions shall receive the care, custody, guidance, control and discipline, preferably in the juvenile's own home, as will best serve the juvenile's rehabilitation and the protection of society. *In no case shall any order, judgment or decree of the district court, in any proceedings under the provisions of this code, be deemed or held to import a criminal act on the part of any juvenile; but all proceedings, orders, judgments and decrees shall be deemed to have been taken and done in the exercise of the parental power of the state.*' (Emphasis supplied.)"

Concluding there was no federal or state constitutional right to a trial by jury under the Kansas Juvenile Offenders Code, the *Findlay* court recognized the unique nature of juvenile proceedings: "'If the formalities of the criminal adjudicative process are to be superimposed upon the juvenile court system, there is little need for its separate existence. Perhaps that ultimate disillusionment will come one day, but for the moment we are disinclined to give impetus to it.'"

Further buttressing this distinction between juvenile proceedings and criminal matters is the language of K.S.A. 38-1683(b), which provides that appeals are to be governed by the Kansas Code of Civil Procedure. This clearly indicates that the legislature intended juvenile matters to have a separate and distinct existence completely apart from criminal procedure. We conclude that juveniles do not have a constitutional right to a speedy trial in matters conducted under the Kansas Juvenile Offenders Code, and K.S.A. 38-1683(a) is not intended as a statutory codification of a right to speedy trial.

Affirmed.

Holdings of *In the Interest of T.K.*: The court held that neither the United States nor the Kansas Constitutions provides a right to a speedy trial for youth accused of committing a delinquent act. The court further held that juvenile delinquency proceedings are not criminal proceedings and so only the juvenile code imposes any deadline for proceeding with a delinquency case.

Discussion Questions

Why should a youth lose the absolute right to a speedy trial just because of his age?

If there is no right to a speedy trial in juvenile court, can the state delay the proceedings to allow the youth to reach an age that would make him subject to adult jurisdiction?

***In the Interest of C.T.F.*:** In *In the Interest of C.T.F.*, the Iowa Supreme Court was asked to determine whether or not the constitutional right to a Speedy Trial was applicable to juvenile delinquency cases. The court acknowledged that some, but not all, due process rights are applicable in juvenile delinquency proceedings and that the United States Supreme Court has not ruled as to whether or not the constitutional right to a speedy trial applies to juvenile proceedings.

As you read *In the Interest of C.T.F.*, look for the following:

1. Consider why the court determined that a speedy trial is essential to justice for a juvenile.

2. Look for what factors must be proven by a youth to support a claim that the youth's right to a speedy trial has been violated.

In the Interest of C.T.F.

316 N.W.2d 865 (Iowa 1982)

The sole issue presented in this appeal is whether a juvenile has a statutory or constitutional right to a speedy trial in a juvenile delinquency proceeding. The juvenile court determined that a juvenile does not have a right to a speedy trial. We hold that a juvenile has a constitutional, but not a statutory, right to a speedy trial. Since the juvenile in this appeal failed to show that he was denied his constitutional right to a speedy trial, however, we affirm the juvenile court.

On July 1, 1980, a petition was filed alleging that on June 16, 1980, C.T.F., a juvenile, committed a delinquent act, second-degree burglary in violation of sections 713.1 and 713.3, The Code. On July 11, a deputy clerk of the juvenile court mailed an original notice, with an attached copy of the petition, to both the juvenile and his father. The notice stated that they would be notified at a later date of the time and place of the hearing on the petition. On July 17 the juvenile's father filed an application on behalf of the juvenile for appointment of counsel. On October 8 the juvenile court appointed the juvenile's present attorney to act as his attorney and guardian ad litem.

On October 11 the attorney filed a motion to dismiss the petition, alleging that the juvenile's right to a speedy trial under the federal and Iowa constitutions and Iowa R.Cr.P. 27(2)(b) had been abridged. On October 15 the juvenile court scheduled a hearing on the petition for November 7. Prior to the commencement of the hearing on the petition, the juvenile court orally overruled the motion to dismiss on the basis that a juvenile does not have a right to a speedy trial in a juvenile delinquency proceeding. No evidence was offered in support of the motion.

Following the hearing the juvenile court, by written order, found the evidence sufficient to establish that the juvenile had committed the delinquent act, as alleged in the petition. After a dispositional hearing, the court entered an order releasing the juvenile, subject to specified conditions of probation, into the custody of his father.

I. *Statutory right to a speedy trial.* The juvenile maintains that the filing of a petition charging a juvenile with commission of a delinquent act is tantamount to filing an indictment or trial information in a criminal prosecution. He argues that since the Juvenile Justice Act, ch. 232, The Code, does not establish a time limit for commencing the formal adjudicatory hearing to determine whether the juvenile committed the alleged delinquent act, it would be reasonable to adopt the speedy trial provisions of Iowa R.Crim.P. 27(2)(b). We disagree.

We have long recognized that a juvenile court proceeding is not a prosecution for crime, but a special proceeding that serves as an ameliorative alternative to a criminal prosecution.

As a result of the enactment of the new Criminal Code, the provisions of section 795.1 are found in Iowa R.Crim.P. 27(2)(a). Rule 27(2)(a), by virtue of a 1980 amendment by this court expressly provides that its speedy indictment requirements are inapplicable to juvenile court proceedings. It would therefore be inconsistent to hold that the speedy trial provisions of rule 27(2)(b) apply to such proceedings. Moreover, rule 27(2)(b) is applicable only when a defendant is "indicted for a public offense." The filing of a petition accusing a juvenile of committing a delinquent act is not equivalent to indictment for a public offense in a criminal prosecution. A juvenile is not amenable to prosecution for a public offense under the provisions of the Criminal Code until it is ordered that the juvenile be transferred to the district court for prosecution as an adult. Since a delinquent act does not constitute a public offense, we hold that rule 27(2)(b) does not provide a juvenile the right to a speedy trial in a juvenile court proceeding.

II. *Constitutional right to a speedy trial.* The sixth amendment to the United States Constitution provides in part: "In all criminal prosecutions, the accused shall enjoy the right to a speedy ... trial ..." Similarly, article one, section ten of the Iowa Constitution provides in part: "In all criminal prosecutions, and in cases involving the life, or liberty of an individual the accused shall have a right to a speedy and public trial ..." The juvenile contends that these provisions guarantee the right to a speedy trial in juvenile court proceedings.

Traditionally, juvenile delinquency proceedings were held to be special proceedings that were not subject to the provisions of either the state or federal constitutions; thus, juveniles did not enjoy the protection of constitutional rights applicable in criminal prosecutions of adults. In 1967, however, the United States Supreme Court decided the landmark case of *In re Gault.* The Court held that when delinquency proceedings may result in the detention of the child, the due process clause of the fourteenth amendment requires states to observe certain fundamental rights. The *Gault* Court found the following constitutional guarantees applicable in such proceedings: the right to written notice of the specific charge in advance of the hearing; notification of the right to counsel, and to appointed counsel in case of indigency; the privilege against self-incrimination; and the right to a hearing based on sworn testimony, with the corresponding right of cross-examination.

The *Gault* Court refrained from stating that all constitutional rights of an adult in a criminal prosecution are available to a juvenile in a delinquency proceeding, however. Instead, the Court prescribed a case-by-case determination of the applicability of constitutional rights available in juvenile proceedings predicated on fair treatment, tempered by the nature of the juvenile hearing.

The Supreme Court has applied its case-by-case due process test on several occasions since *Gault*. In *In re Winship,* a 12-year-old child was charged with a delinquent act for stealing money from a woman's purse, for which the juvenile could have been confined for a maximum period of six years. The Court held that under the due process clause the juvenile had a constitutional right to the beyond-a-reasonable-doubt standard of proof in the adjudicatory hearing. In *McKeiver v. Pennsylvania,* however, the Court held that a juvenile does not have a constitutional right to a jury trial in a delinquency proceeding. A plurality of the Court concluded that because of the impact a constitutionally required jury would have on juvenile proceedings, fundamental fairness did not require a jury trial.

The United States Supreme Court has not addressed the issue whether a juvenile has a constitutional right to a speedy trial in a delinquency proceeding. Nor has this court previously addressed the issue. A juvenile delinquency proceeding has not been held to be a "criminal prosecution" within the meaning of either the sixth amendment to the United States Constitution or article one, section ten of the Iowa Constitution. We hold, however, that the due process clauses of the fourteenth amendment to the Federal Constitution and article one, section nine of the Iowa Constitution provide juveniles the right to a speedy trial in delinquency proceedings.

Although we are not bound to do so, we conclude that the *Gault* due process test should be applied in determining whether the due process clause of article one, section nine requires a speedy trial. We therefore apply the same test under both federal and Iowa constitutional provisions. In balancing the fair treatment of juveniles against the effect that a right to a speedy trial would have on the juvenile justice system, we conclude that fundamental fairness requires that juveniles have the right to speedy trial.

Charging a juvenile with a delinquent act results in family stress and causes concern and anxiety on the part of the juvenile. It often affects the juvenile's relationships with peer groups, school officials, and other adult authorities. Also, unreasonable delay may affect the quality and quantity of evidence presented, impairing the juvenile's defense and preventing a fair hearing. Finally, in the event the juvenile is found to have committed the delinquent act, the delay may be detrimental to the youth's rehabilitation. We therefore conclude that juveniles have a constitutional right to a speedy trial.

The State maintains that even if the juvenile has a constitutional right to a speedy trial there is no evidence in the record that the right was violated in this case. The State bases its contention on the four-factor test enunciated by the United States Supreme Court in *Barker v. Wingo* for determining whether an accused has been denied the right to a speedy trial under the sixth amendment. In *Barker* the Court stated that under the circumstances of each case the following factors must be considered: (1) the length of the delay; (2) the reason for the delay; (3) whether the accused asserted the right; and (4) whether the accused was prejudiced by the delay. The court must balance all of these related factors.

We believe the *Barker* test is appropriate for determining whether a juvenile has been denied the right to a speedy trial under the applicable due process provisions of both the federal and Iowa constitutions. Its application, however, should take into consideration the differences between adult criminal prosecutions and juvenile delinquency proceedings. In this case, as already noted, the juvenile did not offer any evidence to support his motion to dismiss. The record reveals only that the juvenile hearing commenced four months and one week after the petition was filed. There is no evidence concerning the reason for the delay, that the juvenile asserted and was denied the right to a speedy trial prior to the motion to dismiss, or that the juvenile was prejudiced by the delay. We therefore hold that the juvenile failed to prove that he was denied the right to a speedy trial.

Since the juvenile failed to prove that his constitutional right to a speedy trial was violated, we find no reversible error on the part of the juvenile court. Accordingly, we affirm the court's order adjudging that the juvenile committed a delinquent act.

AFFIRMED.

Holdings of *In the Interest of C.T.F.*: The court held that the state and federal constitutions provide a right to a speedy trials for youth accused of committing a delinquent act.

Discussion Questions

What factors help "tip the balance" to cause a court to grant constitutional rights to juveniles in delinquency proceedings?

What other rights guaranteed to adult criminal defendants are still uncertain as to their applicability to juveniles charged with delinquency?

Key Concepts: Right to a Speedy Trial

- The *Gault* decision did not mention the constitutional right to a speedy trial, and no subsequent decision from the high court has determined whether or not such a right is applicable to juvenile delinquency proceedings.

- Some states impose time constraints on juvenile delinquency proceedings by rule or statute, and a few states have found that the constitutional right to a speedy trial is just as applicable to juvenile delinquency cases as to adult criminal cases.

D. Standard of Proof

Overview: One of the issues not addressed by the *Gault* decision was the standard of proof that is applicable to a juvenile delinquency proceeding. It seemed to be a landmark position in criminal law that the state must prove the defendant's guilt by evidence of "beyond a reasonable doubt." However, in 1970, the Supreme Court had not explicitly held that the due process clause of the United States Constitution required such an evidentiary standard. It was time for the Court to determine the burden of proof constitutionally required in juvenile delinquency cases.

As you read *In re: Winship*, look for the following:

1. Consider whether or not the requirement of proof beyond a reasonable doubt was clearly established in adult criminal courts at the time of this ruling.

2. Consider the reasons set forth by the court in support of requiring a heightened standard of proof in juvenile delinquency proceedings.

3. Look for the source in the U.S. Constitution creating the requirement that criminal cases (and juvenile delinquency cases) must be supported by evidence of guilt beyond a reasonable doubt.

In re Winship
397 U.S. 385 (1970)

Mr. Justice BRENNAN delivered the opinion of the Court.

During a 1967 adjudicatory hearing, conducted pursuant to § 742 of the Act, a judge in New York Family Court found that appellant, then a 12-year-old boy, had entered a locker and stolen $112 from a woman's pocketbook. The petition which charged appellant with delinquency alleged that his act, 'if done by an adult, would constitute the crime or crimes of Larceny.' The judge acknowledged that the proof might not establish guilt beyond a reasonable doubt, but rejected appellant's contention that such proof was required by the Fourteenth Amendment. The judge relied instead on § 744(b) of the New York Family Court Act which provides that '(a)ny determination at the conclusion of (an adjudicatory) hearing that a (juvenile) did an act or acts must be based on a preponderance of the evidence.' During a subsequent dispositional hearing, appellant was ordered placed in a training school for an initial period of 18 months, subject to annual extensions of his commitment until his 18th birthday — six years in appellant's case.

The requirement that guilt of a criminal charge be established by proof beyond a reasonable doubt dates at least from our early years as a Nation. Although virtually unanimous adherence to the reasonable-doubt standard in common-law jurisdictions may not conclusively establish it as a requirement of due process, such adherence does 'reflect a profound judgment about the way in which law should be enforced and justice administered.'

Expressions in many opinions of this Court indicate that it has long been assumed that proof of a criminal charge beyond a reasonable doubt is constitutionally required.

The reasonable-doubt standard plays a vital role in the American scheme of criminal procedure. It is a prime instrument for reducing the risk of convictions resting on factual error. The standard provides concrete substance for the presumption of innocence — that bedrock 'axiomatic and elementary' principle whose 'enforcement lies at the foundation of the administration of our criminal law.'

Lest there remain any doubt about the constitutional stature of the reasonable-doubt standard, we explicitly hold that the Due Process Clause protects the accused against conviction except upon proof beyond a reasonable doubt of every fact necessary to constitute the crime with which he is charged.

We turn to the question whether juveniles, like adults, are constitutionally entitled to proof beyond a reasonable doubt when they are charged with violation of a criminal law. The same considerations that demand extreme caution in factfinding to protect the innocent adult apply as well to the innocent child.

We conclude, as we concluded regarding the essential due process safeguards applied in Gault, that the observance of the standard of proof beyond a reasonable doubt 'will not compel the States to abandon or displace any of the substantive benefits of the juvenile process.'

Finally, we reject the Court of Appeals' suggestion that there is, in any event, only a 'tenuous difference' between the reasonable-doubt and preponderance standards. The suggestion is singularly unpersuasive. In this very case, the trial judge's ability to distinguish between the two standards enabled him to make a finding of guilt that he conceded he might not have made under the standard of proof beyond a reasonable doubt.

In sum, the constitutional safeguard of proof beyond a reasonable doubt is as much required during the adjudicatory stage of a delinquency proceeding as are those constitutional safeguards applied in Gault—notice of charges, right to counsel, the rights of confrontation and examination, and the privilege against self-incrimination. We therefore hold, in agreement with Chief Judge Fuld in dissent in the Court of Appeals, 'that, where a 12-year-old child is charged with an act of stealing which renders him liable to confinement for as long as six years, then, as a matter of due process * * * the case against him must be proved beyond a reasonable doubt.'

Reversed.

Mr. Justice HARLAN, concurring.

No one, I daresay, would contend that state juvenile court trials are subject to no federal constitutional limitations. Differences have existed, however, among the members of this Court as to what constitutional protections do apply.

The present case draws in question the validity of a New York statute that permits a determination of juvenile delinquency, founded on a charge of criminal conduct, to be made on a standard of proof that is less rigorous than that which would obtain had the accused been tried for the same conduct in an ordinary criminal case. While I am in full agreement that this statutory provision offends the requirement of fundamental fairness embodied in the Due Process Clause of the Fourteenth Amendment, I am constrained to add something to what my Brother BRENNAN has written for the Court, lest the true nature of the constitutional problem presented become obscured or the impact on state juvenile court systems of what the Court holds today be exaggerated.

Notwithstanding Professor Wigmore's skepticism, we have before us a case where the choice of the standard of proof has made a difference: the juvenile court judge below forthrightly acknowledged that he believed by a preponderance of the evidence, but was not convinced beyond a reasonable doubt, that appellant stole $112 from the complainant's pocketbook. Moreover, even though the labels used for alternative standards of proof are vague and not a very sure guide to decisionmaking, the choice of the standard for a particular variety of adjudication does, I think, reflect a very fundamental assessment of the comparative social costs of erroneous factual determinations.

In this context, I view the requirement of proof beyond a reasonable doubt in a criminal case as bottomed on a fundamental value determination of our society that it is far worse to convict an innocent man than to let a guilty man go free. It is only because of the nearly complete and long-standing acceptance of the reasonable-doubt standard by the States in criminal trials that the Court has not before today had to hold explicitly that due process, as an expression of fundamental procedural fairness, requires a more stringent standard for criminal trials than for ordinary civil litigation.

When one assesses the consequences of an erroneous factual determination in a juvenile delinquency proceeding in which a youth is accused of a crime, I think it must be concluded that, while the consequences are not identical to those in a criminal case, the differences will not support a distinction in the standard of proof. First, and of paramount importance, a factual error here, as in a criminal case, exposes the accused to a complete loss of his personal liberty through a state-imposed confinement away from his home, family, and friends. And, second, a delinquency determination, to some extent at least, stigmatizes a youth in that it is by definition bottomed on a finding that the accused committed a crime. Although there are no doubt costs to society (and possibly even to the youth himself) in letting a guilty youth go free, I think here, as in a criminal case, it is far worse to declare an innocent youth a delinquent. I therefore agree that a juvenile court judge should be no less convinced of the factual conclusion that the accused committed the criminal act with which he is charged than would be required in a criminal trial.

I wish to emphasize, as I did in my separate opinion in *Gault*, that there is no automatic congruence between the procedural requirements imposed by due process in a criminal case, and those imposed by due process in juvenile cases. It is of great importance, in my view, that procedural strictures not be constitutionally imposed that jeopardize 'the essential elements of the State's purpose' in creating juvenile courts. In this regard, I think it worth emphasizing that the requirement of proof beyond a reasonable doubt that a juvenile committed a criminal act before he is found to be a delinquent does not (1) interfere with the worthy goal of rehabilitating the juvenile, (2) make any significant difference in the extent to which a youth is stigmatized as a 'criminal' because he has been found to be a delinquent, or (3) burden the juvenile courts with a procedural requirement that will make juvenile adjudications significantly more time consuming, or rigid. Today's decision simply requires a juvenile court judge to be more confident in his belief that the youth did the act with which he has been charged.

With these observations, I join the Court's opinion, subject only to the constitutional reservations expressed in my opinion in Gault.

Mr. Chief Justice BURGER, with whom Mr. Justice STEWART joins, dissenting.

The Court's opinion today rests entirely on the assumption that all juvenile proceedings are 'criminal prosecutions,' hence subject to constitutional limitations. This derives from earlier holdings, which, like today's holding, were steps eroding the differences between juvenile courts and traditional criminal courts. The original concept of the juvenile court system was to provide a benevolent and less formal means than criminal courts could provide for dealing with the special and often sensitive problems of youthful offenders. Since I see no constitutional requirement of due process sufficient to overcome the legislative judgment of the States in this area, I dissent from further straitjacketing of an already overly restricted system. What the juvenile court system needs is not more but less of the trappings of legal procedure and judicial formalism; the juvenile court system requires breathing room and flexibility in order to survive, if it can survive the repeated assaults from this Court.

My hope is that today's decision will not spell the end of a generously conceived program of compassionate treatment intended to mitigate the rigors and trauma of exposing youthful offenders to a traditional criminal court; each step we take turns the clock back to the pre-juvenile-court era. I cannot regard it as a manifestation of progress to transform juvenile courts into criminal courts, which is what we are well on the way to accomplishing. We can only hope the legislative response will not reflect our own by having these courts abolished.

Mr. Justice BLACK, dissenting.

The majority states that 'many opinions of this Court indicate that it has long been assumed that proof of a criminal charge beyond a reasonable doubt is constitutionally required.' The Court has never clearly held, however, that proof beyond a reasonable doubt is either expressly or impliedly commanded by any provision of the Constitution. The Bill of Rights, which in my view is made fully applicable to the States by the Fourteenth Amendment, does by express language provide for, among other things, a right to counsel in criminal trials, a right to indictment, and the right of a defendant to be informed of the nature of the charges against him. And in two places the Constitution provides for trial by jury, but nowhere in that document is there any statement that conviction of crime requires proof of guilt beyond a reasonable doubt. The Constitution thus goes into some detail to spell out what kind of trial a defendant charged with crime should have, and I believe the Court has no power to add to or subtract from the procedures set forth by the Founders. I realize that it is far easier to substitute individual judges' ideas of 'fairness' for the fairness prescribed by the Constitution, but I shall not at any time surrender my belief that that document itself should be our guide, not our own concept of what is fair, decent, and right. That this old 'shock-the-conscience' test is what the Court is relying on, rather than the words of the Constitution, is clearly enough revealed by the reference of the majority to 'fair treatment' and to the statement by the dissenting judges in the New York Court of Appeals that failure to require proof beyond a reasonable doubt amounts to a 'lack of fundamental fairness.' As I have said time and time again, I prefer to put my faith in the words of the written Constitution itself rather than to rely on the shifting, day-to-day standards of fairness of individual judges.

I admit a strong, persuasive argument can be made for a standard of proof beyond a reasonable doubt in criminal cases—and the majority has made that argument well—but it is not for me as a judge to say for that reason that Congress or the States are without constitutional power to establish another standard that the Constitution does not otherwise forbid. It is quite true that proof beyond a reasonable doubt has long been required in federal criminal trials. It is also true that this requirement is almost universally found in the governing laws of the States. And as long as a particular jurisdiction requires proof beyond a reasonable doubt, then the Due Process Clause commands that every trial in that jurisdiction must adhere to that standard. But when, as here, a State through its duly constituted legislative branch decides to apply a different standard, then that standard, unless it is otherwise unconstitutional, must be applied to insure that persons are treated according to the 'law of the land.' The State of New York has made such a decision, and in my view nothing in the Due Process Clause invalidates it.

Holdings of *In re Winship*: The court held that the constitutional safeguard of proof beyond a reasonable doubt is as much required during the adjudicatory stage of a delinquency proceeding as are those constitutional safeguards that were applied in *Gault*.

Discussion Questions

Does this case extend the constitutional right to proof "beyond a reasonable doubt" to BOTH criminal and juvenile proceedings?

Is this proof standard (beyond a reasonable doubt) applied to all phases of delinquency proceedings by *Winship*?

Key Concepts: Standard of Proof

- In order for a minor to be adjudicated to be a delinquent, the state has the burden to prove its case by evidence beyond a reasonable doubt.

- The same standard of proof for establishing guilt (by evidence of beyond a reasonable doubt) applies to both criminal and juvenile delinquency cases.

E. Suppression of Confessions

Overview: In many cases, the existence of a confession or admission by the juvenile is the most compelling evidence to be used in building a case against the minor in a juvenile delinquency proceeding. As we learned in Chapter III (Interrogation of Minors), the United States Supreme Court has held that the *Miranda* decision is applicable to minors and that a "totality of the circumstances" test is to be used to determine whether or not a confession of a minor is admissible for use against him or her. Some states, either by statute or by court decision, have required that a parent or guardian be present during an interrogation. However, most states have either returned to or continued applying the "totality of the circumstances" test in determining whether or not a confession by a minor is admissible.

Matter of Welfare of S.W.T.: In *Matter of Welfare of S.W.T.,* the Minnesota Supreme Court was confronted with a trial of two juveniles whose confessions were essential to support their adjudication as a delinquent. One of the youth was severely emotionally disturbed and low functioning intellectually. The court was forced to apply the "totality of the circumstances" test to each youth individually.

As you read *Matter of Welfare of S.W.T.,* look for the following:

1. Watch for the ways that the circumstances differed for the two boys.

2. Observe how the court quickly determines that the "totality of the circumstances test" is still applied to determine the admissibility of a confession even when the youth's parent waived the youth's Fifth Amendment rights.

Matter of Welfare of S.W.T.

277 N.W.2d 507 (Minn. 1979)

The incident from which the charges arose occurred on September 22, 1976. At about 10 a.m. on that day, Joseph Antrim, Lawrence Anderson, and Dale Jerry, all age 18 or 19, arrived at Hidden Falls Park, on the St. Paul bank of the Mississippi River. After drinking beer for about an hour, they observed two boys descending the hill on the opposite side of the river. While talking with the boys, they learned that the boys had a rifle. Anderson asked to hear the boys shoot it, and the boys proceeded to fire a number of shots into the middle of the river at such an angle that the bullets ricocheted off the water and into the trees above and behind the adults. At one point, Antrim placed a can 30 to 50 feet to the right of his party for the boys to use as a target and reported the accuracy of the shots to the boys. During this time, Dale Jerry was skipping rocks and did not converse with the boys.

The entire substance of the conversation between the boys and the adults is not clear from the record, but Antrim testified that his group had cautioned the boys not to shoot toward them. After 10 minutes of shooting, the adults decided to leave because the boys seemed to be shooting carelessly. After informing the boys that they were leaving, the adults walked 20 feet up a sandy incline toward their van, which was parked on the River Road among some trees. As Anderson and Antrim got into the van, they heard another shot and then heard Jerry say, "They got me." They helped him into the van and rushed him to a hospital, where he died following surgery.

The police were alerted at around 11:30 a.m., and approximately 25 police officers proceeded to search the riverbank. During their search they found footprints, a .22-caliber rifle buried in the sand, slugs, a beer can which had been shot at, and a chili can. After following the footprints and searching for about 4 hours, the officers found two 12-year-old boys, S. W. T. and N. R. S. The officers did not place the boys under arrest because of the variance between the descriptions the officers had received and the boys' appearance, but there were sufficient similarities to ask the boys to accompany them downtown to talk to juvenile officers.

N. R. S. was taken to the juvenile division of the police department at about 4:00 p.m. and was left alone in a holding room until 5:30 p.m., when Lieutenant Schonnesen took him to an interrogating room. There Schonnesen read a *Miranda* warning to N. R. S. and his mother. After asking N. R. S. and his mother if they understood the rights, Schonnesen proceeded to question N. R. S. and elicited a statement from him in which he stated that he and S. W. T. had skipped school, taken a gun from S. W. T.'s father's closet, and had gone to the riverbank. They were shooting at a culvert when three people across the river asked them to shoot at a can. Both boys shot at the can several times and saw the adults leaving, but they had not known that a shot had hit anyone. N. R. S. indicated that they then walked downriver and began shooting at another culvert and ate some lunch. He said that later he accidentally shot the gun in the direction of a fisherman, who then shut off his engine, ducked down in the boat, and finally got to shore and lay beside his boat. Believing that the shot might have hit this man, the boys buried the gun and ran. He stated that they were caught by a policeman a short time later.

S. W. T. was also taken to the juvenile division about 4:00 p.m. and left in a holding area until 5:30 p.m., when Officer Seliski took him to be fingerprinted. Sometime between 6:00 and 8:00 p.m., Officer Seliski interviewed S. W. T. in the company of his parents. Officer Seliski testified that he told the parents that a person had died, that he did not know whether it was an accident, and that their son was a suspect. However, S. W. T.'s mother testified that she and her husband were given to believe that the police thought it was an accident and that the boy could go home if he talked with the police. After being advised according to *Miranda*, the parents stated that they understood the rights, and S. W. T. nodded his head, indicating that he did. Seliski then proceeded to elicit a statement in which S. W. T. indicated that he hadn't known that they had hit one of the three young adults with whom they had been talking. He stated that after the men left they had eaten a can of chili and had continued their shooting. He admitted that at one point he had shot at a tugboat and that at another point N. R. S. had shot at a fishing boat. He said that after this man jumped out of the boat and lay on the ground on the other side of the river, they buried the gun and ran.

The following day delinquency petitions were filed against both juveniles, charging them with aiding and abetting manslaughter in the second degree. On October 4, 1976, a joint trial was ordered over objection of both counsel for the boys. The statements of the boys, without which the state could not have obtained convictions, were admitted into evidence over objection. Dr. James Gilbertson, the psychologist, testified that S. W. T. was exceedingly emotionally disturbed, had been having difficulties in school for a period of two years which required special teaching, had a mental age of 8 years, 8 months, and, in Gilbertson's opinion could not understandingly, voluntarily, or intelligently waive his right to remain silent, nor could he participate in his own defense in such a way as to help his case or aid his attorney.

The referee found that both juveniles had knowingly and intelligently waived their *Miranda* rights and that, accordingly, their confessions were admissible. Primarily upon the basis of these confessions, and holding the boys to the standard of care required of 12-year-old school children, the referee found that the boys had committed a delinquent act.

The juvenile court, reviewing the case on the record, ruled that the juveniles' parents had properly waived the juveniles' *Miranda* rights and that an adult standard of care applied to the juveniles' acts. Without addressing the issue of competency, the juvenile court then affirmed the referee's decision. This appeal followed.

The second and most crucial issue in the case concerns the validity of the juveniles' waiver of their Fifth Amendment privileges against self-incrimination and the admissibility of the confessions. The referee found that each juvenile had made a voluntary and intelligent waiver of his *Miranda* rights. The trial court, after reviewing the recommended findings of the referee, found that it was unnecessary to determine the capacity of either juvenile to voluntarily and intelligently waive his *Miranda* rights. Citing two Pennsylvania cases, the court held that a parent or guardian's knowledgeable waiver on behalf of the juvenile is legally sufficient.

As the state admitted in its brief at oral argument, the court was in error in so holding. Neither Darden nor Chaney stand for that proposition. The constitutional privilege against self-incrimination is as applicable in the case of juveniles as it is with respect to adults. The rule in the majority of states, including Minnesota, is that the validity of a juvenile's waiver of that privilege is an issue of fact:

> "We hold that the determination whether a waiver of rights is voluntary and intelligently made by a juvenile is a fact question dependent upon the totality of the circumstances. The child's age, maturity, intelligence, education, experience, and ability to comprehend are all factors to be considered in addition to the presence and competence of his parents during waiver."

Because the juvenile court felt that the waivers by the parents were sufficient, it did not address itself to the other factors which it was obliged under our cases to consider in determining the validity of a waiver. The referee, however, did consider these factors and determined that both juveniles had knowingly, voluntarily, and intelligently waived their Fifth Amendment rights. We assume that the juvenile court would have agreed with the referee's decision if it had considered the issue, because it did not disagree with the underlying facts. Counsel for the state and for the juveniles requested in oral argument that this court rule on the admissibility of the written statements on the record before the court rather than to remand the case to the juvenile court for this purpose. We find that the record supports the referee's findings that N. R. S. knowingly, voluntarily, and intelligently waived his Fifth Amendment rights. Thus, his confession was admissible.

The confession of S. W. T., however, presents a different situation. The facts which go to competency go also to the validity of a waiver of Fifth Amendment rights. Dr. James Gilbertson, psychologist, testified that S. W. T. was exceedingly emotionally disturbed and that although he was chronologically 12 years old, he was functioning at an intellectual level of 8 years, 8 months, with an I. Q. in the mid-70s. On the basis of tests, interviews, and a review of school records, Dr. Gilbertson concluded that S. W. T. was incapable of understanding or intelligently waiving his Fifth Amendment rights. S. W. T.'s special learning and behavioral problems teacher and his mother concurred in that assessment. The only evidence that he had knowingly, intelligently, and voluntarily waived his rights was the testimony of the police officer that he had read the *Miranda* card to S. W. T. and his mother, pausing after each statement to ask if it was understood, and that S. W. T. had nodded his head each time. The totality of the circumstances compels a finding of error which renders S. W. T.'s confession inadmissible in the adjudicatory proceeding.

The remaining question of the sufficiency of the evidence is intimately associated with the evidence contained in the juveniles' written admissions. The confessions were critical to establishing the prosecution's case. Without them, the charge on which the petitions were based was not proved beyond a reasonable doubt. No witness was capable of identifying the juveniles as the parties involved in the shooting. The articles discovered by the canine search, including the rifle, could not be connected to the juveniles except for one fingerprint on a car. Although the rifle was identified as the source of the bullet found lodged in the victim, the juveniles' confessions were the only evidence introduced regarding the ownership of the rifle.

Affirmed as to N. R. S., reversed as to S. W. T., and remanded.

Holdings of *Matter of Welfare of S.W.T:* The court affirmed the ruling of the lower court on N.R.S., finding that youth had knowingly and voluntarily waived his Fifth Amendment rights under the totality of the circumstances. The court reversed the adjudication of S.W.T., finding that the state had failed to establish that, under the totality of the circumstances that he had knowingly and voluntarily waived his Fifth Amendment rights.

Discussion Questions

Why would the court not accept the waiver of rights by a parent of a youth who is not capable of making his own decision on waiving those rights?

Is there anything law enforcement can do to accept an admissible confession from a youth who is severely emotionally disturbed and low functioning intellectually?

In re Johnson: In *In re Johnson*, the Ohio appeals court reviewed an adjudication of a 14-year-old youth for murder, rape and kidnapping, using the "totality of the circumstances" to determine if the confession of the youth was voluntary.

As you read *In re Johnson*, look for the following:

1. Look for the various circumstances that the court used to determine the voluntariness of the confession.

In re Johnson

1983 W.L. 2516 (Ohio App. 2d Dist. 1983)

David Rowell, a juvenile, was murdered February 6, 1982. Appellant Michael Johnson (Michael) was adjudicated a delinquent child by Montgomery County Juvenile Court on August 24, 1982 following a hearing to the court.

Michael, then age 14, was found in violation of aggravated murder; rape; abuse of a human corpse; and kidnapping, in connection with the Rowell murder. The juvenile court committed Michael to the legal custody of the Department of Youth Services for care and rehabilitation until age 21. From the adjudication of delinquency Michael has appealed, setting forth three assignments of error.

During their investigation of the Rowell case, Moraine Township police conducted interviews and polygraph examinations of a number of potential witnesses, including Michael. On February 13, and again on March 3, 1983 Michael underwent polygraph examinations at the Centerville police station. He was not a suspect.

Prior to both polygraph exams, an officer came to Michael's home and explained to both he and his mother that Michael did not have to take the polygraph if either of them objected. On each occasion, Michael and his mother signed releases and consent forms in an officer's presence.

Michael was transported on each occasion to the police station where the examinations were administered in the same surroundings by Detective Walker. Before both exams Det. Walker advised Michael of his Miranda rights and asked Michael follow-up questions to insure he understood those rights. Det. Walker also asked Michael to read the pre-interview form containing Miranda warnings which Michael signed on each occasion.

Each examination lasted approximately 3½ hours, which was the usual time for such an interview. Upon conclusion of the first exam, Det. Walker informed Michael the results indicated he was withholding information. Detective Walker asked Michael if he would consider taking another exam at a later date.

After the second polygraph, on March 3, 1982 Det. Walker left the room to analyze the results and Michael slept undisturbed for approximately forty-five minutes. After Michael awoke, Det. Walker informed him the results again indicated deception and that his acquaintance Keith Wampler had implicated himself in the Rowell murder. There-upon, Michael confessed his own involvement.

At Detective Walker's request, Michael reduced his statement to writing in the form of a "letter of apology." Detective Walker asked Michael if he would repeat his statement for Detective Mullins. Michael agreed to a tape-recorded interview with Det. Mullins.

Detective Mullins asked Michael if he understood the rights Det. Walker had explained and that he could refuse to continue. Michael indicated he understood his rights. Michael was offered the use of a telephone, which he declined and food, which he ate.

At the conclusion of the taped interview Michael asked to see his parents. Arrangements were made for a meeting before Michael was taken to juvenile detention.

A suppression hearing was held June 11 and 21, 1982 on Michael's motion to suppress his oral and written statements. By written opinion on June 30, 1982, the juvenile court held that Michael knowingly, intelligently, and voluntarily waived his constitutional rights based on the totality of circumstances reflected in the record, and thus overruled his motion to suppress.

Michael asserts as his first assignment of error that he did not knowingly and intelligently waive his *Miranda* rights and that his oral and written statements were involuntary.

Initially, we need not determine whether Michael's waiver of *Miranda* rights was voluntary or involuntary. Implicit in the claim that Michael did not knowingly and intelligently waive his *Miranda* rights is the assumption that *Miranda* applies to this non-custodial stationhouse polygraph interview. It does not. The touchstone for invoking the protections afforded by Miranda is a "custodial interrogation."

Michael was given *Miranda* warnings, the protections of which he expressly waived. During both polygraphs, Detective Walker was in street clothes rather than in uniform. While at the stationhouse Michael was not charged, arrested, photographed, fingerprinted, nor considered a suspect. Michael asserts he had no transportation to leave the police station. However, Detective Mullins had promised to take Michael to school following the exam. Thus Michael in fact had transportation and could have asked to leave.

Under these circumstances Michael could not have reasonably concluded he was deprived of his freedom so as to constitute a "custodial interrogation." Accordingly Miranda has no application here.

Additionally, Michael claims various factors rendered his subsequent oral and written statements involuntary. He alleges his youth, immaturity, lack of consultation with an adult, length of the interview, and a false statement made by police officers were circumstances which caused his statements to be involuntary.

Admittedly, voluntariness is a special concern in the case of a juvenile's confession. However, even where Miranda does not apply, it is generally established that confessions will be admissible where they are shown to be voluntary. The burden is upon the prosecutor to prove voluntariness.

There were not present in this case some of the gross abuses that have led the Court in other cases to find confessions involuntary, such as beatings, or "truth serums." But "the blood of the accused is not the only hallmark of an unconstitutional inquisition." Determination of whether a statement is involuntary "requires more than a mere color-matching of cases." It requires careful evaluation of all the circumstances of the interrogation.

We note voluntariness is a matter of law to be decided by the court rather than a question of fact, since ultimately it is an admissibility issue. The controlling standard for our review of the voluntariness of Michael's confession is the totality of circumstances test.

Factors which are ordinarily considered in determining voluntariness include the youth of the accused and his opportunity to consult with a parent, guardian, lawyer, or adult friend; his education; intelligence; length of detention; type of questioning, whether constitutional warnings were given and waived, and coercion in the form of deprivation of food or sleep.

At the time of his confession Michael was fourteen. The juvenile court characterized him as a "streetwise youngster" who was "sufficiently familiar with police procedures to be fully cognizant of his rights." With respect to Michael's sophistication, it was shown that prior to this case Michael had been contacted by Moraine police for five other incidents. In one of these instances, Michael made a written statement and on another occasion he filled out and signed a waiver form

Based on two interviews and psychological tests, Barbara Bergman, a psychologist, testified Michael was at the low end of the average I.Q. range, could distinguish degrees of culpability and had nothing in his psychological make-up that would have prevented him from knowingly, intelligently and voluntarily waiving his rights.

Michael's mother, Mary Johnson consented to both polygraphs and attendant interviews, although she did not actively consult with Michael during the questioning. It was shown Mrs. Johnson was functionally illiterate, had a speech impairment and was incapable of thoroughly comprehending the release and consent form which she signed. Although a juvenile's privilege against self-incrimination cannot be waived by a parent, Mary Johnson's allegedly invalid consent to the polygraph does not vitiate the voluntariness of Michael's subsequent confession.

In the case at hand, Michael was not without an adult's assistance. David Caley, a counselor for South Community Mental Health Center was available for consultation during Michael's oral statement. Further, there is no evidence that Michael requested the consultation of his mother (or any adult) at any time during his interview or statement.

Michael further argues the false statement made by Moraine police that Keith Wampler had failed a polygraph and subsequently confessed so frightened Michael that his confession was involuntary. However, confessions obtained by subterfuge are not necessarily involuntary. For instance, even where a police officer falsely relates to a defendant that his accomplice has incriminated him, the deceptive statement does not render a subsequent confession inadmissible or the result of improper coercion.

Applying these principles to the instant case, the fact police confronted Michael with a false statement as to his companion's involvement in the Rowell murder does not render Michael's subsequent statement involuntary.

Additionally, we note Michael was provided with food. When he fell asleep after the second polygraph, he was not disturbed until he awoke. It was shown that 3½ hours was a normal duration for polygraph interviews.

Considering the totality of circumstances surrounding the confession we hold it was in fact voluntary. The trial court did not err in admitting appellant's statements into evidence. Accordingly, the assignment of error is overruled.

A substantial factual basis existed upon which the juvenile court could reasonably adjudicate Michael Johnson a delinquent child. Hence the adjudication of delinquency is affirmed.

Holdings of *In re Johnson:* The court affirmed the adjudication holding that, under the totality of the circumstances, the confession was voluntary.

Discussion Questions

Of what use it is to have a parent present and even sign a waiver of a youth's rights when the parent is functionally illiterate, has a speech impairment and is incapable of thoroughly comprehending the release and consent form which she signed?

Is the fact that the police "lied" to a youth more harmful to the admissibility of a subsequent confession for a minor than it would be for an adult? Doesn't a minor assume that the police have to "follow the rules" and use that assumption to make a decision about waiving his rights?

State v. Presha: In *State v. Presha* the New Jersey Supreme Court reviewed the admissibility of a minor's confession when the 17-year-old asked that the mother not be present during the interrogation, the mother agreed not to be present and where the mother was later denied her request to rejoin her son for the interrogation.

As you read *State v. Presha,* look for the following:

1. Examine the importance that the court places on the presence of a parent during an interrogation of a minor.

2. Observe the way that the court seems to create a "per se" rule of exclusion of a confession of a minor aged 14 or below when the parent was not present for the interrogation.

State v. Presha
163 N.J. 304, 748 A.2d 1108 (2000)

Verniero, J.

In this appeal, we consider the voluntariness of a confession by defendant, a juvenile, in a custodial setting. Defendant confessed to committing certain offenses after waiving his constitutional rights in the presence of his mother and deciding that he did not want her present in the interrogation room. At the outset of the interrogation, the parent agreed she should not be present. At the time, the juvenile was almost seventeen years of age and was familiar with the criminal justice system because of fifteen prior arrests. Defendant's mother wanted to rejoin her son well into the questioning, but the police did not accede to that request.

The trial court and Appellate Division concluded that the juvenile's confession was voluntary based on the totality of circumstances, including the juvenile's age at the time of his statement, his clear desire to speak outside the presence of his mother, his mother's initial agreement to be absent, and his fair treatment by police. We granted defendant's petition for certification, and now affirm.

We hold that courts should consider the totality of circumstances when reviewing the admissibility of confessions by juveniles in custody. Moreover, courts should consider the absence of a parent or legal guardian from the interrogation area as a highly significant fact when determining whether the State has demonstrated that a juvenile's waiver of rights was knowing, intelligent, and voluntary. In the specific circumstances of this case, according enhanced weight to the absence of the parent from the interrogation, we conclude that the State has carried its burden.

We note that a special circumstance exists when a juvenile is under the age of fourteen. We will apply a different standard in that context, namely, the adult's absence will render the young offender's statement inadmissible as a matter of law, unless the parent or legal guardian is truly unavailable. Regardless of the juvenile's age, law enforcement officers must use their best efforts to locate the adult before beginning the interrogation and should account for those efforts to the trial court's satisfaction.

I.

In the early morning hours of February 27, 1995, at approximately 12:30 a.m., the Willingboro home of 70-year-old John Oldham and his 73-year-old wife, Sarah Oldham, was burglarized. There were two perpetrators, armed with knives, who covered their faces with a hood and ski-type mask. After beating John Oldham and cutting both his throat and Sarah Oldham's, the assailants ran from the house carrying Mrs. Oldham's purse. Although seriously injured, the Oldhams survived the attack.

Within an hour, police officers arrived at the scene. The officers observed two sets of footprints in the light snow outside of the Oldham residence. The footprints led the officers to defendant's house, a short distance away. At approximately 1:30 a.m., one of the officers knocked on the door of defendant's home. His mother, Michelle Robinson, answered. The officer explained to Mrs. Robinson that the footprints led them to her front porch. Mrs. Robinson informed the officer that defendant was the last person who had come into the house that evening about fifteen minutes after midnight. She agreed to take both defendant and her other son, who were then present in the house, to the Willingboro Police Station. At the time, defendant was within two weeks of his seventeenth birthday. He had also been arrested on fifteen prior occasions on unrelated charges.

Shortly before 4:00 a.m., with Mrs. Robinson's consent, the officers transported defendant and his brother from the police station to the Burlington County Prosecutor's Office. According to the police, Detective Jay Brown informed defendant of his constitutional rights as required by *Miranda. v. Arizona*. Defendant's mother was present in the same room. At about 4:20 a.m., defendant, who said he had slept until about 1:00 p.m. the day before, indicated that he understood his rights and signed the *Miranda* card. Defendant's mother signed the same *Miranda* card as a witness. Detective Brown thereafter informed Mrs. Robinson that she had the right to be present while he interviewed her son.

After discussing the matter with defendant, Mrs. Robinson and defendant decided that she should leave the room during questioning. After Mrs. Robinson departed, Detective Brown, joined by a second detective, proceeded to interview defendant for approximately forty to fifty minutes. Initially, defendant denied any involvement in the crimes.

After a break, during which defendant was not handcuffed and remained unguarded in the interview room, the detectives resumed questioning for another forty to fifty minutes. During this second session, they confronted defendant with the fact that footprints led them from the house of the victims to his house. In response, defendant stated that he had acted only as a lookout for his 22-year-old cousin and another person, still denying a central role in the robbery and assaults.

The detectives took another ten- to twenty-minute break. After that second break, the detectives informed defendant that they had found two sets of footprints, not three, prompting him to admit that he and his cousin had committed the offenses. The detectives then took another break, during which they escorted defendant to the men's room and gave him a drink of water.

The questioning resumed and defendant provided more details about the night in question, after which the detectives took yet another break. After that fourth break, defendant provided a taped confession beginning at approximately 7:39 a.m. and concluding at 8:11 a.m. Sometime before defendant confessed, his mother asked to see him. She also said to one of the officers, "I think they [her sons] should have a lawyer." The officer replied that he did not think that was necessary, stating "[w]e're just trying to get to the truth." Mrs. Robinson did not see defendant until after he completed his taped statement.

The trial court conducted a four-day *Miranda* hearing, during which defendant and Mrs. Robinson disagreed with the police version of the facts, and disagreed with each other. Defendant testified that he did not see his mother at the Burlington County Prosecutor's Office until after he taped his statement. In contrast, Mrs. Robinson testified that she was brought into the room with her son, witnessed the signing of the *Miranda* card, and then left. The State and defendant disputed other facts as well.

After weighing the credibility of all witnesses, the trial court found as a fact that Detective Brown advised defendant of his *Miranda* rights with his mother present in the same room; that they both understood and signed the *Miranda* card; that they both were aware of Mrs. Robinson's right to be present during the questioning of defendant; that defendant requested that his mother not be present during the interrogation; and that Mrs. Robinson initially agreed to be absent. The court also settled a factual dispute regarding whether Mrs. Robinson asked to reenter the interrogation area. The court found that the parent did, in fact, make that request, notwithstanding the contrary testimony of the officer. For purposes of this appeal, we accept the trial court's findings.

The trial court also concluded that the State had met its burden of proving, beyond a reasonable doubt, that the juvenile's statement was knowing, intelligent, and voluntary. It based that conclusion on the totality of circumstances surrounding the arrest and interrogation. Specifically, the court was persuaded by the juvenile's advanced age, together with his prior experience with law enforcement, and by the fact that defendant himself chose to have his mother out of the room during questioning. The trial court found that under those circumstances the subsequent wishes of defendant's mother "were not controlling … given the age [and] the experience of this particular juvenile." The "bottom line," the trial court noted, was that "[defendant's] will was not overborne by law enforcement."

Reserving his right to appeal, defendant pled guilty, pursuant to a plea agreement, to second-degree conspiracy; first-degree robbery; and second-degree burglary. Consistent with the plea arrangement, the trial court sentenced defendant to a twenty-year term of imprisonment with an eight-year parole disqualifier for the armed robbery; a concurrent term of ten years with a five-year parole disqualifier for the conspiracy; and a concurrent term of ten years with a five-year parole disqualifier for the burglary.

Before the Appellate Division, defendant argued that his rights were violated when his mother was denied access to him during the interrogation, and that the trial court should have merged the conspiracy conviction with the burglary and robbery counts. In an unreported decision, the Appellate Division agreed with the trial court that, considering all factors, defendant's confession was voluntary and thus admissible. The panel specifically noted the following factors as support for its conclusion:

> the fact that defendant was just two weeks shy of his seventeenth birthday; defendant had extensive prior encounters with law enforcement; had been giving [sic] his *Miranda* rights on several of those encounters; defendant had waived those rights on February 27, 1995, in the presence of his mother; defendant had agreed with his mother that she would not be present during his interrogation; and defendant had not attempted to either invoke his right to counsel or expressed a desire to speak to his mother at any time during the interrogation. Further, the interrogation, which occurred in spurts of forty to fifty minute periods, was neither grueling nor strenuous for defendant. Moreover, defendant never challenged the truth of his confession nor claimed that his investigators used tactics that overbore his will.

The Appellate Division agreed with defendant that his conviction for conspiracy should have been merged with his convictions for either robbery or burglary. Consistent with defendant's petition for certification, the voluntariness of his confession is the only issue before us.

II.

A.

The privilege against self-incrimination, as set forth in the Fifth Amendment to the United States Constitution, is one of the most important protections of the criminal law. Although a suspect is always free to waive the privilege and confess to committing crimes, that waiver must never be the product of police coercion. *Ibid.* Accordingly, for a confession to be admissible as evidence, prosecutors must prove beyond a reasonable doubt that the suspect's waiver was knowing, intelligent, and voluntary in light of all the circumstances.

At the root of the inquiry is whether a suspect's will has been overborne by police conduct. In determining whether a suspect's confession is the product of free will, courts traditionally assess the totality of circumstances surrounding the arrest and interrogation, including such factors as "the suspect's age, education and intelligence, advice as to constitutional rights, length of detention, whether the questioning was repeated and prolonged in nature and whether physical punishment or mental exhaustion was involved." Additionally, "[a] suspect's previous encounters with the law has been mentioned as [a] relevant factor." We reaffirm those factors as germane to an evaluation of the admissibility of either adult or juvenile confessions.

B.

The requirement of voluntariness applies equally to adult and juvenile confessions. The role of a parent in the context of a juvenile interrogation takes on special significance. In that circumstance, the parent serves as advisor to the juvenile, someone who can offer a measure of support in the unfamiliar setting of the police station. Thus, we have emphasized that "[w]henever possible and especially in the case of young children no child should be interviewed except in the presence of his parents or guardian."

Earlier in our history, the State's mission in respect of juvenile offenders was predominately one of rehabilitation. Consistent with that purpose, the presence of a parent in the interrogation area served not only to protect the juvenile's interests but, as importantly, to ensure the truthfulness of any statements to the police. Today, the juvenile process is different. A recent government report notes, "[j]uvenile delinquency, or 'youth crime' is recognized as a major social problem in our society. In New Jersey, as elsewhere, juveniles are responsible for a large share of the total amount of crime." As a result, punishment has now joined rehabilitation as a component of the State's core mission with respect to juvenile offenders.

With the State's increased focus on the apprehension and prosecution of youthful offenders, the parent's role in an interrogation setting takes on new significance. When younger offenders are in custody, the parent serves as a buffer between the juvenile, who is entitled to certain protections, and the police, whose investigative function brings the officers necessarily in conflict with the juvenile's legal interests. Parents are in a position to assist juveniles in understanding their rights, acting intelligently in waiving those rights, and otherwise remaining calm in the face of an interrogation.

In view of the changing realities of the juvenile process and the important rights at stake, we reaffirm our belief that a parent or legal guardian should be present in the interrogation room, whenever possible. In respect of confessions by juveniles of any age, courts should consider the adult's absence as a highly significant factor among all other facts and circumstances. By "highly significant factor" we mean that courts should give that factor added weight when balancing it against all other factors. By elevating the significance of the adult's role in the overall balance, we are satisfied that the rights of juveniles will be protected in a manner consistent with constitutional guarantees and modern realities.

As we have suggested in prior cases, younger offenders present a special circumstance in the context of a police interrogation. In respect of a juvenile under the age of fourteen, we believe an evaluation of the totality of circumstances would be insufficient to assure the knowing, intelligent, and voluntary waiver of rights. Accordingly, when a parent or legal guardian is absent from an interrogation involving a juvenile that young, any confession resulting from the interrogation should be deemed inadmissible as a matter of law, unless the adult was unwilling to be present or truly unavailable. That approach is consistent with other jurisdictions that have recently adopted the same or similar rule.

We cannot ignore the immaturity and inexperience of a child under 14 years of age and the obvious disadvantage such a child has in confronting a custodial police interrogation. In such a case, we conclude that the totality of the circumstances is not sufficient to ensure that the child makes an intelligent and knowing waiver of his rights. In other contexts, our State policy reflects the appropriateness of age fourteen as a dividing line. New Jersey statutes and court rules contain numerous provisions creating age-differential standards set at fourteen. Regardless of the juvenile's age, police officers must use their best efforts to locate a parent or legal guardian before beginning the interrogation. Moreover, to sustain the admissibility of incriminating statements made outside of the adult's presence, prosecutors are required to show to the trial court's satisfaction, upon sufficient proofs, that they were unable to locate the adult.

Such an additional showing has been implied by other court decisions; we have expressly noted it here for the sake of completeness. As important, when an adult is unavailable or declines to accompany the juvenile, the police must conduct the interrogation with "the utmost fairness and in accordance with the highest standards of due process and fundamental fairness." That requirement, too, has been a common thread in our jurisprudence and is reaffirmed today.

III.

Defendant was nearly seventeen at the time of the custodial interrogation. Thus, the rule rendering some confessions of juveniles under the age of fourteen inadmissible as a matter of law does not apply to this appeal. Instead, we review defendant's confession in light of the totality of circumstances, viewing as highly significant the fact that defendant's mother was absent from the interrogation area at the time of the juvenile's statement. Under that standard, we are satisfied that the State has carried its burden of demonstrating defendant's voluntary waiver of his rights. We reach that conclusion relying substantially on the factors emphasized by the Appellate Division and trial court.

We emphasize that, because of his advanced age and the fact that he had been arrested on fifteen prior occasions, defendant was familiar with the criminal process at the time of his statement. Further, the police afforded defendant numerous breaks in the interrogation, time enough for him to reevaluate his decision to proceed without a parent. He elected to continue, notwithstanding his mother's absence. Moreover, we view as especially important the fact that Mrs. Robinson was present at the outset of the encounter with the police, before any questioning of her son. She had the opportunity to offer support to defendant, to witness the signing of the *Miranda* card, and she consented to her initial absence from the interrogation area.

All of those facts—defendant's age and familiarity with the criminal process, his clear desire to be interviewed without a parent present, the presence of a parent at the outset of the questioning, and his fair treatment by police—compel us to conclude that defendant's will was not overborne by investigators, the critical factor in this inquiry. Although we have assigned greater weight to Mrs. Robinson's absence than did the trial court and Appellate Division, our conclusion under all the circumstances is consistent with theirs.

We have referred to Mrs. Robinson as being absent from the interrogation, as opposed to being deliberately excluded by the police, because the trial court found that, in concert with defendant, she voluntarily left the interrogation room at the start of the interview. It was only sometime later, the court concluded, that the one officer did not accede to Mrs. Robinson's request to reenter.

It is difficult for us to envision prosecutors successfully carrying their burdens in future cases in which there has been some deliberate exclusion of a juvenile's parent or legal guardian from the interrogation. However, because the proof in the present case is so compelling that defendant's will was not overborne and the police did not have the benefit of our direction at the time of the interrogation, we see no reason to disturb the judgments below. We are satisfied that on this record the police should be judged by the standards prevailing at the time the officers interrogated defendant, not by the stricter standards announced in this opinion.

IV.

In his separate opinion, our colleague confirms that courts in a majority of states apply a totality of circumstances test when considering the voluntariness of a confession by a juvenile. The concurring opinion further observes that "all courts that have applied that standard to a case in which a parent was deliberately excluded have suppressed the confession." That observation reinforces our belief that the totality of circumstances standard as enunciated here will work as it should: namely, when there has been a deliberate exclusion of a parent or legal guardian from the interrogation room and the police thereafter obtain the juvenile's confession, that confession almost invariably will be suppressed.

The concurring opinion also suggests that our holding is out of step with majority case law from around the country. Not so. Upon close scrutiny, the cases cited in the concurring opinion either have stark factual differences making them inapposite to this case or are in harmony with our disposition here. Those facts are far afield from the facts at bar.

Suffice to say, we have no doubt that if the fact patterns in any of the above cases appeared in a New Jersey appeal, the minor's confession would not withstand our totality of circumstances test. But we reiterate that those facts are not before us in this case.

Decisions announced in another group of cases are in complete harmony with our decision. We reiterate that law enforcement officers must use their best efforts to locate a parent or legal guardian before the start of questioning and must account for those efforts to the trial court's satisfaction. That requirement addresses the concern expressed in the eight statutes identified in the concurring opinion, that have codified a similar rule.

The protections set forth in this opinion are similar to the ones found in other jurisdictions and in some instances, exceed them. Although we differ from our colleague in the manner of expression and in the interpretation of cases in this area, we perceive little or no disagreement on this critical point: statements of juveniles in custody in New Jersey must be voluntary and properly obtained, today and in the future.

V.

In sum, a parent or legal guardian should attend a juvenile interrogation whenever possible to help assure that any waiver of rights by the juvenile is the product of free will. Police officers must use their best efforts to locate a juvenile's parent or legal guardian before beginning an interrogation and should be required to account for those efforts to the trial court's satisfaction. We consider the absence of the adult to be a highly significant factor in the overall balance of factors used to determine the admissibility of the juvenile's statement. It would be difficult to envision prosecutors successfully carrying their burdens in cases in which the police deliberately exclude a parent or legal guardian from the interrogation. When the juvenile is under the age of fourteen, the adult's absence will render the young offender's statement inadmissible as a matter of law—unless the adult is truly unavailable, in which case, the voluntariness of the waiver should be determined by considering the totality of circumstances consistent with this opinion.

The judgment of the Appellate Division is affirmed.

Stein, J., concurring.

I join in the Court's determination to sustain the admissibility of the defendant's confession. This record demonstrates that the juvenile defendant had the benefit of a parent's presence during the critical period before questioning began and while defendant was read his *Miranda* rights. Also significant is the fact that defendant's mother left the room voluntarily. However, I believe that the Court errs when it declines to state unequivocally the consequences in future cases of the deliberate exclusion of parents who have not been present at all during their child's interrogation, and does not acknowledge the obvious connection between the exclusion of parents and the availability of a juvenile's right to counsel. The adoption of a bright-line rule rendering inadmissible those statements made by a juvenile whose parent has been deliberately excluded by the police from the interrogation room would be consistent with statutes and judicial decisions throughout the country. There should be no uncertainty within our State's law enforcement community that the same rule will apply in New Jersey's courts.

The critical events of this case occurred in the early hours of the morning of February 27, 1995. Defendant and his mother, Michele Robinson, were at Willingboro police station at about 2:30 a.m. At about 4:00 a.m. defendant was driven to the prosecutor's office by the police. There, he was placed in a waiting room until his mother arrived. After defendant was informed of and indicated that he understood his constitutional rights, he and his mother signed the *Miranda* card at about 4:20 a.m. Mrs. Robinson then voluntarily left the interrogation room.

Sometime between the time of her departure and 7:39 a.m., when her son made a taped confession, Mrs. Robinson told an officer that she wanted to see her son and that she thought he needed a lawyer. At trial, one of the police officers denied that Mrs. Robinson had made those statements. Rejecting that officer's version of the relevant events, the trial court specifically found as a fact "that Michele Robinson was direct, truthful and convincing." The court also found that the police officer, "as to his denial of [Mrs. Robinson's having made the statements], was evasive, unconvincing and disingenuous." Nevertheless, the trial court determined that because of defendant's age, his prior experiences with the police and his decision not to have his mother present during the earlier questioning, his confession was knowing, voluntary and intelligent and therefore admissible into evidence.

II

Courts and legislatures nationwide generally have adopted one of two approaches in deciding whether to admit a minor's confession obtained subsequent to the deliberate exclusion of a parent. Under the first approach, which most states follow, courts consider the totality of the circumstances. Notably, all courts that have applied that standard to a case in which a parent was deliberately excluded have suppressed the confession.

Illinois courts have determined that where a parent desires to be present during the interrogation of his or her minor child, police officers "have an affirmative duty to inform those actually questioning a juvenile of the parents' presence and request to see [his or] her child. And, in order to ensure the true voluntariness of a statement, those actually questioning the juvenile have an affirmative duty to stop the questioning and allow the parent to confer with [his or] her child."

The California Supreme Court, held that the denial by police of a juvenile defendant's request to see his parent rendered his subsequent confession inadmissible. The court found that the defendant's "request to see his parents at or near the commencement of interrogation was an invocation of his Fifth Amendment privilege" against self-incrimination.

Likewise, Florida and Montana have held that a juvenile's request to telephone or otherwise speak to a parent is tantamount to the invocation of his right to remain silent.

The second approach, which mandates that the State demonstrate that an interested adult was present during an interrogation, has been statutorily adopted in ten states. Those statutes render inadmissible any statement made during interrogation by a juvenile outside the presence of an interested adult and prohibit the waiver of the right to counsel by a juvenile unless that waiver is accompanied by a waiver of a parent or other interested adult. Those jurisdictions consistently have held that any statements made during custodial interrogation are inadmissible where a juvenile's parents are absent.

Eight other states statutorily require police to notify a minor's guardian or custodian immediately if a minor is taken into custody. Statements made by juveniles during custodial interrogation where law enforcement authorities have violated those statutes consistently are suppressed. The courts in those states presumably would also suppress statements made where a parent is deliberately excluded from the juvenile's interrogation.

New Jersey courts previously have acknowledged the connection between the right of a juvenile to have a parent present during interrogation and the voluntariness of a confession.

A survey of the law of both this State and those other states that have addressed the issue thus reveals a clear consensus favoring protection of juveniles' rights by requiring the presence and active participation of a parent or guardian during the interrogation of a juvenile.

The Court acknowledges that it finds it "difficult ... to envision prosecutors successfully carrying their burdens in future cases in which there has been some deliberate exclusion of a juvenile's parents or legal guardian from the interrogation." The Court further observes that, applying a totality of the circumstances test, "when there has been a deliberate exclusion of a parent or legal guardian from the interrogation room..., that confession almost invariably will be suppressed." That formulation, however, permits a trial court to conclude under the totality of the circumstances standard that a juvenile's statements were made voluntarily where the juvenile's parents have been deliberately excluded from the interrogation of their child. In my view, that lack of clarity is inexplicable in the context of the consistent rejection by courts throughout the country of statements made where a parent was excluded.

Moreover, the implementation of a bright-line rule that requires the suppression of statements made by a juvenile whose parents have been deliberately excluded from their child's interrogation would discourage police officers from preventing family contact. Such a rule is clear and practical. It explicitly defines limits within which police officials can work, better protects the rights of New Jersey's juveniles and decreases the likelihood that the police will attempt to evade that which the law requires.

III

The Court also neglects to accord adequate significance to the parents' role in assisting juveniles to vindicate their constitutional right to counsel. Parents play a critical role in aiding a juvenile during custodial interrogation. As the majority notes, a parent is "in a position to assist juveniles in understanding their rights, acting intelligently in waiving those rights, and otherwise remaining calm in the face of an interrogation." A juvenile "needs counsel and support if he is not to become the victim first of fear, then of panic. He needs someone on whom to lean lest the overpowering presence of the law, as he knows it, crush him." The adult advice necessary to put juvenile defendants "on a less unequal footing with [their] interrogators," typically will come either from the juvenile's parents or a lawyer. Juveniles would ordinarily be unable to obtain the assistance of counsel without the assistance of their parents.

In my view, a parent holds an equally "critical position in our legal system," a position that is indispensable if a juvenile in custody is to have a realistic opportunity to exercise the right to counsel. A juvenile's right to the assistance of counsel is hollow indeed unless a parent is present to assist the juvenile in retaining and paying for a lawyer. In that context, the deliberate exclusion of parents from a juvenile's interrogation room is the *de facto* equivalent of a denial of the right to counsel.

In *People v. Burton,* the California Supreme Court best expressed the connection between the right to counsel and the right to have a parent present during interrogation:

> It appears to us most likely and most normal that a minor who wants help on how to conduct himself with the police and wishes to indicate that he does not want to proceed without such help would express such desire by requesting to see his parents. For adults, removed from the protective ambit of parental guidance, the desire for help naturally manifests in a request for an attorney. For minors, it would seem that the desire for help naturally manifests in a request for parents. It would certainly severely restrict the "protective devices" required by *Miranda* in cases where the suspects are minors if the only call for help which is to be deemed an invocation of the privilege is the call for an attorney. It is fatuous to assume that a minor in custody will be in a position to call an attorney for assistance and it is unrealistic to attribute no significance to his call for help from the only person to whom he normally looks — a parent or guardian.

Although the Court today adopts a *per se* rule suppressing statements made by those under the age of fourteen whose parents are not present during interrogation, a 16-year-old juvenile is hardly in a better position to get counsel than is a 13-year-old. In the eyes of a juvenile, the request to consult a parent may be essentially equivalent to a request to consult an attorney. Most juveniles do not know how to engage a lawyer without the assistance of a parent. Juveniles typically have neither the financial wherewithal necessary to retain counsel nor the requisite knowledge of the appropriate steps to take to find a lawyer suitable to their needs. Police tactics that deliberately deprive juveniles of contact with their parents effectively deprive them of their right to counsel.

IV

The constitutional rights at stake in juvenile interrogations require clear, unambiguous rules to provide the necessary guidance to law enforcement officials. Although I concur in the Court's judgment, I would hold that in future cases the deliberate exclusion of parents by police officers from a juvenile's interrogation requires suppression of the juvenile's incriminating statements to police officers.

Holdings of *State v. Presha:* The court held: (1) A parent or legal guardian should attend a juvenile interrogation whenever possible to help assure that any waiver of rights by the juvenile is the product of free will. Police officers must use their best efforts to locate a juvenile's parent or legal guardian before beginning an interrogation and should be required to account for those efforts to the trial court's satisfaction. (2) When the juvenile is under the age of fourteen, the adult's absence will render the young offender's statement inadmissible as a matter of law — unless the adult is truly unavailable, in which case, the voluntariness of the waiver should be determined by considering the totality of circumstances

Discussion Questions

Can law enforcement claim unavailability of a parent because the parent is at work and cannot attend the interrogation of the minor for 8 hours?

Why does the court require parental presence for youth aged 14 or under? Why not use the 18-year benchmark set by the juvenile code instead?

Of what relevance is it that the youth in this case "was familiar with the criminal justice system because of fifteen prior arrests"?

Key Concepts: Suppression of Confessions

- Courts generally use the "totality of the circumstances" test to determine whether or not a confession by a minor is voluntary and whether or not the waiver of the Fifth Amendment right is knowing.

- Circumstances such as age, intellectual ability, the presence (or absence) of a parent, and the circumstances of the interrogation itself are important parts of the "totality of the circumstances" analysis.

- Some states, by court decision or by statute, require the presence of a parent or other responsible adult to support the admission of a confession of a minor.

F. Insanity Defense

Overview: Most people are familiar with the insanity defense in adult criminal court. However, that defense is not commonplace in juvenile delinquency proceedings. The *Gault* decision said nothing about the insanity defense. Most states have not recognized the rights of youths in juvenile court to raise the insanity defense. Some states have specifically denied the availability of the insanity defense in juvenile delinquency proceedings, many have not yet been confronted with the issue, and a few states have recognized the defense.

Winburn v. State: In *Winburn v. State*, the Wisconsin Supreme Court was faced with a case of first impression in that state: whether or not the insanity defense is available to youth involved in a juvenile delinquency proceeding.

As you read *Winburn v. State,* look for the following:

1. Note the presence of the old issue that the juvenile justice system are paternalistic in nature and, therefore, should not be a reflection of the criminal justice system.

2. Notice that part of the *Winburn* decision is based upon the fundamental concept in criminal law of requiring the necessary *men rea.*

Winburn v. State
145 N.W.2d 178 (Wis. 1966)

The fundamental question presented in this appeal is whether insanity constitutes a defense to an allegation of juvenile delinquency. We face the additional question in this case, of whether the mental inquiry initiated by the juvenile judge was a sufficient determination of insanity.

The state argues that a juvenile-delinquency procedure is not a criminal prosecution but is merely the state's exercise of its duties *parens patriae* over children—and that the duty of the state is not to prosecute but 'to bring them and their parents or guardians before an experienced and humane judge who shall inquire into the situation, not with the awe-inspiring and frigid methods of a criminal court, but informally and intimately, like a wise and gentle elder (Big?) brother, or like the good Samaritan of Holy Writ, and who shall, when fully advised do that which is best for the child's future, either by way of sending it to an institution or by providing for kind and tactful, but in no sense degrading, surveillance for a limited time at home' and, accordingly, the armor of 'rights' that can be donned by a defendant in a criminal case is not available to the alleged delinquent.

There is much to support this point of view. Our statutes clearly point out that the judicial determination of juvenile delinquency is not a criminal conviction. This court has frequently reiterated this point of view.

The entire philosophy of the children's code is avowedly the antithesis of criminal prosecution. 'For the delinquent child, the aim of the court is to correct, re-educate, re-direct, and rehabilitate, rather than to punish or to seek retribution for misdeeds.' *Wisconsin Handbook for Juvenile Court Services*, p. 2.

The juvenile law is not to be administered as a criminal statute, and the rules of criminal procedure are not to be engrafted upon the children's code. There are many indications in the statutes that the framers of the act did not consider it a criminal code:

'48.01(3) ... The best interests of the child shall always be of paramount consideration ...'

'48.25(1) ... The presence of the child in court may be waived by the court at any stage of the proceeding.'

'48.25(3) ... customary rules of evidence applied to issues of fact in civil trials shall be followed. The finding of fact shall rest on the preponderance of evidence ...'

'48.25(6) ... If any child or his parents desire counsel but are unable to employ it, the court in its discretion may appoint counsel to represent them ...'

'48.38(1) No adjudication upon the status of any child in the jurisdiction of the juvenile court shall operate to impose any of the civil disabilities ordinarily imposed by conviction, nor shall any such child be deemed a criminal by reason of such adjudication, nor shall such adjudication be deemed a conviction.'

The burden of the state's argument then is that, since this is not a criminal action, the child is not entitled to the usual safeguards of the criminal law. The validity of this position has long been questioned. While the avowed purpose of the children's code is that 'the test interests of the child shall always be of paramount consideration,' there is doubt that the strictly civil approach to the problem accomplishes that purpose This was recognized by the child welfare committee of the Wisconsin Legislative council, which in its 1955 report to the legislature said that 'There has been criticism that in certain areas, because the juvenile court does not follow traditional procedures, the rights of the child are diminished rather than increased.' A recent commentary on our juvenile court system by Professor Joel F. Handler of the University of Wisconsin Law School reported criticism that our juvenile courts on a nationwide basis represented 'unfettered official discretion.' He pointed out that '... the system allows intervention by the government into the affairs of people without their consent and without standards and controls.'

The Supreme Court of the United States in *Kent v. United States*, recognized the *parens patriae* theory of juvenile rehabilitation, but went on to recognize the abuses that arise almost inherently from that philosophy:

'The state is *parens patriae* rather than prosecuting attorney and judge. But the admonition to function in a 'parental' relationship is not an invitation to procedural arbitrariness.'

Because the State is supposed to proceed in respect of the child proceeding as *parens patriae* and not as adversary, courts have relied on the premise that the proceedings are 'civil' in nature and not criminal, and have asserted that the child cannot complain of the deprivation of important rights available in criminal cases. It has been asserted that he can claim only the fundamental due process right to fair treatment. For example, it has been held that he is not entitled to bail; to indictment by grand jury; to a speedy and public trial; to trial by jury; to immunity against self-incrimination; to confrontation of his accusers; and in some jurisdictions (but not in the District of Columbia) that he is not entitled to counsel.

'While there can be no doubt of the original laudable purpose of juvenile courts, studies and critiques in recent years raise serious questions as to whether actual performance measures well enough against theoretical purpose to make tolerable the immunity of the process from the reach of constitutional guaranties applicable to adults. There is much evidence that some juvenile courts, including that of the District of Columbia, back the personnel, facilities and techniques to perform adequately as representatives of the State in a *parens patriae* capacity, at least with respect to children charged with law violation. There is evidence, in fact, that there may be grounds for concern that the child receives the worst of both worlds: that he gets neither the protections accorded to adults nor the solicitous care and regenerative treatment postulated for children.'

The United States Supreme Court did not take upon itself the burden of dealing with each issue that it raised, but it did decide specifically in *Kent* that a child was entitled to counsel as a matter of right at the 'critically important' hearing on the waiver of the juvenile court's jurisdiction in favor of the United States District Court. In a broader sense, the Supreme Court, though concluding that the juvenile hearing in question need not conform with all of the requirements of a criminal trial or even of the usual administrative hearing, stated, '(W)e do hold that the hearing must measure up to the essentials of due process and fair treatment.'

The philosophy behind the juvenile act is rehabilitation and treatment, but what may appear to a juvenile worker or judge as treatment may look like punishment to the juvenile. Irrespective of what we call the juvenile procedure, and no matter how benign and well-intended the judge who administers the system, the juvenile procedures, to some degree at least, smack of 'crime and punishment.' While the primary statutory goal is the best interest of the child, that interest is, as it should be, conditioned by the consideration of 'the interest of the public.' The interest of the public is served not only by rehabilitating juveniles when that is possible, but the interest of the public is also served by removing some juveniles from environments where they are likely to harm their fellow citizens. Retribution, in practice, plays a role in the function of the juvenile court. The judgments of juvenile courts do serve as deterrents to the conduct of at least a segment of our juvenile society, not because those juveniles fear rehabilitation, but because they fear incarceration and punishment. Despite all protestations to the contrary, the adjudication of delinquency carries with it a social stigma. This court can take judicial notice that in common parlance 'juvenile delinquent' is a term of opprobrium and it is not society's accolade bestowed on the successfully rehabilitated. It is common knowledge also that juvenile records do not, in fact, have a confidential status. Peace officers' records may be communicated to school authorities and to other law enforcement agencies. The Federal Bureau of Investigation has no difficulty in ascertaining whether an individual has a juvenile record. A juvenile record may be a substantial handicap to one who seeks employment with the United States Government. The confidentiality of records, even if kept inviolate, is no real safeguard to the ex-delinquent for, if asked whether he was ever so adjudged, he will be morally obliged to admit it whether or not that status was adjudicated by due process and fair play. Professor Handler points out:

'These then are some of the consequences of an adjudication of delinquency ... It is true that perhaps in many cases the consequences may not be severe but may even be beneficial. This, however, is beside the point. All that need be recognized is that the consequences are potentially very harsh. There exists the power to take an adolescent from his home and confine him in what amounts to a prison. He will carry the stigma of criminal conviction which may penalize him throughout his life.'

The juvenile may be worse off than merely stigmatized. The adjudication of the rehabilitation status of delinquency may send him to the state prison.

'... while a suspected juvenile offender is not accorded the full protection of traditional due process, this is offset by corresponding concessions by the state in the best interests of the individual child. But after a juvenile is declared delinquent, this distinction may break down; the child, despite the lack of full constitutional protection, may be treated almost exactly as an adult offender.

'This occurs most dramatically when a child, placed in the custody of the state pursuant to an order of a juvenile court, is ultimately confined in an adult correctional institution ... A child may be committed by the court to a juvenile correctional system and subsequently transferred by administrative order to an adult institution; this is essentially the practice authorized in Wisconsin. Whatever the method used, however, the result is the same: a juvenile is placed in the adult correctional system without ever having been extended the full protection of an adult criminal trial.'

In view of the evident consequences of an adjudication of juvenile delinquency, it is difficult to accept the state's argument that the traditional concepts of 'crime and punishment' have been eliminated. It is therefore apparent that the state's consequent argument that the 'old concept of criminal responsibility' has no relevance is not completely acceptable if we are accord to children at least some measure of the 'essentials of due process and fair treatment.'

Intent is a factor in the determination of juvenile delinquency in Wisconsin. In 1921 this court held that a boy was not to be found delinquent as the consequence of his having thrown a dynamite cap toward other children when 'There is nothing to indicate that Arnold intended to do more than frighten his schoolmates'.

We think it would be conceded that juvenile delinquency should not lie where the child's act is purely an accident. As Holmes put it, 'Even a dog distinguishes between being stumbled over and being kicked.'

It seems equally true that the juvenile court in its determination of delinquency should distinguish acts committed by the insane child from those committed by one not so afflicted. This concept, that it is unjust to 'punish' the insane is rooted deep in our law. Mr. Justice Thomas Fairchild in *State v. Esser,* makes an exhaustive study of the historical basis for present day concepts of insanity in the legal sense. He points out that in 1721, a treatise by William Hawkins says, 'The guilt of offending against any law whatsoever, necessarily supposing a willful disobedience, can never justly be imputed to those who are either incapable of understanding it, or of conforming themselves to it.'

The dispute over the proper tests of insanity that has so preoccupied the courts in recent times is essentially concerned with the question of fairness. Is it fair to convict of crime when the defendant, though knowing right from wrong, as the result of mental illness or incapacity, is unable to exercise the restraints upon his conduct that would enable him to conform to acceptable standards. It would seem incongruous that this great outpouring of concern should be lavished only upon adults who may be criminals while the children whom we profess to be particular objects of solicitude are bypassed. We conclude that the defense of insanity must be permitted in a juvenile delinquency procedure if those proceedings are to conform to the minimum *Kent* standards of due process and fair treatment.

The state, however, claims that intent is not required since only the fact that the boy did shoot his mother is necessary to 'trigger' the finding of delinquency—that *mens rea* is irrelevant, that *actus rea* is all that need be proved. The state buttresses this argument by citing *sec. 48.33, Stats.*, that provides for dismissal of the juvenile petition 'if the court finds that the child is not within the jurisdiction of the court, or that the facts alleged in the petition have not been proved ...'

This state, however, has always taken the position that the mental condition is a matter of proof—a 'fact' to be determined if challenged. It is an implied premise of every criminal complaint or juvenile petition that the accused is sane, but when that premise is challenged by evidence raising a reasonable doubt of the defendant's sanity, it becomes the obligation of the state (under *Esser*) to proceed to establish responsibility. "The state of a man's mind," said Lord Bowen in 1882, 'is as much a fact as the state of his digestion." The juvenile petition was based upon the violation of first degree murder—that requires 'intent to kill.' A petition based on a violation that requires criminal intent cannot result in a finding of delinquency when the conduct was either unintended or when, because of insanity, there was a failure to form the requisite intent. Under the statute the juvenile judge had a clear right and duty to dismiss on the merits when the fact of insanity was proved by competent psychiatric testimony and that proof went unchallenged.

We also conclude that the procedure employed by the judge was not incorrect. He is specifically authorized to have an alleged juvenile delinquent, who may be mentally ill, examined by the hearing procedure set forth in ch. 51. The record shows that the corporation counsel was present during the mental hearing and that he as well as the court and guardian ad litem questioned the medical witnesses. The examination included not only the question of the boy's mental condition at the time of hearing but also at the time he shot his mother. The opinion of the court clearly points out that the court not only considered the child mentally ill and therefore subject to commitment to the Winnebago State Hospital but insane under the legal definitions of *Esser*.

The state concedes that if the child is not presently sane he cannot presently be 'tried' as a delinquent. It contends that though insanity should exonerate the child from the responsibility of presently defending himself it should not exonerate him from criminal responsibility for acts committed while insane. Without dwelling on the obviously inconsistent philosophy that underlies these positions, it does appear that the solution proposed by the state—to leave the petition for delinquency pending—hardly serves the paramount interest of the child—or of society. The state would conclude that, in the event that some years hence the child regains his mental health to the extent that he can stand trial, he should then be charged as a juvenile delinquent although the *actus rea* was the result of insanity, and although the child, when finally tried, has been thoroughly rehabilitated and restored to mental health. This hardly seems consonant with the avowed purpose of the law. The state also leaves open the possibility that, should recovery occur after the age of eighteen, and assuming (without deciding) that the juvenile court has lost jurisdiction, the state would then proceed to prosecute criminally a person who as a child allegedly committed first degree murder. Could the child then in the criminal courts be able to raise the defense that was denied to it in the juvenile court? This would hardly be consistent with the avowed policy of showing special solicitude for the child in a juvenile court. The state in its brief asserts that it 'wants the opportunity to prove delinquency even in the face of a strong defense of insanity.' This hardly squares with the original benevolent *parens patriae* concept of the juvenile law.

The juvenile court judge by his finding has preserved a fundamental right — the right not to answer criminally for misdeeds committed under the influence of an insane mind. To hold otherwise would be inconsistent with the *Kent* insistence of fair play. He has by the commitment of the child to a state hospital for rehabilitation and treatment taken the first step to carry out the purpose that the juvenile law is designed to serve — the interest of the child. By that commitment, the additional and extremely important purpose of protecting the interests of the public is also accomplished. Under the conditions of the commitment, the child cannot be released until it appears safe for him and society. Under the provisions of the juvenile code, the dismissal on the merits by reason of insanity is a bar to future criminal prosecution. Accordingly, if the child is restored to health by hospitalization, he can return to society without the possibility of further juvenile or criminal procedures. The action of the county judge effectively implements the legislative purpose.

The order of the circuit court must be reversed, and the order of the children's court dismissing the delinquency petition is reinstated.

Order reversed.

Holdings of *Winburn v. State:* The court held that the defense of insanity must be permitted in a juvenile delinquency procedure if those proceedings are to conform to the minimum *Kent* standards of due process and fair treatment.

Discussion Question

How can the denial of the right to claim lack of responsibility for an act due to insanity ever be consistent with the concept that the juvenile justice system is designed to help the youth and to reform the conduct of the youth?

———————

Golden v. State: In *Golden v. State*, the Arkansas Supreme Court was required to determine whether or not the Due Process Clause and the Equal Protection Clause of the U. S. Constitution requires the recognition of the insanity defense in juvenile delinquency proceedings.

As you read *Golden v. State*, look for the following:

1. Examine the rule established by the United States Supreme Court on the issue of the availability of the insanity defense in adult criminal proceedings.

2. Think about cases previously discussed (including *Gault* and *Winship*) and whether or not the availability of the insanity defense is as fundamental as the rights granted to minors in those cases.

Golden v. State
341 Ark. 656, 341 Ark. 963, 21 S.W.3d 801 (2000)

W.H. "DUB" ARNOLD, Chief Justice.

This case involves the issues of whether a juvenile defendant has a right to have his competency to proceed determined prior to adjudication and, further, whether a juvenile has a right to assert the defense of insanity. We hold that a juvenile does have a due process right to have his competency determined prior to adjudication and, as such, reverse the trial court on this point. However, we hold that neither due process nor equal protection affords a juvenile the right to an insanity defense and, therefore, affirm the trial court on these issues.

On March 24, 1998, appellant Andrew Golden and Mitchell Johnson opened fire on their classmates at Westside Elementary School in Jonesboro, Arkansas. One teacher and four students were killed, and one teacher and nine students were wounded. At the time of the shootings, appellant Andrew Golden was eleven years old.

On March 25, 1998, a petition was filed, charging Golden and Mitchell with five counts of capital murder and ten counts of first-degree battery. At the probable cause hearing held on March 25, 1998, Golden's attorney informed the court that he intended to raise the affirmative defense of insanity and would also be raising issues concerning Golden's competency to proceed to trial. A separate hearing on these issues was later held.

At the hearing on these issues, Golden's attorney argued that if the court denied Golden the right to argue lack of competency and insanity, it would violate Golden's constitutional rights of due process and equal protection. The trial court rejected these arguments, finding that based upon the nature of juvenile proceedings, Golden was not entitled to raise the issue of whether he was competent to stand trial or to assert the insanity defense. The court reasoned that the safeguards present in juvenile proceedings allow a court to consider any alleged mental disease or defect during the disposition phase, when the court is determining the appropriate placement for the juvenile.

Following the issuance of the trial court's order, Golden's attorney informed the court that he wished to proceed to the adjudication hearing in order to preserve Golden's right to argue the competency and insanity issues on appeal. [*Footnote:* Golden's attorney agreed to stipulate to the facts of the case; however, he did not plead guilty; in other words, he did not stipulate to the intent. He chose to proceed to trial rather than appeal interlocutory from the court's order regarding the competency and insanity issues.] An adjudication hearing was subsequently held in which the trial court adjudicated Golden guilty and sentenced him to an indeterminate period of time in the Division of Youth Services Training School. The court also provided that if Golden was released before the age of twenty-one, he would remain in a juvenile detention center for up to ninety days.

I. Due Process Rights

Appellant asserts that the trial court violated his due-process rights by refusing to determine his competency, or fitness to proceed, and that the trial court violated his due-process rights by refusing to allow him to present an insanity defense. We agree in regard to competency and disagree in regard to the insanity defense.

A. Competency to Stand Trial

The law is clear that defendants in criminal cases have a fundamental right not to stand trial while incompetent. This right protects criminal defendants' fundamental interests in their own liberty by ensuring that they are able to participate in their defense in an effort to avoid conviction and incarceration. In regard to juvenile proceedings, while the Arkansas Juvenile Code seems to presume that a defendant being tried in juvenile court is incompetent to some degree, particularly one who is under the age of fourteen, there was no statutory provision for juveniles at the time of appellant's hearing affording juveniles the same fundamental liberty interests as adults where the issue of competency is concerned. [*Footnote:* Although it may not be applied retroactively, it should be noted that when the

General Assembly amended the juvenile code in 1999, it added an entire section on competency. The new language provides for a determination of capacity to stand trial for juveniles charged with certain crimes (capital murder being one of them). Further, it properly provides for an "age appropriate" capacity standard to apply to juveniles, which is different than that of adults.]

Although this issue is one of first impression in Arkansas, the United States Supreme Court held, in the case of *In re Gault*, that while proceedings in a juvenile court need not conform with *all* the requirements of a criminal trial, primarily because of the special nature of the proceedings, essential requirements of due process and fair treatment must be met. The Court, in *Gault*, specifically acknowledged a juvenile's right to constitutionally adequate notice, the right against self-incrimination, and the right to cross-examine witnesses; further, the Court explicitly held that a juvenile must be afforded the right to counsel during these proceedings. Logically, this right to counsel means little if the juvenile is unaware of the proceedings or unable to communicate with counsel due to a psychological or developmental disability. Therefore, applying *Gault*, we hold that a juvenile *must* be allowed to assert incompetency and have his competency determined prior to adjudication. As such, we reverse the trial court on this point.

B. Insanity Defense

Regarding the insanity defense, this Court held that insanity is not a defense in juvenile proceedings because there is no statutory authority or case law for the defense. [*Footnote:* It should be noted that while the applicable juvenile code does not speak in terms of insanity as a defense, the 1999 amendment has included an evaluation of the juvenile's mental state and capacity with regard to mental disease or defect as part of the process of evaluating a juvenile under the age of thirteen who is charged with capital murder or murder in the first degree.] In *K.M.*, we relied upon the U.S. Supreme Court holding in *Medina v. California*, that there is no constitutional right to an insanity defense; therefore, if one is not provided for by statute, then a defendant may not assert the defense.

Clearly, there was no statutory provision in effect in Arkansas at the time of appellant's hearing conferring upon juveniles the right to assert an insanity defense. As such, applying our holding in *K.M. v. State*, we hold that appellant's due process rights were not violated by the trial court's preclusion from allowing him to assert the insanity defense. Therefore, we affirm the trial court on this point.

II. Equal Protection Rights

Appellant asserts that the trial court violated his equal-protection rights by refusing to determine whether he was competent to proceed and that the trial court violated his equal-protection rights by refusing to allow him to present an insanity defense. We decline to address the competency argument; further, we disagree with appellant that his equal-protection rights were violated in regard to the insanity defense.

A. Competency to Stand Trial

Because this case is being reversed on due-process competency grounds, it is unnecessary in this case to address the competency issue with regard to equal protection.

B. Insanity Defense

As discussed above, this Court has already decided the issue of whether juveniles may assert the defense of insanity in *K.M. v. State*. We cited, in support of our decision that juveniles could not assert said defense, the U.S. Supreme Court case of *Medina v. Cali-*

fornia, which held that there is no constitutional right to an insanity defense, so if one is not provided for by statute or case law, then a defendant may not assert it. However, this Court, in *K.M.,* refused to address the issue under an equal protection analysis because it was not raised below. Therefore, this equal-protection argument is one of first impression for this Court.

The appellant contends that no rational basis exists for affording the insanity defense to adult criminal defendants in circuit court while not providing said defense to juvenile defendants; he contends that this undoubtedly amounts to a violation of equal protection. We disagree. Due to the very nature of juvenile proceedings and the difference in purpose of a juvenile proceeding — that being rehabilitative rather than punitive — coupled with the fact that juveniles are neither provided a trial by jury nor various other rights afforded to adult criminal defendants in circuit court, a rational basis *clearly* exists for affording adult criminal defendants in circuit court the right (by statute, not constitutionally), to assert the defense of insanity while not affording the same right to juveniles.

Further, the juvenile code provides a number of alternatives for the judge to consider and recommend in regard to disposition, including treatment, commitment, transfer of legal custody, and other alternatives regarding placement in a community-based program as opposed to a youth services center. Clearly, a rational basis exists for affording juvenile defendants less procedural rights than those charged in criminal circuit court, primarily because of the special nature of the proceedings. After all, criminal defendants in circuit court could potentially face life-imprisonment, or even a death sentence, unlike those charged in juvenile court. For these reasons, we affirm the trial court on this point, as well.

Reversed and remanded in part; affirmed in part.

Smith, J., dissenting.

I concur in the majority's opinion in all points save the issue of Golden's competency to stand trial. I would affirm the trial court's denial of a competency hearing. I do so because the distinctions that exist between juvenile court proceedings and adult criminal proceedings are substantial and are rationally based upon the differences between adults and children. Although according a juvenile the right to a competency hearing appears equitable, it is, I submit, unwise. It reflects the continued erosion of all distinction between juvenile court and adult criminal courts. This erosion could ultimately lead to the irrelevance of juvenile codes in general.

Juveniles do not have a fundamental due process right to not be deprived of their liberty as a result of a hearing during which they were incompetent. The State's *parens patriae* interest, under proper circumstances subordinates the child's liberty interest. A juvenile has a liberty interest, which the U.S. Supreme Court describes as "substantial," but of which they also state that "that interest must be qualified by the recognition that juveniles, unlike adults, are always in some form of custody." The U.S. Supreme Court in this same opinion also states, "Children by definition are not assumed to have the capacity to take care of themselves. They are assumed to be subject to the control of their parents, and if parental control falters, the State must play its role as parens patraie."

The distinctions existing between juveniles and adults are recognized by the legislature in *Ark.Code Ann. § 9-27-102,* which states, "The General Assembly recognizes that children are defenseless and that there is no greater moral obligation upon the General Assembly than to provide for the protection of our children and that our child welfare system needs to be strengthened by establishing a clear policy of the state that the best interests of the children must be paramount and shall have precedence at every stage of juvenile court proceedings...." This is consistent with the *parens patriae* interest as discussed in the U.S. Supreme Court cases. Implicit in the General Assembly's statement is the recognition that juveniles will not be competent in the sense adults would be, because they are assumed not to have the capacity to take care of themselves. In fact, the juvenile proceedings are designed to accomplish its ends without regard to the juvenile's competence because its absence is presumed.

As referenced by the majority, "[T]here is no doubt that the Due Process Clause is applicable in juvenile proceedings." The U.S. Supreme Court went on to note the issue in the application of the Due Process Clause "is to ascertain the precise impact of the due process clause requirement upon such proceedings." The Supreme Court then went on to note it had decided in the past that the Due Process Clause required application of certain constitutional rights enjoyed by adults and did apply to minors. The court listed the rights, including notice of charges, right to counsel, privilege against self-incrimination, right of confrontation, and proof beyond a reasonable doubt. The Supreme Court then notes that the Constitution does not mandate elimination of all differences in the treatment of juveniles. At issue in *Schall* was whether preventative detention of juveniles, as set out in the New York statute, was "compatible with the 'fundamental fairness' required by due process." "We do not mean ... to indicate that the hearing must conform with all of the requirements of a criminal trial or even that of the usual administrative hearing; but we do hold that the hearing must measure up to the essentials of due process and fair treatment." The Supreme Court in *Schall* stated that the inquiry required was twofold: whether the statute served a legitimate State objective, and whether the procedural safeguards are adequate.

Because the U.S. Supreme Court speaks of a 'legitimate State objective,' the applicable test is the 'rational basis test.' That test is whether there is any rational basis connected to a legitimate State purpose. The statute may not be arbitrary or capricious. I would hold that there is a rational basis for the juvenile code not providing for competency hearings in juvenile cases. Therefore, I respectfully dissent.

Holdings of Holdings of *Golden v. State:* The court held that neither due process nor equal protection affords a juvenile the right to an insanity defense

Discussion Questions

Is it consistent for the court to hold (1) that a youth must be competent to stand trial, and (2) that the youth is not entitled to claim insanity as a defense on the merits of the case?

If it is true that the purpose of the juvenile justice system is rehabilitative rather than punitive, how is it rational for the court to hold that insanity is not a defense in juvenile justice proceedings?

If states can deny an insanity defense to an adult criminal defendant but decides to extend that defense to them, how is it rational to deny the same defense to a youth solely because the person is a minor?

Key Concept: Insanity Defense

- State courts differ in their opinions of whether or not a minor has the right to assert an insanity defense in juvenile delinquency proceedings.

G. Right to a Jury Trial

Overview: The *Gault* decision left open the issue of whether or not juveniles charged with delinquency were entitled to a trial by jury. Only four years after *Gault* was decided, the United States Supreme Court was faced with the issue. While the United States Supreme Court found that the United States Constitution did not extend the right to a jury trial to minors in a delinquency case, the evolution of the juvenile delinquency courts into more formal and adversary systems has resulted in state courts reviewing the wisdom of that decision. Today, a vast majority of state courts continue to deny juveniles the right to a jury trial in delinquency cases. However, some states have extended that right to juveniles, often under certain conditions.

McKeiver v. Pennsylvania: In *McKeiver v. Pennsylvania,* the United States Supreme Court was faced with several juvenile delinquency cases (both felony cases and misdemeanor cases) where the juveniles charged with having committed a delinquent act were denied the right to trial by jury.

As you read *McKeiver v. Pennsylvania,* look for the following:

1. Consider why the court does not apply the right to a jury trial to juveniles even though this right is specifically identified in the Constitution after it had extended the right to the standard of proof of "beyond a reasonable doubt" which is not detailed in the Constitution is guaranteed.

2. Consider what concerns were noted by the Court in support of their refusal to extend the right to a jury trial to juveniles.

McKeiver v. Pennsylvania
403 U.S. 528 (1971)

Mr. Justice BLACKMUN announced the judgments of the Court and an opinion in which THE CHIEF JUSTICE, Mr. Justice STEWART, and Mr. Justice WHITE join.

These cases present the narrow but precise issue whether the Due Process Clause of the Fourteenth Amendment assures the right to trial by jury in the adjudicative phase of a state juvenile court delinquency proceeding.

The issue arises understandably, for the Court in a series of cases already has emphasized due process factors protective of the juvenile:

From these six cases — *Haley, Gallegos, Kent, Gault, DeBacker,* and *Winship* — it is apparent that:

1. Some of the constitutional requirements attendant upon the state criminal trial have equal application to that part of the state juvenile proceeding that is adjudicative in nature. Among these are the rights to appropriate notice, to counsel, to confrontation and to cross-examination, and the privilege against self-incrimination. Included, also, is the standard of proof beyond a reasonable doubt.

2. The Court, however, has not yet said that all rights constitutionally assured to an adult accused of crime also are to be enforced or made available to the juvenile in his delinquency proceeding. Indeed, the Court specifically has refrained from going that far.

3. The Court, although recognizing the high hopes and aspirations of Judge Julian Mack, the leaders of the Jane Addams School and the other supporters of the

juvenile court concept, has also noted the disappointments of the system's performance and experience and the resulting widespread disaffection. There have been, at one and the same time, both an appreciation for the juvenile court judge who is devoted, sympathetic, and conscientious, and a disturbed concern about the judge who is untrained and less than fully imbued with an understanding approach to the complex problems of childhood and adolescence. There has been praise for the system and its purposes, and there has been alarm over its defects.

4. The Court has insisted that these successive decisions do not spell the doom of the juvenile court system or even deprive it of its 'informality, flexibility, or speed.' On the other hand, a concern precisely to the opposite effect was expressed by two dissenters in *Winship*.

With this substantial background already developed, we turn to the facts of the present cases:

Joseph McKeiver, then age 16, in May 1968 was charged with robbery, larceny, and receiving stolen goods (felonies under Pennsylvania law) as acts of juvenile delinquency. At the time of the adjudication hearing he was represented by counsel. His request for a jury trial was denied and his case was heard by Judge Theodore S. Gutowicz of the Court of Common Pleas, Family Division, Juvenile Branch, of Philadelphia County, Pennsylvania. McKeiver was adjudged a delinquent upon findings that he had violated a law of the Commonwealth.

Edward Terry, then age 15, in January 1969 was charged with assault and battery on a police officer and conspiracy (misdemeanors under Pennsylvania law) as acts of juvenile delinquency. His counsel's request for a jury trial was denied and his case was heard by Judge Joseph C. Bruno of the same Juvenile Branch of the Court of Common Pleas of Philadelphia County. Terry was adjudged a delinquent on the charges. This followed an adjudication and commitment in the preceding week for an assault on a teacher. He was committed, as he had been on the earlier charge, to the Youth Development Center at Cornwells Heights.

Barbara Burrus and approximately 45 other black children, ranging in age from 11 to 15 years, were the subjects of juvenile court summonses issued in Hyde County, North Carolina, in January 1969.

The charges arose out of a series of demonstrations in the county in late 1968 by black adults and children protesting school assignments and a school consolidation plan. Petitions were filed by North Carolina state highway patrolmen. Except for one relating to James Lambert Howard, the petitions charged the respective juveniles with willfully impeding traffic. The charge against Howard was that he willfully made riotous noise and was disorderly in the O. A. Peay School in Swan Quarter; interrupted and disturbed the school during its regular sessions; and defaced school furniture. The acts so charged are misdemeanors under North Carolina law.

The evidence as to the juveniles other than Howard consisted solely of testimony of highway patrolmen. No juvenile took the stand or offered any witness. The testimony was to the effect that on various occasions the juveniles and adults were observed walking along Highway 64 singing, shouting, clapping, and playing basketball. As a result, there was interference with traffic. The marchers were asked to leave the paved portion of the highway and they were warned that they were committing a statutory offense. They either refused or left the roadway and immediately returned. The juveniles and participating adults were taken into custody. Juvenile petitions were then filed with respect to those under the age of 16.

The evidence as to Howard was that on the morning of December 5, he was in the office of the principal of the O. A. Peay School with 15 other persons while school was in session and was moving furniture around; that the office was in disarray; that as a result the school closed before noon; and that neither he nor any of the others was a student at the school or authorized to enter the principal's office.

In each case the court found that the juvenile had committed 'an act for which an adult may be punished by law.' A custody order was entered declaring the juvenile a delinquent 'in need of more suitable guardianship' and committing him to the custody of the County Department of Public Welfare for placement in a suitable institution 'until such time as the Board of Juvenile Correction or the Superintendent of said institution may determine, not inconsistent with the laws of this State.' The court, however, suspended these commitments and placed each juvenile on probation for either one or two years conditioned upon his violating none of the State's laws, upon his reporting monthly to the County Department of Welfare, upon his being home by 11 p.m. each evening, and upon his attending a school approved by the Welfare Director. None of the juveniles has been confined on these charges.

The right to an impartial jury '(i)n all criminal prosecutions' under federal law is guaranteed by the Sixth Amendment. Through the Fourteenth Amendment that requirement has now been imposed upon the States 'in all criminal cases which—were they to be tried in a federal court—would come within the Sixth Amendment's guarantee.' This is because the Court has said it believes 'that trial by jury in criminal cases is fundamental to the American scheme of justice.'

This, of course, does not automatically provide the answer to the present jury trial issue, if for no other reason than that the juvenile court proceeding has not yet been held to be a 'criminal prosecution,' within the meaning and reach of the Sixth Amendment, and also has not yet been regarded as devoid of criminal aspects merely because it usually has been given the civil label.

The Pennsylvania juveniles' basic argument is that they were tried in proceedings 'substantially similar to a criminal trial.' They say that a delinquency proceeding in their State is initiated by a petition charging a penal code violation in the conclusory language of an indictment; that a juvenile detained prior to trial is held in a building substantially similar to an adult prison; that in Philadelphia juveniles over 16 are, in fact, held in the cells of a prison; that counsel and the prosecution engage in plea bargaining; that motions to suppress are routinely heard and decided; that the usual rules of evidence are applied; that the customary common-law defenses are available; that the press is generally admitted in the Philadelphia juvenile courtrooms; that members of the public enter the room; that arrest and prior record may be reported by the press (from police sources, however, rather than from the juvenile court records); that, once adjudged delinquent, a juvenile may be confined until his majority in what amounts to a prison; and that the stigma attached upon delinquency adjudication approximates that resulting from conviction in an adult criminal proceeding.

The North Carolina juveniles particularly urge that the requirement of a jury trial would not operate to deny the supposed benefits of the juvenile court system; that the system's primary benefits are its discretionary intake procedure permitting disposition short of adjudication, and its flexible sentencing permitting emphasis on rehabilitation; that realization of these benefits does not depend upon dispensing with the jury; that adjudication of factual issues on the one hand and disposition of the case on the other are very different matters with very different purposes; that the purpose of the former is indistinguishable from that of the criminal trial; that the jury trial provides an independent protective factor; that experience has shown that jury trials in juvenile courts are manageable; that no reason exists why protection traditionally accorded in criminal proceedings should be denied young people subject to involuntary incarceration for lengthy periods; and that the juvenile courts deserve healthy public scrutiny.

All the litigants here agree that the applicable due process standard in juvenile proceedings, as developed by *Gault* and *Winship*, is fundamental fairness. As that standard was applied in those two cases, we have an emphasis on factfinding procedures. The requirements of notice, counsel, confrontation, cross-examination, and standard of proof naturally flowed from this emphasis. But one cannot say that in our legal system the jury is a necessary component of accurate factfinding. There is much to be said for it, to be sure, but we have been content to pursue other ways for determining facts. Juries are not required, and have not been, for example, in equity cases, in workmen's compensation, in probate, or in deportation cases.

Despite all these disappointments, all these failures, and all these shortcomings, we conclude that trial by jury in the juvenile court's adjudicative stage is not a constitutional requirement. We so conclude for a number of reasons:

1. The Court has refrained, in the cases heretofore decided, from taking the easy way with a flat holding that all rights constitutionally assured for the adult accused are to be imposed upon the state juvenile proceeding.

2. There is a possibility, at least, that the jury trial, if required as a matter of constitutional precept, will remake the juvenile proceeding into a fully adversary process and will put an effective end to what has been the idealistic prospect of an intimate, informal protective proceeding.

3. The Task Force Report, although concededly pre-*Gault*, is notable for its not making any recommendation that the jury trial be imposed upon the juvenile court system. This is so despite its vivid description of the system's deficiencies and disappointments.

4. The Court specifically has recognized by dictum that a jury is not a necessary part even of every criminal process that is fair and equitable.

5. The imposition of the jury trial on the juvenile court system would not strengthen greatly, if at all, the fact-finding function, and would, contrarily, provide an attrition of the juvenile court's assumed ability to function in a unique manner. It would not remedy the defects of the system. Meager as has been the hoped-for advance in the juvenile field, the alternative would be regressive, would lose what has been gained, and would tend once again to place the juvenile squarely in the routine of the criminal process.

6. The juvenile concept held high promise. We are reluctant to say that, despite disappointments of grave dimensions, it still does not hold promise, and we are particularly reluctant to say, as do the Pennsylvania appellants here, that the system cannot accomplish its rehabilitative goals. So much depends on the availability of resources, on the interest and commitment of the public, on willingness to learn, and on understanding as to cause and effect and cure. In this field, as in so many others, one perhaps learns best by doing. We are reluctant to disallow the States to experiment further and to seek in new and different ways the elusive answers to the problems of the young, and we feel that we would be impeding that experimentation by imposing the jury trial. The States, indeed, must go forward.

If, in its wisdom, any State feels the jury trial is desirable in all cases, or in certain kinds, there appears to be no impediment to its installing a system embracing that feature. That, however, is the State's privilege and not its obligation.

7. Of course there have been abuses. The Task Force Report has noted them. We refrain from saying at this point that those abuses are of constitutional dimension. They relate to the lack of resources and of dedication rather than to inherent unfairness.

8. There is, of course, nothing to prevent a juvenile court judge, in a particular case where he feels the need, or when the need is demonstrated, from using an advisory jury.

9. 'The fact that a practice is followed by a large number of states is not conclusive in a decision as to whether that practice accords with due process, but it is plainly worth considering in determining whether the practice 'offends some principle of justice so rooted in the traditions and conscience of our people as to be ranked as fundamental.'

10. Since Gault and since Duncan the great majority of States, in addition to Pennsylvania and North Carolina, that have faced the issue have concluded that the considerations that led to the result in those two cases do not compel trial by jury in the juvenile court.

11. Stopping short of proposing the jury trial for juvenile proceedings are the Uniform Juvenile Court Act, § 24(a), approved in July 1968 by the National Conference of Commissioners on Uniform State Laws; the Standard Juvenile Court Act, Art. V, § 19, proposed by the National Council on Crime and Delinquency; and the Legislative Guide for Drafting Family and Juvenile Court Acts § 29(a).

12. If the jury trial were to be injected into the juvenile court system as a matter of right, it would bring with it into that system the traditional delay, the formality, and the clamor of the adversary system and, possibly, the public trial.

13. Finally, the arguments advanced by the juveniles here are, of course, the identical arguments that underlie the demand for the jury trial for criminal proceedings. The arguments necessarily equate the juvenile proceeding—or at least the adjudicative phase of it—with the criminal trial. Whether they should be so equated is our issue. Concern about the inapplicability of exclusionary and other rules of evidence, about the juvenile court judge's possible awareness of the juvenile's prior record and of the contents of the social file; about repeated appearances of the same familiar witnesses in the persons of juvenile and probation officers and social workers—all to the effect that this will create the likelihood of pre-judgment—chooses to ignore it seems to us, every aspect of fairness, of concern, of sympathy, and of paternal attention that the juvenile court system contemplates.

If the formalities of the criminal adjudicative process are to be superimposed upon the juvenile court system, there is little need for its separate existence. Perhaps that ultimate disillusionment will come one day, but for the moment we are disinclined to give impetus to it.

Affirmed.

Mr. Justice WHITE, concurring.

Although the function of the jury is to find facts, that body is not necessarily or even probably better at the job than the conscientious judge. Nevertheless, the consequences of criminal guilt are so severe that the Constitution mandates a jury to prevent abuses of official power by insuring, where demanded, community participation in imposing serious deprivations of liberty and to provide a hedge against corrupt, biased, or political justice. We have not, however, considered the juvenile case a criminal proceeding within the meaning of the Sixth Amendment and hence automatically subject to all of the restrictions normally applicable in criminal cases. The question here is one of due process of law and I join the plurality opinion concluding that the States are not required by that clause to afford jury trials in juvenile courts where juveniles are charged with improper acts.

The criminal law proceeds on the theory that defendants have a will and are responsible for their actions. A finding of guilt establishes that they have chosen to engage in conduct so reprehensible and injurious to others that they must be punished to deter them and others from crime. Guilty defendants are considered blameworthy; they are branded and treated as such, however much the State also pursues rehabilitative ends in the criminal justice system.

For the most part, the juvenile justice system rests on more deterministic assumptions. Reprehensible acts by juveniles are not deemed the consequence of mature and malevolent choice but of environmental pressures (or lack of them) or of other forces beyond their control. Hence the state legislative judgment not to stigmatize the juvenile delinquent by branding him a criminal; his conduct is not deemed so blameworthy that punishment is required to deter him or others. Coercive measures, where employed, are considered neither retribution nor punishment. Supervision or confinement is aimed at rehabilitation, not at convincing the juvenile of his error simply by imposing pains and penalties. Nor is the purpose to make the juvenile delinquent an object lesson for others, whatever his own merits or demerits may be. A typical disposition in the juvenile court where delinquency is established may authorize confinement until age 21, but it will last no longer and within that period will last only so long as his behavior demonstrates that he remains an unacceptable risk if returned to his family. Nor is the authorization for custody until 21 any measure of the seriousness of the particular act that the juvenile has performed.

For me there remain differences of substance between criminal and juvenile courts. They are quite enough for me to hold that a jury is not required in the latter. Of course, there are strong arguments that juries are desirable when dealing with the young, and States are free to use juries if they choose. They are also free if they extend criminal court safeguards to juvenile court adjudications, frankly to embrace condemnation, punishment, and deterrence as permissible and desirable attributes of the juvenile justice system. But the Due Process Clause neither compels nor invites them to do so.

Mr. Justice BRENNAN, concurring in the judgment in No. 322 and dissenting in No. 128.

I agree with the plurality opinion's conclusion that the proceedings below in these cases were not 'criminal prosecutions' within the meaning of the Sixth Amendment. For me, therefore, the question in these cases is whether jury trial is among the 'essentials of due process and fair treatment.'

In my view, therefore, the due process question cannot be decided upon the basis of general characteristics of juvenile proceedings, but only in terms of the adequacy of a particular state procedure to 'protect the (juvenile) from oppression by the Government,' and to protect him against 'the complaint, biased, or eccentric judge.'

Examined in this light, I find no defect in the Pennsylvania cases before us. The availability of trial by jury allows an accused to protect himself against possible oppression by what is in essence an appeal to the community conscience, as embodied in the jury that hears his case. To some extent, however, a similar protection may be obtained when an accused may in essence appeal to the community at large, by focusing public attention upon the facts of his trial, exposing improper judicial behavior to public view, and obtaining, if necessary, executive redress through the medium of public indignation. Of course, the Constitution, in the context of adult criminal trials, has rejected the notion that public trial is an adequate substitution for trial by jury in serious cases. But in the context of juvenile delinquency proceedings, I cannot say that it is beyond the competence of a State to conclude that juveniles who fear that delinquency proceedings will mask judicial oppression may obtain adequate protection by focusing community attention upon the trial of their cases. For, however much the juvenile system may have failed in practice, its very existence as an ostensibly beneficent and noncriminal process for the care and guidance of young persons demonstrates the existence of the community's sympathy and concern for the young. Juveniles able to bring the community's attention to bear upon their trials may therefore draw upon a reservoir of public concern unavailable to the adult criminal defendant. In the Pennsylvania cases before us, there appears to be no statutory ban upon admission of the public to juvenile trials. Appellants themselves, without contradiction, assert that 'the press is generally admitted' to juvenile delinquency proceedings in Philadelphia. Most important, the record in these cases is bare of any indication that any person whom appellants sought to have admitted to the courtroom was excluded. In these circumstances, I agree that the judgment in No. 322 must be affirmed.

The North Carolina cases, however, present a different situation. North Carolina law either permits or requires exclusion of the general public from juvenile trials. In the cases before us, the trial judge 'ordered the general public excluded from the hearing room and stated that only officers of the court, the juveniles, their parents or guardians, their attorney and witnesses would be present for the hearing,' notwithstanding petitioners' repeated demand for a public hearing. The cases themselves, which arise out of a series of demonstrations by black adults and juveniles who believed that the Hyde County, North Carolina, school system unlawfully discriminated against black schoolchildren, present a paradigm of the circumstances in which there may be a substantial 'temptation to use the courts for political ends.' Opinion of Mr. Justice WHITE, ante at 1990. And finally, neither the opinions supporting the judgment nor the respondent in No. 128 has pointed to any feature of North Carolina's juvenile proceedings that could substitute for public or jury trial in protecting the petitioners against misuse of the judicial process

Accordingly, I would reverse the judgment in No. 128.

Mr. Justice DOUGLAS, with whom Mr. Justice BLACK and Mr. Justice MARSHALL concur, dissenting.

These cases from Pennsylvania and North Carolina present the issue of the right to a jury trial for offenders charged in juvenile court and facing a possible incarceration until they reach their majority. I believe the guarantees of the Bill of Rights, made applicable to the States by the Fourteenth Amendment, require a jury trial.

Conviction of each of these crimes would subject a person, whether juvenile or adult, to imprisonment in a state institution. In the case of these students the possible term was six to 10 years; it would be computed for the period until an individual reached the age of 21. Each asked for a jury trial which was denied. The trial judge stated that the hearings were juvenile hearings, not criminal trials. But the issue in each case was whether they had violated a state criminal law. The trial judge found in each case that the juvenile had committed 'an act for which an adult may be punished by law' and held in each case that the acts of the juvenile violated one of the criminal statutes cited above.

The trial judge thereupon ordered each juvenile to be committed to the state institution for the care of delinquents and then placed each on probation for terms from 12 to 24 months.

Just as courts have sometimes confused delinquency with crime, so have law enforcement officials treated juveniles not as delinquents but as criminals.

Even when juveniles are not incarcerated with adults the situation may be no better. One Pennsylvania correctional institution for juveniles is a brick building with barred windows, locked steel doors, a cyclone fence topped with barbed wire, and guard towers. A former juvenile judge described it as 'a maximum security prison for adjudged delinquents.'

In the present cases imprisonment or confinement up to 10 years was possible for one child and each faced at least a possible five-year incarceration. No adult could be denied a jury trial in those circumstances. The Fourteenth Amendment, which makes trial by jury provided in the Sixth Amendment applicable to the States, speaks of denial of rights to 'any person,' not denial of rights to 'any adult person'; and we have held indeed that where a juvenile is charged with an act that would constitute a crime if committed by an adult, he is entitled to be tried under a standard of proof beyond a reasonable doubt.

These cases should be remanded for trial by jury on the criminal charges filed against these youngsters.

Holdings of *McKeiver v. Pennsylvania:* The court held that trial by jury in the juvenile court's adjudicative stage is not a constitutional requirement.

Discussion Questions

Would a jury trial be the one thing that would deal a "fatal blow" to the entire juvenile process adding undue formality to the system?

Does the fact that a juvenile with a jury trial would not have a real "jury of his peers" anyway have anything to do with this opinion?

In re Jeffrey C.: In *In re Jeffrey C.,* the 16-year-old youth involved (who turned 17 just 6 days after the dispositional hearing) was ordered to be committed to an adult correctional facility upon reaching age 17. New Hampshire had a statue that allowed minors to be sentenced to an adult correctional facility. The New Hampshire Supreme Court was asked to hold that a juvenile subject to confinement in an adult facility should be afforded the right to trial by jury.

As you read *In re Jeffrey C.,* look for the following:

1. Consider the basis used by the court to grant a limited right to a jury trial for minors.

2. Consider whether or not a juvenile who would be denied a jury trial in juvenile court might be advised to agree to waive jurisdiction to adult court where a jury trial would be assured.

In re Jeffrey C.

781 A.2d 4 (N.H. 2001)

The juvenile, Jeffrey C., appeals a decision of the District Court for Southern Carroll County (*Albee,* J.) finding that RSA 169-B:19, III and III-a (Supp.1999), which authorize the confinement of juveniles to adult facilities without a jury trial, are constitutional. We vacate the dispositional order and remand.

The relevant facts follow. In September 1999, three juvenile delinquency petitions were filed with the district court alleging that Jeffrey C., then sixteen years old, had committed one count of first degree assault and two counts of criminal threatening. The court entered a finding of true on the first degree assault petition. On the criminal threatening petitions, the court entered a finding of true on one count and found that the juvenile committed the lesser-included offense of reckless conduct on the other petition.

Prior to the dispositional hearing, the juvenile filed a motion arguing that he could not be committed to the house of correction because he was not afforded a jury trial. The court denied his motion and sentenced him to the house of correction for a total of twenty-four months, with six months stand committed, nine months suspended and nine months deferred. The court ordered that the juvenile be held at the Youth Services Detention Unit and transferred to the house of correction upon his seventeenth birthday, which occurred six days after the dispositional hearing. This appeal followed.

On appeal, the juvenile asserts that RSA 169-B:19, III and III-a violate his right to a trial by jury pursuant to Part I, Article 15 of the New Hampshire Constitution and the Sixth Amendment to the United States Constitution.

We consider the defendant's argument first under the State Constitution. Because we grant relief under the State Constitution, we need not undertake a separate federal analysis.

Pursuant to statute, delinquency petitions are heard in the district court and a right to a jury trial is not provided. The court is authorized to commit juveniles to adult correctional facilities in certain instances. Specifically, RSA 169-B:19, III provides:

> A minor found to be a delinquent on a petition filed after the minor's sixteenth birthday ... may be committed to a county correctional facility for no greater term than an adult could be committed for a like offense; provided, however, that during minority the minor shall not be confined in a county correctional facility and provided further that the term shall not extend beyond the minor's eighteenth birthday.

Further, pursuant to RSA 169-B:19, III-a, if a minor has committed certain violent crimes or has been adjudicated delinquent on four or more occasions, the court may extend jurisdiction over the minor until he attains the age of twenty-one. If the court extends jurisdiction over the minor until age twenty-one, it can order that the minor be placed in an adult facility under the supervision of the department of corrections.

Part I, Article 15 of the State Constitution provides, "No subject shall be arrested, imprisoned, despoiled, or deprived of his property, immunities, or privileges, put out of the protection of the law, exiled or deprived of his life, liberty, or estate, but by the judgment of his peers, or the law of the land...." "This right to trial by jury has long been held to be the same as that enjoyed by criminal defendants at common law at the time of the adoption of the constitution." We have held that the right to a jury trial extends to all criminal defendants facing the possibility of incarceration.

We hold that RSA 169-B:19, III and RSA 169-B:19, III-a, to the extent that they authorize incarceration of juveniles in adult correctional facilities without first affording the juvenile the right to a jury trial, are unconstitutional. This conclusion is mandated by the well-settled principle that all defendants facing the possibility of incarceration are entitled to a trial by jury. Imprisonment in an adult facility fundamentally changes the nature of the underlying proceedings.

The State contends that juveniles facing imprisonment in adult correctional facilities are not entitled to jury trials because juvenile proceedings are fundamentally different from adult criminal trials. "Juvenile proceedings are designed to be more protective of minors than the adult criminal justice system, because, under the juvenile system, the purpose is not that the child shall be punished for breach of a law or regulation, but that he shall have a better chance to become a worthy citizen." Thus, "juvenile adjudications do not require jury trials because they are not criminal prosecutions." Here, the State relies on that analysis to assert that the juvenile is not entitled to a jury trial because a juvenile delinquency proceeding is not a criminal proceeding. When commitment to an adult criminal facility is permitted, however, the juvenile is constitutionally entitled to a trial by jury.

The State further asserts that the statute does provide the juvenile with the right to obtain a jury trial because RSA 169-B:26 permits a juvenile to petition the court to be tried as an adult, and thus have his case dealt with in the same manner as any other criminal prosecution. Here, the court found that the juvenile "was well counseled and had an opportunity to request that he be certified as an adult to enable him to have a jury trial." Thus, the State argues that the juvenile's failure to seek certification constitutes a waiver of the juvenile's right to a jury trial. We disagree. Should the juvenile seek certification, he would be subject to adult penalties, which would generally expose him to a significantly longer period of incarceration. We decline to hold that a juvenile who does not choose to expose himself to the possibility of many years of incarceration in the New Hampshire State Prison has waived his fundamental right to a trial by jury.

Accordingly, we hold that RSA 169-B:19, III and III-a, are unconstitutional to the extent that they authorize commitment of juveniles to adult correctional facilities without first affording them the right to a jury trial.

Dispositional order vacated; remanded.

Holdings of *In re Jeffrey C.*: The court held that the New Hampshire Constitution required the right of trial by jury in the juvenile court when the court commits the youth to an adult correctional facility.

Discussion Questions

Does the youth have a right to a jury trial any time that the court has the option to commit the minor to an adult correctional facility or is that right only present when the court actually commits the youth to such an institution?

Does the juvenile have to make a demand for a jury trial or is that right automatically extended to him by the New Hampshire court?

––––––––––

***In re L.M.*:** In *In re L.M.,* the Kansas Supreme Court was faced with a claim that the holding in *McKeiver* was no longer applicable to the juvenile delinquency proceedings in that state because the juvenile delinquency system in Kansas has become akin to the criminal system in that state.

As you read *In re L.M.,* look for the following:

1. Consider what factors are most important in finding that the juvenile system and the adult system are similar.

2. Look for anything that sheds light on whether or not the juvenile delinquency system in Kansas is adversarial in nature.

In re L.M.

286 Kan. 460, 186 P.3d 164 (2008)

L.M. seeks review of the Court of Appeals decision affirming his juvenile adjudication for aggravated sexual battery and being a minor in possession of alcohol. L.M. claims that he should have received a jury trial and argues that sweeping changes to juvenile justice procedures in Kansas since 1984 merit renewed scrutiny under applicable constitutional protections.

Sixteen-year-old L.M. was charged and prosecuted as a juvenile offender on one count of aggravated sexual battery and one count of minor in possession of alcohol. The facts leading up to these charges involve a sexually suggestive confrontation between L.M. and a neighbor who was walking home. Further discussion of the facts is not relevant to the issue on appeal and will not be discussed herein. L.M. requested a jury trial, and the district court denied his request. After a trial to the bench, the district court found L.M. guilty as charged. The district court sentenced L.M. as a Serious Offender I to a term of 18 months in a juvenile correctional facility but stayed his sentence and ordered L.M. to be placed on probation until he was 20 years old. In addition, the district court ordered L.M. to complete sex offender treatment and register as a sex offender.

L.M. appealed to the Court of Appeals, claiming that he had a constitutional right to a jury trial, that his statements to police should have been suppressed, and that the evidence was insufficient to support his convictions.

L.M. is challenging the constitutionality of K.S.A.2006 Supp. 38-2344(d), which provides that a juvenile who pleads not guilty is entitled to a "trial to the court," and K.S.A.2006 Supp. 38-2357, and which gives the district court complete discretion in determining whether a juvenile should be granted a jury trial.

United States Constitution

L.M.'s first argument relies on the Sixth Amendment to the United States Constitution, which provides in pertinent part:

"In all criminal prosecutions, the accused shall enjoy the right to a speedy and public trial, by an impartial jury of the State and district wherein the crime shall have been committed...."

L.M. further relies on the United States Constitution's Fourteenth Amendment Due Process Clause, which provides in relevant part:

"No State shall make or enforce any law which shall abridge the privileges or immunities of citizens of the United States; nor shall any State deprive any person of life, liberty, or property without due process of law...."

Kansas has previously resolved this issue against L.M.'s position. Twenty-four years ago, under the statutes then controlling the disposition of juvenile offender cases, this court held that juveniles do not have a constitutional right to a jury trial under either the federal or state constitutions. Acknowledging that the Sixth Amendment applies only to criminal prosecutions, the *Findlay* court concluded that juvenile adjudications then were not criminal prosecutions based on K.S.A.1982 Supp. 38-1601, which provided:

"'K.S.A.1982 Supp. 38-1601 through 38-1685 shall be known and may be cited as the Kansas juvenile offenders code and shall be liberally construed to the end that each juvenile coming within its provisions shall receive the care, custody, guidance, control and discipline, preferably in the juvenile's own home, as will best serve the juvenile's rehabilitation and the protection of society. In no case shall any order, judgment or decree of the district court, in any proceedings under the provisions of this code, be deemed or held to import a criminal act on the part of any juvenile; but all proceedings, orders, judgments and decrees shall be deemed to have been taken and done in the exercise of the parental power of the state.'

The Findlay court also adopted the United States Supreme Court's reasoning in *McKeiver v. Pennsylvania,* where a plurality of the Court held that juveniles are not entitled to a jury trial under the Sixth and Fourteenth Amendments to the Constitution.

L.M. recognizes the import of *Findlay* and *McKeiver* but asks us to overturn *Findlay*. L.M. raises three arguments to support his request. First, L.M. claims that the changes in the Revised Kansas Juvenile Justice Code (KJJC) have eroded the child-cognizant, paternal, and rehabilitative purposes of the juvenile offender process, thereby requiring us to recognize a juvenile's right to a jury trial under the federal Constitution. Second, L.M. argues that juveniles are entitled to a jury trial under the Kansas Constitution. Third, L.M. asserts that regardless of whether all juveniles are constitutionally entitled to a jury, he should have received one because he ran the risk of having to register as a sex offender.

We begin our analysis by noting that the Kansas Legislature has significantly changed the language of the Kansas Juvenile Offender Code (KJOC) since the *Findlay* court decided this issue 24 years ago. The juvenile code is now called the Revised Kansas Juvenile Justice Code. L.M. asserts that these changes to the code negated the rehabilitative purpose set forth in the KJOC. According to L.M., the negating of the rehabilitative purpose is evidenced by the replacement of nonpunitive terminology with criminal terminology similar to the adult criminal code, the alignment of the KJJC sentencing provisions with the adult sentencing guidelines, and the removal of the protections that the McKeiver Court relied on to distinguish juvenile systems from the adult criminal systems.

In 1982, the KJOC was focused on rehabilitation and the State's parental role in providing guidance, control, and discipline. However, under the KJJC, the focus has shifted to protecting the public, holding juveniles accountable for their behavior and choices, and making juveniles more productive and responsible members of society. These purposes are more aligned with the legislative intent for the adult sentencing statutes, which include protecting the public by incarcerating dangerous offenders for a long period of time, holding offenders accountable by prescribing appropriate consequences for their actions, and encouraging offenders to be more productive members of society by considering their individual characteristics, circumstances, needs, and potentialities in determining their sentences.

In addition to being more aligned with the purpose of the criminal sentencing statutes, the KJJC also incorporates language similar to that found in the Kansas Criminal Code.

The legislature also emulated the structure of the Kansas Sentencing Guidelines when it established a sentencing matrix for juveniles based on the level of the offense committed and, in some cases, the juvenile's history of juvenile adjudications.

In addition to reflecting the provisions of the sentencing guidelines, the KJJC also establishes sentencing options that are similar to those available for adult offenders.

Besides amending the 1982 version of the KJOC to reflect the purpose and provisions included in the adult criminal code, the legislature has removed some of the protective provisions that made the juvenile system more child-cognizant and confidential, a key consideration in the *McKeiver* plurality decision. In 1982, juvenile proceedings were confidential. The official court file and all police records of any juvenile under the age of 16 were not open to the public. Likewise, any hearing involving a juvenile under the age of 16 was confidential and the court could exclude anyone except the juvenile; his or her parents; the attorneys of any interested parties; officers of the court; and any testifying witness.

However, under the KJJC, the official file must be open to the public unless a judge orders it to be closed for juveniles under the age of 14 based on finding that it is in the best interests of the juvenile. Similarly, law enforcement records and municipal court records for any juvenile age 14 and over are subject to the same disclosure restrictions as the records for adults. Only juveniles under the age of 14 may have their law enforcement and municipal records kept confidential. The legislature has also eliminated the presumption of confidentiality for hearings, opening all hearings to the public unless the juvenile is under the age of 16 and the judge concludes that a public hearing would not be in the juvenile's best interests.

These changes to the juvenile justice system have eroded the benevolent parens patriae character that distinguished it from the adult criminal system. The United States Supreme Court relied on the juvenile justice system's characteristics of fairness, concern, sympathy, and paternal attention in concluding that juveniles were not entitled to a jury trial. Likewise, this court relied on that parens patriae character in reaching its decision in *Findlay*. However, because the juvenile justice system is now patterned after the adult criminal system, we conclude that the changes have superseded the *McKeiver* and *Findlay* Courts' reasoning and those decisions are no longer binding precedent for us to follow. Based on our conclusion that the Kansas juvenile justice system has become more akin to an adult criminal prosecution, we hold that juveniles have a constitutional right to a jury trial under the Sixth and Fourteenth Amendments. As a result, K.S.A.2006 Supp. 38-2344(d), which provides that a juvenile who pleads not guilty is entitled to a "trial to the court," and K.S.A.2006 Supp. 38-2357, which gives the district court discretion in determining whether a juvenile should be granted a jury trial, are unconstitutional.

In reaching this conclusion, we are mindful of decisions in other jurisdictions rejecting the argument that changes to the juvenile justice system have altered its parens patriae character.

We are also mindful that many of the state courts that have addressed this issue in one form or another have declined to extend the constitutional right to a jury trial to juveniles.

While there is wide variability in the juvenile offender laws throughout the country, it nevertheless seems apparent to us that the KJJC, in its tilt towards applying adult standards of criminal procedure and sentencing, removed the paternalistic protections previously accorded juveniles while continuing to deny those juveniles the constitutional right to a jury trial. Although we do not find total support from the courts in some of our sister states, we are undaunted in our belief that juveniles are entitled to the right to a jury trial guaranteed to all citizens under the Sixth and Fourteenth Amendments to the United States Constitution.

Kansas Constitution

In addition to claiming a federal constitutional right to a jury trial, L.M. asserts that he has a right to a jury trial under the Kansas Constitution. L.M. relies on the Kansas Constitution Bill of Rights, Sections 1, 5, and 10, which provide:

§ 1. "All men are possessed of equal and inalienable natural rights, among which are life, liberty, and the pursuit of happiness."

§ 5. "The right of trial by jury shall be inviolate."

§ 10. "In all prosecutions, the accused shall be allowed to appear and defend in person, or by counsel; to demand the nature and cause of the accusation against him; to meet the witness face to face, and to have compulsory process to compel the attendance of the witnesses in his behalf, and a speedy public trial by an impartial jury of the county or district in which the offense is alleged to have been committed. No person shall be a witness against himself, or be twice put in jeopardy for the same offense." (Emphasis added.)

The plain language of § 10 extends the right to a jury trial to "all prosecutions." This court has previously interpreted the phrase "all prosecutions" to "mean all criminal prosecutions for violations of the laws of the state."

The KJJC repeatedly refers to its proceedings as a prosecution. In addition, proceedings under the KJJC are based on allegations that juveniles have violated the criminal laws of this State. Because the KJJC has lost the parens patriae character of the former KJOC and has transformed into a system for prosecuting juveniles charged with committing crimes, we conclude that the proceedings under the KJJC fit within the meaning of the phrase "all prosecutions" as set forth in § 10, and juveniles have a right to a jury trial under the Kansas Constitution. Consequently, K.S.A.2006 Supp. 38-2344(d) and K.S.A.2006 Supp. 38-2357 are also unconstitutional under the Kansas Constitution.

As a third argument, L.M. asserts that even if all juveniles are not entitled to a jury trial, he should have received a jury trial because he was subject to registering as a sex offender, an adult sanction. Given our decision that juveniles have a right to a jury trial under the Sixth and Fourteenth Amendments to the federal Constitution and the Kansas Constitution, we decline to analyze this argument.

Because L.M. was tried without a jury, his adjudication is reversed and this matter is remanded to the district court for a new trial before a jury.

Reversed.

LUCKERT, J., concurring:

I concur in the majority's conclusion that L.M. has a constitutional right to trial by jury, but I base this conclusion on the rights guaranteed by § 5 of the Kansas Constitution Bill of Rights rather than the Sixth Amendment to the United States Constitution or § 10 of the Kansas Constitution Bill of Rights, which are relied upon by the majority.

McFARLAND, C.J., dissenting:

I respectfully dissent from the majority's decision holding that changes to the juvenile offender system over the last couple of decades have eroded the protective, rehabilitative features of that system to the point that it has become akin to the adult criminal system and, therefore, juvenile offenders are now constitutionally entitled to a jury trial.

In *McKeiver v. Pennsylvania*, the United States Supreme Court held that the Due Process Clause of the Fourteenth Amendment does not require the states to provide a jury trial in a juvenile offender proceeding. The decision was based on the recognition that the juvenile system is fundamentally different from the adult criminal system in that its focus is rehabilitation, not punishment. This goal is pursued through less formal, more individualized, paternalistic, protective proceedings than those in the adult criminal system.

Thirteen years after *McKeiver*, the newly enacted Kansas Juvenile Offenders Code was the subject of a challenge similar to the one presently before the court.

The majority acknowledges this precedent, but holds that the benevolent, protective, parens patriae characteristics of the juvenile system that the United States Supreme Court relied on in *McKeiver* to distinguish it from adult criminal prosecutions have been so eroded by legislative changes over the years that the current system is more geared toward prosecuting and punishing juveniles in a manner akin to the adult criminal system. Thus, the rationale underlying *McKeiver* and *Findlay* no longer applies and juveniles therefore must be afforded the right to trial by jury under the Sixth and Fourteenth Amendments to the United States Constitution and under § 10 of the Kansas Constitution Bill of Rights.

I disagree. Although it cannot be disputed that in the 20-plus years since *Findlay*, the juvenile system has become more punitive and has incorporated some of the terminology and mechanisms of the adult criminal system, the majority overstates and overemphasizes the changes while ignoring the many features of the current system that remain consistent with the benevolent, protective, rehabilitative, child-cognizant characteristics that distinguish the juvenile system from the criminal system. The protective, rehabilitative focus that has distinguished the juvenile system from the punitive, retributive adult criminal system is still very much alive.

The majority contends that the current juvenile system has changed to be more in line with the adult criminal system in four ways: (1) the policy goals of the juvenile system have shifted from rehabilitation to protection of the public and accountability, goals more akin to those underlying the criminal system; (2) the current juvenile code uses language similar to that used in the criminal codes; (3) juveniles are now subject to determinative sentencing that closely resembles the sentencing guidelines for adults, and the sentencing options available for juvenile offenders are analogous to those available in the adult sentencing system; and (4) some of the protective confidentiality features of the former juvenile system have been eliminated.

First, the majority points to changes in the policy goals of the juvenile system. The majority contends the amendments in the stated goals evidence a shift from rehabilitation and the State's parental role in providing care, custody, guidance, control, and discipline to protecting the public, holding juveniles accountable, and making juveniles more productive and responsible members of society. What the majority disregards, however, is that in 1982, protection of the public, along with rehabilitation, was an express goal of the juvenile system.

Although the new statute is much more specific about how its goals will be accomplished, the basic goals of protecting the public and rehabilitating juvenile offenders, i.e., improving the ability of juveniles to live more productively and responsibly in the community, remain consistent.

That statute makes it clear that in the adult sentencing system, the focus is on the protection of the public through long terms of confinement for dangerous offenders, with imposition of lesser sanctions only where consistent with public safety and the welfare of the offender. There is no language suggesting that rehabilitation is one of the goals of the adult sentencing system.

The majority concludes that the current juvenile code incorporates language similar to that found in the adult system, thus stressing the similarities between juvenile and adult offenders over their differences.

Clearly some of the terminology has changed. And labels are important to some extent — hence the retention of the term adjudication instead of the term conviction. Nevertheless, form must not be placed over substance. If a change in terminology does not reflect any substantive change in the thing or process described, then too much emphasis should not be placed on that terminology. The facilities denominated as state youth centers, and now juvenile correctional facilities, are one and the same. Regardless of their names, these facilities have always been institutions where juvenile offenders are sent to serve a period of court-ordered confinement.

The majority contends that the sentencing scheme and the options available are now more like those in the adult criminal system. Specifically, the majority notes that juveniles now have determinate presumptive sentencing under a matrix that is based on the offense committed and the juvenile's unique adjudicatory history. And, the majority notes that, like the adult sentencing scheme under the guidelines grid, the current allows the juvenile judge to depart upward from the presumptive matrix upon finding that substantial and compelling reasons support departure. In determining whether to depart, the court may consider the nonexclusive list of aggravating factors set forth in the adult guidelines.

Significant differences remain between the two systems that are overlooked by the majority. First, the majority's analysis fails to take into account the difference in the severity of the sentences juveniles face under the matrix for the same crime committed by an adult offender. The KJJC also does not allow imposition of consecutive sentences. Additionally, the maximum term of commitment of any juvenile to a juvenile correctional facility is age 22 years, 6 months.

Second, in contrast to the adult sentencing guidelines, the sentences provided under the juvenile sentencing matrix are not mandatory. Commitment to a juvenile correctional facility for a term under the matrix is only one of a number of sentencing alternatives available to a juvenile judge. Thus, the judge has discretion in deciding whether to sentence a juvenile to a juvenile correctional facility. If that option is chosen, however, the court must impose the applicable sentence specified in the matrix. While the court may depart upward, downward departures are not authorized, presumably because a commitment to a juvenile correctional facility is discretionary in the first instance.

Another compelling difference is the power given to the juvenile judge to modify the sentence after it has been imposed — a power that does not exist under the adult sentencing guidelines.

The discretionary sentencing provisions and the modification provisions are unique to the juvenile system and are a clear expression of the legislature's continued belief in the juvenile system as an individualized, protective, and rehabilitative process.

Additionally, the majority notes that the current juvenile code imposes a term of aftercare on juveniles sentenced to a term of confinement under the matrix. This, the majority contends, reflects the adult sentencing guidelines postrelease provisions. A postrelease period of supervision is not new to the juvenile system.

The majority also mentions that the KJJC now provides the opportunity for good time credits, just like the adult system. I fail to see how providing a benefit to juveniles — even if it is the same benefit provided to incarcerated adult offenders — is really relevant to the issue of whether the new juvenile system is no longer the individualized, protective, rehabilitative system that it was when *Findlay* was decided. How would denying juveniles good time credits better serve a benevolent, paternalistic purpose?

The majority also fails to consider the importance of extended jurisdiction juvenile prosecution. Extended jurisdiction juvenile prosecution became effective in 1997 and is a mechanism whereby serious or repeat juvenile offenders who might otherwise have been waived up to adult court may remain in the juvenile sentencing system. In an extended jurisdiction juvenile prosecution, the court imposes both a juvenile and an adult sentence. The adult sentence is stayed as long as the juvenile complies with and completes the conditions of the juvenile sentence. If, however, the juvenile violates the conditions of the juvenile sentence, the juvenile sentence is revoked, the adult sentence is imposed, and the juvenile court transfers jurisdiction of the case to adult court. Because a juvenile in an extended jurisdiction prosecution may end up in adult court with an adult sentence, the right to trial by jury is provided by statute. Extended jurisdiction juvenile prosecution is important to the issue at hand because it evidences a last-ditch effort to extend the favorable protections of juvenile court and the benefits of its less severe sentences to juvenile offenders who previously would have been waived to adult court.

The majority contends that the sentencing options available to the juvenile judge are much more akin to those available for adult offenders. The court notes that juvenile offenders, like adult offenders, may be sentenced to probation; a community-based program; house arrest; a sanctions house, which the majority likens to conservation camps; placement in an out-of-home facility; and incarceration. In addition, the court may order both adults and juveniles to attend counseling; drug and alcohol evaluations; mediation; and educational programs. The court may also order both juveniles and adults to perform charitable or community service, pay restitution, and pay fines.

This broad overview overlooks the many unique features of the juvenile system that emphasize family and community involvement, early intervention diversionary procedures, flexibility to accommodate individualized needs of juveniles upon intake into the system, preference for noncustodial placements, graduated sanctions with preferences for the least-restrictive alternatives, and, above all, rehabilitation.

The juvenile system has unique pre-charge intake and intervention procedures: the Juvenile Intake and Assessment Program and the intermediate intervention program.

The importance of these unique intake and intervention procedures to the issue at hand cannot be dismissed. As Justice White noted in *McKeiver*: "To the extent that the jury is a buffer to the corrupt or overzealous prosecutor in the criminal law system, the distinctive intake policies and procedures of the juvenile court system to a great extent obviate this important function of the jury."

A dispositional feature unique to the juvenile system is its preference for maintaining the family unit. Under the KJJC, the court must make specific findings that reasonable efforts were made to maintain the family unit or that an emergency exists before a juvenile may be removed from the home, whether for detention, placement in the custody of the commissioner, or commitment to a juvenile correctional facility. An order removing a juvenile from the home may be made if the juvenile presents a risk to public safety.

It appears the legislature required these findings in an effort to comply with the provisions of the federal Adoption and Safe Families Act of 1997. However, it must be noted that this statutory preference for maintaining the family unit is consistent with the policy stated in K.S.A.1982 Supp. 38-1601: "[The code] shall be liberally construed to the end that each juvenile coming within its provisions shall receive the care, custody, guidance, control and discipline, preferably in the juvenile's own home, as will best serve the juvenile's rehabilitation and the protection of society."

In line with this emphasis on maintaining the family unit, the KJJC also requires that when a juvenile is placed out of the home, a permanency plan must be prepared which provides for reintegration or, if reintegration is not a viable option, for some other permanent placement. The court must conduct a review every 6 months of the progress being made toward permanency.

Another significant difference between the adult system and the juvenile system is the court-appointed special advocate (CASA). In 1994, the legislature provided for the appointment of a CASA—formerly a feature unique to child in need of care cases—in juvenile offender cases. The CASA's primary duty is to advocate for the juvenile's bests interests.

The addition of local citizen review boards to the juvenile process is also a feature not found in the adult criminal system. Under K.S.A.2006 Supp. 38-2308(a), judges may refer juvenile offender cases to the local citizen review board for the purpose of determining the progress that has been made toward rehabilitation and making recommendations regarding further actions on the case.

Additionally, and most importantly, the KJJC not only emphasizes, but requires, parental involvement in the entire process. Intake and assessment workers may require parents to participate in programs and services as a condition of the juvenile's release back home. The county or district attorney is authorized to require parents to be a part of any immediate intervention program. Parents served with a summons are required to attend all proceedings involving the juvenile unless excused by the court. The court has the power to require parents to participate in counseling, mediation, alcohol and drug evaluations and treatment programs, and parenting classes. The court also has the power to order parents to report violations of conditions of probation or conditional release and may order them to aid the court in enforcing the court's orders. Violation may result in contempt sanctions.

This emphasis on parental involvement is not merely incidental to the fact the juvenile offender is a child, but is, instead, part of the family and community centered approach to juvenile rehabilitation.

The majority also contends that juvenile proceedings and records no longer have the confidentiality protections they did in 1982. The majority points to provisions concerning public access to juvenile court hearings and confidentiality of records. With respect to juvenile hearings, there is little practical difference between the KJOC provisions in 1982 and the current KJJC provisions. The KJOC required that juvenile court hearings be open to the public if the juvenile was 16 years of age or older at the time of the alleged offense. For a juvenile under age 16, the court had discretion to close the hearing. Under the current KJJC, all hearings are open to the public, but in the case of juveniles under the age of 16, the court has discretion to close the hearing.

With respect to confidentiality of juvenile records, there are only two differences between the KJOC and the KJJC. First, the age of protection was lowered from 15 to 13.

Second, with respect to the official court file only, the file is now open for public inspection unless, in the case of a juvenile who is under age 14, the judge determines that public inspection is not in the juvenile's best interests. Previously, the official file of a juvenile under the age of 16 was privileged and not subject to disclosure to anyone other than the court, the parties and their attorneys, an agency or institution with custody of the juvenile, law enforcement, or upon court order.

The changes to the juvenile code cited by the majority have not so eroded the features of the juvenile system that distinguish it from the adult system that it can be said that the rationale underlying *McKeiver* and *Findlay* is no longer valid. The new system continues to further the goals that have always characterized the modern juvenile system: protection of the public and rehabilitation. As the Criminal Justice Coordinating Council's Juvenile Task Force noted in its report to the legislature in 1995, these two goals are not incompatible. Given the fact that the juvenile system must deal with serious, violent, and habitual offenders, it is entirely appropriate that the juvenile system balance rehabilitation with protection of the public.

The incorporation of certain aspects of the adult sentencing scheme for the most violent and chronic juvenile offenders is a critical part of meeting the obligation to protect the community from these offenders. However, the legislature, in choosing to make sentencing under the matrix a discretionary sentencing option, kept in place the individualized sentencing flexibility that has always been characteristic of the juvenile system. In addition, in creating extended juvenile jurisdiction, the legislature extended the protective net of the juvenile system as a last-ditch effort for those juveniles who would otherwise be prosecuted and sentenced as adults. These key features demonstrate the legislature's effort to carefully balance protection of the public with the goal of rehabilitating youthful offenders.

The dual goals of the juvenile system that commanded its process in 1982 are very much alive and well. The juvenile system still retains significant individualized, protective, rehabilitative, child-cognizant features that distinguish it from the adult system and which allow it to operate toward achieving those goals.

I must also note that the majority's decision is contrary to the weight of authority. The argument the majority accepts in this case has been rejected by the overwhelming majority of courts that have considered it.

With no persuasive authority from other jurisdictions, and a less than comprehensive analysis of the current system, the majority concludes that the Kansas juvenile justice system is the essential equivalent of the adult criminal justice system and, thus, the right to trial by jury must be afforded. To what end? As the United States Supreme Court recognized in *McKeiver*, imposing the constitutional right to trial by jury on the juvenile court system would not greatly strengthen the fact-finding function, but would erode the juvenile court's ability to function in a unique manner, and "remake the juvenile proceeding into a fully adversary process and ... put an effective end to what has been the idealistic prospect of an intimate, informal protective proceeding." "If the formalities of the criminal adjudicative system are to be superimposed upon the juvenile court system, there is little need for its separate existence."

The experiment has not failed. The majority has overlooked the most significant features of the juvenile system that distinguish it from the adult system—features that promote protection of the public while not only preserving, but furthering, the individualized, protective, rehabilitative character unique to the juvenile system. It does not embrace a purely punitive or retributive philosophy. Instead, it attempts to tread an equatorial line somewhere midway between the poles of rehabilitation and retribution.

For these reasons, I dissent.

Holdings of *In re L.M.*: The court held that the Kansas juvenile justice system has become more akin to an adult criminal prosecution, and, therefore, juveniles have a constitutional right to a jury trial under the Sixth and Fourteenth Amendment, as well as under the Kansas Constitution.

Discussion Questions

If the juvenile system really has moved away from a benevolent *parens patriae* system to a more adversarial system, should age alone be enough to deny the right to a jury trial?

If a juvenile is constitutionally entitled to a "jury of his peers," would that mean that the jurors must also be minors or can a juvenile's right to a jury trial be protected if only adults are allowed to serve on the jury?

Key Concepts: Right to a Jury Trial

• The United States Supreme Court, in *McKeiver v. Pennsylvania,* held that the Constitution does not require that a minor have the right to a jury trial in delinquency proceedings.

• While the vast majority of states follow the *McKeiver* ruling and deny a minor a jury trial in delinquency proceedings, some states have given minors such rights when the state proceedings or sanctions have become virtually identical to adult criminal proceedings.

Key Concepts: Court Hearings: Constitutional Minimums for Delinquency Hearings

• Juveniles are entitled to some due process protections in delinquency hearings, but their due process rights are not identical to the rights of adults in criminal cases.

• Juveniles are entitled to notice of charges which must be given sufficiently in advance of scheduled court proceedings so that reasonable opportunity to prepare will be afforded, and it must set forth the alleged misconduct with particularity.

• In cases where the youth may be committed to an institution, a juvenile is entitled to the right to counsel, and, if unable to afford counsel, that counsel will be appointed to represent the child.

• The constitutional privilege against self-incrimination is applicable in the case of juveniles.

• Absent a valid plea, confrontation and sworn testimony by witnesses available for cross-examination are essential for a finding of delinquency.

• Juveniles are not entitled to trial by jury in juvenile delinquency cases.

• In order to adjudicate a juvenile to be a delinquent, the state must establish the guilt of the juvenile by proof of beyond a reasonable doubt.

• Juveniles may be subject to preventive detention so long as procedures are afforded that provide sufficient protection against erroneous and unnecessary deprivations of liberty.

Practical Questions: Court Hearings: Constitutional Minimums for Delinquency Hearings

1. Michael Swanson, age 16, comes into your office asking you to represent him on two offenses filed in juvenile court: the first is a theft charge (shoplifting) that occurred 3 weeks ago; and the second was a possession of a controlled substance (marijuana) charge that occurred two years ago. You ask him about the drug charge, and he tells you that two years ago he was at a concert where he was caught with a "joint." At the time, he was arrested, handcuffed, and taken to detention for two days when he was released. The case was "adjusted" with a juvenile officer telling him that if he "stayed clean" until he reached 18, no charges would ever be filed. Because of the shoplifting charge, they have now also

charged him with the old marijuana charge. Has Michael's Sixth and Fourteenth Amendment constitutional rights to a "speedy trial" been violated?

2. In your city, someone has been painting swastikas on all of the Jewish Synagogues. A 17-year-old self-proclaimed "skinhead" has been charged with a hate crime in juvenile court. State law declares juvenile actions to be confidential and the public is not allowed to attend adjudicatory hearings. A newspaper editor contacts you to represent them in an action to allow a reporter to attend and report on the trial. The editor tells you, "We have a right to be there. The Sixth Amendment guarantees that trials are 'public.'" What do you tell him?

Chapter X

Dispositional Options Available in Juvenile Court

Overview: Once a juvenile has been adjudicated a delinquent, the three primary options available to a juvenile court judge for disposition are: probation, out-of-home placement and institutional confinement. Courts have also begun to use "blended" sentencing (a combination of dispositional alternatives from both the juvenile courts and the criminal courts). Most states have statutory requirements that the court order the least restrictive alternative that is appropriate for the case and for the youth. The most common dispositional option is probation, and juvenile courts have been granted great leeway in fashioning terms of probation that the court feels is appropriate for the particular offense and the particular youth involved. Some of the terms of probation ordered by the courts have been extremely creative. More common terms of probation include school attendance, community service and restitution. If the juvenile violates the terms of probation, a probation revocation hearing is held. The standard of proof for a probation violation varies among states from preponderance of the evidence, to clear and convincing evidence, and even to proof beyond a reasonable doubt. Courts may also sanction violation of the terms of probation by means of contempt of court.

In the Matter of Janice Westbrooks: In *In the Matter of Janice Westbrooks*, the South Carolina Supreme Court was asked to decide whether or not a juvenile could be sentenced to "indefinite probation" as a dispositional order.

As you read *In the Matter of Janice Westbrooks,* look for the reasoning of the lower court in failing to set a term for the probationary period.

In the Matter of Janice Westbrooks
277 S.C. 410, 288 S.E.2d 395 (1982)

Appellant was adjudicated delinquent as a result of a shoplifting charge filed against her in Family Court. The judge ordered her to perform thirty (30) hours of community service and placed her on indefinite probation. Appellant contends the lower court erred by placing her on indefinite probation. We disagree and affirm.

Section 14-21-620 of the 1976 Code sets forth the alternative dispositions available to a family court judge after a minor has been adjudicated delinquent. When a child is adjudicated delinquent by the Family Court, he may be punished only as prescribed by the Family Court Act.

According to Section 14-21-620, the court may place the child on probation or under supervision in his own home or in the custody of a suitable person, upon such conditions as the court may determine. Section 14-21-620 further provides that probation shall be ordered and administered as a measure for the protection, guidance and well-being of the child and his family.

The family court is vested with broad discretion in imposing the conditions of probation. The length of the probationary period constitutes a condition of probation within the lower court's discretion. We find no abuse of that discretion. Clearly, the court could not impose probation to extend beyond appellant's twenty-first birthday because the jurisdiction of the Family Court terminates when a child becomes twenty-one. Therefore, the probationary period would end on appellant's twenty-first birthday.

While we find no abuse of discretion in this instance, we are of the opinion that the better practice would be to set a definite period of probation. The order of the lower court is affirmed.

Holdings of *In the Matter of Janice Westbrooks:* The court affirmed the ruling of the lower court and found that, while it would be better for a court to set a term for a probation period, the court does have the power to order "indefinite probation."

Discussion Questions

Why would the court have the power to keep a youth on probation for years when the crime is minor (in this case, shoplifting)?

J.R.D. v. Commonwealth: In *J.R.D. v. Commonwealth,* the Kentucky Court of Appeals was faced with a case where the juvenile, beginning at the age of 14 was charged with a number of juvenile charges, many being status offenses (such as being "beyond the control of her parents" and being an "habitual truant"). Some of the orders of the court in response to the allegations included such things as completing 40 hours of community service, not leaving home without custodial permission, copying the entire driver's manual by hand, having no unexcused absences from school, complying with a "zero-hour curfew," and obeying all home rules. The court found her in contempt on the habitual truant violation and ordered the minor to long term residential treatment. The youth appealed the decision.

As you read *J.R.D. v. Commonwealth,* look for the following:

1. Observe the unusual options that the court imposed on the minor for violations of status offense laws.

2. Consider whether the Court has the power to sentence a youth into placement even though the acts of the juvenile were not "criminal" in nature.

3. Notice the use of contempt powers to "sidestep" restrictions on penalties for commission of a status offense.

J.R.D. v. Commonwealth
2006 WL 3040845 (Ky. App. 2006)

J.R.D., a juvenile status offender, has appealed from the Boyle Family Court's December 7, 2006, order committing her to the Cabinet for Families and Children with the recommendation that she complete a residential treatment program at Ramey-Estep Homes. J.R.D. asserts that the family court improperly committed her to the Cabinet for finding her in contempt of a status offender order, while the Commonwealth maintains that her commitment was as a result of her being a habitual truant. We affirm.

The record in this case consists of four separate juvenile complaints/petitions filed against J.R.D. The mother filed the first complaint/petition on May 1, 2003, when J.R.D.

was fourteen years old. The mother called the police after J.R.D. attacked her sister, as a result of which she was taken into custody and later charged with Assault 4th-Domestic pursuant to KRS 508.030. She was conditionally released after a detention hearing, and the matter was eventually resolved. The mother also filed the second complaint the same date, alleging that J.R.D. was beyond the control of her parents in violation of KRS 630.020(2) and citing J.R.D.'s disrespectful attitude and her refusal to obey house rules. That status offense charge was later dismissed without prejudice on the Commonwealth's motion.

The third, two-part petition was filed by a Danville police officer on September 5, 2003. The grounds for the petition were an August 22, 2003, motor vehicle accident during which J.R.D. hit a parked van in a parking lot and left the scene of the accident. J.R.D. did not have an operator's license at the time. She was cited for both offenses. At a later conference, J.R.D. admitted to the offense of leaving the scene of the accident, and was ordered to complete forty hours of community service and to pay restitution to the owner of the van she damaged. The charge of not having an operator's license was to be dismissed if she copied the driver's manual by hand. A docket order dated December 4, 2003, indicated that J.R.D. had been suspended from school, in violation of the conditions of her release. For this reason, we assume, the family court stated that any violation of the conditions of release before the next scheduled hearing date in January 2004 would result in her immediate pick-up.

On December 18, 2003, Chuck Stallard of Danville Schools filed an affidavit stating that J.R.D. had continued to be defiant to authority and had skipped class. Based upon this affidavit, the family court entered a pick-up order that day. A detention hearing was held on December 29, 2003, when J.R.D. admitted to the two pending allegations of contempt. The family court imposed a zero-hour curfew and scheduled a disposition hearing for January 15, 2004. At the disposition hearing, the family court probated J.R.D. to the court until she reached her eighteenth birthday. A third contempt affidavit was filed on October 19, 2004, which indicated that J.R.D. had been kicked out of school, but the summons was never successfully served. At one of the scheduled show cause hearings, the family court learned that J.R.D. was being home-schooled.

Prior to the filing of the contempt charges resulting from the third petition, Chuck Stallard filed the fourth complaint/petition on November 25, 2003, for which J.R.D. was charged with the status offense of Habitual Truancy pursuant to KRS 630.020(3). J.R.D. obtained appointed counsel and denied the allegations at her arraignment on January 7, 2004. At the conclusion of the January 7th court appearance, the family court entered a Juvenile Status Offender Order, stating that J.R.D. was alleged to be a status offender relating to Habitual Truancy, found that it had jurisdiction over her, and ordered her to comply with several conditions. These conditions required her to not leave home without custodial permission; to obey all home rules (including the imposition of a zero hour curfew); to attend school on time, have no unexcused absences, and have no behavior problems at school; to not violate the law; and to not consume alcohol, or to use or possess any alcohol, tobacco products or illegal drugs. The Status Offender Order also warned that "[f]ailure to abide by this Order may result in a contempt finding being made against you by the court which could result in a fine and/or your being placed in a secure detention or other alternative placement[.]" An adjudication hearing was scheduled for February 25, 2004.

By February 11, 2004, J.R.D. had already violated the terms of the Status Offender Order. Her father filed an affidavit that day indicating that she was "running the streets, skipping school, staying gone for days and according to the police associating with the 'wrong' people." The family court ordered J.R.D. to be picked up and detained, and held a detention hearing on February 16th. J.R.D. admitted to the contempt, and the family court sentenced her to 10 days in detention, credited her for two days served, and probated the balance on the condition that she abide by the terms of the Status Offender Order.

At the February 25, 2004, adjudication hearing on the habitual truancy charge, J.R.D. admitted to being a habitual truant. The family court ordered the Cabinet to complete and file a Pre-Dispositional Investigation Report, and set the matter for a disposition hearing on March 31, 2004. Pursuant to the order, the Cabinet filed the PDI report in which it recommended that J.R.D. enter a long-term residential treatment program. According to its recommendation, such treatment would provide her with the means to become more responsible for her behavior, and would allow her to develop and demonstrate a healthy sense of respect for social norms and the rights of others. At the disposition hearing, the family court indicated that it was ready to remove J.R.D. from her home based upon the Cabinet's report. However, the Cabinet amended its recommendation, stating that it wanted to open a six-month case on the family and have J.R.D. probated to the Cabinet as opposed to placed into its custody. Based upon this amended recommendation, the family court opted to probate J.R.D. to the Cabinet until her eighteenth birthday under the terms of the previously entered Status Offender Order. The family court specifically stated that if the situation did not improve, she could be removed from her family.

On September 14, 2004, the family court heard this case on a second contempt charge, this one arising from information the court had recently learned in a domestic violence action involving J.R.D.'s estranged parents. During the domestic violence hearing, a social worker testified that J.R.D. had been drinking alcohol. During the course of the juvenile court appearance, the family court learned that J.R.D. had been removed from Danville High School, was in a GED program and was being home-schooled (all which would technically be violations of the status offender order.) The mother also indicated that a few days earlier J.R.D. had returned home drunk. She filed an affidavit to this effect later that day. At the conclusion of the hearing, the family court found that the Status Offender Order was in full force and effect and adopted the terms of a Prevention Plan entered a few days previously in the domestic violence case. The family court then entered a new Juvenile Status Offender Order, adding several additional conditions, including that J.R.D. enroll in and attend day treatment/GED track, that she be permitted to work at her mother's discretion, and that she be assessed for drug/alcohol abuse through Comprehensive Care. The Status Offender Order again warned that any failure to abide by its terms may result in a finding of contempt.

As J.R.D.'s mother was driving them home from the September 14th court appearance, J.R.D. became upset when she was not permitted to visit with her father that evening. As a result, J.R.D. punched the windshield while her mother was driving, causing it to break. The mother pulled over, called the police, had J.R.D. placed into detention, and returned to court to file a new affidavit detailing J.R.D.'s actions.

The family court held a detention hearing on September 15, 2004, on the new contempt charge. At the conclusion of the hearing, the family court entered the following order:

> Court finds probable cause to believe that child has committed the offense of contempt of court for violation of Status Offender Order. The Court further finds based upon the fact, that if found ultimately to be in contempt it would be the child's third contempt allegation and second finding. Further, the child is alleged to have committed the offense within an hour of her court appearance on 9/14/2005. Accordingly, the Court finds that detention at this time is in the child's best interests. In so finding the Court has determined that there was a

valid status offender order in place at the time the alleged offense was committed. The Court has also directed that CHFS file a written report, copy to court and counsel by Tues., September 20, 2005 as required in KRS 610.265(2)(b)4.c. PTC set for October 12, 2005.

At the October 12, 2005, pretrial conference, the family court ordered the Cabinet to open a case on the family, stated that all prior orders were to remain in effect, and reset the case on the contempt issue for December 7, 2005.

On October 31, 2005, Cabinet employee Scott Helm filed an affidavit stating that J.R.D. tested positive for marijuana during an October 18th drug test. J.R.D. was again picked up and placed in detention. At the detention hearing on November 3, 2005, J.R.D. admitted the contempt and that there was probable cause for the pick up. As an alternate to detention, and pursuant to the parties' agreement, the family court placed J.R.D. in the temporary custody of the Cabinet for transportation that day to Ramey-Estep Homes for in-patient treatment. The family court then set a disposition hearing on this contempt charges for the previously set December 7th show cause hearing on the other two pending contempt charges, and ordered the Cabinet to file another PDI report.

At the December 7, 2005, court date, the Cabinet filed the PDI report as ordered, in which it recommended that J.R.D. be committed to the Cabinet, that she complete the program at Ramey-Estep Homes and earn her GED, that the parents continue with their case plans, that J.R.D. and her father continue to submit to random drug tests, and that J.R.D. follow the status probationary orders as well as other orders and recommendations of the court and the Cabinet. During the hearing, counsel for J.R.D. asserted that her family did not realize that the treatment program would last several months and requested that she be returned home to continue with her treatment. At the conclusion of the hearing, the family court merged the three pending contempt charges and adopted the recommendations of the Cabinet. The family court decided to conditionally permit J.R.D. to spend two days with her family over the Christmas holiday, adding an amendment to this effect to the adopted recommendations. Finally, the family court entered a Juvenile Status Disposition order, in which it found that J.R.D. was a habitual truant and in contempt of court, and committed her to the Cabinet with the recommendation that she complete the treatment program at Ramey-Estep Homes. It is from this order that J.R.D. has taken the present appeal.

On appeal, J.R.D. argues that the family court erred by committing her to the Cabinet for contempt of court and because commitment to the Cabinet was not the last restrictive alternative. In response, the Commonwealth counters J.R.D.'s arguments, pointing out (as did J.R.D.) that the first argument was unpreserved, but that any error did not rise to the level of palpable error, and that the family court committed her for being a status offender, rather than for contempt of court. The Commonwealth also asserts that commitment to the Cabinet was the least restrictive alternative in this case.

1) COMMITMENT TO THE CABINET

J.R.D. concedes that this argument was not preserved for appeal, but nevertheless asserts that this argument must be reviewed as it is akin to sentencing in a criminal matter, or that it should be reviewed under the palpable error rule pursuant to RCr 10.26. She argues that the statutes applicable to status offenders do not permit a court to delegate a decision on confinement to the Cabinet, and that it was fundamentally unfair to her for the family court to bootstrap a commitment order to a contempt finding as she was never told that this could be a possible outcome of violating a status offender order. The Commonwealth, on the other hand, asserts that this is not a true criminal matter and that this is not a case involving palpable error. Furthermore, the Commonwealth argues that the family court's order of commitment was both authorized and lawful.

We agree with the Commonwealth that commitment to the Cabinet was the appropriate ruling in this matter, and we can identify no error, palpable or otherwise. By the terms of the order relating to the habitual truancy charge, J.R.D. was probated to the Cabinet until her eighteenth birthday, and the family court specifically stated that she could be removed from her family if the situation did not improve. Furthermore, the Cabinet recommended in its PDI report that J.R.D. would benefit from long-term residential treatment. As revealed by the numerous contempt charges and detentions that followed, J.R.D. clearly violated the terms of her probation, meaning that she was subject to removal to the Cabinet. By committing J.R.D. to the Cabinet, the family court was simply following its order resolving the habitual truancy charge; J.R.D. was not committed solely for her contemptuous actions.

We perceive no error in the family court's decision to commit J.R.D. to the Cabinet.

2) LEAST RESTRICTIVE ALTERNATIVE

J.R.D. next argues that commitment to the Cabinet to be placed into a treatment center was not the least restrictive alternative available. On the other hand, the Commonwealth points out that the many other alternatives attempted had not worked and that J.R.D.'s removal from her home served her best interests.

While we agree with J.R.D.'s statement of the law that a court must impose the least restrictive method of treatment, we ultimately agree with the Commonwealth that the family court properly committed her to the Cabinet. The Legislature has made it clear that "[t]he court shall show that other less restrictive alternatives have been attempted or are not feasible in order to insure that children are not removed from families except when absolutely necessary[.]" KRS 600.010(2)(c). But the Legislature also provided that "[w]hen all appropriate resources have been reviewed and considered insufficient to adequately address the needs of the child and the child's family, the court may commit the child to the cabinet for such services as may be necessary." KRS 630.120(6). In the present case, the family court obviously expended a tremendous amount of time and effort through numerous court proceedings over several years to remedy the situation without removing J.R.D. from her home. Nothing was effective. Both the Cabinet and the family court recognized that J.R.D. needed to be removed from her home in order for her to get the appropriate treatment.

Again, we perceive no error or abuse of discretion in the family court's decision to commit J.R.D. to the Cabinet, or in its recommendation that she be required to complete the treatment plan at Ramey-Estep Homes.

For the foregoing reasons, the judgment of the Boyle Family Court is affirmed.

Holdings of *J.R.D. v. Commonwealth*: The court affirmed the ruling of the family court and found that commitment to a long-term residential facility is an appropriate sentencing option for juveniles in response to a status offense.

Discussion Questions

Why are courts allowed to commit a juvenile for "treatment" purposes for extended periods of time when the "offense" involved is not even criminal activity?

Does the possibility of long-term placement as a juvenile court response to a minor's violation of a status offense make the juvenile court petition more criminal in nature?

In re McDonald: In *In re McDonald*, the North Carolina Court of Appeals reviewed a juvenile dispositional order granting probation with one of the terms of that probation being that the juvenile was prohibited from watching television for a year. Among other things, the youth argued that such a probationary condition violated her First Amendment rights.

As you read *In re McDonald*, notice how quickly the court found that the prohibition on television viewing was "related to" the delinquent conduct and was, therefore, within the judge's power.

In re McDonald

133 N.C.App. 433, 515 S.E.2d 719 (N.C.Ct.App. 1999)

Between 25 December 1997 and 5 January 1998, defendant Shannon McDonald and two other 14-year-old girls spent part of their Christmas break playing in what they believed to be an abandoned boat house. At some point, the girls decided to transform the boat house into a "clubhouse" and accordingly rearranged some items and spray painted words and pictures on the boat house walls. McDonald spray painted, *inter alia*, the words "Charles Manson Rules." The other two girls spray painted words such as "Nicole and Deanna Best Friends."

Ultimately, the three girls were found "responsible" for the charge of injury to real property. All three girls were given twelve months of juvenile probation with virtually identical conditions; including the condition that they pay the boat house custodian restitution in the amount of two hundred dollars.

During the disposition phase, McDonald informed the judge that she spray painted the words "Charles Manson" because she had recently watched a documentary on television about him. This revelation led the judge to believe that McDonald was "too susceptible to impression to be watching television" and accordingly he ordered an additional condition of probation, to wit, that she not watch television for one year. McDonald appeals both this additional condition and the judge's restitution order.

On appeal, McDonald first contends that the judge's decision to place an additional condition on her probation — that she not watch television for a year — violates her First Amendment rights. Specifically, McDonald contends that Judge Barnes singled her out for special punishment because of the content of her writings rather than her conduct in spray painting the structure.

Initially, we note that under N.C. Gen.Stat. §7A-649(8) a judge may place a juvenile on probation and "shall specify conditions of probation that are related to the needs of the juvenile." In deciding the conditions of probation, the trial judge is free to fashion alternatives which are in harmony with the individual child's needs. Indeed, the statutory framework was designed to provide flexible treatment in the best interests of both the juvenile and the State.

In the case *sub judice*, the judge found that McDonald's susceptibility to the influences of television contributed to her delinquent conduct. Accordingly, the judge concluded that it was in her best interests to avoid those influences for one year. Because this condition of probation was related to both McDonald's unlawful conduct and her needs, it was within the judge's power to impose this condition. Therefore, we need only determine whether the judge, by imposing a greater sentence upon McDonald based upon the content of her words, violated McDonald's First Amendment rights.

We find the United States Supreme Court case of *Wisconsin v. Mitchell* controlling. In *Mitchell,* the Court confronted the constitutionality of a penalty-enhancing statute which provides for an increased penalty if a person commits the underlying offense "because of" the race of the victim. The Court began by noting that "sentencing judges have considered a wide variety of factors in addition to evidence bearing on guilt in determining what sentence to impose on a convicted defendant" including their motive for committing the crime. Thereafter, the Court noted that although a defendant's abstract beliefs, no matter how obnoxious, cannot be considered, those beliefs can be permissibly taken into account when they are relevant to underlying crime or the weighing of aggravating or mitigating circumstances. That is, the Court held that a judge may consider a defendant's underlying motives and beliefs so long as they are relevant to the proceedings.

In the case *sub judice,* the judge's consideration of McDonald's words were directly relevant to the proceedings. Specifically, the judge took McDonald's words into account only to determine what factors influenced her delinquent conduct and the best way to remove those factors from her life. Moreover, the judge sentenced McDonald differently not because his beliefs about Charles Manson differed from hers, but rather because he felt that she was too susceptible to the influences of television. Indeed, it has not been argued nor has there been any evidence that McDonald even believed in the teachings of Charles Manson. Rather, it appears that she was emulating what she observed on television and the judge was merely trying to alleviate some of those potentially damaging influences. This is evidenced by the fact that the judge's order in no way prohibits McDonald from learning about Charles Manson or any other figure through other means. Accordingly, this assignment of error is rejected.

McDonald also contends that the trial court erred in ordering her to pay restitution because it failed to make appropriate findings of fact. This Court has previously stated that "[a]n order of restitution must be supported by appropriate findings of fact, and those findings must in turn be supported by some evidence in the record." In the case *sub judice,* it is undisputed that the State failed to provide any evidence about the monetary amount of damages suffered by the boat house owner. The State's only evidence regarding the extent of damage consisted of pictures of the spray-painted walls. These pictures, however, did not provide the trial court with factual support for its determination that the boat house suffered six hundred dollars damage. Indeed, it appears that the trial court looked at these pictures and simply speculated as to the extent of damage. Accordingly, because there is no factual support underlying the trial court's restitution order, we must reverse this aspect of its ruling.

Affirmed in part, reversed in part.

Holdings of *In re McDonald:* The court affirmed the ruling of the family court and found that, because the prohibition on television viewing was "related to" the delinquent conduct, the condition of probation was within the judge's power. The court also held that the condition did not violate the youth's First Amendment rights because "... the judge's consideration of McDonald's words were directly relevant to the proceedings."

Discussion Questions

If the minor had read a book about Charles Manson instead of seeing a story on television, could the court have prohibited her from reading all books for a year without violating her First Amendment Rights?

Could the court have ordered the other juvenile, who wrote "Nicole and Deanna Best Friends," not to associate with any friends during the term of her probation?

In re Gerald B: In *In re Gerald B*, the California Appeals Court reviewed a case where a minor was adjudicated a delinquent for petty theft (a bottle of whiskey) and one of the terms of the probation was regular school attendance. The offense was totally unrelated to school.

As you read *In re Gerald B*, consider whether or not it is appropriate for juvenile courts to make regular school attendance a condition of every probation granted.

In re Gerald B
105 Cal.App.3d 119,164 Cal.Rptr. 193 (Ct.App. 1980)

This appeal raises two issues: (1) whether a juvenile court may impose regular school attendance as a condition of probation following a wardship adjudication under section 602 of the Welfare and Institutions Code; and (2) whether such condition may validly require summary detention in the event of noncompliance. We conclude that while school attendance is an appropriate condition of probation, its violation may not be summarily enforced.

On February 28, 1979, Gerald, then 16 years of age, was adjudicated a ward of the court. The offense charged was petty theft (a bottle of whiskey). On March 14, 1979, a dispositional hearing was held. The probation report considered by the court revealed prior contacts with authorities for curfew violation and public intoxication as well as an unspecified criminal charge pending in another jurisdiction; the report further disclosed a record of irregular school attendance and marked academic underachievement. The probation department recommended that Gerald be placed on formal probation for a period of six months in the custody of his mother, subject to alcohol abuse and family counseling and regular school attendance pursuant to a "special school order" imposing limited juvenile hall confinement in the event of one or more unexcused school absences. Following declaration of wardship, the juvenile court placed Gerald on probation subject to the recommended conditions, including the questioned order. In granting probation, the court stated that the special order would become self-executing without further hearing.

At a subsequent hearing clarifying the manner in which the order would be enforced, it was established that the probation department routinely monitored similar orders by periodically contacting the schools involved and obtaining a list of those affected juveniles with unexcused absences. In the event of such absence, the juvenile is advised to spend the following weekend in juvenile hall; if there has been a second absence, the juvenile is arrested and without benefit of prior notice to counsel (if any) or hearing taken directly to juvenile hall to spend the remainder of the week. The parents are routinely notified and responsible for providing any existing medical excuse.

Gerald renews his challenge below based upon the statutory and constitutional grounds discussed herein.

Validity of School Attendance as a Probation Condition

Gerald first argues that the special order conflicts with the statutory scheme implementing a preliminary school board review of habitual truancy. The argument must be rejected.

While it is relatively clear that truants are no longer subject to the original jurisdiction of the juvenile court under the amended provisions of section 601, the basis of wardship jurisdiction herein was not Gerald's truancy but rather the determination of a penal violation under the provisions of section 602 a wholly independent basis of jurisdiction. Thus, the statutory directives of prior referral to the local school attendance review board are inapplicable.

Upon an adjudication of wardship under section 602, the court may place the juvenile in parental custody subject to the supervision of the probation officer and may impose "any and all reasonable conditions that it may determine fitting and proper" in the interests of justice and successful rehabilitation. Such a condition is valid and enforceable unless it bears no reasonable relationship to the underlying offense or prohibits conduct neither itself criminal in nature nor related to future criminality. In light of the minor's history of irregular school attendance, his disobedience of a previous court order to enroll in school and the fact that the theft occurred during normal school hours, we conclude that the section 602 probation order requiring school attendance was both "fitting and proper" and reasonably calculated to serve the ends of justice and to enhance the likelihood of "reformation and rehabilitation of the ward." Nor does Gerald contend otherwise.

Gerald next argues that the special order violates the statutory provision prohibiting locked detention for noncriminal conduct. He argues that the net effect of the order is to convert a section 601 status offense into a section 602 criminal offense by impermissibly "bootstrapping" an unexcused school absence into a punishable violation. We find the argument unconvincing.

The limitation on secured detention contained in section 207, subdivision (b) applies where the minor is "taken into custody solely upon the ground that he is a person described by Section 601 or adjudged to be such or made a ward of the juvenile court solely upon that ground, ..." (Emphasis added.) As noted, Gerald was made a ward of the court by virtue of his criminal conduct under section 602; his potential confinement to juvenile hall arises not from the fact of truancy alone, but as the result of a condition of probation stemming from such criminal conduct. And it is generally recognized that there is no legal impediment to the imposition of brief periods of juvenile hall detention as a condition of probation in section 602 proceedings.

Summary Enforcement

Gerald's principal challenge is directed to the provisions of the order calling for summary detention in juvenile hall on account of a reported absence from school. Relying upon an analogy to establish principles applicable to revocation proceedings, Gerald claims that the self-executing order invoking automatic confinement without opportunity for hearing is in flagrant disregard of fundamental principles of due process. The analogy is misplaced since the potential confinement herein is based not upon probation revocation or modification proceedings but upon the summary implementation of a condition involving an otherwise appropriate subject matter of probation. Yet the effect of such implementation resulting in a term of involuntary confinement with almost mechanical certitude solely by reason of an uncharged, unproved and noncriminal act is of doubtful validity. Had the order of probation been limited to compulsory school attendance without more, the prescribed statutory procedure in the event of noncompliance would have been a modification or revocation proceeding "subject to ... procedural requirements", including the filing of a supplemental petition and a noticed hearing to determine whether the previous order of disposition has proven ineffectual. Moreover, if the juvenile court thereafter concluded that probation should be revoked, the court would have been expressly prohibited from ordering the minor's commitment to the county juvenile hall unless a less restrictive facility was unavailable. Thus, the special order would operate to completely circumvent the statutory procedural requirements by triggering automatic juvenile hall confinement merely upon a reported unexcused absence from school. Such summary disposition and resultant incarceration would indirectly nullify the legislative intent that juvenile hall detention be employed as a last resort and in principle would tend to frustrate the parallel legislative scheme which accords prior noncustodial treatment to habitual truants. We therefore conclude that the challenged order, insofar as it purports to authorize automatic confinement in the county juvenile hall simply upon a reported school absence without medical excuse, is invalid and must be stricken.

We reverse and remand for such further proceedings as may be appropriate consistent with the views expressed herein.

Holdings of *In re Gerald B:* The California Appeals Court held: (1) school attendance is an appropriate condition of probation in juvenile delinquency court; and (2) a violation of a condition of probation cannot be summarily enforced.

Discussion Questions

Why are courts allowed to make school attendance a condition of probation when the youth is beyond the age of compulsory school attendance?

Why are courts allowed to make school attendance a condition of probation when the youth committed a delinquent act that is totally unrelated to school (in this case the delinquent act was petty theft of a bottle of whiskey)?

———————

In re Shannon A.: In *In re Shannon A.*, the Maryland Appeals Court reviewed the dispositional order for a juvenile who was adjudicated a delinquent as a result of a manslaughter. The dispositional order required, as a term of the probation, that the youth complete 1,000 hours of community service in the form of working with a brain-damaged child.

As you read *In re Shannon A.,* consider whether or not the imposition of such a large number of hours (1,000 — equal to approximately 20 hours per week for a year) can be appropriate for a youth who was only 13 years old.

In re Shannon A.
60 Md.App. 399, 483 A.2d 363 (1984)

The Circuit Court for Anne Arundel County, after an adjudicatory hearing on November 21, 1983, determined the appellant, Shannon A., to be a delinquent child. The court found that Shannon had committed acts which, if committed by an adult, would have constituted the crimes of manslaughter, assault and battery, and illegal use of a handgun. Following a disposition hearing on December 16, 1983, the court placed Shannon on probation under supervision of the Department of Juvenile Services and, among other conditions of probation, ordered him to perform 1000 hours of community services providing physical therapy to a brain-damaged child.

FACTS

On August 11, 1983, appellant, then 13 years old, his sister Tracey, 10, and Jeffrey Talbot, 10, were playing at appellant's house in Millersville, Anne Arundel County. Neither of appellant's parents was at home. At approximately noon on that day, the paramedic unit of the fire department responded to a call at appellant's home where they found young

Jeffrey outside on the lawn bleeding profusely. Jeffrey was transported to the hospital and pronounced dead at 4:14 p.m.; his cause of death was later determined to be a gunshot to the head.

After the paramedics arrived at the hospital, they notified their central dispatcher, who in turn notified the police that a possible shooting had occurred. Several officers arrived on the scene around 1:00, among them Officer Malloy, a neighbor of appellant. Officer Malloy spoke to Shannon outside of the house and asked him what had happened. Another officer spoke with appellant's sister. Shannon told Malloy that Jeffrey had fallen and hit his head on a chest of drawers. Shannon then showed Malloy the bedroom in which Jeffrey was hurt. Shannon's mother returned home, and by this time a crowd of neighbors had gathered. Malloy took Shannon and his mother into his squad car to discuss the incident more privately.

Shortly thereafter, Malloy was notified by one of the other officers present that a bullet had been recovered from Tracey's bedroom. Malloy informed appellant that physical evidence had been located which contradicted his story. Shannon then broke down and amended his story. He claimed that he had found a gun in his parents' bedroom while cleaning, that the gun had accidentally cocked, and that he and Jeffrey were trying to uncock it when the gun went off. Two guns, one of which was loaded, were subsequently retrieved from the bedroom of appellant's parents.

Around 3:30 that afternoon, appellant was taken to the Winterrode Building in Crownsville for further questioning. His mother and sister were present in the building during the inquiry, as was his father who arrived later. Appellant was then advised of his rights by Detective Moore. He installed the standard *Miranda* form utilized by the police department, indicated to Detective Moore that he understood the rights explained to him, and stated that he had no questions about them. Moore also asked Shannon if he wanted to answer questions without an attorney present, and Shannon agreed.

Appellant was then given a polygraph examination by Detective Moore. Apparently Shannon repeated the story he had given to Officer Moore and Officer Malloy earlier, that the gun had accidentally cocked and the two boys were trying to disengage the hammer when the gun discharged. Moore turned off the machine and explained the difficulties with Shannon's story—namely, that a gun such as the one which killed Jeffrey could not accidentally cock. While the polygraph machine was still turned off, appellant changed his story again and told Moore that he went into his parents' bedroom, got the gun, cocked it intentionally, took it back into his sister's room where Jeffrey and Tracey were playing, pointed it at Jeffrey and it fired. At no time during the questioning did Shannon ask to speak to an attorney or his mother or father.

PROPRIETY OF SENTENCING

At the disposition hearing, the court placed appellant on probation and enunciated five special conditions of probation. Among those special conditions was a requirement that Shannon perform 1000 hours of community service, under the supervision of Juvenile Services, in the form of working with a brain-damaged child in Severna Park, Maryland. Appellant contends that this aspect of the disposition was improper. We disagree.

Maryland Cts. & Jud.Proc.Code Ann. § 3-820 (1984) lists the options available to a judge at a juvenile disposition hearing. The statute controlling at the time of the disposition stated, in part:

(c) In making a disposition on a petition, the court may:

(1) Place the child on probation or under supervision in his own home or in the custody or under the guardianship of a relative or other fit person, upon terms the court deems appropriate;

(2) Commit the child to the custody or under the guardianship of the Juvenile Services Administration, a local department of social services, the Department of Health and Mental Hygiene, or a public or licensed private agency; or

(3) Order the child, parents, guardian, or custodian of the child to participate in rehabilitative services that are in the best interest of the child and the family.

Subsection (d) then provided:

(2) In addition to the dispositions under subsection (c)(1) of this section, the court also may:

(i) Counsel the child or the parent or both;

(ii) Impose a civil fine of not more than $25 for the first violation and a civil fine of not more than $100 for the second and subsequent violations;

(iii) Order the child to participate in a supervised work program for not more than 20 hours for the first violation and not more than 40 hours for the second and subsequent violations.

Appellant maintains that the disposition of this proceeding was made pursuant to § 3-820(c)(1) as Shannon was placed on probation and that 1000 hours of community service was one of the "terms the court deems appropriate" of that probation. Appellant further contends that § 3-820(d)(2)(iii) specifically provided an additional disposition to (c)(1) in the form of community service and the existence of § 3-820(d)(2)(iii) necessarily precludes an interpretation that community services may be one of the probationary terms generally imposable.

While appellant's argument is logical, we find that the 1000 hours of community service imposed on Shannon comes under the ambit of § 3-820(c)(3). Such service certainly may be viewed as "rehabilitative services that are in the best interest of the child...." The comments of the trial judge clearly indicate that he imposed the condition for its rehabilitative effect, not as punishment. Accordingly, we affirm the disposition order.

JUDGMENT AFFIRMED.

Holdings of *In re Shannon A.*: The court affirmed the ruling of the lower court finding that community service may be viewed as rehabilitative services that are in the best interest of the child.

Discussion Questions

In this case, the terms of probation for a 13-year-old included imposition of 1,000 hours of community service (equal to approximately 20 hours per week for a year). Is there some "reasonableness" requirement for the terms of probation in the juvenile delinquency court?

In the prior case, we found that courts routinely find that regular school attendance is in the best interest of the child. Can a court impose a condition of probation (such as here) that could interfere with the youth regularly attending school?

Key Concepts: Dispositional Options Available in Juvenile Court

- Once a juvenile has been adjudicated a delinquent, the three primary options available to a juvenile court judge for disposition are: probation, out-of-home placement and institutional confinement.

- The most common dispositional option is probation, and juvenile courts have been granted great leeway in fashioning terms of probation that the court feels are appropriate for the particular offense and the particular youth involved.

- Common terms of probation include regular school attendance, community service and restitution.

- Normally, states require that courts select the least restrictive alternative when making a dispositional decision, with remaining home under probationary requirements being the least restrictive placement and placement in a secure facility being the most restrictive placement.

- Generally, courts do not allow juveniles adjudicated on a status offense to be placed in a secure facility and, in those few exceptions (such as for contempt) they must be segregated from juveniles adjudicated for offenses that would constitute a crime in adult court.

Chapter XI

Double Jeopardy in Juvenile Court

Overview: As has been seen in the previous cases, the courts have struggled to define what constitutional protections guaranteed for adults charged with criminal offenses by the United States Constitution are also guaranteed to minors charged with committing a delinquent act. Double Jeopardy concerns have confronted the courts both when juveniles are charged and tried in juvenile court and subsequently waived to adult court, as well as when states employ more informal statutory schemes using Referees or Masters that are unique to juvenile courts.

Breed v. Jones: In *Breed v. Jones*, the United States Supreme Court was faced the issue of whether or not the Constitution's prohibition against double jeopardy applies in juvenile delinquency proceedings. In the case, a 17-year-old youth was charged in juvenile court with robbery with a deadly weapon. He was adjudicated a delinquent on the charge and, after the adjudication, the court held a waiver hearing and granted jurisdiction to the adult criminal court where he was subsequently found guilty of first degree robbery. The youth claimed that the waiver of his case to adult court after adjudication as a delinquent violated his rights against twice being placed in jeopardy.

As you read *Breed v. Jones,* look for the following:

1. Consider the reasons for the court's decision finding that a waiver hearing must occur prior to the adjudicatory hearing.

2. Look at the dilemma in which the court finds that a juvenile is placed at a waiver hearing and consider whether or not the court's ruling relative to that dilemma is really based on fundamental fairness rather than the double jeopardy clause of the constitution.

3. Consider why the court says that some states may need to require that, if transfer is rejected, a different judge preside at the adjudicatory hearing

Breed v. Jones
421 U.S. 519 (1975)

Mr. Chief Justice BURGER delivered the opinion for a unanimous Court.

We granted certiorari to decide whether the prosecution of respondent as an adult, after Juvenile Court proceedings which resulted in a finding that respondent had violated a criminal statute and a subsequent finding that he was unfit for treatment as a juvenile, violated the Fifth and Fourteenth Amendments to the United States Constitution.

On February 9, 1971, a petition was filed in the Superior Court of California, County of Los Angeles, Juvenile Court, Alleging that respondent, then 17 years of age, was a person described by Cal. Welf. & Inst'ns Code s 602 (1966), in that, on or about February 8, while armed with a deadly weapon, he had committed acts which, if committed by an adult, would constitute the crime of robbery. The following day, a detention hearing was held, at the conclusion of which respondent was ordered detained pending a hearing on the petition.

The jurisdictional or adjudicatory hearing was conducted on March 1. After taking testimony from two prosecution witnesses and respondent, the Juvenile Court found that the allegations in the petition were true, and it sustained the petition. The proceedings were continued for a dispositional hearing, pending which the court ordered that respondent remain detained.

At a hearing conducted on March 15, the Juvenile Court indicated its intention to find respondent 'not … amenable to the care, treatment and training program available through the facilities of the juvenile court.' Respondent's counsel orally moved 'to continue the matter on the ground of surprise,' contending that respondent 'was not informed that it was going to be a fitness hearing.' The court continued the matter for one week, at which time, having considered the report of the probation officer assigned to the case and having heard her testimony, it declared respondent 'unfit for treatment as a juvenile,' and ordered that he be prosecuted as an adult.

Thereafter, respondent filed a petition for a writ of habeas corpus in Juvenile Court, raising the same double jeopardy claim now presented

After a preliminary hearing respondent was ordered held for trial in Superior Court, where an information was subsequently filed accusing him of having committed robbery while armed with a deadly weapon, on or about February 8, 1971. Respondent entered a plea of not guilty, and he also pleaded that he had 'already been placed once in jeopardy and convicted of the offense charged, by the judgment of the Superior Court of the County of Los Angeles, Juvenile Court, rendered … on the 1st day of March, 1971.' The court found respondent guilty of robbery in the first degree and ordered that he be committed to the California Youth Authority.

The parties agree that, following his transfer from Juvenile Court, and as a defendant to a felony information, respondent was entitled to the full protection of the Double Jeopardy Clause of the Fifth Amendment, as applied to the States through the Fourteenth Amendment. In addition, they agree that respondent was put in jeopardy by the proceedings on that information, which resulted in an adjudication that he was guilty of robbery in the first degree and in a sentence of commitment. Finally, there is no dispute that the petition filed in Juvenile Court and the information filed in Superior Court related to the 'same offence' within the meaning of the constitutional prohibition. The point of disagreement between the parties, and the question for our decision, is whether, by reason of the proceedings in Juvenile Court, respondent was 'twice put in jeopardy.'

Although the juvenile-court system had its genesis in the desire to provide a distinctive procedure and setting to deal with the problems of youth, including those manifested by antisocial conduct, our decisions in recent years have recognized that there is a gap between the originally benign conception of the system and its realities. With the exception of *McKeiver v. Pennsylvania,* the Court's response to that perception has been to make applicable in juvenile proceedings constitutional guarantees associated with traditional criminal prosecutions. In so doing the Court has evinced awareness of the threat which such a process represents to the efforts of the juvenile court system, functioning in a unique manner, to ameliorate the harshness of criminal justice when applied to youthful offenders. That the system has fallen short of the high expectations of its sponsors in no way detracts from the broad social benefits sought or from those benefits that can survive constitutional scrutiny.

We believe it is simply too late in the day to conclude, as did the District Court in this case, that a juvenile is not put in jeopardy at a proceeding whose object is to determine whether he has committed acts that violate a criminal law and whose potential consequences include both the stigma inherent in such a determination and the deprivation of liberty for many years. For it is clear under our cases that determining the relevance of constitutional policies, like determining the applicability of constitutional rights, in juvenile proceedings, requires that courts eschew 'the 'civil' label-of-convenience which has been attached to juvenile proceedings.'

We cannot agree with petitioner that the trial of respondent in Superior Court on an information charging the same offense as that for which he had been tried in Juvenile Court violated none of the policies of the Double Jeopardy Clause.

Respondent was subjected to the burden of two trials for the same offense; he as twice put to the task of marshaling his resources against those of the State, twice subjected to the 'heavy personal strain' which such an experience represents.

The possibility of transfer from juvenile court to a court of general criminal jurisdiction is a matter of great significance to the juvenile. At the same time, there appears to be widely shared agreement that not all juveniles can benefit from the special features and programs of the juvenile-court system and that a procedure for transfer to an adult court should be available. This general agreement is reflected in the fact that an overwhelming majority of jurisdictions permits transfer in certain circumstances. As might be expected, the statutory provisions differ in numerous details. Whatever their differences, however, such transfer provisions represent an attempt to impart to the juvenile-court system the flexibility needed to deal with youthful offenders who cannot benefit from the specialized guidance and treatment contemplated by the system.

We do not agree with petitioner that giving respondent the constitutional protection against multiple trials in this context will diminish flexibility and informality to the extent that those qualities relate uniquely to the goals of the juvenile-court system. We agree that such a holding will require, in most cases, that the transfer decision be made prior to an adjudicatory hearing. To the extent that evidence concerning the alleged offense is considered relevant, it may be that, in those cases where transfer is considered and rejected, some added burden will be imposed on the juvenile courts by reason of duplicative proceedings. Finally, the nature of the evidence considered at a transfer hearing may in some States require that, if transfer is rejected, a different judge preside at the adjudicatory hearing.

A requirement that transfer hearings be held prior to adjudicatory hearings affects not at all the nature of the latter proceedings. More significantly, such a requirement need not affect the quality of decisionmaking at transfer hearings themselves. In *Kent v. United States,* the Court held that hearings under the statute there involved 'must measure up to the essentials of due process and fair treatment.' However, the Court has never attempted to prescribe criteria for, or the nature and quantum of evidence that must support, a decision to transfer a juvenile for trial in adult court. We require only that, whatever the relevant criteria, and whatever the evidence demanded, a State determine whether it wants to treat a juvenile within the juvenile-court system before entering upon a proceeding that may result in an adjudication that he has violated a criminal law and in a substantial deprivation of liberty, rather than subject him to the expense, delay, strain, and embarrassment of two such proceedings.

What concerns us here is the dilemma that the possibility of transfer after an adjudicatory hearing presents for a juvenile, a dilemma to which the Court of Appeals alluded.

Because of that possibility, a juvenile, thought to be the beneficiary of special consideration, may in fact suffer substantial disadvantages. If he appears uncooperative, he runs the risk of an adverse adjudication, as well as of an unfavorable dispositional recommendation. If, on the other hand, he is cooperative, he runs the risk of prejudicing his chances in adult court if transfer is ordered. We regard a procedure that results in such a dilemma as at odds with the goal that, to the extent fundamental fairness permits, adjudicatory hearings be informal and nonadversary. Knowledge of the risk of transfer after an adjudicatory hearing can only undermine the potential for informality and cooperation which was intended to be the hallmark of the juvenile-court system. Rather than concerning themselves with the matter at hand, establishing innocence or seeking a disposition best suited to individual correctional needs, the juvenile and his attorney are pressed into a posture of adversary wariness that is conductive to neither.

We hold that the prosecution of respondent in Superior Court, after an adjudicatory proceeding in Juvenile Court, violated the Double Jeopardy Clause of the Fifth Amendment, as applied to the States through the Fourteenth Amendment.

Judgment vacated and case remanded.

Holdings of *Breed v. Jones:* The court held that the prosecution of a juvenile in adult criminal court after an adjudicatory proceeding in Juvenile Court violated the Double Jeopardy Clause of the Fifth Amendment as applied to the States through the Fourteenth Amendment.

Discussion Questions

How does the Double Jeopardy clause apply to this juvenile proceeding?

Is there a "magic" time when a waiver decision must be made to avoid violating a youth's double jeopardy rights?

———————

Swisher v. Brady: In *Swisher v. Brady,* the United States Supreme Court was faced with a Maryland statute which codified the use of Masters in Juvenile Court and required that hearings before a master be recorded and that, at their conclusion, the master submit to the Juvenile Court Judge written findings of fact, conclusions of law, and recommendations. Either party was authorized to file exceptions and could elect a hearing on the record or a de novo hearing before the judge. The statute specified that the master's "proposals and recommendations ... for juvenile causes do not constitute orders or final action of the court." Accordingly, the judge could, even in the absence of exceptions, reject a master's recommendations and conduct a de novo hearing or, if the parties agreed, a hearing on the record. Nine minors brought a § 1983 action claiming that such a procedure violated their rights against double jeopardy.

As you read *Swisher v. Brady,* look for the following:

1. Consider whether the dissent is right that the Maryland statute would not be constitutional if it were applied to adult criminal trials.

2. Consider whether the mere fact that the statute says that the decisions of a Master are not "final decisions" is enough to make the double jeopardy clause inapplicable.

3. Look for anything that would justify treating juveniles charged with a delinquent act differently that adults charged with a crime.

Swisher v. Brady

438 U.S. 204 (1978)

Mr. Chief Justice BURGER delivered the opinion of the Court.

Nine minors, appellees here, brought an action under 42 U.S.C. § 1983, seeking a declaratory judgment and injunctive relief to prevent the State from filing exceptions with the Juvenile Court to proposed findings and recommendations made by masters of that court. The minors' claim was based on an alleged violation of the Double Jeopardy Clause of the Fifth Amendment, as applied to the States through the Fourteenth Amendment.

In order to understand the present Maryland scheme for the use of masters in juvenile court proceedings, it is necessary to trace briefly the history both of antecedent schemes and of this and related litigation.

Prior to July 1975, the use of masters in Maryland juvenile proceedings was governed by Rule 908(e), Maryland Rules of Procedure. It provided that a master "shall hear such cases as may be assigned to him by the court." The Rule further directed that, at the conclusion of the hearing, the master transmit the case file and his "findings and recommendations" to the Juvenile Court. If no party filed exceptions to these findings and recommendations, they were to be "promptly ... confirmed, modified or remanded by the judge." If, however, a party filed exceptions — and in delinquency hearings, only the State had the authority to do so — then, after notice, the Juvenile Court judge would "hear the entire matter or such specific matters as set forth in the exceptions de novo."

Before either the three-judge District Court or the single judge reviewing the habeas corpus petitions could act, the Maryland Legislature enacted legislation which, for the first time, provided a statutory basis for the use of masters in juvenile court proceedings. In doing so, it modified slightly the scheme previously operative under Rule 908(e). The new legislation required that hearings before a master be recorded and that, at their conclusion, the master submit to the Juvenile Court judge written findings of fact, conclusions of law, and recommendations. Either party was authorized to file exceptions and could elect a hearing on the record or a de novo hearing before the judge. The legislature specified that the master's "proposals and recommendations ... for juvenile causes do not constitute orders or final action of the court." Accordingly, the judge could, even in the absence of exceptions, reject a master's recommendations and conduct a de novo hearing or, if the parties agreed, a hearing on the record.

In the application of these general principles, the narrow question here is whether the State in filing exceptions to a master's proposals, pursuant to Rule 911, thereby "require[s] an accused to stand trial" a second time. We hold that it does not. Maryland has created a system with Rule 911 in which an accused juvenile is subjected to a single proceeding which begins with a master's hearing and culminates with an adjudication by a judge.

A Rule 911 proceeding does not provide the prosecution that forbidden "second crack." The State presents its evidence once before the master. The record is then closed, and additional evidence can be received by the Juvenile Court judge only with the consent of the minor.

To the extent the Juvenile Court judge makes supplemental findings in a manner permitted by Rule 911 — either sua sponte, in response to the State's exceptions, or in response to the juvenile's exceptions, and either on the record or on a record supplemented by evidence to which the parties raise no objection — he does so without violating the constraints of the Double Jeopardy Clause.

Accordingly, we reverse and remand for further proceedings consistent with this opinion.

It is so ordered.

Mr. Justice MARSHALL, with whom Mr. Justice BRENNAN and Mr. Justice POWELL join, dissenting.

Appellees are a class of juveniles who, following adjudicatory hearings on charges of criminal conduct, were found nondelinquent by a "master." Because the State has labeled the master's findings as "proposed," the Court today allows the State in effect to appeal those findings to a "judge," who is empowered to reverse the master's findings and convict the juvenile. The Court's holding is at odds with the constitutional prohibition against double jeopardy, made applicable to the States by the Due Process Clause of the Fourteenth Amendment, and specifically held to apply to juvenile proceedings in *Breed v. Jones.*

The majority does not purport to retreat from our holding in *Breed.* Yet the Court reaches a result that it would not countenance were this a criminal prosecution against an adult, for the juvenile defendants here are placed twice in jeopardy just as surely as if an adult defendant, after acquittal in a trial court, were convicted on appeal. In addition to violating the Double Jeopardy Clause, Maryland's scheme raises serious due process questions because the judge making the final adjudication of guilt has not heard the evidence and may reverse the master's findings of nondelinquency based on the judge's review of a cold record. For these reasons, I dissent.

Viewing the master and judge in terms of their relative functions, I think the appropriate analogy is between a trial judge and an appellate court with unusually broad powers of review. In the cases before us, the masters had made unequivocal findings, on the facts, that the State had not proved its case, and the State sought to have the judge overturn these findings. By ignoring these functional considerations, the Court permits the State to circumvent the protections of the Double Jeopardy Clause by a mere change in the formal definitions of finality.

The decision today might well be read to hold that the Double Jeopardy Clause is no bar to structuring a juvenile justice system or, for that matter, an adult criminal justice system so as to have several layers of adjudication, none of which is final until the State has exhausted its last appeal. This proliferation of levels at which a defendant—juvenile or adult—must defend himself against an adjudication of guilt is precisely the kind of evil that the Double Jeopardy Clause was designed to forbid. Yet under the Court's rationale, this is seemingly permissible so long as the State takes care to define the lower levels of decisionmaking as only "proposed" or "tentative" in nature, thereby commingling traditional trial and appellate functions.

Even if the master's findings are not regarded as an acquittal, the Double Jeopardy Clause does more than simply protect acquittals from review on direct appeal. It also protects the defendant's right to go to judgment before a "particular tribunal" once jeopardy has attached, absent a "'manifest necessity'" justifying termination of the first proceeding. This rule is designed in part to ensure that the government not be able to bolster its case by additional evidence or arguments, once it believes that its evidence has not persuaded the first tribunal. But the Maryland system is structured so as to give the State precisely this type of proscribed opportunity, where it disagrees with the favorable rulings of the first trier of fact.

For these reasons, I conclude that the Maryland Rule, insofar as it permits a judge to review and set aside a master's findings favorable to the defendant on the facts of the case, violates the Double Jeopardy Clause.

As the majority accurately states, the only issue raised in the complaints or focused upon in the parties' briefs was that of double jeopardy. It is argued by amicus, however, that the Maryland system, even if it were found to avoid double jeopardy problems, violates the Due Process Clause by permitting ultimate factfinding by a judge who did not actually conduct the trial. The Court does not reach this issue, apparently believing that it is not properly presented here. It is thus important to emphasize that the Maryland system and ones like it have not been held constitutional today; the Court's only holding is that such systems are not unconstitutional under the Double Jeopardy Clause. It is entirely open to this Court, and lower courts, to find in another case that a system like that in Maryland violates the Due Process Clause.

It would thus appear that the Maryland system of splitting the hearing of evidence from the final adjudication violates the Due Process Clause.

It is no answer to this problem that the juvenile defendant may elect to submit additional material to the judge when the State takes an exception to the master's finding. In the first place, the State apparently must agree to the supplementation of the record, and can thus stymie a defendant's efforts to persuade the judge that he is not guilty. But more importantly, when a juvenile seeks to reopen the proceeding before the judge—in order to avoid having a case decided against him on the basis of a cold record in violation of the Due Process Clause—he is being subjected to a second trial of the sort clearly prohibited by the Double Jeopardy Clause. The constitutionality of forcing a juvenile to such a choice between fundamental rights is questionable at best.

That the current Maryland scheme cannot pass constitutional muster does not necessarily mean that the idea of using masters, or some other class of specially trained or selected personnel for juvenile court adjudications, is either unconstitutional or unwise. Using masters to adjudicate the more common charges may save scarce judicial resources for the more difficult cases. It may also aid the ultimate goals of a juvenile justice system by ensuring that the decisionmakers have some familiarity with the special problems of juvenile dispositions. But the State must find a way of implementing this concept without jeopardizing the constitutional rights of juveniles. Whether it does so by endowing masters with the power to make final adjudications or by some other means, matters not. What does matter is that, absent compelling circumstances not present here, the system of juvenile justice in this country must not be permitted to fall below the minimum constitutional standards set for adult criminal proceedings. Accordingly, I dissent.

Holding of *Swisher v. Brady:* The court held that allowing the Juvenile Court judge to make supplemental findings—either *sua sponte*, in response to the State's exceptions, or in response to the juvenile's exceptions, and either on the record or on a record supplemented by evidence to which the parties raise no objection—to the findings of the Master in a manner permitted by the Maryland statute does not violate the constraints of the Double Jeopardy Clause.

Discussion Questions

Would a similar procedure be upheld in an adult criminal action, or is the majority decision based on the unique nature of a juvenile proceeding?

How does the procedure used in Maryland juvenile courts differ from a de novo appeal from a trial to an appellate court?

Key Concepts: Double Jeopardy in Juvenile Court

- The Double Jeopardy Clause of the United States Constitution applies, at least to some extent, to juvenile delinquency actions.

- Jeopardy "sets in" at the point of adjudication and, as such, a juvenile cannot be waived to adult court after adjudication without violating the Double Jeopardy Clause of the United States Constitution.

- Some procedures, such as the use of Masters or Referees, that would not be acceptable in adult criminal court, may be constitutional in juvenile delinquency proceedings due to the unique nature of the juvenile court system.

Practical Questions: Double Jeopardy in Juvenile Court

1. Your jurisdiction follows the "one child, one judge" model where the same judge is always assigned to the same youth in juvenile court. You successfully represented a youth charged with possession of stolen property and drug possession in a waiver hearing where you argued that he was "fencing" stolen property to support his drug habit and that the juvenile court has more resources to treat your client's drug addiction than does the adult court. Since you have successfully kept the case in juvenile court, what arguments would you make that a different judge should be assigned to the case for the adjudicatory hearing?

2. You represent a youth charged with aggravated assault in juvenile court. At the beginning of the case, your client was 16 years old, and the state filed a motion to waive jurisdiction to adult court. You resisted the motion arguing that your client has serious mental health issues that are more amenable to treatment in juvenile court. The judge agreed with you, and denied the motion to waive jurisdiction to adult court. Your client's condition deteriorated and required him to be mentally committed for almost one year, delaying the juvenile proceedings. After his release, the state filed a second motion to waive jurisdiction arguing that your client will be 18 (and, thus, beyond the jurisdiction of the juvenile court) in only 2 months. Another Waiver Hearing is scheduled. Does the Double Jeopardy Clause prevent this second hearing when the conditions have changed substantially since the first hearing?

Chapter XII

Sentencing of Juvenile Offenders in Adult Court

A. Death Penalty

Overview: Over a century ago, courts approved sentences of death for minors. At least two minors aged 12 and under were put to death between 1806 and 1882. [See *Godfrey v. State*, 31 Ala. 323 (1858); *State v. Guild*, 10 N.J.L. 163 (1828)]. The United States Supreme Court began the process of evaluating whether or not the execution of a minor constitutes "Cruel and Unusual Punishment" as prohibited by the 8th Amendment of the U.S. Constitution in 1988. The reasoning of the court in the series of cases dealing with the death penalty for minors continues to affect the application of the 8th Amendment to other sentences of minors.

Thompson v. Oklahoma: In *Thompson v. Oklahoma*, the United States Supreme Court was required to determine whether or not imposition of the death penalty on 15-year-old William Wayne Thompson was a violation of the 8th Amendment's prohibition on cruel and unusual punishment. Thompson, in concert with three older persons, was accused of actively participating in the brutal murder of his former brother-in-law. The Juvenile Court waived jurisdiction of Thompson's case to adult criminal court, where he was convicted of first degree murder and sentenced to death.

As you read *Thompson v. Oklahoma*, look for the following:

1. Consider why the court believes that minors should be treated differently than adults when it comes to the death penalty.

2. Consider whether the court is saying that the mere fact that the death penalty is rarely used on defendants who were under age sixteen is reason enough to find the use of it in such cases to be cruel and unusual.

3. Look for reasoning as to why the court limited its ruling to youth under the age of 16 rather than just drawing the line at age 18.

Thompson v. Oklahoma
487 U.S. 815 (1988)

Justice STEVENS announced the judgment of the Court and delivered an opinion in which Justice BRENNAN, Justice MARSHALL, and Justice BLACKMUN join.

Petitioner was convicted of first-degree murder and sentenced to death. The principal question presented is whether the execution of that sentence would violate the constitutional prohibition against the infliction of "cruel and unusual punishments" because petitioner was only 15 years old at the time of his offense.

Because there is no claim that the punishment would be excessive if the crime had been committed by an adult, only a brief statement of facts is necessary. In concert with three older persons, petitioner actively participated in the brutal murder of his former brother-in-law in the early morning hours of January 23, 1983. The evidence disclosed that the victim had been shot twice, and that his throat, chest, and abdomen had been cut. He also had multiple bruises and a broken leg. His body had been chained to a concrete block and thrown into a river where it remained for almost four weeks. Each of the four participants was tried separately and each was sentenced to death.

Because petitioner was a "child" as a matter of Oklahoma law, the District Attorney filed a statutory petition seeking an order finding "that said child is competent and had the mental capacity to know and appreciate the wrongfulness of his [conduct]." After a hearing, the trial court concluded "that there are virtually no *reasonable* prospects for rehabilitation of William Wayne Thompson within the juvenile system and that William Wayne Thompson should be held accountable for his acts as if he were an adult and should be certified to stand trial as an adult."

The Court of Criminal Appeals affirmed the conviction and sentence, citing its earlier opinion for the proposition that "once a minor is certified to stand trial as an adult, he may also, without violating the Constitution, be punished as an adult." We granted certiorari to consider whether a sentence of death is cruel and unusual punishment for a crime committed by a 15-year-old child, as well as whether photographic evidence that a state court deems erroneously admitted but harmless at the guilt phase nevertheless violates a capital defendant's constitutional rights by virtue of its being considered at the penalty phase.

The authors of the Eighth Amendment drafted a categorical prohibition against the infliction of cruel and unusual punishments, but they made no attempt to define the contours of that category. They delegated that task to future generations of judges who have been guided by the "evolving standards of decency that mark the progress of a maturing society." In performing that task the Court has reviewed the work product of state legislatures and sentencing juries, and has carefully considered the reasons why a civilized society may accept or reject the death penalty in certain types of cases. Thus, in confronting the question whether the youth of the defendant—more specifically, the fact that he was less than 16 years old at the time of his offense—is a sufficient reason for denying the State the power to sentence him to death, we first review relevant legislative enactments, then refer to jury determinations, and finally explain why these indicators of contemporary standards of decency confirm our judgment that such a young person is not capable of acting with the degree of culpability that can justify the ultimate penalty.

Justice Powell has repeatedly reminded us of the importance of "the experience of mankind, as well as the long history of our law, recognizing that there *are* differences which must be accommodated in determining the rights and duties of children as compared with those of adults. Examples of this distinction abound in our law: in contracts, in torts, in criminal law and procedure, in criminal sanctions and rehabilitation, and in the right to vote and to hold office." Oklahoma recognizes this basic distinction in a number of its statutes. Thus, a minor is not eligible to vote, to sit on a jury, to marry without parental consent, or to purchase alcohol or cigarettes. Like all other States, Oklahoma has developed a juvenile justice system in which most offenders under the age of 18 are not held criminally responsible. Its statutes do provide, however, that a 16- or 17-year-old charged with murder and other serious felonies shall be considered an adult. Other than the special certification procedure that was used to authorize petitioner's trial in this case "as an adult," apparently there are no Oklahoma statutes, either civil or criminal, that treat a person under 16 years of age as anything but a "child."

The line between childhood and adulthood is drawn in different ways by various States. There is, however, complete or near unanimity among all 50 States and the District of Columbia in treating a person under 16 as a minor for several important purposes. In no State may a 15-year-old vote or serve on a jury. Further, in all but one State a 15-year-old may not drive without parental consent, and in all but four States a 15-year-old may not marry without parental consent. Additionally, in those States that have legislated on the subject, no one under age 16 may purchase pornographic materials (50 States), and in most States that have some form of legalized gambling, minors are not permitted to participate without parental consent (42 States). Most relevant, however, is the fact that all States have enacted legislation designating the maximum age for juvenile court jurisdiction at no less than 16. All of this legislation is consistent with the experience of mankind, as well as the long history of our law, that the normal 15-year-old is not prepared to assume the full responsibilities of an adult.

Most state legislatures have not expressly confronted the question of establishing a minimum age for imposition of the death penalty. In 14 States, capital punishment is not authorized at all, and in 19 others capital punishment is authorized but no minimum age is expressly stated in the death penalty statute. One might argue on the basis of this body of legislation that there is no chronological age at which the imposition of the death penalty is unconstitutional and that our current standards of decency would still tolerate the execution of 10-year-old children. We think it self-evident that such an argument is unacceptable; indeed, no such argument has been advanced in this case. If, therefore, we accept the premise that some offenders are simply too young to be put to death, it is reasonable to put this group of statutes to one side because they do not focus on the question of where the chronological age line should be drawn. When we confine our attention to the 18 States that have expressly established a minimum age in their death-penalty statutes, we find that all of them require that the defendant have attained at least the age of 16 at the time of the capital offense.

The conclusion that it would offend civilized standards of decency to execute a person who was less than 16 years old at the time of his or her offense is consistent with the views that have been expressed by respected professional organizations, by other nations that share our Anglo-American heritage, and by the leading members of the Western European community.

The second societal factor the Court has examined in determining the acceptability of capital punishment to the American sensibility is the behavior of juries.

While it is not known precisely how many persons have been executed during the 20th century for crimes committed under the age of 16, a scholar has recently compiled a table revealing this number to be between 18 and 20. All of these occurred during the first half of the century, with the last such execution taking place apparently in 1948. In the following year this Court observed that this "whole country has traveled far from the period in which the death sentence was an automatic and commonplace result of convictions." The road we have traveled during the past four decades—in which thousands of juries have tried murder cases—leads to the unambiguous conclusion that the imposition of the death penalty on a 15-year-old offender is now generally abhorrent to the conscience of the community.

Department of Justice statistics indicate that during the years 1982 through 1986 an average of over 16,000 persons were arrested for willful criminal homicide (murder and non-negligent manslaughter) each year. Of that group of 82,094 persons, 1,393 were sentenced to death. Only 5 of them, including the petitioner in this case, were less than 16 years old at the time of the offense. Statistics of this kind can, of course, be interpreted in different ways, but they do suggest that these five young offenders have received sentences that are "cruel and unusual in the same way that being struck by lightning is cruel and unusual."

"Although the judgments of legislatures, juries, and prosecutors weigh heavily in the balance, it is for us ultimately to judge whether the Eighth Amendment permits imposition of the death penalty" on one such as petitioner who committed a heinous murder when he was only 15 years old. In making that judgment, we first ask whether the juvenile's culpability should be measured by the same standard as that of an adult, and then consider whether the application of the death penalty to this class of offenders "measurably contributes" to the social purposes that are served by the death penalty.

It is generally agreed "that punishment should be directly related to the personal culpability of the criminal defendant." There is also broad agreement on the proposition that adolescents as a class are less mature and responsible than adults.

Thus, the Court has already endorsed the proposition that less culpability should attach to a crime committed by a juvenile than to a comparable crime committed by an adult. The basis for this conclusion is too obvious to require extended explanation. Inexperience, less education, and less intelligence make the teenager less able to evaluate the consequences of his or her conduct while at the same time he or she is much more apt to be motivated by mere emotion or peer pressure than is an adult. The reasons why juveniles are not trusted with the privileges and responsibilities of an adult also explain why their irresponsible conduct is not as morally reprehensible as that of an adult.

"The death penalty is said to serve two principal social purposes: retribution and deterrence of capital crimes by prospective offenders." In *Gregg* we concluded that as "an expression of society's moral outrage at particularly offensive conduct," retribution was not "inconsistent with our respect for the dignity of men." Given the lesser culpability of the juvenile offender, the teenager's capacity for growth, and society's fiduciary obligations to its children, this conclusion is simply inapplicable to the execution of a 15-year-old offender.

For such a young offender, the deterrence rationale is equally unacceptable. The Department of Justice statistics indicate that about 98% of the arrests for willful homicide involved persons who were over 16 at the time of the offense. Thus, excluding younger persons from the class that is eligible for the death penalty will not diminish the deterrent value of capital punishment for the vast majority of potential offenders. And even with respect to those under 16 years of age, it is obvious that the potential deterrent value of the death sentence is insignificant for two reasons. The likelihood that the teenage offender has made the kind of cost-benefit analysis that attaches any weight to the possibility of execution is so remote as to be virtually nonexistent. And, even if one posits such a cold-blooded calculation by a 15-year-old, it is fanciful to believe that he would be deterred by the knowledge that a small number of persons his age have been executed during the 20th century. In short, we are not persuaded that the imposition of the death penalty for offenses committed by persons under 16 years of age has made, or can be expected to make, any measurable contribution to the goals that capital punishment is intended to achieve. It is, therefore, "nothing more than the purposeless and needless imposition of pain and suffering," and thus an unconstitutional punishment.

Petitioner's counsel and various *amici curiae* have asked us to "draw a line" that would prohibit the execution of any person who was under the age of 18 at the time of the offense. Our task today, however, is to decide the case before us; we do so by concluding that the Eighth and Fourteenth Amendments prohibit the execution of a person who was under 16 years of age at the time of his or her offense.

The judgment of the Court of Criminal Appeals is vacated, and the case is remanded with instructions to enter an appropriate order vacating petitioner's death sentence.

It is so ordered.

Holdings of *Thompson v. Oklahoma:* The court held that the Eighth and Fourteenth Amendments prohibit the execution of a person who was under 16 years of age at the time of his or her offense.

Discussion Questions

Why (based on what factors) does the court "draw the line" at 16 in this case?

How does the court support the claim that a juvenile under the age of 16 is not as culpable as an adult?

Stanford v. Kentucky: In *Stanford v. Kentucky,* the court was faced with a case that forced them to decide whether or not the *Thompson* holding concerning the constitutionality of the imposition of the death penalty on a minor should be extended beyond the age of 16. In this case, two defendants had been sentenced to death in separate cases. *Kevin Stanford* was age 17 and 4 months old at the time when he and his accomplice repeatedly raped and sodomized a 20-year-old woman during and after their commission of a robbery at a gas station where she worked as an attendant. They then drove her to a secluded area near the station, where Stanford shot her pointblank in the face and then in the back of her head. Jurisdiction of Stanford's case was waived by the juvenile court to adult criminal court where Stanford was convicted of murder, first-degree sodomy, first-degree robbery, and receiving stolen property, and was sentenced to death and 45 years in prison. *Heath Wilkins,* who was approximately 16 years and 6 months of age at the time, during the course of a robbery, repeatedly stabbed a woman and left her on the floor to bleed to death. Wilkins was waived to adult court, where he was charged with first-degree murder, armed criminal action, and carrying a concealed weapon. After the court found him competent, Wilkins entered guilty pleas to all charges. A punishment hearing was held, at which both the State and Wilkins himself urged imposition of the death sentence. The court sentenced Wilkins to death.

As you read *Stanford v. Kentucky,* look for the following:

1. Consider why the court takes a different approach in applying the 8th Amendment to youth aged 16 and 17 at the time of their offense than applied in the case of youth under the age of 16.

2. Look for any analysis of the factors that the court used to arrive at their decision in *Thompson v. Oklahoma* decision and how that analysis support holding 16 and 17-year-old youth to a different standard that youth under the age of 16.

Stanford v. Kentucky
492 U.S. 361 (1989)

Justice SCALIA announced the judgment of the Court and delivered the opinion of the Court with respect to Parts I, II, III, and IV-A, and an opinion with respect to Parts IV-B and V, in which THE CHIEF JUSTICE, Justice WHITE, and Justice KENNEDY join.

These two consolidated cases require us to decide whether the imposition of capital punishment on an individual for a crime committed at 16 or 17 years of age constitutes cruel and unusual punishment under the Eighth Amendment.

The first case involves the shooting death of 20-year-old Barbel Poore in Jefferson County, Kentucky. Petitioner Kevin Stanford committed the murder on January 7, 1981, when he was approximately 17 years and 4 months of age. Stanford and his accomplice repeatedly raped and sodomized Poore during and after their commission of a robbery at a gas station where she worked as an attendant. They then drove her to a secluded area near the station, where Stanford shot her pointblank in the face and then in the back of her head. The proceeds from the robbery were roughly 300 cartons of cigarettes, two gallons of fuel, and a small amount of cash. A corrections officer testified that petitioner explained the murder as follows: "'[H]e said, I had to shoot her, [she] lived next door to me and she would recognize me.... I guess we could have tied her up or something or beat [her up] ... and tell her if she tells, we would kill her.... Then after he said that he started laughing.'"

After Stanford's arrest, a Kentucky juvenile court conducted hearings to determine whether he should be transferred for trial as an adult under. That statute provided that juvenile court jurisdiction could be waived and an offender tried as an adult if he was either charged with a Class A felony or capital crime, or was over 16 years of age and charged with a felony. Stressing the seriousness of petitioner's offenses and the unsuccessful attempts of the juvenile system to treat him for numerous instances of past delinquency, the juvenile court found certification for trial as an adult to be in the best interest of petitioner and the community.

Stanford was convicted of murder, first-degree sodomy, first-degree robbery, and receiving stolen property, and was sentenced to death and 45 years in prison.

The second case before us today involves the stabbing death of Nancy Allen, a 26-year-old mother of two who was working behind the sales counter of the convenience store she and David Allen owned and operated in Avondale, Missouri. Petitioner Heath Wilkins committed the murder on July 27, 1985, when he was approximately 16 years and 6 months of age. The record reflects that Wilkins' plan was to rob the store and murder "whoever was behind the counter" because "a dead person can't talk." While Wilkins' accomplice, Patrick Stevens, held Allen, Wilkins stabbed her, causing her to fall to the floor. When Stevens had trouble operating the cash register, Allen spoke up to assist him, leading Wilkins to stab her three more times in her chest. Two of these wounds penetrated the victim's heart. When Allen began to beg for her life, Wilkins stabbed her four more times in the neck, opening her carotid artery. After helping themselves to liquor, cigarettes, rolling papers, and approximately $450 in cash and checks, Wilkins and Stevens left Allen to die on the floor.

Because he was roughly six months short of the age of majority for purposes of criminal prosecution, Wilkins could not automatically be tried as an adult under Missouri law. Before that could happen, the juvenile court was required to terminate juvenile court jurisdiction and certify Wilkins for trial as an adult under § 211.071, which permits individuals between 14 and 17 years of age who have committed felonies to be tried as adults. Relying on the "viciousness, force and violence" of the alleged crime, petitioner's maturity, and the failure of the juvenile justice system to rehabilitate him after previous delinquent acts, the juvenile court made the necessary certification.

Wilkins was charged with first-degree murder, armed criminal action, and carrying a concealed weapon. After the court found him competent, petitioner entered guilty pleas to all charges. A punishment hearing was held, at which both the State and petitioner himself urged imposition of the death sentence. Evidence at the hearing revealed that petitioner had been in and out of juvenile facilities since the age of eight for various acts of burglary, theft, and arson, had attempted to kill his mother by putting insecticide into Tylenol capsules, and had killed several animals in his neighborhood. Although psychiatric testimony indicated that Wilkins had "personality disorders," the witnesses agreed that Wilkins was aware of his actions and could distinguish right from wrong.

We granted certiorari in these cases, to decide whether the Eighth Amendment precludes the death penalty for individuals who commit crimes at 16 or 17 years of age.

"[F]irst" among the "'objective indicia that reflect the public attitude toward a given sanction'" are statutes passed by society's elected representatives. Of the 37 States whose laws permit capital punishment, 15 decline to impose it upon 16-year-old offenders and 12 decline to impose it on 17-year-old offenders. This does not establish the degree of national consensus this Court has previously thought sufficient to label a particular punishment cruel and unusual. In invalidating the death penalty for rape of an adult woman, we stressed that Georgia was the sole jurisdiction that authorized such a punishment. In striking down capital punishment for participation in a robbery in which an accomplice takes a life, we emphasized that only eight jurisdictions authorized similar punishment. In finding that the Eighth Amendment precludes execution of the insane and thus requires an adequate hearing on the issue of sanity, we relied upon (in addition to the common-law rule) the fact that "no State in the Union" permitted such punishment. And in striking down a life sentence without parole under a recidivist statute, we stressed that "[i]t appears that [petitioner] was treated more severely than he would have been in any other State."

Twenty-nine States, including both Kentucky and Missouri, have codified this constitutional requirement in laws specifically designating the defendant's age as a mitigating factor in capital cases. Moreover, the determinations required by juvenile transfer statutes to certify a juvenile for trial as an adult ensure individualized consideration of the maturity and moral responsibility of 16- and 17-year-old offenders before they are even held to stand trial as adults. The application of this particularized system to the petitioners can be declared constitutionally inadequate only if there is a consensus, not that 17 or 18 is the age at which most persons, or even almost all persons, achieve sufficient maturity to be held fully responsible for murder; but that 17 or 18 is the age before which no one can reasonably be held fully responsible. What displays society's views on this latter point are not the ages set forth in the generalized system of driving, drinking, and voting laws cited by petitioners and their amici, but the ages at which the States permit their particularized capital punishment systems to be applied.

We discern neither a historical nor a modern societal consensus forbidding the imposition of capital punishment on any person who murders at 16 or 17 years of age. Accordingly, we conclude that such punishment does not offend the Eighth Amendment's prohibition against cruel and unusual punishment.

The judgments of the Supreme Court of Kentucky and the Supreme Court of Missouri are therefore

Affirmed.

Justice O'CONNOR, concurring in part and concurring in the judgment.

Last Term, in *Thompson v. Oklahoma,* I expressed the view that a criminal defendant who would have been tried as a juvenile under state law, but for the granting of a petition waiving juvenile court jurisdiction, may only be executed for a capital offense if the State's capital punishment statute specifies a minimum age at which the commission of a capital crime can lead to an offender's execution and the defendant had reached that minimum age at the time the crime was committed. As a threshold matter, I indicated that such specificity is not necessary to avoid constitutional problems if it is clear that no national consensus forbids the imposition of capital punishment for crimes committed at such an age. Applying this two-part standard in Thompson, I concluded that Oklahoma's imposition of a death sentence on an individual who was 15 years old at the time he committed a capital offense should be set aside. Applying the same standard today, I conclude that the death sentences for capital murder imposed by Missouri and Kentucky on petitioners Wilkins and Stanford respectively should not be set aside because it is sufficiently clear that no national consensus forbids the imposition of capital punishment on 16- or 17-year-old capital murderers.

Justice BRENNAN, with whom Justice MARSHALL, Justice BLACKMUN, and Justice STEVENS join, dissenting.

I believe that to take the life of a person as punishment for a crime committed when below the age of 18 is cruel and unusual and hence is prohibited by the Eighth Amendment.

The Court's discussion of state laws concerning capital sentencing gives a distorted view of the evidence of contemporary standards that these legislative determinations provide. Currently, 12 of the States whose statutes permit capital punishment specifically mandate that offenders under age 18 not be sentenced to death. When one adds to these 12 States the 15 (including the District of Columbia) in which capital punishment is not authorized at all, it appears that the governments in fully 27 of the States have concluded that no one under 18 should face the death penalty. A further three States explicitly refuse to authorize sentences of death for those who committed their offense when under 17, making a total of 30 States that would not tolerate the execution of petitioner Wilkins. Congress' most recent enactment of a death penalty statute also excludes those under 18.

I do not suggest, of course, that laws of these States cut against the constitutionality of the juvenile death penalty — only that accuracy demands that the baseline for our deliberations should be that 27 States refuse to authorize a sentence of death in the circumstances of petitioner Stanford's case, and 30 would not permit Wilkins' execution; that 19 States have not squarely faced the question; and that only the few remaining jurisdictions have explicitly set an age below 18 at which a person may be sentenced to death.

Both in absolute and in relative terms, imposition of the death penalty on adolescents is distinctly unusual. Adolescent offenders make up only a small proportion of the current death-row population: 30 out of a total of 2,186 inmates, or 1.37 percent. Eleven minors were sentenced to die in 1982; nine in 1983; six in 1984; five in 1985; seven in 1986; and two in 1987. Forty-one, or 2.3 percent, of the 1,813 death sentences imposed between January 1, 1982, and June 30, 1988, were for juvenile crimes. And juvenile offenders are significantly less likely to receive the death penalty than adults. During the same period, there were 97,086 arrests of adults for homicide, and 1,772 adult death sentences, or 1.8 percent; and 8,911 arrests of minors for homicide, compared to 41 juvenile death sentences, or 0.5 percent.

Our cases recognize that objective indicators of contemporary standards of decency in the form of legislation in other countries is also of relevance to Eighth Amendment analysis. Many countries, of course—over 50, including nearly all in Western Europe—have formally abolished the death penalty, or have limited its use to exceptional crimes such as treason. Twenty-seven others do not in practice impose the penalty. Of the nations that retain capital punishment, a majority—65—prohibit the execution of juveniles. Sixty-one countries retain capital punishment and have no statutory provision exempting juveniles, though some of these nations are ratifiers of international treaties that do prohibit the execution of juveniles. Since 1979, Amnesty International has recorded only eight executions of offenders under 18 throughout the world, three of these in the United States. The other five executions were carried out in Pakistan, Bangladesh, Rwanda, and Barbados. In addition to national laws, three leading human rights treaties ratified or signed by the United States explicitly prohibit juvenile death penalties. Within the world community, the imposition of the death penalty for juvenile crimes appears to be overwhelmingly disapproved.

Together, the rejection of the death penalty for juveniles by a majority of the States, the rarity of the sentence for juveniles, both as an absolute and a comparative matter, the decisions of respected organizations in relevant fields that this punishment is unacceptable, and its rejection generally throughout the world, provide to my mind a strong grounding for the view that it is not constitutionally tolerable that certain States persist in authorizing the execution of adolescent offenders. It is unnecessary, however, to rest a view that the Eighth Amendment prohibits the execution of minors solely upon a judgment as to the meaning to be attached to the evidence of contemporary values outlined above, for the execution of juveniles fails to satisfy two well-established and independent Eighth Amendment requirements—that a punishment not be disproportionate, and that it make a contribution to acceptable goals of punishment.

Proportionality analysis requires that we compare "the gravity of the offense," understood to include not only the injury caused, but also the defendant's culpability, with "the harshness of the penalty." In my view, juveniles so generally lack the degree of responsibility for their crimes that is a predicate for the constitutional imposition of the death penalty that the Eighth Amendment forbids that they receive that punishment.

Legislative determinations distinguishing juveniles from adults abound. These age-based classifications reveal much about how our society regards juveniles as a class, and about societal beliefs regarding adolescent levels of responsibility.

The participation of juveniles in a substantial number of activities open to adults is either barred completely or significantly restricted by legislation. All States but two have a uniform age of majority, and have set that age at 18 or above. No State has lowered its voting age below 18. Nor does any State permit a person under 18 to serve on a jury. Only four States ever permit persons below 18 to marry without parental consent. Thirty-seven States have specific enactments requiring that a patient have attained 18 before she may validly consent to medical treatment. Thirty-four States require parental consent before a person below 18 may drive a motor car. Legislation in 42 States prohibits those under 18 from purchasing pornographic materials. Where gambling is legal, adolescents under 18 are generally not permitted to participate in it, in some or all of its forms. In these and a host of other ways, minors are treated differently from adults in our laws, which reflects the simple truth derived from communal experience that juveniles as a class have not the level of maturation and responsibility that we presume in adults and consider desirable for full participation in the rights and duties of modern life.

To be sure, the development of cognitive and reasoning abilities and of empathy, the acquisition of experience upon which these abilities operate and upon which the capacity to make sound value judgments depends, and in general the process of maturation into a self-directed individual fully responsible for his or her actions, occur by degrees. But the factors discussed above indicate that 18 is the dividing line that society has generally drawn, the point at which it is thought reasonable to assume that persons have an ability to make, and a duty to bear responsibility for, their judgments. Insofar as age 18 is a necessarily arbitrary social choice as a point at which to acknowledge a person's maturity and responsibility, given the different developmental rates of individuals, it is in fact "a conservative estimate of the dividing line between adolescence and adulthood. Many of the psychological and emotional changes that an adolescent experiences in maturing do not actually occur until the early 20s."

There may be exceptional individuals who mature more quickly than their peers, and who might be considered fully responsible for their actions prior to the age of 18, despite their lack of the experience upon which judgment depends. In my view, however, it is not sufficient to accommodate the facts about juveniles that an individual youth's culpability may be taken into account in the decision to transfer him or her from the juvenile to the adult court system for trial, or that a capital sentencing jury is instructed to consider youth and other mitigating factors. I believe that the Eighth Amendment requires that a person who lacks that full degree of responsibility for his or her actions associated with adulthood not be sentenced to death. Hence it is constitutionally inadequate that a juvenile offender's level of responsibility be taken into account only along with a host of other factors that the court or jury may decide outweigh that want of responsibility.

It is thus unsurprising that individualized consideration at transfer and sentencing has not in fact ensured that juvenile offenders lacking an adult's culpability are not sentenced to die. Quite the contrary. Adolescents on death row appear typically to have a battery of psychological, emotional, and other problems going to their likely capacity for judgment and level of blameworthiness. A recent diagnostic evaluation of all 14 juveniles on death rows in four States is instructive. Seven of the adolescents sentenced to die were psychotic when evaluated, or had been so diagnosed in earlier childhood; four others had histories consistent with diagnoses of severe mood disorders; and the remaining three experienced periodic paranoid episodes, during which they would assault perceived enemies. Eight had suffered severe head injuries during childhood, and nine suffered from neurological abnormalities, Psychoeducational testing showed that only 2 of these death-row inmates had IQ scores above 90 (that is, in the normal range) — and both individuals suffered from psychiatric disorders — while 10 offenders showed impaired abstract reasoning on at least some tests. All but two of the adolescents had been physically abused, and five sexually abused. Within the families of these children, violence, alcoholism, drug abuse, and psychiatric disorders were commonplace.

Juveniles very generally lack that degree of blameworthiness that is, in my view, a constitutional prerequisite for the imposition of capital punishment under our precedents concerning the Eighth Amendment proportionality principle. The individualized consideration of an offender's youth and culpability at the transfer stage and at sentencing has not operated to ensure that the only offenders under 18 singled out for the ultimate penalty are exceptional individuals whose level of responsibility is more developed than that of their peers. In that circumstance, I believe that the same categorical assumption that juveniles as a class are insufficiently mature to be regarded as fully responsible that we make in so many other areas is appropriately made in determining whether minors may be subjected to the death penalty. As we noted in *Thompson*, it would be ironic if the assumptions we so readily make about minors as a class were suddenly unavailable in conducting proportionality analysis. I would hold that the Eighth Amendment prohibits the execution of any person for a crime committed below the age of 18.

"[R]etribution as a justification for executing [offenders] very much depends on the degree of [their] culpability." I have explained why I believe juveniles lack the culpability that makes a crime so extreme that it may warrant, according to this Court's cases, the death penalty; and why we should treat juveniles as a class as exempt from the ultimate penalty. These same considerations persuade me that executing juveniles "does not measurably contribute to the retributive end of ensuring that the criminal gets his just deserts." A punishment that fails the Eighth Amendment test of proportionality because disproportionate to the offender's blameworthiness by definition is not justly deserved.

Nor does the execution of juvenile offenders measurably contribute to the goal of deterrence. Excluding juveniles from the class of persons eligible to receive the death penalty will have little effect on any deterrent value capital punishment may have for potential offenders who are over 18: these adult offenders may of course remain eligible for a death sentence. The potential deterrent effect of juvenile executions on adolescent offenders is also insignificant. The deterrent value of capital punishment rests "on the assumption that we are rational beings who always think before we act, and then base our actions on a careful calculation of the gains and losses involved." First, juveniles "have less capacity ... to think in long-range terms than adults," Task Force 7, and their careful weighing of a distant, uncertain, and indeed highly unlikely consequence prior to action is most improbable. In addition, juveniles have little fear of death, because they have "a profound conviction of their own omnipotence and immortality." Because imposition of the death penalty on persons for offenses committed under the age of 18 makes no measurable contribution to the goals of either retribution or deterrence, it is "nothing more than the purposeless and needless imposition of pain and suffering."

There are strong indications that the execution of juvenile offenders violates contemporary standards of decency: a majority of States decline to permit juveniles to be sentenced to death; imposition of the sentence upon minors is very unusual even in those States that permit it; and respected organizations with expertise in relevant areas regard the execution of juveniles as unacceptable, as does international opinion. These indicators serve to confirm in my view my conclusion that the Eighth Amendment prohibits the execution of persons for offenses they committed while below the age of 18, because the death penalty is disproportionate when applied to such young offenders and fails measurably to serve the goals of capital punishment.

I dissent.

Holding of *Stanford v. Kentucky:* The court held that the imposition of the death penalty on individuals who were 16 or 17 at the time of the commission of the offense does not offend the Eighth Amendment.

Discussion Questions

What are some of the facts of these cases that distinguish them from each other?

How does a survey of state laws on capital punishment of minors have any impact on the decision?

Does the majority consider any particular conditions important in supporting its decision that capital punishment of minors is constitutional?

———

Roper v. Simmons: In *Roper v. Simmons,* the United States Supreme Court was asked to revisit their ruling in the *Stanford* case. At the age of 17, when he was still a junior in high school, Christopher Simmons, committed murder. About nine months later, after he had turned 18, he was tried and sentenced to death. Before its commission, Simmons said he wanted to murder someone. He described his plan in detail to two friends, then aged 15 and 16 respectively, and assured his friends they could "get away with it" because they were minors. After confessing to the murder, Simmons was waived to adult court where he was charged with burglary, kidnaping, stealing, and murder in the first degree. A jury returned a guilty verdict of murder and Simmons was sentenced to death.

As you read *Roper v. Simmons,* look for the following:

1. Consider what had changed between the time that *Stanford* was decided and the time of this decision.

2. Look for the arguments supporting the claim that the imposition of the death penalty on juveniles is (a) cruel; and (b) unusual.

Roper v. Simmons
543 U.S. 551 (2005)

Justice KENNEDY delivered the opinion of the Court.

This case requires us to address, for the second time in a decade and a half, whether it is permissible under the Eighth and Fourteenth Amendments to the Constitution of the United States to execute a juvenile offender who was older than 15 but younger than 18 when he committed a capital crime. In *Stanford v. Kentucky,* a divided Court rejected the proposition that the Constitution bars capital punishment for juvenile offenders in this age group. We reconsider the question.

At the age of 17, when he was still a junior in high school, Christopher Simmons, the respondent here, committed murder. About nine months later, after he had turned 18, he was tried and sentenced to death. There is little doubt that Simmons was the instigator of the crime. Before its commission Simmons said he wanted to murder someone. In chilling, callous terms he talked about his plan, discussing it for the most part with two friends, Charles Benjamin and John Tessmer, then aged 15 and 16 respectively. Simmons proposed to commit burglary and murder by breaking and entering, tying up a victim, and throwing the victim off a bridge. Simmons assured his friends they could "get away with it" because they were minors.

The three met at about 2 a.m. on the night of the murder, but Tessmer left before the other two set out. (The State later charged Tessmer with conspiracy, but dropped the charge in exchange for his testimony against Simmons.) Simmons and Benjamin entered the home of the victim, Shirley Crook, after reaching through an open window and unlocking the back door. Simmons turned on a hallway light. Awakened, Mrs. Crook called out, "Who's there?" In response Simmons entered Mrs. Crook's bedroom, where he recognized her from a previous car accident involving them both. Simmons later admitted this confirmed his resolve to murder her.

Using duct tape to cover her eyes and mouth and bind her hands, the two perpetrators put Mrs. Crook in her minivan and drove to a state park. They reinforced the bindings, covered her head with a towel, and walked her to a railroad trestle spanning the Meramec River. There they tied her hands and feet together with electrical wire, wrapped her whole face in duct tape and threw her from the bridge, drowning her in the waters below.

By the afternoon of September 9, Steven Crook had returned home from an overnight trip, found his bedroom in disarray, and reported his wife missing. On the same afternoon fishermen recovered the victim's body from the river. Simmons, meanwhile, was bragging about the killing, telling friends he had killed a woman "because the bitch seen my face."

The next day, after receiving information of Simmons' involvement, police arrested him at his high school and took him to the police station in Fenton, Missouri. They read him his Miranda rights. Simmons waived his right to an attorney and agreed to answer questions. After less than two hours of interrogation, Simmons confessed to the murder and agreed to perform a videotaped reenactment at the crime scene.

The State charged Simmons with burglary, kidnaping, stealing, and murder in the first degree. As Simmons was 17 at the time of the crime, he was outside the criminal jurisdiction of Missouri's juvenile court system. He was tried as an adult. At trial the State introduced Simmons' confession and the videotaped reenactment of the crime, along with testimony that Simmons discussed the crime in advance and bragged about it later. The defense called no witnesses in the guilt phase. The jury having returned a verdict of murder, the trial proceeded to the penalty phase.

The State sought the death penalty.

During closing arguments, both the prosecutor and defense counsel addressed Simmons' age, which the trial judge had instructed the jurors they could consider as a mitigating factor. Defense counsel reminded the jurors that juveniles of Simmons' age cannot drink, serve on juries, or even see certain movies, because "the legislatures have wisely decided that individuals of a certain age aren't responsible enough." Defense counsel argued that Simmons' age should make "a huge difference to [the jurors] in deciding just exactly what sort of punishment to make." In rebuttal, the prosecutor gave the following response: "Age, he says. Think about age. Seventeen years old. Isn't that scary? Doesn't that scare you? Mitigating? Quite the contrary I submit. Quite the contrary."

The jury recommended the death penalty after finding the State had proved each of the three aggravating factors submitted to it. Accepting the jury's recommendation, the trial judge imposed the death penalty.

After these proceedings in Simmons' case had run their course, this Court held that the Eighth and Fourteenth Amendments prohibit the execution of a mentally retarded person. Simmons filed a new petition for state postconviction relief, arguing that the reasoning of Atkins established that the Constitution prohibits the execution of a juvenile who was under 18 when the crime was committed.

The Missouri Supreme Court agreed. It held that since Stanford,

"a national consensus has developed against the execution of juvenile offenders, as demonstrated by the fact that eighteen states now bar such executions for juveniles, that twelve other states bar executions altogether, that no state has lowered its age of execution below 18 since Stanford, that five states have legislatively or by case law raised or established the minimum age at 18, and that the imposition of the juvenile death penalty has become truly unusual over the last decade."

On this reasoning it set aside Simmons' death sentence and resentenced him to "life imprisonment without eligibility for probation, parole, or release except by act of the Governor."

We granted certiorari, and now affirm.

In *Thompson v. Oklahoma*, a plurality of the Court determined that our standards of decency do not permit the execution of any offender under the age of 16 at the time of the crime.

The next year, in *Stanford v. Kentucky*, the Court, over a dissenting opinion joined by four Justices, referred to contemporary standards of decency in this country and concluded the Eighth and Fourteenth Amendments did not proscribe the execution of juvenile offenders over 15 but under 18.

The same day the Court decided *Stanford*, it held that the Eighth Amendment did not mandate a categorical exemption from the death penalty for the mentally retarded.

Three Terms ago the subject was reconsidered in *Atkins*. We held that standards of decency have evolved since *Penry* and now demonstrate that the execution of the mentally retarded is cruel and unusual punishment.

Just as the *Atkins* Court reconsidered the issue decided in *Penry*, we now reconsider the issue decided in *Stanford*. The beginning point is a review of objective indicia of consensus, as expressed in particular by the enactments of legislatures that have addressed the question. These data give us essential instruction. We then must determine, in the exercise of our own independent judgment, whether the death penalty is a disproportionate punishment for juveniles.

The evidence of national consensus against the death penalty for juveniles is similar, and in some respects parallel, to the evidence *Atkins* held sufficient to demonstrate a national consensus against the death penalty for the mentally retarded. When *Atkins* was decided, 30 States prohibited the death penalty for the mentally retarded. This number comprised 12 that had abandoned the death penalty altogether, and 18 that maintained it but excluded the mentally retarded from its reach. By a similar calculation in this case, 30 States prohibit the juvenile death penalty, comprising 12 that have rejected the death penalty altogether and 18 that maintain it but, by express provision or judicial interpretation, exclude juveniles from its reach. *Atkins* emphasized that even in the 20 States without formal prohibition, the practice of executing the mentally retarded was infrequent. Since *Penry*, only five States had executed offenders known to have an IQ under 70. In the present case, too, even in the 20 States without a formal prohibition on executing juveniles, the practice is infrequent. Since *Stanford*, six States have executed prisoners for crimes committed as juveniles. In the past 10 years, only three have done so: Oklahoma, Texas, and Virginia. In December 2003 the Governor of Kentucky decided to spare the life of Kevin Stanford, and commuted his sentence to one of life imprisonment without parole, with the declaration that "'[w]e ought not be executing people who, legally, were children.'" By this act the Governor ensured Kentucky would not add itself to the list of States that have executed juveniles within the last 10 years even by the execution of the very defendant whose death sentence the Court had upheld in *Stanford v. Kentucky*.

There is, to be sure, at least one difference between the evidence of consensus in Atkins and in this case. Impressive in *Atkins* was the rate of abolition of the death penalty for the mentally retarded. Sixteen States that permitted the execution of the mentally retarded at the time of *Penry* had prohibited the practice by the time we heard *Atkins*. By contrast, the rate of change in reducing the incidence of the juvenile death penalty, or in taking specific steps to abolish it, has been slower. Five States that allowed the juvenile death penalty at the time of Stanford have abandoned it in the intervening 15 years—four through legislative enactments and one through judicial decision.

Though less dramatic than the change from *Penry to Atkins*, we still consider the change from *Stanford* to this case to be significant. The number of States that have abandoned capital punishment for juvenile offenders since *Stanford* is smaller than the number of States that abandoned capital punishment for the mentally retarded after *Penry*; yet we think the same consistency of direction of change has been demonstrated. Since *Stanford*, no State that previously prohibited capital punishment for juveniles has reinstated it. This fact, coupled with the trend toward abolition of the juvenile death penalty, carries special force in light of the general popularity of anticrime legislation, and in light of the particular trend in recent years toward cracking down on juvenile crime in other respects. Any difference between this case and *Atkins* with respect to the pace of abolition is thus counterbalanced by the consistent direction of the change.

The slower pace of abolition of the juvenile death penalty over the past 15 years, moreover, may have a simple explanation. When we heard *Penry*, only two death penalty States had already prohibited the execution of the mentally retarded. When we heard *Stanford*, by contrast, 12 death penalty States had already prohibited the execution of any juvenile under 18, and 15 had prohibited the execution of any juvenile under 17. If anything, this shows that the impropriety of executing juveniles between 16 and 18 years of age gained wide recognition earlier than the impropriety of executing the mentally retarded.

As in *Atkins*, the objective indicia of consensus in this case—the rejection of the juvenile death penalty in the majority of States; the infrequency of its use even where it remains on the books; and the consistency in the trend toward abolition of the practice—provide sufficient evidence that today our society views juveniles, in the words *Atkins* used respecting the mentally retarded, as "categorically less culpable than the average criminal."

A majority of States have rejected the imposition of the death penalty on juvenile offenders under 18, and we now hold this is required by the Eighth Amendment.

Three general differences between juveniles under 18 and adults demonstrate that juvenile offenders cannot with reliability be classified among the worst offenders. First, as any parent knows and as the scientific and sociological studies respondent and his amici cite tend to confirm, "[a] lack of maturity and an underdeveloped sense of responsibility are found in youth more often than in adults and are more understandable among the young. These qualities often result in impetuous and ill-considered actions and decisions." It has been noted that "adolescents are overrepresented statistically in virtually every category of reckless behavior." In recognition of the comparative immaturity and irresponsibility of juveniles, almost every State prohibits those under 18 years of age from voting, serving on juries, or marrying without parental consent.

The second area of difference is that juveniles are more vulnerable or susceptible to negative influences and outside pressures, including peer pressure. This is explained in part by the prevailing circumstance that juveniles have less control, or less experience with control, over their own environment.

The third broad difference is that the character of a juvenile is not as well formed as that of an adult. The personality traits of juveniles are more transitory, less fixed.

These differences render suspect any conclusion that a juvenile falls among the worst offenders. The susceptibility of juveniles to immature and irresponsible behavior means "their irresponsible conduct is not as morally reprehensible as that of an adult." Their own vulnerability and comparative lack of control over their immediate surroundings mean juveniles have a greater claim than adults to be forgiven for failing to escape negative influences in their whole environment. The reality that juveniles still struggle to define their identity means it is less supportable to conclude that even a heinous crime committed by a juvenile is evidence of irretrievably depraved character. From a moral standpoint it would be misguided to equate the failings of a minor with those of an adult, for a greater possibility exists that a minor's character deficiencies will be reformed. Indeed, "[t]he relevance of youth as a mitigating factor derives from the fact that the signature qualities of youth are transient; as individuals mature, the impetuousness and recklessness that may dominate in younger years can subside."

In *Thompson*, a plurality of the Court recognized the import of these characteristics with respect to juveniles under 16, and relied on them to hold that the Eighth Amendment prohibited the imposition of the death penalty on juveniles below that age. We conclude the same reasoning applies to all juvenile offenders under 18.

Once the diminished culpability of juveniles is recognized, it is evident that the penological justifications for the death penalty apply to them with lesser force than to adults. We have held there are two distinct social purposes served by the death penalty: "'retribution and deterrence of capital crimes by prospective offenders.'" As for retribution, we remarked in *Atkins* that "[i]f the culpability of the average murderer is insufficient to justify the most extreme sanction available to the State, the lesser culpability of the mentally retarded offender surely does not merit that form of retribution." The same conclusions follow from the lesser culpability of the juvenile offender. Whether viewed as an attempt to express the community's moral outrage or as an attempt to right the balance for the wrong to the victim, the case for retribution is not as strong with a minor as with an adult. Retribution is not proportional if the law's most severe penalty is imposed on one whose culpability or blameworthiness is diminished, to a substantial degree, by reason of youth and immaturity.

As for deterrence, it is unclear whether the death penalty has a significant or even measurable deterrent effect on juveniles, as counsel for petitioner acknowledged at oral argument. Here, however, the absence of evidence of deterrent effect is of special concern because the same characteristics that render juveniles less culpable than adults suggest as well that juveniles will be less susceptible to deterrence. In particular, as the plurality observed in *Thompson*, "[t]he likelihood that the teenage offender has made the kind of cost-benefit analysis that attaches any weight to the possibility of execution is so remote as to be virtually nonexistent." To the extent the juvenile death penalty might have residual deterrent effect, it is worth noting that the punishment of life imprisonment without the possibility of parole is itself a severe sanction, in particular for a young person.

In concluding that neither retribution nor deterrence provides adequate justification for imposing the death penalty on juvenile offenders, we cannot deny or overlook the brutal crimes too many juvenile offenders have committed. Certainly it can be argued, although we by no means concede the point, that a rare case might arise in which a juvenile offender has sufficient psychological maturity, and at the same time demonstrates sufficient depravity, to merit a sentence of death. A central feature of death penalty sentencing is a particular assessment of the circumstances of the crime and the characteristics of the offender. The system is designed to consider both aggravating and mitigating circumstances, including youth, in every case. Given this Court's own insistence on individualized consideration, petitioner maintains that it is both arbitrary and unnecessary to adopt a categorical rule barring imposition of the death penalty on any offender under 18 years of age.

We disagree. The differences between juvenile and adult offenders are too marked and well understood to risk allowing a youthful person to receive the death penalty despite insufficient culpability. An unacceptable likelihood exists that the brutality or cold-blooded nature of any particular crime would overpower mitigating arguments based on youth as a matter of course, even where the juvenile offender's objective immaturity, vulnerability, and lack of true depravity should require a sentence less severe than death. In some cases a defendant's youth may even be counted against him. In this very case, as we noted above, the prosecutor argued Simmons' youth was aggravating rather than mitigating. While this sort of overreaching could be corrected by a particular rule to ensure that the mitigating force of youth is not overlooked, that would not address our larger concerns.

It is difficult even for expert psychologists to differentiate between the juvenile offender whose crime reflects unfortunate yet transient immaturity, and the rare juvenile offender whose crime reflects irreparable corruption. As we understand it, this difficulty underlies the rule forbidding psychiatrists from diagnosing any patient under 18 as having antisocial personality disorder, a disorder also referred to as psychopathy or sociopathy, and which is characterized by callousness, cynicism, and contempt for the feelings, rights, and suffering of others. If trained psychiatrists with the advantage of clinical testing and observation refrain, despite diagnostic expertise, from assessing any juvenile under 18 as having antisocial personality disorder, we conclude that States should refrain from asking jurors to issue a far graver condemnation — that a juvenile offender merits the death penalty. When a juvenile offender commits a heinous crime, the State can exact forfeiture of some of the most basic liberties, but the State cannot extinguish his life and his potential to attain a mature understanding of his own humanity.

Drawing the line at 18 years of age is subject, of course, to the objections always raised against categorical rules. The qualities that distinguish juveniles from adults do not disappear when an individual turns 18. By the same token, some under 18 have already attained a level of maturity some adults will never reach. For the reasons we have discussed, however, a line must be drawn. The plurality opinion in *Thompson* drew the line at 16. In the intervening years the *Thompson* plurality's conclusion that offenders under 16 may not be executed has not been challenged. The logic of *Thompson* extends to those who are under 18. The age of 18 is the point where society draws the line for many purposes between childhood and adulthood. It is, we conclude, the age at which the line for death eligibility ought to rest.

These considerations mean *Stanford v. Kentucky* should be deemed no longer controlling on this issue. To the extent *Stanford* was based on review of the objective indicia of consensus that obtained in 1989, it suffices to note that those indicia have changed. It should be observed, furthermore, that the *Stanford* Court should have considered those States that had abandoned the death penalty altogether as part of the consensus against the juvenile death penalty; a State's decision to bar the death penalty altogether of necessity demonstrates a judgment that the death penalty is inappropriate for all offenders, including juveniles. Last, to the extent *Stanford* was based on a rejection of the idea that this Court is required to bring its independent judgment to bear on the proportionality of the death penalty for a particular class of crimes or offenders, it suffices to note that this rejection was inconsistent with prior Eighth Amendment decisions. It is also inconsistent with the premises of our recent decision in *Atkins*.

In holding that the death penalty cannot be imposed upon juvenile offenders, we take into account the circumstance that some States have relied on *Stanford* in seeking the death penalty against juvenile offenders. This consideration, however, does not outweigh our conclusion that *Stanford* should no longer control in those few pending cases or in those yet to arise.

Our determination that the death penalty is disproportionate punishment for offenders under 18 finds confirmation in the stark reality that the United States is the only country in the world that continues to give official sanction to the juvenile death penalty. This reality does not become controlling, for the task of interpreting the Eighth Amendment remains our responsibility.

As respondent and a number of amici emphasize, Article 37 of the United Nations Convention on the Rights of the Child, which every country in the world has ratified save for the United States and Somalia, contains an express prohibition on capital punishment for crimes committed by juveniles under 18. No ratifying country has entered a reservation to the provision prohibiting the execution of juvenile offenders. Parallel prohibitions are contained in other significant international covenants.

Respondent and his amici have submitted, and petitioner does not contest, that only seven countries other than the United States have executed juvenile offenders since 1990: Iran, Pakistan, Saudi Arabia, Yemen, Nigeria, the Democratic Republic of Congo, and China. Since then each of these countries has either abolished capital punishment for juveniles or made public disavowal of the practice. In sum, it is fair to say that the United States now stands alone in a world that has turned its face against the juvenile death penalty.

It is proper that we acknowledge the overwhelming weight of international opinion against the juvenile death penalty, resting in large part on the understanding that the instability and emotional imbalance of young people may often be a factor in the crime. The opinion of the world community, while not controlling our outcome, does provide respected and significant confirmation for our own conclusions.

The Eighth and Fourteenth Amendments forbid imposition of the death penalty on offenders who were under the age of 18 when their crimes were committed. The judgment of the Missouri Supreme Court setting aside the sentence of death imposed upon Christopher Simmons is affirmed.

It is so ordered.

Justice O'CONNOR, dissenting.

The Court's decision today establishes a categorical rule forbidding the execution of any offender for any crime committed before his 18th birthday, no matter how deliberate, wanton, or cruel the offense. Neither the objective evidence of contemporary societal values, nor the Court's moral proportionality analysis, nor the two in tandem suffice to justify this ruling.

Although the Court finds support for its decision in the fact that a majority of the States now disallow capital punishment of 17-year-old offenders, it refrains from asserting that its holding is compelled by a genuine national consensus. Indeed, the evidence before us fails to demonstrate conclusively that any such consensus has emerged in the brief period since we upheld the constitutionality of this practice in *Stanford v. Kentucky*.

Instead, the rule decreed by the Court rests, ultimately, on its independent moral judgment that death is a disproportionately severe punishment for any 17-year-old offender. I do not subscribe to this judgment. Adolescents as a class are undoubtedly less mature, and therefore less culpable for their misconduct, than adults. But the Court has adduced no evidence impeaching the seemingly reasonable conclusion reached by many state legislatures: that at least some 17-year-old murderers are sufficiently mature to deserve the death penalty in an appropriate case. Nor has it been shown that capital sentencing juries are incapable of accurately assessing a youthful defendant's maturity or of giving due weight to the mitigating characteristics associated with youth.

On this record—and especially in light of the fact that so little has changed since our recent decision in *Stanford*—I would not substitute our judgment about the moral propriety of capital punishment for 17-year-old murderers for the judgments of the Nation's legislatures. Rather, I would demand a clearer showing that our society truly has set its face against this practice before reading the Eighth Amendment categorically to forbid it.

It is by now beyond serious dispute that the Eighth Amendment's prohibition of "cruel and unusual punishments" is not a static command. Its mandate would be little more than a dead letter today if it barred only those sanctions—like the execution of children under the age of seven—that civilized society had already repudiated in 1791.

Although the general principles that guide our Eighth Amendment jurisprudence afford some common ground, I part ways with the Court in applying them to the case before us. As a preliminary matter, I take issue with the Court's failure to reprove, or even to acknowledge, the Supreme Court of Missouri's unabashed refusal to follow our controlling decision in Stanford. The lower court concluded that, despite *Stanford*'s clear holding and historical recency, our decision was no longer binding authority because it was premised on what the court deemed an obsolete assessment of contemporary values. Quite apart from the merits of the constitutional question, this was clear error.

Because the Eighth Amendment "draw[s] its meaning from … evolving standards of decency," significant changes in societal mores over time may require us to reevaluate a prior decision. Nevertheless, it remains "this Court's prerogative alone to overrule one of its precedents." That is so even where subsequent decisions or factual developments may appear to have "significantly undermined" the rationale for our earlier holding. The Eighth Amendment provides no exception to this rule. On the contrary, clear, predictable, and uniform constitutional standards are especially desirable in this sphere. By affirming the lower court's judgment without so much as a slap on the hand, today's decision threatens to invite frequent and disruptive reassessments of our Eighth Amendment precedents.

Seventeen-year-old murderers must be categorically exempted from capital punishment, the Court says, because they "cannot with reliability be classified among the worst offenders." That conclusion is premised on three perceived differences between "adults," who have already reached their 18th birthdays, and "juveniles," who have not. First, juveniles lack maturity and responsibility and are more reckless than adults. Second, juveniles are more vulnerable to outside influences because they have less control over their surroundings. And third, a juvenile's character is not as fully formed as that of an adult. Based on these characteristics, the Court determines that 17-year-old capital murderers are not as blameworthy as adults guilty of similar crimes; that 17-year-olds are less likely than adults to be deterred by the prospect of a death sentence; and that it is difficult to conclude that a 17-year-old who commits even the most heinous of crimes is "irretrievably depraved."

It is beyond cavil that juveniles as a class are generally less mature, less responsible, and less fully formed than adults, and that these differences bear on juveniles' comparative moral culpability. But even accepting this premise, the Court's proportionality argument fails to support its categorical rule.

First, the Court adduces no evidence whatsoever in support of its sweeping conclusion that it is only in "rare" cases, if ever, that 17-year-old murderers are sufficiently mature and act with sufficient depravity to warrant the death penalty. The fact that juveniles are generally less culpable for their misconduct than adults does not necessarily mean that a 17-year-old murderer cannot be sufficiently culpable to merit the death penalty. At most, the Court's argument suggests that the average 17-year-old murderer is not as culpable as the average adult murderer. But an especially depraved juvenile offender may nevertheless be just as culpable as many adult offenders considered bad enough to deserve the death penalty. Similarly, the fact that the availability of the death penalty may be less likely to deter a juvenile from committing a capital crime does not imply that this threat cannot effectively deter some 17-year-olds from such an act. Surely there is an age below which no offender, no matter what his crime, can be deemed to have the cognitive or emotional maturity necessary to warrant the death penalty. But at least at the margins between adolescence and adulthood—and especially for 17-year-olds such as respondent—the relevant differences between "adults" and "juveniles" appear to be a matter of degree, rather than of kind. It follows that a legislature may reasonably conclude that at least some 17-year-olds can act with sufficient moral culpability, and can be sufficiently deterred by the threat of execution, that capital punishment may be warranted in an appropriate case.

Indeed, this appears to be just such a case. Christopher Simmons' murder of Shirley Crook was premeditated, wanton, and cruel in the extreme. Well before he committed this crime, Simmons declared that he wanted to kill someone. On several occasions, he discussed with two friends (ages 15 and 16) his plan to burglarize a house and to murder the victim by tying the victim up and pushing him from a bridge. Simmons said they could "'get away with it'" because they were minors. In accord with this plan, Simmons and his 15-year-old accomplice broke into Mrs. Crook's home in the middle of the night, forced her from her bed, bound her, and drove her to a state park. There, they walked her to a railroad trestle spanning a river, "hog-tied" her with electrical cable, bound her face completely with duct tape, and pushed her, still alive, from the trestle. She drowned in the water below. One can scarcely imagine the terror that this woman must have suffered throughout the ordeal leading to her death. Whatever can be said about the comparative moral culpability of 17-year-olds as a general matter, Simmons' actions unquestionably reflect "'a consciousness materially more "depraved" than that of'... the average murderer." And Simmons' prediction that he could murder with impunity because he had not yet turned 18—though inaccurate—suggests that he did take into account the perceived risk of punishment in deciding whether to commit the crime. Based on this evidence, the sentencing jury certainly had reasonable grounds for concluding that, despite Simmons' youth, he "ha[d] sufficient psychological maturity" when he committed this horrific murder, and "at the same time demonstrate[d] sufficient depravity, to merit a sentence of death."

The Court's proportionality argument suffers from a second and closely related defect: It fails to establish that the differences in maturity between 17-year-olds and young "adults" are both universal enough and significant enough to justify a bright-line pro-phylactic rule against capital punishment of the former. The Court's analysis is premised on differences in the aggregate between juveniles and adults, which frequently do not hold true when comparing individuals. Although it may be that many 17-year-old mur-derers lack sufficient maturity to deserve the death penalty, some juvenile murderers may be quite mature. Chronological age is not an unfailing measure of psychological devel-opment, and common experience suggests that many 17-year-olds are more mature than the average young "adult." In short, the class of offenders exempted from capital punish-ment by today's decision is too broad and too diverse to warrant a categorical prohibition. Indeed, the age-based line drawn by the Court is indefensibly arbitrary — it quite likely will protect a number of offenders who are mature enough to deserve the death penalty and may well leave vulnerable many who are not.

For purposes of proportionality analysis, 17-year-olds as a class are qualitatively and materially different from the mentally retarded. "Mentally retarded" offenders, as we un-derstood that category in Atkins, are defined by precisely the characteristics which ren-der death an excessive punishment. A mentally retarded person is, "by definition," one whose cognitive and behavioral capacities have been proved to fall below a certain min-imum. There is no such inherent or accurate fit between an offender's chronological age and the personal limitations which the Court believes make capital punishment exces-sive for 17-year-old murderers. Moreover, it defies common sense to suggest that 17-year-olds as a class are somehow equivalent to mentally retarded persons with regard to culpability or susceptibility to deterrence. Seventeen-year-olds may, on average, be less ma-ture than adults, but that lesser maturity simply cannot be equated with the major, life-long impairments suffered by the mentally retarded.

The proportionality issues raised by the Court clearly implicate Eighth Amendment concerns. But these concerns may properly be addressed not by means of an arbitrary, cat-egorical age-based rule, but rather through individualized sentencing in which juries are required to give appropriate mitigating weight to the defendant's immaturity, his suscep-tibility to outside pressures, his cognizance of the consequences of his actions, and so forth.

I turn, finally, to the Court's discussion of foreign and international law. Without ques-tion, there has been a global trend in recent years toward abolishing capital punishment for under-18 offenders. Very few, if any, countries other than the United States now per-mit this practice in law or in fact. Because I do not believe that a genuine national con-sensus against the juvenile death penalty has yet developed, and because I do not believe the Court's moral proportionality argument justifies a categorical, age-based constitu-tional rule, I can assign no such confirmatory role to the international consensus de-scribed by the Court. In short, the evidence of an international consensus does not alter my determination that the Eighth Amendment does not, at this time, forbid capital pun-ishment of 17-year-old murderers in all cases.

Nevertheless, I disagree with Justice SCALIA's contention that foreign and international law have no place in our Eighth Amendment jurisprudence. Over the course of nearly half a century, the Court has consistently referred to foreign and international law as relevant to its assessment of evolving standards of decency. But this Nation's evolving understand-ing of human dignity certainly is neither wholly isolated from, nor inherently at odds with, the values prevailing in other countries. On the contrary, we should not be surprised to find congruence between domestic and international values, especially where the interna-tional community has reached clear agreement — expressed in international law or in the domestic laws of individual countries — that a particular form of punishment is inconsistent with fundamental human rights. At least, the existence of an international consensus of this nature can serve to confirm the reasonableness of a consonant and genuine American consensus. The instant case presents no such domestic consensus, however, and the recent emergence of an otherwise global consensus does not alter that basic fact.

Reasonable minds can differ as to the minimum age at which commission of a serious crime should expose the defendant to the death penalty, if at all. Many jurisdictions have abolished capital punishment altogether, while many others have determined that even the most heinous crime, if committed before the age of 18, should not be punishable by death. Indeed, were my office that of a legislator, rather than a judge, then I, too, would be inclined to support legislation setting a minimum age of 18 in this context. But a significant number of States, including Missouri, have decided to make the death penalty potentially available for 17-year-old capital murderers such as respondent. Without a clearer showing that a genuine national consensus forbids the execution of such offenders, this Court should not substitute its own "inevitably subjective judgment" on how best to resolve this difficult moral question for the judgments of the Nation's democratically elected legislatures.

I respectfully dissent.

Justice SCALIA, with whom THE CHIEF JUSTICE and Justice THOMAS join, dissenting.

In urging approval of a constitution that gave life-tenured judges the power to nullify laws enacted by the people's representatives, Alexander Hamilton assured the citizens of New York that there was little risk in this, since "[t]he judiciary ... ha[s] neither FORCE nor WILL but merely judgment." But Hamilton had in mind a traditional judiciary, "bound down by strict rules and precedents which serve to define and point out their duty in every particular case that comes before them." Bound down, indeed. What a mockery today's opinion makes of Hamilton's expectation, announcing the Court's conclusion that the meaning of our Constitution has changed over the past 15 years—not, mind you, that this Court's decision 15 years ago was wrong, but that the Constitution has changed. The Court reaches this implausible result by purporting to advert, not to the original meaning of the Eighth Amendment, but to "the evolving standards of decency," of our national society. It then finds, on the flimsiest of grounds, that a national consensus which could not be perceived in our people's laws barely 15 years ago now solidly exists. Worse still, the Court says in so many words that what our people's laws say about the issue does not, in the last analysis, matter: "[I]n the end our own judgment will be brought to bear on the question of the acceptability of the death penalty under the Eighth Amendment." The Court thus proclaims itself sole arbiter of our Nation's moral standards—and in the course of discharging that awesome responsibility purports to take guidance from the views of foreign courts and legislatures. Because I do not believe that the meaning of our Eighth Amendment, any more than the meaning of other provisions of our Constitution, should be determined by the subjective views of five Members of this Court and like-minded foreigners, I dissent.

Words have no meaning if the views of less than 50% of death penalty States can constitute a national consensus. Our previous cases have required overwhelming opposition to a challenged practice, generally over a long period of time.

Consulting States that bar the death penalty concerning the necessity of making an exception to the penalty for offenders under 18 is rather like including old-order Amishmen in a consumer-preference poll on the electric car. Of course they don't like it, but that sheds no light whatever on the point at issue. That 12 States favor no executions says something about consensus against the death penalty, but nothing—absolutely noth-ing—about consensus that offenders under 18 deserve special immunity from such a penalty. In repealing the death penalty, those 12 States considered none of the factors that the Court puts forth as determinative of the issue before us today—lower culpabil-ity of the young, inherent recklessness, lack of capacity for considered judgment, etc. What might be relevant, perhaps, is how many of those States permit 16- and 17-year-old offenders to be treated as adults with respect to noncapital offenses. (They all do; in-deed, some even require that juveniles as young as 14 be tried as adults if they are charged with murder.) The attempt by the Court to turn its remarkable minority consensus into a faux majority by counting Amishmen is an act of nomological desperation.

I also doubt whether many of the legislators who voted to change the laws in those four States would have done so if they had known their decision would (by the pro-nouncement of this Court) be rendered irreversible. After all, legislative support for cap-ital punishment, in any form, has surged and ebbed throughout our Nation's history.

If the Eighth Amendment set forth an ordinary rule of law, it would indeed be the role of this Court to say what the law is. But the Court having pronounced that the Eighth Amendment is an ever-changing reflection of "the evolving standards of decency" of our society, it makes no sense for the Justices then to prescribe those standards rather than discern them from the practices of our people. On the evolving-standards hypothesis, the only legitimate function of this Court is to identify a moral consensus of the Ameri-can people. By what conceivable warrant can nine lawyers presume to be the authorita-tive conscience of the Nation?

Today's opinion provides a perfect example of why judges are ill equipped to make the type of legislative judgments the Court insists on making here. To support its opinion that States should be prohibited from imposing the death penalty on anyone who com-mitted murder before age 18, the Court looks to scientific and sociological studies, pick-ing and choosing those that support its position. It never explains why those particular studies are methodologically sound; none was ever entered into evidence or tested in an adversarial proceeding.

Moreover, the cited studies describe only adolescents who engage in risky or antiso-cial behavior, as many young people do. Murder, however, is more than just risky or an-tisocial behavior. It is entirely consistent to believe that young people often act impetuously and lack judgment, but, at the same time, to believe that those who commit premedi-tated murder are—at least sometimes—just as culpable as adults. Christopher Simmons, who was only seven months shy of his 18th birthday when he murdered Shirley Crook, described to his friends beforehand—"[i]n chilling, callous terms," as the Court puts it, ante, at 1187—the murder he planned to commit. He then broke into the home of an innocent woman, bound her with duct tape and electrical wire, and threw her off a bridge alive and conscious. In their amici brief, the States of Alabama, Delaware, Oklahoma, Texas, Utah, and Virginia offer additional examples of murders committed by individu-als under 18 that involve truly monstrous acts. In Alabama, two 17-year-olds, one 16-year-old, and one 19-year-old picked up a female hitchhiker, threw bottles at her, and kicked and stomped her for approximately 30 minutes until she died. They then sexually assaulted her lifeless body and, when they were finished, threw her body off a cliff. They later returned to the crime scene to mutilate her corpse. Other examples in the brief are equally shocking. Though these cases are assuredly the exception rather than the rule, the studies the Court cites in no way justify a constitutional imperative that prevents leg-islatures and juries from treating exceptional cases in an exceptional way—by determining that some murders are not just the acts of happy-go-lucky teenagers, but heinous crimes deserving of death.

Though the views of our own citizens are essentially irrelevant to the Court's decision today, the views of other countries and the so-called international community take center stage.

Unless the Court has added to its arsenal the power to join and ratify treaties on behalf of the United States, I cannot see how this evidence favors, rather than refutes, its position. That the Senate and the President—those actors our Constitution empowers to enter into treaties, see Art. II, § 2—have declined to join and ratify treaties prohibiting execution of under-18 offenders can only suggest that our country has either not reached a national consensus on the question, or has reached a consensus contrary to what the Court announces. That the reservation to the ICCPR was made in 1992 does not suggest otherwise, since the reservation still remains in place today. It is also worth noting that, in addition to barring the execution of under-18 offenders, the United Nations Convention on the Rights of the Child prohibits punishing them with life in prison without the possibility of release. If we are truly going to get in line with the international community, then the Court's reassurance that the death penalty is really not needed, since "the punishment of life imprisonment without the possibility of parole is itself a severe sanction," gives little comfort.

More fundamentally, however, the basic premise of the Court's argument—that American law should conform to the laws of the rest of the world—ought to be rejected out of hand. In fact the Court itself does not believe it. In many significant respects the laws of most other countries differ from our law—including not only such explicit provisions of our Constitution as the right to jury trial and grand jury indictment, but even many interpretations of the Constitution prescribed by this Court itself. The Court-pronounced exclusionary rule, for example, is distinctively American.

The Court should either profess its willingness to reconsider all these matters in light of the views of foreigners, or else it should cease putting forth foreigners' views as part of the reasoned basis of its decisions. To invoke alien law when it agrees with one's own thinking, and ignore it otherwise, is not reasoned decisionmaking, but sophistry.

To add insult to injury, the Court affirms the Missouri Supreme Court without even admonishing that court for its flagrant disregard of our precedent in Stanford. Until today, we have always held that "it is this Court's prerogative alone to overrule one of its precedents."

One must admit that the Missouri Supreme Court's action, and this Court's indulgent reaction, are, in a way, understandable. In a system based upon constitutional and statutory text democratically adopted, the concept of "law" ordinarily signifies that particular words have a fixed meaning. Such law does not change, and this Court's pronouncement of it therefore remains authoritative until (confessing our prior error) we overrule. The Court has purported to make of the Eighth Amendment, however, a mirror of the passing and changing sentiment of American society regarding penology. The lower courts can look into that mirror as well as we can; and what we saw 15 years ago bears no necessary relationship to what they see today. Since they are not looking at the same text, but at a different scene, why should our earlier decision control their judgment?

However sound philosophically, this is no way to run a legal system. We must disregard the new reality that, to the extent our Eighth Amendment decisions constitute something more than a show of hands on the current Justices' current personal views about penology, they purport to be nothing more than a snapshot of American public opinion at a particular point in time (with the timeframes now shortened to a mere 15 years). We must treat these decisions just as though they represented real law, real prescriptions democratically adopted by the American people, as conclusively (rather than sequentially) construed by this Court. Allowing lower courts to reinterpret the Eighth Amendment whenever they decide enough time has passed for a new snapshot leaves this Court's decisions without any force—especially since the "evolution" of our Eighth Amendment is no longer determined by objective criteria. To allow lower courts to behave as we do, "updating" the Eighth Amendment as needed, destroys stability and makes our case law an unreliable basis for the designing of laws by citizens and their representatives, and for action by public officials. The result will be to crown arbitrariness with chaos.

Holdings of *Roper v. Simmons:* The court held that the Eighth and Fourteenth Amendments forbid imposition of the death penalty on offenders who were under the age of 18 when their crimes were committed.

Discussion Questions

How does the Court's holding in Atkins (holding imposing the death penalty on the mentally retarded is unconstitutional) affect this case?

Does the majority draw a "red line" at the age of 18 and hold that capital punishment can NEVER be imposed for the act of a person under the age of 18 at the time of the crime?

What are the three differences between Juveniles and adults that the court finds warrant a different holding for the two groups concerning the imposition of the death penalty (that they are not among the "worst offenders")?

How does the majority reason that the two justifications for the imposition of the death penalty (retribution and deterrence) are not as applicable to minors as to adults?

Key Concepts: Death Penalty for Juvenile Offenders

- There are three perceived differences between adults, who have already reached their 18th birthdays, and juveniles, who have not, all of which impact the decision of sentencing juveniles to death: First, juveniles lack maturity and responsibility and are more reckless than adults. Second, juveniles are more vulnerable to outside influences because they have less control over their surroundings. And third, a juvenile's character is not as fully formed as that of an adult.

- The Eighth and Fourteenth Amendments forbid imposition of the death penalty on offenders who were under the age of 18 when their crimes were committed.

Practical Questions: Death Penalty for Juvenile Offenders

1. You have agreed to represent a number of defendants on death row in death penalty cases. One of the defendants was 17 at the time of the murder he committed in 1993 (between the dates *Standford* decision and the *Roper* decision). His last appeal was concluded in 2003. Which of these decisions applies to your client? Can he be executed?

2. You represent an undocumented youth who committed a murder on March 15, 2016. He does not have a birth certificate and is uncertain of his birthday. He knows that he was born sometime in March of 1998. Neither you nor the state is able to determine whether he was 17 or 18 at the time of the offense. Who has the burden of proof as to age in order to support the imposition of the death penalty—the state or the defendant?

B. Life Without Parole for Juvenile Offenders

Overview: Courts have been faced with challenges to the constitutionality of sentences of life imprisonment without parole (LWOP) for juveniles on some of the same grounds that were used to attack the imposition of the death penalty on juveniles: juveniles lack maturity and responsibility and are more reckless than adults; juveniles are more vulnerable to outside influences because they have less control over their surroundings; a juvenile's character is not as fully formed as that of an adult and are therefore capable of reform. As a result, the United States Supreme Court has been asked to determine if sentences of LWOP violate the prohibition against cruel and unusual punishment contained in the 8th Amendment.

Graham v. Florida: In *Graham v. Florida,* the United States Supreme Court was faced with a case where a 16-year-old youth (Graham) was arrested for an attempted robbery. In Florida, the prosecutor could elect to try Graham in adult court, which he did. The charges against Graham included armed burglary with assault or battery (a first-degree felony carrying a maximum penalty of life imprisonment without the possibility of parole). Graham pleaded guilty, and the trial court withheld adjudication of guilt as to both charges and sentenced Graham to concurrent 3-year terms of probation. Graham was required to spend the first 12 months of his probation in the county jail. Less than 6 months after his release from jail, Graham was arrested for robbery. The night that Graham allegedly committed the robbery, he was "34 days short of his 18th birthday." The trial court found Graham guilty of the earlier armed burglary and attempted armed robbery charges. It sentenced him to the maximum sentence authorized by law on each charge: life imprisonment for the armed burglary and 15 years for the attempted armed robbery. Because Florida had abolished its parole system, a life sentence gives a defendant no possibility of release unless he is granted executive clemency.

As you read *Graham v. Florida,* look for the following:

1. Consider why the court limited its ruling to non-homicide offenders.

2. Consider the factors relied on by the court to prohibit LWOP for juvenile non-homicide offenders and determine which of those factors would not apply to juvenile homicide offenders.

Graham v. Florida
560 U.S. 48 (2010)

JUSTICE KENNEDY delivered the opinion of the Court.

The issue before the Court is whether the Constitution permits a juvenile offender to be sentenced to life in prison without parole for a nonhomicide crime. The sentence was imposed by the State of Florida. Petitioner challenges the sentence under the Eighth Amendment's Cruel and Unusual Punishments Clause, made applicable to the States by the Due Process Clause of the Fourteenth Amendment.

Petitioner is Terrance Jamar Graham. He was born on January 6, 1987. Graham's parents were addicted to crack cocaine, and their drug use persisted in his early years. Graham was diagnosed with attention deficit hyperactivity disorder in elementary school. He began drinking alcohol and using tobacco at age 9 and smoked marijuana at age 13. In July 2003, when Graham was age 16, he and three other school-age youths attempted to rob a barbeque restaurant in Jacksonville, Florida. One youth, who worked at the restaurant, left the back door unlocked just before closing time. Graham and another youth, wearing masks, entered through the unlocked door. Graham's masked accomplice twice struck the restaurant manager in the back of the head with a metal bar. When the manager started yelling at the assailant and Graham, the two youths ran out and escaped in a car driven by the third accomplice. The restaurant manager required stitches for his head injury. No money was taken.

Graham was arrested for the robbery attempt. Under Florida law, it is within a prosecutor's discretion whether to charge 16- and 17-year-olds as adults or juveniles for most felony crimes. Graham's prosecutor elected to charge Graham as an adult. The charges against Graham were armed burglary with assault or battery, a first-degree felony carrying a maximum penalty of life imprisonment without the possibility of parole and attempted armed-robbery, a second-degree felony carrying a maximum penalty of 15 years' imprisonment.

On December 18, 2003, Graham pleaded guilty to both charges under a plea agreement.

The trial court accepted the plea agreement. The court withheld adjudication of guilt as to both charges and sentenced Graham to concurrent 3-year terms of probation. Graham was required to spend the first 12 months of his probation in the county jail, but he received credit for the time he had served awaiting trial, and was released on June 25, 2004. Less than 6 months later, on the night of December 2, 2004, Graham again was arrested. The State's case was as follows: Earlier that evening, Graham participated in a home invasion robbery. His two accomplices were Meigo Bailey and Kirkland Lawrence, both 20-year-old men. According to the State, at 7 p.m. that night, Graham, Bailey, and Lawrence knocked on the door of the home where Carlos Rodriguez lived. Graham, followed by Bailey and Lawrence, forcibly entered the home and held a pistol to Rodriguez's chest. For the next 30 minutes, the three held Rodriguez and another man, a friend of Rodriguez, at gunpoint while they ransacked the home searching for money. Before leaving, Graham and his accomplices barricaded Rodriguez and his friend inside a closet.

The State further alleged that Graham, Bailey, and Lawrence, later the same evening, attempted a second robbery, during which Bailey was shot. Graham, who had borrowed his father's car, drove Bailey and Lawrence to the hospital and left them there. As Graham drove away, a police sergeant signaled him to stop. Graham continued at a high speed but crashed into a telephone pole. He tried to flee on foot but was apprehended. Three handguns were found in his car.

When detectives interviewed Graham, he denied involvement in the crimes. He said he encountered Bailey and Lawrence only after Bailey had been shot. One of the detectives told Graham that the victims of the home invasion had identified him. He asked Graham, "Aside from the two robberies tonight how many more were you involved in?" Graham responded, "Two to three before tonight." The night that Graham allegedly committed the robbery, he was 34 days short of his 18th birthday.

On December 13, 2004, Graham's probation officer filed with the trial court an affidavit asserting that Graham had violated the conditions of his probation by possessing a firearm, committing crimes, and associating with persons engaged in criminal activity. The trial court held hearings on Graham's violations about a year later, in December 2005 and January 2006. The judge who presided was not the same judge who had accepted Graham's guilty plea to the earlier offenses.

Graham maintained that he had no involvement in the home invasion robbery; but, even after the court underscored that the admission could expose him to a life sentence on the earlier charges, he admitted violating probation conditions by fleeing. The State presented evidence related to the home invasion, including testimony from the victims. The trial court noted that Graham, in admitting his attempt to avoid arrest, had acknowledged violating his probation. The court further found that Graham had violated his probation by committing a home invasion robbery, by possessing a firearm, and by associating with persons engaged in criminal activity.

The trial court held a sentencing hearing. Under Florida law the minimum sentence Graham could receive absent a downward departure by the judge was 5 years' imprisonment. The maximum was life imprisonment. Graham's attorney requested the minimum nondeparture sentence of 5 years. A presentence report prepared by the Florida Department of Corrections recommended that Graham receive an even lower sentence—at most 4 years' imprisonment. The State recommended that Graham receive 30 years on the armed burglary count and 15 years on the attempted armed robbery count.

The trial court found Graham guilty of the earlier armed burglary and attempted armed robbery charges. It sentenced him to the maximum sentence authorized by law on each charge: life imprisonment for the armed burglary and 15 years for the attempted armed robbery. Because Florida has abolished its parole system, a life sentence gives a defendant no possibility of release unless he is granted executive clemency.

The analysis begins with objective indicia of national consensus. Six jurisdictions do not allow life without parole sentences for any juvenile offenders. Seven jurisdictions permit life without parole for juvenile offenders, but only for homicide crimes. Thirty-seven States as well as the District of Columbia permit sentences of life without parole for a juvenile nonhomicide offender in some circumstances. Federal law also allows for the possibility of life without parole for offenders as young as 13.

Here, an examination of actual sentencing practices in jurisdictions where the sentence in question is permitted by statute discloses a consensus against its use. Although these statutory schemes contain no explicit prohibition on sentences of life without parole for juvenile nonhomicide offenders, those sentences are most infrequent. According to a recent study, nationwide there are only 109 juvenile offenders serving sentences of life without parole for nonhomicide offenses.

The numbers cited above reflect all current convicts in a jurisdiction's penal system, regardless of when they were convicted. It becomes all the more clear how rare these sentences are, even within the jurisdictions that do sometimes impose them, when one considers that a juvenile sentenced to life without parole is likely to live in prison for decades. Thus, these statistics likely reflect nearly all juvenile nonhomicide offenders who have received a life without parole sentence stretching back many years. It is not certain that this opinion has identified every juvenile nonhomicide offender nationwide serving a life without parole sentence, for the statistics are not precise. The available data, nonetheless, are sufficient to demonstrate how rarely these sentences are imposed even if there are isolated cases that have not been included in the presentations of the parties or the analysis of the Court.

It must be acknowledged that in terms of absolute numbers juvenile life without parole sentences for nonhomicides are more common than the sentencing practices at issue in some of this Court's other Eighth Amendment cases.

Many States have chosen to move away from juvenile court systems and to allow juveniles to be transferred to, or charged directly in, adult court under certain circumstances. Once in adult court, a juvenile offender may receive the same sentence as would be given to an adult offender, including a life without parole sentence. But the fact that transfer and direct charging laws make life without parole possible for some juvenile non-homicide offenders does not justify a judgment that many States intended to subject such offenders to life without parole sentences.

Community consensus, while "entitled to great weight" is not itself determinative of whether a punishment is cruel and unusual. In accordance with the constitutional design, "the task of interpreting the Eighth Amendment remains our responsibility." The judicial exercise of independent judgment requires consideration of the culpability of the offenders at issue in light of their crimes and characteristics, along with the severity of the punishment in question. In this inquiry the Court also considers whether the challenged sentencing practice serves legitimate penological goals.

Roper established that because juveniles have lessened culpability they are less deserving of the most severe punishments. As compared to adults, juveniles have a "'lack of maturity and an underdeveloped sense of responsibility'"; they "are more vulnerable or susceptible to negative influences and outside pressures, including peer pressure"; and their characters are "not as well formed." These salient characteristics mean that "[i]t is difficult even for expert psychologists to differentiate between the juvenile offender whose crime reflects unfortunate yet transient immaturity, and the rare juvenile offender whose crime reflects irreparable corruption." Accordingly, "juvenile offenders cannot with reliability be classified among the worst offenders." A juvenile is not absolved of responsibility for his actions, but his transgression "is not as morally reprehensible as that of an adult."

No recent data provide reason to reconsider the Court's observations in *Roper* about the nature of juveniles. As petitioner's *amici* point out, developments in psychology and brain science continue to show fundamental differences between juvenile and adult minds. For example, parts of the brain involved in behavior control continue to mature through late adolescence. Juveniles are more capable of change than are adults, and their actions are less likely to be evidence of "irretrievably depraved character" than are the actions of adults. It remains true that "[f]rom a moral standpoint it would be misguided to equate the failings of a minor with those of an adult, for a greater possibility exists that a minor's character deficiencies will be reformed." These matters relate to the status of the offenders in question; and it is relevant to consider next the nature of the offenses to which this harsh penalty might apply.

It follows that, when compared to an adult murderer, a juvenile offender who did not kill or intend to kill has a twice diminished moral culpability. The age of the offender and the nature of the crime each bear on the analysis.

As for the punishment, life without parole is "the second most severe penalty permitted by law."

It is true that a death sentence is "unique in its severity and irrevocability," yet life without parole sentences share some characteristics with death sentences that are shared by no other sentences. The State does not execute the offender sentenced to life without parole, but the sentence alters the offender's life by a forfeiture that is irrevocable. It deprives the convict of the most basic liberties without giving hope of restoration, except perhaps by executive clemency—the remote possibility of which does not mitigate the harshness of the sentence. As one court observed in overturning a life without parole sentence for a juvenile defendant, this sentence "means denial of hope; it means that good behavior and character improvement are immaterial; it means that whatever the future might hold in store for the mind and spirit of [the convict], he will remain in prison for the rest of his days."

Life without parole is an especially harsh punishment for a juvenile. Under this sentence a juvenile offender will on average serve more years and a greater percentage of his life in prison than an adult offender. A 16-year-old and a 75-year-old each sentenced to life without parole receive the same punishment in name only. This reality cannot be ignored. It does not follow, however, that the purposes and effects of penal sanctions are irrelevant to the determination of Eighth Amendment restrictions. A sentence lacking any legitimate penological justification is by its nature disproportionate to the offense. With respect to life without parole for juvenile nonhomicide offenders, none of the goals of penal sanctions that have been recognized as legitimate—retribution, deterrence, incapacitation, and rehabilitation—provides an adequate justification.

Retribution is a legitimate reason to punish, but it cannot support the sentence at issue here. Society is entitled to impose severe sanctions on a juvenile nonhomicide offender to express its condemnation of the crime and to seek restoration of the moral imbalance caused by the offense. But "[t]he heart of the retribution rationale is that a criminal sentence must be directly related to the personal culpability of the criminal offender." And as *Roper* observed, "[w]hether viewed as an attempt to express the community's moral outrage or as an attempt to right the balance for the wrong to the victim, the case for retribution is not as strong with a minor as with an adult." The case becomes even weaker with respect to a juvenile who did not commit homicide. Deterrence does not suffice to justify the sentence either. *Roper* noted that "the same characteristics that render juveniles less culpable than adults suggest ... that juveniles will be less susceptible to deterrence." Because juveniles' "lack of maturity and underdeveloped sense of responsibility ... often result in impetuous and ill-considered actions and decisions," they are less likely to take a possible punishment into consideration when making decisions. This is particularly so when that punishment is rarely imposed. That the sentence deters in a few cases is perhaps plausible, but "[t]his argument does not overcome other objections." Even if the punishment has some connection to a valid penological goal, it must be shown that the punishment is not grossly disproportionate in light of the justification offered. Here, in light of juvenile nonhomicide offenders' diminished moral responsibility, any limited deterrent effect provided by life without parole is not enough to justify the sentence.

Incapacitation, a third legitimate reason for imprisonment, does not justify the life without parole sentence in question here. Recidivism is a serious risk to public safety, and so incapacitation is an important goal. But while incapacitation may be a legitimate penological goal sufficient to justify life without parole in other contexts, it is inadequate to justify that punishment for juveniles who did not commit homicide. To justify life without parole on the assumption that the juvenile offender forever will be a danger to society requires the sentencer to make a judgment that the juvenile is incorrigible. The characteristics of juveniles make that judgment questionable.

Here one cannot dispute that this defendant posed an immediate risk, for he had committed, we can assume, serious crimes early in his term of supervised release and despite his own assurances of reform. Graham deserved to be separated from society for some time in order to prevent what the trial court described as an "escalating pattern of criminal conduct," but it does not follow that he would be a risk to society for the rest of his life. Even if the State's judgment that Graham was incorrigible were later corroborated by prison misbehavior or failure to mature, the sentence was still disproportionate because that judgment was made at the outset. A life without parole sentence improperly denies the juvenile offender a chance to demonstrate growth and maturity. Incapacitation cannot override all other considerations, lest the Eighth Amendment's rule against disproportionate sentences be a nullity.

A sentence of life imprisonment without parole, however, cannot be justified by the goal of rehabilitation. The penalty forswears altogether the rehabilitative ideal. By denying the defendant the right to reenter the community, the State makes an irrevocable judgment about that person's value and place in society. This judgment is not appropriate in light of a juvenile nonhomicide offender's capacity for change and limited moral culpability. A State's rejection of rehabilitation, moreover, goes beyond a mere expressive judgment.

For juvenile offenders, who are most in need of and receptive to rehabilitation, the absence of rehabilitative opportunities or treatment makes the disproportionality of the sentence all the more evident.

In sum, penological theory is not adequate to justify life without parole for juvenile nonhomicide offenders. This determination; the limited culpability of juvenile nonhomicide offenders; and the severity of life without parole sentences all lead to the conclusion that the sentencing practice under consideration is cruel and unusual. This Court now holds that for a juvenile offender who did not commit homicide the Eighth Amendment forbids the sentence of life without parole. This clear line is necessary to prevent the possibility that life without parole sentences will be imposed on juvenile nonhomicide offenders who are not sufficiently culpable to merit that punishment. Because "[t]he age of 18 is the point where society draws the line for many purposes between childhood and adulthood," those who were below that age when the offense was committed may not be sentenced to life without parole for a nonhomicide crime.

A State is not required to guarantee eventual freedom to a juvenile offender convicted of a nonhomicide crime. What the State must do, however, is give defendants like Graham some meaningful opportunity to obtain release based on demonstrated maturity and rehabilitation. It is for the State, in the first instance, to explore the means and mechanisms for compliance. It bears emphasis, however, that while the Eighth Amendment forbids a State from imposing a life without parole sentence on a juvenile nonhomicide offender, it does not require the State to release that offender during his natural life. Those who commit truly horrifying crimes as juveniles may turn out to be irredeemable, and thus deserving of incarceration for the duration of their lives. The Eighth Amendment does not foreclose the possibility that persons convicted of nonhomicide crimes committed before adulthood will remain behind bars for life. It does forbid States from making the judgment at the outset that those offenders never will be fit to reenter society.

Finally, a categorical rule gives all juvenile nonhomicide offenders a chance to demonstrate maturity and reform. The juvenile should not be deprived of the opportunity to achieve maturity of judgment and self-recognition of human worth and potential. In *Roper*, that deprivation resulted from an execution that brought life to its end. Here, though by a different dynamic, the same concerns apply. Life in prison without the possibility of parole gives no chance for fulfillment outside prison walls, no chance for reconciliation with society, no hope. Maturity can lead to that considered reflection which is the foundation for remorse, renewal, and rehabilitation. A young person who knows that he or she has no chance to leave prison before life's end has little incentive to become a responsible individual. In some prisons, moreover, the system itself becomes complicit in the lack of development. As noted above, it is the policy in some prisons to withhold counseling, education, and rehabilitation programs for those who are ineligible for parole consideration. A categorical rule against life without parole for juvenile nonhomicide offenders avoids the perverse consequence in which the lack of maturity that led to an offender's crime is reinforced by the prison term.

Terrance Graham's sentence guarantees he will die in prison without any meaningful opportunity to obtain release, no matter what he might do to demonstrate that the bad acts he committed as a teenager are not representative of his true character, even if he spends the next half century attempting to atone for his crimes and learn from his mistakes. The State has denied him any chance to later demonstrate that he is fit to rejoin society based solely on a nonhomicide crime that he committed while he was a child in the eyes of the law. This the Eighth Amendment does not permit.

There is support for our conclusion in the fact that, in continuing to impose life without parole sentences on juveniles who did not commit homicide, the United States adheres to a sentencing practice rejected the world over. This observation does not control our decision. The judgments of other nations and the international community are not dispositive as to the meaning of the Eighth Amendment. But "'[t]he climate of international opinion concerning the acceptability of a particular punishment'" is also "'not irrelevant.'"

Today we continue that longstanding practice in noting the global consensus against the sentencing practice in question. A recent study concluded that only 11 nations authorize life without parole for juvenile offenders under any circumstances; and only 2 of them, the United States and Israel, ever impose the punishment in practice. An updated version of the study concluded that Israel's "laws allow for parole review of juvenile offenders serving life terms," but expressed reservations about how that parole review is implemented. But even if Israel is counted as allowing life without parole for juvenile offenders, that nation does not appear to impose that sentence for nonhomicide crimes; all of the seven Israeli prisoners whom commentators have identified as serving life sentences for juvenile crimes were convicted of homicide or attempted homicide. Thus, as petitioner contends and respondent does not contest, the United States is the only Nation that imposes life without parole sentences on juvenile nonhomicide offenders.

The question before us is not whether international law prohibits the United States from imposing the sentence at issue in this case. The question is whether that punishment is cruel and unusual. In that inquiry, "the overwhelming weight of international opinion against" life without parole for nonhomicide offenses committed by juveniles "provide[s] respected and significant confirmation for our own conclusions."

The Constitution prohibits the imposition of a life without parole sentence on a juvenile offender who did not commit homicide. A State need not guarantee the offender eventual release, but if it imposes a sentence of life it must provide him or her with some realistic opportunity to obtain release before the end of that term. The judgment of the First District Court of Appeal of Florida is reversed, and the case is remanded for further proceedings not inconsistent with this opinion.

It is so ordered.

CHIEF JUSTICE ROBERTS, concurring in the judgment.

I agree with the Court that Terrance Graham's sentence of life without parole violates the Eighth Amendment's prohibition on "cruel and unusual punishments." Unlike the majority, however, I see no need to invent a new constitutional rule of dubious provenance in reaching that conclusion. Instead, my analysis is based on an application of this Court's precedents, in particular (1) our cases requiring "narrow proportionality" review of noncapital sentences and (2) our conclusion in *Roper* v. *Simmons* that juvenile offenders are generally less culpable than adults who commit the same crimes.

These cases expressly allow courts addressing allegations that a noncapital sentence violates the Eighth Amendment to consider the particular defendant and particular crime at issue. The standards for relief under these precedents are rigorous, and should be. But here Graham's juvenile status—together with the nature of his criminal conduct and the extraordinarily severe punishment imposed—lead me to conclude that his sentence of life without parole is unconstitutional.

The second line of precedent relevant to assessing Graham's sentence consists of our cases acknowledging that juvenile offenders are *generally*—though not necessarily in every case—less morally culpable than adults who commit the same crimes.

Today, the Court views *Roper* as providing the basis for a new categorical rule that juveniles may never receive a sentence of life without parole for nonhomicide crimes. I disagree. In *Roper*, the Court tailored its analysis of juvenile characteristics to the specific question whether juvenile offenders could constitutionally be subject to capital punishment. Our answer that they could not be sentenced to death was based on the explicit conclusion that they "cannot with reliability be classified among the *worst* offenders."

This conclusion does not establish that juveniles can never be eligible for life without parole. A life sentence is of course far less severe than a death sentence, and we have never required that it be imposed only on the very worst offenders, as we have with capital punishment. Treating juvenile life sentences as analogous to capital punishment is at odds with our longstanding view that "the death penalty is different from other punishments in kind rather than degree." It is also at odds with *Roper* itself, which drew the line at capital punishment by blessing juvenile sentences that are "less severe than death" despite involving "forfeiture of some of the most basic liberties." Indeed, *Roper* explicitly relied on the possible imposition of life without parole on some juvenile offenders. But the fact that *Roper* does not support a categorical rule barring life sentences for all juveniles does not mean that a criminal defendant's age is irrelevant to those sentences. On the contrary, our cases establish that the "narrow proportionality" review applicable to noncapital cases itself takes the personal "culpability of the offender" into account in examining whether a given punishment is proportionate to the crime. There is no reason why an offender's juvenile status should be excluded from the analysis. Indeed, given *Roper*'s conclusion that juveniles are typically less blameworthy than adults, an offender's juvenile status can play a central role in the inquiry.

But *Roper*'s conclusion that juveniles are typically less culpable than adults has pertinence beyond capital cases, and rightly informs the case-specific inquiry I believe to be appropriate here.

In short, our existing precedent already provides a sufficient framework for assessing the concerns outlined by the majority. Not every juvenile receiving a life sentence will prevail under this approach. Not every juvenile should. But all will receive the protection that the Eighth Amendment requires.

Applying the "narrow proportionality" framework to the particular facts of this case, I conclude that Graham's sentence of life without parole violates the Eighth Amendment.

I begin with the threshold inquiry comparing the gravity of Graham's conduct to the harshness of his penalty. There is no question that the crime for which Graham received his life sentence — armed burglary of a nondomicil with an assault or battery — is "a serious crime deserving serious punishment." So too is the home invasion robbery that was the basis of Graham's probation violation. But these crimes are certainly less serious than other crimes, such as murder or rape. As for Graham's degree of personal culpability, he committed the relevant offenses when he was a juvenile — a stage at which, *Roper* emphasized, one's "culpability or blameworthiness is diminished, to a substantial degree, by reason of youth and immaturity." Graham's youth made him relatively more likely to engage in reckless and dangerous criminal activity than an adult; it also likely enhanced his susceptibility to peer pressure. There is no reason to believe that Graham should be denied the general presumption of diminished culpability that *Roper* indicates should apply to juvenile offenders. If anything, Graham's in-court statements — including his request for a second chance so that he could "do whatever it takes to get to the NFL" — underscore his immaturity. The fact that Graham committed the crimes that he did proves that he was dangerous and deserved to be punished. But it does not establish that he was *particularly* dangerous — at least relative to the murderers and rapists for whom the sentence of life without parole is typically reserved. On the contrary, his lack of prior criminal convictions, his youth and immaturity, and the difficult circumstances of his upbringing noted by the majority, all suggest that he was markedly less culpable than atypical adult who commits the same offenses.

Despite these considerations, the trial court sentenced Graham to life in prison without the possibility of parole. This is the second-harshest sentence available under our precedents for *any* crime, and the most severe sanction available for a nonhomicide offense. Indeed, as the majority notes, Graham's sentence far exceeded the punishment proposed by the Florida Department of Corrections (which suggested a sentence of four years), and the state prosecutors (who asked that he be sentenced to 30 years in prison for the armed burglary). No one in Graham's case other than the sentencing judge appears to have believed that Graham deserved to go to prison for life.

Based on the foregoing circumstances, I conclude that there is a strong inference that Graham's sentence of life imprisonment without parole was grossly disproportionate in violation of the Eighth Amendment. I therefore proceed to the next steps of the proportionality analysis.

Both intrajurisdictional and interjurisdictional comparisons of Graham's sentence confirm the threshold inference of disproportionality. Graham's sentence was far more severe than that imposed for similar violations of Florida law, even without taking juvenile status into account.

Finally, the inference that Graham's sentence is disproportionate is further validated by comparison to the sentences imposed in other domestic jurisdictions. As the majority opinion explains, Florida is an outlier in its willingness to impose sentences of life without parole on juveniles convicted of nonhomicide crimes.

So much for Graham. But what about Milagro Cunningham, a 17-year-old who beat and raped an 8-year-old girl before leaving her to die under 197 pounds of rock in a recycling bin in a remote landfill? Or Nathan Walker and Jakaris Taylor, the Florida juveniles who together with their friends gang-raped a woman and forced her to perform oral sex on her 12-year-old son? The fact that Graham cannot be sentenced to life without parole for his conduct says nothing whatever about these offenders, or others like them who commit nonhomicide crimes far more reprehensible than the conduct at issue here.

The Court uses Graham's case as a vehicle to proclaim a new constitutional rule—applicable well beyond the particular facts of Graham's case—that a sentence of life without parole imposed on *any* juvenile for *any* nonhomicide offense is unconstitutional. This categorical conclusion is as unnecessary as it is unwise.

A holding this broad is unnecessary because the particular conduct and circumstances at issue in the case before us are not serious enough to justify Graham's sentence. In reaching this conclusion, there is no need for the Court to decide whether that same sentence would be constitutional if imposed for other more heinous nonhomicide crimes.

Those under 18 years old may as a general matter have "diminished" culpability relative to adults who commit the same crimes, but that does not mean that their culpability is always insufficient to justify a life sentence. It does not take a moral sense that is fully developed in every respect to know that beating and raping an 8-year-old girl and leaving her to die under 197 pounds of rocks is horribly wrong. The single fact of being 17 years old would not afford Cunningham protection against life without parole if the young girl had died—as Cunningham surely expected she would—so why should it do so when she miraculously survived his barbaric brutality?

Terrance Graham committed serious offenses, for which he deserves serious punishment. But he was only 16 years old, and under our Court's precedents, his youth is one factor, among others, that should be considered in deciding whether his punishment was unconstitutionally excessive. In my view, Graham's age—together with the nature of his criminal activity and the unusual severity of his sentence—tips the constitutional balance. I thus concur in the Court's judgment that Graham's sentence of life without parole violated the Eighth Amendment. I would not, however, reach the same conclusion in every case involving a juvenile offender. Some crimes are so heinous, and some juvenile offenders so highly culpable, that a sentence of life without parole may be entirely justified under the Constitution. As we have said, "successful challenges" to noncapital sentences under the Eighth Amendment have been—and, in my view, should continue to be—"exceedingly rare." But Graham's sentence presents the exceptional case that our precedents have recognized will come along. We should grant Graham the relief to which he is entitled under the Eighth Amendment. The Court errs, however, in using this case as a vehicle for unsettling our established jurisprudence and fashioning a categorical rule applicable to far different cases.

JUSTICE THOMAS, with whom JUSTICE SCALIA joins, and with whom JUSTICE ALITO joins as to Parts I and III, dissenting.

The Court holds today that it is "grossly disproportionate" and hence unconstitutional for any judge or jury to impose a sentence of life without parole on an offender less than 18 years old, unless he has committed a homicide. Although the text of the Constitution is silent regarding the permissibility of this sentencing practice, and although it would not have offended the standards that prevailed at the founding, the Court insists that the standards of American society have evolved such that the Constitution now requires its prohibition.

The news of this evolution will, I think, come as a surprise to the American people. Congress, the District of Columbia, and 37 States allow judges and juries to consider this sentencing practice in juvenile nonhomicide cases, and those judges and juries have decided to use it in the very worst cases they have encountered.

The Court does not conclude that life without parole itself is a cruel and unusual punishment. It instead rejects the judgments of those legislatures, judges, and juries regarding what the Court describes as the "moral" question of whether this sentence can ever be "proportionat[e]" when applied to the category of offenders at issue here.

I am unwilling to assume that we, as members of this Court, are any more capable of making such moral judgments than our fellow citizens. Nothing in our training as judges qualifies us for that task, and nothing in Article III gives us that authority.

I respectfully dissent.

The Court has nonetheless adopted categorical rules that shield entire classes of offenses and offenders from the death penalty on the theory that "evolving standards of decency" require this result. The Court has offered assurances that these standards can be reliably measured by "'objective indicia'" of "national consensus," such as state and federal legislation, jury behavior, and (surprisingly, given that we are talking about "national" consensus) international opinion. Yet even assuming that is true, the Framers did not provide for the constitutionality of a particular type of punishment to turn on a "snapshot of American public opinion" taken at the moment a case is decided. By holding otherwise, the Court pretermits in all but one direction the evolution of the standards it describes, thus "calling a constitutional halt to what may well be a pendulum swing in social attitudes," and "stunt[ing] legislative consideration" of new questions of penal policy as they emerge.

Remarkably, the Court today does more than return to *Solem*'s case-by-case proportionality standard for noncapital sentences; it hurtles past it to impose a *categorical* proportionality rule banning life-without-parole sentences not just in this case, but in *every* case involving a juvenile nonhomicide offender, no matter what the circumstances. Neither the Eighth Amendment nor the Court's precedents justify this decision.

Our society tends to treat the average juvenile as less culpable than the average adult. But the question here does not involve the average juvenile. The question, instead, is whether the Constitution prohibits judges and juries from *ever* concluding that an offender under the age of 18 has demonstrated sufficient depravity and incorrigibility to warrant his permanent incarceration.

The Court equates the propensity of a fairly substantial number of youths to engage in "risky" or antisocial behaviors with the propensity of a much smaller group to commit violent crimes.

The Court responds that a categorical rule is nonetheless necessary to prevent the "'unacceptable likelihood'" that a judge or jury, unduly swayed by "'the brutality or cold-blooded nature'" of a juvenile's nonhomicide crime, will sentence him to a life-without-parole sentence for which he possesses "'insufficient culpability.'" I find that justification entirely insufficient. The integrity of our criminal justice system depends on the ability of citizens to stand between the defendant and an outraged public and dispassionately determine his guilt and the proper amount of punishment based on the evidence presented. That process necessarily admits of human error. But so does the process of judging in which we engage. As between the two, I find far more "unacceptable" that this Court, swayed by studies reflecting the general tendencies of youth, decree that the people of this country are not fit to decide for themselves when the rare case requires different treatment.

That is especially so because, in the end, the Court does not even believe its pronouncements about the juvenile mind. If it did, the categorical rule it announces today would be most peculiar because it leaves intact state and federal laws that permit life-without-parole sentences for juveniles who commit homicides. The Court thus acknowledges that there is nothing inherent in the psyche of a person less than 18 that prevents him from acquiring the moral agency necessary to warrant a life-without-parole sentence. Instead, the Court rejects overwhelming legislative consensus only on the question of which *acts* are sufficient to demonstrate that moral agency.

The Court is quite willing to accept that a 17-year-old who pulls the trigger on a firearm can demonstrate sufficient depravity and irredeemability to be denied reentry into society, but insists that a 17-year-old who rapes an 8-year-old and leaves her for dead does not.

The ultimate question in this case is not whether a life-without-parole sentence 'fits' the crime at issue here or the crimes of juvenile nonhomicide offenders more generally, but to whom the Constitution assigns that decision. The Florida Legislature has concluded that such sentences should be available for persons under 18 who commit certain crimes, and the trial judge in this case decided to impose that legislatively authorized sentence here. Because a life-without-parole prison sentence is not a "cruel and unusual" method of punishment under any standard, the Eighth Amendment gives this Court no authority to reject those judgments. It would be unjustifiable for the Court to declare otherwise even if it could claim that a bare majority of state laws supported its independent moral view. The fact that the Court categorically prohibits life-without-parole sentences for juvenile nonhomicide offenders in the face of an overwhelming legislative majority *in favor* of leaving that sentencing option available under certain cases simply illustrates how far beyond any cognizable constitutional principle the Court has reached to ensure that its own sense of morality and retributive justice pre-empts that of the people and their representatives.

I agree with JUSTICE STEVENS that "[w]e learn, sometimes, from our mistakes." Perhaps one day the Court will learn from this one.

I respectfully dissent.

JUSTICE ALITO, dissenting.

I join Parts I and III of JUSTICE THOMAS's dissenting opinion. I write separately to make two points.

First, the Court holds only that "for a juvenile offender who did not commit homicide the Eighth Amendment forbids the sentence of *life without parole*." Nothing in the Court's opinion affects the imposition of a sentence to a term of years without the possibility of parole. Indeed, petitioner conceded at oral argument that a sentence of as much as 40 years without the possibility of parole "probably" would be constitutional.

Second, the question whether petitioner's sentence violates the narrow, as-applied proportionality principle that applies to noncapital sentences is not properly before us in this case. Although petitioner asserted an as-applied proportionality challenge to his sentence before the Florida courts, he did not include an as-applied claim in his petition for certiorari or in his merits briefs before this Court. Instead, petitioner argued for only a categorical rule banning the imposition of life without parole on *any* juvenile convicted of a nonhomicide offense. Because petitioner abandoned his as-applied claim, I would not reach that issue.

Holdings of *Graham v. Florida*: The court held that the Constitution prohibits the imposition of a life without parole sentence on a juvenile offender who did not commit homicide. A State need not guarantee the offender eventual release, but if it imposes a sentence of life it must provide him or her with some realistic opportunity to obtain release before the end of that term.

Discussion Questions

Is the outcome of this case solely limited to non-homicide cases?

Of all the arguments made by the majority to justify their decision, which ones, if any, would not apply to homicide cases as well?

Does this opinion mean that no minor can be sentenced to life in prison in non-homicide cases?

Does this opinion mean that no minor can be forced to serve life in prison in non-homicide cases?

———

Miller v. Alabama: In *Miller v. Alabama,* the court was faced with a case that forced them to decide whether or not the *Graham v. Florida* holding concerning the constitutionality of the imposition of a mandatory sentence of life without parole (LWOP) on a minor should be extended to all cases (including where the minor committed a homicide.)

As you read *Miller v. Alabama,* look for the following:

1. Consider what will be required of trial courts when sentencing a minor for homicide cases.

2. Consider what limitations the court has put on its decision and what options are still available for a sentencing court in homicide cases where the defendant was a minor at the time of the crime.

3. Look for anything that distinguishes this case from the *Roper v. Simmons* cases involving the death penalty.

Miller v. Alabama

567 U.S. ___, 132 S.Ct. 2455 (2012)

Justice KAGAN delivered the opinion of the Court.

The two 14-year-old offenders in these cases were convicted of murder and sentenced to life imprisonment without the possibility of parole. In neither case did the sentencing authority have any discretion to impose a different punishment. State law mandated that each juvenile die in prison even if a judge or jury would have thought that his youth and its attendant characteristics, along with the nature of his crime, made a lesser sentence (for example, life with the possibility of parole) more appropriate. Such a scheme prevents those meting out punishment from considering a juvenile's "lessened culpability" and greater "capacity for change," and runs afoul of our cases' requirement of individualized sentencing for defendants facing the most serious penalties. We therefore hold that mandatory life without parole for those under the age of 18 at the time of their crimes violates the Eighth Amendment's prohibition on "cruel and unusual punishments."

In November 1999, petitioner Kuntrell Jackson, then 14 years old, and two other boys decided to rob a video store. En route to the store, Jackson learned that one of the boys, Derrick Shields, was carrying a sawed-off shotgun in his coat sleeve. Jackson decided to stay outside when the two other boys entered the store. Inside, Shields pointed the gun at the store clerk, Laurie Troup, and demanded that she "give up the money." Troup refused. A few moments later, Jackson went into the store to find Shields continuing to demand money. At trial, the parties disputed whether Jackson warned Troup that "[w]e ain't playin'," or instead told his friends, "I thought you all was playin'." When Troup threatened to call the police, Shields shot and killed her. The three boys fled empty-handed.

Arkansas law gives prosecutors discretion to charge 14-year-olds as adults when they are alleged to have committed certain serious offenses. The prosecutor here exercised that authority by charging Jackson with capital felony murder and aggravated robbery. Jackson moved to transfer the case to juvenile court, but after considering the alleged facts of the crime, a psychiatrist's examination, and Jackson's juvenile arrest history (shoplifting and several incidents of car theft), the trial court denied the motion, and an appellate court affirmed. A jury later convicted Jackson of both crimes. Noting that "in view of [the] verdict, there's only one possible punishment," the judge sentenced Jackson to life without parole.

Like Jackson, petitioner Evan Miller was 14 years old at the time of his crime. Miller had by then been in and out of foster care because his mother suffered from alcoholism and drug addiction and his stepfather abused him. Miller, too, regularly used drugs and alcohol; and he had attempted suicide four times, the first when he was six years old.

One night in 2003, Miller was at home with a friend, Colby Smith, when a neighbor, Cole Cannon, came to make a drug deal with Miller's mother. The two boys followed Cannon back to his trailer, where all three smoked marijuana and played drinking games. When Cannon passed out, Miller stole his wallet, splitting about $300 with Smith. Miller then tried to put the wallet back in Cannon's pocket, but Cannon awoke and grabbed Miller by the throat. Smith hit Cannon with a nearby baseball bat, and once released, Miller grabbed the bat and repeatedly struck Cannon with it. Miller placed a sheet over Cannon's head, told him "'I am God, I've come to take your life,'" and delivered one more blow. The boys then retreated to Miller's trailer, but soon decided to return to Cannon's to cover up evidence of their crime. Once there, they lit two fires. Cannon eventually died from his injuries and smoke inhalation.

Alabama law required that Miller initially be charged as a juvenile, but allowed the District Attorney to seek removal of the case to adult court. The D.A. did so, and the juvenile court agreed to the transfer after a hearing. The State accordingly charged Miller as an adult with murder in the course of arson. That crime (like capital murder in Arkansas) carries a mandatory minimum punishment of life without parole.

Relying in significant part on testimony from Smith, who had pleaded to a lesser offense, a jury found Miller guilty. He was therefore sentenced to life without the possibility of parole. The Alabama Court of Criminal Appeals affirmed, ruling that life without parole was "not overly harsh when compared to the crime" and that the mandatory nature of the sentencing scheme was permissible under the Eighth Amendment.

The Eighth Amendment's prohibition of cruel and unusual punishment "guarantees individuals the right not to be subjected to excessive sanctions." That right, we have explained, "flows from the basic 'precept of justice that punishment for crime should be graduated and proportioned'" to both the offender and the offense. As we noted the last time we considered life-without-parole sentences imposed on juveniles, "[t]he concept of proportionality is central to the Eighth Amendment." And we view that concept less through a historical prism than according to "'the evolving standards of decency that mark the progress of a maturing society.'"

The cases before us implicate two strands of precedent reflecting our concern with proportionate punishment. The first has adopted categorical bans on sentencing practices based on mismatches between the culpability of a class of offenders and the severity of a penalty. So, for example, we have held that imposing the death penalty for non-homicide crimes against individuals, or imposing it on mentally retarded defendants, violates the Eighth Amendment. Several of the cases in this group have specially focused on juvenile offenders, because of their lesser culpability. Thus, *Roper* held that the Eighth Amendment bars capital punishment for children, and *Graham* concluded that the Amendment also prohibits a sentence of life without the possibility of parole for a child who committed a nonhomicide offense. *Graham* further likened life without parole for juveniles to the death penalty itself, thereby evoking a second line of our precedents. In those cases, we have prohibited mandatory imposition of capital punishment, requiring that sentencing authorities consider the characteristics of a defendant and the details of his offense before sentencing him to death. Here, the confluence of these two lines of precedent leads to the conclusion that mandatory life-without-parole sentences for juveniles violate the Eighth Amendment.

To start with the first set of cases: *Roper* and *Graham* establish that children are constitutionally different from adults for purposes of sentencing. Because juveniles have diminished culpability and greater prospects for reform, we explained, "they are less deserving of the most severe punishments." Those cases relied on three significant gaps between juveniles and adults. First, children have a "'lack of maturity and an underdeveloped sense of responsibility,'" leading to recklessness, impulsivity, and heedless risk-taking. Second, children "are more vulnerable ... to negative influences and outside pressures," including from their family and peers; they have limited "contro[l] over their own environment" and lack the ability to extricate themselves from horrific, crime-producing settings. And third, a child's character is not as "well formed" as an adult's; his traits are "less fixed" and his actions less likely to be "evidence of irretrievabl[e] deprav[ity]."

Our decisions rested not only on common sense—on what "any parent knows"—but on science and social science as well.

Roper and *Graham* emphasized that the distinctive attributes of youth diminish the penological justifications for imposing the harshest sentences on juvenile offenders, even when they commit terrible crimes. Because "'[t]he heart of the retribution rationale'" relates to an offender's blameworthiness, "'the case for retribution is not as strong with a minor as with an adult.'" Nor can deterrence do the work in this context, because "'the same characteristics that render juveniles less culpable than adults'"—their immaturity, recklessness, and impetuosity—make them less likely to consider potential punishment. Similarly, incapacitation could not support the life-without-parole sentence in Graham: Deciding that a "juvenile offender forever will be a danger to society" would require "mak[ing] a judgment that [he] is incorrigible"—but "'incorrigibility is inconsistent with youth.'" And for the same reason, rehabilitation could not justify that sentence. Life without parole "forswears altogether the rehabilitative ideal." It reflects "an irrevocable judgment about [an offender's] value and place in society," at odds with a child's capacity for change.

Graham concluded from this analysis that life-without-parole sentences, like capital punishment, may violate the Eighth Amendment when imposed on children. To be sure, *Graham*'s flat ban on life without parole applied only to nonhomicide crimes, and the Court took care to distinguish those offenses from murder, based on both moral culpability and consequential harm. But none of what it said about children—about their distinctive (and transitory) mental traits and environmental vulnerabilities—is crime-specific. Those features are evident in the same way, and to the same degree, when (as in both cases here) a botched robbery turns into a killing. So *Graham*'s reasoning implicates any life-without-parole sentence imposed on a juvenile, even as its categorical bar relates only to nonhomicide offenses.

Most fundamentally, *Graham* insists that youth matters in determining the appropriateness of a lifetime of incarceration without the possibility of parole. In the circumstances there, juvenile status precluded a life-without-parole sentence, even though an adult could receive it for a similar crime. And in other contexts as well, the characteristics of youth, and the way they weaken rationales for punishment, can render a life-without-parole sentence disproportionate. "An offender's age," we made clear in *Graham*, "is relevant to the Eighth Amendment," and so "criminal procedure laws that fail to take defendants' youthfulness into account at all would be flawed."

But the mandatory penalty schemes at issue here prevent the sentencer from taking account of these central considerations. By removing youth from the balance—by subjecting a juvenile to the same life-without-parole sentence applicable to an adult—these laws prohibit a sentencing authority from assessing whether the law's harshest term of imprisonment proportionately punishes a juvenile offender. That contravenes *Graham*'s (and also *Roper*'s) foundational principle: that imposition of a State's most severe penalties on juvenile offenders cannot proceed as though they were not children.

And *Graham* makes plain these mandatory schemes' defects in another way: by likening life-without-parole sentences imposed on juveniles to the death penalty itself. Life-without-parole terms, the Court wrote, "share some characteristics with death sentences that are shared by no other sentences." Imprisoning an offender until he dies alters the remainder of his life "by a forfeiture that is irrevocable." And this lengthiest possible incarceration is an "especially harsh punishment for a juvenile," because he will almost inevitably serve "more years and a greater percentage of his life in prison than an adult offender." The penalty when imposed on a teenager, as compared with an older person, is therefore "the same … in name only." All of that suggested a distinctive set of legal rules: In part because we viewed this ultimate penalty for juveniles as akin to the death penalty, we treated it similarly to that most severe punishment. We imposed a categorical ban on the sentence's use, in a way unprecedented for a term of imprisonment. And the bar we adopted mirrored a proscription first established in the death penalty context—that the punishment cannot be imposed for any nonhomicide crimes against individuals.

In light of *Graham*'s reasoning, these decisions too show the flaws of imposing mandatory life-without-parole sentences on juvenile homicide offenders. Such mandatory penalties, by their nature, preclude a sentencer from taking account of an offender's age and the wealth of characteristics and circumstances attendant to it. Under these schemes, every juvenile will receive the same sentence as every other—the 17-year-old and the 14-year-old, the shooter and the accomplice, the child from a stable household and the child from a chaotic and abusive one. And still worse, each juvenile (including these two 14-year-olds) will receive the same sentence as the vast majority of adults committing similar homicide offenses—but really, as *Graham* noted, a greater sentence than those adults will serve. In meting out the death penalty, the elision of all these differences would be strictly forbidden. And once again, *Graham* indicates that a similar rule should apply when a juvenile confronts a sentence of life (and death) in prison.

So *Graham* and *Roper* and our individualized sentencing cases alike teach that in imposing a State's harshest penalties, a sentencer misses too much if he treats every child as an adult. To recap: Mandatory life without parole for a juvenile precludes consideration of his chronological age and its hallmark features—among them, immaturity, impetuosity, and failure to appreciate risks and consequences. It prevents taking into account the family and home environment that surrounds him—and from which he cannot usually extricate himself—no matter how brutal or dysfunctional. It neglects the circumstances of the homicide offense, including the extent of his participation in the conduct and the way familial and peer pressures may have affected him. Indeed, it ignores that he might have been charged and convicted of a lesser offense if not for incompetencies associated with youth—for example, his inability to deal with police officers or prosecutors (including on a plea agreement) or his incapacity to assist his own attorneys. And finally, this mandatory punishment disregards the possibility of rehabilitation even when the circumstances most suggest it.

Both cases before us illustrate the problem. Take Jackson's first. As noted earlier, Jackson did not fire the bullet that killed Laurie Troup; nor did the State argue that he intended her death. Jackson's conviction was instead based on an aiding-and-abetting theory; and the appellate court affirmed the verdict only because the jury could have believed that when Jackson entered the store, he warned Troup that "[w]e ain't playin,'" rather than told his friends that "I thought you all was playin.'" To be sure, Jackson learned on the way to the video store that his friend Shields was carrying a gun, but his age could well have affected his calculation of the risk that posed, as well as his willingness to walk away at that point. All these circumstances go to Jackson's culpability for the offense. And so too does Jackson's family background and immersion in violence: Both his mother and his grandmother had previously shot other individuals. At the least, a sentencer should look at such facts before depriving a 14-year-old of any prospect of release from prison.

That is true also in Miller's case. No one can doubt that he and Smith committed a vicious murder. But they did it when high on drugs and alcohol consumed with the adult victim. And if ever a pathological background might have contributed to a 14-year-old's commission of a crime, it is here. Miller's stepfather physically abused him; his alcoholic and drug-addicted mother neglected him; he had been in and out of foster care as a result; and he had tried to kill himself four times, the first when he should have been in kindergarten. Nonetheless, Miller's past criminal history was limited—two instances of truancy and one of "second-degree criminal mischief." That Miller deserved severe punishment for killing Cole Cannon is beyond question. But once again, a sentencer needed to examine all these circumstances before concluding that life without any possibility of parole was the appropriate penalty.

We therefore hold that the Eighth Amendment forbids a sentencing scheme that mandates life in prison without possibility of parole for juvenile offenders. By making youth (and all that accompanies it) irrelevant to imposition of that harshest prison sentence, such a scheme poses too great a risk of disproportionate punishment. Because that holding is sufficient to decide these cases, we do not consider Jackson's and Miller's alternative argument that the Eighth Amendment requires a categorical bar on life without parole for juveniles, or at least for those 14 and younger. But given all we have said in *Roper, Graham,* and this decision about children's diminished culpability and heightened capacity for change, we think appropriate occasions for sentencing juveniles to this harshest possible penalty will be uncommon. That is especially so because of the great difficulty we noted in Roper and Graham of distinguishing at this early age between "the juvenile offender whose crime reflects unfortunate yet transient immaturity, and the rare juvenile offender whose crime reflects irreparable corruption." Although we do not foreclose a sentencer's ability to make that judgment in homicide cases, we require it to take into account how children are different, and how those differences counsel against irrevocably sentencing them to a lifetime in prison.

Alabama and Arkansas offer two kinds of arguments against requiring individualized consideration before sentencing a juvenile to life imprisonment without possibility of parole. The States (along with the dissents) first contend that the rule we adopt conflicts with aspects of our Eighth Amendment caselaw. And they next assert that the rule is unnecessary because individualized circumstances come into play in deciding whether to try a juvenile offender as an adult. We think the States are wrong on both counts.

We have by now held on multiple occasions that a sentencing rule permissible for adults may not be so for children. Capital punishment, our decisions hold, generally comports with the Eighth Amendment — except it cannot be imposed on children. So too, life without parole is permissible for nonhomicide offenses — except, once again, for children. Nor are these sentencing decisions an oddity in the law. Indeed, it is the odd legal rule that does not have some form of exception for children. In that context, it is no surprise that the law relating to society's harshest punishments recognizes such a distinction.

Alabama and Arkansas (along with THE CHIEF JUSTICE and Justice ALITO) next contend that because many States impose mandatory life-without-parole sentences on juveniles, we may not hold the practice unconstitutional. In considering categorical bars to the death penalty and life without parole, we ask as part of the analysis whether "'objective indicia of society's standards, as expressed in legislative enactments and state practice,'" show a "national consensus" against a sentence for a particular class of offenders. By our count, 29 jurisdictions (28 States and the Federal Government) make a life-without-parole term mandatory for some juveniles convicted of murder in adult court. The States argue that this number precludes our holding.

We do not agree; indeed, we think the States' argument on this score weaker than the one we rejected in *Graham*. For starters, the cases here are different from the typical one in which we have tallied legislative enactments. Our decision does not categorically bar a penalty for a class of offenders or type of crime — as, for example, we did in *Roper* or *Graham*. Instead, it mandates only that a sentencer follow a certain process — considering an offender's youth and attendant characteristics — before imposing a particular penalty. And in so requiring, our decision flows straightforwardly from our precedents: specifically, the principle of *Roper*, *Graham*, and our individualized sentencing cases that youth matters for purposes of meting out the law's most serious punishments. When both of those circumstances have obtained in the past, we have not scrutinized or relied in the same way on legislative enactments.

In any event, the "objective indicia" that the States offer do not distinguish these cases from others holding that a sentencing practice violates the Eighth Amendment. In *Graham*, we prohibited life-without-parole terms for juveniles committing nonhomicide offenses even though 39 jurisdictions permitted that sentence. That is 10 more than impose life without parole on juveniles on a mandatory basis. And in *Atkins*, *Roper*, and *Thompson*, we similarly banned the death penalty in circumstances in which "less than half" of the "States that permit[ted] capital punishment (for whom the issue exist[ed])" had previously chosen to do so.

Almost all jurisdictions allow some juveniles to be tried in adult court for some kinds of homicide. But most States do not have separate penalty provisions for those juvenile offenders. Of the 29 jurisdictions mandating life without parole for children, more than half do so by virtue of generally applicable penalty provisions, imposing the sentence without regard to age. And indeed, some of those States set no minimum age for who may be transferred to adult court in the first instance, thus applying life-without-parole mandates to children of any age — be it 17 or 14 or 10 or 6. As in Graham, we think that "underscores that the statutory eligibility of a juvenile offender for life without parole does not indicate that the penalty has been endorsed through deliberate, express, and full legislative consideration." That Alabama and Arkansas can count to 29 by including these possibly (or probably) inadvertent legislative outcomes does not preclude our determination that mandatory life without parole for juveniles violates the Eighth Amendment.

Discretionary sentencing in adult court would provide different options: There, a judge or jury could choose, rather than a life-without-parole sentence, a lifetime prison term with the possibility of parole or a lengthy term of years. It is easy to imagine a judge deciding that a minor deserves a (much) harsher sentence than he would receive in juvenile court, while still not thinking life-without-parole appropriate. For that reason, the discretion available to a judge at the transfer stage cannot substitute for discretion at post-trial sentencing in adult court — and so cannot satisfy the Eighth Amendment.

Graham, Roper, and our individualized sentencing decisions make clear that a judge or jury must have the opportunity to consider mitigating circumstances before imposing the harshest possible penalty for juveniles. By requiring that all children convicted of homicide receive lifetime incarceration without possibility of parole, regardless of their age and age-related characteristics and the nature of their crimes, the mandatory sentencing schemes before us violate this principle of proportionality, and so the Eighth Amendment's ban on cruel and unusual punishment. We accordingly reverse the judgments of the Arkansas Supreme Court and Alabama Court of Criminal Appeals and remand the cases for further proceedings not inconsistent with this opinion.

It is so ordered.

Justice BREYER, with whom Justice SOTOMAYOR joins, concurring.

I join the Court's opinion in full. I add that, if the State continues to seek a sentence of life without the possibility of parole for Kuntrell Jackson, there will have to be a determination whether Jackson "kill[ed] or intend[ed] to kill" the robbery victim. In my view, without such a finding, the Eighth Amendment as interpreted in Graham forbids sentencing Jackson to such a sentence, regardless of whether its application is mandatory or discretionary under state law.

In *Graham* we said that "when compared to an adult murderer, a juvenile offender who did not kill or intend to kill has a twice diminished moral culpability." For one thing, "compared to adults, juveniles have a lack of maturity and an underdeveloped sense of responsibility; they are more vulnerable or susceptible to negative influences and outside pressures, including peer pressure; and their characters are not as well formed." ("[P]sychology and brain science continue to show fundamental differences between juvenile and adult minds" making their actions "less likely to be evidence of 'irretrievably depraved character' than are the actions of adults". For another thing, Graham recognized that lack of intent normally diminishes the "moral culpability" that attaches to the crime in question, making those that do not intend to kill "categorically less deserving of the most serious forms of punishment than are murderers." And we concluded that, because of this "twice diminished moral culpability," the Eighth Amendment forbids the imposition upon juveniles of a sentence of life without parole for nonhomicide cases.

Given *Graham's* reasoning, the kinds of homicide that can subject a juvenile offender to life without parole must exclude instances where the juvenile himself neither kills nor intends to kill the victim. Quite simply, if the juvenile either kills or intends to kill the victim, he lacks "twice diminished" responsibility. But where the juvenile neither kills nor intends to kill, both features emphasized in Graham as extenuating apply. The dissent itself here would permit life without parole for "juveniles who commit the worst types of murder," but that phrase does not readily fit the culpability of one who did not himself kill or intend to kill.

I recognize that in the context of felony-murder cases, the question of intent is a complicated one. The felony-murder doctrine traditionally attributes death caused in the course of a felony to all participants who intended to commit the felony, regardless of whether they killed or intended to kill. This rule has been based on the idea of "transferred intent"; the defendant's intent to commit the felony satisfies the intent to kill required for murder.

But in my opinion, this type of "transferred intent" is not sufficient to satisfy the intent to murder that could subject a juvenile to a sentence of life without parole. As an initial matter, this Court has made clear that this artificially constructed kind of intent does not count as intent for purposes of the Eighth Amendment. We do not rely on transferred intent in determining if an adult may receive the death penalty. Thus, the Constitution forbids imposing capital punishment upon an aider and abettor in a robbery, where that individual did not intend to kill and simply was "in the car by the side of the road..., waiting to help the robbers escape." Given *Graham*, this holding applies to juvenile sentences of life without parole a fortiori. Indeed, even juveniles who meet the Tison standard of "reckless disregard" may not be eligible for life without parole. Rather, Graham dictates a clear rule: The only juveniles who may constitutionally be sentenced to life without parole are those convicted of homicide offenses who "kill or intend to kill."

Moreover, regardless of our law with respect to adults, there is no basis for imposing a sentence of life without parole upon a juvenile who did not himself kill or intend to kill. At base, the theory of transferring a defendant's intent is premised on the idea that one engaged in a dangerous felony should understand the risk that the victim of the felony could be killed, even by a confederate. Yet the ability to consider the full consequences of a course of action and to adjust one's conduct accordingly is precisely what we know juveniles lack capacity to do effectively.

This is, as far as I can tell, precisely the situation present in Kuntrell Jackson's case. Jackson simply went along with older boys to rob a video store. On the way, he became aware that a confederate had a gun. He initially stayed outside the store, and went in briefly, saying something like "We ain't playin'" or "I thought you all was playin,'" before an older confederate shot and killed the store clerk. Crucially, the jury found him guilty of first-degree murder under a statute that permitted them to convict if, Jackson "attempted to commit or committed an aggravated robbery, and, in the course of that offense, he, or an accomplice, caused [the clerk's] death under circumstance manifesting extreme indifference to the value of human life." Thus, to be found guilty, Jackson did not need to kill the clerk (it is conceded he did not), nor did he need to have intent to kill or even "extreme indifference." As long as one of the teenage accomplices in the robbery acted with extreme indifference to the value of human life, Jackson could be convicted of capital murder.

The upshot is that Jackson, who did not kill the clerk, might not have intended to do so either. In that case, the Eighth Amendment simply forbids imposition of a life term without the possibility of parole. If, on remand, however, there is a finding that Jackson did intend to cause the clerk's death, the question remains open whether the Eighth Amendment prohibits the imposition of life without parole upon a juvenile in those circumstances as well.

Chief Justice ROBERTS, with whom Justice SCALIA, Justice THOMAS, and Justice ALITO join, dissenting.

Determining the appropriate sentence for a teenager convicted of murder presents grave and challenging questions of morality and social policy. Our role, however, is to apply the law, not to answer such questions. The pertinent law here is the Eighth Amendment to the Constitution, which prohibits "cruel and unusual punishments." Today, the Court invokes that Amendment to ban a punishment that the Court does not itself characterize as unusual, and that could not plausibly be described as such. I therefore dissent.

The parties agree that nearly 2,500 prisoners are presently serving life sentences without the possibility of parole for murders they committed before the age of 18. The Court accepts that over 2,000 of those prisoners received that sentence because it was mandated by a legislature. And it recognizes that the Federal Government and most States impose such mandatory sentences. Put simply, if a 17-year-old is convicted of deliberately murdering an innocent victim, it is not "unusual" for the murderer to receive a mandatory sentence of life without parole. That reality should preclude finding that mandatory life imprisonment for juvenile killers violates the Eighth Amendment.

Here the number of mandatory life without parole sentences for juvenile murderers, relative to the number of juveniles arrested for murder, is over 5,000 times higher than the corresponding number in *Graham*. There is thus nothing in this case like the evidence of national consensus in *Graham*.

The Court also advances another reason for discounting the laws enacted by Congress and most state legislatures. Some of the jurisdictions that impose mandatory life without parole on juvenile murderers do so as a result of two statutes: one providing that juveniles charged with serious crimes may be tried as adults, and another generally mandating that those convicted of murder be imprisoned for life. According to the Court, our cases suggest that where the sentence results from the interaction of two such statutes, the legislature can be considered to have imposed the resulting sentences "inadvertent[ly]."

It is a fair question whether this Court should ever assume a legislature is so ignorant of its own laws that it does not understand that two of them interact with each other, especially on an issue of such importance as the one before us. But in *Graham* and *Thompson* it was at least plausible as a practical matter. In *Graham*, the extreme rarity with which the sentence in question was imposed could suggest that legislatures did not really intend the inevitable result of the laws they passed. In *Thompson*, the sentencing practice was even rarer—only 20 defendants had received it in the last century. Perhaps under those facts it could be argued that the legislature was not fully aware that a teenager could receive the particular sentence in question. But here the widespread and recent imposition of the sentence makes it implausible to characterize this sentencing practice as a collateral consequence of legislative ignorance.

Nor do we display our usual respect for elected officials by asserting that legislators have accidentally required 2,000 teenagers to spend the rest of their lives in jail. This is particularly true given that our well-publicized decision in *Graham* alerted legislatures to the possibility that teenagers were subject to life with parole only because of legislative inadvertence. I am aware of no effort in the wake of *Graham* to correct any supposed legislative oversight. Indeed, in amending its laws in response to *Graham* one legislature made especially clear that it does intend juveniles who commit first-degree murder to receive mandatory life without parole. See Iowa Code Ann. § 902.1.

In any event, the Court's holding does not follow from *Roper* and *Graham*. Those cases undoubtedly stand for the proposition that teenagers are less mature, less responsible, and less fixed in their ways than adults—not that a Supreme Court case was needed to establish that. What they do not stand for, and do not even suggest, is that legislators—

who also know that teenagers are different from adults—may not require life without parole for juveniles who commit the worst types of murder.

Today's decision does not offer *Roper* and *Graham*'s false promises of restraint. Indeed, the Court's opinion suggests that it is merely a way station on the path to further judicial displacement of the legislative role in prescribing appropriate punishment for crime. The Court's analysis focuses on the mandatory nature of the sentences in this case. But then—although doing so is entirely unnecessary to the rule it announces—the Court states that even when a life without parole sentence is not mandatory, "we think appropriate occasions for sentencing juveniles to this harshest possible penalty will be uncommon." Today's holding may be limited to mandatory sentences, but the Court has already announced that discretionary life without parole for juveniles should be "uncommon"—or, to use a common synonym, "unusual."

Indeed, the Court's gratuitous prediction appears to be nothing other than an invitation to overturn life without parole sentences imposed by juries and trial judges. If that invitation is widely accepted and such sentences for juvenile offenders do in fact become "uncommon," the Court will have bootstrapped its way to declaring that the Eighth Amendment absolutely prohibits them.

It is a great tragedy when a juvenile commits murder—most of all for the innocent victims. But also for the murderer, whose life has gone so wrong so early. And for society as well, which has lost one or more of its members to deliberate violence, and must harshly punish another. In recent years, our society has moved toward requiring that the murderer, his age notwithstanding, be imprisoned for the remainder of his life. Members of this Court may disagree with that choice. Perhaps science and policy suggest society should show greater mercy to young killers, giving them a greater chance to reform themselves at the risk that they will kill again. But that is not our decision to make. Neither the text of the Constitution nor our precedent prohibits legislatures from requiring that juvenile murderers be sentenced to life without parole. I respectfully dissent.

Justice THOMAS, with whom Justice SCALIA joins, dissenting.

Today, the Court holds that "mandatory life without parole for those under the age of 18 at the time of their crimes violates the Eighth Amendment's prohibition on 'cruel and unusual punishments.'" To reach that result, the Court relies on two lines of precedent. The first involves the categorical prohibition of certain punishments for specified classes of offenders. The second requires individualized sentencing in the capital punishment context. Neither line is consistent with the original understanding of the Cruel and Unusual Punishments Clause. The Court compounds its errors by combining these lines of precedent and extending them to reach a result that is even less legitimate than the foundation on which it is built. Because the Court upsets the legislatively enacted sentencing regimes of 29 jurisdictions without constitutional warrant, I respectfully dissent.

As I have previously explained, "the Cruel and Unusual Punishments Clause was originally understood as prohibiting torturous methods of punishment—specifically methods akin to those that had been considered cruel and unusual at the time the Bill of Rights was adopted." The clause does not contain a "proportionality principle." In short, it does not authorize courts to invalidate any punishment they deem disproportionate to the severity of the crime or to a particular class of offenders. Instead, the clause "leaves the unavoidably moral question of who 'deserves' a particular nonprohibited method of punishment to the judgment of the legislatures that authorize the penalty."

The legislatures of Arkansas and Alabama, like those of 27 other jurisdictions have determined that all offenders convicted of specified homicide offenses, whether juveniles or not, deserve a sentence of life in prison without the possibility of parole. Nothing in our Constitution authorizes this Court to supplant that choice.

As discussed above, the Cruel and Unusual Punishments Clause, as originally understood, prohibits "torturous methods of punishment." It is not concerned with whether a particular lawful method of punishment—whether capital or noncapital—is imposed pursuant to a mandatory or discretionary sentencing regime. Accordingly, the idea that the mandatory imposition of an otherwise-constitutional sentence renders that sentence cruel and unusual finds "no support in the text and history of the Eighth Amendment."

Thus, there is no basis for concluding that a mandatory capital sentencing scheme is unconstitutional. Because the Court's cases requiring individualized sentencing in the capital context are wrongly decided, they cannot serve as a valid foundation for the novel rule regarding mandatory life-without-parole sentences for juveniles that the Court announces today.

In any event, this Court has already declined to extend its individualized-sentencing rule beyond the death penalty context.

Today, the Court makes clear that, even though its decision leaves intact the discretionary imposition of life-without-parole sentences for juvenile homicide offenders, it "think[s] appropriate occasions for sentencing juveniles to [life without parole] will be uncommon." That statement may well cause trial judges to shy away from imposing life without parole sentences and embolden appellate judges to set them aside when they are imposed. And, when a future petitioner seeks a categorical ban on sentences of life without parole for juvenile homicide offenders, this Court will most assuredly look to the "actual sentencing practices" triggered by this case. The Court has, thus, gone from "merely" divining the societal consensus of today to shaping the societal consensus of tomorrow.

Today's decision invalidates a constitutionally permissible sentencing system based on nothing more than the Court's belief that "its own sense of morality ... pre-empts that of the people and their representatives." Because nothing in the Constitution grants the Court the authority it exercises today, I respectfully dissent.

Justice ALITO, with whom Justice SCALIA joins, dissenting.

The Court now holds that Congress and the legislatures of the 50 States are prohibited by the Constitution from identifying any category of murderers under the age of 18 who must be sentenced to life imprisonment without parole. Even a 17½-year-old who sets off a bomb in a crowded mall or guns down a dozen students and teachers is a "child" and must be given a chance to persuade a judge to permit his release into society. Nothing in the Constitution supports this arrogation of legislative authority.

The Court long ago abandoned the original meaning of the Eighth Amendment, holding instead that the prohibition of "cruel and unusual punishment" embodies the "evolving standards of decency that mark the progress of a maturing society." Both the provenance and philosophical basis for this standard were problematic from the start. (Is it true that our society is inexorably evolving in the direction of greater and greater decency? Who says so, and how did this particular philosophy of history find its way into our fundamental law? And in any event, aren't elected representatives more likely than unaccountable judges to reflect changing societal standards?) But at least at the start, the Court insisted that these "evolving standards" represented something other than the personal views of five Justices.

In this search for objective indicia, the Court toyed with the use of public opinion polls, and occasionally relied on foreign law. In the main, however, the staple of this inquiry was the tallying of the positions taken by state legislatures.

While the tally in these early cases may be characterized as evidence of a national consensus, the evidence became weaker and weaker in later cases.

The importance of trend evidence, however, was not long lived. In *Roper,* which outlawed capital punishment for defendants between the ages of 16 and 18, the lineup of the States was the same as in *Atkins,* but the trend in favor of abolition—five States during the past 15 years—was less impressive. Nevertheless, the Court held that the absence of a strong trend in support of abolition did not matter.

Two years after *Kennedy,* in *Graham v. Florida,* any pretense of heeding a legislative consensus was discarded. In *Graham,* federal law and the law of 37 States and the District of Columbia permitted a minor to be sentenced to life imprisonment without parole for nonhomicide crimes, but despite this unmistakable evidence of a national consensus, the Court held that the practice violates the Eighth Amendment. The Court, however, drew a distinction between minors who murder and minors who commit other heinous offenses, so at least in that sense the principle that death is different lived on.

Today, that principle is entirely put to rest, for here we are concerned with the imposition of a term of imprisonment on offenders who kill. The two (carefully selected) cases before us concern very young defendants, and despite the brutality and evident depravity exhibited by at least one of the petitioners, it is hard not to feel sympathy for a 14-year-old sentenced to life without the possibility of release. But no one should be confused by the particulars of the two cases before us. The category of murderers that the Court delicately calls "children" (murderers under the age of 18) consists overwhelmingly of young men who are fast approaching the legal age of adulthood. Evan Miller and Kuntrell Jackson are anomalies; much more typical are murderers like Donald Roper, who committed a brutal thrill-killing just nine months shy of his 18th birthday.

Seventeen-year-olds commit a significant number of murders every year, and some of these crimes are incredibly brutal. Many of these murderers are at least as mature as the average 18-year-old. Congress and the legislatures of 43 States have concluded that at least some of these murderers should be sentenced to prison without parole, and 28 States and the Federal Government have decided that for some of these offenders life without parole should be mandatory. The majority of this Court now overrules these legislative judgments.

It is true that, at least for now, the Court apparently permits a trial judge to make an individualized decision that a particular minor convicted of murder should be sentenced to life without parole, but do not expect this possibility to last very long. The majority goes out of its way to express the view that the imposition of a sentence of life without parole on a "child" (i.e., a murderer under the age of 18) should be uncommon. Having held in *Graham* that a trial judge with discretionary sentencing authority may not impose a sentence of life without parole on a minor who has committed a nonhomicide offense, the Justices in the majority may soon extend that holding to minors who commit murder. We will see.

What today's decision shows is that our Eighth Amendment cases are no longer tied to any objective indicia of society's standards. Our Eighth Amendment case law is now entirely inward looking. After entirely disregarding objective indicia of our society's standards in *Graham,* the Court now extrapolates from *Graham.* Future cases may extrapolate from today's holding, and this process may continue until the majority brings sentencing practices into line with whatever the majority views as truly evolved standards of decency.

Unless our cases change course, we will continue to march toward some vision of evolutionary culmination that the Court has not yet disclosed. The Constitution does not authorize us to take the country on this journey.

Holdings of *Miller v. Alabama*: The court held that sentences of mandatory life without parole for those under the age of 18 at the time of their crimes violates the Eighth Amendment's prohibition on 'cruel and unusual punishments. The court held that a youth's age should be considered as a mitigating factor in a sentencing decision. The court also held that, while it is still possible for a court to sentence a minor to life without parole in a homicide case, such a sentence should be "uncommon."

Discussion Questions

What does the majority find unconstitutional about a sentencing scheme that mandates life in prison without possibility of parole for juvenile offenders?

Can a juvenile be sentenced to life in prison and, after being given an "individualized treatment" be denied parole for life?

Key Concepts: Life without Parole for Juvenile Offenders

- Juveniles who were under the age of 18 at the time of their offense, cannot be subject to a statutory scheme that mandates that they be sentenced to life without parole.

- Although the court does not foreclose a sentence of life without parole in a homicide case, the judge issuing the sentence must take into account how children are different, and how those differences counsel against irrevocably sentencing them to a lifetime in prison.

- Sentencing decisions for minors must include an individual review of the minor's circumstances before the minor can be sentenced to life without parole.

Practical Questions: Life without Parole for Juvenile Offenders

1. Your friend, a member of the state legislature, proposes to amend the state statute to provide that, in the case of juveniles charged with "Class A" Felonies, a juvenile can provide evidence of mitigation to overcome a presumption that the sentence should be life without parole. He asks you whether or not you think this proposed statute will comply with *Miller v. Alabama*. What do you tell him?

2. You are appointed to represent a defendant who wants to plead guilty to first degree murder, an offense that, prior to *Miller v. Alabama*, would have carried a mandatory life sentence without parole. What kind of issues will you explore "in mitigation" of a life sentence without parole?

Simulation Exercise V

Characters: Prosecuting attorney, defense attorney, and a panel of 3 Appellate Judges.

Facts: Jeffrey Ragland was seventeen years old when he committed a murder in Iowa. He was convicted, and sentenced to life without parole, as mandated by the state statute. After the United States Supreme Court decided *Miller v. Alabama,* the Governor of Iowa commuted Ragland's sentence, as well as the sentences of every other inmate in Iowa's prison system who, like Ragland, had received statutorily mandated sentences of life without parole for crimes committed as juveniles. For all such defendants, the Governor commuted the sentences to life with no possibility for parole for sixty years and directed that no credit be given for earned time. Ragland must serve sixty years of his sentence before he may be considered for parole. Under the commutation order of the Governor, Ragland will not be eligible for parole until he is 78-years-old. Ragland's attorney has filed a motion claiming that the action of the Governor makes his sentence the functional equivalent of life without parole. Evidence is in the record that under standard mortality tables, his life expectancy is 78.6 years.

Simulation: The exercise is for both attorneys to conduct oral arguments on the motion to set aside the Governor's commutation order and to order a hearing on mitigating factors for all defendants currently serving time under a sentence of mandatory life without parole for crimes committed while they were juveniles. The judges should be prepared to ask any questions necessary to arrive at a ruling, the attorneys shall be prepared to answer any questions posed to them, and the judges will conference the case in order to arrive at a ruling on the motion.

C. Future Applications of *Miller v. Alabama*

Overview: The progression of cases leading to the prohibition of the application of the death penalty to minors, as well as the prohibition of statutes mandating life without parole for minors causes courts to use the analysis of the Supreme Court in those strings of cases to other areas that may have long-term or permanent impact on juveniles. The courts must ask the question of how the inherent difference between minors and adults should impact other issues.

In re C.P.: In *In re C.P.,* the Ohio court was faced with a case where a youth who was 15 years old at the time, was charged with two counts of rape and one count of kidnapping with sexual motivation. The victim was a 6-year-old boy, a relative of C.P. A statue in Ohio created a new class of juvenile sex-offender registrants: public-registry qualified juvenile-offender registrants. These offenders were automatically subject to mandatory, lifetime sex-offender registration and notification requirements, including notification on the Internet. C.P. was found guilty in juvenile court. Pursuant to the statute, the court classified C.P. a public-registry-qualified juvenile-offender registrant ("PRQJOR"). C.P. was automatically classified as a Tier III sex-offender/child-victim offender. The court was forced to decide whether or not this automatic life-time impact on the youth violated the 8th Amendment by constituting "cruel and unusual punishment."

As you read *In re C.P.,* look for the following:

1. In this case, the court held that "fundamental fairness is not a one-way street that allows only for an easing of due process requirements for juveniles; instead, fundamental fairness may require, as it does in this case, additional procedural safeguards for juveniles in order to meet of the juvenile system's goals of rehabilitation and reintegration into society." Look for examples the court uses to show this dichotomy.

2. Look for similarities between the factors supporting this court's ruling to those that supported the rulings in the *Roper v. Simmons* case and the *Miller v. Alabama*

case (such as the finding that juvenile offenders are less culpable and more amenable to reform than adult offenders).

In re C.P.

131 Ohio St.3d 513, 967 N.E.2d 729 (2012)

PFEIFER, J.

In this case we determine the constitutionality of R.C. 2152.86, which creates a new class of juvenile sex-offender registrants: public-registry qualified juvenile-offender registrants. These offenders are automatically subject to mandatory, lifetime sex-offender registration and notification requirements, including notification on the Internet. We hold that to the extent that it imposes such requirements on juvenile offenders tried within the juvenile system, R.C. 2152.86 violates the constitutional prohibition against cruel and unusual punishment contained in the Eighth Amendment to the United States Constitution and the Ohio Constitution, Article I, Section 9, and the Due Process Clause of the Fourteenth Amendment to the United States Constitution and the Ohio Constitution, Article I, Section 16.

On June 26, 2009, a multicount complaint was filed in Athens County Juvenile Court against appellant, C.P., who was 15 years old at the time. The complaint alleged that C.P. was a delinquent child and charged him with two counts of rape and one count of kidnapping with sexual motivation, each count a first-degree felony if committed by an adult. The victim was a six-year-old boy, a relative of C.P.

The state immediately moved the juvenile court to transfer jurisdiction to the Athens County Court of Common Pleas, General Division. On July 29, 2009, the juvenile court held a hearing pursuant to R.C. 2152.12(B) to determine whether to retain jurisdiction over C.P.'s case. The parties stipulated that there was probable cause to believe that C.P. had committed the alleged offenses. The court learned that at age 11, C.P. had been adjudicated delinquent in Utah for sexually abusing his half-sister, who was two years younger than C.P., and that C.P. had undergone over two years of sex-offender treatment there as a result of his adjudication.

At a hearing held on August 24, 2009, the court denied the state's motion to transfer jurisdiction over C.P. to the general division to be tried as an adult. The judge stated, "I think we can have our best chance of working with [C.P.] in the juvenile system and I don't think everything has been exhaustively tried there. It doesn't mean that there won't be consequences and it doesn't mean that there won't be loss of freedom there certainly will be if convicted of this offense [sic], but I think we have time within the juvenile system and we have resources within the juvenile system to work with this boy. So, I deny the state's motion for transfer and we'll continue to work with this within the juvenile system."

On September 23, 2009, C.P. entered an admission to each charge in the indictment; because of the nature of his offenses, he was eligible for a discretionary SYO dispositional sentence pursuant to R.C. 2152.11(D)(2)(b). At a subsequent hearing, the court found C.P. to be a delinquent child and designated him an SYO in relation to each offense, imposing a three-year minimum commitment to the Ohio Department of Youth Services on each count, to run concurrently. As part of the SYO disposition, the court imposed three concurrent five-year prison terms, which were stayed pending C.P.'s successful completion of his juvenile dispositions.

Further, the court advised C.P. of the duties and classification automatically imposed upon him by R.C. 2152.86. Pursuant to R.C. 2152.86(A)(1), the court classified C.P. a juvenile-offender registrant and informed him of his duty to abide by the registration and notification requirements of R.C. Chapter 2950. The court also classified C.P. a public-registry-qualified juvenile-offender registrant ("PRQJOR"). Pursuant to R.C. 2152.86(B)(1), C.P. was automatically classified as a Tier III sex-offender/child-victim offender. The judge further informed C.P. of his registration requirements: You are required to register in person with the sheriff of the county in which you establish residency within three days of coming into that county, or if temporarily domiciled for more than three days. If you change residence address you shall provide written notice of that residence change to the sheriff with whom you are most recently registered and to the sheriff in the county in which you intend to reside at least 20-days prior to any change of residence address ... You are required to provide to the sheriff temporary lodging information including address and length of stay if your absence will be for seven days or more. Since you are a public registry qualified juvenile offender registrant you are also required to register in person with the sheriff of the county in which you establish a place of education immediately upon coming to that county ... You are also required to register in person with the sheriff of the county in which you establish a place of employment if you have been employed for more than three days or for an aggregate of 14 days in a calendar year ... Employment includes voluntary services. As a public registry qualified juvenile offender registrant, you ... also shall provide written notice of a change of address or your place of employment or your place of education at least 20 days prior to any change and no later than three days after the change of employment ... [Y]ou shall provide written notice within three days of any change in vehicle information, e-mail addresses, internet identifiers or telephone numbers registered to or used by you to the sheriff with whom you are most recently registered ... [Y]ou are required to abide by all of the above described requirements ... for your lifetime as a Tier III offender with in person verification every 90-days. That means for the rest of your life ... every three months you're going to be checking in with [the] sheriff where you live or work or both ... Failure to register, failure to verify on the specific notice and times as outlined here will result in criminal prosecution.

C.P. appealed his automatic classification as a Tier III juvenile offender registrant and PRQJOR to the Fourth District Court of Appeals, arguing that R.C. 2152.86 violated his rights to due process and equal protection and his right against cruel and unusual punishment. The court of appeals affirmed the judgment of the trial court.

This court has recently held, in a case involving an adult offender, that the enhanced sex-offender reporting and notification requirements contained in R.C. Chapter 2950 enacted by Am.Sub.S.B. No. 10 ("S.B. 10") are punitive in nature, making their retroactive application unconstitutional: "Following the enactment of S.B. 10, all doubt has been removed: R.C. Chapter 2950 is punitive." In this case we consider the constitutionality of the prospective, automatic application of those reporting and notification requirements to certain juvenile offenders.

Pursuant to changes brought about by S.B. 10, R.C. 2152.86 creates a new class of juvenile sex-offender registrants: public-registry-qualified juvenile-offender registrants. PRQJORs are subject to more stringent registration and notification requirements than other juvenile-offender registrants. Moreover, the requirements are imposed automatically rather than at the discretion of a juvenile judge.

Pursuant to R.C. 2152.86, PRQJOR status is assigned to juveniles who (1) were 14 through 17 years old when the offense was committed, (2) have been adjudicated a delinquent child for committing certain specified sexually oriented offenses, including rape, gross sexual imposition when the victim is under 12, sexual battery of a child under age 12, and aggravated murder, murder, or kidnapping with a purpose to gratify the sexual needs or desires of the offender, and (3) have had a court impose on them a serious youthful offender ("SYO") dispositional sentence under R.C. 2152.13.

As we explained in *State v. D.H.*, the nature of an SYO disposition requires that the juvenile remain under the continuing jurisdiction of a juvenile judge: A juvenile charged as a potential serious youthful offender does not face bindover to an adult court; the case remains in the juvenile court. Under R.C. 2152.11(A), a juvenile defendant who commits certain acts is eligible for "a more restrictive disposition." That "more restricted disposition" is a "serious youthful offender" disposition and includes what is known as a blended sentence—a traditional juvenile disposition coupled with the imposition of a stayed adult sentence. R.C. 2152.13. The adult sentence remains stayed unless the juvenile fails to successfully complete his or her traditional juvenile disposition.

Theoretically, the threat of the imposition of an adult sentence encourages a juvenile's cooperation in his own rehabilitation, functioning as both carrot and stick.

R.C. 2152.86 changes the very nature of an SYO disposition, imposing an adult penalty immediately upon the adjudication. The juvenile is not given the opportunity to avoid the adult portion of his punishment by successfully completing his juvenile rehabilitation. Instead, he must comply with all of S.B. 10's reporting and notification requirements for Tier III sexual offenders contained in R.C. Chapter 2950.

Both the method of assignment and the obligations of PRQJORs assigned to Tier III differ from those juveniles placed in Tier III as juvenile offender registrants ("JORs"). For juveniles adjudicated delinquent through a traditional juvenile disposition and who were age 14 or older at the time of their delinquent act, an assignment to Tier III is not automatic. Instead, if the juvenile court finds that the child is a JOR under R.C. 2152.82(A), the court holds a hearing to determine the JOR's tier classification. Which tier such an offender is placed in rests within the juvenile court's discretion. If the court finds that the JOR is a Tier III sex-offender/childvictim offender, then the court may impose certain notification requirements contained in R.C. 2950.10 and 2950.11.

Though all JORs must register personally with the sheriff within three days of entering into a county where they will reside or be temporarily domiciled, a PRQJOR must comply with additional registration requirements.

Notification requirements also differ significantly. JORs assigned to Tier III are subject to community notification only if the juvenile court orders it, and to victim notification only if the victim requests it. The registration information of JORs is not disseminated on the Internet. For PRQJORs, on the other hand, the community and victim notification requirements are automatic. Further, the state must place PRQJORs on its public Internet database.

The potential for reclassification varies greatly depending on whether the juvenile is a PRQJOR or a JOR. For JORs, the juvenile court must conduct a hearing "upon completion of the disposition of that child" to determine whether the child should be reclassified. Additionally, a JOR may file a petition for reclassification three years after the court issues its order pursuant to that mandatory hearing, a second petition three years later, and further petitions every five years thereafter. PRQJORs, in contrast, do not receive a reclassification hearing upon the completion of their juvenile disposition. Instead, they are placed on a reclassification track similar to that of adult Tier III offenders. They are not eligible for a reclassification hearing until 25 years after their statutory registration duties begin.

In sum, for PRQJORs, Tier III classification imposes a lifetime penalty that extends well beyond the age at which the juvenile court loses jurisdiction. It is a consequence that attaches immediately and leaves a juvenile with no means of avoiding the penalty by demonstrating that he will benefit from rehabilitative opportunities.

That the Eighth Amendment prohibits torture is elemental. But the bulk of Eighth Amendment jurisprudence concerns not whether a particular punishment is barbaric, but whether it is disproportionate to the crime. Central to the Constitution's prohibition against cruel and unusual punishment is the "precept of justice that punishment for crime should be graduated and proportioned to [the] offense."

Proportionality review falls within two general classifications: the first involves "challenges to the length of term-of-years sentences given all the circumstances in a particular case." The second, which until recently was applied only in capital cases, involves "cases in which the Court implements the proportionality standard by certain categorical restrictions."

In this case, we address the second classification of cases. Within that classification, there are two subsets, "one considering the nature of the offense, the other considering the characteristics of the offender." In regard to the nature of the offense, for instance, the court has held that capital punishment is impermissible for nonhomicide crimes against individuals. In this juvenile case, we are dealing with the second subset, the characteristics of the offender.

In recent years, the court has established categorical rules prohibiting certain punishments for juveniles. In *Roper v. Simmons*, the court prohibited the death penalty for defendants who committed their crimes before the age of 18. In *Graham*, the court held that the Eighth Amendment prohibits imposition of a life-without-parole sentence on a juvenile offender who did not commit homicide. It is important to note that in both *Roper* and *Graham*, the court addressed the cases of juveniles who had been tried as adults. Here, we address the imposition of a sentence upon a child who remains under the jurisdiction of the juvenile court.

The court engages in a two-step process in adopting categorical rules in regard to punishment: first, the court considers whether there is a national consensus against the sentencing practice at issue, and second, the court determines "in the exercise of its own independent judgment whether the punishment in question violates the Constitution."

In 2006, Congress passed the Adam Walsh Child Protection and Safety Act ("Adam Walsh Act"). Section 16912(a) of the Adam Walsh Act "directs every jurisdiction to maintain a sex-offender registry conforming to the requirements of the Act. And to ensure compliance, Congress directed that states that did not adopt the Adam Walsh Act risked losing ten percent of certain federal crime control funds that would otherwise be allocated to them. These registry requirements are contained in the Sex Offender Registration and Notification Act ("SORNA"), Title I of the Adam Walsh Act.

Ohio was the first state to implement SORNA. By the start of 2011, only three other states were in substantial compliance with SORNA.

In 2008, the Council of State Governments promulgated a resolution against the application of SORNA to juveniles, stating that "[t]he Council of State Governments strongly opposes SORNA's application to juvenile sex offenders and urges Congress to revise the law to more accurately address the needs of juvenile offenders."

In January 2011, because of that resistance by the states, the attorney general exercised his authority under 42 U.S.C. 16918(c)(4) "to provide that jurisdictions need not publicly disclose information concerning persons required to register on the basis of juvenile delinquency adjudications."

Thus, the attorney general acknowledged that to be SORNA compliant in January 2011 required less in the area of publication of a juvenile's status than it had previously: Given this change, the effect of the remaining registration requirements under SORNA for certain juvenile delinquent sex offenders is, in essence, to enable registration authorities to track such offenders following their release and to make information about them available to law enforcement agencies. There is no remaining requirement under SORNA that jurisdictions engage in any form of public disclosure or notification regarding juvenile delinquent sex offenders. Jurisdictions are free to do so, but need not do so to any greater extent than they may wish.

This declaration is a major shift in policy, reflective of a national consensus against the very policy that Ohio imposed as part of its attempt to comply with SORNA. In short, outside of three other states, the rest of the nation dealt with an entirely different landscape vis-à-vis SORNA. The goalposts had been moved — after Ohio and other states had already instituted a system the rest of the nation resisted. The assumption that a national consensus favored publication of juvenile sex offenders' personal information had collapsed. Even after the Supplemental Guidelines, as of December 2011, the United States Justice Department has reported that only 15 states are in substantial compliance with SORNA.

Although national consensus is an important factor in the determination of whether a punishment is cruel or unusual, this court must also conduct an independent review of the sentencing practice in question to determine whether it fits within the constraints of the Eighth Amendment. "The judicial exercise of independent judgment requires consideration of the culpability of the offenders at issue in light of their crimes and characteristics, along with the severity of the punishment in question, * * * [and] whether the challenged sentencing practice serves penological goals." We thus undertake our own independent review addressing these factors.

In regard to the culpability of the offenders, we note that Ohio has developed a system for juveniles that assumes that children are not as culpable for their acts as adults. The court's decision in *Graham* supports this self-evident principle: *Roper* established that because juveniles have lessened culpability they are less deserving of the most severe punishments. As compared to adults, juveniles have a "lack of maturity and an underdeveloped sense of responsibility"; they "are more vulnerable or susceptible to negative influences and outside pressures, including peer pressure"; and their characters are "not as well formed."

Not only are juveniles less culpable than adults, their bad acts are less likely to reveal an unredeemable corruptness: Juveniles are more capable of change than are adults, and their actions are less likely to be evidence of "irretrievably depraved character" than are the actions of adults.

In this case we address a lifetime penalty — albeit open to review after 25 years — making the offender's potential for redemption particularly relevant. Juvenile offenders are more susceptible of change than adult offenders. And again, we are dealing in this case with juveniles who remain under the jurisdiction of the juvenile court. Based on the review of a juvenile judge, juveniles deemed serious youthful offenders have been determined to be amenable to the rehabilitative aims of the juvenile system. They are in a category of offenders that does not include the worst of those who commit crimes as juveniles.

An important consideration in addressing culpability in an independent review of a punishment for Eighth Amendment purposes is the nature of the offenses to which the penalty may apply. In this case, R.C. 2152.86 applies to sex offenses, including rape. In *Graham*, the court stated that "defendants who do not kill, intend to kill, or foresee that life will be taken are categorically less deserving of the most serious forms of punishment than are murderers." The court bluntly noted, "Although an offense like robbery or rape is 'a serious crime deserving serious punishment,' those crimes differ from homicide crimes in a moral sense."

Thus, as the court pointed out in *Graham*, a juvenile who did not kill or intend to kill has "twice diminished moral culpability" on account of his age and the nature of his crime. Thus, when we address the constitutionality of the penalties resulting from an application of R.C. 2152.86, we first recognize that those punishments apply to juveniles with a reduced degree of moral culpability.

The next step in the Eighth Amendment analysis is a consideration of the punishment. In this case, as opposed to *Roper* and *Graham*, we are not dealing with the harshest and next-harshest possible sentences, death and life without possibility of parole. Indeed, in this case, if C.P.'s behavior does not warrant the imposition of the adult portion of his SYO sentence, he will not spend time in an adult prison cell. When his juvenile commitment is complete, he will no longer be confined. However, his punishment will continue. Registration and notification requirements for life, with the possibility of having them lifted only after 25 years, are especially harsh punishments for a juvenile. In *Graham*, the court wrote that a life sentence for a juvenile is different from such a sentence for an adult; the juvenile will spend a greater percentage of his life in jail than the adult.

Here, too, the registration and notification requirements are different from such a penalty for adults. For juveniles, the length of the punishment is extraordinary, and it is imposed at an age at which the character of the offender is not yet fixed. Registration and notification necessarily involve stigmatization. For a juvenile offender, the stigma of the label of sex offender attaches at the start of his adult life and cannot be shaken. With no other offense is the juvenile's wrongdoing announced to the world. Before a juvenile can even begin his adult life, before he has a chance to live on his own, the world will know of his offense. He will never have a chance to establish a good character in the community. He will be hampered in his education, in his relationships, and in his work life. His potential will be squelched before it has a chance to show itself. A juvenile—one who remains under the authority of the juvenile court and has thus been adjudged redeemable—who is subject to sex-offender notification will have his entire life evaluated through the prism of his juvenile adjudication. It will be a constant cloud, a once-every-three-month reminder to himself and the world that he cannot escape the mistakes of his youth. A youth released at 18 would have to wait until age 43 at the earliest to gain a fresh start. While not a harsh penalty to a career criminal used to serving time in a penitentiary, a lifetime or even 25-year requirement of community notification means everything to a juvenile. It will define his adult life before it has a chance to truly begin.

Finally, in an Eighth Amendment analysis, we must consider the penological justifications for the sentencing practice. Since we are deciding a case involving a juvenile who has not been bound over to adult court, the goals of juvenile disposition are relevant to our analysis. R.C. 2152.01 establishes the purposes of any juvenile disposition: (A) The overriding purposes for dispositions under this chapter are to provide for the care, protection, and mental and physical development of children subject to this chapter, protect the public interest and safety, hold the offender accountable for the offender's actions, restore the victim, and rehabilitate the offender. These purposes shall be achieved by a system of graduated sanctions and services.

Lifetime registration and notification requirements run contrary to R.C. 2152.01's goals of rehabilitating the offender and aiding his mental and physical development. Instead, lifetime registration and notification ensure that PRQJORs will encounter continued difficulties because of their offenses, long into adulthood. Notification and registration anchor the juvenile offender to his crime.

As for protecting the public interest and safety, some might argue that the registration and notification requirements further those aims. However, it is difficult to say how much the public interest and safety are served in individual cases, because the PRQJOR statutory scheme gives the juvenile judge no role in determining how dangerous a child offender might be or what level of registration or notification would be adequate to preserve the safety of the public.

The PRQJOR penalties do meet the statutory objective of accountability. However, a major issue in this case is whether the depth and duration of the accountability that R.C. 2152.86 requires of a juvenile offender are excessive. Another statutory goal, restoring the victim, is advanced only minimally by the requirements of R.C. 2152.86.

In addition to the penological considerations laid out by Ohio's legislature, the *Graham* court set forth "the goals of penal sanctions that have been recognized as legitimate—retribution, deterrence, incapacitation, and rehabilitation" and considered whether any of those goals justified a sentence of life without parole for juveniles committing nonhomicide crimes.

As the court recognized in *Graham*, retribution does not justify imposing the same serious penalty on a less culpable defendant.

The court in *Graham* also discounted the penological goal of deterrence for the same reason we do in this case: [B]ecause juveniles "lack of maturity and underdeveloped sense of responsibility ... often result in impetuous and ill-considered actions and decisions," they are less likely to take a possible punishment into consideration when making decisions. Further, in this case, the significance of the particular punishment and its effects are less likely to be understood by the juvenile than the threat of time in a jail cell. Juveniles are less likely to appreciate the concept of loss of future reputation. Incapacitation as a penological goal is not relevant in this case. The focus here is what happens to a juvenile once he has emerged from confinement.

Finally, as to the final penological goal—rehabilitation—we have already discussed the effect of forcing a juvenile to wear a statutorily imposed scarlet letter as he embarks on his adult life. "Community notification may particularly hamper the rehabilitation of juvenile offenders because the public stigma and rejection they suffer will prevent them from developing normal social and interpersonal skills—the lack of those traits have been found to contribute to future sexual offenses."

In addition to increasing the likelihood of reoffense, publication of a juvenile's offense makes reintegration into society more difficult, due in part to the personal economic impact: Sex offender registration constitutes an additional form of punishment for juvenile sex offenders, perhaps more substantial than that experienced by adult sex offenders. Many juvenile sex offenders are released back into society after completion of their court-imposed disposition at an age when they would ordinarily first be entering the workforce and find themselves unable to obtain employment due to their publicized "sex offender" label. Any job in education, health care, or the military is virtually impossible to get. Any job that requires a background check is placed virtually out of reach. And although a PRQJOR's employer's name is not made public under R.C. 2950.11(B)(2), the employer's address is. That fact can only harm a juvenile offender's employment prospects.

The social response to publication of a juvenile's sexual offenses also affects rehabilitation: When a sex offender registration and notification law requires door-to-door neighborhood notification, public announcements, or listing on a sex offender website, the likelihood that a juvenile offender's peers and community will discover the offense is very high. Public disclosure may inspire "vigilantism, public shame, social ostracism, and various types of adverse legal action, including loss of employment and eviction."

We conclude that the social and economic effects of automatic, lifetime registration and notification, coupled with an increased chance of reoffense, do violence to the rehabilitative goals of the juvenile court process. As the court decided in *Graham* in regard to a life sentence without parole for juvenile offenders, we find that penological theory "is not adequate to justify" the imposition of the lifetime registration and notification requirements of R.C. 2152.86 for juveniles.

In sum, the limited culpability of juvenile nonhomicide offenders who remain within the jurisdiction of the juvenile court, the severity of lifetime registration and notification requirements of PRQJOR status, and the inadequacy of penological theory to justify the punishment all lead to the conclusion that the lifetime registration and notification requirements in R.C. 2152.86 are cruel and unusual. We thus hold that for a juvenile offender who remains under the jurisdiction of the juvenile court, the Eighth Amendment forbids the automatic imposition of lifetime sex-offender registration and notification requirements.

The Ohio Constitution, Article I, Section 9, contains its own prohibition against cruel and unusual punishment.

For juveniles who remain in the juvenile system, R.C. 2152.86 is striking in the disproportionate way it treats PRQJORs. We trust judges to make the important calls in imposing the adult portion of the SYO sentence. In discretionary SYO cases, juvenile judges determine whether an SYO denomination is appropriate. But under R.C. 2152.86, the juvenile judge is given absolutely no discretion over the portion of the juvenile's penalty that could extend for a lifetime. There is none of the important, individualized work that juvenile judges do. Instead, a lifetime punishment is imposed with no chance for reconsideration of its appropriateness for 25 years. Compared to punishments for other juvenile offenders, whose cases are reevaluated when their juvenile disposition ends and at regularly scheduled intervals thereafter, this punishment is disproportionate.

Lack of proportionality is also evidenced by the very public nature of the penalty. The punishment of lifetime exposure for a wrong committed in childhood runs counter to the private nature of our juvenile court system. Confidentiality has always been at the heart of the juvenile justice system. That core principle is trampled by any requirement of public notification. Publicity is even more of a concern for PRQJORs, whose information is disseminated on the Internet.

Ohio's juvenile system is designed to shield children from stigmatization based upon the bad acts of their youth: For delinquent children, "it is the law's policy 'to hide youthful errors from the full gaze of the public and bury them in the graveyard of the forgotten past.'" In Ohio, we are required to liberally interpret the juvenile delinquency provisions to "protect the public interest in removing the consequences of criminal behavior and the taint of criminality from children committing delinquent acts and to substitute therefor a program of supervision, care, and rehabilitation."

"[T]raditionally juveniles have been shielded from the stigma of the proceedings by keeping hearings private and not publishing juveniles' names.

In this case, for instance, we refer to the juvenile by his initials, rather than by his full name. But if R.C. 2152.86 is enforced, his name, offense, and addresses will be published on the Internet.

Registration and notification requirements frustrate two of the fundamental elements of juvenile rehabilitation: confidentiality and the avoidance of stigma. Confidentiality promotes rehabilitation by allowing the juvenile to move into adulthood without the baggage of youthful mistakes. Public exposure of those mistakes brands the juvenile as an undesirable wherever he goes.

The publication required by S.B. 10 causes the greatest possible stigmatization: Operating directly contrary to the rehabilitative goals of the juvenile justice system, sex offender registration and notification laws can publicly and permanently mark juvenile sex offenders as deviant criminals who should be feared and shunned. While many juvenile proceedings are confidential and sealed, sex offender registration and notification laws, by creating a public record, place the sexual offense of a juvenile directly and prominently in the public eye.

[F]ew labels are as damaging in today's society as "convicted sex offender." Sex offenders are, as one scholar put it, "the lepers of the criminal justice system," with juveniles listed in the sex offender registry sharing this characterization. The state's interest in and responsibility for a juvenile's well-being and rehabilitation is not promoted by a practice that makes a juvenile's sex offenses public.

S.B. 10 forces registration and notification requirements into a juvenile system where rehabilitation is paramount, confidentiality is elemental, and individualized treatment from judges is essential. The public punishments required by R.C. 2152.86 are automatic, lifelong, and contrary to the rehabilitative goals of the juvenile system. We conclude that they "shock the sense of justice of the community" and thus violate Ohio's prohibition against cruel and unusual punishments.

Appellant also argues that R.C. 2152.86 violates a juvenile's right to due process guaranteed by the Fourteenth Amendment to the United States Constitution and the Ohio Constitution, Article I, Section 16. We agree.

From a due process perspective, both this court and the United States Supreme Court have held that juveniles may be treated differently from adults.

In *D.H.*, this court applied a fundamental-fairness standard in addressing due process concerns, holding that a balanced approach is required to preserve the special nature of the juvenile process. We recognized the state's stake in the rehabilitation of juvenile offenders and the state's paternal role: The State has "a *parens patriae* interest in preserving and promoting the welfare of the child," which makes a juvenile proceeding fundamentally different from an adult criminal trial. We have tried, therefore, to strike a balance— to respect the "informality" and "flexibility" that characterize juvenile proceedings, and yet to ensure that such proceedings comport with the "fundamental fairness" demanded by the Due Process Clause.

In *D.H.*, we held that fundamental fairness does not demand the same Sixth Amendment jury-trial rights for juveniles as required by *Foster* for adults. This court based its decision on the special role of juvenile courts and juvenile judges. The court's dispositional role is at the heart of the remaining differences between juvenile and adult courts. It is there that the expertise of a juvenile judge is necessary. The judge, given the factors set forth in R.C. 2152.13(D)(2)(a)(i), must assess the strengths and weaknesses of the juvenile system vis-à-vis a particular child to determine how this particular juvenile fits within the system and whether the system is equipped to deal with the child successfully. That assessment requires as much familiarity with the juvenile justice system as it does familiarity with the facts of the case. To leave that determination to an expert, given the juvenile system's goal of rehabilitation, does not offend fundamental fairness, especially since the adult portion of the blended sentence that the judge imposes upon a jury verdict is not immediately, and may never be, enforced.

Thus, this court held that the discretionary role of the judge in the disposition of a juvenile case overrides the importance of the role of the jury. The disposition of a child is so different from the sentencing of an adult that fundamental fairness to the child demands the unique expertise of a juvenile judge.

R.C. 2152.86 eliminates the discretion of the juvenile judge, this essential element of the juvenile process, at the most consequential part of the dispositional process. R.C. 2152.86 requires the automatic imposition of a lifetime punishment—with no chance of reconsideration for 25 years—without benefit of a juvenile judge weighing its appropriateness. It is contrary to the juvenile system's core emphasis on individual, corrective treatment and rehabilitation. Punishment is not the goal of the juvenile system, except as necessary to direct the child toward the goal of rehabilitation.

R.C. 2152.86(B)(1) requires the imposition of an adult penalty for juvenile acts without input from a juvenile judge. Under R.C. 2152.86, the court cannot consider individual factors about a child or his background, cannot have a say in how often a child must register or where he must register, or determine how publication of the offense might affect rehabilitation. An SYO offender remains within the jurisdiction of the juvenile court, but R.C. 2152.86 removes the juvenile court's ability to exercise its most important role in rehabilitation. Fundamental fairness requires that the judge decide the appropriateness of any such penalty.

Thus, for the bulk of Ohio's SYO scheme, the juvenile court retains discretion to deal individually with juvenile offenders, and procedural protections are in place before adult punishment can be invoked. Even after additional bad acts by a juvenile, the judge has the discretion not to invoke the adult sentence, or to lessen the one imposed at the time of the juvenile disposition. On the other hand, even for a juvenile who is amenable to rehabilitation and commits no further bad acts during his juvenile disposition, the adult consequences of registration and notification attach immediately. PRQJORs have no right to present evidence or even be heard on the issue of their classification.

Once the juvenile court makes its SYO determination, the juvenile judge never gets an opportunity to determine whether the juvenile offender has responded to rehabilitation or whether he remains a threat to society. Even if the adult portion of his sentence is not invoked, the sex-offender classification is irrevocable. The timing of the classification— immediately upon the imposition of SYO status—leaves no room for the judge to determine whether the juvenile offender has been rehabilitated. And the automatically imposed punishment lasts far longer than the jurisdiction of the juvenile court.

Again, we are dealing with juveniles who remain in the juvenile system through the decision of a juvenile judge—a decision made through the balancing of the factors set forth in R.C. 2152.12(B) — that the juvenile at issue is amenable to the rehabilitative purpose of the juvenile system. The protections and rehabilitative aims of the juvenile process must remain paramount; we must recognize that juvenile offenders are less culpable and more amenable to reform than adult offenders.

The requirement in R.C. 2152.86 of automatic imposition of Tier III classification on a juvenile offender who receives an SYO dispositional sentence undercuts the rehabilitative purpose of Ohio's juvenile system and eliminates the important role of the juvenile court's discretion in the disposition of juvenile offenders and thus fails to meet the due process requirement of fundamental fairness. In *D.H.*, we held that because of the central role of the juvenile judge in a juvenile's rehabilitative process, fundamental fairness did not require the same jury-trial rights for juveniles as we required for adults in *Foster*. In this case, we determine that fundamental fairness is not a one-way street that allows only for an easing of due process requirements for juveniles; instead, fundamental fairness may require, as it does in this case, additional procedural safeguards for juveniles in order to meet of the juvenile system's goals of rehabilitation and reintegration into society.

R.C. 2152.86 creates a classification of juvenile offenders called public-registry-qualified juvenile-offender registrants. R.C. 2152.86 imposes upon that classification of juvenile offenders an automatic, lifetime requirement of sex-offender registration and notification, including placement on a public Internet registry. Such requirements are imposed upon juveniles without the participation of a juvenile judge. We conclude that R.C. 2152.86 is unconstitutional because the penalty it imposes violates the prohibitions against cruel and unusual punishment contained in the Eighth Amendment to the United States Constitution and the Ohio Constitution, Article I, Section 9. Further, we hold that R.C. 2152.86 is unconstitutional because the procedure involved in imposing the punishments violates the Due Process Clause of the Fourteenth Amendment to the United States Constitution and the Ohio Constitution, Article I, Section 16.

Accordingly, we reverse the judgment of the court of appeals and remand the cause to the trial court for further proceedings in accordance with this opinion.

Judgment reversed and cause remanded.

O'DONNELL, J., dissenting.

Respectfully, I dissent.

In *State v. Williams*, I expressed my view in a dissenting opinion, that consistent with prior holdings of this court, the registration and notification requirements of S.B. 10 are civil in nature and part of a regulatory scheme designed to protect the public from known sex offenders. Because application of those requirements to juveniles pursuant to R.C. 2152.86 does not alter S.B. 10's nonpunitive purpose, that view also applies to juveniles such as C.P.

In 2005, the state of Utah filed a petition charging C.P., then age 11, with destruction of property, sodomy, aggravated sexual abuse of a child, and rape of a child. The three latter charges stemmed from allegations that when C.P. was nine and ten years old, he had engaged in sexual conduct with his halfsister — three years younger — for several years. That conduct included making his sister perform strip acts, forcing her to perform and receive oral sex, exposing himself, and forcibly raping her. C.P. admitted to the charges of destruction of property, sodomy, and sexual abuse of a child, a charge which the state had reduced from aggravated sexual abuse of a child. The Utah juvenile court placed C.P. in the temporary custody of the Division of Child and Family Services for foster care, committed him to the Department of Juvenile Justice Services for 30 days, and ordered him to obtain sex-specific counseling. During a neuropsychological evaluation conducted in 2006, C.P. admitted the allegations involving his half-sister and also admitted to having "touched five or six other young girls inappropriately."

While in foster care in Utah, C.P. left his second foster home after being accused of touching a girl's breast at school. He was then placed in the Youth Track residential program for juvenile sex offenders, where he received inpatient residential care from June 1, 2006, through November 3, 2008, when he returned home to live with his mother. C.P. participated in outpatient counseling, but discontinued taking his medications because he did not like how they made him feel.

Thereafter, C.P.'s parents agreed that he might benefit from living with his father in Ohio, and in June 2009 he moved to Ohio. Within nine days of his arrival, C.P., then age 15, secluded himself with his 6-year-old nephew and orally and anally raped him.

The day after the incident, the state filed a complaint against C.P. in the Athens County Juvenile Court, charging him with two counts of child rape and one count of kidnapping with sexual motivation, each count a first-degree felony if committed by an adult. The state filed a motion pursuant to R.C. 2152.10(A)(1)(b), which sought to transfer jurisdiction of the case to the common pleas court to prosecute C.P. as an adult. After holding an amenability hearing, the trial court denied the state's motion. The state then obtained an indictment against C.P. that contained a serious-youth-offender ("SYO") specification for each count.

C.P. subsequently entered an admission to each charge in the indictment, and due to his age and the nature of his offenses, he was eligible for a discretionary SYO dispositional sentence pursuant to R.C. 2152.11(D)(2)(b). The court found him to be a delinquent child and designated him an SYO in relation to each offense. It committed C.P. to the Ohio Department of Youth Services for concurrent commitments on each count of a minimum period of three years and a maximum period not to exceed age twenty-one. As part of the SYO disposition, the court imposed three concurrent five-year prison terms that were stayed pending C.P.'s successful completion of his juvenile dispositions. The court further classified C.P. as a public-registry-qualified juvenile-offender registrant ("PRQJOR") pursuant to R.C. 2152.86(A)(1) and a Tier III sex-offender/childvictim offender pursuant to R.C. 2152.86(A)(1), and advised him of the duties imposed by that statute.

C.P. appealed his classification as a Tier III offender and PRQJOR to the Fourth District Court of Appeals, arguing that R.C. 2152.86 violated his rights to due process and equal protection, as well as his right against cruel and unusual punishment. The court of appeals affirmed the judgment of the trial court.

The majority reverses the judgment of the court of appeals, finding that the registration and notification requirements of R.C. 2152.86 constitute cruel and unusual punishment in violation of the Eighth Amendment to the United States Constitution and the Ohio Constitution, Article I, Section 9. The majority further finds that because the statute imposes those requirements automatically rather than at the discretion of a juvenile judge, it also violates the Due Process Clause of the Fourteenth Amendment to the United States Constitution and the Ohio Constitution, Article I, Section 16.

The Ohio General Assembly passed 2007 Am.Sub.S.B. No. 10 ("S.B. 10") in accordance with legislation enacted by the United States Congress in an effort to create a national, uniform system of sex-offender registration. It is undisputed that the General Assembly is "the ultimate arbiter of public policy" and the only branch of government charged with fulfilling that role. And prior to this court's abandonment of precedent in the majority opinion in *Williams*, we have historically construed registration statutes as part of a civil regulatory scheme and nonpunitive in nature.

Accordingly, in my view, the General Assembly constitutionally enacted R.C. 2152.86 and imposed registration and notification requirements on certain juvenile sex offenders based on concerns for public safety and public welfare. Those requirements are not punitive and do not offend the Constitution. To the extent that any policy concern exists regarding the registration of juvenile sex offenders, it is within the sole province of the legislature to address that issue.

The majority opinion begins with the premise that R.C. Chapter 2950 is punitive, and then it applies the two-part analysis discussed by the Supreme Court in *Graham v. Florida*. The majority opinion today relies on *Graham* to conclude that the registration and notification requirements of R.C. 2152.86 constitute cruel and unusual punishment.

The majority bases its conclusion on several factors: the lack of a national consensus favoring the publication of juvenile sex offenders' personal information, its belief that juvenile sex offenders are less culpable and more susceptible to change than adult sex offenders, and its position that the requirements of the statute are especially harsh because a juvenile offender will begin adulthood with the stigma associated with being labeled a sex offender, which in turn will hamper education, relationships, and employment opportunities. The majority further finds that R.C. 2152.86 does not advance penological goals. Under the guise of exercising the independent judgment permitted by the test in *Graham*, the majority impermissibly supplants the judgment of the General Assembly with its own beliefs.

Registration has historically been viewed as a regulatory measure and not as a form of punishment.

As applied to juveniles, courts have rejected the argument that statutes subjecting juveniles to public registration are punitive because of the unpleasant consequences that may flow from registration or the length of time a juvenile may be required to report. The requirement that juveniles register in a sex offender database for at least 25 years because they committed the equivalent of aggravated sexual abuse is not a disproportionate punishment.

Although the majority finds juvenile sex offenders less culpable than their adult counterparts, juveniles commit more than 25 percent of all sex offenses and more than 35 percent of all sex offenses against children. In fact, C.P. was a repeat offender and all of his victims were other juveniles; by invalidating R.C. 2152.86, as applied to juveniles such as C.P., the majority leaves the public unaware of a significant number of sex offenders who are capable of reoffending, directly contrary to the intent of the General Assembly and contrary to our precedent and determinations of constitutionality that exist in our sister states.

Moreover, this court has previously recognized that an offense committed as a juvenile may have adverse consequences on the offender as an adult.

With respect to the argument that public registration constitutes punishment because of the potential for adversely affecting a juvenile's future employment, the Supreme Court of the United States has held occupational debarment to be regulatory, and therefore civil in nature.

For the foregoing reasons, the requirements of R.C. 2152.86 are not punitive and do not constitute cruel and unusual punishment. The General Assembly enacted R.C. 2152.86

pursuant to its authority and with the intent to protect the safety and welfare of the public. Moreover, it cannot be disputed that preventing crime "persists undiluted in the juvenile context." Thus, the statute is not unconstitutional.

As applied here, C.P. cannot establish a due process violation based on the fact that R.C. 2152.86 imposes *automatic* registration, as opposed to registration imposed by an exercise of judicial discretion, because whether a juvenile sex offender has been sufficiently rehabilitated is not material to the statute's operation; it is the adjudication that triggers the duty to register. There is no constitutional requirement that juveniles must receive greater due process than adults.

Discretion is a matter of grace and not of right. Thus, the General Assembly was within its authority to impose automatic registration on juvenile sex offenders when it enacted R.C. 2152.86. Accordingly, the statute meets the requirements of due process and does not offend notions of fundamental fairness.

R.C. 2152.86 is constitutional and does not violate the prohibition against cruel and unusual punishment contained in the Eighth Amendment to the United States Constitution or the Ohio Constitution, Article I, Section 9, nor does it violate the Due Process Clause of the Fourteenth Amendment to the United States Constitution or the Ohio Constitution, Article I, Section 16.

For these reasons, I would affirm the judgment of the court of appeals and hold that R.C. 2152.86 is constitutional.

CUPP, J., dissenting.

For a violation of the Eighth Amendment's prohibition against cruel and unusual punishment, as a general matter the punishment in question must be "grossly disproportionate" to the crime's severity. This "narrow proportionality" standard is highly deferential and strongly favors upholding a punishment that has been imposed as authorized by a particular statute. It sets a very high bar for a challenger claiming a violation of the Eighth Amendment's ban to overcome. Judges do not possess blanket authority to second guess decisions of legislatures or sentencing courts. Successful Eighth Amendment challenges to noncapital sentences are " 'exceedingly rare.' "

When reviewing a particular juvenile punishment for an Eighth Amendment violation, an offender's status as a juvenile must be taken into account because juveniles are typically less culpable than adults due to their youth and immaturity. However, the general standards of gross disproportionality and substantial deference to the legislative judgment expressed within the relevant statute are not to be abandoned merely because the offender is a juvenile.

But the sex-offender registration and notification provisions at issue in this case are so significantly different from the punishment at issue in *Graham*—lifetime imprisonment with no chance of parole, with its fundamental loss of liberty—that I am left wondering how the two can possibly be considered comparable for constitutional purposes.

Although the provisions of R.C. 5152.86 subjecting certain juveniles to automatic lifetime registration and notification requirements, with a potential for reclassification after 25 years, may be viewed as highly burdensome or even onerous, they do not reach that high level of punishment that the United States Supreme Court has held categorically unconstitutional. The punishments held by the United States Supreme Court to violate the Eighth Amendment ban when applied to juveniles are the death penalty, and lifetime imprisonment without the possibility of parole for serious, but non-homicide, crimes. I do not find the requirements at issue here pertaining to registration and notification to rise to such a level as to be even remotely comparable.

The statutory requirements at issue apply only to a small and select category of juvenile offenders — those who have committed the most serious sex offenses after reaching the age of 14 and who have ultimately received a disposition as a serious youthful offender ("SYO") after all the procedural steps of the SYO process have been fulfilled. The General Assembly has determined that these offenders pose a special danger to public safety that separates them from all other juvenile offenders. R.C. 2152.86 assigns only offenders of this type to the special category of public-registry-qualified juvenile-offender registrants, or PRQJORs.

Under R.C. 2152.86, all juveniles who commit sex offenses before their fourteenth birthday, those juvenile sex offenders over the age of 14 who commit less serious offenses than C.P. committed, and those offenders who have not received a SYO disposition are not considered PRQJORs. The General Assembly's differentiations in this regard are not unreasonable in light of its objective of protecting the public, and the determinations are entitled to substantial deference.

In the present case, however, the majority unjustifiably relies on the offender's juvenile status to minimize the substantial bar the challenger must surmount to establish cruel and unusual punishment. In place of that substantial bar, the majority substitutes a threshold that bears no resemblance to the threshold applied in the review of the death penalty in *Roper* or the review of the sentence of life imprisonment with no possibility of parole in *Graham*. The punishment of life without parole under scrutiny in *Graham* deprived the juvenile offender in that case of "the most basic liberties without giving hope of restoration" because the offender was to be unconditionally imprisoned for life with absolutely no prospect of parole. In contrast, most courts have held that sex-offender requirements of the type at issue in this case are not even "punishment" for purposes of the Eighth Amendment, even if the requirements do place heavy burdens on an offender.

The sex-offender notification and registration requirements at issue here, while burdensome, simply do not approach the severity of the punishments at issue in *Graham* or *Roper*.

The majority opinion, unfortunately, fails to acknowledge this fundamental difference, even as it repeatedly compares the requirements in this case to the punishment of lifetime imprisonment in *Graham*. Instead, it appears to stage-manage the *Graham* factors in order to reach its own preferred policy result.

Additionally, I am unable to agree with the majority's determination that R.C. 2152.86 violates due process principles. The majority's finding of fundamental unfairness fails to take into account that PRQJORs such as C.P. reach that status only by undergoing a rigorous narrowing process designed to eliminate most juvenile sex offenders. The statute at issue provides adequate procedural safeguards for those offenders who are not eliminated, and who are ultimately assigned PRQJOR status, to satisfy due process concerns.

Finally, the majority's analysis leaves unanswered a multitude of additional issues that its conclusions generate. As a result, the trial court will be forced to guess what is actually required in this case upon remand. I note just two of these unanswered questions.

First, the majority opinion concludes that the lack of discretion afforded to a juvenile judge by R.C. 2152.86 in assigning the PRQJOR designation is a significant infirmity in the statute bearing upon its constitutionality. Does this mean that a juvenile judge may now, notwithstanding the statute, exercise discretion as to whether to impose sex-offender notification and reporting requirements on PRQJOR-status offenders such as C.P.? If so, what are the boundaries of that discretion?

Second, another constitutional infirmity of the statute, according to the majority opinion, is that the registration and notification requirements are lifelong (with a possibility for adjustment after 25 years). May a juvenile judge in the exercise of discretion now impose requirements of shorter duration on offenders such as C.P. and overcome the constitutional deficiencies? If so, what duration will satisfy the majority's concerns?

I am unable to agree that the provisions of R.C. 2152.86 at issue violate either the United States or Ohio constitutional prohibitions against cruel and unusual punishment and the requirements of due process. I would hold that the provisions under consideration survive constitutional scrutiny and would affirm the judgment of the court of appeals. Therefore, I respectfully dissent.

Holdings of *In re: C.P.*: The court held that the statute which automatically placed certain minors on a sex offender registry for the rest of their life violated the constitutional prohibition against cruel and unusual punishment contained in the Eighth Amendment and the Due Process Clause of the Fourteenth Amendment to the United States Constitution as well as similar provisions of the Ohio Constitution.

Discussion Questions

How does the majority analyze the "culpability of offenders" in this case?

How do the courts justify finding that juveniles are less culpable than adults for their acts? What about juveniles that are only days from the age of majority?

Are ALL juveniles capable of "redemption" or "rehabilitation"? If not, wouldn't the court be better off looking at each case individually?

State v. Lyle: In *State v. Lyle*, the Iowa Supreme Court was faced with the case of a 17-year-old who had been waived to adult court. In adult court, the youth was convicted of second degree robbery. The Iowa statute required that the judge sentence any defendant convicted of this offense to prison for a term not to exceed 10 years and furthermore that the defendant not be eligible for parole until his has served at least 70% (7 years) of the sentence. The judge sentenced the youth as required by the statute, and the youth appealed on the grounds that the mandatory sentence and the "mandatory minimum" violated the 8th Amendment prohibition against cruel and unusual punishment.

As you read *State v. Lyle*, look for the following:

1. Consider what reasoning by the court supports finding that the "mandatory minimum" provisions qualify as "cruel" under the cruel and unusual punishment prohibition embodied in the 8th Amendment.

2. Consider whether the court is objecting to the mandatory imprisonment requirement, the mandatory minimum time served before parole requirement, or both.

3. Consider whether or not the sentence imposed would have survived the scrutiny of the Iowa Supreme Court if it had not been mandated by the statute but was determined by the judge in the case after hearing all of the individual facts of the case.

State v. Lyle

854 N.W.2d 378 (Iowa 2014)

CADY, Chief Justice.

In this appeal, a prison inmate who committed the crime of robbery in the second degree as a juvenile and was prosecuted as an adult challenges the constitutionality of a sentencing statute that required the imposition of a mandatory seven-year minimum sentence of imprisonment. The inmate was in high school at the time of the crime, which involved a brief altercation outside the high school with another student that ended when the inmate took a small plastic bag containing marijuana from the student. He claims the sentencing statute constitutes cruel and unusual punishment in violation of the State and Federal Constitutions when applied to all juveniles prosecuted as adults because the mandatory sentence failed to permit the court to consider any circumstances based on his attributes of youth or the circumstances of his conduct in mitigation of punishment. For the reasons expressed below, we hold a statute mandating a sentence of incarceration in a prison for juvenile offenders with no opportunity for parole until a minimum period of time has been served is unconstitutional under article I, section 17 of the Iowa Constitution. Accordingly, we vacate the sentence and remand the case to the district court for resentencing. Importantly, we do not hold that juvenile offenders cannot be sentenced to imprisonment for their criminal acts. We do not hold juvenile offenders cannot be sentenced to a minimum term of imprisonment. We only hold juvenile offenders cannot be mandatorily sentenced under a mandatory minimum sentencing scheme.

Andre Lyle Jr. was convicted following a jury trial of the crime of robbery in the second degree on June 29, 2011. He was a 17-year-old high school student when he committed the crime. The conviction resulted from an incident in October 2010 when Lyle and a companion punched another young man and took a small bag of marijuana from him. The altercation between the boys occurred outside the high school they attended after the victim failed to deliver marijuana to Lyle and his companion in exchange for $5 they had given the victim the previous day. Lyle videoed the confrontation on his cell phone. Prior to trial, Lyle unsuccessfully sought to transfer jurisdiction of the matter to the juvenile court.

Lyle grew up in Des Moines with little family support and few advantages. His father was in prison, and he was raised by his grandmother after his mother threatened him with a knife. His grandmother permitted him to smoke marijuana, and he was frequently tardy or absent from school. Lyle had frequent contact with law enforcement and first entered the juvenile justice system at twelve years of age. He was involved in many criminal acts as a teenager, including assaults and robberies. Lyle was known to record his criminal behavior with his cell phone and post videos on the Internet.

Lyle appeared before the district court for sentencing on his eighteenth birthday. The district court sentenced him to a term of incarceration in the state corrections system not to exceed ten years. Pursuant to Iowa statute, the sentence was mandatory, and he was required to serve seventy percent of the prison term before he could be eligible for parole.

Lyle objected to the seventy percent mandatory minimum sentence. He claimed it was unconstitutional as applied to juvenile offenders. The district court overruled Lyle's objection.

During the pendency of the appeal, the United States decided *Miller v. Alabama*. In *Miller*, the Court held a statutory schema that mandates life imprisonment without the possibility of parole cannot constitutionally be applied to a juvenile. Subsequently, we held the rule contemplated by *Miller* was retroactive. We then applied the reasoning in *Miller* to sentences that effectively deprived a juvenile offender of a meaningful opportunity for early release on parole during the offender's lifetime based on demonstrated maturity and rehabilitation. In a trilogy of cases, our reasoning applied not just to a de facto life sentence or one "that is the practical equivalent of a life sentence without parole," but also to a "lengthy term-of-years sentence."

Lyle contends the prohibition against cruel and unusual punishment in the Iowa Constitution does not permit a statutory scheme that mandates a person sentenced for a crime committed as a juvenile to serve a minimum period of time prior to becoming eligible for parole or work release. The State argues a mandatory minimum sentence of the term of years for the crime committed in this case is not cruel and unusual.

Time and experience have taught us much about the efficacy and justice of certain punishments. As a consequence, we understand our concept of cruel and unusual punishment is "not static." "This is because '[t]he standard of extreme cruelty is not merely descriptive, but necessarily embodies a moral judgment. The standard itself remains the same, but its applicability must change as the basic mores of society change.'" In other words, punishments once thought just and constitutional may later come to be seen as fundamentally repugnant to the core values contained in our State and Federal Constitutions as we grow in our understanding over time. As with other rights enumerated under our constitution, we interpret them in light our understanding of today, not by our past understanding.

Importantly, *Miller* added to this jurisprudence by conjoining two sets of caselaw: outright categorical prohibitions on certain punishments for certain crimes or against certain offenders, with another line of cases requiring a sentencer have the ability to consider certain characteristics about the offender as mitigating circumstances in favor of not sentencing the offender to death.

By importing the line of cases represented by *Lockett*, *Miller* effectively crafted a new subset of categorically unconstitutional sentences: sentences in which the legislature has forbidden the sentencing court from considering important mitigating characteristics of an offender whose culpability is necessarily and categorically reduced as a matter of law, making the ultimate sentence categorically inappropriate.

The analysis of a categorical challenge to a sentence normally entails a two-step inquiry. First, we consider "'objective indicia of society's standards, as expressed in legislative enactments and state practice' to determine whether there is a national consensus against the sentencing practice at issue. Second, we exercise our own "independent judgment" "guided by 'the standards elaborated by controlling precedents and by [our] own understanding and interpretation of the [Iowa Constitution's] text, history, meaning, and purpose.'"

Beginning with the first prong of the analysis, we recognize no other court in the nation has held that its constitution or the Federal Constitution prohibits a statutory schema that prescribes a mandatory minimum sentence for a juvenile offender. Further, most states permit or require some or all juvenile offenders to be given mandatory minimum sentences. This state of the law arguably projects a consensus in society in favor of permitting juveniles to be given mandatory minimum statutory sentences.

Yet, "[c]onsensus is not dispositive." Moreover, as *Miller* demonstrates, constitutional protection for the rights of juveniles in sentencing for the most serious crimes is rapidly evolving in the face of widespread sentencing statutes and practices to the contrary.

Nevertheless, the absence of caselaw does not necessarily support the presence of a consensus contrary to the challenge by Lyle in this case. Our legislature has already started to signal its independent concern with mandatory prison sentences for juveniles.

Here, the legislative decision to back away from mandatory sentencing for most crimes committed by juveniles weakens the notion of a consensus in favor of the practice of blindly sentencing juveniles based on the crime committed. In fact, it helps illustrate a building consensus in this state to treat juveniles in our courts differently than adults.

Actually, the statutory recognition of the need for some discretion when sentencing juveniles is consistent with our overall approach in the past in dealing with juveniles. Primarily, the juvenile justice chapter of our Code gives courts considerable discretion to take action in the best interests of the child.

All of these statutes reflect a pair of compelling realities. First, children lack the risk-calculation skills adults are presumed to possess and are inherently sensitive, impressionable, and developmentally malleable. Second, the best interests of the child generally support discretion in dealing with all juveniles.

Overall, it is becoming clear that society is now beginning to recognize a growing understanding that mandatory sentences of imprisonment for crimes committed by children are undesirable in society. If there is not yet a consensus against mandatory minimum sentencing for juveniles, a consensus is certainly building in Iowa in the direction of eliminating mandatory minimum sentencing.

We next turn to the second step in the analysis of the Cruel and Unusual Punishment Clause. We must decide if the mandatory minimum sentence for a youthful offender violates the Cruel and Unusual Punishment Clause in light of its text, meaning, purpose, and history.

In doing so, we cannot ignore that over the last decade, juvenile justice has seen remarkable, perhaps watershed, change. This evolution must be cast in its proper place in the history of juvenile justice. This history is particularly salient given the categorical nature of Lyle's challenge. It reveals children and juveniles have been viewed as constitutionally different from adults in this country for more than a century.

The nub of at least some of these cases is that juveniles are not fully equipped to make "important, affirmative choices with potentially serious consequences." "[D]uring the formative years of childhood and adolescence, minors often lack the experience, perspective, and judgment to recognize and avoid choices that could be detrimental to them."

Upon exercise of our independent judgment, as we are required to do under the constitutional test, we conclude that the sentencing of juveniles according to statutorily required mandatory minimums does not adequately serve the legitimate penological objectives in light of the child's categorically diminished culpability. First and foremost, the time when a 17-year-old could seriously be considered to have adult-like culpability has passed. Of course, scientific data and the opinions of medical experts provide a compelling and increasingly ineluctable case that from a neurodevelopment standpoint, juvenile culpability does not rise to the adult-like standard the mandatory minimum provision of section 902.12(5) presupposes. Thus, this prevailing medical consensus continues to inform and influence our opinion today under the constitutional analysis we are required to follow. As demonstrated by our prior opinions and the recent opinions of the United States Supreme Court, however, we can speak of youth in the common-sense terms of what any parent knows or what any former child knows, and so, surely, we do not abdicate our constitutional duty to exercise independent judgment when we determine Lyle does not have adult-like culpability.

We understand and appreciate that harm to a victim is not diluted by the age of the offender. Yet, justice requires us to consider the culpability of the offender in addition to the harm the offender caused. A constitutional framework that focused only on the harm the defendant caused would never have produced *Roper*, which involved a profoundly heinous crime.

Simply put, attempting to mete out a given punishment to a juvenile for retributive purposes irrespective of an individualized analysis of the juvenile's categorically diminished culpability is an irrational exercise.

Rehabilitation and incapacitation *can* justify criminally punishing juveniles, but mandatory minimums do not further these objectives in a way that adequately protects the rights of juveniles within the context of the constitutional protection from the imposition of cruel and unusual punishment for a juvenile. As much as youthful immaturity has sharpened our understanding to use care in the imposition of punishment of juveniles, it also reveals an equal understanding that reform can come easier for juveniles without the need to impose harsh measures. Sometimes a youthful offender merely needs time to grow. As with the lack of maturity in youth, this too is something most parents know.

The greater likelihood of reform for juveniles also substantially undermines an incapacitation rationale.

In the end, we conclude all mandatory minimum sentences of imprisonment for youthful offenders are unconstitutional under the cruel and unusual punishment clause in article I, section 17 of our constitution. Mandatory minimum sentences for juveniles are simply too punitive for what we know about juveniles. Furthermore, we do not believe this conclusion is inconsistent with the consensus of Iowans. Although most parents fortunately will never find themselves in a position to be in court to see their teenage child sentenced to a mandatory minimum term of imprisonment for committing a forcible felony, we think most parents would be stunned to learn this state had a sentencing schema for juvenile offenders that required courts to imprison all youthful offenders for conduct that constituted a forcible felony without looking behind the label of the crime into the details of the particular offense and the individual circumstances of the child. Additionally, we think the jolt would be compounded once parents would further discover that their child must serve at least seventy percent of the term of the mandatory sentence before becoming eligible for parole. This shock would only intensify when it is remembered how some serious crimes can at times be committed by conduct that appears less serious when the result of juvenile behavior. This case could be an illustration.

Consequently, the mandatory minimum sentences applicable to adult offenders apply, with no exceptions, to juvenile offenders, including those who engage in inane juvenile schoolyard conduct. At least for those juveniles, our collective sense of humanity preserved in our constitutional prohibition against cruel and unusual punishment and stirred by what we all know about child development demands some assurance that imprisonment is actually appropriate and necessary. There is no other area of the law in which our laws write off children based only on a category of conduct without considering all background facts and circumstances. In other words, the protection of article I, section 17 applies across the board to all crimes. Thus, if mandatory sentencing for the most serious crimes that impose the most serious punishment of life in prison without parole violates article I, section 17, so would mandatory sentences for less serious crimes imposing the less serious punishment of a minimum period of time in prison without parole. All children are protected by the Iowa Constitution. The constitutional prohibition against cruel and unusual punishment does not protect all children if the constitutional infirmity identified in mandatory imprisonment for those juveniles who commit the most serious crimes is overlooked in mandatory imprisonment for those juveniles who commit less serious crimes. *Miller* is properly read to support a new sentencing framework that reconsiders mandatory sentencing for all children. Mandatory minimum sentencing results in cruel and unusual punishment due to the differences between children and adults. This rationale applies to all crimes, and no principled basis exists to cabin the protection only for the most serious crimes.

Ultimately, we hold a mandatory minimum sentencing schema, like the one contained in section 902.12, violates article I, section 17 of the Iowa Constitution when applied in cases involving conduct committed by youthful offenders. The keystone of our reasoning is that youth and its attendant circumstances and attributes make a broad statutory declaration denying courts this very discretion categorically repugnant to article I, section 17 of our constitution.

It is important to be mindful that the holding in this case does not prohibit judges from sentencing juveniles to prison for the length of time identified by the legislature for the crime committed, nor does it prohibit the legislature from imposing a minimum time that youthful offenders must serve in prison before being eligible for parole. Article I, section 17 only prohibits the one-size-fits-all mandatory sentencing for juveniles. Our constitution demands that we do better for youthful offenders—all youthful offenders, not just those who commit the most serious crimes. Some juveniles will deserve imprisonment, but others may not. A statute that sends all juvenile offenders to prison for a minimum period of time under all circumstances simply cannot satisfy the standards of decency and fairness embedded in article I, section 17 of the Iowa Constitution.

We also recognize the remedy in this case is to resentence Lyle so a judge can at least consider a sentencing option other than imprisonment. We also recognize our decision will apply to all juveniles currently serving a mandatory sentence of imprisonment. Thus, this case will require all juvenile offenders who are in prison under a mandatory sentence to be returned to court for resentencing. Furthermore, our holding today has no application to sentencing laws affecting adult offenders. Lines are drawn in our law by necessity and are incorporated into the jurisprudence we have developed to usher the Iowa Constitution through time. This case does not move any of the lines that currently exist in the sentencing of adult offenders. On remand, judges will do what they have taken an oath to do. They will apply the law fairly and impartially, without fear. They will sentence those juvenile offenders to the maximum sentence if warranted and to a lesser sentence if warranted.

Accordingly, article I, section 17 of the Iowa Constitution forbids a sentencing schema for juvenile offenders that deprives the district court the discretion to consider youth and its attendant circumstances as a mitigating factor and to impose a lighter punishment, including one that suspends all or part of the sentence, including any mandatory minimum.

V. Conclusion.

For the above reasons, we vacate Lyle's sentence and remand the case to the district court for further proceedings.

DECISION OF COURT OF APPEALS VACATED; DISTRICT COURT SENTENCE VACATED; CASE REMANDED.

WATERMAN, Justice (dissenting).

I respectfully dissent for the reasons set forth in Justice Zager's dissent, which I join. I write separately because I would go further to overrule as plainly erroneous our court's juvenile sentencing decisions in *Pearson* and *Null* for the reasons explained in the dissents in those cases.

And, I would follow Eighth Amendment decisions of our nation's highest court when applying the cruel-and-unusual-punishment provision of the Iowa Constitution because our state's founders intended those provisions to have the same meaning.

The trial judge found Lyle, then nearly age eighteen, "poses a serious danger to the community at present." In denying Lyle's motion for transfer to juvenile court, the trial judge noted Lyle's "cell phone contained numerous videos which showed [him] engaging in unprovoked, cowardly and vicious attacks against several different individuals" on or near school property. The trial judge personally observed Lyle's defiant demeanor in open court. I have no reason to disagree with the trial judge's firsthand assessment of Lyle. But, even if we accept Lyle as a merely misguided, immature schoolyard bully, the mandatory sentence he received falls well short of being unconstitutionally cruel and unusual punishment. More importantly, the majority's sweeping, unprecedented holding today precludes mandatory minimum sentences for *any* violent felon who was under age eighteen at the time of the offense.

By holding Lyle's seven-year mandatory minimum sentence for his violent felony is cruel and unusual punishment and unconstitutional under article I, section 17 of the Iowa Constitution, rather than under the Eighth Amendment, the majority evades review by the United States Supreme Court. As Justice Zager observes, no other appellate court in the country has gone this far. Our court stands alone in taking away the power of our elected legislators to require even a seven-year mandatory sentence for a violent felony committed by a 17-year-old.

Will the majority stop here? Under the majority's reasoning, if the teen brain is still evolving, what about 19-year-olds? If the brain is still maturing into the mid-20s, why not prohibit mandatory minimum sentences for any offender under age 26? As judges, we do not have a monopoly on wisdom. Our legislators raise teenagers too. Courts traditionally give broad deference to legislative sentencing policy judgments.

Our trial judges have day-to-day experience adjudicating thousands of juvenile cases. Why not continue to trust the trial judges to make the right individualized judgments in deciding whether a youthful offender should be adjudicated in juvenile court or adult court? Why make today's categorical decision invalidating any mandatory minimum sentence for juveniles when no other appellate court has gone that far? We are not writing on a clean slate. Courts across the country are appropriately concluding that only mandatory life without parole or its de facto equivalent constitute cruel and unusual punishment for juveniles who commit violent felonies.

This is much more than an interesting intellectual debate over jurisprudential philosophies and the proper role for independent state constitutional adjudication. Today's decision will have dramatic realworld consequences. Justice Zager has identified the burdens imposed on the judicial system by the scores of resentencing hearings and has noted the trauma to victims who must testify and relive what the defendant did to them. These hearings will reopen the wounds of the victims and their families. And, some of the offenders will gain release from prison earlier than under the mandatory minimum sentences. Some of those violent felons will commit new crimes. I would instead trust the legislative judgment of our elected branches that required a seven-year mandatory minimum prison term for second-degree robbery, a class "C" felony. A 17-year-old offender would still be eligible for release by age twenty-five. But, that offender would be incarcerated during the late teens and early twenties—the ages when violent crimes are most likely to be committed.

The majority opines that the resentencing hearings to be required of our district court judges "will honor the decency and humanity embedded within article I, section 17 of the Iowa Constitution and, in turn, within every Iowan." I believe our elected representatives—not the members of this court—are best equipped to decide what values are embedded within every Iowan.

It is easy in the abstract to say we do not put constitutional rights to a vote. It is the role of the courts to say where constitutional lines are drawn. But, we must remember rights, by definition, are restrictions on governmental power—the government elected by the people. If our court misinterprets a statute, the legislature can amend the statute the next session. But, if we misinterpret our state constitution, the people are stuck with the decision unless the decision is overruled or the constitution is amended. That is why judges must be extraordinarily careful with constitutional interpretation. Adherence to settled Federal Eighth Amendment precedent would avoid today's aberrational judicial decision-making on sentencing policy.

I therefore dissent for the reasons set forth above and in Justice Zager's dissent.

ZAGER, Justice (dissenting).

I respectfully dissent. I do not believe a seven-year mandatory minimum sentence imposed on an individual who was a juvenile at the time the offense was committed is cruel and unusual punishment under either the Federal or our Iowa Constitution. This mandatory minimum sentence is not grossly disproportional, and there is no recognized categorical challenge for a juvenile's "categorically diminished culpability." There is no authority for holding such. By holding all mandatory minimum sentences imposed on juveniles constitutes cruel and unusual punishment, the majority abandons any semblance of our previous constitutional analysis of cruel and unusual punishment and creates a new category for the sentencing of juveniles to achieve a perceived "best practice" in sentencing. The majority expands article I, section 17 of the Iowa Constitution to a point supported by neither our own caselaw nor by any caselaw of the United States Supreme Court. Neither does such an expansive interpretation find support in the caselaw of any other appellate court in the nation. Contrary to the majority's reasoning, the United States Supreme Court's interpretation of the Federal Constitution does not support this expansive interpretation. I would apply the reasoning of *Miller v. Alabama*, and *State v. Pearson*, to the facts of this case and hold this mandatory minimum sentence is not cruel or unusual under the Iowa Constitution.

The majority's reason for applying *Graham* is that juveniles are categorically less culpable, and so a categorical analysis and categorical rules are appropriate here. On its own, the majority now creates a new constitutional category under our Iowa Constitution, but we need to be clear that there is no judicial authority for creating this new constitutional category. Up to this point, in most cases, the fact of a juvenile's diminished culpability only required the sentencing court "to take into account how children are different, and how those differences counsel against irrevocably sentencing them to a lifetime in prison." Were a categorical rule appropriate based solely on a juvenile's diminished culpability, the Supreme Court in *Miller* would have imposed a categorical rule. Instead, it expressly declined to consider the "argument that the Eighth Amendment requires a categorical bar on life without parole for juveniles, or at least for those 14 and younger." Nevertheless, the majority in this case deems the juvenile's diminished culpability alone is of sufficient constitutional magnitude to impose a categorical rule against mandatory minimum sentences and holds the sentence cruel and unusual.

To be clear, the majority cannot cite to any case of any court that used the *Graham-Miller* line of jurisprudence to strike down as cruel and unusual punishment any sentence imposed on anyone under the age of eighteen when the individual still had a substantial life expectancy left at the time of eligibility for parole. Finding no support in a national survey on mandatory minimum sentences for juveniles, apart from legislation limiting the use of mandatory sentences to certain circumstances, the majority elects to give little weight to the strong national consensus approving juvenile mandatory minimum sentences. Instead, the majority turns to this state's body of unrelated statutory law concerning juveniles.

But, if this court is to give deference to legislative judgments concerning punishment enacted after an offender is sentenced, then surely this court must also give deference to legislative judgments that were in effect when the offender was sentenced. The statute in effect at that time of sentencing is at least as good an objective indicium of society's standards as a statute enacted two years later.

The statute in effect when Lyle was sentenced mandated he serve seventy percent of his ten-year sentence. Assuming both the new sentencing statute and the older sentencing statute should be considered as indicators of society's standards, they are entitled to equal amounts of deference. Nonetheless, the majority analysis discounts one legislative judgment, because they apparently don't agree with it, by elevating the other with which they do agree. This is not the role of an appellate court.

Nothing in the majority's survey of the objective indicia of our society's standards suggests our society believes violent juvenile offenders are constitutionally different for purposes of sentencing, except for life without parole and its functional equivalent. Thus, this court should not interfere with the legislature's selected sentencing scheme.

Juveniles' attributes undermine the four "penological justifications for imposing the harshest sentences on juvenile offenders, even when they commit terrible crimes." First, juveniles are less blameworthy than adults, so the case for retribution is weak. Second, deterrence does not justify the harshest sentences; juveniles are immature, reckless, and impetuous, and so "less likely to consider potential punishment." Third, to justify incapacitating a juvenile for life, it would need to be found that the juvenile was incorrigible. Incorrigibility, however, is not consistent with youth. Finally, rehabilitation does not justify a life sentence. In fact, such a long sentence "is at odds with a child's capacity for change." The Court found imposing a sentence on a juvenile that "alters the remainder of his life" advances none of these penological justifications. No one can reasonably argue that a seven-year mandatory minimum sentence imposed on Lyle will "alter the remainder of his life" or that it serves no penological purpose.

While relying heavily on the other two factors, the Court's holding in *Miller* primarily focused on the mandatory nature of the juvenile's life without parole sentence. Mandatory life without parole sentencing schemes prevent judges and juries from considering the juvenile's diminished culpability, the juvenile's capacity for change, and the justifications for a particular sentence. Indeed, by subjecting teens and children to the same sentences as adults, mandatory life without parole sentencing laws "prohibit a sentencing authority from assessing whether the law's harshest term of imprisonment proportionately punishes a juvenile offender." Mandatory life without parole sentencing risks disproportionate sentencing. But, again, we are not talking about our law's harshest term of imprisonment, nor does the majority opinion now base its decision on a disproportionality analysis.

Like Null and Pearson, Andre Lyle was a juvenile at the time he committed his crime, but he was subject to the same mandatory minimum sentence as an adult. In this case, however, the sentence is not harsh, it is not cruel, and it is not unusual. Lyle was sentenced to a maximum prison term of ten years, and he is required to serve seventy percent of that term, or seven years, before being eligible for parole. There is clearly no reasonable correlation between adult death sentences, juvenile life sentences without the possibility of parole, and this seven-year mandatory minimum sentence. As a chronological fact, Lyle's sentence is significantly shorter than all the sentences with which this court or the United States Supreme Court has previously dealt.

If Lyle served the maximum of ten years, he would be released in his late twenties, about twenty-five years younger than Pearson would have been if she been released when she first became parole eligible. If released when he first becomes parole eligible, Lyle will be in his mid-twenties, which would leave him ample time for hitting major life milestones.

As in the case of any juvenile, deterrence and retribution offer little support for Lyle's sentence because of his immaturity and diminished culpability. Despite Lyle's youth, however, one cannot dispute that he poses a risk to public safety. Incapacitating him, therefore, protects the public. Incapacitation is thus an appropriate justification for Lyle's sentence.

So too with rehabilitation; it is the "penological goal that forms the basis of parole systems." Lyle's sentence does not deny him the right to reenter society, as was the case in *Graham* and *Miller*. Imprisoning Lyle until his middle or late twenties does not forswear the "rehabilitative ideal." Lyle's comparatively short sentence does not, unlike the life without parole sentence meted out to the juvenile in *Graham*, deny Lyle "the right to reenter the community." And it does not reflect "an irrevocable judgment about [Lyle's] value and place in society." Rehabilitation therefore also justifies Lyle's sentence.

Here, Lyle does not face the prospect of geriatric release after decades of incarceration. In fact, Lyle faces at most a single decade behind bars. Lyle will be provided a "meaningful opportunity to obtain release based on demonstrated maturity and rehabilitation" and reenter society as required by *Graham* and *Null*. I would apply the rationale of *Miller*, *Null*, and *Pearson* and hold the sentence imposed on Lyle is not cruel and unusual under our Iowa Constitution, and thus no individualized sentencing hearing is required.

I also strenuously disagree with the majority's conclusion, in the exercise of its independent judgment, that sentencing juveniles according to a statutorily required mandatory minimum, regardless of the length of the sentence, does not adequately serve legitimate penological objectives in light of the child's categorically diminished culpability. As stated previously, a short-term period of incarceration clearly serves penological goals of rehabilitation and incapacitation, both goals considered important in *Graham* and all of the later cases. There is simply no authority for this blanket proposition.

But, perhaps most troubling to me is the majority's recognition that every case so far employing this principle of a child's categorically diminished culpability involved harsh, lengthy sentences—even death. In fact, there is no authority cited by the majority, nor did my research disclose any authority, that would extend the principle employed by the majority to all mandatory minimum sentences for juveniles.

The majority now holds that, in order to meet our constitutional prohibition against cruel and unusual punishment, every juvenile facing a mandatory minimum sentence of any length must have an individualized sentencing hearing utilizing the *Miller* factors. This is wrong and has no constitutional support in federal jurisprudence or our own jurisprudence.

Finally, several observations need to be made in this area of juvenile sentencing. First, no court in the land has followed our opinions in *Pearson* and *Null*, which dramatically extended the circumstances under which a *Miller*-type sentencing hearing was constitutionally required. In my opinion, such an extension was far beyond that contemplated by the United States Supreme Court, and clearly, no other federal court or state supreme court has felt it constitutionally required to extend it either. Second, no federal court, no state supreme court, nor any court for that matter has used a categorical analysis employed by the majority in this case to strike down all mandatory minimum sentences for a juvenile. In reaching this conclusion, the majority contorts our constitutional jurisprudence under the guise of independently analyzing our Iowa Constitution. Third, the majority justifies its decision in this case by declaring that its decision is based on its desire to return to the district courts its rightful discretion in sentencing juveniles. What the majority fails to comprehend is that these constitutionally unnecessary resentencings come paired with significant practical difficulties for the district courts. Based on the majority's opinion, all of those juveniles must be resentenced and have an individualized sentencing hearing. It will take hundreds, if not thousands, of hours to perform this task. And, of course, there will be expert witnesses: social workers, psychologists, psychiatrists, substance-abuse counselors, and any number of related social scientists. And, other witnesses: mothers, fathers, sisters, and brothers. Finally, and most importantly, victims will again have to testify and relive the trauma they experienced at the hands of the juvenile offender.

I agree that time and expense should be irrelevant if constitutional rights are affected. However, these should be primary considerations when deciding to impose on the courts and the corrections systems a new sentencing practice that has no basis in this state's constitution. I also question whether the ultimate decisions by our district courts will be qualitatively better given this unnecessary time, money, and effort. And, so more time and money will be spent trying to determine the appropriate sentence for a juvenile offender. According to the majority, this is what our constitution requires of any juvenile offender.

I understand that the majority believes that an individualized sentencing hearing is the "best practice" for the sentencing of juveniles: "[A]pplying the teachings of *Miller* irrespective of the crime or sentence is simply the right thing to do, whether or not required by our Constitution." I do not necessarily disagree. I would hold that the mandatory minimum sentence imposed under Iowa Code section 902.12(5), under these facts, does not constitute cruel and unusual punishment and accordingly does not violate article I, section 17 of the Iowa Constitution.

I would affirm the sentence imposed by the district court.

Holdings of *State v. Lyle:* The court held that a statute mandating a sentence of incarceration in prison for juvenile offenders with no opportunity for parole until a minimum period of time has been served is unconstitutional under the Iowa Constitution.

Discussion Questions

The court says, "We do not hold juvenile offenders cannot be sentenced to a minimum term of imprisonment. We only hold juvenile offenders cannot be mandatorily sentenced under a mandatory minimum sentencing scheme." What is the difference?

Lyle was sentenced on his 18th birthday. Why should the result be so different if the crime had just occurred just a little later?

Key Concepts: Application of Miller v. Alabama to Other Issues

- Some state courts apply the analysis of *Miller v. Alabama* to cases other than mandatory life without parole sentences to require that sentencing of defendants who were minors at the time of their offense must be subject to individualized findings and decision-making by the judge rather than statutory mandatory sentences.

- While minors may not be entitled to all of the rights or protections accorded to adults, the mere fact that the defendant is a minor affects culpability and, as such, some courts hold that sentences must be individualized making allowances for the infirmities of a youth.

Practical Questions: Application of Miller v. Alabama to Other Issues

1. You have a client who was adjudicated a delinquent for a sexual offense that resulted in his being placed on the state's sex abuse registry for a period of 5 years. There is no mechanism to allow the period to be shortened. Is that provision constitutional as applied to your client who was a minor at the time of his offense?

2. Your state statute requires a minimum sentence of 2 days in jail for a first drunk driving offense. Is this constitutional when applied to a minor?

Simulation Exercise VI

Characters: Prosecuting attorney, defense attorney, and Judge.

Facts: Steven Smith, a 12-year-old, attempted to steal a bag of candy from a local gas station. He was caught and charged with misdemeanor theft (shoplifting). The evidence of guilt is overwhelming, and the youth is willing to plead guilty to the charge. However, once he is adjudicated a delinquent (either by plea or by trial), the conviction will appear online in the "Courts Online" website operated by the court system. If Steven is not convicted of any additional charges by the age of 18, he can apply to the court to "seal" his records and remove his name from the "Courts Online" website. Prior to entering a plea at the adjudicatory hearing, Steven's attorney calls an employment expert as a witness to establish that there are companies who "fish" the "Courts Online" website on a continuous basis to gather information about any convictions involving honesty (such as theft). The expert further testified that, once those companies have captured a conviction, it remains in their records permanently regardless of whether or not a judge subsequently seals the records, and, consequently, the conviction will "haunt" convicted persons for the rest of their lives. Finally, the expert testified that even an old shoplifting conviction will reduce the employability of a person by at least 45%. Steven's attorney has filed a motion to "seal" the record before entering an adjudication order, arguing that the lifetime impediment on employment for such minor acts of a 12-year-old is "cruel and unusual punishment," citing the *Miller v. Alabama* decision. The prosecuting attorney has argued that there is no provision for the sealing of a juvenile record before age 18 in the state and that the effect of appearance on the "Courts Online" website is not such a hardship as to implicate constitutional concerns.

Simulation: The exercise is for both attorneys to conduct oral arguments on the motion to seal Steven's record prior to adjudication to prevent appearance on the "Courts Online" website. The judge should be prepared to ask any questions necessary to arrive at a ruling, the attorneys shall be prepared to answer any questions posed to them, and the judge will enter an oral ruling on the motion specifying findings and reasons for the ruling.

Table of Cases

Index